Communication in a Civil Society

Communication in a Civil Society

Shelley D. Lane
University of Texas—Dallas

Ruth Anna Abigail
Azusa Pacific University

John Casey Gooch
University of Texas—Dallas

Routledge
Taylor & Francis Group

LONDON AND NEW YORK

First published 2014 by Pearson Education, Inc.

Published 2016 by Routledge
2 Park Square, Milton Park, Abingdon, Oxon OX14 4RN
711 Third Avenue, New York, NY 10017, USA

Routledge is an imprint of the Taylor & Francis Group, an informa business

Copyright © 2014 Taylor & Francis. All rights reserved.

All rights reserved. No part of this book may be reprinted or reproduced or utilised in any form or by any electronic, mechanical, or other means, now known or hereafter invented, including photocopying and recording, or in any information storage or retri eval system, without permission in writing from the publishers.

Notice:
Product or corporate names may be trademarks or registered trademarks, and are used only for identification and explanation without intent to infringe.

Cover Design: Bruce Kenselaar

Credits and acknowledgments borrowed from other sources and reproduced, with permission, in this textbook appear on appropriate page within text (or on page 346).

Library of Congress Cataloging-in-Publication Data
Lane, Shelley D.
　Communication in a civil society / Shelley D. Lane, Ruth Anna Abigail, John Gooch.
　　pages cm
　Includes bibliographical references and index.
　ISBN-13: 978-0-205-77021-2
　ISBN-10: 0-205-77021-5
1. Communication--Moral and ethical aspects. 2. Interpersonal communication. 3. Courtesy. I. Abigail, Ruth Anna. II. Gooch, John, 1971- III. Title.
　P94.L356 2013
　302.2--dc23
　　　　　　　　　　2013012701

ISBN-13: 978-0-205-77021-2 (pbk)

SHELLEY D. LANE

*To my husband, Dr. Lawrence Warren Miller,
who supported and encouraged me from the initial idea for
Communication in a Civil Society to its publication*

RUTH ANNA ABIGAIL

*To my children, Kathryn and David
Lulofs, who continue to be my inspiration*

JOHN CASEY GOOCH

*To all my friends and family who have supported
me in my academic endeavors*

BRIEF CONTENTS

PART I FOUNDATIONS OF COMMUNICATION 1

1. A First Look at Civil Communication 2
2. Perceiving the Self and Others 26
3. Civil Verbal Communication 47
4. Civil Nonverbal Communication 67
5. Civil Listening and Responding with Confirmation 90

PART II CIVIL INTERPERSONAL COMMUNICATION 111

6. Interpersonal Relationships and Civil Communication 111
7. Intimate Relationships, Romantic Relationships, and Civil Communication 129
8. Civil Communication in Conflicts 150

PART III CIVIL SMALL GROUP COMMUNICATION 172

9. Civil Communication in Groups 172
10. Group Processes and Civil Communication 195

PART IV CIVIL PUBLIC SPEAKING 221

11. Preparing Civil Public Speeches 221
12. Delivering Public Speeches with Civility 251
13. Giving Civil Informative and Special Occasion Speeches 272
14. Giving Persuasive Speeches with Civility 293

CONTENTS

Preface xxii

PART I FOUNDATIONS OF COMMUNICATION 1

1 A First Look at Civil Communication 1

CIVIL AND ETHICAL COMMUNICATION 2
  Civility and Civil Communication 3
  Trends In Technology and Social Media Civility Initiatives 5
  Ethics and Ethical Communication 6
  Ask the Ethicist What's Ethical? 6
  The Relationship Between Civil and Ethical Communication 8
  A Case Study Ethics "Marriage Is So Gay" 9

DEFINING COMMUNICATION 11

TYPES OF COMMUNICATION 11
  Intrapersonal Communication 11
  Interpersonal Communication 12
  Small Group Communication 14
  Public Communication 14
  Mediated and Technology-Based Communication 14
  Trends In Technology and Social Media How Do New Media Affect Us? 15

MODELS OF COMMUNICATION 17
  Action and Interaction Feedback Models of Communication 17
  A Transactional Model of Communication 18

CONTEXTS OF COMMUNICATION 20
  The Culture Context 20
  The Workplace Context 21
  The Gender Context 21

IMPROVING OUR ABILITY TO COMMUNICATE CIVILLY AND EFFECTIVELY: PRINCIPLES OF COMMUNICATION 21
  Communication Is Irreversible 22
  Communication Is an Ongoing Process 22
  Communication Is Inevitable 22
  Understanding the Principles of Communication 23
  Tech Check Assessing Your Self-Perceived Communication Competence 23

CHAPTER SUMMARY 24
CIVILITY SUMMARY 25
REVIEW QUESTIONS 25

2 Perceiving the Self and Others 26

DEFINITION OF PERCEPTION AND SELF-CONCEPT 27
    What Is Perception? 28
    What Is Self-Concept? 28

PERCEPTION, SELF-CONCEPT, AND CIVILITY 29

STAGES IN THE PERCEPTION PROCESS 30
    Selection 30
    Organization 30
    Interpretation 32
    Differences in Perception 33
    Ask the Ethicist Influencing Others' Perceptions of Me 35

THEORETICAL PERSPECTIVES ABOUT PERCEPTION 35
    Attribution Theory 35
    Implicit Personality Theory 36
    Cultural Influences on Perception 37

CHARACTERISTICS OF THE SELF-CONCEPT 38
    Self-Image 39
    Self-Esteem 39
    Tech Check Assessing Your Ability to Self-Monitor 39
    Trends In Technology and Social Media Perception, Self-Concept, and Computer-Mediated Communication 40
    The Influence of Others on the Self-Concept 41
    The Influence of Culture on Self-Concept 41
    The Influence of the Workplace on Self-Concept 42
    The Influence of Gender on the Self-Concept 42
    A Case Study in Ethics "I'm a Loser..." 43

IMPROVING OUR ABILITY TO COMMUNICATE CIVILLY AND EFFECTIVELY ABOUT OUR PERCEPTIONS 44

CHAPTER SUMMARY 45
CIVILITY SUMMARY 46
REVIEW QUESTIONS 46

3 Civil Verbal Communication 47

DEFINITION OF VERBAL COMMUNICATION 48

VERBAL COMMUNICATION AND MEANING 49
    The Triangle of Meaning 49
    Denotative and Connotative Meanings 50
    Shortcuts in Communication: Jargon and Slang 51
    Verbal Communication and Gender 52
    Trends In Technology and Social Media "GR8 Tweet!" 53
    The Coordinated Management of Meaning 54

VERBAL COMMUNICATION AND THOUGHT 55
  Words That Strongly Influence Thought 55
  Words That Subtly Influence Thought 56
  Verbal Communication and Culture 57
IMPROVING OUR ABILITY TO ENGAGE IN CIVIL AND EFFECTIVE VERBAL COMMUNICATION 59
  Abstraction 59
  Ask the Ethicist Why Can't I Just Say What I Want? 60
  Civil Communication: Using Specific and Concrete Words 61
  Allness 61
  Civil Communication: Indexing and Owning Thoughts and Feelings 62
UNCIVIL LANGUAGE: PROFANITY AND CURSING 63
  A Case Study in Ethics The Cursing Prof and "Conservative Coming Out Week" 64

CHAPTER SUMMARY 65
CIVILITY SUMMARY 66
REVIEW QUESTIONS 66

4 Civil Nonverbal Communication 67

DEFINITION OF NONVERBAL COMMUNICATION 68
FUNCTIONS OF NONVERBAL COMMUNICATION 69
  Repeating 69
  Substituting 69
  Accenting 70
  Complementing 71
  Regulating 71
  Ask the Ethicist "Mandatory" Social Gatherings 71
  Trends in Technology and Social Media Email, "Second Life," and Nonverbal Communication 72
  Nonverbal Communication and Culture 72
TYPES OF NONVERBAL COMMUNICATION 74
  Kinesics 74
  Paralanguage 76
  Physical Characteristics 77
  A Case Study in Ethics Hair Today, Gone from School Tomorrow 78
  Environment 79
  Nonverbal Communication and Gender 81
ROAD RAGE: NONVERBAL COMMUNICATION AND INCIVILITY 82
DECEPTION AND NONVERBAL COMMUNICATION 83
  Lab Studies 83
  Naturalistic Studies 83

x Contents

IMPROVING OUR ABILITY TO COMMUNICATE WITH CIVIL AND EFFECTIVE NONVERBAL IMMEDIACY BEHAVIORS 84
    Tech Check The Nonverbal Immediacy Scale 86
    Immediacy and Your Career 87

CHAPTER SUMMARY 87
CIVILITY SUMMARY 88
REVIEW QUESTIONS 89

5 Civil Listening and Responding with Confirmation 90

DEFINITION OF LISTENING 91
    Tech Check Listening Preference Profile 92

LISTENING, CIVILITY, AND ETHICS 92
    Uncivil Listening: Disconfirming Others 92
    Civil Listening: Confirming Others 93
    Ask the Ethicist Do I Have to Listen? 94

STAGES AND TYPES OF LISTENING 94
    Stage 1: Hearing and Appreciative Listening 95
    A Case Study in Ethics Cochlear Implants 96
    Stage 2: Understanding and Comprehensive Listening 97
    Stage 3: Remembering 97
    Stage 4: Interpreting and Empathic Listening 98
    Stage 5: Evaluating and Critical Listening 98
    Stage 6: Responding and Active Listening 98

IMPROVING OUR ABILITY TO ENGAGE IN CIVIL AND EFFECTIVE LISTENING 99
    Stage 1: Improving the Ability to Hear Messages and Engage in Appreciative Listening 99
    Stage 2: Improving the Ability to Understand Messages and Engage in Comprehensive Listening 100
    Stage 3: Improving the Ability to Remember Messages 100
    Stage 4: Improving the Ability to Interpret Messages and Engage in Empathic Listening 100
    Stage 5: Improving the Ability to Evaluate Messages and Engage in Critical Listening 101
    Stage 6: Improving the Ability to Respond to Messages and Engage in Active Listening 101

CONFIRMING LISTENING RESPONSE STYLES 101
    Prompting and Questioning 102
    Reassuring and Expressing Concern 103
    Paraphrasing Thoughts and Feelings 103
    Trends in Technology and Social Media Supportive Communication 106

LISTENING, CONFIRMING RESPONSES, AND CONTEXTS 107
    Listening, Confirming Responses, and Culture 107

Contents **xi**

    Listening, Confirming Responses, and Your Career   108
    Listening, Confirming Responses, and Gender   108

CHAPTER SUMMARY   109
CIVILITY SUMMARY   110
REVIEW QUESTIONS   110

PART II   CIVIL INTERPERSONAL COMMUNICATION   111

6 Interpersonal Relationships and Civil Communication   111

DEFINITION AND TYPES OF INTERPERSONAL RELATIONSHIPS   112
    Impersonal and Personal Relationships   113
    Ask the Ethicist Is It Okay to Be Impersonal with Others?   114
    Family Relationships   114
    Friendships   115
    Tech Check Friendship Inventory   116
    Interpersonal Relationships and Culture   116
    Trends in Technology and Social Media Facebook and Friendship   117
    Interpersonal Relationships and Gender   118

INTERPERSONAL RELATIONSHIPS AND CIVILITY   119
    Interpersonal Relationships and Your Career   120

THEORETICAL PERSPECTIVES ABOUT INTERPERSONAL RELATIONSHIPS   120
    Attraction Theory   120
    Uncertainly Reduction Theory   122

RELATIONAL COMMUNICATION   124
    Content and Relational Levels of Communication   124
    Relational-Level Messages   124

IMPROVING OUR ABILITY TO COMMUNICATE CIVILLY AND EFFECTIVELY WITH METACOMMUNICATION   125
    Metacommunication at the Content Level of Meaning   126
    A Case Study in Ethics Cell Phone Subterfuge   126
    Metacommunication at the Relational Level of Meaning   127

CHAPTER SUMMARY   127
CIVILITY SUMMARY   128
REVIEW QUESTIONS   128

7 Intimate Relationships, Romantic Relationships, and Civil Communication 129

DEFINITION OF INTIMATE AND ROMANTIC RELATIONSHIPS 130
- Intimate Relationships 131
- Romantic Relationships 131
- Intimate Relationships, Romantic Relationships, and Gender 132
- Intimate Relationships, Romantic Relationships, and Culture 132
- Intimate Relationships, Romantic Relationships, and Your Career 133

COMMUNICATION IN INTIMATE AND ROMANTIC RELATIONSHIPS 134

SELF-DISCLOSURE AND SOCIAL PENETRATION THEORY 135
- Self-Disclosure 135
- Social Penetration Theory 135

STAGE MODELS 137
- Knapp and Vangelisti's Staircase Model of Relationship Development 137
- Improving Our Ability to Communicate Civilly and Effectively in Stages of Relationship Development 139
- *Tech Check* Relational Maintenance Strategies 140
- *Trends in Technology and Social Media* The Internet, Social Media, and Relationship Initiation and Maintenance 141

DIALECTICAL TENSIONS MODEL 143
- Baxter's Model of Dialectical Tensions in Relationships 143
- *Ask the Ethicist* "To Lie or Not to Lie; That Is the Question" 144
- Improving Our Ability to Communicate Civilly and Effectively When Contending with Relational Dialectics 145

INTIMATE RELATIONSHIPS, ROMANTIC RELATIONSHIPS, AND CIVILITY 146
- *A Case Study in Ethics* The Secret Lover Collection 147

CHAPTER SUMMARY 148
CIVILITY SUMMARY 149
REVIEW QUESTIONS 149

8 Civil Communication in Conflicts 150

DEFINITION OF CONFLICT 151
- Situation 152
- Interdependence 152
- Incompatible Goals or Means 152
- Emotional Residues 153
- Sense of Urgency 153

THEORETICAL PERSPECTIVES ON CONFLICT BEHAVIOR 153
- Social Exchange Theory 153
- Styles Theory 154

Tech Check Conflict Management Styles 156
Phase Theory 157

CAUSES OF CONFLICT 158
Conflict in Organizations and Groups 158
Conflict in Relationships 159

OPTIONS IN CONFLICT MANAGEMENT 160
A Case Study in Ethics Parents, Pixels, and Political Parties 161
The Other-Oriented, Nonassertive Approach 162
The Self-Oriented, Aggressive Approach 162
The Relationship-Oriented, Assertive Approach 162
Identifying Your Options 163
Trends in Technology and Social Media What's the Best Way to Do a Conflict? 163

IMPROVING OUR ABILITY TO COMMUNICATE IN CONFLICT SITUATIONS 164
The S-TLC Conflict Resolution System 164
Civility and Effective Conflict Messages 165

AVOIDING VIOLENCE IN CONFLICTS 165

IMPROVING OUR ABILITY TO COME TOGETHER AFTER CONFLICT 166
Understanding Forgiveness and Reconciliation 167
Communicating Forgiveness and Reconciliation 167
Asking for Forgiveness with Apologies 169
Ask the Ethicist What's So Bad About Revenge? 169

CHAPTER SUMMARY 170
CIVILITY SUMMARY 171
REVIEW QUESTIONS 171

PART III CIVIL SMALL GROUP COMMUNICATION 172

9 Civil Communication in Groups 172

GROUP COMMUNICATION AND CIVILITY 174
Trends in Technology and Social Media Flaming and Group Communication 175

WHAT CHARACTERIZES GROUPS? 176
Distinguishing Groups from Teams 176
Identifying the Goal of a Group 177
Short-Term, Task-Oriented Groups 177
Long-Term, Relationship-Oriented Groups 178
Virtual Groups 178
Group Work and Productivity 179

HOW GROUPS DEVELOP 179
Forming 179
Storming 180
Norming 180
Performing 181
Terminating 181

CREATING GROUP CLIMATE 181
    Group Norms 181
    A Case Study in Ethics The Politics of Exclusion 182
    Responding to One Another 183
    Roles Members Play 184
    Cohesiveness: Balancing Fit and Diversity 185
    Ask the Ethicist Is Diversity a Matter of Ethics? 188

POWER AND LEADERSHIP IN GROUPS 188
    Power in Groups 188
    Leadership in Groups 189
    The Importance of Following 191
    Leadership Emergence in Groups 191
    How Do Men and Women Respond Differently to Group Situations? 191

CHAPTER SUMMARY 192

CIVILITY SUMMARY 193

REVIEW QUESTIONS 194

10 Group Processes and Civil Communication 195

GROUP PROBLEM SOLVING, CIVILITY, AND ETHICS 196

COMMUNICATION AND DECISION MAKING IN GROUPS 197
    A Case Study in Ethics Are You Decision Fatigued? 198
    Patterns of Communication 198
    Trends in Technology and Social Media Twitter and Group Communication 200
    Decision-Making Patterns in Groups 200

INTRODUCTION TO GROUP PROCESSES 202
    Group Problem Solving and Your Career 202

PROBLEM-SOLVING: THE HEART OF GROUP PROCESSES 202
    Steps in Problem Solving 202
    Creativity and Problem Solving 205

IMPROVING OUR ABILITY TO ENGAGE IN CIVIL AND EFFECTIVE PROBLEM SOLVING 206
    Vertical and Lateral Thinking 206
    Standard Problem-Solving Techniques 207
    Mind Mapping 208

BARRIERS TO EFFECTIVE PROBLEM SOLVING 209
    Groupthink 210
    The Abilene Paradox 210
    Ask the Ethicist Why Should I Speak Up? 211
    The Lucifer Effect 212

HANDLING CONFLICT IN GROUPS 213
    Instrumental/Task-Oriented Conflict 213
    Relationship-Oriented Conflict 214
    Identity-Oriented Conflict 214
    Process-Oriented Conflict 214

Contents   XV

IMPROVING OUR ABILITY TO CREATE CIVIL AND EFFECTIVE GROUP MEETINGS 215
Questions and Guidelines Related to Running Meetings 215
Roles Members Play in Meetings 216
Culture and Meeting Behavior 217
Gender and Meeting Behavior 218

CHAPTER SUMMARY 219
CIVILITY SUMMARY 220
REVIEW QUESTIONS 220

PART IV   CIVIL PUBLIC SPEAKING   221

11 Preparing Civil Public Speeches 221

ENGAGING YOUR AUDIENCE WITH CIVILITY 222
Considering Your Audience's Psychographics 223
Considering Your Audience's Demographics 225
Types of Audiences 227
The Occasion 227
A Case Study in Ethics "Discouraging Jeerers" 228

PLANNING YOUR SPEECH TOPIC 229
Determining the General Purpose of a Speech 229
Selecting Your Topic and Generating Ideas 231
Creating a Specific Speech Purpose 232
Formulating the Thesis Statement 234

ORGANIZING YOUR INFORMATION 234
Topical Organization 235
Chronological Organization 235
Spatial Organization 235
Familiar to Unfamiliar Organization 236
Comparing Advantages and Disadvantages 236
Narration or Story-Telling 237
Trends in Technology and Social Media YouTube and Public Speaking 238

WRITING A SPEECH OUTLINE 238
Creating the Body of the Speech First 239
Creating a Formal Outline 240

FORMULATING THE INTRODUCTION, TRANSITIONS, AND CONCLUSION 241
Introduction 241
Transitions 244
Conclusion 245

GATHERING AND USING SUPPORTING MATERIAL 246
Planning Your Supporting Material 246
Gathering and Selecting Information 246

   Using Supporting Material   247
    Ask the Ethicist   Sharing Resources   249
  CHAPTER SUMMARY   249
  CIVILITY SUMMARY   250
  REVIEW QUESTIONS   250

12 Delivering Public Speeches with Civility   251

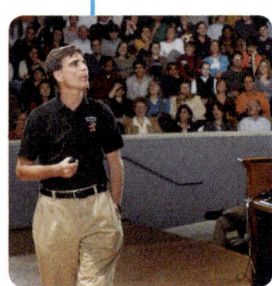

 DELIVERY, CIVILITY, AND ETHICS   252
  A Case Study in Ethics   Uncivil Delivery   252
 CONTROLLING ANXIETY   253
  Understanding Communication Apprehension   253
  Tech Check   Personal Report of Public Speaking Anxiety   253
  Techniques for Handling Nervousness   254
  Trends in Technology and Social Media   Virtual Reality Therapy (VRT) and Communication Apprehension   255
 METHODS OF DELIVERY   255
  Speaking from a Manuscript   256
  Speaking from Notes or an Outline   256
  Speaking from Memory   256
  Speaking with Little or No Preparation   256
  Speaking Extemporaneously   256
 TECHNIQUES FOR EFFECTIVE DELIVERY   257
  Effective Vocal Delivery   257
  Good Use of Gestures and Nonverbal Communication   259
  Appropriate Eye Contact and Visual Delivery   259
  Proper Attire   260
  Communicating Emotions   261
 PLANNING, PREPARING, AND USING PRESENTATION AIDS   261
  The Purpose of Presentation Aids   261
  When to Use Presentation Aids   262
  Using Presentation Software   263
  Ask the Ethicist   Should Two Different Speakers Use the Same Visual Aids?   265
  Conveying Information on Slides   265
 PRACTICING YOUR SPEECH   267
  Using a Speech or Presentation Outline   268
  Practicing with Presentation Aids   269
  Simulating the Situation   269
  Practicing Delivery   270

 CHAPTER SUMMARY   270
 CIVILITY SUMMARY   271
 REVIEW QUESTIONS   271

Contents   xvii

13 Giving Civil Informative and Special Occasion Speeches   272

WHAT IS INFORMATION?   273

INFORMATIVE SPEECH PURPOSES   274
- Raising Awareness   275
- Providing New Information   275
- Making a Decision   276

THE PROCESS OF INFORMING AUDIENCES   276
- Motivating the Audience   276
- Making the Information Accessible   277
  - Trends in Technology and Social Media Taking Words Out of Context   278
- Using Clear Language   279

COMPOSING AN INFORMATIVE SPEECH   279
- Choosing a Strategy for Communicating Information   279
- Using Appropriate Supporting Material   280
- Using Visual Aids for Informative Speeches   280

SPECIAL OCCASION SPEECHES   281
- Types of Special Occasion Speeches   281
- Strategies for Giving Special Occasion Speeches   282
  - A Case Study in Ethics "You're Not Special!"   283

INFORMATIVE SPEECHES, SPECIAL OCCASION SPEECHES, AND CIVILITY: AVOIDING PLAGIARISM   284
- Forms of Plagiarism   284
- Ask the Ethicist Paying for Online Research   285
- Attributing Ideas to an Original Source   286

SAMPLE STUDENT SPEECH HIV Home Testing   288

CHAPTER SUMMARY   291
CIVILITY SUMMARY   291
REVIEW QUESTIONS   292

14 Giving Persuasive Speeches with Civility   293

WHAT IS PERSUASION?   294
- Rhetoric and Argumentation   294
  - A Case Study in Ethics Uncivil Persuasion   295
- The Persuasive Appeals   295

PERSUASIVE SPEECH PURPOSES   296
- To Strengthen Commitment   296
- To Weaken Commitment   297
- To Convert the Audience   297
- To Induce a Specific Action   297

THE PROCESS OF PERSUADING AUDIENCES   297
- The Nature of Persuasive Arguments: The Toulmin Model   298
- Types of Claims   299
- Persuasion as an Interactive Process: The Elaboration Likelihood Model   300
- Directness of Approach   301
- Trends in Technology and Social Media   Twitter and the Political Process   302
- Persuasive Outcomes   303

COMPOSING A PERSUASIVE SPEECH   303
- Establishing Credibility   304
- Adapting to an Audience   304
- Structuring the Message   305

PERSUASIVE SPEAKING AND INCIVILITY: LOGICAL FALLACIES   307
- Definition and Types of Fallacies   308
- Avoiding Logical Fallacy   309
- Ask the Ethicist   Using Fear Appeals and Personal Attacks   310

PERSUASIVE SPEAKING AND CIVILITY: INVITATIONAL RHETORIC   310

SAMPLE STUDENT SPEECH   Mandatory Minimums   312

CHAPTER SUMMARY   314
CIVILITY SUMMARY   315
REVIEW QUESTIONS   315

Notes   316
Glossary   335
Credits   346
Index   348

SPECIALIZED CONTENTS

CONTEXTS

1 A First Look at Civil Communication 1
Culture 20 • Workplace (your career) 21 • Gender 21

2 Perceiving the Self and Others 26
Culture 37–38, 41–42 • Workplace (your career) 34, 42 • Gender 33–34, 42–43

3 Civil Verbal Communication 47
Culture 57–59 • Workplace (your career) 51–52 • Gender 52–54

4 Civil Nonverbal Communication 67
Culture 72–73 • Workplace (your career) 87 • Gender 81–82

5 Civil Listening and Responding with Confirmation 90
Culture 107 • Workplace (your career) 108 • Gender 108–109

6 Interpersonal Relationships and Civil Communication 111
Culture 116–118 • Workplace (your career) 120 • Gender 118

7 Intimate Relationships, Romantic Relationships, and Civil Communication 129
Culture 132–133 • Workplace (your career) 133–134 • Gender 132

8 Civil Communication and Conflicts 150
Culture 155–156 • Workplace (your career) 156 • Gender 156–157

9 Civil Communication in Groups 172
Gender 192

10 Group Processes and Civil Communication 195
Culture 217–218 • Workplace (your career) 202 • Gender 218

11 Preparing Civil Public Speeches 221
Culture 225–226, 242 • Workplace 237, 239–241 • Gender 225–226, 242

12 Delivering Public Speeches With Civility 251
Culture 261–62 • Workplace 262, 266–269

13 Giving Civil Informative and Special Occasion Speeches 272
Culture 275–276 • Workplace 273, 278–281 • Gender 272–273, 275–276, 288–290

14 Giving Persuasive Speeches with Civility 293
Culture 301, 308 • Workplace 303–304, 306–308 • Gender 293–294

xix

SKILLS AND STRATEGIES FOR CIVIL COMMUNICATION

- (Using) Alliteration and Assonance in lieu of Profanity and Cursing 65
- Apologies and Asking for Forgiveness 169–170
- (Expressing) Appreciation 140
- Assertive Communication 162
- Avoiding Interpersonal Violence 165–166
- Becoming Aware of and Monitoring Our Behavior 64–65, 100
- Brainstorming and Reverse Brainstorming for Problem-Solving 207
- Brainstorming for Writing Speeches 232
- Civil Listening Strategies 99–101
- (Managing) Communication Apprehension 253–255
- (Strategies to improve) Comprehensive Listening 100
- Confirming Responses 101–105
- Conflict Confrontation Steps 165
- Conflict Management Styles 154–155
- Content Paraphrase 105
- Critical Listening and Thinking Skills 98, 101
- Decision-Making Patterns 199–200
- Empathic Listening 98, 100
- Feelings Paraphrase 105
- Five-Person Network Patterns 198–200
- Five Second Strategy to Remember Names 100
- (Communicating) Forgiveness and Reconciliation 167–168
- Fractionation for Problem-Solving 207
- Followership 199
- (Strategies for Effective) Group Meetings 215–218
- Indexing and Owning Thoughts and Feelings 62
- Information Seeking Behaviors to Reduce Uncertainty about Others 123
- Metacommunication 126–127

- Mind-Mapping for Problem-Solving 208–209
- (Using) Nonverbal Immediacy Behaviors 84–86
- (Using) Open-Ended and Closed-Ended Questions 102
- Paraphrasing Thoughts and Feelings 103–105
- Perception-Checking 44–45
- Perspective-Taking 27, 34
- (Strategies to Develop a) Positive Group Climate 181–183
- (Strategies for Using) Presentation Aids Effectively 261–267
- (Strategies for) Presenting an Interesting Informative Speech 279–281
- (Strategies for) Presenting Information in a Speech 276–280
- Prompting and Questioning 102-103
- Reassurance and Expressing Concern 103
- Reducing Distractions and Recognizing our Propensity to Listen Selectively 99
- Reflective Thinking System for Problem-Solving 203
- Relational Feedback 103
- (Strategies to Contend with) Relationship Dialectics 144–145
- Relationship Initiation Strategies 138–139
- Relationship Maintenance Strategies and Skills 139–140
- Relationship Termination Strategies 140, 142
- Responding to Others in Groups 183–184
- SCRIPTS for Problem-Solving 203–205
- Self-Disclosure Strategies 136
- Six Hats Method of Problem-Solving 207–208
- (Using) Specific and Concrete Words 61
- (Strategies for Effective) Speech Delivery 255–261
- STLC Conflict Resolution System 164–165

MODELS AND THEORIES OF COMMUNICATION

- Action Model of Communication 17
- Attraction Theory 120–122
- Attribution Theory 35–36
- Coordinated Management of Meaning 54–55
- Cues Filtered Out Approach 72
- Dialectical Tensions Model 142–145
- Elaboration Likelihood Model 300–301
- Group Development Model 179–181
- HyperPersonal Approach 72, 141
- Implicit Personality Theory 36–37
- Interaction Model of Communication 18
- Theory of Invitational Rhetoric 310–311
- Maslow's Hierarchy of Needs 222–223
- Monroe's Motivated Sequence 306–307
- Phase Theory of Conflict 157–158
- Relational Communication 124–125
- Sapir-Whorf Hypothesis 58–59
- Social Exchange Theory 153–154
- Social Penetration Theory 135–137
- Stages in the Listening Process 94–99
- Stages in the Perception Process 30–33
- Staircase Stage Model of Relationship Development 137–138
- Styles Theory of Conflict 154–157
- Symbolic Interactionism 41
- Theoretical Approaches to Leadership 189–190
- Toulmin Model of Argumentation 298–299
- Transactional Model of Communication 19
- Triangle of Love 131–132
- Triangle of Meaning 49–50
- Uncertainty Reduction Theory 122–124

PREFACE

IN TODAY'S WORLD, where uncivil acts and messages too often color our experiences with others, *Communication in a Civil Society* offers an alternative way to teach and learn about communication. We have written this book as a response to the challenges students face today to communicate effectively in a complex society. The content in every chapter is framed in terms of communication based on respect, restraint, responsibility, and ethical choices that can bind people together.

Historically, the study of civil behavior was focused on communication that engaged the democratic process and enabled us to be good citizens. We believe that fostering civil communication across the spectrum of our interactions with others is the key to societal transformation. We need not engage in violent protest or communication that attacks others in the course of working out important issues in both our personal lives and the community. We can foster a civil society and concern for our community by choosing to engage in civil and ethical communication that is trustworthy, responsible, respectful, fair, and caring.

CIVILITY, TECHNOLOGY, AND SOCIAL MEDIA

The changes in today's communication technology have dramatically altered the way we communicate with each other and have made the challenges of communicating civilly ever more complex. We welcome the ability technology has given us to stay in touch with many more people than we ever could through face-to-face or traditional communication media and to conveniently send messages and respond, even as we go our separate ways in our busy lives. But we pay a price for these conveniences. We may experience misinterpretations and failed messages that result in uncivil messages because we have fewer cues than we would have in a face-to-face communication encounter. Our well-intentioned messages may make their way into the wrong person's hands without our ever knowing it, giving an easy opportunity to misuse the information in an uncivil manner. Our online time may impinge upon the time we spend in our face-to-face encounters, resulting in bad feelings and uncivil responses. As you read and study this book, you will learn research-based strategies for coping with these and other challenges of today's fast-paced life so that you can civilly, ethically, efficiently, and effectively send and receive messages.

CIVILITY AND THE CONTEXTS OF COMMUNICATION

Another challenge is the ability to communicate civilly in the context of today's increasingly diverse world. Because we must communicate on a daily basis with people who are different from us, we must make a special effort to make the choice to communicate on behalf of others, based on the ideas of respect, restraint, and civility and a firm foundation in ethics. Every chapter in *Communication in a Civil Society* offers research to help you understand the cultural and gender differences among people and help you learn to communicate effectively with people who are different from you. Many introductory communication texts cover the contexts of communication in a separate chapter. We have chosen to cover these contexts in every chapter to reinforce the idea that these factors are a part of our everyday lives.

UNIQUE FEATURES

Communication in a Civil Society offers a distinctly different approach from the typical "hybrid" communication textbook. We cover all the expected topics that make up the core curriculum of introduction to communication—intrapersonal, interpersonal, small group, public, and mediated communication—using an integrated approach throughout each chapter, but we also go beyond this core. Although many communication textbooks claim to be based on a theme (for instance, the first chapter may introduce a goals-oriented approach or emphasize uncertainty reduction), the chapters that follow often present the skills and concepts without regard to unifying the content around their stated theme. *Communication in a Civil Society*, in contrast, makes use of a framework of civility and ethics to unite all the content—skills, concepts, and theory—throughout each chapter.

In addition to the unique framework of civility and ethics, *Communication in a Civil Society* includes the following special features that unify the theme:

- Each chapter opens with a **current cultural reference** that models civil and ethical communication. These vignettes tell the stories of how real people have used civil and ethical messages to share their beliefs and opinions, and then a special "Why It Matters" section goes on to explain the importance of the story to our everyday communication. These vignettes include the MTV Music Awards ceremony during which Beyonce Knowles acknowledged Taylor Swift after Kanye West interrupted her acceptance speech; Kansas teenager Emma Sullivan's tweet offering her opinion about Governor Brownback's political speech—and the governor's civil reply; the wounding of Arizona Representative Gabrielle Giffords and the resulting pleas for civil communication; and former Secretary of State Hillary Rodham Clinton's speech on Internet freedom and the importance of information networks in bringing people together.

- *Communication in a Civil Society* offers **cutting-edge information about how emerging media and technology** are intertwined with civil and ethical communication through "Trends in Technology and Social Media" features and integrated discussions in each chapter. Rather than having a single chapter that may lead students to believe that new media has little impact on intrapersonal, interpersonal, small group, and public speaking, *Communication in a Civil Society* clarifies the relationship between technology and each communication context included in the text. Emerging media and technology topics include gender swapping in MMORPGs; perceptions of others based on personal websites and Facebook profiles; nonverbal communication and Second Life; the implications of millennials multitasking in class; using Twitter to facilitate group communication; and using virtual reality therapy to help students overcome communication apprehension. This cutting-edge information will resonate with today's computer-savvy students.

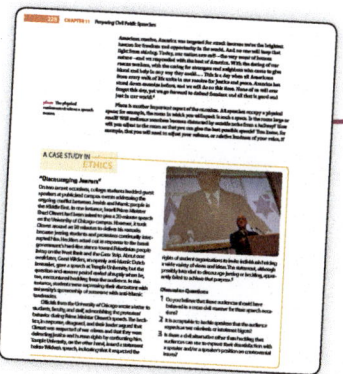

- Each chapter includes an ethics-based feature called "A Case Study in Ethics." The feature describes **real-life situations related to chapter material that involve questions of ethics**. Students are asked to critically analyze the situations, based on chapter material and their knowledge of ethical communication and behavior. Topics include a woman who was asked to leave the Dollywood theme park for wearing a t-shirt that said "marriage is so gay," a professor who sent a profanity-laced email to students and others associated with the university's "Conservative Coming Out Week," The Hastings Law School's Christian Legal Society's exclusionary politics that conflicted with the university's open-access policy, and protesters who heckled Israeli Prime Minister Olmert at the University of Chicago about Jewish–Islamic differences.

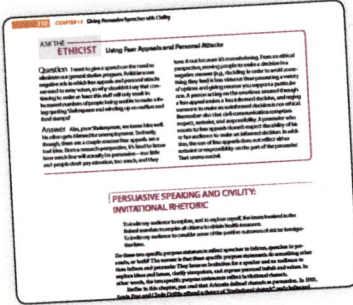

- Each chapter includes an additional ethics feature called "Ask the Ethicist." Written in an advice column format, "Ask the Ethicist" **poses questions of ethics related to chapter content and provides readers with suggestions** regarding ethical communication behavior. "Ask the Ethicist" questions include "What is ethical?" "Why can't I just say what I want?" "Do I have to listen to others?" and "Do I have to tell the truth when s/he asks me if I like her new boy/girlfriend?"

- Selected chapters include a **self-assessment activity** that students can take online. By better understanding their own communication preferences, these "Tech Check" features will give them tools they can use to become more effective civil communicators. Topics include "Listing Preference Profile," "Styles of Conflict Profile," and "Personal Report of Personal Report of Public Speaking Anxiety."

- In keeping with the organizing theme of civility and ethics, *Communication in a Civil Society* **includes the topic of "forgiveness" and "apology"** in Chapter 8. Studies indicate that college-age students have a difficult time forgiving others. In addition, the ability to forgive is connected to both mental and physical benefits and can facilitate the ability to communicate in a civil manner. This section offers strategies and language students can use to effectively cope with difficult times in their lives.

PEDAGOGY

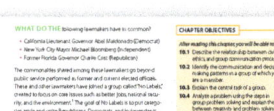

Communication in a Civil Society provides study and learning tools to help you in your journey to become a civil communicator:

- Each chapter begins with a set of **learning objectives** that will help you focus on the key information and skills that you will learn. These objectives form a pathway that will lead you through the text and the supplemental resources that are provided.

- To help you get started learning the essential vocabulary, **key terms** are formatted in boldface type, and the definition of each one is printed in the margin, near the term. These terms are also gathered together in a glossary at the end of the book for easy reference.

- A chapter summary is organized by learning objective to help you confirm that you have learned the essential content for the chapter.

- A civility summary reminds you of the specific civility and ethics strategies that you can use in your everyday life to communicate effectively and with civility.

- Review questions can serve as a springboard to class discussions, as homework assignments, or as a final test to be sure you have learned the essential content.

ACKNOWLEDGMENTS

Few books are written in isolation, and this text is no exception. As authors, we are grateful to the community of scholars in the National Communication Association, as well as in our individual universities, who have enriched our ideas through conversation and critique. In particular, we'd like to thank the many colleagues around the country who generously offered their feedback and suggestions for how to shape this book.

Kaylene Barbe, *Oklahoma Baptist University*
Cristina Doda Cárdenas, *San Jacinto College*
Pete Croisant, *Geneva College*
Alice L. Crume, *Kent State University, Tuscarawas*
E. K. Daufin, *Alabama State University*
Deborah Ford, *St. Petersburg College*
Jim Hikins, *University of Central Arkansas*
Kyle B. Heuett, *Southern Utah University*
Charles Livings, *Auburn University, Montgomery*
Audrey E. Kali, *Framingham State University*
Kay Neal, *University of Wisconsin, Oshkosh*
Travice Baldwin Obas, *Georgia Highlands*
Janice E. Panella, *Arkansas State University, Heber Springs*
John Parrish, *Texas Christian University*
Elizabeth Ribarsky, *University of Illinois, Springfield*
Dan Rogers, *Cedar Valley College*
Esther Rumsey, *Sul Ross State University*
Martha Shoemaker, *University of Houston, Downtown*
Kate Simcox, *Messiah College*
Erica Simpson, *Georgia Highlands College*
Christopher Smejkal, *St Louis Community College, Meramec*
Denise Speruzza, *St. Louis Community College, Meramec*
Jason J. Teven, *California State, Fullerton*
Becca Turner, *Abraham Baldwin Agricultural College*
Ann Vogel, *University Wisconsin, Oshkosh*
Curt Van Geison, *St. Charles Community College*
Amy Wolfson, *Spokane Falls Community College*

We are especially grateful to those at Pearson who have nurtured this text from the beginning and worked so hard to turn our manuscript into a book: Carol Alper, senior development editor; Karon Bowers, publisher; Blair Zoe Tuckman, senior marketing manager; Raegan Keida Heerema, project manager; Anne Ricigliano, program manager; Jennifer Nolan, editorial assistant; and Cordes Hoffmann, photo researcher.

We hope that you will enjoy entering into this rich discussion of communication. And we would like to hear from you personally if you have comments on what we've written here. Most of all, we hope that you will communicate, civilly.

SHELLEY D. LANE
Associate Dean of Undergraduate Studies, School of Arts and Humanities
Associate Professor, University of Texas–Dallas

RUTH ANNA ABIGAIL
Faculty Emeritus, Azusa Pacific University

JOHN GOOCH
Director of Rhetoric, School of Arts and Humanities
Assistant Professor, University of Texas–Dallas

ABOUT THE AUTHORS

SHELLEY D. LANE (Ph.D., University of Southern California, 1982) is the Associate Dean for Undergraduate Education in the School of Arts and Humanities at the University of Texas at Dallas. She has approximately 35 years of university and college experience that combines publication, teaching and administration. She is the author of *Interpersonal Communication: Competence and Contexts*, 2nd Edition, also published by Pearson Education, and a memoir, *A Stirling Diary: An intercultural Story of Communication, Connection, and Coming-of-Age*. Lane was selected as a Minnie Stevens Piper Professor, which is the most distinguished higher education teaching award in Texas.

RUTH ANNA ABIGAIL (Ph.D., University of Southern California, 1982) taught at Azusa Pacific University for 30 years, retiring in 2012 as faculty emeritus. She is the author (with Dudley D. Cahn) of *Managing Conflict through Communication,* 5th Edition, also published by Pearson Education. In addition to her research in the area of communication, Abigail is an artist whose textile work has been displayed both in the US and abroad. She recently accepted a position with the State of New Mexico as a trainer. One of her most frequently taught classes is on civility and ethics in the workplace.

JOHN CASEY GOOCH (Ph.D., Texas Tech University, 2002) is Director of Rhetoric and Writing and Assistant Professor of Literary Studies at the University of Texas at Dallas. For almost 20 years, he has taught courses in professional speaking, technical writing, and rhetoric. He has published articles in *IEEE Transactions on Professional Communication* and *Rhetor: Journal of the Canadian Society for the Study of Rhetoric*; his piece on rhetoric pedagogy will appear in the forthcoming *Oxford Studies in Rhetoric: A Report from the Interactive Seminar on Rhetoric and the 21st Century* from Cambridge Scholars Press.

PART I FOUNDATIONS OF COMMUNICATION

1 A First Look at Civil Communication

THE ANNUAL MTV VIDEO MUSIC AWARDS are notable for outrageous dress and behavior, and the 2009 awards show included its share of "anything goes" moments. One memorable occurrence involved hip-hop singer Kanye West disrupting Taylor Swift's acceptance speech for the Best Female Video and beginning a tirade about Beyonce Knowles being more deserving of the award. The audience gasped (some booed) and Swift appeared stunned. Later in the ceremony, Knowles invited Swift onstage and said that she remembered being a teenage member of the group Destiny's Child and being nominated for an MTV award. Knowles recalled how excited she had been as a nominee and eventual winner and that she wanted Taylor to have her moment in the spotlight. The two then shared a warm embrace, and Swift completed her acceptance speech. Knowles was widely lauded for the compassion and generosity she showed toward Swift.[1]

CHAPTER OBJECTIVES

After reading this chapter, you will be able to:

1.1 Explain how choosing civil communication and relying on ethical principles can help you make good communication-related choices.

1.2 Define communication.

1.3 Differentiate among five types of communication: intrapersonal, interpersonal, small group, public, and mediated/technology based.

1.4 Compare the ways three models of communication—action, interaction, and transaction—explain the communication process.

1.5 Explain three contexts of communication: culture, workplace, and gender.

1.6 Apply three principles of communication that can improve your ability to communicate civilly; communication is irreversible; communication is an ongoing process; and communication is inevitable.

WHY IT MATTERS

The different communication styles exhibited by West, Knowles, and Swift at the MTV Video Music Awards ceremony illustrate how civil and uncivil communication can affect our and others' thoughts, feelings, and behavior. You most likely have never experienced a situation similar to the MTV Awards show during which Kanye West uncivilly snatched the microphone away from Taylor Swift, but you probably have experienced a situation in which someone communicated to you in an uncivil manner. When communicators fail to engage in civil communication, it creates more than hurt feelings or communication problems. Civil and uncivil communication can also influence how others perceive us and our behavior. Whether you are in the audience at a live event such as the MTV Video Music Awards; engaging in conversation or debate; reading tweets, texts, blogs, or websites; watching television; or driving along a highway, it's important to remember that how we communicate affects how others communicate with us. These are compelling reasons to study communication and to attempt to improve our communication.

Researchers have found that individuals and society experience costs associated with uncivil communication. By choosing civility, we can:[2]

- Lower our stress levels, thus avoiding the health issues associated with it
- Increase productivity at work
- Avoid accidents caused by aggressive driving (road rage)
- Avoid personal injury caused by sidewalk rage, parking lot rage, and air rage
- Contribute to the well-being of the human spirit

President Barack Obama has emphasized the importance of civil communication at various times during his presidency. Speaking at the 2010 National Prayer Breakfast, Obama urged Americans to avoid needless political attacks and personal insults. In his University of Michigan 2010 commencement address, the president warned that uncivil communication diminishes the possibility of compromise, undermines democratic deliberation, and prevents us from learning about legitimate but bridgeable differences.[3] In 2011, after the politically motivated shootings in Tucson, Arizona, where 6 people were killed and 12 were wounded, President Obama remarked:

> At a time when our discourse has become so sharply polarized, at a time when we are far too eager to lay the blame for all that ails the world at the feet of those who think differently than we do, it's important for us to pause for a moment and make sure that we are talking with each other in a way that heals, not a way that wounds. . . . Only a more civil and honest public discourse can help us face up to our challenges as a nation, in a way that would make . . . [the shooting victims] proud. . . . We may not be able to stop all evil in the world, but I know that how we treat one another is entirely up to us.[4]

CIVIL AND ETHICAL COMMUNICATION

We'll begin our study of communication with a discussion of the theme of this text—that civility and ethics are critical for responsible thinking, decision-making, and communication choices. We believe that civil and ethical communication is necessary across all types of communication (i.e., intrapersonal, interpersonal, small group, public, and mediated and technology-related communication) and across all contexts of communication (e.g., cultural, the workplace, and gender contexts).

Research bears out the importance of civility. For example, the 2010 Allegheny College Survey of Civility and Compromise in American Politics found that more than 95 percent of their respondents agree that civility in politics is important for a healthy democracy, and 87 percent of respondents believe that it is possible to disagree in a civil manner.[5] In addition, people believe that social networking sites should be places of civility and should leave the sites when they encounter incivility. A 2010 poll released by Weber Shandwick, Powell Tate, and KRC Research has found that almost one-third of Americans are "tuning out" of social networking sites because of uncivil communication. Specifically, 45 percent have blocked or unfriended someone because of uncivil comments, 38 percent have stopped visiting an online site because of incivility there, and 25 percent have dropped out of an online community because of uncivil discourse.[6] Finally, while many people have been targets of uncivil communication, about 6 in 10 Americans also admit that they have occasionally engaged in uncivil communication.[7] The point we are making is that most people want to engage in communication that is civil. Sometimes we fail, and when we do, it's often because we don't have the skills to be civil. This book is designed to provide you with the skills to engage in civil communication—communication that enriches the lives of those involved in it.

Civility and Civil Communication

Much of the civility content we refer to throughout this book is based on the work of two scholars: P. M. Forni, author of *Choosing Civility: The Twenty-Five Rules of Considerate Conduct* and founder of the Johns Hopkins Civility Project; and Stephen L. Carter, Professor of Law at Yale University and author of *Civility: Manners, Morals, and the Etiquette of Democracy*. Forni's definition of civility focuses on ideas such as abiding by rules, compassion, consideration, courtesy, decency, honesty, manners, politeness, and tact.[8] Carter's definition focuses on civility as a choice we make on behalf of others—disciplining our passions for the sake of cooperation and limiting our language to create community.[9] Civil communication is the application of civility to our everyday communication encounters and will be the focus of this book. According to Forni, this means communicating with respect, restraint, and responsibility.[10] He believes we do not need to abandon who we are or what we believe in to engage in civil behavior. Instead, Forni says, civil communication involves being "aware of others and weaving restraint, respect, and consideration into the very fabric of this awareness."[11] For example, imagine that you and a classmate are engaged in a debate about politics in which you hold very different viewpoints. Civil communication does not call for you to give up your beliefs or remain silent in response to your conversation partner's comments. Instead, civil communication allows you to speak your mind in a way that is respectful (e.g., you listen well and acknowledge your partner's points), demonstrates restraint (e.g., you refrain from name-calling and insults), and is responsible (e.g., you remember that your comments have the potential to affect your community—in this case, your debate partner and classmates). Carter further describes civil communication as:[12]

- Reflecting the realization that we don't have to like others to act in a civil manner
- Illustrating good manners, politeness, and courtesy
- Doing good rather than harm
- Disagreeing respectfully and listening to others knowing that they may be right and we may be wrong
- Forgoing the urge to say anything that comes to mind; instead, thinking carefully about how our comments will affect others

civility The choice we make to consider others' thoughts and feelings in our communication and general behavior.

We combine elements of both Forni's and Carter's definitions in our definition of civility and civil communication. While **civility** reflects a choice we make to consider

Americans frequently experience uncivil behavior while driving or shopping.

civil communication The choice we make to communicate on the basis of respect, restraint, and responsibility.

others' thoughts and feelings in our communication and general behavior, **civil communication** refers to the choice we make to communicate on the basis of respect, restraint, and responsibility.

Criticism of Civil Communication While civil communication fosters cooperation and community-building, sometimes disadvantaged groups perceive that they are not being heard. As a result, some scholars have concerns about the unintended consequences of civil communication. For example, expecting civil communication from others may be perceived as a way for those in power to maintain social order, preserve discriminatory actions, and leave unspoken important comments that may disturb pleasant social interaction. Similarly, powerful groups tend to be the ones who define what is considered civil communication.[13]

The issue of civility being used as a tool by the powerful arose recently at Queens University in Ontario, Canada. Students of one professor there filed a complaint against the "civility clause" in her syllabus, which links grade penalties to perceived breaches of civility.[14] Her definition encompasses a wide range of behaviors, including "inappropriate behavior and language." One spokesperson for the university was concerned that the policy didn't really distinguish between annoying behavior and offensive behavior. Would it be disruptive for a student to question the validity of a test item? Would it be offensive for a student to disagree with a point the professor made? Would the professor be permitted to be inappropriate without some kind of sanction? Critics of the policy argue that it violates academic freedom.

A goal for civil communication is for people with conflicting viewpoints to live peacefully and enable different groups to get along.[15] However, there are times when incivility may be warranted. For example, in the United States for much of the twentieth century, it was considered acceptable for those in power (typically white males) to refer to adult African-American males as *boys*. At the time, some white males would have considered it uncivil (and worse) for an adult African-American male to assert that he did not want to be addressed in this way. During the civil rights era of the 1960s, after civil communication failed to work, minority groups used civil disobedience *and* violent (uncivil) protest to change the status quo. Violent protest may have been avoided if all parties had instead engaged in civil communication and respectful dialogue, which bind people together and improve conditions in society. In other words, civil communication can "be a way of interacting that turns individual interest into group interest, enabling people to move across barriers of difference into common cause."[16]

Some criticize civil communication as merely "good manners" and believe that this type of communication is superficial and trivial. Civility as "good manners" is said to gloss over symptoms of deeper problems, such as inequality and injustice. However, using good manners is a way to communicate that we care about a conversation partner and how she or he may perceive us. Good manners are not merely superficial because they "do the everyday busywork of goodness."[17] Similarly, there may be a connection between subtle forms of disrespect (i.e., bad manners) and costs to humanity. For example, people who are denied the respect associated with good manners may begin to feel dehumanized and degraded, and the rejection of

TRENDS IN TECHNOLOGY AND SOCIAL MEDIA

Civility Initiatives

In response to the call for a more civil society, several groups have used the Internet to launch and/or sustain projects to build networks of civil communication. The Anti-Defamation League (ADL) is an organization that calls for more respect and civility in national discourse; it has promoted thoughtful and reasoned debate about contentious issues such as health care and immigration. ADL delegates have asked elected officials, candidates for office, civic leaders, and media personalities to sign a statement on civility in national public discourse, which you can find by searching for "ADL Statement on Civility in National Public Discourse." You can also follow the ADL on Facebook.

The Workplace Bullying Institute (WBI), founded in 1997 by Drs. Gary and Ruth Namie, is dedicated to the elimination of on-the-job bullying. Workplace bullying includes behaviors such as abusive conduct, repeated mistreatment, verbal abuse, and threatening conduct. The WBI supports research about workplace bullying, promotes anti-bullying legislation, and designs and delivers training programs. The WBI also provides bullied targets with coaching from licensed mental health professionals. You can find additional information about the WBI by searching for its website. You can also follow the WBI on Facebook and Twitter.

Ron Barber, Congressman Gabrielle Giffords's district director, created the Fund for Civility, Respect, and Understanding, which is sponsored by the Community Foundation for Southern Arizona. The purpose of the fund is to maintain and build on the compassion and good will that resulted from the January 8, 2011, shootings of Giffords and others in Tucson, Arizona. The fund supports nonprofit organizations and programs that encourage respect for differing points of view, promote the understanding of differences, endorse civil discourse about public policy issues, and create anti-bullying campaigns. You can learn more about the Fund for Civility, Respect, and Understanding by searching for its website.

Civil communication can foster cooperation and community building.

In February 2011, the University of Arizona established an institute to promote civility in public discourse, civic engagement and leadership, and politics. The honorary chairpersons of the National Institute for Civil Discourse (NICD) include former Presidents Bill Clinton and George H. W. Bush. One of the first goals of the NICD is to characterize best practices and corrosive practices in national discourse in order to nurture constructive debate that promotes democracy. The NICD is developing educational programs and encouraging research that supports the expression of First Amendment freedoms in a manner that respects the ideas of others and those who expound such ideas. For more information about the NICD, search for its website.

Discussion Questions

1. Are you aware of other civility initiatives?
2. What would you add to the list?
3. Do you think civility initiatives will make a difference in the long run?

"superficial" forms of civility may reflect concealed disdain or malevolence that can erupt into outward displays of prejudice and bigotry.[18] We can use good manners to communicate respect for the dignity of others and our belief that a conversation partner is of value.[19]

Ethics and Ethical Communication

Being aware of how our communication affects others when we choose to communicate on the basis of respect, restraint, and responsibility can foster cooperation and smooth interactions. However, civil communication alone does not guarantee that the outcomes of cooperative exchanges will be "right" or "good." Therefore, civil communication should also be ethical. Civil communication and ethical communication are overlapping concepts, both of which are necessary to foster accountability in thinking, decision-making, and communication choices.

deontological ethics Ethics concerning principles, rules, and duties.

consequentialist ethics Ethics that examine the relationship between the ends and the means.

Ethics Many people think of civility in terms of politeness, but politeness alone does not define civility; civility also needs to be considered in terms of ethical values. Consider the

---

ASK THE ETHICIST What's Ethical?

Question How do I know what's ethical and what's not?

Answer Generally, people make ethical decisions in two ways: based on important principles or by judging the effects of a situation. Philosophers refer to these as **deontological ethics**, or ethics concerning principles, rules, and duties, and **consequentialist ethics**, or ethics that examine the relationship between the ends and the means. People who adhere steadfastly to deontological ethics argue that a person should do his or her duty whether or not it benefits self or others. Those on the consequentialist ethics side of the fence might say, "The end justifies the means." The fact is that most of us use a combination of the two approaches. We have principles that are important to us but often consider the effects of the situation as we make a decision.

For example, a principle that most people accept is the "golden rule": Do to and for others what you would have done to and for yourself. If you want others to treat you with respect, then you should treat others with respect. If you don't want others to lie to you, then you shouldn't lie to them. On the other hand, even if you think it is wrong to lie, you might hedge when someone asks you an uncomfortable question such as "How do you like my outfit?"

A third approach is to look at a situation and consider what result will create the greatest amount of good for the largest number of people. Few people taking a situational approach really argue that "the ends justifies the means" because what we do in the present has such a significant effect on the outcome. If you lie about yourself in an online dating environment, chances are that whoever you finally meet face-to-face is going to be angry about being misled. Your means (lying) will have gotten you to the ends (meeting someone special) but will not have created a good result. On the other hand, many parents "lie" about the existence of Santa Claus in order to create a better holiday experience for their children. Few people would condemn those parents for the deception.

Is one means better than another? Certainly, philosophers have filled books trying to argue the merits of one kind of ethical decision-making over another, but most of us use several frames of reference when making a decision. You might try asking yourself these questions when trying to decide whether a particular kind of communication act is ethical:

- Would I like everyone to act the same way I am planning to act? Do I want my actions to become a blueprint for what other people should do?
- Who will benefit from the action I am about to take? Will only I benefit? Will someone else be harmed? Most people would say that it is acceptable for only your only benefit, but it is questionable to benefit at the expense of others.
- How would I feel if I were secretly videotaped after I made my decision and it were the top video on YouTube tomorrow?

Is the best answer to all these questions "It depends"? Not really. The best answer lies within you. What are your values? What do you think is good? Despite your best intentions, you'll make some ethical mistakes. It is easy to say what we believe, but it is hard to live it.

example of a World War II concentration camp guard who commits a horrifically unethical act at the same time as he expresses good manners when he asks, "Excuse me, sir; could you please step into the gas chamber?"[20] As you can see from this example, simply acting in a polite manner is not enough; our communication choices must be linked to ethics.[21] **Ethics** is a system of standards that defines what behaviors are "right" or "good"; ethics allow us to evaluate situations and then decide among various behavioral options. Whereas civility focuses more on how we communicate, ethics allow us to make good choices about what we communicate.[22] Michael Josephson, co-director of the Joseph and Edna Josephson Institute of Ethics, mentions six ethical principles to guide our behavior: trustworthiness, responsibility, respect, fairness, caring, and concern for the community.[23] These principles are applicable to a number of different cultures, and they are also integral to civil communication.

ethics A system of standards that defines what behaviors are "right" or "good" and that allows us to evaluate and decide among behavioral options. In terms of civil communication, ethics allow us to make good choices about what and how we communicate.

Ethical Communication
If the best way to determine what is ethical lies within ourselves, then one way we can engage in ethical communication is by considering our answers to the following questions that deal with everyday behavior:[24]

- *Have I demonstrated trustworthiness and responsibility?* For example, if someone tells you a secret, do you disclose the confidential information if the disclosure can bring you personal benefit? Do you cheat on a romantic partner without telling her or him about it? You can also consider whether you have communicated in a responsible manner. Think about the consequences of your actions and realize that your comments and behavior have the potential to affect others (your community). Your community can be your neighborhood, apartment building, family, company, or place of worship. For example, do you consider others' thoughts and feelings when listening to music, using a cell phone, or talking in a public place?

- *Have I treated people with dignity and respect?* Respect refers to showing consideration to people's beliefs, attitudes, values, and rights. We can show respect by listening to others and acknowledging their viewpoints even if we disagree with them. Do you belittle or contradict beliefs, attitudes, and values that differ from your own? Do you call people names or yell needlessly when angered?

- *Have I been fair and just today?* Do you ask your relationship partner to engage in activities such as cleaning the apartment or taking care of the car merely because of her or his sex? Do you communicate to those with less power than yourself (e.g., a little brother or sister) the same way that you communicate to someone with equal power (e.g., a friend)?

- *Have I done more good than harm today by demonstrating that I care about others?* For example, do you make it a point to show that you are concerned about your relationship partner(s)? Do you express appreciation or compliment people close to you, knowing that your expressions of appreciation and compliments have the ability to bolster their self-esteem?

- *Have I made my community stronger because of my actions?* The word *civility* derives from the Latin *civitas*, which means "city." The historical assumption behind civility is that we are to be good citizens.[25] We can practice our citizenship by engaging in the community

One component of ethical communication is fairness.

in a political and moral manner (e.g., by voting and doing volunteer work).[26] For our purposes, concern for the community means that, as with responsibility, we are aware that our communication has the potential to positively or negatively affect others. We therefore choose to engage in ethical communication that is trustworthy, responsible, respectful, fair, and caring.

Each chapter of this book presents and explains civil and ethical communication skills as they relate to intrapersonal communication, interpersonal communication, small group communication, public speaking, and mediated and technology-based communication. In addition, you will strengthen your ability to engage in ethical judgments and decision-making when you answer questions associated with true-life case studies in ethics.

Ethical communication includes the consideration of well-based standards of right and wrong. Read the Case Study in Ethics on the next page, about a T-shirt deemed offensive at the Dollywood theme park, and evaluate whether Dollywood and the person wearing the T-shirt acted in an ethical manner.

The Relationship Between Civil and Ethical Communication

In general, ethics are a critical component of communication because "questions of right or wrong arise whenever people communicate."[27] This is true whether the communication occurs between two people, in small groups, in public speeches, or via media and technology.[28] The relationship between civil and ethical communication is manifested in codes of ethics that specify what type of civil behavior is expected of employees and members of professional organizations. It doesn't matter whether we work for a company that manufactures semiconductors, peanut butter, or clothing; businesses create codes of ethics that govern on-the-job communication and behavior. The same holds true for professionals in fields such as banking, law, medicine, and real estate; "civil communication is part of all such codes."[29]

The inherent interconnection between civil and ethical communication is evidenced in the National Communication Association's (NCA's) "Credo for Ethical Communication." The NCA is the largest nonprofit national organization that promotes communication education and scholarship. The NCA creates publications, sponsors conferences and conventions, and provides resources and services to more than 8,000 practitioners, educators, and students who reside in all of 50 U.S. states and in more than 20 other countries.[30]

The NCA principles of ethical communication include the following:[31]

- We advocate truthfulness, accuracy, honesty, and reason as essential to the integrity of communication.
- We endorse freedom of expression, diversity of perspective, and tolerance of dissent to achieve the informed and responsible decision-making fundamental to a civil society.
- We strive to understand and respect other communicators before evaluating and responding to their messages.
- We promote access to communication resources and opportunities as necessary to fulfill human potential and contribute to the well-being of families, communities, and society.
- We promote communication climates of caring and mutual understanding that respect the unique needs and characteristics of individual communicators.

A CASE STUDY IN ETHICS

"Marriage Is So Gay"

Olivier Odom and her partner, Jennifer Tipton, expected a day of family fun when they visited the Dollywood amusement park with friends and their friends' children. Odom didn't expect to be stopped at the theme park entrance because of what was deemed an "offensive" T-shirt. However, an attendant asked Odom to turn her "marriage is so gay" T-shirt inside-out to avoid offending others at the family-oriented theme park. Odom agreed so as not to make a scene in front of the children, but *she* entered the park feeling offended. Odom contends that the situation reflects discrimination against the gay/lesbian/bisexual/transgender (GLBT) community and wondered what specifically was offensive about the shirt—the word *gay*? the word *gay* used in conjunction with the word *marriage*?[32]

Dollywood spokesperson Pete Owens said that while Dollywood is open to families of all shapes and sizes, the park's dress code requires front gate attendants to ask guests to remove clothing or cover up tattoos that may be considered offensive. However, Odom said that she was offended not only by the request to turn her T-shirt inside out but also because the reason for the request was that Dollywood is a family park. Odom countered that there are many different types of families and that she was with her family and her friends' family. In addition, after entering the park, she noticed guests with tattoos and T-shirts that she deemed offensive, such as those sporting the Confederate flag and other political sayings. The Dollywood spokesperson replied that these visitors would have been asked to cover up if another patron had complained. Odom and Tipton have subsequently asked Dollywood to make their policies clear and to train employees about determining what is or isn't offensive. She also wrote a letter to the park in which she requested that Dollywood implement policies that are inclusive of GLBT people, conduct staff sensitivity training, and issue a statement that the park is open to all kinds of families.[33]

Discussion Questions

1 Do you think that Dollywood officials acted in an ethical manner when they asked Odom to turn her T-shirt inside-out and in the subsequent explanation for the request? (That is, did Dollywood act in a manner that is trustworthy, responsible, respectful, fair, just, and caring and that makes the community stronger?)

2 Do you think Odom acted in an ethical manner when she chose to wear the "marriage is so gay" T-shirt to Dollywood and in her request for changes at Dollywood?

3 Do you think that some people would consider a pro-"Defense of Marriage Act" (anti-gay marriage) T-shirt to be offensive? If so, should Dollywood also ban such a shirt?

4 If you believe that offensive communication is present in this incident, whose communication is offensive (Dollywood guest Odom, the front gate attendant, and/or spokesperson Pete Owens, who operated under the guise of enforcing the theme park dress code)?

5 Do you believe it's possible to define what is and what isn't "offensive communication"?

6 Have you ever worn a T-shirt or jewelry or sported a tattoo that others might find offensive? Did you consider the impact your choice might have on others when you decided to wear the shirt, jewelry, or tattoo? How might your future behavior change after reading this case study and considering its implications?

- We condemn communication that degrades individuals and humanity through distortion, intimidation, coercion, and violence, and through the expression of intolerance and hatred.

- We are committed to the courageous expression of personal convictions in pursuit of fairness and justice.
- We advocate sharing information, opinions, and feelings when facing significant choices while also respecting privacy and confidentiality.
- We accept responsibility for the short- and long-term consequences for our own communication and expect the same of others.

The relationship between civil communication and ethical communication is illustrated in Figure 1.1. Civility, civil communication, ethics, and ethical communication involve "choice"; *civility* reflects a choice we make to consider others in our communication, and *civil communication* refers to the choice we make to communicate on the basis of respect, restraint, and responsibility. *Ethics* are standards that allow us to choose among behavioral options, and *ethical communication* allows us to make good choices about what and how we communicate. In addition, just as civil communication is based on respect and responsibility (along with restraint), ethical communication is also based on respect and responsibility (along with trustworthiness, fairness, caring, and concern for the community). In sum, in all types of communication and across all communication contexts, civil and ethical behavior facilitates accountability in thinking and decision-making, as well as in making communication choices.

Let's return to the chapter-opening example of Beyonce Knowles and Taylor Swift at the 2009 MTV Video Music Awards. Knowles engaged in civil communication because she *chose* to acknowledge Swift by inviting her onstage (*respect*), refrained from insulting Kanye West during the presentation (*restraint*), and most likely was aware that her comments about being a young nominee would positively affect Swift, those in attendance at the ceremony, and the viewing audience (*responsibility*). Knowles also engaged in ethical communication because she illustrated *trustworthiness*, *fairness*, *caring*, and *concern for the community* when she invited Swift to return to the stage to finish her acceptance speech. Knowles's communication illustrates that "we can reclaim civility; one act at a time."[34]

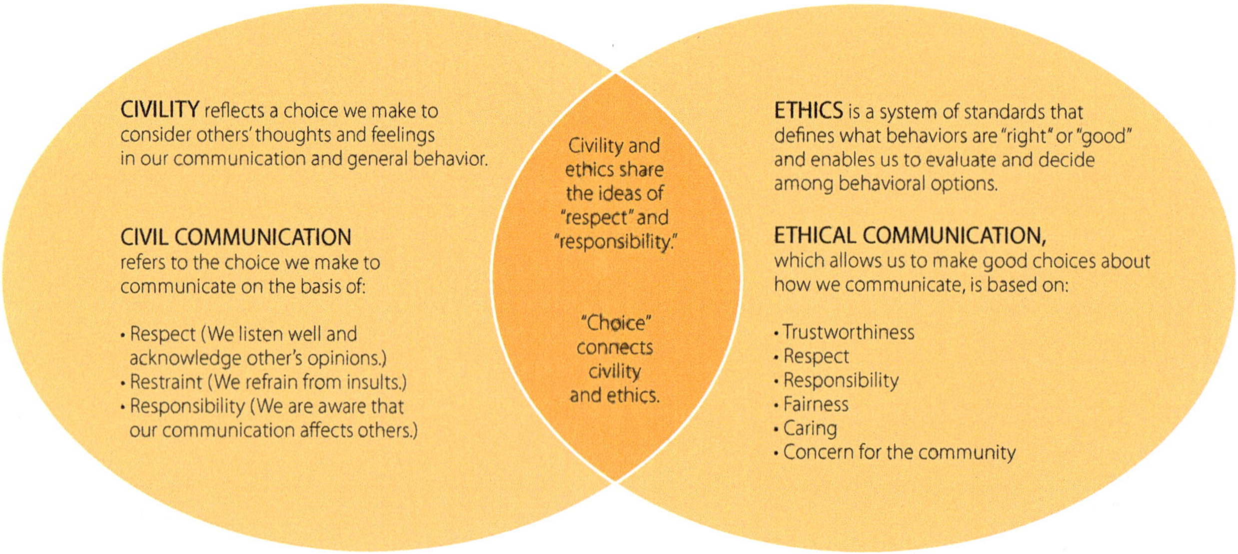

CIVILITY reflects a choice we make to consider others' thoughts and feelings in our communication and general behavior.

CIVIL COMMUNICATION refers to the choice we make to communicate on the basis of:

- Respect (We listen well and acknowledge other's opinions.)
- Restraint (We refrain from insults.)
- Responsibility (We are aware that our communication affects others.)

Civility and ethics share the ideas of "respect" and "responsibility."

"Choice" connects civility and ethics.

ETHICS is a system of standards that defines what behaviors are "right" or "good" and enables us to evaluate and decide among behavioral options.

ETHICAL COMMUNICATION, which allows us to make good choices about how we communicate, is based on:

- Trustworthiness
- Respect
- Responsibility
- Fairness
- Caring
- Concern for the community

FIGURE 1.1 Civil and Ethical Communication
By paying attention to the principles of civility and ethics, we can communicate both civilly and ethically.

DEFINING COMMUNICATION

Now that we understand the relationship between civility and ethics, let's take a step back and look at the definition of *communication*. Communication means different things to different people, but most communication scholars agree that it involves people who create and share meaning. Some of their definitions of communication include the words "**symbols**" (e.g., words that stand for tangible objects or abstract concepts), "nonverbal communication" (messages that often don't depend on the presence of language), "**transaction**" (meaning that verbal and nonverbal communication occur simultaneously among conversation partners), and "**process**" (suggesting that communication is ongoing and continuous). Because communication is so broad and multi-faceted, many of its various definitions highlight only a few specific characteristics and/or functions. Therefore, in this book we broadly define **communication** as "the process of creating and sharing meaning." However, we need to remember that this is just one of many possible definitions of communication.

Suppose a college friend asks you for an in-depth description and explanation of communication. One way to comprehend this complex phenomenon is to think of it in terms of a jigsaw puzzle. When we first attempt to assemble the puzzle pieces, they appear unrelated and disjointed. After some time and effort, we begin to see connections between the pieces, and they fit together to create an overall picture. As illustrated in Figure 1.2, our study of communication is similar to putting together a jigsaw puzzle. At first, the various "pieces" of the puzzle (i.e., the types, contexts, models, and principles of communication) appear unrelated and disjointed. In the remainder of this chapter, we will look at connections between the pieces and will get an overall picture of what the communication process is all about. The overall picture will provide a thorough description and explanation of communication.

symbols Words that stand for tangible objects or abstract concepts.

transaction The simultaneous communication between individuals who participate in face-to-face conversation and listen as a conversation unfolds.

process Communication that is ongoing and continuous.

communication The process of creating and sharing meaning.

intrapersonal communication Communication that takes place within us. Internal dialog and self-talk are examples of this form of communication.

self-talk Communication within us that is specifically about ourselves. Positive self-talk offers encouragement, support, reassurance, and sometimes a pat on the back. Negative self-talk is critical, evaluative, and devaluing.

TYPES OF COMMUNICATION

One way to make the study of communication manageable and understandable is to categorize the situations in which it takes place. We'll therefore look now at the first puzzle piece, types of communication, which encompasses intrapersonal, interpersonal, small group, public, and mediated (or technology-based) communication.

FIGURE 1.2 Communication as a Jigsaw Puzzle
The connections between the puzzle pieces become clear as we begin to understand the various elements of communication.

Intrapersonal Communication

Intrapersonal communication is communication that takes place within us. Our self-talk and internal dialog are examples of this form of communication.

Self-Talk One kind of intrapersonal communication is **self-talk**, or communication within us that is specifically about ourselves. Positive self-talk offers encouragement, support, reassurance, and sometimes a pat on the back. As a student, you've probably used positive self-talk when you've performed well on a test, written a thoughtful essay, or solved a difficult problem. Examples of positive self-talk are "I didn't do as well as I would have liked on that test, but I know what the instructor wants," "I'll do better next time," and "I did great on that essay, and I knew I could solve that problem. I'm so relieved!" On the other hand, negative self-talk is critical, evaluative, and devaluing. This form of self-talk tends to occur when we end a relationship, fail to master a skill, or feel we are unworthy of friendship or love. Some examples of negative self-talk are "I knew I'd be dumped; no one wants to spend time with me," "I'm so stupid I'll never find a boyfriend/girlfriend," and "There must be something wrong with me." Negative self-talk can be extremely destructive, and we will learn that it can affect our self-concept and our relationships.

Internal Dialogue A second kind of intrapersonal communication occurs when we think about a conversation we might have with another person. Suppose you are searching for your new friend's house and feel frustrated because you are lost. As you search, you are likely to have a conversation like this with yourself: "She told me to go to the third house. I'll never find this place. I'm going to tell her how bad her directions are. She's probably going to tell me I can't follow them." This kind of intrapersonal communication is called **internal dialogue**. It's a natural and normal form of intrapersonal communication that helps us solve problems and work out our feelings.

Intrapersonal communication allows us to consider the association between civility and communication as we plan and prepare to interact with others. We can use internal dialog to think about how our comments may affect others, and we can phrase our messages to illustrate respect.[35]

Interpersonal Communication

Whereas intrapersonal communication is communication within us, **interpersonal communication** involves at least two people who establish a communicative relationship. Interpersonal communication involves partners who have the power to simultaneously affect each other through their behavior, either positively or negatively. For example, you might communicate interpersonally with a salesperson at a local department store, an instructor at your college, a business associate, a casual friend, or a family member. Through interpersonal communication, our needs can be met, we can meet the needs of others, and, if appropriate, we can build on our communication interactions to establish healthy relationships.

As illustrated in Figure 1.3, interpersonal communication can be further characterized along a continuum from impersonal to personal, depending on how we perceive our conversation partners. As you read about the following types of communication, think about your typical interactions and where you might place them on the impersonal communication–personal communication continuum shown in Figure 1.3.

Impersonal Communication At one end of the continuum shown in Figure 1.3 is impersonal communication. When we communicate with others as if they are objects or roles and when we communicate in stereotypic ways, we engage in **impersonal communication**. For example, suppose you decide to go to a restaurant one evening. At the beginning of the meal, you interact with the server for the sole purpose of meeting

---

internal dialogue A natural and normal form of intrapersonal communication that helps us solve problems and work out our feelings.

interpersonal communication Communication between at least two people who establish a communicative relationship. Interpersonal communication involves partners who have the power to simultaneously affect each other through their behavior, either positively or negatively.

impersonal communication Communication with others as if they are objects or roles.

FIGURE 1.3 Impersonal Communication–Personal Communication Continuum

The nature of our relationships with others determines where each relationship falls on this continuum.

IMPERSONAL COMMUNICATION	PERSONAL COMMUNICATION
Communication based on a person's role	Communication based on a person's uniqueness

your immediate needs—obtaining the food you desire. The server introduces himself, asks how you're doing, and attempts to interact with you through small talk. You answer with a curt "fine" and turn away, only acknowledging the server when he returns with your meal. This behavior meets the criteria for impersonal communication. In this situation, you are treating this person as a role (i.e., a server) rather than as a unique individual with distinct characteristics.

You have also probably been the recipient of impersonal communication. Suppose you receive a sales call at home. The salesperson calls you by your first name, which suggests that you may have a personal relationship, and then begins the sales pitch. You respond by saying that you're not interested in the product. However, the salesperson is trained to override your objections and continues to talk, even though you have expressed a desire to end the conversation. You might find yourself feeling uncomfortable at first and then angry because you believe that you are being treated as an object, or a means to an end.

Obviously, we cannot engage in personal communication with everyone we meet, either face-to-face, via the phone, or on a computer. We can, however, be civil, which means treating others with respect whether they are personally known to us. Disrespecting a person's individuality and uniqueness has the potential to foster ineffective communication interactions.

personal communication
Communication that occurs when we interact with others on the basis of their uniqueness.

Personal Communication At the other end of the continuum shown in Figure 1.3 is personal communication. **Personal communication** occurs when we interact with others on the basis of their uniqueness. At the extreme end of the impersonal–personal communication continuum, personal communication in an intimate relationship entails a high degree of self-disclosure. However, personal communication can also occur among friends and acquaintances. For example, suppose your best friend asks, "What's up?" You respond that you feel stupid because you yelled at a family member. Your friend says, "Come on, I know how smart you are. You usually communicate well, and I know you'll be able to explain why you yelled." This exchange can be characterized as personal communication because of your self-disclosure (saying that you feel stupid and that you yelled at a family member) and your best friend's acknowledgment of your unique characteristics (being smart; usually a good communicator; being able to explain yourself).

Would it be appropriate to communicate about our feelings at a restaurant to a server who asks, "How are you doing today?" Of course not. But it would be appropriate to move from a highly impersonal response such as "Fine. I'm ready to order now" to a more personal response like "I've had better days. How about you?" We need not be completely impersonal or completely personal in our communication interactions; we can choose to communicate at a midpoint on the impersonal–personal communication continuum. In addition, not only is it important to communicate in a civil manner with strangers and acquaintances, it is also important to communicate civilly in our intimate relationships.[36] The role of civil communication in our relationships will be discussed in Chapter 6, "Interpersonal Relationships and Civil Communication," and Chapter 7, "Intimate Relationships, Romantic Relationships, and Civil Communication."

We need not be completely impersonal or completely personal in our communication interactions.

Small Group Communication

small group communication Communication that occurs when a small number of people (sometimes characterized as 5 to 7 people or 3 to 12 people) share a common purpose and interact for a reason.

Small group communication occurs when a small number of people share a common purpose and interact for a reason. Some researchers characterize a small group as 5 to 7 people; others characterize a small group as 3 to 12 people. A small group may interact for a number of reasons, such as to solve a problem, share information, complete a task, or make a decision. Think about some of the occasions when you've been involved in small group communication. Perhaps you and members of your family once got together for the specific purpose of planning an event such as a family reunion or vacation. You also have most likely engaged in small group communication when working on group projects in some of your college or university classes. Maybe you are a member of a team in your place of employment and you attend regularly scheduled meetings to solve workplace problems. Small group communication has been described as being more complex than interpersonal communication because the dynamics of interaction change as the number of people involved increases. You will learn about complexity of small group communication when you read about types of small groups, group roles and climate, effective group problem-solving, group conflict, and leadership in Chapters 8, "Civil Communication in Conflicts," and 9, "Civil Communication in Groups." For now, understand that "civil communication skills can help to ease and smooth the interaction that takes place among members in groups and contribute to the success and the effectiveness of a group."[37]

Public Communication

public communication Communication that occurs when a speaker delivers a message to an audience.

Public communication occurs when a speaker delivers a message to an audience. Many people fear public speaking and try to avoid it at all costs. However, speaking in front of an audience, whether large or small, is an activity most people must participate in at some point. You've probably given presentations in your classes or perhaps in a religious setting. You may be asked to give a toast at a wedding, nominate a club member for an elected office, or present information and/or persuade others in your future occupation. In Chapters 11, "Preparing Civil Public Speeches," through 14, "Giving Persuasive Speeches with Civility," you will learn that civil communication with an audience is crucial for a successful public presentation.

Mediated and Technology-Based Communication

mediated and technology-based communication Communication that is transmitted by some kind of technology, such as television, radio, mobile devices, or the Internet.

Mediated and technology-based communication occur when communication is transmitted by some kind of technology, such as television, radio, mobile devices, or the Internet. Recent statistics reveal that approximately 93 percent of young U.S. Americans (ages 12 to 17) use the Internet, and 79 percent of all adults (18 and older) go online.[38] Six in 10 Americans (59 percent) go online wirelessly using a cell phone or laptop; 72 percent of adult cell phone users send and receive text messages, as do 87 percent of teens.[39] While young adults between the ages of 18 and 29 are the heaviest users of social media (83 percent), two-thirds of adult Internet users (65 percent) use social networking sites.[40] In September

"Public communication" and "mediated and technology-based communication" overlap when using websites as visual aids while delivering a speech.

TRENDS IN
TECHNOLOGY AND SOCIAL MEDIA

How Do New Media Affect Us?

The dramatic increase in the use of the Internet, social networking sites, and mobile technology has been hailed as a way for us to connect with more people and create stronger relationships. At the same time, new media have been criticized for creating communication that is increasingly shallow and for threatening personal relationships. Both viewpoints underscore the idea that new media are somehow changing our social connections.[41]

Many studies about the effect of new media ask what new media do to us and whether the results are good or bad. Interestingly, research results are mixed and/or inconclusive. For example, while earlier studies of social interaction and the Internet suggested that time online caused people to feel lonely, recent studies dispute that conclusion.[42] One study of high school students found that the amount of time communicating online and the total time spent online failed to correlate with increased loneliness.[43] The same result was also found in a study of university students. In fact, research illustrates that loneliness is diminished when older adults use social networking cites to support existing friendships.[44] While more time browsing and communicating online may be correlated with more loneliness, we can't conclude that time online *causes* loneliness. It may be that increased loneliness may actually encourage people to spend more time online.[45]

Do new media allow us to avoid opinions and beliefs contrary to our own? New media allow us to personalize the news so we can see only the stories that interest us and visit websites that confirm our prejudices.[46] However, research reveals that most Internet users spend their time on large integrated sites, such as Yahoo! News, which is accessed by a varied audience. When users leave integrated websites, they actually visit sites read by users who are not like themselves (e.g., people who spend time on liberal sites are also likely to visit foxnews.com). Of course, viewing a particular website says nothing about how we evaluate and use the information presented to us, but those on the Internet typically seek out opposing information and don't stay within their communities.[47] This research suggests that if there is increased polarization, it is not caused by the Internet.

Throughout history, new forms of media have been disruptive and have led to social reflection. "When they are new, technologies affect how we see the world, our communities, our relationships, and ourselves."[48] In truth, new media are tools that people can use to connect with others—tools that cannot be understood without taking into consideration who we are and our personal, social, cultural and historical background. We typically come to new media with our identity and worldviews in place, and we replicate and enact them via technology.[49] Therefore, to ask questions regarding how new media affect us and our relationships misses the point. This is because we bring who we are and our relationships to new media. "Digital media aren't saving us or ruining us. They aren't reinventing us. But they are changing the ways we relate to others and ourselves in countless, pervasive ways."[50]

Discussion Questions

1 Do you use new media? If so, has your use changed the nature of your social connections?

2 In terms of your friends' use of social media, do you see a connection between social media use and loneliness and news isolation? If so, do you perceive that those friends are lonely offline? Do those friends tend to read newspapers and magazines that reinforce their views?

3 Some scholars contend that civility is at least partially based on an agreed-upon set of norms (i.e., guidelines for appropriate behavior) and that norms are currently changing because of the rapid growth of new media.[51] Could the perceived decline in civility be due to confusion about changing norms rather than any faults associated with individual personalities or generations?

2012, Facebook reported that its active users had surpassed 1 billion.[52] In addition, according to statistics gathered in 2012, Twitter has more than 500 million users, although only 170 million of those users are active.[53] The seemingly constant demands of social media can sometimes result in uncivil behavior. Maybe you've had a meal with someone who constantly answered his cell phone, tweeted, or engaged in text messaging.

In addition, the lack of visual context and other clues that help us frame and interpret messages can result in communication that lacks civility. Perhaps you know of someone who has been "flamed" while participating in a chat room discussion or while engaged in a MMORPG or massively multiplayer online role-playing game (e.g., World of Warcraft, Dungeons and Dragons Online) in a virtual reality environment.

While this book devotes specific chapters to intrapersonal, interpersonal, small group, and public communication, information about mediated and technology-related communication is included in all chapters. For example, you will read that perception (i.e., selecting, organizing, and interpreting stimuli from the environment) is considered a form of intrapersonal communication. One study of computer-mediated communication and perception found that readers can accurately perceive personality characteristics of extroversion and introversion from the text of someone's email messages.[54] In terms of interpersonal communication, personal communication on the Internet has been found to be more sociable, personal, and intimate than what is found in face-to-face interaction.[55] Regarding small group communication, research illustrates that group norms and social contexts contribute to levels of flaming. In other words, flaming is not found universally across every newsgroup, bulletin board, and social network; flaming occurs if it is accepted among the social norms of the group in which it happens.[56] In addition, media and technology affect public speaking. For example, speech topics can be easily accessed on library databases and online sites, and we may create, use, and discuss PowerPoint or Prezi slides while presenting a speech. We may also access, display, and talk about websites during a presentation.

Figure 1.4 illustrates that the boundaries that distinguish intrapersonal, interpersonal, small group, public, and mediated and technology-based communication are fluid. This means that it may sometimes be difficult to categorize the type of communication in which we engage. The broken lines that surround the intrapersonal communication circle illustrate that we also engage in mediated communication when we play Solitaire on our computer and intrapersonally communicate about our next move. The intersecting broken lines

Mediated and Technology-Related Communication

Public Communication

Intrapersonal Communication

Interpersonal Communication

Small Group Communication

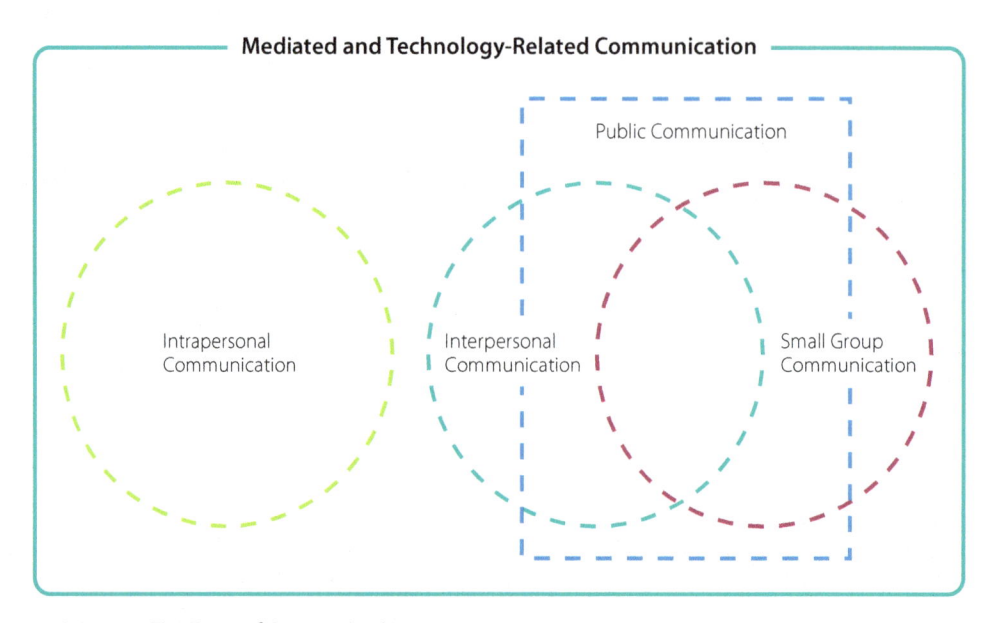

FIGURE 1.4 Five Types of Communication

Because the boundaries that distinguish intrapersonal, interpersonal, small group, public, and mediated and technology-based communication are fluid, it is sometimes difficult to categorize the type of communication in which we engage.

between the interpersonal and small group circles and the broken lines that form the public speaking box that surrounds the circles indicate that it may be difficult to pinpoint when interpersonal communication becomes small group communication, when small group communication becomes public communication, and when interpersonal communication becomes public communication. For example, does interpersonal communication become small group communication when a third person joins what was originally a two-person conversation? Does small group communication become public communication when an employee stands up in a meeting and addresses his or her coworkers without interruption? Does interpersonal communication become public communication when someone shouts loudly enough to be heard by others when talking on a cell phone in a public area? The boundaries between interpersonal communication and mediated communication are also blurred when we gather to talk about a television show in an online space. The people gathered are considered a mass communication audience, and their communication is mediated because it is available for anyone to read. However, the communication these people have with one another is also interpersonal.[57] Rod L. Troester and Cathy Sargent Mester, directors of the Janet Neff Sample Center for Manners and Civility at Penn State University, assert that "civility can and should play a crucial role in shaping the message-related behavior that takes place," regardless of the type of communication in which we engage.[58]

MODELS OF COMMUNICATION

Types of communication comprise the first piece in the communication jigsaw puzzle; the second piece of the jigsaw puzzle concerns models of communication. These first two jigsaw puzzle pieces fit with the other puzzle pieces to create an overall picture of human communication.

communication models
Pictures of the structure and key components of communication. Models define and isolate specific elements in the communication process and show their relationship to each other and to the communication process itself.

Communication models are diagrams of the structure and key components of communication. They define and isolate specific elements in the communication process and show their relationship to each other and to the communication process itself. Specifically, communication models are useful because they enable us to locate the particular components of a communication exchange and determine how their relationship to each other can affect the outcome of a communication episode. Think about how each component can affect others as you read the information about the elements involved in the communication process. Consider as well how the relationships between the components can positively or negatively affect the outcome of a conversation.

Action and Interaction Feedback Models of Communication

Early models of communication that were popular in the mid-1900s pictured communication as a one-way, linear action. These models depicted communication as involving one person who spoke and another person who listened. This type of model is illustrated in Figure 1.5. As indicated by the arrow that points in one direction, in this model, only one person talks to another. The unidirectional arrow makes it clear that the listener does not communicate with the speaker.

While this type of model may be accurate when it illustrates times we yell in frustration at the computer or scream excitedly at a television character, it is not accurate when it depicts communication between two individuals. After all, the computer can't yell at us in return, and the TV character can't react to our excitement. When people communicate with each other, they provide a response, or "feedback," whether that feedback is verbal or nonverbal (e.g., facial expressions, vocal characteristics).

Interaction models, which were popular in the 1960s and 1970s, improve on action-oriented models in that they illustrate the give-and-take nature of communication, as

FIGURE 1.5 An Action Model of Communication

In this one-way model, one person (the sender) communicates a message to another person (the receiver).

evidenced by feedback. This type of model is shown in Figure 1.6.

The two-way character of communication is illustrated by the two arrows that point in opposite directions. As in the action model, one person speaks and the other listens in the interaction model. But unlike the action model, the interaction model shows that the person who originally listened now communicates feedback, while the person who originally spoke now listens. An interaction model depicts the turn-taking that occurs when speaker turns to listener and listener turns to speaker.

This type of model may be accurate when it illustrates the turn-taking that occurs when we speak on the telephone, engage in text messaging on our cell, and participate in an instant messaging (IM) conversation with someone on the computer. However, it is not accurate when it depicts individuals who communicate in a face-to-face situation, whether or not they share the same physical space or communicate via Skype software. In face-to-face situations, communicators both speak and listen simultaneously. For example, while you tell your friend about the argument you had with a roommate, you see your friend nodding her or his head up and down and making a "tsk" sound at the same time as you speak. Your friend is communicating with you nonverbally while you are communicating verbally. Similarly, when your friend responds to your comments with verbal feedback, he or she notices that you grimace and listens to your "mmm" sounds while she or he communicates. In face-to-face situations, speakers don't take turns communicating with each other; instead, they communicate simultaneously with verbal and nonverbal communication.

sender A person who conveys thoughts, feelings, or ideas to others.

A Transactional Model of Communication

Recall that our definition of *communication* is "the process of creating and sharing meaning." Transactional models of communication illustrate that conversation partners send and receive messages (i.e., create and share meaning) in a concurrent manner. The idea of "process" is also shown in transactional models in that we can't tell when communication begins and when it ends. You will learn more about process when you read about principles of communication, the fourth and final piece of the communication jigsaw puzzle. For now, the ideas of transaction and process are illustrated in Figure 1.7

The double-headed arrow pictured in Figure 1.7 illustrates that communication occurs simultaneously when people interact face-to-face. Figure 1.7 also depicts the particular components that are often included in transaction communication models. In terms of the components of a transactional model of communication, a **sender** is a person who conveys thoughts, feelings, or ideas to others. The process of translating thoughts, feelings, and ideas into symbols

FIGURE 1.6 An Interaction Model of Communication

In this two-way model, the individuals take turns functioning as the sender and the receiver of the message.

Models of Communication 19

encoding The process of translating thoughts, feelings, and ideas into symbols (words and nonverbal cues).

receiver A person who receives a message conveyed by a sender. The receiver is responsible for interpreting or assigning meaning to the message and for responding to the sender.

decoding The mental process of interpreting a message.

message The information (e.g., thoughts, feelings, ideas) a sender wishes to convey to a receiver. Both verbal (words) and nonverbal (e.g., body language, vocal behavior) communication are used to convey meaning.

feedback The response to a sender's message, which can be verbal, nonverbal, or both. It is through feedback that the sender learns whether her or his message has been received as intended.

channel The pathway used to convey a message between a sender and a receiver.

noise Any force that can interfere with the communication process in any communication context or situation.

context The environment surrounding communication, including the physical environment, interpretation of a particular situation (e.g., the formality or informality of an occasion), frame of reference (e.g., culture, gender, expectations, past history, beliefs, attitudes, values), and significant others. It's easiest to communicate with others when our contexts overlap.

FIGURE 1.7 A Transactional Model of Communication
In this model of communication, the double-headed arrow illustrates that communication occurs simultaneously when interacting face-to-face.

(words and nonverbal cues) is called **encoding**. This is a mental process generated by the sender to convey meaning to the receiver of the communication.

A **receiver** is a person who receives the message conveyed by a sender. The receiver is responsible for interpreting or assigning meaning to the message and for responding to the sender. The mental process of interpreting the message is called **decoding**.

The **message** contains the information (e.g., thoughts, feelings, ideas) the sender wishes to convey to the receiver. We use both verbal (words) and nonverbal (e.g., body language, vocal behavior) communication to convey meaning.

A response to a sender's message is called **feedback**. Feedback can be verbal, nonverbal, or both. It is through feedback that the sender learns whether her or his message has been received as intended.

A **channel** is a pathway used to convey the message between a sender and a receiver. Usually our five senses assist us in the transfer and interpretation of a message. However, technology such as telephones, intercoms, IM on personal computers, and text messaging on cell phones also provide channels to convey messages.

Noise is any force that can interfere with the communication process in any communication context or situation. Noise can occur anytime during an interaction and can be external or internal. Distractions such as loud voices at another table in a restaurant, a jet plane flying overhead, or a student arriving late to class are examples of external noise. Internal noise can be physiological or psychological. Physiological factors include illness, fatigue, pain, and hunger. Psychological factors are mental or emotional distractions such as daydreaming about upcoming weekend events, feeling bored by the speaker's message, and feeling annoyed while replaying an argument in your mind.

The **context** in which communication takes place is another factor that can affect how you communicate and how others communicate with you; it refers to the environment surrounding the communication. The context can be as simple as the physical environment—the noise level, aesthetics, familiarity, and so on—in which the communication takes place. The context also goes beyond the physical environment to include many other factors that can affect the communication, such as interpretations of a particular situation (e.g., the formality or informality of an occasion), frame of reference (e.g., culture, our gender, expectations, past history, beliefs, attitudes), and significant others. It's easiest to communicate with people when our contexts overlap, and interaction becomes increasingly difficult as our contexts diverge. This occurs because contexts may provide us with assumptions and standards for effective and appropriate communication that differ from those of our conversation partner(s). Contexts also significantly influence the transactional nature of communication—that is, how you simultaneously communicate and interpret communication from others.

We will examine three contexts throughout this book because they influence and/or are influenced by communication in significant ways: the culture context, the workplace context, and the gender context. On a daily basis, you may communicate with people who differ from you based on country of origin and/or race and ethnicity. Similarly, you may have a full- or part-time job that influences how you communicate with coworkers and how coworkers communicate with you. You also probably spend some time communicating with members of the opposite gender. These contexts will be presented throughout this book in terms of why it is important to understand how they affect specific types of communication (i.e., intrapersonal, interpersonal, small group, public, and mediated/technology-based communication) and why knowing this information is important in your everyday life. In this chapter we explain contexts in general as part of the communication jigsaw puzzle.

culture The shared assumptions, values, and beliefs of a group of people, which result in characteristic behaviors.

Some politicians criticized President Barack Obama for bowing deeply to Japanese Emperor Akihito during a State visit. However, the State Department described the nonverbal behavior as "respectful" rather than "inappropriate" and "deferential."

CONTEXTS OF COMMUNICATION

The third piece of the communication jigsaw puzzle is communication contexts. At this point, you may still be thinking that the jigsaw puzzle pieces are more unrelated and disjointed than they are related. However, soon you will begin to see connections between the pieces and will get a general idea of what the communication process is all about.

The Culture Context

Culture refers to the "shared assumptions, values, and beliefs of a group of people which result in characteristic behaviors."[59] Although the concept of civility is cross-cultural, what is considered civil communication can differ according to the culture in which we find ourselves. Our culture teaches us which verbal and nonverbal behaviors are civil and uncivil and when it is appropriate and inappropriate to communicate verbally and/or display nonverbal behaviors. Because what we are taught may differ cross-culturally, misinterpretations can arise about the civil and ethical use of such behaviors. For example, some politicians criticized President Barack Obama for bowing deeply to Japanese Emperor Akihito during a state visit. Obama's bow was described as inappropriate, overly-deferential, groveling, and a symbol of the weakness of the United States. However, the State Department responded that the bow was within protocol guidelines and that the Protocol Office ensures that presidents respect the traditions and customs of a host country. In other words, the president's bow was a show of respect.[60]

Improving our Ability to Communicate Civilly and Effectively: Principles of Communication

Men typically engage in "agonism," or ritualistic fighting, more frequently than women, whose conversations tend to be more relationship oriented.

workplace incivility On-the-job behaviors that are rude, discourteous, and disrespectful and display a lack of regard for others.

gender The influence of the environment and socially constructed meaning of the similarities and difference between men and women.

agonism A ritualistic form of insult and nonliteral fighting. Agonism occurs among those who enjoy fighting for its own sake and who perceive trading insults as a type of game.

The Workplace Context

In each chapter, we highlight the workplace context in terms of how a particular communication theory, concept, or skill might relate to your (future) career. In regard to civil communication, **workplace incivility**—characterized by on-the-job behaviors that are rude, discourteous, and disrespectful and display a lack of regard for others—is common. In a survey of more than 1,100 respondents, 71% experienced uncivil behaviors at work during a five-year period.[61] Examples of workplace incivility include interrupting a conversation, talking loudly in a common area, not introducing a newcomer, failing to return a phone call, and showing little interest in someone's opinion.[62] However, workplace incivility can be diminished if managers become aware of the nature and costs of uncivil behavior and encourage open discussion about it. When workers become aware of on-the-job incivility and realize that they will be held accountable for uncivil communication, they may be better able to monitor their behavior and prevent themselves from demonstrating uncivil behavior.[63]

The Gender Context

Although many people use the terms interchangeably, *gender* and *sex* are not the same thing. Whereas *sex* is based on anatomy, endocrinology, and neurology, **gender** refers to the influence of the environment and socially constructed meaning and is the context we are referring to here. The perception of and participation in uncivil communication often depend on our gender. Some people participate in a ritualistic form of insult and nonliteral fighting called **agonism**. Agonism occurs among those who enjoy fighting for its own sake and who perceive trading insults as a type of game. Agonistic exchanges occur when communicators try to top each other with clever insults in a war or words. Although it's not unheard of for women to participate in such rituals, typically men engage in agonism more than women. In addition, the topics associated with agonistic exchanges are different for men and women. While men may boast of their sexual prowess and insult the prowess of other men, women may engage in ritual laments and display their creativity and skill in making up verses.[64]

IMPROVING OUR ABILITY TO COMMUNICATE CIVILLY AND EFFECTIVELY: PRINCIPLES OF COMMUNICATION

Read the following statements and consider whether they are true or false:

- The statement "Disregard what I've just said" will cause us to ignore or forget an utterance.
- It is easy to pinpoint when communication begins and ends.
- One cannot *not* communicate.

These statements correspond to the fourth piece of the communication jigsaw puzzle: principles of communication. Communication is irreversible, communication is an ongoing process, and communication is inevitable are principles that can increase our knowledge of communication and help us improve our ability to communicate effectively. As you read about the three principles, you will be able to determine whether the previous statements are true or false.

Communication Is Irreversible

"I'm sorry; please forget that I ever said it!" How often have you or someone you know uttered a similar plea? No matter how sincerely we apologize for our uncivil behavior, our communication may be forgiven, but it will not likely be forgotten. This is because communication is irreversible; we can't "take it back" once a listener has interpreted something we've said. This principle is particularly applicable to computer mediated communication (CMC). It's impossible to take back our thoughts and feelings when we engage in IM, and email may provide someone with a permanent message that we wish we had never sent. The principle of irreversibility underscores the importance of the civil component of restraint.

Communication Is an Ongoing Process

Communication is an ongoing process; it is not static. Although communication occurs in distinct episodes with various individuals, it is difficult or even impossible to determine when communication begins and when it ends. We may think communication begins when we initiate interaction by speaking to a conversation partner. However, although we can determine when a verbal interaction begins and ends, communication is more than verbal interaction. It can be argued that communication begins in the intrapersonal domain—with a thought or a feeling. In addition, it can be said that a communication episode begins on the basis of a previous interaction. For example, have you ever become angry at someone and taken it out on someone else? Suppose you have an argument with a coworker in the morning, and you replay the argument in your mind while driving home in the late afternoon. Preoccupied, you don't respond to your partner's question, "How was your day?" when you arrive at your home. Annoyed, your partner sarcastically asks, "What's the matter with you?" You respond with an angry, "Give me a break!" Even though you're mad at your coworker for the morning's argument, you direct your anger at your partner. When did this communication episode with your partner begin? Did it begin when you responded with silence to her or his "How was your day?" Did it begin with the intrapersonal communication in the car? Did it begin with the argument with your coworker? Or did it begin with your thoughts prior to the argument? Clearly, this example illustrates that communication is ongoing and process oriented. It also demonstrates the importance of responsibility in our communication, choosing the appropriate time and place to say what is on our minds.

Communication Is Inevitable

All communication has the potential to convey meaning to someone else. Actually, we cannot *not* communicate. Even when we think we are not communicating, we are. As human beings, we are constantly perceiving and interpreting other people's behavior. Whether we are frowning or laughing, speaking or being silent, expressing joy or anger, we are communicating. Take a moment and think about a time when you were riding in a car with a friend. Perhaps your friend talked for several miles and then stopped talking. After a few moments, you may have begun to feel uncomfortable because you were not sure why she or he stopped talking. You may have turned to your friend and asked, "What's wrong?" Surprised, your friend may have answered, "Nothing." She or he may have merely been paying attention to the road, but you interpreted the silence to mean something else. This is an example of how a person's silence can convey meaning even though it's not intended to communicate. On the

We communicate even when we don't say a word.

other hand, if no one notices what we are doing, we haven't communicated anything. Communication is inevitable, and it is important for us to respect those around us and pay attention to the way our nonverbal behavior may be interpreted.

Understanding the Principles of Communication

The three principles of communication can help you improve your ability to communicate civilly and effectively. Knowing that communication is irreversible may influence you to civilly refrain from uttering a hurtful comment to a relationship partner because a subsequent apology will not "erase" the utterance. Understanding that communication is an ongoing process may influence you to communicate respectfully to an angry customer because you know that she or he may be upset about a conversation that occurred earlier in the day rather than at something you just said. Knowing that communication is inevitable, even when we're not speaking directly to others, can help us pay attention to the way our behavior may be interpreted. For example, we may illustrate responsible behavior by lowering our voice when using a cell phone in a public place so as not to disturb passersby.

You are now familiar with the various pieces of the communication jigsaw puzzle. While at first the jigsaw puzzle pieces appeared unrelated and disjointed, you can now see that they provide an overall picture of what constitutes communication:

- Types of communication (i.e., intrapersonal, interpersonal, small group, public, and mediated and technology-related)
- Action, interaction, and transaction communication models and their components, such as a sender who encodes a message that travels via a channel and is decoded by a receiver who provides feedback
- Contexts that influence and/or can be influenced by communication, such as those associated with culture, the workplace, and gender
- Communication principles, which explain that communication is irreversible, an ongoing process, and inevitable

TECH CHECK

Assessing Your Self-Perceived Communication Competence

The Self-Perceived Communication Competence (SPCC) scale is designed to help obtain information concerning how competent you believe you are in a variety of communication contexts and with a variety of types of receivers. Higher SPCC scores indicate higher self-perceived communication competence with basic communication contexts (e.g., interpersonal, small group, public) and receivers (e.g., strangers, acquaintances, friends).

Once you have obtained your scores, consider what you can do to improve them. Might you give yourself higher scores when you begin to regularly communicate on the basis of civility and ethics? Can you apply the information included in this chapter to your everyday life in an attempt to improve your self-perceived communication competence?

Now that you have completed the communication jigsaw puzzle and can describe and explain what communication is about, you have the foundation to examine the various communication concepts, theories, and skills that are covered in more detail in the remaining chapters.

CHAPTER SUMMARY

Now that you have read this chapter you can:

1.1 Explain how choosing civil communication and relying on ethical principles can help you make good communication-related choices.

Civil communication requires us to be respectful, demonstrates restraint, and illustrates responsibility and is grounded in ethics. Ethics is a system of standards that defines what behaviors are "right" or "good" and that allows us to evaluate and decide among behavioral options. Ethical communication is based on the principles of trustworthiness, respect, responsibility, fairness, caring, and concern for the community. Civility, civil communication, ethics, and ethical communication involve "choice." Civility and ethics are critical for responsible thinking, decision-making, and communication choices. Civil and ethical communication is necessary across all types of communication and across all contexts of communication.

1.2 Define communication.

Communication is the process of creating and sharing meaning

1.3 Differentiate among five types of communication: intrapersonal, interpersonal, small group, public, and mediated/technology based.

Intrapersonal communication is communication that takes place within us. Our internal dialog and self-talk are examples of this form of communication. Interpersonal communication involves at least two people who establish a communicative relationship. Interpersonal communication can be characterized along a continuum from impersonal to personal, depending on how we perceive our conversation partners. Small group communication occurs when a small number of people (sometimes characterized as 5 to 7 people or 3 to 12 people) share a common purpose and interact for a reason. Public communication occurs when a speaker delivers a message to an audience. Mediated and technology-based communication occurs when communication is transmitted by some kind of technology, such as television, radio, mobile devices, or the Internet.

1.4 Compare the ways three models of communication—action, interaction, and transaction – explain the communication process.

Communication models are pictures of the structure and key components of communication. They define and isolate specific elements in the communication process and show their relationship to each other and to the communication process itself. Action models depict communication as a one-way, linear route of communication from speaker to listener. Interaction models show communication as a turn-taking process in which feedback causes the speaker and listener to switch roles. Transactional models of communication illustrate that conversation partners send and receive messages simultaneously, and such models display various components in the communication process. A transactional model of communication includes a sender who encodes, a receiver who decodes, a message, a channel, feedback, noise, and contexts that influence and/or are influenced by the communication process.

1.5 Explain three contexts of communication: culture, workplace, and gender.

It's easiest to communicate with others when our contexts overlap, and interaction becomes increasingly difficult as our contexts diverge because they may provide us with assumptions and standards for effective and appropriate communication that differ from those of our conversation partner(s). The culture context refers to shared assumptions, values, and beliefs that influence communication and behavior. Our culture teaches us which verbal and nonverbal behaviors are civil and uncivil and when it is appropriate and inappropriate to communicate verbally and/or display nonverbal behaviors. Because what we are taught may differ cross-culturally, misinterpretations can arise about the civil and ethical use of such behaviors. The workplace context is often a site for uncivil communication, but such communication can be diminished if managers become aware of the nature and costs of uncivil behavior and encourage open discussion about it. The gender context influences the perception of and participation in uncivil communication, especially as it relates to agonism, a ritualistic form of insult and nonliteral fighting.

1.6 **Apply three principles of communication that can improve your ability to communicate civilly; communication is irreversible; communication is an ongoing process; and communication is inevitable.**

"Communication is irreversible" refers to the idea that we can't take back our messages once they are interpreted by a listener. "Communication is an ongoing process" suggests that communication is not static. "Communication is inevitable" means that all communication has the potential to convey meaning to someone else (i.e., we cannot *not* communicate). Knowing that communication is irreversible may influence you to civilly refrain from uttering a hurtful comment to a relationship partner because a subsequent apology will not "erase" the utterance. Understanding that communication is an ongoing process may influence you to communicate respectfully to an angry customer because you know that she or he may be upset about a conversation that occurred earlier in the day rather than at something you just said. Knowing that communication is inevitable, even when we're not speaking directly to others, can help us pay attention to the way our behavior may be interpreted

CIVILITY SUMMARY

Overall, remember that civility and basic communication characteristics involve the following:

- Intrapersonal communication allows us to consider the association between civility and communication as we plan and prepare to interact with others. We can think about how our comments may affect others, and we can phrase our messages to illustrate respect.
- We cannot engage in personal communication with everyone we meet, either face-to-face, via the phone, or using a computer. We can, however, be civil, which means treating others with respect whether or not we personally know them.
- The seemingly constant demands of social media can sometimes result in uncivil behavior. However, public opinion polls reveal that most Americans believe that social networking sites should be places of civility, and many people leave those sites when they encounter incivility.

REVIEW QUESTIONS

1. Identify the benefits of civil communication.
2. How can we define *civil communication*?
3. How can we characterize ethical communication? How can we improve the possibility of engaging in ethical communication?
4. What is the relationship between civil communication and ethical communication?
5. Define *communication* and categorize the situations in which it takes place (i.e., types of communication).
6. Describe that transaction model of communication and the components that are typically included in such models.
7. Describe three communication contexts and how they are associated with civil and/or uncivil communication.
8. What are three principles of communication? Describe and explain them.

2 Perceiving the Self and Others

CHAPTER OBJECTIVES

After reading this chapter, you will be able to:

2.1 Define *perception* and *self-concept*.
2.2 Describe the relationship among perception, self-concept, and civility.
2.3 Identify the three stages that make up the perception process.
2.4 Explain two theoretical perspectives about perception.
2.5 Describe two characteristics of the self-concept – self-image and self-esteem – and explain the importance of several environmental influences.
2.6 Use the skill of perception-checking to improve your civil communication.

IN JUNE 2010, baseball player Armando Galarraga was about to celebrate the first perfect game in the history of the Detroit Tigers. However, Umpire Jim Joyce called Cleveland's Jason Donald "safe" at first base, which meant Galarraga did not pitch a perfect game. But Joyce admitted freely that his perception of the situation was wrong and that he had made a mistake. "It was the biggest call of my career, and I kicked the @#$%! out of it. I just cost that kid a perfect game."[1] Although upset, Galarraga refrained from using harsh words or condemning Joyce after the call was made. In addition, Joyce personally apologized to Galarraga and hugged him after the game. They shook hands the following day, and a tearful Joyce gave Galarraga a pat on the shoulder. Galarraga commented, "There's no doubt he feels bad and terrible. I have a lot of respect for the man. It takes a lot to say you're sorry and to say in interviews he made a mistake."[2]

In this situation, both Galarraga and Joyce exhibited communication that was civil and ethical. Galarraga and Joyce were civil because they acknowledged each other's thoughts, feelings, and actual communication (*respect*). In fact, Galarraga engaged in **perspective-taking**—that is, imagining oneself in the place of another to understand how she or he perceives the self, others, and the world. Specifically, Galarraga imagined that Joyce felt "terrible" and that it required much effort to apologize during interviews. Galarraga and Joyce also refrained from name-calling and exchanging insults (*restraint*), and they realized that their comments had the potential to affect the community—in particular, other baseball players, umpires, fans, and just about anyone knowledgeable about the incident (*responsibility*). They were ethical because they demonstrated trustworthiness, responsibility, respect, fairness, caring, and concern for the community. Hampton Stevens, a writer for *The Atlantic* and ESPN, wrote that the incident illustrates values that go beyond the dedication needed to play major league baseball and beyond the skills of a team and a pitcher: "The men at the eye of the storm stayed calm, comporting themselves with nothing but dignity and mutual respect."[3]

WHY IT MATTERS

Have you, like Jim Joyce, ever perceived a situation differently than others? Have you ever perceived a helpful comment as criticism in disguise? If so, did you respond to the person who made the comment in an angry and defensive manner? Could Armando Garralaga's perception of himself have influenced him to engage in civil communication? Do you believe that *your* self-concept influences your communication and behavior?

The study of perception and communication deserves merit because we often communicate with people who hold different perceptions than we do. Although we all tend to perceive the same things differently, we assume that our perceptions are true reflections of reality, and we communicate on the basis of this assumption. This creates the potential for situations in which we may argue about the "correct" version of reality. Civil conversation partners realize that while their own perspectives may be accurate, they can see the validity in the perspectives of others. Knowing that our perceptions may not correspond to the perceptions of others can help us improve our relationships and enhance our ability to communicate in a civil and ethical manner.

In addition, understanding the relationship between the self-concept and communication can motivate us to communicate in a civil manner. For example, suppose you must frequently interact with someone you consider a braggart. If you engage in perspective-taking, you might see that the braggart is using boasting to overcome feelings of low self-esteem. You can exhibit restraint by refraining from rolling your eyes and/or uttering a sarcastic comment about the braggart that is just loud enough for him to hear. You might be motivated to communicate with respect, restraint, and responsibility if you realize that the braggart may be trying to contend with a poor self-concept rather than merely impress others.

In this chapter, you'll learn about perception and the self-concept. You will learn about the relationship among perception, self-concept, civility, and ethics. In addition, you will read about the stages in the perception process and theoretical perspectives about perception. You will learn about the characteristics of the self-concept and how to communicate civilly about your perceptions.

perspective-taking
Imagining oneself in the place of another to understand how she or he perceives the self, others, and the world.

DEFINITION OF PERCEPTION AND SELF-CONCEPT

No matter how we perceive ourselves or how others perceive us, our self-concept is inextricably entwined with perception. The way we perceive ourselves, how we perceive others, and how we perceive the stimuli around us influence how we communicate and interpret others' communication. In turn, perceptions help create one's self-concept, as beliefs about oneself are confirmed or disconfirmed in interactions with others.

What Is Perception?

Have you ever misjudged the distance between you and another person or something that is inanimate—and therefore accidentally bumped into the person or walked into something? Have you ever thought that someone "looked" unintelligent but revised your opinion after speaking with her or him? These questions relate to perception. **Perception** occurs when sense data—or what we see, hear, smell, taste, and/or touch—is transmitted to the brain. The brain almost instantly transforms the sensory messages into conscious perceptions by attaching meaning to the sense data. As discussed later in this chapter, this process occurs in three stages.

Our perceptions are not always shared by others. For example, perhaps one semester you are forced to enroll in a professor's course that a friend describes as "boring" and requiring "too many assignments." Maybe you are surprised when you perceive the course as "interesting" and find the number of required assignments to be reasonable. You might wonder what caused your friend to have such a "distorted" perception of the class. This example illustrates that one person's truth or reality isn't another's.

perception A process that occurs when sense data—or what we see, hear, smell, taste, and/or touch—is transmitted to the brain. Perception occurs in three stages: selection, organization, and interpretation.

What Is Self-Concept?

If you could describe yourself in just a few words, which words would you choose? Quite simply, **self-concept** refers to how we perceive ourselves. Communication scholars contend that our self-concept is formed, sustained, and changed by our interactions with others.[4] This means that the self-concept is primarily a social phenomenon that is influenced by our relationships. Of course, just as others affect our self-concept, our communication can significantly influence the self-concept of others. Even a comment not intended to affect a person's sense of self, such as a mild put-down said as a joke, has the potential to impact a person's self-concept. However, it may be impossible to say that the formation of the self is entirely social because research suggests that biologically influenced personality traits are a major component of our self-concept.[5]

self-concept How we perceive ourselves.

Our self-concept can be placed on a continuum that ranges from "healthy" or "strong" to "unhealthy" or "poor." A healthy self-concept can result in a realistic acknowledgement of our strengths and weaknesses, and therefore we may accept praise and defend viewpoints even when they are opposed by others. An unhealthy self-concept can result in exaggerated and unrealistic perceptions of our strengths and weaknesses, and therefore we may:[6]

Knowing that our perceptions may not correspond to the perceptions of others can help us improve our relationships and enhance our ability to communicate in a civil and ethical manner.

- Downplay our strengths
- Exaggerate our accomplishments
- Fail to value our successes
- Expect to be perceived negatively by others

An individual with an unhealthy self-concept might be overly self-critical because it may be easier and less painful to criticize himself or herself than to hear the criticism of others. People who have an unhealthy self-concept may also boast about their accomplishments to mask feelings of insecurity and inadequacy.[7]

PERCEPTION, SELF-CONCEPT, AND CIVILITY

"Whatever happened to freedom of speech?"
"I can do and say what I want!"

How many times have you heard, read, or communicated these or similar sentiments? Although we have a right to wear offensive phrases on our T-shirts, is it *right* to do so? Is it acceptable for people to boom four-letter obscenities from car speakers? Some scholars contend that there is a connection between uncivil discourse and words used to describe the self. These scholars maintain that today's "vocabulary of the self" reflects the overemphasis on individualism as a societal value and is devoid of responsibility and accountability. People today tend to talk about themselves with words such as *self-expression*, *self-assertion*, *self-realization*, *self-approval*, and *self-acceptance*, which reflect their focus on individualism; people tend to avoid words such as *self-denial*, *self-discipline*, *self-control*, *self-reproach*, and *self-sacrifice*, which reflect responsibility and accountability.[8] This vocabulary implies that "the old ethic of self-discipline has given way to a new ethic of self-esteem and self-expression. This has endangered the practice of traditional civility."[9] Recall that civil communication is based on respect, restraint, and responsibility. Roy F. Baumeister, a leading researcher in the area of self-esteem, recommends that we shift our focus from the extreme individualistic sense of self (i.e., the Western view of the overall importance of the self) to self-control (restraint) and self-discipline in order to truly benefit self and society.[10]

Self-control occurs when an individual overrides, inhibits, or stops a response to avoid a temptation, reach a goal, or follow a rule.[11] A recent study about self-control and social norms found that people with low levels of self-control tend to lie, cheat, and engage in uncivil behavior, such as neglecting to say "thank you." In addition, survey respondents rate these individuals as "disagreeable" and "rude."[12] It's important to note that self-control or restraint doesn't mean that we must restrict our everyday behaviors or that we must eliminate self-expression. However, it does mean that we should realize that everything we want to express may not be worthy of expression. It also means that "we can choose to express one part of ourselves rather than another. Although it may appear that we give up self-expression when we exercise [civility], in truth, restraint can be much an expression of ourselves as is unfettered behavior."[13]

Because we may perceive that we have minimal, if any, obligations to others, it is easy to confuse desires with "rights" and turn to the U.S. Constitution to protect offensive speech and behavior. Although the First Amendment protects a variety of our rights, our norms, or rules of conduct, provide us with the discipline to exercise these rights with respect for others and the larger social community we are part of. This means that although uncivil communication may reflect constitutionally protected rights, it doesn't mean that it is "right" to communicate in an uncivil manner. Simply put, just because we *can* engage in uncivil communication doesn't mean that we *should*.

self-control A process that occurs when an individual overrides, inhibits, or stops a response to avoid a temptation, reach a goal, or follow a rule.

selection The first stage of the perception process, during which we select from the environment the stimuli to which we will attend.

salience A characteristic of stimuli that are selected from the environment based on their interest, use, and meaning to us.

vividness A characteristic of stimuli that are selected from the environment because they are noticeable.

organization The second stage of the perception process, during which we categorize the stimuli we have selected from the environment to make sense of the environment.

schemas Mental templates that enable us to organize and classify stimuli into manageable groups or categories.

STAGES IN THE PERCEPTION PROCESS

Perception involves the process of selecting, organizing, and interpreting sensory information. These three stages occur almost simultaneously and concern attending to stimuli in our environment, organizing stimuli in our environment, and attaching meaning to the stimuli we attend to and organized.

Selection

Imagine the most recent walk to your communication class. Can you describe all the people you passed on your way to class? Do you remember the smells you encountered and the sounds you heard? Of course you don't; it's impossible to perceive all the stimuli in your environment. Therefore, during **selection**, the first stage of the perception process, we choose from the environment the stimuli to which we will attend. We tend to choose two types of stimuli from all the stimuli that bombard our senses and compete for attention: stimuli that are salient and stimuli that are vivid.

Salience **Salience** refers to stimuli that we select from the environment based on their interest, use, and meaning to us. For example, think about a time when you were in a crowded restaurant or store. In that situation, you may have been aware of others' conversations but didn't pay attention to what was being said until, suddenly and without warning, someone from across the room mentioned your name. The reason you selected that particular stimulus from the environment is because your name is meaningful to you. You wouldn't pick out someone else's name from the low-level noise of conversation unless that particular name was also meaningful to you.

Vividness **Vividness** refers to stimuli that we select from the environment because they are noticeable. We tend to pay attention to stimuli that are intense, large, and repetitious, as well as to stimuli that move. You are likely to notice a girl who raises her voice, a guy who is 6′10″, a friend who uses broad gestures and talks with his hands, and a student who peppers her speech with too many "ya knows?"

Once you have selected material from the environment to attend to, you next organize the material to help in its interpretation.

Organization

Organization occurs when we categorize the stimuli we have selected from the environment to make sense of it. Researchers have discovered that we tend to organize stimuli in certain ways, particularly on the basis of schemas, figure–ground, proximity, and similarity patterns. These patterns influence how we organize the stimuli we attend to.

Schemas **Schemas** are mental templates that enable us to organize and classify stimuli into manageable groups or categories. Schemas typically are general views of people and their social roles. For example, we may categorize others based on their appearance (e.g., pretty, ugly, fat, thin) or their group membership (e.g., Jewish, Republican, Junior League member). We may also categorize people according to roles, such as parent, student, or doctor. We use schemas to determine the origin of a memory when we can't recall the source (e.g., we may attribute a comment about a flu epidemic to a particular person only because she or he belongs in the schema of "medical students").[14]

We may use the schema of "young children typically have short attention spans" to predict that a child will need a variety of activities to occupy her or his time when we babysit.

stereotypes Generalizations that lack validity because they ignore individual differences and contribute to perceptual inaccuracies.

proximity The basis for perceptual organization of grouping together stimuli that are physically close to each other.

FIGURE 2.1 Figure–Ground Organization

Defining the figure versus the ground is just as significant in communication as in this drawing: Where you focus determines what you perceive.

The various schemas we use each day help us make sense of the world and enable us to make generalizations and predictions about others. For example, we may be asked to babysit a friend's five-year-old child. We may therefore use the schema "young children typically have short attention spans" to predict that the child will need a variety of activities to occupy her or his time. We risk engaging in **stereotypes**, or generalizations that lack validity, when our perceptions of others based on schemas ignore the possibility of individual differences. We create stereotypes as a way to quickly organize and remember information that we might need in order to achieve our goals in our daily lives. But because stereotypes ignore individual differences, they contribute to perceptual inaccuracies.

You may be thinking, "I just read that the second step in the perception process is 'organization' and that we can organize on the basis of schemas. Isn't that a form of stereotyping?" The difference between organizing and stereotyping is that stereotypes are exaggerated generalizations. They may be based on partial truths, but they may also include beliefs that go beyond the facts. For example, the stereotypes "all men are pigs" and "all blondes are dumb" obviously go beyond the facts and leave no room for individual differences. On the other hand, "careful generalizations" (such as the schema example mentioned earlier, about young children typically having short attention spans) point out the possibility of individual differences. However, we usually don't consciously consider individual differences when we stereotype.[15] Unfortunately, without our realizing it, stereotyping can blind us to the unique attributes and perceptions of a person and to the diversity and variety of people within a culture. However, we can minimize our stereotypic perceptions by revising or discarding them when we discover an "exception to the rule" (in other words, we can change the rule instead of declaring an exception).[16] We can also use clarifying terms such as *often*, *sometimes*, and *generally* when talking about groups of people. In sum, when we become consciously aware that we may be thinking about people based on a stereotype, we will be "less likely to put others at a disadvantage based solely on a label that can be attached to them."[17]

Figure–Ground Organization Figure–ground organization occurs when a portion of the stimuli selected from the environment is the focal point of our attention (the figure) and the rest is placed in the background (the ground). For example, before reading on, look at Figure 2.1. What do you perceive? You might at first see a silhouette of a man playing a saxophone. But if you look again, you might see a woman's face on the right side of the figure. Our focus easily shifts back and forth between the two images. The figure–ground organization also applies to communication situations. Have you ever been in a crowded room and paid attention to various conversations? When we begin to focus on one particular conversation and others recede into the background, we are organizing based on the figure–ground pattern. In addition, one overheard word in a conversation we are not attending to may shift our focus toward the conversation. Shifts in figure and ground can happen rapidly when we are communicating.

Proximity We organize stimuli selected from the environment on the basis of proximity and similarity. We organize on the basis of **proximity** when we group stimuli that are physically close to each other. Before reading on, describe what you perceive in Figure 2.2. Do you describe this illusion as four pairs of parallel lines or as eight parallel lines?

If you perceive four pairs of parallel lines in Figure 2.2, you are organizing based on the principle of proximity. Organization based on proximity also applies to communication situations. Suppose your professor begins class by saying that far too many students failed the last exam. Your professor then calls your name and asks to speak with you after class. Because these messages occur in close temporal proximity, you may believe that your professor wants to speak to you about your poor test grade. However, your professor may want to talk to you about a topic totally unrelated to the test.

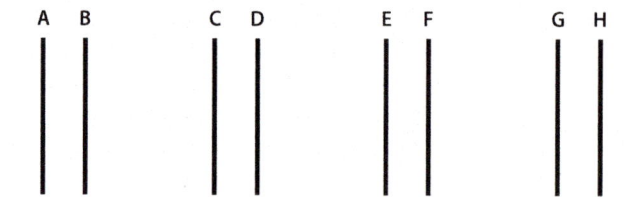

FIGURE 2.2 Organization Based on Proximity

As with these parallel lines, we tend to interpret messages that occur around the same time as being related, but they may not be.

Similarity We also tend to group elements together based on size, color, shape, and other characteristics. When this occurs, we organize on the basis of **similarity**. For example, follow the directions and look at the words listed in the following "Memory Test."

similarity The basis for perceptual organization of grouping together elements based on size, color, shape, and other characteristics.

Memory Test

Directions: Read the following words and prepare to remember as many as possible. Turn the page once you have read the words and write as many words as you can on a piece of scratch paper. Return to the text on this page when you are finished writing the words that you remembered.

Cat	Sun	Square	Apple
Lemon	Bird	Planet	Dog
Triangle	Plum	Fish	Moon
Star	Circle	Orange	Rectangle

The point of the memory test is not to remember as many words as possible but to uncover the method you use to remember the words. Most likely you grouped the words into categories of items that share something similar. You may have grouped items that relate to pets, the solar system, shapes, and fruits. This illustrates the idea that we tend to group similar elements together. Organization based on similarity also applies to communication situations. Think back to your days in high school. Were your high school classmates organized into various cliques based on similar interests, activities, and communication styles? Did your high school include the jocks who were typically loud and aggressive, the popular people who tended to be talkative and happy, and the artists who were often introverted and quiet? The proverb "birds of a feather flock together" describes organization based on similarity.

Interpretation

interpretation The third stage of the perception process, during which we assign meaning to the stimuli that we have selected and organized from the environment.

The final stage in the perception process is interpretation. **Interpretation** occurs when we assign meaning to the stimuli that we have selected and organized from the environment. For example, you may select from the environment your roommate standing in the middle of a crowd (*selection*), focus on the frown on her face as being in the foreground (*organization*), and believe that your roommate is unhappy (*interpretation*). However, friends standing next to you tell you that they didn't see a frown on your roommate's face. Later that day, you ask your roommate about the sad look and learn that she was merely deep in thought. This example illustrates that our interpretations of sensory data may be incorrect and that we may select and organize stimuli from the environment (e.g., a frown) that others fail to perceive. You will later learn about the skill of perception-checking, which enables you to determine whether your interpretation

Makers of game consoles use high definition graphics and surround sounds to give players a more realistic perception of actually playing the game.

expectancy The basis for perceptual interpretation when we perceive what we expect to perceive.

familiarity The basis for perceptual interpretations of perceiving or failing to perceive what we are familiar with.

of stimuli is correct. For now, note that the interpretation of stimuli is also influenced by both expectancy and familiarity.

Expectancy Our interpretation of stimuli is influenced by **expectancy**, or what we expect to perceive. In other words, we become accustomed to seeing stimuli in certain ways and therefore often don't perceive the obvious. For example, have you ever written a paper and, even after proofreading it, later discovered that you overlooked some obvious misspellings? You are likely to focus on your meaning and not the written words while you proofread. However, after your instructor returns your paper to you, you might be surprised to see misspelled words that you didn't expect to find because you proofread the paper and didn't see them.

Familiarity Our interpretation of stimuli is also influenced by **familiarity**—that is, the level of experience we have with stimuli. This idea is evidenced in Figure 2.3. Look at it now before you read on, and read the phrases out loud, very slowly, one word at a time.

Sometimes familiarity adds to what we expect to perceive. Did you perceive a second "a" in "Birds of a a feather"? Did you see a second "the" in "Paris in the the spring" and a second "a" in "Happy as a a lark"? Familiarity with stimuli can explain why your professors sometimes hand back your assignments with words, clauses, or even sentences circled in red because you have typed them twice. It may be that you are so familiar with what you have written that you fail to perceive anything other than what you expect.

Expectancy and familiarity also affect communication situations. Have you ever failed to notice a change in a friend's appearance (a form of nonverbal communication)? You may have been so familiar with your friend that you failed to notice any change. Perhaps you once got your braces off, had your ears pierced, or shaved off a moustache. Did any of your friends fail to notice the change in your appearance? If so, your friends didn't perceive the difference in your appearance because they didn't expect to see a change.

Differences in Perception

Perhaps you once talked about a difficult day to an opposite-gender partner and found that instead of communicating sympathy and understanding, your partner told you how to deal with the day's problems. Maybe you became upset because you didn't want solutions; maybe your partner became upset and thought, "What's the point of talking about problems if you don't want to know how to fix them?!" What influences us to perceive that we should respond to a comment with understanding rather than advice? The answer to this question concerns how gender affects perception.

Birds of a a feather

Paris in the the spring

Happy as a a lark

FIGURE 2.3 Do You Know These Phrases?
Look closely. Did you assume that these are the phrases you are already familiar with?

Past research in gender and communication has found that boys and men tend to perceive communication as a means to an end. Boys are taught that talk is used to achieve instrumental goals, such as negotiating power and position on a status hierarchy, to assert identities, to solve problems, and to argue points of view. Conversation is viewed as a way to demonstrate knowledge and superiority and as a method to gain respect. On the other hand, girls are taught that communication functions to build and maintain harmonious relationships that take priority over instrumental goals; communication is perceived to foster intimacy and is the crux of relationships. In general, girls and women tend to perceive communication as an end in and of itself. Research about social networking sites and mobile communication supports the idea that women and men perceive communication differently. In particular, women use social networking sites such as Facebook and MySpace to make and maintain social connections more so than men. In addition, women use social networking sites for enjoyment, while men search sites for information.[18] Similarly, women use mobile chat services (such as texting on a cell phone) for the intrinsic motive of "perceived enjoyment," while men use mobile chat services for the extrinsic motive of "perceived usefulness."[19] Of course, not all men perceive communication as a way to achieve instrumental goals and not all women perceive communication as functioning primarily to establish and maintain relationships. However, such views of communication can influence women and men to perceive the same situation differently.[20]

Gender isn't the only factor that can lead to differences in perception. Can you think of a situation in which your perception of a person, a place, or an event was affected by your employment? Your career or place of employment also has an effect on your perceptions.

Imagine that three people decide to view a film together. One person, a speech pathologist, noticing the actors' accents and how they pronounce their words, decides that, overall, the film is "realistic." The second person, an aerobics instructor, watches the actors chase the bad guys, jump from buildings, and escape from near-death situations without once catching their breath. The aerobics instructor therefore concludes that the film is "ridiculous." The third person, a computer specialist, notices the advanced software, complicated gadgets, and modern technological devices used in the film. The computer specialist believes that the development of the futuristic technology used in the movie is extremely plausible and therefore perceives the film to be "cutting edge." "Realistic," "ridiculous," and "cutting-edge"—these varying perceptions of the same movie are from observers with different careers, focusing on different facets of the film.

Just as our careers can influence our perceptions, our position in an organizational hierarchy can affect our ability to engage in perspective-taking. Research demonstrates that people who hold powerful positions within an organization, such as supervisors and managers, are less likely to take their subordinates' perspectives. People in management positions may not need to understand how their subordinates perceive the world because they have control over valuable resources and are less dependent on others to accomplish their goals. Also, people in positions of authority may have increased demands on their attention, and therefore it may be difficult for them to engage in perspective-taking with their subordinates. Persons who hold powerful positions typically don't make conscious decisions to ignore the perspectives of others. When people in powerful positions engage in perspective-taking, they tend to make less accurate estimations of how others think and perceive the world than do those in less powerful positions.[21]

We often believe that what we perceive is reality or the truth; however, one person's reality may not match the reality of others, even if they all perceive the same stimuli. Attribution theory and implicit personality theory help explain why others' realities may not be the same as our own.

ASK THE ETHICIST

Influencing Others' Perceptions of Me

Question Is it ethical for me to do things that will affect the perceptions others have of me? What's the line between trying to look my best and manipulating others?

Answer Most of us try to look our best for others, whether it means we dress appropriately for an occasion or speak in particular ways with others. There's nothing wrong with doing so. Some would even say that our efforts to be our best are a mark of respect toward others (e.g., recognizing the importance or prestige of a potential employer by dressing appropriately for a job interview). In general, speaking politely to others will likely result in them perceiving you positively.

The questions you have to ask yourself are "What's my motive?" "Why am I trying to look so good?" and "Am I trying to appear to be something I am not?" The fiery crash-and-burn scenarios of the 1980s surrounding prominent religious figures were largely driven by constituents perceiving these figures as hypocrites. People felt duped when they had been told to sacrifice and send gifts so that people like Tammy Faye and Jim Bakker could live a life of luxury. Similarly, if you are polite to someone face-to-face and then ridicule that person later, your politeness is not going to endear you to others.

Creating a resume presents us with one of the greatest temptations to make ourselves look better than we really are. Resume puffery is common, but it is not a good idea. If you claim to have experiences or skills that you do not, you either will be spending lots of late nights at the office trying to catch up, or you'll end up failing.

The important thing is to be someone you are comfortable with. If you try to create an impression for others but you can't sustain it, you're likely to be seen as unethical.

THEORETICAL PERSPECTIVES ABOUT PERCEPTION

Suppose an employee is tagged for low productivity. A supervisor may perceive the employee's low productivity to be a result of a personal defect or a negative personality characteristic such as being irresponsible. The supervisor may also perceive that the employee is lazy, inconsiderate, or stupid. These perceptions may influence the supervisor to deny the employee a salary increase or consider terminating her or his employment. However, something in the employee's work situation, such as malfunctioning equipment or unreliable team members, may be the cause of the productivity problem.[22] The attribution that a personality flaw is the cause of poor job performance is an example of how we perceive others versus how we perceive ourselves; this perceptual difference can be explained in terms of attribution theory. Furthermore, assuming that an employee is lazy, inconsiderate, and stupid because she or he is perceived to be irresponsible can be explained in terms of implicit personality theory.

Attribution Theory

Psychologist Fritz Heider, known as the "father of attribution theory," determined that we make interpretations about someone's personality based on his or her behavior.[23] **Attribution theory** explains how we create explanations or attach meaning to our own or another's behavior. Attributions answer the question of "why" when we look at our own and another's behavior. We tend to overemphasize inherent characteristics or personality and underemphasize situational factors when we explain the reasons for others' behavior. This is called the **fundamental attribution error**. For example, have you ever thought that a friend's lack of preparedness and study, and her or his "slacker" tendencies were why she or he failed a test? You committed the fundamental attribution error if you ignored some situational factors that also may have explained the poor grade, such as the

---

attribution theory A theory that explains how we create explanations or attach meaning to our own or another's behavior.

fundamental attribution error Reasons for others' behavior that overemphasize inherent characteristics or personality and underemphasize situational factors.

self-serving bias Reasons for our actions that include attributing our successful behavior to inherent characteristics or our personality and our unsuccessful behavior to situational factors.

implicit personality theory A theory that explains one way to perceive others. According to implicit personality theory, we tend to perceive others based on a set of beliefs that tell us which characteristics relate to other characteristics.

friend's illness or need to study for a major test in another class. Besides assigning reasons for others' behavior, we also provide explanations for our own behavior. Specifically, we tend to attribute our successful behavior to inherent characteristics or our personality and our unsuccessful behavior to situational factors. This is called the **self-serving bias**. Have you ever done poorly on a test and attributed your results to tricky test questions, questions that covered material that wasn't supposed to be on the test, or a professor who deliberately included difficult questions in order to fail as many students as possible? Have you ever done well on a test and attributed your grade to preparedness and good study habits? If so, you demonstrated the self-serving bias. Perception problems such as the fundamental attribution error and the self-serving bias occur in virtual groups when members are geographically distant and lack common interests.[24] These perceptual errors may lead us to incorrectly perceive that someone is personally responsible for her or his misfortunes, take unrealistic credit for what we do well, and minimize personal responsibility for what we do poorly.

Implicit Personality Theory

Complete the following sentence with your choice of words from the parentheses:

> Her financial advisor is generous, charismatic, honest, and (trustworthy, a 'fraudster,' affable, a chameleon, realistic, a swindler).

If you chose the words *trustworthy*, *affable*, and/or *realistic*, you're not alone. In June 2009, 71-year-old financier Bernard Madoff was sentenced to 150 years in prison for swindling thousands of investors in a $65 billion Ponzi scheme that wiped out their life savings. Instead of responsibly investing the funds, Madoff used money from new investors to pay returns to existing investors and to finance his lavish lifestyle. Madoff's friends and clients described him as "charming, generous, realistic, affable, and charismatic." His employees said that Madoff treated them like family. Many of his victims trusted Madoff because he was a part of their social circle.[25] However, Gregg O. McCrary, a former FBI agent, said that people like Madoff are like chameleons because "they manage the impression you receive of them. They know what people want, and they give it to them." One of Madoff's employees said that he appeared to believe in "family, loyalty, and honesty." The employee commented that no one would ever have guessed that Madoff was a "fraudster."[26]

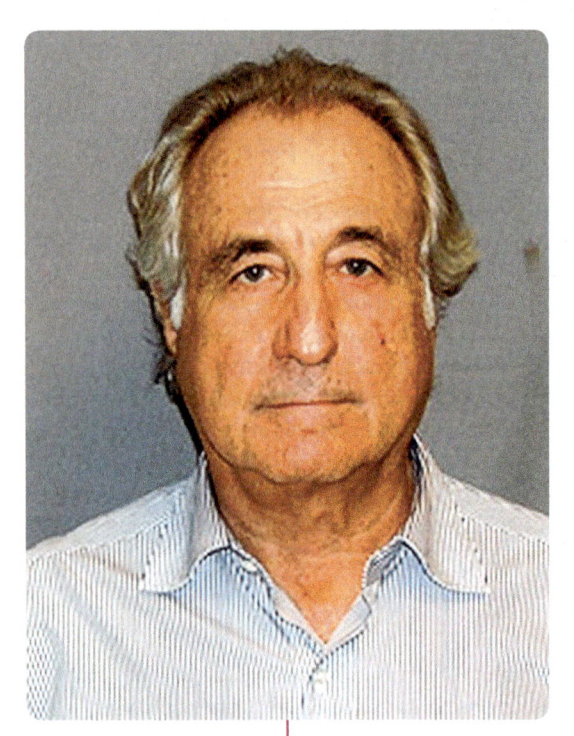

Financier Bernie Madoff was sentenced to 150 years in prison for multiple fraud and securities violations when he masterminded a massive Ponzi scheme that defrauded thousands of investors of billions of dollars.

One theory that can explain why thousands of clients entrusted Madoff with their life savings is **implicit personality theory**. Implicit personality theory explains that we tend to perceive others based on a set of beliefs that tell us which characteristics relate to other characteristics. We typically believe that personality traits cluster together; therefore, if we perceive a person to have one characteristic or trait, we assume that he or she will have a number of other similar traits or characteristics.[27] Implicit personality theory contributes to the **halo effect**, which causes us to perceive that a person holds many positive qualities if we believe she or he possesses one or a few positive qualities. On the other hand, the reverse halo effect implies that we perceive a person to hold many negative qualities if we believe her or him to possess one or a few negative qualities.[28] Implicit personality theory and the halo/reverse halo effect have the potential to

halo effect A perception influenced by positive qualities. The halo effect causes us to perceive that a person holds many positive qualities if we believe she or he possesses one or a few positive qualities.

culture The shared assumptions, values, and beliefs of a group of people that result in characteristic behaviors.

cultural pattern The particular beliefs and values associated with a specific culture.

individualist culture A culture that focuses more on the individual than the group. Individual needs come before group needs, and people take care of themselves before they take care of others.

collectivist culture A culture that focuses more on the group (e.g., the family, village, or organization) than the individual.

bias our perceptions of others. Therefore, we should judge others with care and recognize that, as in the case of Bernie Madoff, a person who appears to be generous and honest is not necessarily trustworthy, and someone we perceive to be untrustworthy may actually be honest and worthy of our trust.

Cultural Influences on Perception

Scholars who study culture have created theories that help explain differences in perception. **Culture** creates characteristic behaviors based on shared beliefs, values, and assumptions associated with a group of people.[29] We perceive the world based on **cultural patterns**, or the particular beliefs and values associated with our specific culture.[30] Members of cultural groups learn to perceive similarly based on their shared experiences and what their culture teaches them. In general, our perceptions are comparable to those of other individuals who belong to the same cultural groups as we do.[31]

Social scientists create cultural pattern taxonomies to understand cultural similarities and differences. Such taxonomies, or "belief systems," can be represented on a grid with a cultural belief or value at one end and an opposing cultural belief or value at the other. Although there are many cultural pattern taxonomies, we present one in this section: individualism and collectivism, the most powerful and fundamental dimension of cultural difference (see Table 2.1).[32]

The broken line bordered by arrowheads in Table 2.1 illustrates that the individualist–collectivist belief system can be placed on a continuum, and no culture is 100 percent individualist or collectivist. Both patterns exist in all cultures, although one pattern usually dominates. **Individualist cultures** focus more on the individual than the group. Individual needs come before group needs, and people take care of themselves before they take care of others, if at all.[33] Members of cultures that are primarily individualist tend to be self-reliant and competitive and perceive that they should be rewarded for personal achievement or blamed for personal failure. In addition, members of cultures that are primarily individualist typically have friends based on shared activities and interests and associate with groups whose memberships are flexible.[34] The dominant cultures in Australia, the Netherlands, Belgium, and the United States are highly individualist.[35] In contrast, **collectivist cultures**

Table 2.1 Individualist and Collectivist Cultures
Individualism and collectivism are two ends of a continuum that describe powerful cultural differences.

Individualist Cultures	Collectivist Cultures
• Individual needs come before group needs.	• Group needs come before individual needs.
• Individuals are expected to take care of themselves.	• Groups are expected to take care of their members.
• Individuals are self-reliant and competitive.	• Group opinion (e.g., opinions of significant others) is more important than individual opinion.
• Individuals are rewarded for personal achievement or blamed for personal failure.	• Group contributions are rewarded, and credit and blame are shared.
• Friendships may be short term and are based on shared activities and interests.	• Friendships are long-lasting and are maintained regardless of shared activities and interests.
• Individuals belong to a variety of groups, and membership is flexible.	• Group membership is limited and long-lasting.

Although both the individualist and collectivist cultural patterns exist in all cultures, one pattern usually dominates.

Our perceptions tend to be similar to those of other individuals who belong to the same cultural and co-cultural groups as we do.

focus more on the group (e.g., family, village, organization) than the individual. Decisions are made based on what is best for the group, and the group is expected to take care of its members. Members of cultures that are primarily collectivist are more concerned with the opinion of group members than are members of individualist cultures. In addition, members of cultures that are primarily collectivist typically have long-lasting friendships, regardless of shared interests and activities. Similarly, members of collectivist cultures belong to fewer groups than do members of individualist cultures, and group membership is long-lasting.[36] The dominant cultures in Indonesia, West Africa, Guatemala, and Pakistan are primarily collectivist.[37]

Culture and Perception   People in cultures such as the United States typically believe that individuals are responsible for their lot in life and may perceive individual weakness and poor choices as the reasons for poverty or crime. Similarly, Americans find it difficult to fully understand that people in collectivist cultures may not perceive themselves as distinct from others. Americans perceive that everyone has an individual identity and contend that people's different preferences, styles, and interests should be recognized by others.[38] On the other hand, people from other cultural backgrounds typically don't make judgments about individuals when they attempt to explain causal relationships or reasons for behavior.[39] For example, people in cultures such as Africa and the Middle East tend to perceive that life is determined by forces outside our control, such as fate or destiny, and typically do not blame an individual and her or his choices and actions for undesirable life outcomes.[40]

Co-Cultures and Perception   Members of the same culture may perceive an identical phenomenon differently because of the influence of the co-cultures(s) to which they belong. A **co-culture** is a group within a larger dominant culture that has its own values and beliefs, which sometimes may be at odds with the dominant culture. Co-cultures are based on ethnicity, race, sexual orientation, gender, class, ability, and age.[41] For example, one study of Mexican Americans and Anglo Americans illustrates how co-cultural beliefs can affect a work group's communication and success. When asked what can be done to improve success at work, the Mexican-American respondents perceived that a focus on socio-emotional aspects of interactions with coworkers (e.g., social harmony, graciousness, and collegiality) are more important than a focus on task-related considerations. However, the Anglo-American respondents perceived that an increased task focus would increase work group success. These findings illustrate that Mexican Americans and Anglo Americans may perceive and evaluate work groups, coworkers, and communication differently, based on the beliefs associated with their co-cultural groups.[42]

co-culture   A group within a larger dominant culture that has its own values and beliefs, which sometimes may be at odds with the dominant culture.

CHARACTERISTICS OF THE SELF-CONCEPT

As we discussed previously, our self-concept is made up of the perceptions we have of ourselves, which we create as a result of interacting with others. Our self-concept is comprised of both our self-image, or the characteristics we believe we possess (e.g., strengths and

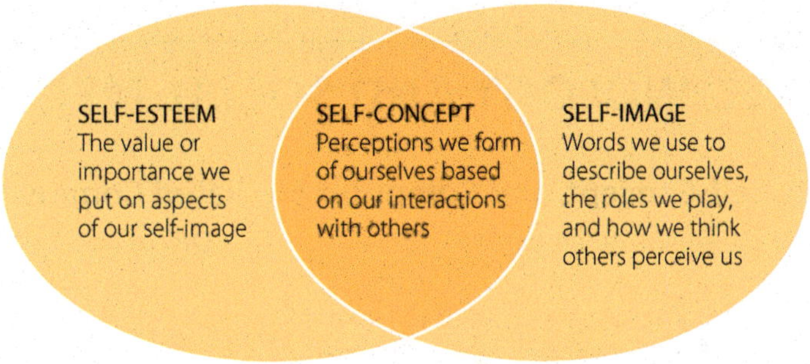

SELF-ESTEEM The value or importance we put on aspects of our self-image

SELF-CONCEPT Perceptions we form of ourselves based on our interactions with others

SELF-IMAGE Words we use to describe ourselves, the roles we play, and how we think others perceive us

FIGURE 2.4 The Relationship Among Self-Concept, Self-Image, and Self-Esteem
Our self-concept comprises both our self-image and our self-esteem.

weaknesses, personality traits), and our self-esteem, or how we evaluate these characteristics. The relationship between self-concept, self-image, and self-esteem is shown in Figure 2.4.

Self-Image

self-image The characteristics we believe we possess.

Self-image refers to the characteristics we believe we possess. Our self-image may include the roles we perceive we inhabit, the words we use when we describe ourselves, and how we believe others perceive us. For example, if you describe yourself as a student who does volunteer work and who is looking for a mate, you have communicated several aspects of your self-image (i.e., the roles of student, giving citizen, and someone who desires a relationship). Our self-image also involves how others see us. We use other people's comments to check our self-perceptions, and they reinforce or change the perception of what and who we are. For instance, you may perceive yourself as someone who is altruistic and giving. However, this self-perception may change when a coworker mentions the volunteer work he does or the charities to which she donates.

Self-Esteem

self-esteem The value or importance we place on our perceived characteristics.

Our **self-esteem** depends on what we perceive to be worthwhile and/or valuable. In other words, self-esteem places value or importance on aspects of our self-image. While we may evaluate some aspect of our self-image as positive or negative, it may not have a large impact on our self-concept. For example, you may perceive that your bowling ability is poor. However, this belief may be an inconsequential component of your self-concept. It

TECH CHECK

Assessing Your Ability to Self-Monitor

As a part of your self-image, do you believe that you can easily adapt to various social situations and the people with whom you interact? Do you think that others see you as someone who effectively manages how you are perceived in social situations? The Self-Monitoring Scale assesses the degree to which you adjust your behavior to situational demands. Overall, people rate those who have the ability to engage in self-monitoring as being better at emotional self-control and better at figuring out how to behave appropriately in new social situations.

TRENDS IN
TECHNOLOGY AND SOCIAL MEDIA

Perception, Self-Concept, and Computer-Mediated Communication

Can you accurately perceive others based on their personal websites? Researchers have compared personal websites with other places where personality is expressed, such as bedrooms and offices. We tend to be deliberate when we include information on our website that illustrates our personality, but we are less deliberate and sometimes don't realize that we express ourselves in other contexts, such as the tidiness (or lack thereof) of our car's interior. Studies document that observers can learn at least as much about others by viewing the photos, fonts, colors, and language used on websites as they can from viewing bedrooms and offices.[43]

How a person uses social networking sites also influences others' perceptions. For example, a teacher who allows students access to her or his Facebook page may be perceived as more accessible and similar to students, which may result in higher student participation.[44] Perceptions people have of others are influenced by the number of Facebook friends a person has, the descriptions that a person makes about herself or himself, and the comments posted by others. Researchers say that the number of friends a person has is related to perceptions of popularity but only up to a certain point. If you have fewer than 100 friends or more than 300 friends, you will be viewed as less popular than those in the middle, but for different reasons. Specifically, people with too many friends may be perceived as focusing on Facebook because they are desperate to make connections in an environment in which they feel more comfortable (i.e., in a computer-mediated environment rather than a face-to-face environment).[45]

A variety of studies have established a relationship between the self-concept and use of computer-mediated communication and social networking sites. In terms of social networking sites, users typically control information about themselves to project to others a self that is socially desirable.[46] In particular, users attempt to create a self-presentation that is authentic; is current, positive, and professional; and is socially literate.[47] However, projecting a socially desirable self to others also influences our self-concept. Research reveals that reviewing and editing information on one's Facebook profile can enhance self-esteem. This occurs because Facebook users typically present positive information about the self and therefore enhance awareness of an "optimal self."[48]

Discussion Questions

1 What type of information, fonts, colors, and/or photos that illustrate facets of your personality do you have on your website, Facebook profile page, and so on? If you don't have a website or Facebook profile page, what information and photos would you include?

2 How would you compare a private space (such as a bedroom) you have decorated to one of your social networking site pages in terms of its ability to say something about you? Which do you think is more accurate? Why?

3 Have you been accepted as a Facebook "friend" by any of your instructors? If so, has that instructor's posts influenced your perceptions of her or him? Explain.

4 Might there be other ways of enhancing our self-esteem that don't involve reviewing and editing information on our Facebook profile?

may be that your perceived weakness is not very important to you and doesn't negatively affect your overall self-concept. In addition, you might believe that you are a sensitive and kind person (*self-image*) and that sensitivity and kindness are valuable and worthwhile characteristics to possess (*self-esteem*). In this instance, your belief about yourself and your positive evaluation of that belief are likely to contribute to a healthy self-concept.

The Influence of Others on the Self-Concept

The theory of **symbolic interactionism**, developed by sociologist George Herbert Mead in the 1920s, posits that our view of self is shaped by those with whom we communicate. The influence of others on our self-concept also occurs in mediated settings when we comment about our homepage, when we receive responses in discussion groups and blogs, and even when we receive responses to our "all about me" page on eBay.[49] Two processes, the Pygmalion effect and social comparison, strongly influence how we perceive ourselves.

symbolic interactionism A theory developed by sociologist George Herbert Mead which posits that our view of self is shaped by those with whom we communicate.

Pygmalion effect An effect that illustrates the way our significant others influence our self-concept.

significant others People who are important to us.

The Pygmalion Effect
The **Pygmalion effect** illustrates the way our **significant others** (people who are important to us) influence our self-concept. Significant others may include family members, friends, employers, coaches, and teachers. In the classic study "Pygmalion in the Classroom," psychologists Robert Rosenthal and Lenore Jacobson describe an experiment in which certain teachers had been informed that they had exceptionally intelligent students. In reality, the students who were identified as exceptional were no different from any other students in their grade. At the end of the school year, the students who were described as extremely bright actually did perform at a high level and even improved their IQ scores. The researchers concluded that these children performed well because of their teachers' expectations. The teachers communicated their high expectations to their students by providing them with extra verbal and nonverbal reinforcement. Furthermore, the teachers didn't react negatively when their students answered questions incorrectly. The teachers directly and indirectly communicated to their students that they were high achievers, and the students actually came to believe that they were high achievers. In other words, the expectations of their teachers influenced the students' self-concepts.[50]

social comparison A comparison that provides us with knowledge about ourselves in terms of how we measure up to others.

Social Comparison
Our self-concept is also influenced when we engage in **social comparison** with others. Comparing our athletic ability or relationship success to others is an example of social comparison, as is asking classmates about their scores on a test. These examples illustrate that social comparison provides us with knowledge about ourselves in terms of how we measure up to others.[51] Research illustrates that social comparison is an important determinant of self-perception in Western cultures. Specifically, we tend to respond negatively when others perform better than we do on a consequential task, even when we receive positive above-average feedback about our performance. We compensate by comparing ourselves with people who perform with average ability and subsequently evaluate ourselves much higher than we evaluate the average performers.[52] For example, we may be dissatisfied when we receive a "B" on an important test because we know that classmates received an "A." However, it is probable that we will also compare ourselves with classmates who receive a "C" and decide that we really performed much better on the test than those who received the average scores.

The Influence of Culture on Self-Concept

Just as a person's culture affects the way in which he or she perceives the world, the culture to which we belong influences the ideas we have about our self-concept. One study about the effect of culture on the self-concept revealed that people who associate with a culture that is more individualist make more "I am" statements that illustrate autonomy and separation from others (e.g., "I am honest," "I am intelligent," and "I am happy"). On the other hand, people who associate with a culture that is more collectivist make more "I am" statements that illustrate connections to groups and other individuals (e.g., "I am a Roman Catholic," "I am a daughter," and "I am a person who wants to help others").[53] These divergent ideas of the self are illustrated by comparing how a U.S. corporation and a Japanese corporation attempted to elevate productivity in their grocery stores. The U.S. corporation had its employees begin the day by saying "I am beautiful" 100 times while looking in a mirror; the Japanese corporation had its employees start the day by holding hands with other employees and telling them that they are beautiful.[54]

Co-Cultures and Self-Concept Who we are and how we see ourselves are influenced not only by the dominant culture in which we live but also by the co-cultures with which we identify. The gay, lesbian, bisexual, and transgender (GLBT) community is also sometimes considered to be a co-culture. The process of "coming out" includes exploring one's sexual identity and sharing that identity with others. Achieving self-acceptance is a crucial step in coming out, and the process is easier when we are less reliant on others for our self-concept and self-esteem. A healthy level of self-esteem has also been found to be important after the coming-out process in that it can mitigate the harmful psychological effects (e.g., depression) of societal oppression.[55]

For the gay, lesbian, bisexual, and transgender (GLBT) community, achieving self-acceptance is a crucial step in coming out. The coming out process is easier when we are less reliant on others for our self-concept and self-esteem.

The Influence of the Workplace on Self-Concept

People with whom we work affect our self-concept in terms of our perceived **self-efficacy**, the belief in our ability to manage prospective situations.[56] Our self-efficacy perceptions are influential in choosing a career and are highly significant in career persistence and success. For example, the low number of women in technical vocations is linked to their perceived self-efficacy about their ability to engage in problem solving that involves technical skills.[57] However, role models and persons who can provide us with on-the-job encouragement help us dispel doubts about our self-efficacy perceptions. Therefore, female role models who work in technical fields can significantly influence the self-efficacy perceptions of young women and encourage them to become computer scientists or engineers.[58]

The Influence of Gender on the Self-Concept

The way women and men describe themselves is influenced by gender expectations. Women typically mention characteristics such as generosity, sensitivity, and care and concern for others when asked to describe themselves. Women also tend to be more concerned about their body image and physical appearance than are men, perhaps because women receive conflicting messages about their appearance. On the one hand, they are expected to make

Role models who can provide us with on-the-job encouragement help us dispel doubts about our self-efficacy perceptions.

self-efficacy One's belief in his or her ability to manage prospective situations.

themselves attractive. On the other hand, they can be blamed for provoking violence that responds to their attractiveness. Women frequently experience anxiety about their appearance, wondering if they are attractive but worrying whether their attractiveness will harm or help them.[59] When men describe themselves, however, they don't tend to comment about their physiques. Instead.[60]

Of course, many men have self-concepts that include care and concern for others, just as many women have self-concepts that include power and control. Studies of MMORPGs such as Ever Quest reveal that many people play a different-gendered character. Players engage in "gender swapping" to change the way they are perceived and to try out different ways of presenting themselves.[61] Similarly, a recent study of gender, self-esteem, and group membership illustrates that both women and men possess an equal sense of self-worth based on their relational group memberships.[62] Therefore, it is best to think of gendered self-concepts as a matter of degree rather than as polar opposites.

We have learned that civil communication entails respect, restraint, and responsibility and ethical communication involves trustworthiness, responsibility, respect, fairness, caring, and citizenship. Read the situation in "A Case Study in Ethics: 'I'm a Loser . . .'" and consider whether requiring students to write "I'm a loser . . ." sentences is an ethical way to influence perception, self-concept, and behavior.

A CASE STUDY IN ETHICS

"I'm a Loser . . ."

Think back to your days in middle school. How would you perceive yourself if a teacher made you write "I am a loser because . . ." if you didn't complete your homework? This is far from a hypothetical situation. Spanish teacher Julie Barrentine had students write "loser sentences" over and over on a piece of paper if they failed to complete their assignments. The idea to use the word *loser* in the sentences, which came from Barrentine's students, was intended to be a humorous way to motivate them to finish their homework. However, parents complained to school officials when they found out about the loser sentences. In addition to insisting that Barrentine stop the practice, officials sent letters of apology to all of her 137 students.

The loser sentences story was exposed in the media, and many people indicated that they thought the teacher crossed the line between "discipline" and "humiliation." Some parents asked that Barrentine be disciplined so that she would be perceived as a "loser." However, others responded that they were happy to see a teacher who held students accountable for completing their assignments. Emails to the *Dallas Morning News* about the incident included the following:

- "God forbid that kids get disciplined because they don't do their homework . . . or for anything else, for that matter."

- "None of the parents or principals addressed the real issue—the students not turning in their work."
- "The teacher was wrong in applying the term 'loser' to any student. While it is fine when one kid says it to another, it takes on an entirely different meaning when coming from a teacher."

One parent in particular said that the loser sentences could have a damaging effect on students' self-concept. "People in authority don't realize that little things like this make a big difference in someone's self-esteem. Negativity is destroying our young children."[63]

Discussion Questions

1. Do you believe having students write "I'm a loser . . ." sentences is an ethical way to motivate students to complete their homework?
2. Do you believe that writing loser sentences effectively influences self-concept and behavior?
3. Is it acceptable for students to call each other "loser"? Is it acceptable for teachers to apply this term to their pupils?

IMPROVING OUR ABILITY TO COMMUNICATE CIVILLY AND EFFECTIVELY ABOUT OUR PERCEPTIONS

Recall that we all perceive different realities because of the way we subjectively select, organize, and interpret stimuli. Knowing that we can perceive the same things differently than others and engaging in perspective-taking are the first steps in improving our ability to perceive and to communicate civilly about our perceptions. Specifically, our knowledge of perception can motivate us to acknowledge another person's perception with which we disagree (*respect*), influence us to refrain from comments that denigrate another person's perception (or the person her- or himself), and cause us to realize that our comments may affect the "community"—that is, the other person and anyone else involved in the conversation (*responsibility*). We can further improve our ability to communicate civilly about our perceptions by engaging in perception-checking.

Perception-checking illustrates that we recognize that no one has a corner on the truth and that each stage in the perception process is influenced by our own biases. Perception-checking is civil because it promotes cooperation with others; similarly, perception-checking is ethical because it communicates respect for others and recognition that we are responsible for our perceptions. As illustrated in Table 2.2, a **perception check** has three elements: a description of sense data, at least one interpretation (perception) of the sense data, and a request for feedback.

The first step in a perception check is to communicate facts based on sense data. A **fact** is independently verifiable by others, such as "She wore a red dress" or "He left for the airport at 7:15 A.M." Facts are often, but not always, based on sense data, such as what we see, hear, taste, smell, and touch. On the other hand, an **inference** is an interpretation based on a fact, such as "She wore an *ugly* red dress" or "He left for the airport *a long time ago*." Although everyone you ask may agree that her dress was red or that 7:15 A.M. was the time he left for the airport, not all would share the inferences that her dress was ugly or that he left a long time ago. The second step of the perception check includes one or two inferences or interpretations about what the sense data mean. We offer our interpretations in a tentative manner to illustrate that we realize that our perception(s) may be incorrect. In the third step, we follow our interpretation(s) with a question (e.g., "Am I on the right track?" or "Is it one of these?") or a rising inflection to indicate that we desire feedback about our interpretation(s). For example, instead of asking, "Why are you so crabby?" you can use a perception check:

> "I haven't seen you smile this morning (*sense data*). Is anything wrong?" (*The request for feedback is included in the interpretation that "something may be wrong."*)

perception check A communication skill that includes three elements: a description of sense data, at least one interpretation (perception) of the sense data, and a request for feedback.

fact Information that is independently verifiable by others. Facts are often, but not always, based on sense data, such as what we see, hear, taste, smell, and touch.

inference An interpretation based on a fact.

Table 2.2 Perception Checking
This process involves three steps to ensure that your perceptions are accurate.

Element	Example
A description of sense data	"You slammed the door when you got home."
At least one interpretation (perception) of the sense data	"I'm thinking something bad happened at work, or maybe you're mad at me."
A request for feedback	"Am I completely off-base here?"

Instead of sarcastically saying, "Thanks for forgetting to help me with my assignment," you can use a perception check:

> "When you didn't show up to help me with my assignment (*sense data*), I thought that either you forgot or that something bad had happened (*two interpretations*). Am I right?" (*request for feedback*)

Similarly, instead of angrily remarking, "I guess you're just too busy to text," you can use a perception check:

> "I sent you a text yesterday, and I haven't received an answer from you (*sense data*). Have you been busy, or is something else going on?" (*This perception check communicates that the perception may be incorrect because it's possible that "something else is going on."*)

CHAPTER SUMMARY

Now that you have read this chapter you can:

2.1 Define *perception* and *self-concept*.

Perception occurs when sense data—or what we see, hear, smell, taste, and/or touch—is transmitted to the brain. The *self-concept* refers to how we perceive ourselves. No matter how we perceive ourselves or how others perceive us, the self-concept is inextricably entwined with perception and communication.

2.2 Describe the relationship among perception, self-concept, and civility.

Some scholars contend that there is a connection between uncivil discourse and words used to describe the self. These scholars maintain that today's "vocabulary of the self" reflects the overemphasis on individualism as a societal value and is devoid of responsibility and accountability. Shifting our perception from the extreme individualistic sense of self to self-control (restraint) and self-discipline will promote civil interaction and benefit society.

2.3 Identify the three stages that make up the perception process.

Perception is the process of selecting, organizing, and interpreting sensory information. During selection, we select from the environment the stimuli to which we will attend. Organization occurs when we categorize the stimuli we have selected from the environment to make sense of it. Interpretation occurs when we assign meaning to the stimuli that we have selected and organized from the environment and is influenced by expectancy and familiarity.

2.4 Explain two theoretical perspectives about perception.

Attribution theory explains exactly how we create explanations or attach meaning to our own or another's behavior. The fundamental attribution error occurs when we tend to overemphasize inherent characteristics or personality and underemphasize situational factors when we explain the reasons for others' behavior. The self-serving bias occurs when we tend to attribute our successful behavior to inherent characteristics or our personality and our unsuccessful behavior to situational factors. Implicit personality theory illustrates that we tend to perceive others based on a set of beliefs that tell us which characteristics relate to other characteristics. We typically believe that personality traits cluster together; therefore, if we perceive a person to have one characteristic or trait, we assume that the person will have a number of other similar traits or characteristics. Implicit personality theory contributes to the halo effect, which causes you to perceive that a person holds many positive qualities if you believe she or he possesses one or a few positive qualities.

2.5 Describe two characteristics of the self-concept – self-image and self-esteem – and explain the importance of several environmental influences.

Our self-concept is affected by our self-image, or the characteristics we believe we possess (e.g., strengths and weaknesses, personality traits) and our self-esteem, or how we evaluate those characteristics. A healthy self-concept can result in a realistic acknowledgment of our strengths and weaknesses, but an unhealthy self-concept can cause us to downplay our strengths or exaggerate our accomplishments. The Pygmalion effect illustrates the way our significant others influence our self-concept. Our self-concept is also influenced when we engage in social comparison with others.

2.6 Use the skill of perception-checking to improve your civil communication.

Knowing that we can perceive the same things differently than others and engaging in perspective-taking are the first steps in improving our ability to perceive and to communicate civilly about our perceptions. We can also improve our perceptions by learning the difference between sense data and interpretations—that is, "fact" and "inference." In addition, we can improve the civil communication of our perceptions by engaging in perception-checking, which includes a description of sense data, at least one interpretation (perception) of the sense data, and a request for feedback.

CIVILITY SUMMARY

Overall, remember that civility, self-concept, and perception involve the following:

- Civil conversation partners realize that while their own perspectives may be accurate, they can see the validity in the perspectives of others.
- Although uncivil communication may be constitutionally protected, it doesn't mean it is "right" or that we should engage in such behavior.
- Self-control or restraint doesn't mean that we must restrict our everyday behaviors or that we must eliminate self-expression. However, it does mean that we should realize that everything we want to express may not be worthy of expression.
- Although it may appear that we give up self-expression when we exercise civility, in truth, restraint can be as much an expression of ourselves as is unfettered behavior.

REVIEW QUESTIONS

1. Define *perception* and *self-concept*. What is the relationship between the two?
2. What are some ways that self-concept affects communication?
3. Why is understanding perception and the self-concept important to our lives?
4. Define *culture* and *co-culture*. Describe cultures that are primarily individualistic and those that are primarily collectivistic.
5. How do culture, the workplace and your career, and gender influence perception and the self-concept?
6. What is the relationship among perception, self-concept, civility, and ethics?
7. What are the three stages in the perception process, and what influences how we engage in the three stages?
8. How do the fundamental attribution error and the self-serving bias influence perception?
9. Describe implicit personality theory and the halo effect and how they affect perception.
10. What are *self-image* and *self-esteem*, and how do they influence the perception of self?
11. What is *fact*, and what is *inference*? How can we distinguish fact from inference?
12. What is a perception check? How can perception checks help us communicate our perceptions in a civil manner?

3 Civil Verbal Communication

CHAPTER OBJECTIVES

After reading this chapter, you will be able to:

3.1 Define *verbal communication*.
3.2 Explain the relationship between verbal communication and meaning.
3.3 Explain how verbal communication can influence thought.
3.4 Use verbal communication skills that can improve your ability to communicate civilly.
3.5 Describe why profanity and cursing are uncivil and practice curbing their use.

ON JANUARY 8, 2011, one day after she sent an email in which she expressed a desire to promote civil discourse in politics, Arizona Democratic congresswoman Gabrielle Giffords was grievously wounded at a Tucson shopping center political rally. Giffords, whose office door was shot at in response to her support of national health care, was concerned about polarization and inflammatory political rhetoric. During the shooter's rampage, 11 others were wounded, and 6 people, including a nine-year-old child, were killed.

Soon after the tragedy, media pundits and politicians began searching for a reason for the carnage. Some blamed the uncivil political rhetoric that Congresswoman Giffords sought to mediate. Some said that the shooter was incited by uncivil communication associated with the Tea Party and the anti-immigration movements. Others contended that the shooter was mentally ill and that there was no evidence that his actions were politically motivated or influenced by uncivil rhetoric.[1] Still others suggested that it was the combination of anti-government feelings, uncivil discourse, and mental illness that influenced the shooter to specifically target Congresswoman Giffords.

The shooter could have responded to a number of different messages concerning Giffords and government in general. The shooter read books such as *Animal Farm*, *Brave New World*, and *The Communist Manifesto*; these works share the theme of institutions and governments trying to take away individual control. At the same time, Sarah Palin, a former vice presidential nominee, had placed a graphic on her website that put Giffords's district and other political opponents in the crosshairs of a gun sight. Giffords's recent political opponent had urged voters to "Get on target for victory in November. Help remove Gabrielle Giffords from office. Shoot a fully automatic M16 with Jesse Kelly."[2] While it was acknowledged that the shooter suffered from mental illness, some analysts argued that the shooting was not an isolated event and that it was associated with the uncivil political climate of the nation.[3] Others asserted that while the shooter may have been mentally ill, his political leanings and the normalization of uncivil and violent political rhetoric demonstrates that he targeted an officeholder.[4] Even President Obama expressed the hope that the tragedy in Tucson would help "usher in more civility in our public discourse."[5]

WHY IT MATTERS

Do you think uncivil communication may have contributed to the shootings in Tucson? Is it possible to link uncivil rhetoric, whether it occurs in politics, sports, entertainment, education, or our interpersonal relationships, to specific outcomes? In terms of interpersonal communication, do you know someone who engages in uncivil discourse? Do you or someone you know ever call people names, curse, and/or use incendiary speech? Have you ever struggled to find just the right word to express what you were thinking? Have you ever regretted your choice of words or used words incorrectly?

If you are familiar with such experiences, you have firsthand knowledge of the fact that effective verbal communication is difficult without the words needed to express our meanings. Maybe you once told your parents that you "love" them, told your roommate that you "love" your car, and told a friend that you "love" pepperoni pizza. Obviously, the word *love* has many meanings and may not be the best word to use in all situations to describe positive feelings toward someone or something. If *love* is the only word you can think of to describe your feelings, your communication may be ineffective because you may fail to get your precise meaning across to a conversation partner. Verbal communication enables us to interact with others—and that's an important reason verbal communication deserves study.

In this chapter, you will learn about the definition and characteristics of verbal communication and why understanding verbal communication is important in your everyday life. You will also read about the relationship between verbal communication and meaning and between verbal communication and thought. In addition, you will learn how to improve your ability to engage in civil verbal communication by using specific and concrete words and by owning your thoughts and feelings. You will also learn about uncivil verbal communication in the form of cursing and profanity and how to curb its use. Finally, you will read about the association between verbal communication and culture, workplace (your career), and gender contexts.

DEFINITION OF VERBAL COMMUNICATION

Can you recall a time when you were unable to communicate verbally with others? Perhaps you had your tonsils removed, experienced a bad sore throat, or were hoarse from too much shouting. If you are not fluent in ASL - American Sign Language (a signed language of symbols and a grammar for their use) or if you grew tired of using paper and pen to communicate, you probably found it difficult to convey your thoughts and feelings.

Verbal Communication and Meaning   49

Perhaps you appreciated what you had once taken for granted—the ability to use words to engage in verbal interaction.

Verbal communication is the use of words to create and convey meaning. We communicate verbally with **symbols** that stand for something else (i.e., words). The words used in verbal communication enable us to:

- Define and classify
- Express our beliefs, attitudes, thoughts, and feelings
- Organize our perceptions
- Talk about hypothetical events, events that occurred in the past, and events that may occur in the future

verbal communication The use of words to create and convey meaning.

symbols Verbal (i.e., words) and nonverbal communication that stands for something else.

VERBAL COMMUNICATION AND MEANING

Our ability to speak is not enough to communicate. We also need to share with others an understanding of what words mean. Misunderstandings can arise from not knowing what a word means or from not sharing the same meaning for a particular word. The triangle of meaning, denotative and connotative meanings, and the Coordinated Management of Meaning theory can help you understand how you attach meaning to verbal communication.

The Triangle of Meaning

Suppose a being from outer space beams down to Earth and somehow winds up in your bedroom. Looking around your environment, the space creature stares at an object it has never seen before: a clock. The being does not know what the object is, what the object is used for, or how to label the object. Your uninvited guest cannot even guess the name of the object because there's no apparent connection between what something is called (the symbol) and what something is (the referent).

The idea that words are symbolic and representative of something else is illustrated in the triangle of meaning, shown in Figure 3.1. Originally developed by linguists C. K. Ogden and I. A. Richards, the triangle of meaning shows that the relationship between words and what they stand for is arbitrary.[6] The line that connects a symbol (word) and its corresponding thought illustrates that we have our own meaning for a word, which may or may not be the same meaning that someone else uses for that word. The line that

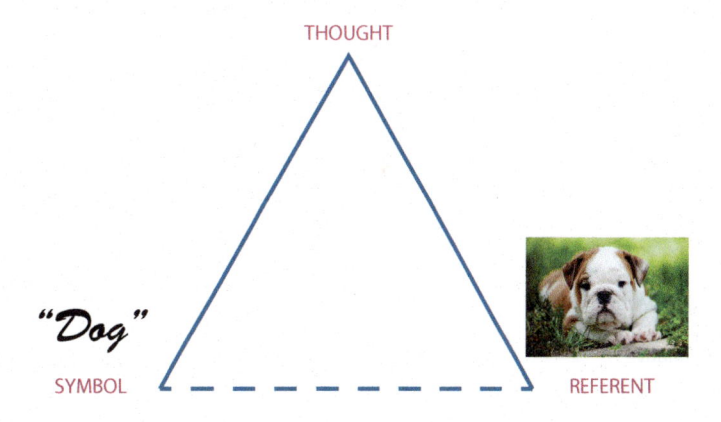

FIGURE 3.1 Ogden's Triangle of Meaning

The connection we make between the symbol and referent is unique to each person.

connects the referent (thing) and thought shows that we create mental images of the things we actually encounter. The broken line between the symbol and referent illustrates that there is an arbitrary relationship between a symbol and what it represents. There is no connection between the symbol and referent except the one we make with our thoughts.

Denotative and Connotative Meanings

Do you experience a strong emotional reaction when you read the word *jihad*? Zayed Yasin, a senior at Harvard University, sought to deliver a commencement address he titled "My American Jihad." Yasin asserted that his use of the word *jihad* referred to what the Quran defines as an "internal struggle," such as the struggle to do right, even at a personal cost. He also said that he wanted to reclaim the word from its incorrect interpretation as a "holy war." However, Harvard students began two online petitions in which they suggested that his use of the word was offensive and insensitive. One petition demanded that Yasin include an explicit condemnation of violent jihad in his speech, and the other insisted that a more appropriate graduation speaker be chosen to present the commencement address. In the end, Yasin agreed to Harvard's suggestion to change the title of his speech to "Of Faith and Citizenship," and he presented the otherwise unchanged speech without incident.[7] The different meanings for the word *jihad* in this scenario illustrate denotative and connotative meaning.

The broken line in Figure 3.2 illustrates that the words that make up a language can be placed on a continuum that ranges from highly denotative to highly connotative. **Denotative meaning** is what people think of when they ask what the "real meaning" of a word is—the "dictionary definition."

Denotative meanings tend to change very slowly, if at all. For example, when we look up the meaning for the word *jihad* in the dictionary, we find a definition similar to "a struggle, contest, or effort."[8] This definition is general and probably hasn't changed over the centuries. On the other hand, **connotative meaning** is emotional and personal and may engender disagreement. Connotative meanings are typically not found in dictionaries, and connotative meanings often change very quickly. The word *jihad*, for example, has a highly negative connotative meaning if we associate *jihad* with a doctrinal crusade or holy war. However, our connotative meaning for a word can change rapidly, depending on the context in which meaning occurs. Furthermore, our connotative meanings vary according to our experiences, beliefs, and attitudes. Whether or not we agree with Yasin's positive connotative meaning for the word *jihad* or the meanings held by Harvard petitioners, the point is that connotative meanings can produce strong emotional reactions.

Advertisers, speechwriters, editors, and others engaged in "word craft" realize that connotative meanings may produce highly negative reactions. To avoid such negative

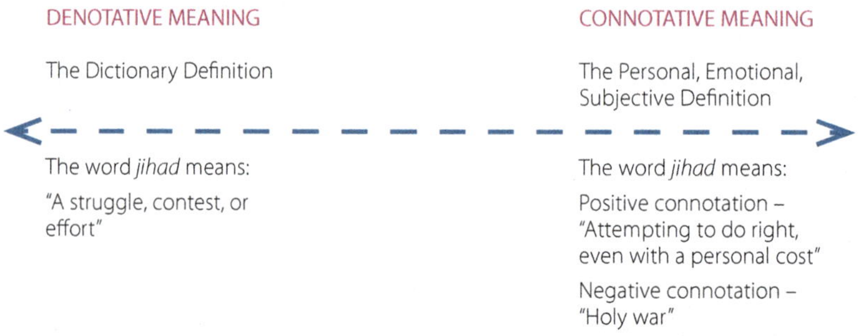

denotative meaning
Meaning that is considered to be "correct" and that is found in dictionaries.

connotative meaning
Meaning that is emotional and personal and that engenders disagreement.

FIGURE 3.2 Denotative and Connotative Meaning

To understand another person's meaning, we must consider the dictionary definition (denotative meaning) and the personal, emotional, and subjective definition (connotative meaning).

DENOTATIVE MEANING	CONNOTATIVE MEANING
The Dictionary Definition	The Personal, Emotional, Subjective Definition
The word *jihad* means: "A struggle, contest, or effort"	The word *jihad* means: Positive connotation – "Attempting to do right, even with a personal cost" Negative connotation – "Holy war"

Verbal Communication and Meaning

euphemisms Words with positive or neutral connotations that are used to replace words associated with unpleasant and negative connotations. Many euphemisms in the English language concern natural body functions and taboo topics such as death and sex.

reactions, they often use **euphemisms**, or words that are more pleasant, less distasteful, or neutral, to replace words that are associated with unpleasant and negative connotations. Many euphemisms in the English language concern natural body functions and taboo topics such as death and sex. For example, some people attempt to avoid the unpleasant connotations associated with the words *death* and *died* by using terms they find less bothersome, such as *passed away*, *deceased*, and *gone to a better place*.

Most words don't produce automatic, emotional reactions and include both connotative and denotative meanings. However, imagine that your friends use words such as *patriotism*, *liberal*, *money*, and *love* in a particular conversation. Will you and your friends implicitly share the same definitions for these words? Probably not. The use of these words can lead to misinterpretations, demonstrating that even words that are not associated with highly negative connotative meanings can contribute to misunderstandings and miscommunication.

Shortcuts in Communication: Jargon and Slang

Different groups tend to create shortcuts in communication that allow them to share meaning more quickly between themselves than they may be able to with people outside the group. These shortcuts take the form of slang and jargon.

Slang
Can you define the following words according to their slang meanings?

- Bling
- Homey
- Thirsty

slang A specialized vocabulary shared by people with similar experiences and interests. Slang establishes a sense of belonging and commonality among its users.

Slang is a specialized vocabulary shared by people with similar experiences and interests, including those related to the workplace. Slang establishes a sense of belonging and commonality among its users, whether users share an occupation or whether they share the enjoyment of a particular type of music, television show, or computer game. Occupations related to technology often fuel slang words used by the general public, such as the word *app* (short for "computer application"; *killer app* refers to an extremely good program).[9] Other slang words are influenced by youth, oppression, sports, and vice. Young people are the most powerful stimulus for creation of slang and use slang to define status, establish bonds with peers, and confound adults. As of this writing, current slang words include *bling* (anything that's shiny or new, such as jewelry), *homey* (friend), and *thirsty* (to really want something). As you may have guessed, slang changes very quickly and often "dies" from disuse or becomes a part of the common language. Lexicographers (people who compile dictionaries) maintain that the majority of new words included in dictionaries come from technological inventions and from slang.[10] However, slang changes so rapidly that the words compiled for a printed dictionary could possibly be out-of-date by the time the dictionary goes to press.

jargon A specialized vocabulary shared and understood by members of particular occupational groups. Jargon often functions as a "shorthand code" or quick method for sharing meaning.

Jargon
One source of jargon is the workplace. People who share your occupation may use special words that people outside your field may not use or understand. The workplace context influences verbal communication in terms of special words used by members of particular occupations and occupations that have influenced words used by the general public. Like slang, jargon is influenced by specific occupations.

Jargon is a specialized vocabulary shared and understood by members of particular occupational groups. Jargon often functions as a shorthand code or quick method for sharing meaning.[11] Perhaps you've watched a television medical show in which an emergency room doctor shouts instructions that end with "stat!" Saying "stat" is much easier and quicker than saying "This patient may die if you don't immediately do what I say!"

Read the following examples of jargon and guess which occupations they refer to. Then try to guess the meaning of the jargon:

- Behavior adjustment unit
- Flotation support system
- Manually operated humus excavator
- Therapeutic misadventures

Prison officials use the jargon "behavior adjustment unit" for solitary confinement. Furniture salespersons say "flotation support system" when they're talking about a waterbed. Government officials may use the term "manually operated humus excavator" to refer to a shovel. And doctors use the term "therapeutic misadventures" to refer to malpractice cases.

The correct use of jargon is an important element in computer games. A former member of the Delta Force and a former Navy SEAL (both part of the U.S. Special Operations Command) consulted with Electronic Arts on the Medal of Honor computer game to ensure that game details were specific and realistic and that jargon was used correctly. (Although the two retired soldiers did not receive official permission to work with Electronic Arts, sources inside the Special Operations community must have received at least tacit permission from their commanders to cooperate with Electronic Arts.) One portion of the Medal of Honor game featured a Navy SEAL instructing his teammates to look up at the second floor of a building. The former Navy SEAL told staff at Electronic Arts that the dialogue needed to be rewritten because SEALs wouldn't use the word *floor*. The dialogue was subsequently changed to reflect the correct use of jargon used by Navy SEALs: "Look up at the second *deck*."[12]

Jargon can provide us with a sense of belonging to a particular occupation and can make it easier to communicate with coworkers. Jargon can also cause someone to feel left out of a conversation and make it difficult for people to understand each other. In addition, sometimes you might perceive that jargon is being used in an uncivil manner to simply "show off"[13] or even mislead. Therefore, it can be a good idea to limit the use of jargon to those who share an occupation.

Physicians have a vast vocabulary of medical terminology and jargon that help them communicate in an efficient manner, but not everyone will be able to interpret this communication.

Verbal Communication and Gender

The effect of gender on our verbal communication reflects learned expectations . . . to a point. In general, both men and women tend to talk about work, movies, and television, and both talk about sex and sexuality with members of the same sex. Female friends tend to talk about people, feelings, problems, relationships, family, food, fashion, and men. Male friends tend to talk about music, sports, work, hobbies, and women.[14]

In a study about relating to spouses and strangers in which respondents were asked to describe dramatic or interesting life experiences, women made more reference to emotions, motivations, and themselves, and men made more references to destructive actions, time, and space.[15] Moreover, a group of men often begin conversation by establishing who is best informed about movies, books, current events, or other topics, perhaps because men tend to view communication primarily in terms of status and hierarchy.

TRENDS IN TECHNOLOGY AND SOCIAL MEDIA

"GR8 Tweet!"

Technology has dramatically changed our vocabulary, and the more technology evolves, the more our language changes. Some researchers contend that the Internet allows language users to be inventive and adaptive because it is a new medium that blends speaking and writing. Internet-mediated language is different from writing because of its immediacy and changeability, and it's different from speech because of the absence of nonverbal cues such as pitch, rhythm, and loudness. "Net lingo" blends aspects of speech and writing and yet is not completely either one. The same is true of communication produced by text messaging. Users regard this form of textual communication as something other than writing. Texting lingo is described as a hybrid of speech and writing in which people try to speak with their fingers. People who are interrupted while text messaging don't say, "Hold on, I'm writing." Instead, they say, "Hold on, I'm talking to someone."[16]

In addition, text messaging has added a wide variety of acronyms and new words to verbal communication. Acronyms include "RUOK" ("Are you OK?") and "CUL8R" ("See you later"). Shorthand terms such as BBLR ("Be back later"), GR8 ("great"), and HAND ("Have a nice day") that originated in text messaging have been included in the *Oxford English Dictionary*, as have the following:[17]

- Unfriend—To remove someone as a friend on a social networking site
- Netbook—A small laptop computer
- Going viral—A video or photo continuously forwarded to many people
- Intexticated—Distracted while driving because of texting on a cell phone
- Hashtag—A sign added to a word or phrase that enables Twitter users to search for postings

For those who are not tech savvy, online dictionaries are available to provide the meanings of many new words related to technology and social media.

Discussion Questions

1. What text messaging acronyms do you habitually use?
2. Have you ever not known the meaning of a text messaging acronym? What online dictionaries are available to help learn the meaning of new technology- and social media–related terms?
3. Have you ever used a text messaging acronym in an email? Have you ever used a text messaging acronym in a written assignment? Is it appropriate to use such acronyms in these channels of communication?
4. Have you ever used an Internet, technology, or social media–related term in casual conversation and not been understood? Were you civil and ethical in response to the misunderstanding?

---

gossip Communication about people (not necessarily against them).

Talking about such topics at the beginning of a gathering enables men to size up the competition and negotiate where they stand in relation to each other.

Interestingly, both men and women talk about people and the details of everyday life. Although the term **gossip** has negative connotations, this word also refers to talking about people (rather than talking against them). Both men and women gossip; however, they gossip about different topics. Men's interest in the details of politics, news, and sports is parallel to women's interest in the details of the personal lives of others and their relationships.[18]

A few caveats are in order when it comes to the relationship between gender and verbal communication. Many researchers assert that there are more similarities than there are differences in gender communication and that an overemphasis on differences doesn't paint a realistic picture of gender and communication.[19] In addition, research on gender communication typically fails to account for the relationship between the communicators, the topic under discussion, and the overall context. For example, one study found that women use "feminine language" (characterized by questions, intensive adverbs such as *very* and *so*, and personal pronouns) when talking to their husbands or other men. However, men generally use "masculine language" (characterized by interruptions and directives) when talking to women but change their styles when speaking with their wives.[20] Remember that our language patterns don't typically follow one particular gender style to the exclusion of the other. We can choose whether to communicate verbally in a manner that reflects a masculine style, a feminine style, or a style that reflects aspects of both.

The Coordinated Management of Meaning

Even though it may be difficult to assign specific meaning to our verbal communication, we attempt to coordinate the various meanings of the words through the application of communication rules. Communication theorists W. Barnett Pearce and Vernon Cronen developed the theory of **Coordinated Management of Meaning (CMM)** to explain how people are able to come to agree on the meaning of verbal communication. According to this theory, the application of syntactic, semantic, and pragmatic rules enables conversation partners to experience meaning from their communication.[21]

Syntactic rules refer to how symbols are arranged, and **semantic rules** refer to what symbols mean. **Pragmatic rules** help us interpret verbal communication in a given context. Pragmatic rules also enable us to determine how to respond or behave within that context. As illustrated in Figure 3.3, all three types of rules work together to help us understand verbal communication.

For example, suppose someone says to you, "From vacation just I back got a great." Would you understand the comment? Probably not. Would you understand the statement in the following format: "I just got back from a great vacation"? Because it follows the accepted syntactic rules, you have a better understanding of the utterance.

Although we understand the words, however, we may still struggle to communicate exactly what we mean and to understand others' comments. What do you think of when you hear the words *great vacation*? Our shared semantic rules tell us that *great* means something "positive" and that *vacation* means something "out of the ordinary." However, each person's own specific meanings for *great vacation* will vary. For example, do you think *great vacation* means basking in the sun on a deserted beach? Do you think of camping and hiking as activities that occur during a *great vacation*? Maybe you think a *great vacation* includes dancing till dawn at popular nightclubs in exciting cities.

Coordinated Management of Meaning A theory which says that the application of syntactic, semantic, and pragmatic rules enables conversation partners to experience meaning based on coherence, coordination, and mystery.

syntactic rules Rules that specify how symbols are arranged (e.g., a grammar).

semantic rules Rules that specify what symbols stand for or mean. Semantic rules are found in dictionaries and concern denotative meanings.

pragmatic rules Rules that help us interpret verbal communication in a given context.

Syntactic Rules – the way symbols are arranged
For example, unlike Spanish, English requires that adjectives precede nouns:
English - *"She is a smart woman."*
Spanish - *"Es una mujer intelligente."*

Semantic Rules – what symbols mean
For example: Meanings can be denotative or connotative. Consider again:
   "She is a smart woman"
Does this mean she gets good grades, has "street smarts," or has emotional intelligence (EQ)?

Pragmatic Rules – what symbols mean in a given context
For example, a statement may be related to those that precede it:
Preceding sentences in a conversation about empathy indicate that *"smart"* refers to EQ.

FIGURE 3.3 Pearce and Cronen's the Coordinated Management of Meaning

Syntactic, semantic, and pragmatic rules work together to enable conversation partners to experience meaning.

According to the theory of the Coordinated Management of Meaning, getting a job may be based on the meaning the interviewer experiences during the interview that is invisible and "mysterious" to you.

coherence In terms of the Coordinated Management of Meaning theory, "making meaning" is the goal of conversation.

coordination In terms of the Coordinated Management of Meaning theory, how meaning is created by the rules we use to manage talk and create our social realities.

mystery In terms of the Coordinated Management of Meaning theory, mystery refers to the idea that coherence and coordination are arbitrary and are created by language. Mystery also suggests that the words we use not only create and name things in our experience of reality but also limit them and can make them invisible.

Pragmatic rules can help us understand meaning by attending to the context or overall topic of a conversation when meanings are unclear. For instance, if you and a conversation partner are talking about the world's best beaches, it's likely (but not definite) that the statement "I just got back from a great vacation!" refers to the topic of discussion—beaches—and that the "great vacation" somehow involved sand and surf. Taken alone, "I just got back from a great vacation!" may indicate "climbing high mountains" to one person and "visiting historic museums" to another person. Our pragmatic rules tell us that meaning is situational; if your conversation had instead been focused on great cities in Europe, a "great vacation" comment would possibly concern London or Paris.

According to the theory of Coordinated Management of Meaning, participants in conversations experience meaning through coherence, coordination, and mystery. **Coherence** refers to our goal of "making meaning" through conversation. This meaning is **coordinated** by the rules of conversation we use to manage talk and create our social realities. **Mystery** refers to the idea that coherence and coordination are arbitrary and are created by language. Mystery also suggests that the words we use not only create and name things in our experience of reality but also limit them and can make them invisible. If we realize that words limit our experience of reality, we can understand that there may be something *more* to reality than what we can communicate by using words. Although what is "more" is unknown and mysterious, this knowledge can help us transcend the power of words to limit our perceptions of the world.[22] For example, suppose you are feeling anxious about an upcoming job interview. You can attempt to alleviate your fears by thinking about the fact that you and your interviewer will probably share syntactic and semantic rules that will help you experience coherence and coordinate meaning. Pragmatic rules will help you predict that most, if not all, interview questions will concern job-related topics. Similarly, pragmatic rules will help you predict that your answers will be interpreted in terms of how well you meet the job requirements and whether you appear to be a good fit with the company. However, you may realize that there's more to reality than words can communicate and that getting the job may be based on the meaning the interviewer experiences during the interview that is invisible and "mysterious" to you.

VERBAL COMMUNICATION AND THOUGHT

The symbols used in verbal communication influence our perceptions of the world. For example, an Oxford University study had respondents smell a cheesy aroma while one of two labels simultaneously flashed on a screen. Respondents who read the "cheddar cheese" label rated the aroma as "pleasant," and respondents who read the "body odor" label did not.[23] How we react to others' communication and how others react to our communication are significantly based on the words that are expressed during verbal communication.

Words That Strongly Influence Thought

Words are often specifically used to influence thought and action. For example, microbiologist and former USDA meat inspector Gerald Zirnstein wanted to find a new name for the "lean finely textured beef" filler that had been used in "100% ground beef" products for decades. Zirnstein thought this description was misleading and believed that the filler, made of fatty bits of beef scrap, sinew, fat, and connective tissue that are heated and treated with ammonium to kill bacteria, should not be mixed into beef. His new label, "pink slime," was quoted in a 2009 *New York Times* article. The article influenced celebrity chef Jamie Oliver to criticize the filler, and major fast food companies and grocery store chains promised to stop selling beef that included pink slime. One food blogger received more than 200,000 signatures within one week when she posted a petition to ban pink slime in school lunches. Beef Products, which makes the filler, eventually had to close plants in four states and blamed the closings on unfounded attacks. Whether or not the attacks were unfounded, the label "pink slime" raised awareness of the filler that most Americans hadn't previously known or cared about. In fact, "pink slime" has been described as the nickname that dramatically changed the entire beef industry.[24]

Another example of how words can influence thought occurs in the form of an analogy; pay particular attention to the italicized words here: "An *undeveloped fertilized egg* doesn't describe a baby any more than a seed describes a rose bush." What did you envision when you read the italicized words "undeveloped fertilized egg"? How might the overall terminology used in this analogy influence your thoughts? Whether you agree or disagree with the analogy, you can see that words have the power to influence beliefs and behavior in our conversations with others. Suppose you find yourself in a discussion about abortion. Would you use one of the labels of "pro-life" or "pro-choice"? How might you react to hearing the word *murder* versus *prevention*? Would you use labels such as "fetus" or "zygote," or would you use labels such as "baby" or "pre-born child"? Even if you've never engaged in a discussion about abortion, you can probably understand how the phrases "eliminating a product of conception" and "fighting for the rights of the unborn" can influence thought.

The powerful influence of words on thought is recognized by governments that have "information ministries" and political candidates who have "media advisors."[25] In fact, the government, military, and big business have been accused of deliberately using language that conceals the truth and/or shifts responsibility to influence people's perceptions. Just as euphemisms are used to make unpleasant people, places, and things appear more palatable, **doublespeak** is used deliberately by those in the government, big business, and the media to mislead and to manipulate.[26] For example, in 2006 the U.S. Department of Agriculture used the phrase "low food security" to describe persons with low incomes who can't afford to buy food and who go hungry.[27] The CIA used the phrase "enhanced interrogation techniques" when describing tactics used to elicit information from al-Qaeda detainees; others described the tactics as "torture."[28] In an effort to neutralize the loaded terms used to describe the economic crisis, businesspeople and politicians substituted "synergy-related head-count adjustments" for the layoffs that occurred at Nokia, "global economic restructuring" for "global financial crisis," and "exceptional assistance" for "bailout."[29]

doublespeak Language used deliberately to mislead and to manipulate.

Words That Subtly Influence Thought

You may believe that you are aware of how words are used to influence perceptions; however, many words you hear, read, and use to describe people, things, and events can subtly influence your perceptions in ways you're unaware of. For example, have you ever read that Christopher Columbus "discovered" America? Reflect on this idea for a moment. How might the word *discovered* subtly influence thought? This terminology implies that Native Americans were invisible or insignificant until a European recognized their existence.[30] Another example of the ability of words to subtly influence thought concerns how we label co-cultures or racial or ethnic groups. For example, do you label people of color "non-white"? The label "non-white" implies that "whiteness" is the standard and norm; consider why white people aren't labeled people of "non-color." Have you ever heard people of color labeled "minority group"? How does the label "minority group" subtly affect our thoughts? Some people believe that "minority group" suggests insignificance or something that is negligible.[31] Will U.S. citizens of European ancestry accept the label "minority group" when "non-whites" outnumber "whites" in the year 2050?[32] The words used to describe people, places, and things can, unbeknownst to us, affect our thoughts.

Verbal Communication and Culture

The relationship between culture and language is reciprocal. Changes in language affect culture, and changes in culture affect language.[33] Culture influences our language (and therefore how we perceive the world), and the language we speak reflects cultural values. The relationships between language and culture are illustrated by the low- and high-context belief systems and by the Sapir-Whorf hypothesis.

Low- and High-Context Belief Systems

What would you think if you asked someone a question, and the person didn't respond but remained silent? Would you think your conversation partner was rude and acting in an uncivil manner? Or would you consider that the lack of response is civil because the situation required politeness and restraint? These interpretations may relate to the differences between low-context and high-context cultures.

Recall that social scientists create cultural pattern taxonomies, or belief systems, to understand cultural similarities and differences. One cultural taxonomy that is relevant to verbal communication involves low-context and high-context cultures. Characteristics of low-context and high-context cultures are illustrated in Table 3.1. Much like individualist

Table 3.1 Low-Context and High-Context Cultures

People who tend to gather meaning from the environment use a high-context style of communication. People who gather meaning from the actual words spoken use a low-context communication style.

Low-Context Cultures	High-Context Cultures
• Communication is direct.	• Communication is indirect.
• The focus is on verbal communication for meaning rather than on situational factors.	• The focus is on situational factors and nonverbal communication for meaning rather than relying solely on verbal communication.
• Communication in individualist cultures tend to be low context.	• Communication in collectivist cultures tend to be high context.
• Members of low-context cultures tend to focus on individual personality to explain communication behavior.	• Members of high-context cultures tend to focus on the situation to explain communication behavior.
• Verbal fluency and self-expression are admired, regardless of whether they cause someone to stand out from the crowd or lose "face" (dignity).	• Communication that contributes to harmonious relationships is admired, such as talk that enables others to save "face" (dignity).

low-context cultures Cultures that tend to communicate in a very direct manner. Members of low-context cultures focus on verbal communication for meaning and do not rely on situational factors when communicating or interpreting messages.

high-context cultures Cultures that tend to communicate in an indirect manner. Members of high-context cultures focus on situational factors for meaning and do not rely solely on verbal communication when communicating or interpreting messages.

Sapir-Whorf hypothesis A hypothesis which illustrates that culture influences language and language influences cultural differences in thought.

and collectivist cultures, no culture is 100 percent low-context or high-context and both patterns exist in all cultures, although one pattern usually dominates.

People who are members of primarily **low-context cultures** tend to communicate in a very direct manner. Members of low-context cultures focus on verbal communication for meaning and tend not to rely on situational factors when communicating or interpreting messages. In addition, verbal fluency and self-expression are admired in low-context cultures, whether or not they cause someone to stand out from the crowd or lose "face" (dignity).[34] Examples of low-context cultures include the United States, Canada, Australia, Israel, and most of northern Europe.[35] Individualist cultures tend to also be low-context cultures, and like members of individualist cultures, members of low-context cultures may focus on an individual's personality to explain communication behavior. In the case of a conversation partner who fails to answer a question, a member of a low-context culture may attribute the "uncivil behavior" to her or his "rude personality." In contrast, members of primarily **high-context cultures** tend to communicate in an indirect manner. Members of high-context cultures focus on situational factors for meaning and tend not to rely solely on verbal communication when communicating or interpreting messages. Situational factors can include the relationship between the communicators, the place where the conversation occurs, and the nonverbal communication (e.g., eye contact, tone of voice, the amount of time that passes before a response is uttered) displayed by those involved in the conversation. In addition, communication that contributes to harmonious relationships is admired in high-context cultures, such as talk that enables others to save "face."[36] Examples of high-context cultures include Japan, China, Korea, and many African and Latin American countries.[37] Collectivist cultures tend to also be high-context cultures. In the case of a conversation partner who fails to answer a question, a member of a high-context culture isn't likely to attribute the behavior to personality; instead, the lack of response will be perceived as civil communication that is sensitive to the situation.

Overall, the communication characteristics associated with low- and high-context cultures can influence the perception of civility and can cause incidents of miscommunication. Can you imagine someone from a low-context culture becoming impatient with a person from a high-context culture who doesn't "get to the point" or who appears to be evasive? Can you imagine someone from a high-context culture feeling insulted because of direct communication uttered by someone from a low-context culture? These examples illustrate that knowledge of low- and high-context cultures can help us avoid mistaken perceptions of incivility and that this knowledge is important in our everyday lives.

The Sapir-Whorf Hypothesis

Linguists Edward Sapir and Benjamin Lee Whorf hypothesized that culture significantly affects how people think and communicate. Although it lacks hard evidence, the **Sapir-Whorf hypothesis** posits that culture influences language and that language influences cultural differences in thought. The original version of their hypothesis, sometimes labeled the "deterministic" or "firm" version, compared language to a prison to indicate that we are trapped by our language and cannot escape its influence on how we perceive the world. The deterministic position holds that we cannot perceive something unless we have the words to describe it. The "relativistic" or "softer" version of the Sapir-Whorf hypothesis, which is more widely accepted than the deterministic position, posits that language reflects what we need to know to cope in our culture and reinforces our culturally influenced patterns of thought, beliefs, attitudes, values, and rules for behavior. The relativistic version also posits that the language we use influences us to perceive and label certain things in our environment.[38]

Sapir and Whorf explained their hypothesis with a hypothetical story of a guard who walks into a warehouse that contains gasoline barrels labeled "empty." The guard decides to light a cigarette, and the result is an explosion. Sapir and Whorf explained that the guard thought it was safe to light a cigarette because the English language has no word for "empty-of-original-gas-content-but-incendiary-fumes-may-remain." Does this story sound unrealistic? Unfortunately, Sapir and Whorf's hypothetical example became all too real for the passengers aboard a ValuJet flight. Although potentially flammable oxygen generators aboard the jet had been labeled "Oxygen canisters—empty," they were suspected as the source of a fire and subsequent crash. While the canisters were empty of their original contents, they contained a trace of a chemical considered to be "hazardous waste" that requires special handling.[39] However, the English language is based on a cultural assumption of linear cause–effect thinking that is typical of individualist cultures. Consequently, English influences speakers to think and speak according to polar opposites or dichotomies.[40] It is therefore much easier to think and speak in English in terms of the polar opposites of "full" and "empty" than in terms of words that can more accurately reflect the true nature of a situation—that is, words that describe a middle ground between two extremes.

IMPROVING OUR ABILITY TO ENGAGE IN CIVIL AND EFFECTIVE VERBAL COMMUNICATION

"Engineering students are 'nerds.'"
"I know what you really mean."
"Liz never wants to do anything fun."

Can you see how these sentences may cause misinterpretations if we use them in conversations with others? These sentences illustrate two categories of problematic verbal communication: abstraction and allness. We can reduce the misinterpretations caused by these types of problematic talk when we communicate civilly with specific and concrete words, by engaging in indexing, and by owning our thoughts and feelings.

abstraction The levels of specificity in language. In general, highly connotative words tend to be highly abstract.

The use of abstract language, indiscrimination, allness, and other problematic communication behaviors can lead to socially awkward situations.

Abstraction

Abstraction refers to levels of specificity in language. In general, words with many connotations also tend to be highly abstract. On the one hand, abstract language helps people avoid the necessity of constantly "overexplaining" what they mean. For example, if we tell a good friend that we think she or he is "a good listener," we have eliminated the need for a wordy overexplanation. We need not overexplain by saying, "You let me say what I need to say before you respond" (meaning that our friend doesn't interrupt), "You support me by saying 'Uh-huh' and 'go on'" (meaning that our friend encourages us to continue speaking), or "You give me good advice" (meaning our friend offers excellent solutions to problems). However, which meaning—"listener who doesn't interrupt," "listener who is encouraging," or "listener who provides excellent solutions to problems"—will our friend apply to our compliment about being a good listener? Our friend might possibly have her or his own interpretation of what we mean by "good listener."

ASK THE ETHICIST: Why Can't I Just Say What I Want?

Question Why do I have to make an effort to speak the way other people expect me to? Why can't I just say what I want and let them say what they want? Isn't trying to adapt my language to others just indulging in political correctness?

Answer We're always free to make choices. But there are consequences associated with those choices. If you choose to use bad language with a customer service representative on the phone or face to face, it is likely that person will choose to terminate the conversation; more companies are supporting the right of their representatives to say "no" to verbal abuse. Using jargon that shuts other people out of your conversation, or using obscenities, or telling crude jokes will affect how people perceive your competence, your civility, and your ethics. It's difficult simply to "be yourself" (whatever that is) and live with the fallout.

Almost all world religions contain statements of ethics concerning how people should treat one another. The Council for Secular Humanism, which espouses no religion, has created a statement that includes expectations concerning the way we should respond to each other.[41] There's a saying that everyone brings joy to a situation—some when they come, and some when they leave. Speaking in a way that pleases only yourself is likely to put you in the latter category.

But it goes beyond that. If you are only worried about how people will perceive you because of your language use, you are focused too narrowly. It's hard to live in isolation. For the most part, we live in community, and community is sustained through words that reinforce the idea that we're all in this together. More importantly, the words we use can be life giving or spirit killing. Think of the way you have felt when you have received praise for a job well done or criticism that wasn't deserved. The power of our words is enormous. It's probably a good idea to use them wisely.

The following two examples show how the use of abstract language can lead to serious consequences:

- On January 25, 1990, 73 people were killed as a result of a Boeing 707 crashing in New York. The National Transportation Safety Board asserted that miscommunication between the air traffic controllers and the flight crew was involved in the crash. Although the airline pilots used the words "running out of fuel" when communicating with the controllers, they failed to use specific language such as "fuel emergency" that would have resulted in immediate clearance for landing.[42]

- In a week of televised reruns of the World Trade Center attacks on September 11, 2001, Eunice Stone called the police from a roadside diner in Georgia. She had listened to what she had thought were terrorist-sounding plans discussed by three men who looked like they were from the Middle East. Stone overheard the men use sentences such as "Do you think we have enough to bring it down?" and "If we don't have enough, I have contacts. We can get enough to bring it down." But what did the abstract language in the phrase "bring it down" actually refer to? Were the men talking about "bringing down" a building like the World Trade Center? Were the men talking about "bringing down" an airplane? In reality, the three men, all medical students in clinical training at Larkin Hospital in Florida, were talking about bringing a car to Miami, yet they were the subject of a two-state, nationally televised search.[43]

You may think that these examples are atypical and that you will never experience such abstraction-related problems when you talk to others. Although the consequences of your abstract language use may not be as dire as these examples, they may cause problems in your interpersonal communication and relationships.

Civil Communication: Using Specific and Concrete Words

Abstract language can cause problems in our communication and relationships. For example, have you ever called someone a "jerk" (or worse)? What was your conversation partner's response? Instead of using an abstract word with negative connotations, we can use civil and ethical communication that is concrete and specific. The idea that language can move from highly abstract to highly specific and concrete is illustrated in Figure 3.4. Near the top of the ladder of abstraction, where language is the most abstract, is the sentence "You're a jerk." *Jerk* is a word that is so abstract that it can mean just about anything negative. Moving down the ladder of abstraction is the sentence "You're lazy." This sentence is more specific than "You're a jerk" (it implies something to do with physical activity), but it still is open to a myriad of meanings. The sentence near the middle of the ladder, "You don't help around the house," is even more specific than the previous sentence, but what is the meaning of the word *help*? Does *help* mean doing our fair share of dusting, vacuuming, and washing, or does it mean that we lift our legs while someone else vacuums underneath them? Moving on, perhaps you once communicated at the next level of specificity when you told a roommate or partner, "You don't clean up after yourself around the house." Maybe you thought that you clearly communicated your meaning and were surprised when you discovered articles of clothing scattered across the floor. Because "clean up after yourself" is an abstract phrase, your roommate or partner could have interpreted it to mean putting the dishes in the dishwasher after a meal. The lowest level of the ladder of abstraction includes the most specific and behaviorally oriented language, with **concrete words** based on sense data, such as "You leave your shoes, socks, and books near the door instead of taking them to your room." This sentence is civil, ethical, and so specific that there is no doubt as to its meaning.

concrete words Words based on sense data.

Allness

Do you know people who think they know everything about everything and who think their meanings and interpretations are the only ones that are correct? **Allness** refers to the incorrect assumption that it is possible to know everything about a person, place, or thing. Maybe you have an acquaintance who is characterized as a "know-it-all," someone who believes she

allness The incorrect idea that it is possible to know everything about a person, place, or thing. Allness results from the first stage in the perception process, during which we attend to some stimuli and filter out the rest. Allness also results from the multiple factors that can affect meaning.

FIGURE 3.4 The Ladder of Abstraction

When our message is that we want to get more help around the house, the ladder of abstraction can help us frame our communication in an effective way.

Source: Shelley D. Lane, *Interpersonal Communication: Competence and Contexts*, 2nd ed. Boston: Allyn & Bacon, 2010, p. 127.

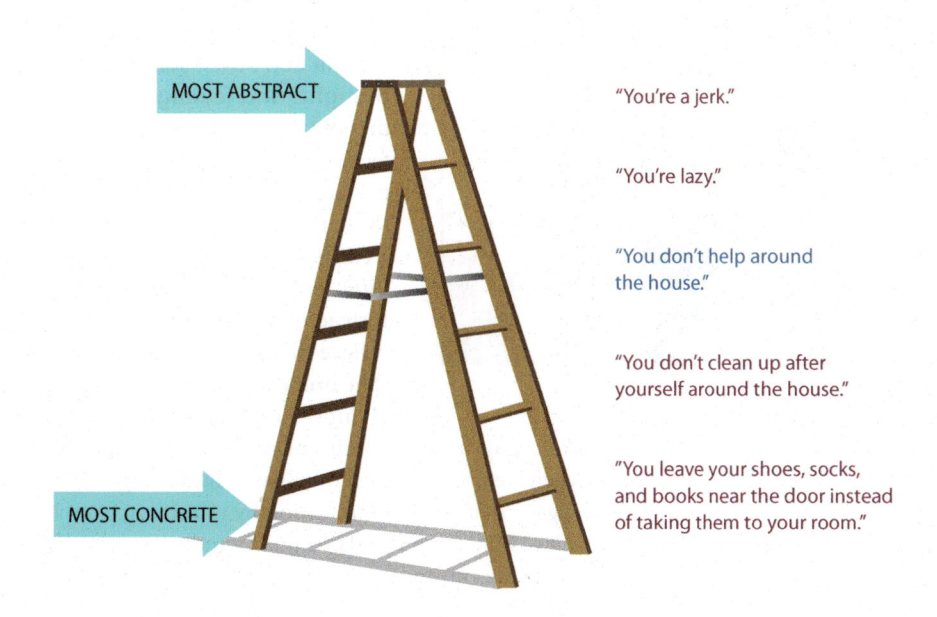

MOST ABSTRACT

"You're a jerk."

"You're lazy."

"You don't help around the house."

"You don't clean up after yourself around the house."

"You leave your shoes, socks, and books near the door instead of taking them to your room."

MOST CONCRETE

or he can say all there is that can be said about a subject. "Know-it-alls" erroneously assume that they cannot learn anything new about a subject and therefore are unwilling to acknowledge that their meanings may change upon learning new information. The perception process occurs in three stages: selection, organization, and interpretation. Allness results from the first stage in the perception process, during which we attend to some stimuli and filter out the rest. Once we organize the stimuli we attend to, we interpret or attach meaning to the stimuli we've selected from the environment. Because we cannot attend to all the stimuli that bombard us for attention, we fail to attend to stimuli that have the potential to change our meanings and interpretations. Thus, allness can occur when we draw conclusions based on insufficient stimuli or evidence.[44] Allness also results from the multiple factors that can affect meaning. Sometimes the words we use indicate that our meanings or versions of "truth" are *the* only meanings or versions of "truth." However, as you have read in this chapter, our meanings and interpretations vary according to our experiences, beliefs, and attitudes. We have also learned that another person's meanings may be invisible, or "mysterious," to others. Allness occurs when we fail to acknowledge that we don't have a corner on the truth and that others' meanings may be as valid as our own.[45]

Civil Communication: Indexing and Owning Thoughts and Feelings

Because one person's meaning is not the same as another's, we can engage in indexing and owning our thoughts and feelings to demonstrate that we acknowledge and respect the others' meanings. Both indexing and owning thoughts and feelings are civil and ethical because they acknowledge that we realize that we don't know "everything" and that our meanings and interpretations are influenced by many factors, including culture, careers, gender, and experiences. **Indexing** recognizes differences in thought and opinion that may be based on insufficient evidence. Indexing also communicates that we are open to different meanings and interpretations. Indexing-related words and phrases include *maybe*, *it could be*, and *perhaps*. For example, instead of saying, "He failed his classes because he partied too much," we can say, "Maybe he failed his classes because he partied too much." Instead of saying, "Your parents trust you but don't trust your friends," we can say, "It could be that your parents trust you but don't trust your friends." In addition, **owning our thoughts and feelings** is a way to accept responsibility for our thoughts and feelings and recognize that others may not think and feel as we do. When we own our thoughts and feelings, we communicate respect for others' meanings and that we may be willing to change our opinions. One way we can own our thoughts and feelings is by using the pronouns *I* and *my* with words such as *think*, *believe*, *feel*, *perceive*, *thoughts*, *beliefs*, and *perception*. Instead of saying, "The death penalty is immoral," we can say, "I believe the death penalty is immoral." Similarly, instead of saying, "She broke up with him because she got tired of him," we can say "I think she broke up with him because she got tired of him."

We engage in civil communication when we use concrete words to avoid abstraction and when we use indexing and owning our thoughts and feelings to avoid allness. We can also engage in civil communication by refraining from the use of curse words. Some people believe that cursing adds emphasis and power to an utterance; however, there are other ways we can communicate emphatically in a civil and ethical manner.

---

indexing A communication skill that recognizes differences in thought and opinion that may be based on insufficient evidence. Indexing also communicates that we are open to different meanings and interpretations. Indexing-related words and phrases include *maybe*, *it could be*, and *perhaps*.

owning our thoughts and feelings A way to accept responsibility for our thoughts and feelings and recognize that others may not think and feel as we do.

We can remain civil in a heated exchange when we use concrete words to avoid abstraction and when we use indexing and owning our thoughts and feelings to avoid allness.

UNCIVIL LANGUAGE: PROFANITY AND CURSING

Can you think of a famous person or celebrity who uses foul language? What about an elected official? While it may be easy for you to name one or more creative artists who engage in cursing, it may be more difficult for you to think of a respected public servant who curses . . . or maybe not. For example, former Republican Vice President Dick Cheney cursed Democratic Senator Patrick Leahy on the Senate floor after a group photo shoot. Leahy said hello to Cheney after the Senate photo, and a confrontation began as Cheney criticized Leahy's remarks about alleged war profiteering in Iraq. Cheney told Leahy to "@#$%! off," and Leahy later told reporters that he "was kind of shocked to hear that kind of language on the floor."[46] Current Democratic Vice President Joe Biden was also caught using foul language. After the vice president introduced President Obama prior to signing the health care reform bill, Biden shook the president's hand and said, "You did it. It's a big @#$%! deal."[47]

While people may curse to express anger, to make a point, or to merely "fill up space," some people believe that profanity, cursing, and other forms of crude language illustrate uncivil and ethical behavior. *Cursing*, *profanity*, and *crude language* are often defined synonymously. This type of verbal communication is described as "vulgar" and "irreverent," and words such as "obscene" and "foul" are associated with such language.[48] No matter the label, cursing is a common occurrence. Approximately one-third of the respondents in a Public Agenda poll admitted that they use foul language in public.[49] A 2006 Associated Press-Ipsos poll found that 74 percent of respondents frequently or occasionally hear profanity in public, 67 percent believe people curse more today than 20 years ago, and 64 percent admit to using the "F-word." Swearing and foul language occur in schools and at sporting events, are overheard in shopping malls, are flaunted by radio "shock-jocks," are found on TV and in the movies, are emblazoned on clothing, and are used in public by politicians.[50]

Do you become uncomfortable when you hear others curse? In the Associated Press-Ipsos poll mentioned earlier, 74 percent of the women and 60 percent of the men questioned said they are bothered by cursing. Although we might believe that swearing may help us "let off some steam" every now and then, it can become habit forming, and we may begin to pepper our speech with crude language no matter what the occasion. In addition, our venting behavior may result in displacing our anger toward an innocent victim of our curse words. Swearing may also lead to physical violence; arguments that escalate into physical assault almost always involve cursing.[51]

Overall, cursing and profanity reflect uncivil and unethical behavior. Civil communication involves respect, restraint, and responsibility. Ethical behavior is trustworthy, responsible, respectful, fair, and kind, and it illustrates concern for the community. This means that cursing and profanity are uncivil and unethical because such language entails expressing ourselves without concern for others and our community. Some cities (e.g., Raritan, New Jersey; Fostoria, Ohio; and Middleborough, Massachusetts) recognize cursing as uncivil, and they have enacted ordinances that ban swearing in public. In addition, restaurant and shop owners recognize the uncivil and unethical nature of cursing and profanity and can ask customers to leave if they use words that other patrons find offensive.[52] Institutions of higher learning also

Both Republican Dick Cheney and Democrat Joe Biden used the "F-word" in pubic while Vice President of the United States.

A CASE STUDY IN ETHICS

The Cursing Prof and "Conservative Coming Out Week"

Evaluate the following scenario, where a professor uses profanity to protest a campus activity she found offensive in terms of ethical communication (including trustworthiness, responsibility, respect, fairness, caring, and citizenship) and civil communication (including respect, restraint, and responsibility). Keep these definitions in mind as you read the following case study and answer the discussion questions.

University of Iowa professor of anthropology and women's studies Ellen Lewin sent a "@#$%! off" email in response to the College Republicans' university-wide invitation to Conservative Coming Out Week. Conservative Coming Out Week was advertised on the University of Iowa College Republicans website as an opportunity for conservatives in Iowa City to "come out of the closet." Events included an animal rights barbecue and an invitation to "pick up your doctor's notes to miss class for 'sick-of-stress,' just like the Wisconsin public employees during the union protests."[53] Lewin later apologized for her remarks and explained that her email was prompted by the College Republicans' disrespect toward union workers, animal-rights activists, and the gay, lesbian, bisexual, and transgender (GLBT) community.

Lewin received close to 400 email responses, many laced with vulgarities, protesting her message to the members of the College Republicans. Although Democrat and Republican student leaders disagreed about the appropriateness of Conservative Coming Out Week, leaders from both sides expressed concern about Lewin's language. Students, alumni, and community members wrote that they were outraged over Lewin's communication, that they no longer planned to support the university financially, and that Lewin deserved to be fired. One professor blogged that Lewin had engaged in unethical communication, based on the American Association of University Professors (AAUP) "Statement of Principles on Academic Freedom and Tenure," which informs professors that the public will judge them and their university/college on their communication. Specifically, professors are told that "they should at all times be accurate, should exercise appropriate restraint, [and] should show respect for the opinions of others."[54]

On the other hand, Lewin received some support for her actions. A graduate student in the anthropology department said that he completely and utterly agreed with Lewin's comment, and the student government director of sustainability thanked her for sending her initial email and the subsequent email of apology. The president-elect of the University of Iowa College Democrats said that while Lewin's comments were disrespectful, the College Republicans' "coming out" campaign was offensive. H. Brinton Milward, director of the National Institute for Civil Discourse, pointed out that Lewin used just one profane word and that her remarks alone don't qualify as civil or uncivil discourse.[55]

Discussion Questions

1. Do you think communicating in an unethical and uncivil manner is justified, particularly when responding to perceived unethical and uncivil behavior?
2. Are the responses that Lewin received any more or less unethical than her one-word profane comment?
3. Which do you think was least ethical or civil—the College Republicans' "coming out" event, Lewin's email, or the responses from students, alumni, and members of the community?
4. Should college professors be held to higher standards of ethics and civil communication than others?
5. Do you agree with the idea that one profane word doesn't necessarily qualify as civil or uncivil discourse?

---

recognize cursing as being uncivil and unethical. For example, Hinds Community College can fine students up to $50 for "public profanity, cursing and vulgarity."[56] Rather than using a code of conduct to limit cursing, officials at Onondaga Community College use peer pressure to limit the expression of vulgarities. The "Create Change" campaign encourages students to take ownership of bad behavior and to discourage bad behavior among themselves.[57]

It is possible for us to communicate emphatically without the use of curse words or profane language. One way to do this is by monitoring our own behavior. This doesn't mean that we completely abandon the use of profanity or crude language, but it does mean that we reflect on the time and place that we use such language. For example, we can refrain from swearing in front of young people who may be influenced to imitate the crude language they hear. Even if parents teach their children not to use profanity and crude language, the children may be confused if they hear it in public and may mimic the use of curse words to appear "adult."[58] We can also curb our use of curse words by finding civil and ethical substitutes. We can make up our own cuss words or use words that reflect alliteration or assonance (e.g., "Everything I touch turns to *trash*"). However, breaking the habit of using curse words and profanity may be difficult. Realistic goals can motivate a person to keep this type of uncivil speech at bay. For example, you may initially set a goal to drop a couple of curse words every few days before working your way up to your desired state.[59] Another way to avoid the use of curse words is to learn how to communicate in an assertive manner rather than an aggressive manner; you will learn assertive communication skills when you read about conflict and communication in Chapter 8. If we recognize that free speech should be tempered by the norm of civility and ethical communication, we can be motivated to rein in our impulses to swear and use hurtful words.[60]

CHAPTER SUMMARY

Now that you have read this chapter you can:

3.1 Define *verbal communication*.

Verbal communication is the use of words to create and convey meaning. We communicate verbally with symbols that stand for something else (i.e., words). Verbal communication enables us to interact with others—an important reason verbal communication deserves study.

3.2 Explain the relationship between verbal communication and meaning.

Our ability to speak is not enough to communicate. We also need to share with others an understanding of what words mean. Misunderstandings can arise from not knowing what a word means or from not sharing the same meaning for a particular word. The triangle of meaning, denotative and connotative meanings, and the Coordinated Management of Meaning theory can help us understand how we attach meaning to verbal communication.

3.3 Explain how verbal communication can influence thought.

The symbols used in verbal communication influence our perceptions of the world. Words are often specifically used to influence thought and action, such as when the government, military, and big business use doublespeak—language that conceals the truth and/or shifts responsibility to influence people's perceptions. Words can also subtly influence thought in ways we're unaware of (e.g., words used to label co-cultures or racial or ethnic groups).

3.4 Use verbal communication skills that can improve your ability to communicate civilly.

Abstraction refers to levels of specificity in language; highly abstract (vague) words may cause problems in interpersonal communication and relationships. However, concrete words based on sense data can help reduce the problems associated with abstract language. Allness refers to the incorrect idea that it is possible to know everything about a person, place, or thing, and allness may result when we draw conclusions based on insufficient stimuli or evidence. We minimize the problems associated with allness by indexing and owning our thoughts and feelings to demonstrate that we acknowledge and respect the others' meanings. Indexing recognizes differences in thought and opinion that may be based on insufficient evidence. Owning our thoughts and feelings is a way to accept responsibility for our thoughts and feelings and recognize that others may not think and feel as we do.

3.5 Describe why profanity and cursing are uncivil and practice curbing their use.

Cursing, *profanity*, and *crude language* are often defined synonymously and reflect uncivil and unethical behavior because such language entails expressing ourselves without concern for others and our community. We can monitor our behavior and reflect on the time and place that we utter profanity and curse words to curb their use. We can refrain from swearing in front of young people who may be influenced to imitate the crude language they hear. We can also curb our use of curse words by finding civil and ethical substitutes, such as making up our own "cuss words" based on alliteration or assonance.

CIVILITY SUMMARY

Overall, remember that civility and verbal communication involve the following:

- Knowledge of low- and high-context cultures can help us avoid mistaken perceptions of incivility.
- We engage in civil communication when we use concrete words to avoid abstraction and when we use indexing and owning our thoughts and feelings to avoid allness.
- By reining in our impulses, including the impulse to swear and use hurtful words, we temper free speech with the norm of civility and ethical communication.

REVIEW QUESTIONS

1. What is verbal communication?
2. Why is verbal communication important in your everyday life?
3. What is the triangle of meaning, and how does it describe verbal communication?
4. What are denotative and connotative meanings?
5. Describe and explain the Coordinated Management of Meaning.
6. How do symbols influence our perceptions of the world?
7. Describe abstract words and a civil and ethical alternative.
8. Describe allness and a civil and ethical alternative.
9. Why are profanity, cursing, and crude verbal communication considered to be uncivil? What can we do to curb their use?
10. What are low-context and high-context cultures, and how do they approach verbal communication?
11. What is the difference between the deterministic and relativistic versions of the Sapir-Whorf hypothesis?
12. Describe jargon and slang and provide examples of them.
13. How does gender affect verbal communication? In what way does gossip relate to gender and verbal communication?

4 Civil Nonverbal Communication

CHAPTER OBJECTIVES

After reading this chapter, you will be able to:

4.1 Define *nonverbal communication*.
4.2 Explain the functions of nonverbal communication.
4.3 Identify the types of nonverbal communication.
4.4 Recognize why road rage is an example of uncivil nonverbal communication.
4.5 Explain the role of nonverbal behavior in the communication of deception.
4.6 Use nonverbal immediacy behaviors to improve your ability to communicate civilly.

ACTOR JOHNNY DEPP, star of the *Pirates of the Caribbean* films, is known for communicating civilly with his fans, both verbally and nonverbally. Depp repeatedly makes *Autographs* magazine's annual list of the "10 Best Hollywood Signers" and is described as someone who talks to his fans to get to know them while signing autographs.[1] Unlike some other celebrities, Depp signs more than one item if he has the time and also signs autographs for crowds in airports, even while carrying luggage.[2] However, Depp's civil communication goes beyond signing autographs. For example, Depp received a letter from nine-year-old Beatrice Delap, who asked if he could help her and other "budding young pirates" mutiny against her primary school teachers. The actor visited the primary school in full make-up and *Pirates* costume and gave the child a hug in front of a joyous crowd of students and teachers.[3] Depp also visited young patients at the Great Ormond Street Hospital for Children, dressed in his *Pirates* costume.[4] In addition, the actor added his handprint to a book of celebrity handprints and photos used to raise money for children's charities, and he wears a Children's Hospice Coalition bracelet in memory of a deceased child. Depp has also donated a shirt he wore in the film *The Libertine* and a pair of his briefs to charity auctions.[5]

WHY IT MATTERS

Reaching out to sign autographs, wearing and donating items of clothing, displaying make-up, wearing jewelry, and giving a hug—these are all forms of nonverbal communication. Depp communicates nonverbally in a civil manner that demonstrates respect, restraint, and responsibility. Do you know someone who exhibits civil nonverbal behavior? On the other hand, do you know someone who exhibits uncivil nonverbal behavior? Perhaps a person you know screams loudly, gets in "someone's face" (invades another's personal space), or even gives others "the finger." Have *you* ever demonstrated uncivil nonverbal communication?

Although nonverbal messages are ambiguous, nonverbal communication is nonetheless worthy of study because it is powerful. Research demonstrates that between 65 percent and 93 percent of the meaning of messages comes from nonverbal communication.[6] For example, suppose you are arguing with a younger sibling, relative, or child. The child screams and stomps her or his feet, and you demand an apology for the inappropriate behavior. The child puts hands on hips, sticks out her or his tongue, and shouts, "I'm sorry!" Do you think the child is truly sorry for the behavior? The reason you probably answered "no" to this question is because the nonverbal communication caused you to believe that the child wasn't truly sorry, although the verbal communication suggested otherwise. Studies have found that nonverbal communication is 12 to 13 times more powerful than the verbal messages it accompanies.[7] Overall, when nonverbal messages contradict verbal messages, we tend to believe the nonverbal communication.

In this chapter, you'll learn why understanding nonverbal communication is important in your everyday life. In addition, you'll become aware of the functions and types of nonverbal communication. You'll read about a particular form of uncivil nonverbal communication, "road rage," and learn about specific types of civil nonverbal communication called "immediacy behaviors." You'll also understand the association between nonverbal communication and culture, workplace (your career), and gender contexts.

DEFINITION OF NONVERBAL COMMUNICATION

Imagine that you and a friend are attending a party. Your friend notices an extremely attractive person and wants to strike up a conversation with that individual. However, your friend notices that this person is looking down at the floor and sitting with arms and legs folded. Your friend interprets the attractive person's nonverbal communication as meaning "Don't bother me. I want to be left alone!" A short time later, you walk by the attractive person and hear the person mutter, "I don't know anyone here; it would be great if someone would talk to me." This example illustrates that nonverbal communication is ambiguous (i.e., can have many meanings) and powerful (e.g., can influence our behavior).

Now imagine yourself sitting in a restaurant. If you need to speak to your server, you will generally make eye contact and perhaps nod your head or raise your hand slightly to let the server know you'd like some attention. This is also an example of nonverbal communication. **Nonverbal communication** refers to all forms of communication other than words themselves. Nonverbal communication occurs via facial expression and eye contact, gestures, posture and body orientation, clothing and artifacts (e.g., jewelry, tattoos), tone of voice, touch, and the environment in which both verbal and nonverbal

nonverbal communication
All forms of communication other than words themselves.

communication take place. Even time, smell, and color are considered to be forms of nonverbal communication.

The interpretation of nonverbal behavior isn't always straightforward because nonverbal communication is ambiguous. A person's downcast eyes and folded arms and legs may mean "leave me alone." On the other hand, these behaviors may suggest that the person is lonely and wants some attention. It's also possible that these behaviors may mean nothing at all. In addition, consider the various meanings associated with a pat on the back. A pat on the back can be interpreted as an expression of sympathy ("I'm so sorry"), encouragement ("Way to go!"), or merely an attempt to engage someone's attention ("Hey!"). Because nonverbal communication is ambiguous, it's best to interpret nonverbal behavior in conjunction with verbal communication.

FUNCTIONS OF NONVERBAL COMMUNICATION

We have read that nonverbal communication is characterized as communication that occurs without words. Have you ever nodded your head and used words to suggest that you agree with a conversation partner? Perhaps you have nodded your head in agreement without the use of verbal communication. Maybe you can recall a time when you communicated a nonverbal message by staring at someone in anger, used animated gestures while telling a story, or couldn't stop a tear from trickling down your face. Have you ever had to shout loudly to enter a conversation? These questions and examples illustrate that nonverbal communication can repeat, substitute for, accent, complement, and regulate what we state verbally.

Repeating

repeating A function of nonverbal communication. This type of nonverbal communication can stand alone and convey the verbal meaning without the necessity of accompanying words.

One function of nonverbal communication is to merely **repeat** what is communicated verbally. For example, you might point your index finger at something as you say, "It's over there," and lift your hand in the air with the palm facing down as you say, "She's about this high." You may also shrug our shoulders as you say, "I don't know" when answering a question. Consider how your nonverbal communication might repeat the statement "It stinks!" You most likely would wrinkle your nose and perhaps purse your lips while conveying this message. Nonverbal behavior that repeats what is stated verbally can often stand alone and convey the verbal meaning without the necessity of accompanying words.

Substituting

substituting A function of nonverbal communication; nonverbal behavior can function as a substitute for verbal communication.

Nonverbal communication can function as a **substitute** for verbal communication. For example, what nonverbal behaviors might express the following?

- "A-OK"
- "I don't know"
- "borrrrrring!"

Touching your thumb with your index finger (or lifting your thumb in the air and curling your fingers), shrugging your shoulders, and yawning are nonverbal behaviors that can take the place of these verbal communications.

emblems Nonverbal behaviors that can be translated directly in a word or two of verbal communication.

Emblems are a category of nonverbal behaviors that often function to substitute for verbal communication. An **emblem** is a nonverbal behavior that can be translated

FIGURE 4.1 Nonverbal Emblems

The meanings people attribute to emblems are culture specific.

Thumbs–Up Gesture
United States: "good, positive, or OK"
Middle East: obscene gesture

Fig Gesture (thumb inserted between index and 3rd finger)
United States: unknown (gesture isn't emblematic)
Germany, Holland, Denmark: an invitation to have sex
Portugal and Brazil: a wish for good luck or protection

"V" Sign
United States: "peace" or "victory"
Great Britain: insult if palm faces inward toward body (e.g., "up yours")

Vertical Horn
United States: University of Texas "Hook 'em Horns" salute
Portugal, Spain, Italy: "cuckold"

accenting A function of nonverbal communication. Nonverbal communication can accent or emphasize the spoken word.

illustrators Speech-related gestures that are directly tied to speech. Pointing movements, movements that depict spatial relationships, and rhythmic chopping gestures are examples of illustrators.

complementing A function of nonverbal communication. Complementing nonverbal communication adds meaning to verbal communication. Examples of complementing nonverbal behaviors include weeping while telling a sad story and blushing when communicating embarrassment.

regulating A function of nonverbal communication. Subtle shifts in nonverbal behavior which signal that a speaker is finished with her or his turn and/or a listener desires a turn to speak.

directly in a word or two of verbal communication. Although we use emblems consciously, it's important to note that emblems are culturally specific; that is, a particular emblem in one culture will not have the same meaning in another. For example, the "A-OK" emblem of the index finger touching the thumb refers to "money" in Japan; means "you're worth zero" in France and Belgium; is an insult in parts of southern Italy; and is a vulgar sexual reference in Greece and Turkey. Americans shake their head back and forth as the emblem for "no," but this particular emblem means "I don't understand" in Turkey.[8] As illustrated in Figure 4.1, using the wrong emblem in the wrong place can create a problematic situation.

Accenting

In addition to repeating and substituting for verbal communication, nonverbal communication also functions to **accent**, or emphasize, the spoken word. We can accent the spoken word by pounding our fist on a table, thrusting an index finger close to someone's face, and changing the volume of certain words as we speak them (e.g., "I said that I'd THINK about it!"). Sometimes illustrators are used to accent the spoken word. **Illustrators** are typically speech-related gestures that are directly tied to what we say. For example, pointing movements can help identify a specific person, place, or thing. Illustrators can also depict spatial relationships and can accent or organize important parts of an utterance. These gestures may be in the form of rhythmic chopping gestures (e.g., "We must first do this [gesture], then this [gesture], and then this" [gesture]). However, illustrators need not always be gestures. For example, our eyes may widen momentarily and accent

Speakers can use an illustrator to emphasize (accent) a point during a presentation.

the spoken words "I don't believe it!" (or the slang "Shut up!") when we hear something that is difficult to believe.⁹

Complementing

In addition to accenting, nonverbal communication functions to **complement** verbal communication. Like nonverbal behaviors that accent the spoken word, complementing nonverbal communication intensifies the meaning of verbal communication. Examples of complementing nonverbal behaviors include weeping while telling a sad story and blushing when communicating embarrassment. Sometimes it's difficult to distinguish nonverbal behaviors that accent verbal communication from nonverbal behaviors that complement the spoken word. However, we usually have less control over complementing nonverbal behaviors than we have over accenting nonverbal behaviors.

Regulating

Nonverbal communication also functions to **regulate** the flow of verbal behavior. Why is it that people who engage in face-to-face conversation need not say "over" or "I'm finished talking now; it's your turn" when switching the roles of verbal sender and receiver? It's because subtle shifts in nonverbal behavior signal that a speaker is finished with her/his turn and/or a listener desires a turn to speak. We tend to increase our eye contact with a conversation partner to signal that we are finished speaking. We also tend to decrease eye contact and raise our voices if our partner tries to speak and we're not ready to give up

ASK THE ETHICIST — "Mandatory" Social Gatherings

Question There are times when I really don't want to be in a certain place. For example, I had to attend a mandatory social gathering with people at work. Most of them were having lots of fun, but all I could think of was the amount of work on my desk that was piling up while we played team-building games. I was pretty withdrawn and didn't participate much. I thought I was just being honest, but one of my colleagues told me that my nonverbal behavior was offensive and rude. Was it?

Answer There are times when I think "mandatory social gathering" is a contradiction in terms. Most of us don't want to be told to do something, especially when it seems frivolous. On the other hand, there are many times in our lives when we need to show some interest for the sake of others. As a parent, I can't say I really looked forward to musical concerts in which my kids participated, but my attendance and enthusiasm were important to them. Likewise, attending an important event (such as a wedding) for a person who is important to us demands that we make an effort to appear sociable and friendly.

So you find yourself at a mandatory social event and think "What a waste of time." Why not let your opinion show in your nonverbal behavior? A very good reason not to is that your lack of enjoyment dims the enthusiasm of others. It makes them anxious. They may wonder if they are responsible for your reaction; they may be stressed trying to figure out ways to make you feel better. Honesty is important, but even more important is how we communicate our caring to others. Letting your boredom be overtly visible may be honest, but it doesn't seem civil.

TRENDS IN TECHNOLOGY AND SOCIAL MEDIA

Email, "Second Life," and Nonverbal Communication

With the exception of computer-based innovations such as Skype software, webcams, and virtual reality environments, computer-mediated communication (CMC) is primarily textual and limits the exchange of nonverbal information. Early research about CMC was based on the assumption that CMC is primarily a verbal medium that lacks the benefit of nonverbal cues—the "cues-filtered-out approach." The cues-filtered-out approach assumes that the functions served by nonverbal communication in face-to-face interaction are not met because nonverbal cues are absent in CMC.

In contrast to the cues-filtered-out approach, more recent CMC research tends to reflect a "hyperpersonal approach," where communicators attempt to find a way to use nonverbal cues to their advantage. The hyperpersonal approach assumes that CMC users strategically manipulate their identities and plan and edit their communication to achieve relational goals. For example, a person writing an email message to a stranger may be careful to create a greeting and explain the purpose of the email before making some kind of request. And because CMC users don't have cues that demonstrate the physical attractiveness of their conversation partners, CMC can facilitate relational development by having people focus on what the other says, not what the other looks like. Consistent with the assumptions that underlie the hyperpersonal approach, research has found that the reduced nonverbal cues associated with email messages and the ability to plan, edit, and control "performance" result in the creation of more socially desirable messages.[10]

On the other hand, various types of nonverbal behavior *can* be communicated online. For example, 3-D virtual environments such as Second Life have been used to study expression and the interpretation of touch. In one study, a networked "force-feedback haptic device" similar to a joystick was used to transmit emotion through a virtual interpersonal handshake. Participants were asked to generate seven different emotions using the device, and others were asked to recognize emotions on the basis of virtual touch. Study results demonstrated that participants in a virtual reality context are able to express emotions by using different touch-related movements, and those differences enable others to interpret the various emotions with a haptic device. The researchers concluded that people who engage in virtual communication can transmit and interpret touch-related emotional cues with accuracy in a manner similar to face-to-face communication.[11]

Discussion Questions

1. Do you strategically "plan, edit, and control your performance" when you write an email, engage in text messaging, or post on a social networking site such as Facebook or Twitter?

2. What types of nonverbal cues are communicated when we read an email message, a text message, or a tweet? What types of nonverbal cues can be communicated when we view a Facebook profile page?

3. What types of nonverbal cues might we *unintentionally* communicate when we write an email message, a text message, or a tweet? What types of nonverbal cues might we *unintentionally* communicate when we put together a Facebook profile page or create an avatar and virtual environment in Second Life?

a turn. To signal that we're ready to speak, we may straighten our posture, raise our index finger, and perhaps take an audible inhalation of breath.

Nonverbal Communication and Culture

display rules Rules that tell people how and when to display nonverbal behaviors. They vary by culture.

Culture has an impact on the function of nonverbal communication and the rules that guide their display. **Display rules** govern when and under which circumstances nonverbal behaviors are considered appropriate. People from Mediterranean cultures are likely to believe that intense displays of emotion are appropriate, whereas Americans of northern

European background tend to believe that people should display neutral or calm emotions in public.[12] Furthermore, cultures differ in terms of meanings that are attributed to nonverbal communication. Specifically, interpretations of nonverbal communication are based on whether the behavior is considered to be random (i.e., it has no meaning whatsoever), idiosyncratic (i.e., when only partners understand the relational meaning), or shared (i.e., when people collectively understand that a shrug of the shoulders means "I don't understand").[13]

Because repertoires, display rules, and interpretations of nonverbal communication differ from one culture to another, misperceptions about the civility of such behaviors are common. Nonverbal display rules are usually learned via cultural observation and experience and remain out of our awareness unless our expectations have been violated. This means that members of a specific culture typically use their own display rules to judge the civility of nonverbal behavior associated with other cultures. Negative judgments of others' personalities, attitudes, and intelligence often result when members of one culture use their own rules to interpret and evaluate the nonverbal communication of persons of other cultures.[14] In other words, judging another's nonverbal behavior based on our own cultural rules may cause us to make misinterpretations about nonverbal civility.

Behaviors understood as civil for Americans vary in terms of the various co-cultures that exist within the United States. For example, Latinos may avoid direct eye contact with others as a sign of respect or may perceive touch to be normal and appropriate during conversation. However, other people may perceive indirect eye contact as an indication of inattentiveness and touching behavior as a violation of personal space. Similarly, Native Americans typically use silence as a sign of respect, thoughtfulness, and/or uncertainty, while other people may perceive this behavior as an indication of boredom, disagreement, or a refusal to provide feedback. African Americans generally perceive that speaking with intensity is appropriate when disagreeing with others, but other people may perceive this behavior to be a precursor to violence.[15] Of course, not all Latinos avoid direct eye contact, not all Native Americans use silence to communicate respect, and not all African Americans speak with intensity while disagreeing with others. Remember that cultures and co-cultures are fluid and are influenced by immigration patterns, by other cultural values disseminated through the media and technology, and by factors such as class, socioeconomic status, and gender.

Interestingly, the makers of virtual environments such as Second Life have programmed cultural rules regarding the appropriateness of nonverbal communication into the behavior of avatars. For example, avatars communicate with other avatars within the range of 18 inches to 4 feet, the desired amount of space between people who converse in Western cultures. An avatar that is positioned 0 to 18 inches away from another avatar is perceived as committing a personal space invasion. In addition, as in actual face-to-face communication, avatars positioned closely together adhere to the nonverbal communication rule of exhibiting limited mutual eye gaze (so as not to stare) compared to avatars that are positioned far apart.[16] This attention to detail makes the Second Life experience realistic.

Avatars in "Second Life" adhere to culturally-based rules for the appropriate use of personal space.

TYPES OF NONVERBAL COMMUNICATION

In this chapter, you have read that nonverbal communication repeats, substitutes for, accents, complements, and regulates the spoken word. Four general categories of nonverbal communication are used to carry out these functions: kinesics (i.e., gestures, body orientation and posture, touch, facial expression and eye behavior), paralanguage (i.e., vocal qualities and accents), physical characteristics (i.e., attractiveness, body shape, and artifacts), and the environment (i.e., the physical environment, time, territoriality, and proxemics). Although the types of nonverbal communication are divided into categories in this chapter and are explained as if they are separate and distinct, the various types work together to communicate meaning. For example, to demonstrate surprise, you may lift your eyebrows, open your eyes wide, open your mouth, and make an audible gasp. It is therefore important to remember that nonverbal communication occurs in clusters when conveying a message, with or without accompanying words.

Kinesics

Kinesics, or the category of body movement and position, includes gestures, body orientation and posture, touch, and facial expressions and eye behavior.

Gestures. **Gestures** are movements of the body that are used to communicate thoughts, feelings, and/or intentions. Gestures appear to naturally accompany speech, and people need not learn hand gestures by watching and modeling others' behavior. Researchers have discovered that children and adolescents who are blind from birth gesture as often and in the same manner as sighted people. Therefore, people don't need to see gestures in order to know how to gesture on their own.

Recent research suggests that people not only gesture to communicate information to others and to acknowledge interaction partners but also to help retrieve language. For example, stroke patients gesture more when they attempt to name or label objects, and people who don't even realize they gesture in fact do so when asked to come up with words that match particular definitions. In general, people gesture more when they refer to words and concepts with spatial connotations such as "under" and "adjacent" than when they refer to abstract concepts such as "thought" or "evil." One interesting study demonstrated that people have difficulty finding words when they can't gesture freely. Gestures precede spoken words by as much as three seconds, and gestures may aid in accessing words. Just as memories are retrieved when the senses are activated, words may be retrieved with gestures.[17]

Body Orientation and Posture. In addition to gestures, **body orientation and posture** can communicate meaning. Body orientation involves the extent to which we face or lean toward or away from others. Both body orientation and posture can indicate whether we are open to interaction. For example, the positioning of the arms and legs while standing can indicate that we are available to talk with some people but not others, and the positioning of the arms, legs, and torso while seated can inhibit other people from entering our conversations.

---

kinesics Nonverbal behaviors that are associated with movement.

gestures Movements of the body used to communicate thoughts, feelings, and/or intentions.

body orientation and posture The extent to which we face or lean toward or away from others. Both body orientation and posture can indicate whether or not we are open to interaction.

Gestures naturally accompany speech. To become effective at gesturing, we need not learn hand gestures by modeling others' behavior.

Types of Nonverbal Communication

haptics Touch. The meanings that are associated with touching behavior depend on what body part is touched, the intensity of the touch, the duration of the touch, the method of the touch (such as closed or open fist), and the frequency of the touch.

facial expression and eye behavior Nonverbal communication that is involved in opening, closing, and regulating the channels of interaction and that functions as the prime communicator of emotion.

affect blends A combination of one emotion evidenced in one facial area and another emotion shown in a different area; two different emotions illustrated in one part of the face; and a facial display that results from muscle action that is associated with two emotions.

microexpressions Extremely fast facial movements that last less than one-fifth of a second and that can reveal emotions, especially those we are trying to conceal.

Posture and body orientation can also indicate status and power. More relaxed and expansive postures are typically associated with high status and dominant individuals. Although most studies of responses to emotional situations focus on facial expressions, recent research demonstrates that posture can communicate fear. Fear contagion, or the rapid spread of fright that occurs in crowds, often occurs when people view others who adopt fearful postures.[18] Body orientation and posture can also help us retrieve certain memories. One theory of memory suggests that activating a "sensory fragment" such as a sight, sound, odor, or body position can facilitate memory retrieval. For example, we will more easily recall an event that happened while we were golfing if we stand as if we are holding a golf club.[19]

Haptics.
Haptics, or touch, is related to the development of emotional and mental adjustment. Touch provides infants with comfort and protection and helps young children develop their identities. Adults also need touch and may turn to professionals such as massage therapists to fulfill the need for touch. The meanings that are associated with touching behavior depend on what body part is touched, the intensity of the touch, the duration of the touch, the method of the touch (e.g., closed or open fist), and the frequency of the touch. The meaning of touch is also dependent on the physical context (e.g., the home, the university setting, an airport) and the age, sex, and relationship between the person who is touched and the person who does the touching.[20]

Facial Expression and Eye Behavior.
Facial expression and eye behavior are difficult to describe and measure because there are so many configurations and types of face and eye behavior. However, the face and eyes are an extremely potent source of nonverbal communication in that they are involved in opening, closing, and regulating the channels of interaction, and they function as the prime communicator of emotion.

In the 1970s, Paul Ekman established that seven emotions have universal facial expressions: sadness, surprise, disgust, happiness, anger, fear, and contempt. Ekman has also researched how the face illustrates multiple emotions all at once. These **affect blends** may be one emotion evidenced in one facial area and another emotion shown in a different area, two different emotions illustrated in one part of the face, or a facial display that results from muscle action that is associated with two emotions. For example, we can raise our eyebrows in surprise and, at the same time, lift the corners of our mouth to smile with happiness. We can also show anger and surprise when we raise one eyebrow and lower the other toward the eye.[21]

Microexpressions, which are extremely fast facial movements that last less than one-fifth of a second, can reveal emotions, especially those we are trying to conceal.[22] Imagine someone who eagerly anticipates a holiday present such as a gift card, an iPod, or a cell phone. After opening the box expected to contain the desired gift, the recipient instead finds a pair of socks. Although she or he may attempt to hide the emotion felt on seeing the socks, others may perceive a brief and fleeting expression of disappointment. The microexpression of disappointment may give the people near the recipient some insight about what the person truly feels.

Ekman's research has been used to teach police officers and judges how to read clues in facial expressions, and it has also been used by airport security officers, the FBI, and CIA agents to size up potential terrorists. The Department of Defense is using Ekman's

People who display a "poker face," like poker players who don't allow their facial expressions to communicate the type of "hand" they hold during a card game, reveal few emotions on their face.

research to develop computer technology that will scan and analyze videotaped facial movements. Ekman is also researching whether specific expressions of anger made of subtle facial movements can signal a forthcoming attack. The results of these investigations will not be publicized but instead will be made available only to law enforcement and security agents.[23]

Facial expression and eye behavior are related to **interaction management**, or the regulation of communication. For example, we open our mouths and simultaneously inhale as a sign of our readiness to speak. Making eye contact with someone also indicates that communication channels are open, whereas avoiding eye contact suggests that communication channels are closed. Eye contact also regulates the flow of communication with turn-taking signals. Glancing at grammatical breaks and the end of thought units enables us to obtain feedback about how we are being received, to see if our conversation partner will allow us to continue, and to signal to our partner that we are ready to switch to the role of the listener. When the speaking and listening roles change, the speaker will gaze at the listener as the utterance comes to a close. The listener will maintain gaze until he or she assumes the speaking role, at which time the new speaker will look away.

> **interaction management** How we control the channels of communication. For example, making eye contact with someone indicates that communication channels are open, while avoiding eye contact suggests that communication channels are closed.

Paralanguage

The second category of nonverbal communication is **paralanguage**, also known as *vocalics*. This category includes vocal qualities (e.g., volume, pitch, inflection, speed, silence) and accents. Paralanguage concerns *how* we say something rather than *what* we say.

> **paralanguage** Also known as vocalics, a category of nonverbal communication that includes tone of voice, accents, pauses, and silence. Vocalics refers to *how* something is said instead of *what* is actually said.

Vocal Qualities.   Vocal qualities include:

- Volume (loudness or softness)
- Pitch (highness or lowness)
- Inflection (vocal emphasis)
- Speed (rate)
- Silence

Our vocal qualities affect how others perceive us and interpret our messages. We can alter our vocal qualities to sound assertive, sympathetic, or sarcastic. Say the following italicized sentence out loud, and see if you can alter your voice to express assertion, sympathy, and sarcasm: *"I'm so sorry."*

In general, attractive voices are resonant, not too nasal, not too monotonous, and midrange in terms of pitch. We also associate personality characteristics with vocal qualities. For example, a low pitch, especially in males, is perceived to be sophisticated, sexy, appealing, and masculine. Vocal qualities can communicate emotions and elicit corresponding emotional feelings in listeners. University of Southern California researchers have developed software that recognizes "irritation" from vocal cues. The software is designed for commercial use and can read increasing levels of frustration in the voices of people using telephones to communicate with others. Depending on the level of frustration detected, callers are offered a soothing computerized response or are immediately routed to a human operator.[24]

Silence is a vocal quality that can communicate many meanings. Giving someone "the silent treatment" can communicate our displeasure. Silence can also communicate uneasiness, such as when we cannot find words to express ourselves. It can also communicate contentment and the pleasure we feel in the company of someone we care for.

Types of Nonverbal Communication 77

accents The particular way that words are pronounced. Accents vary according to ethnicity, age, and geographic location.

Accents. Another component of paralanguage is **accents**, the particular way that words are pronounced. Accents vary according to ethnicity, age, and geographic location. There is no universal standard regarding the correct ways to pronounce words in "American English." Some people believe that the way Midwesterners pronounce words is accentless and therefore "standard," but even people in the Midwest communicate with an accent. In general, we tend to stereotype others on the basis of their accents. One common stereotype is that Southerners sound friendly but are not as intelligent as Northerners. Another common stereotype is that New York and New Jersey accents sound "rude" and "unpleasant" and that New Yorkers pronounce words "incorrectly." However, linguists assert that pronunciation isn't associated with intelligence or personality. What is considered "standard" pronunciation is based on nothing more than social processes; that is, groups with status and power impose their standards on others, and their standards dictate what is considered to be the proper and improper pronunciation of words.[25]

general attractiveness and body shape A type of nonverbal communication used to judge others' backgrounds, characters, personalities, talents, and potential future behavior.

Physical Characteristics

The nonverbal category of physical characteristics includes general attractiveness (e.g., height, weight, hair, skin color), body shape, and artifacts such as clothing, jewelry, and other accessories and personal objects.

artifacts Items such as clothing, jewelry, and accessories that communicate about the person who wears them.

General Attractiveness and Body Shape. What is the first question often asked when we learn that a friend is attracted to someone? We probably ask, "What does she or he look like?" In general, we use appearance, such as **general attractiveness and body shape**, to judge others' backgrounds, characters, personalities, talents, and potential future behavior. Studies demonstrate that physical attractiveness can help people obtain employment and receive high salaries. In addition, judges and juries are less likely to perceive attractive defendants as guilty, and such defendants receive shorter sentences than unattractive defendants.[26]

Recent changes in clothing mannequins and fashion dolls suggest that the characterization of physical attractiveness is undergoing transformation, at least for women. Goddess clothing mannequins, which reflect various faces, skin tones, and body proportions and sizes, are a response to the time and culture in which we live. Goddess mannequins represent people of various ethnic backgrounds and recognize different body types and standards of beauty. Even the idealized blond-haired, blue-eyed fashion doll is becoming obsolete. The Bratz line of fashion dolls not only illustrates cutting-edge fashion trends but also comes in a variety of skin tones and hair colors and textures. The Bratz dolls were introduced in 2001 and are extremely popular worldwide because of their multicultural appeal.[27]

Singer Lady GaGa communicates as much about herself with her outrageous outfits as she does with her songs.

Artifacts **Artifacts**, including clothing, jewelry, accessories, and personal objects such as briefcases and backpacks, communicate about the person who wears them. Clothes are an important aspect of first impressions, and we infer personal attributes such as age, nationality, socioeconomic status, group identification, occupation, personality, and interests from clothing.[28] Clothing is also related to civility. People who wear clothes that sport foul language and who dress sloppily have been described as contributing to the "decline in civility because they don't

A CASE STUDY IN ETHICS

Hair Today, Gone from School Tomorrow

Ethical communication reflects trustworthiness, responsibility, respect, fairness, caring, and concern for the community. Keep the components of ethical communication in mind as you read the following case study and answer the discussion questions.

Taylor Pugh, a preschooler at Floyd Elementary School in Mesquite, Texas, was considered a typical student until October 2009. At that time, the school principal told his mother, Elizabeth Taylor, that Taylor's hair would have to be cut, or he would be withdrawn from school. Taylor's hair fell just below his ears, touched his shirt collar, and could cover his eyes. The Mesquite Independent School District elementary dress code includes the regulation that hair is to be clean and well groomed; it prohibits unusual coloring and "excessive styles" (such as "tails," "designs," and "puffs"). Additional guidelines for elementary boys include the rule that hair is to be out of the eyes, not extend below the bottom of the earlobes, and cut so that it does not extend over the collar of a dress shirt.[29] Ms. Taylor trimmed Taylor's hair along the sides and back but was told it was still too long in front. She then offered to put it in a ponytail and slick back the front to keep his hair out of his eyes and off his forehead. School officials placed Taylor in in-school suspension, away from his classmates, and told his mother that Taylor would most likely be dismissed from school.[30]

Taylor's parents fought the decision to separate him from his friends and pleaded their case to the school board. Taylor's parents asserted that their son's choice of long hair should be accepted as an expression of his individuality and maintained that his hair was not a distraction.[31] Furthermore, Taylor was planning to donate his hair to a charity that makes wigs for cancer patients. Mr. Pugh argued that his family is part Cherokee, and although he isn't registered as part of the tribe, there's a strong Native American influence in their home. Both parents complained to the school board that their son was being singled out and showed photos of Mesquite students with hair longer than Taylor's receiving awards from the school.[32]

The school board responded to Taylor's parents by presenting a compromise: Taylor could return to his classroom if he wore his hair in cornrow braids placed close to his head, over his ears, and not gathered in a bun on his neck. Ms. Taylor subsequently braided Taylor's hair and found that cornrow braids caused his scalp to bleed. Taylor then returned to school with a ponytail and was again placed in in-school suspension. After a return visit to the school board, Taylor's father said that the district was being unreasonable and compared their actions to those that occurred in Nazi Germany.[33]

In the end, the school district agreed to adjust its grooming policy, and Taylor was allowed back into his prekindergarten class after his mother put his long hair in two French braids. "He looks a little like Princess Leia," his mother said.[34]

Discussion Questions

1. Do you think that the Mesquite Independent School District's dress code and the enforcement of the dress code are ethical?
2. Is placing a four-year-old in in-school suspension an ethical punishment for a preschooler?
3. Is it ethical to break a rule if the cause is just (e.g., donating to charity)?
4. Is it ethical to use a child's individual likes and dislikes to justify noncompliance with school dress code regulations?
5. Did Taylor's father communicate in an ethical manner when he suggested that his Native American heritage should be taken into account in the controversy about Taylor's hair?
6. Did Taylor's father communicate in an ethical manner when he suggested that the Mesquite Independent School District's "braid compromise" was similar to actions taken in Nazi Germany?

---

believe they are responsible for their community."[35] Badges, tattoos, and jewelry also have communicative value. A ring with a single diamond worn on the fourth finger of a woman's left hand communicates that she is engaged; a man's forearm tattoo may communicate love for a specific person or affiliation with a particular group.

Physical characteristics and artifacts also have political and cultural meanings. For example, although the headscarf, or *hijab*, is a symbol of piety for millions of Muslim women, several European nations have banned the wearing of headscarves based on the belief that they symbolize a particular political ideology or radical activism.[36] Moreover, former French President Nicolas Sarkozy asserted the Islamic *burqa*, which is a body-length robe that covers the entire face (except for the eyes) is not welcome in France.[37] To minimize non-Islamic influences in universities and cultural institutions, Iranian "morality squads" have cracked down on men who wear hairstyles and watches that are "too Western."[38]

Environment

The final category of nonverbal communication concerns the environment, which includes features such as architectural style, lighting, color, temperature, and time. The environment also includes the territory that we claim as our own and proxemics, or the distance between interactants.

Physical Environment. The physical environment in which we communicate influences the quality of our interactions. We tend to perceive our environments in particular ways and to include such perceptions in the messages we develop and encode. Perceptions of formality based on furniture, decorations, color, and other factors can influence communication behavior. Perceptions of extreme formality typically result in communication that is less relaxed, more hesitant, and more stylized. Perceptions of privacy, based on the number of people the environment can accommodate, can also influence communication behavior. Perceptions of privacy can result in close speaking distances and messages designed for a particular person instead of a general group.[39]

Chronemics. **Chronemics**, or *time*, is an environmental factor that influences nonverbal behavior. **Monochronic time** refers to time perceived as a commodity. Individuals who have a sense of urgency, believe that time shouldn't be wasted, and feel that people should do things one at a time adhere to a monochromic time system. **Polychronic time** refers to time perceived as limitless and not quantifiable. Individuals who believe that time should be adjusted to people's needs, that it's acceptable to change schedules and deadlines, and that people can do several things simultaneously adhere to a polychronic time system.

One way that time influences nonverbal communication is in terms of standing in line. Do you and your friends stand in line while waiting for a bus or taxi or do you gather in a disorganized group? Standing in line is a characteristic of individuals and cultures, such as those in Scandinavia and the United States, that are primarily monochromic time oriented. Gathering in a group without standing in line is a characteristic of individuals and cultures, such as those in Latin American and Mediterranean countries, that are primarily polychronic time oriented. People who adhere to a monochromic time orientation expect to be waited on one at a time; people who adhere to a polychronic time orientation expect to be waited on en masse.[40]

Territoriality. **Territoriality** refers to a stationary area or fixed geographic location to which we lay claim and protect from invasion by others. Your territory may include your room, your bathroom, your car, and even your particular seat at the dinner table. Interestingly, we also claim places to which we have no legal ownership rights. Do you "own" chairs in which you habitually sit during classes? Are you surprised or perturbed when someone sits in "your" seat? Parking spots, library desks, and even places in line are staked out as our territories. In addition, we prevent territorial invasion in a number of ways. We place nameplates on the outside of our domiciles and office doors, and we hope that others will recognize that we "own" a parking spot or seat in a classroom if we use it long enough or often enough. Sometimes we use markers such as books, coats, and

---

chronemics An environmental factor, *time*, that influences nonverbal behavior.

monochronic time A time orientation that considers time as commodity. Individuals who have a sense of urgency, believe that time shouldn't be wasted, and believe that people should do things one at a time adhere to a monochromic time system.

polychronic time A time orientation that considers time as limitless and not quantifiable. Individuals who believe that time should be adjusted to peoples' needs; that it's acceptable to change schedules and deadlines; and that people can do several things simultaneously adhere to a polychronic time system.

territoriality A stationary area or fixed geographic location to which one lays claim and that one protects from invasion by others. Your territory may include your room, your bathroom, and even your particular seat at the dinner table.

A large gate in front of a private residence can protect the property from territorial invasion.

proxemics How people use space and distance. Also called *personal space*, proxemics can reveal how we feel about ourselves and how we feel about others.

intimate distance The distance used for touching and intimacy as well as physical aggression and threat (i.e., contact to 18 inches).

notebooks to communicate the ownership of territory such as a table in the library.

Territory is often related to status and power. High-status individuals in the workplace often have offices with windows and larger offices than low-status individuals. High-status workers also may have more barriers, such as outer offices and secretaries, to prevent territorial invasion. On the other hand, low-status workers may often be victims of "prairie-dogging," a type of territorial invasion that occurs when coworkers pop over cubicle partitions to begin or barge in on conversations.[41]

Proxemics Unlike the physical environment or our territory, **proxemics** refers to how people use space and distance. Also called *personal space*, proxemics can reveal how we feel about ourselves and how we feel about others. Anthropologist Edward T. Hall identified the four distances of personal space used by most people in Western cultures. These distances, illustrated in Figure 4.2, also imply the relationship between the interactants and the kind of interaction in which they may be involved:[42]

- **Intimate distance** is contact to 18 inches. This distance is sometimes called our "personal space bubble" and is used for touching and intimacy, as well as physical aggression and threat. People who communicate within the range of intimate distance may have close relationships and may communicate confidential information. On the other hand, enemies may use intimate distance to threaten each other and "get in each other's face." Sometimes we are forced to endure personal space invasion and share intimate distances with people we do not know. Have you ever squeezed into a crowded elevator, bus, or subway? If so, you probably felt discomfort and tried to cope by avoiding eye contact, backing away (if possible), and/or changing your body orientation. Interestingly, South Americans, Arabs, and Southern Europeans prefer smaller distances when communicating compared with North Americans, Native Americans, Northern Europeans,

FIGURE 4.2 Hall's Personal Space Distances (Proxemics)
The comfortable personal space a person inhabits may depend partly on culture.

Pakistanis, and Asians.[43] How might a North American feel, and what might she or he think if a South American invaded her or his personal space bubble? How might a South American interpret the North American's response to the space invasion?

- **Personal distance** is 18 inches to 4 feet. This distance is preferred for informal conversation and to keep people "at arm's length." Most Americans prefer personal distance when interacting with others.
- **Social distance** is 4 to 12 feet. This distance is appropriate for business discussions and conversations that are neither personal nor private. The inner range (4 to 7 feet) is appropriate for people who work together and for conversations that involve conducting business. Because we typically stand or sit at farther distances the more formal our interaction becomes, the outer range (7 to 12 feet) is appropriate for communicating respect and the recognition of status.
- **Public distance** is 12 feet and beyond. This distance is used by instructors in their classrooms and for other public speaking situations. This distance is also sometimes used to communicate with strangers.

personal distance The preferred distance for informal conversation and to keep people "at arm's length" (i.e., 18 inches to 4 feet).

social distance The distance that is appropriate for business discussions and conversations that are neither personal nor private (i.e., 4 to 12 feet).

public distance The distance that is used by instructors in their classrooms and for other public speaking situations (i.e., 12 feet and beyond).

Nonverbal Communication and Gender

Nonverbal communication serves different functions and comes in a variety of types. Often, the way we interpret nonverbal communication is based on the expectations and stereotypes that we think are appropriate for our gender.

Gender Stereotypes and Expectations.
Adhering to gender stereotypes is generally more comfortable for most people than deviating from the norm. Girls and women may learn to use softer and higher voices to communicate a positive gender message of femininity. Boys and men may learn to use a loud volume while speaking in order to communicate authority and power. In fact, feminine-sounding job candidates are judged as less competent potential employees, even if their resumes are as strong as those of male candidates.[44] Gender expectations about vocal qualities have even found their way into the realm of technology. For example, German drivers of BMWs reacted negatively to female-sounding GPS artificial voices that communicated directions, even though the drivers knew the voices were computer generated. BMW responded to drivers' discomfort according to gender stereotypes and switched to a male-sounding synthetic voice.[45]

Similarly, although the evidence regarding touching behavior is mixed, the meaning of touch can be linked to power and dominance. Studies have revealed that men respond negatively to women of equal status who engage in touching, but women do not respond negatively to men of greater, equal, or lesser status who touch them. It may be that masculine expectations teach men to find touch acceptable only from someone of higher status.[46]

Furthermore, as a means of expressing status and control, men tend to expand their personal space while receiving messages. Women tend to hold their limbs nearer their bodies than do men and often appear to use a small amount of personal space. Women's use of space may derive from instructions about femininity. It is rare to see women lean

Some women defy nonverbal gender stereotypes to communicate that that they are assertive.

back in chairs, clasp their hands behind their heads, and rest their feet upon their desks; these are considered masculine nonverbal behaviors.[47]

Interpretations of Nonverbal Communication. Overall, women are more skilled than men at interpreting nonverbal behaviors. A review of 75 studies regarding the ability to ascertain others' feelings from facial and vocal expressiveness resulted in the finding that women possess better decoding skills. Women may be more nonverbally sensitive than men because they are perceived to have a less dominant role in society (and therefore must be better able to read nonverbal cues of the dominant group to enhance survival), because they are more attuned to the nonverbal rules that guide communication and are expected to be more nonverbally sensitive, and because they have more opportunities to practice nonverbal sensitivity in occupations that are stereotypically perceived as "feminine" (e.g., teachers, nurses).[48]

Research has also discovered that with the exception of anger, women's faces are more emotionally expressive than men's in both artificial and natural settings.[49] Research also illustrates that women smile more than men as a way to be polite and to promote pleasant conversations. However, men may misinterpret women's smiles as a signal that indicates sexual interest. Similarly, when women display dominance gestures to men, they are rated higher on sexuality and lower in dominance than are men who use the same gestures when speaking with women.[50]

Not only can nonverbal communication be clustered into four categories concerning kinesics, vocal behavior, physical characteristics, and the environment, nonverbal communication can be associated with (un)civil and (un)ethical behavior. One particular type of nonverbal behavior, road rage, is an extreme form of uncivil communication.

ROAD RAGE: NONVERBAL COMMUNICATION AND INCIVILITY

According to an Associated Press-Ipsos poll, many people believe that uncivil and unethical behavior may be increasing in our culture because of our high-tech, fast-paced existence. The poll revealed that the most commonly cited example of incivility was nonverbal: aggressive or reckless driving. Of the poll respondents, 91 percent cited road rage as the most frequent complaint.[51]

Communication researchers Daniel J. Canary and Melissa A. Tafoya view road rage as symbolic interpersonal communication. The symbolic behavior associated with road rage involves using vehicles to nonverbally express anger (which the researchers label "vehicular communication"). The most common form of vehicular communication is cutting off other drivers, followed by speeding, not allowing drivers to merge, and tailgating. Overall, the researchers found that vehicular communication is used much more often than human communication in episodes of road rage.[52]

Canary and Tafoya also discovered that persons who instigate road rage incidents tend to blame the other drivers. These individuals typically believe that internal characteristics of other drivers contribute to road rage incidents and are unable to see that their own behaviors influence road rage. This self-serving bias is exacerbated by de-individuation, in which drivers relate to others on the road as "cars" instead of "people." De-individuation subsequently causes them to aggress even more and feel that their actions are justified.

The fact that our attributions have been found to strongly influence incidents of road rage suggests that intervention programs that focus on perceptions have the potential to reduce this form of uncivil nonverbal behavior. For example, research conducted

An Associated Press-Ipsos poll revealed that the most commonly cited example of nonverbal incivility is road rage.

at SUNY-Albany studied the effect of training on voluntary aggressive drivers and drivers whom the court system mandated to attend the program. Drivers were educated about the ramifications of aggressive driving and learned motivational techniques, progressive muscle relaxation training, alternative coping strategies, and strategies for dealing with problematic perceptions. Such strategies included targeting faulty assumptions and challenging distorted and maladaptive thoughts. Many of the drivers in the study didn't perceive the extent of their problem; therefore, they were taught to perceive themselves as "aggressive drivers," which was a difficult attribution change for some respondents. Study results indicated that as a group, the respondents averaged a 64 percent reduction in aggressive driving behaviors. These results indicate that cognitive-behavioral interventions can significantly decrease this dangerous and potentially fatal form of uncivil and unethical nonverbal communication.[53]

DECEPTION AND NONVERBAL COMMUNICATION

Do you know how to spot a liar? What nonverbal cues tell you that someone is trying to deceive you or hide something? When scientists asked such questions to more than 2,000 people from nearly 60 countries, the most frequent answer involved eye contact. Most people believe that liars avert their gaze. Additional nonverbal **deception cues**, or behaviors that people typically associate with lying, include fidgeting behaviors and throat clearing. However, there is no general telltale sign of a lie. Past research on deception detection has traditionally taken place in laboratories, under highly controlled conditions. Conversely, recent research has been conducted in naturalistic settings (e.g., hospitals, police stations) and focused on whether the deception cues in the controlled studies mirror those outside the lab.

deception cues Behaviors that are typically associated with lying, such as fidgeting behaviors and throat clearing.

Lab Studies

Lab studies suggest that a number of general behaviors are exhibited by people engaged in deception. Liars tend to:

- Move their arms, hands and fingers less than truth tellers
- Blink less than people telling the truth
- Communicate with high-pitched or tense voices
- Fill their speech with more pauses than truth tellers

However, researchers caution that not all liars exhibit these behaviors and that they may be natural behaviors for certain individuals.[54]

Naturalistic Studies

Current studies that take place outside the lab suggest that deception cues associated with lying do not result from actually telling lies but from the experience of emotion, content complexity, and impression management. A liar may speak with a higher-pitched voice,

Cyclist Lance Armstrong admitted that he used performance-enhancing drugs during his successful career. Prior to his admission, Armstrong vehemently denied he used such drugs, and his nonverbal communication didn't suggest otherwise.

which may be the result of feeling guilty, excited, or afraid while lying. A liar may include few details in an explanation because of the complex content of the lie. A liar may also exhibit few illustrators while lying because of her or his attempt to control the situation and to engage in impression management. Researchers who study deception in naturalistic settings not only suggest that there is no single nonverbal behavior that is associated with lying but also propose that typical lab studies do not take individual differences into account. For example, researchers have coded the deception cues of videotaped suspects speaking to police in interrogation rooms and have studied their nonverbal behavior in relation to forensic evidence, witness accounts, and actual suspect confessions. In contrast to results found in some lab studies, the crime suspects didn't fill their speech with disturbances (e.g., stuttering, false starts and stops), and there was no decrease in the use of illustrators. The researchers further concluded that the differences between lying and truth telling depended on each individual. Some suspects increased their eye contact when lying; others averted their gaze. In fact, stressed truth tellers may exhibit the same nonverbal behaviors as liars because of the intense conditions of police interrogations. The only differences found between liars and truth tellers in this real-life situation was that liars paused longer and blinked less frequently than did suspects who told the truth.[55]

A number of obstacles prevent us from accurately interpreting nonverbal communication that is reliably associated with deception. These obstacles include:[56]

- *The determination of what the observed nonverbal behavior means*—Some nervous gestures are merely a sign of anxiety and emotion that can be displayed while lying as well as while telling the truth.
- *The ability to alter nonverbal communication*—Liars who are knowledgeable about nonverbal deception cues can avoid demonstrating particular behaviors, mask the behaviors, or create distractions so they won't be noticed.
- *The circumstances that can affect the nonverbal deception cues that are displayed*—The expectations of a situation (i.e., whether lies are expected), the consequences associated with deception detection, and the target of the lie affect the nonverbal communication that will be displayed during a deception episode.
- *The motivation for lying*—Experienced liars and those not concerned with detection may possess heightened motivation, which can facilitate deception with signs of deception cues.

immediacy In terms of nonverbal communication, physical or psychological closeness between people involved in interaction.

IMPROVING OUR ABILITY TO COMMUNICATE WITH CIVIL AND EFFECTIVE NONVERBAL IMMEDIACY BEHAVIORS

Immediacy refers to the physical or psychological closeness between people involved in interaction. Nonverbal immediacy behaviors have primarily been studied in college classrooms. Research suggests that immediacy behaviors are associated with more positive evaluations of instructors by their students and increased perceptions of learning.[57] Nonverbal immediacy behaviors and increased perceptions of learning have also been related to students' willingness to talk during class discussions and in out-of-class communication.[58] Overall, studies illustrate that the more we make use of immediacy behaviors, the more others tend to like us, evaluate us highly, and prefer communicating with us. Conversely, the less we make use of immediacy behaviors, the more others tend to dislike us, evaluate us negatively, and avoid communicating with us. Table 4.1 presents specific immediacy behaviors.

A number of positive communication-related outcomes result from the use of immediacy behaviors. Immediacy behaviors contribute to perceptions of approachability, responsiveness, and understanding; are associated with decreased anxiety on the part of a conversation partner; and enhance the perception of communication competence. Interestingly, students whose professors communicate with them via Twitter are perceived to display a high degree of nonverbal immediacy behaviors.[59]

On the other hand, immediacy behaviors are associated with some disadvantages. Specifically, some people mistake immediacy behaviors for cues that communicate a desire for intimacy. Immediacy behaviors also promote communication between people that isn't always rewarding. However, the advantages of using immediacy behaviors outnumber and outweigh the disadvantages.[60] In particular, nonverbal immediacy behaviors reflect ethical and civil communication because they communicate respect, responsibility, and caring. When we use immediacy behaviors, we signal our openness to the other person, helping that person to feel acknowledged and appreciated.

Table 4.1 Immediacy and Nonimmediacy Behaviors
You can use immediacy behaviors to make your communication more civil.

Category	Immediacy Behaviors	Nonimmediacy Behaviors
Verbal immediacy	Using pronouns such as *we* and *us* Talking with others Statements that infer liking: *I like your dress. I really like that. You are right.*	Using pronouns such as *you*, *your*, and *I* Talking to or at others Guarded statements of liking or statements that infer disliking: *Your dress is okay. That's dumb. That's a stupid idea.*
Appearance	Attractive Clean, neat Informal clothing but not sloppy Appropriate hairstyle	Unattractive Dirty, unkempt Formal clothing Inappropriate or unusual hairstyle
Gestures and body movement	Leaning toward another Open body position More gestures More positive-affect displays Relaxed body position Calm movements Positive head movements	Leaning away from another Closed body position Fewer gestures More negative-affect displays Tense body position Nervous movements Negative head movements
Face and eye	Eye contact and mutual gaze Facial expressions that show pleasure Smiles a lot	Limited eye contact Averted eye gaze Facial expressions that show displeasure Frowns a lot

continued

Table 4.1 Immediacy and Nonimmediacy Behaviors (*continued*)

Category	Immediacy Behaviors	Nonimmediacy Behaviors
Voice	Short pauses Few silences Positive vocal inflections Vocal variety Relaxed tones (calm) Sound confident Dynamic, animated, interested Friendly vocal cues	Lengthy pauses and silences Sarcasm Monotonous, dull, irritated tones Nasal Harsh sounding Sneering sounds Bored, unfriendly vocal cues
Space	Moving closer to a person Standing closer to a person Sitting closer Orienting more directly Leaning forward while seated	Leaning away from a person Sitting farther away Leaning away or back while seated Standing farther away Indirect body orientation
Touch	Touch on hand, forearm, shoulder Pat Friendly handshake Frequent touch Hugging	Avoiding or withdrawing from touch Clammy or distant handshake Infrequent touch Slapping, hitting, striking another
Environment	Warm, secure, pleasant environments Soft colors Movable chairs Moderate to soft illumination	Cold, distant, ugly environments Bright illumination Fixed seating Ugly rooms Ugly colors
Scent	Pleasant, inoffensive scents Familiar scents Scents of one's own culture	Unpleasant, offensive scents Unfamiliar scents Scents from other cultures
Time	Short lag before response Promptness Spending more time with another Spending time with another when they choose	Long lag before response Delinquent about being on time Spending little time with another Often glancing at watch or clock

From Virginia Richmond and James McCroskey, *Nonverbal Behavior in Interpersonal Relations*, 5th ed. Published by Allyn & Bacon, Boston. Copyright © 2000 by Pearson Education.

TECH CHECK

The Nonverbal Immediacy Scale

Research demonstrates that the more we make use of immediacy behaviors, the more others tend to like us, evaluate us highly, and prefer communicating with us. Conversely, the less we make use of immediacy behaviors, the more others tend to dislike us, evaluate us negatively, and avoid communicating with us. Think about someone you like and evaluate highly and with whom you enjoy communicating. Use the Nonverbal Immediacy scale to rate the person's nonverbal behaviors. According to research about nonverbal immediacy, this person should receive a high score on the scale. After completing the assessment, ask yourself whether you believe the person's nonverbal communication is related to your perceptions of him or her—specifically, how you like and evaluate that person and whether you enjoy communicating with him or her.

Immediacy and Your Career

Research reveals that supervisors who exhibit nonverbal immediacy behaviors can communicate liking, positive evaluation, and positive affect for their subordinates. In addition, supervisors who are perceived as immediate are seen as credible and interpersonally attractive by their employees. Subordinates who perceive their supervisors as immediate express positive attitudes about their supervisors and their supervisors' communication. These employees also reciprocate their supervisors' immediacy behaviors.[61]

Supervisor immediacy is also positively related to motivation and job satisfaction. Employees who are highly motivated and satisfied are typically more productive than those who are not, and they are less likely to leave their jobs. These findings are particularly relevant to modern organizations because of the high cost of training new workers in today's technologically oriented economy.[62]

On the other hand, nonverbal immediacy is associated with perceived supervisor Machiavellianism. Machiavellian supervisors often attempt to achieve interpersonal goals in terms of manipulation, strategic self-presentation, and ingratiation tactics. That is, they may purposely display immediacy behaviors, which their subordinates, in turn, perceive as phony. Subordinates' perceptions of supervisor Machiavellianism are strongly associated with a lack of nonverbal immediacy, and employees tend to hold negative attitudes about such supervisors, as well as low levels of motivation and job satisfaction.[63]

CHAPTER SUMMARY

Now that you have read this chapter you can:

4.1 Define *nonverbal communication*.

Nonverbal communication refers to all forms of communication other than words. Nonverbal communication is worthy of study because it is powerful. Research demonstrates that between 65 percent and 93 percent of the meaning of messages comes from nonverbal communication. Studies have found that nonverbal communication is 12 to 13 times more powerful than the verbal messages it accompanies. When nonverbal messages contradict verbal messages, we tend to believe the nonverbal communication.

4.2 Explain the functions of nonverbal communication.

One function of nonverbal communication is to repeat what is communicated verbally. For example, you might point your index finger at something as you say, "It's over there." Nonverbal communication can substitute for verbal communication. For example, an emblem is a nonverbal behavior that can be translated directly in a word or two of verbal communication. Nonverbal communication also functions to accent or emphasize the spoken word. Sometimes illustrators, speech-related gestures that are directly tied to what we say, are used to accent the spoken word. In addition, nonverbal communication functions to complement verbal communication. Like nonverbal behaviors that accent the spoken word, complementing nonverbal communication intensifies the meaning of verbal communication. Nonverbal communication also functions to regulate the flow of verbal behavior.

4.3 Identify the types of nonverbal communication.

Nonverbal communication is typically organized and studied in terms of four categories: kinesics (i.e., gestures, body orientation and posture, touch, facial expression and eye behavior), paralanguage (i.e., vocal qualities and accents), physical characteristics (i.e., attractiveness, body shape, and artifacts), and the environment (i.e., the physical environment, chronemics, territoriality, and proxemics). Although the types of nonverbal communication are divided into categories and are explained as if they are separate and distinct, the various types work together to communicate meaning. It is therefore important to remember that nonverbal communication occurs in clusters when conveying a message, with or without accompanying words.

4.4 Recognize why road rage is an example of uncivil nonverbal communication.

According to an Associated Press-Ipsos poll, the most commonly cited example of incivility is nonverbal—aggressive or reckless driving. The symbolic behavior associated with road rage involves using vehicles to nonverbally express anger. People who instigate road rage incidents tend to blame the other drivers. These individuals typically believe that internal characteristics of other drivers contribute to road rage incidents and are unable to see that their own behaviors influence road rage. It appears that cognitive-behavioral interventions can significantly decrease this dangerous and potentially fatal form of uncivil and unethical nonverbal communication.

4.5 Explain the role of nonverbal behavior in the communication of deception.

Nonverbal deception cues, or behaviors that people typically associate with lying, include fidgeting behaviors and throat clearing. However, there is no general telltale sign of a lie. Current studies that take place outside a laboratory suggest that deception cues associated with lying do not result from actually telling lies but from the experience of emotion, content complexity, and impression management. A liar may speak with a higher-pitched voice, which may be the result of feeling guilty, excited, or afraid while lying. A liar may include few details in an explanation because of the complex content of the lie. And a liar may also exhibit few illustrators while lying because of her or his attempt to control the situation and to engage in impression management.

4.6 Use nonverbal immediacy behaviors to improve your ability to communicate civilly.

Immediacy refers to the physical or psychological closeness between people involved in interaction. Studies illustrate that the more we make use of immediacy behaviors, the more others tend to like us, evaluate us highly, and prefer communicating with us. Conversely, the less we make use of immediacy behaviors, the more others tend to dislike us, evaluate us negatively, and avoid communicating with us. Nonverbal immediacy behaviors include appearance (i.e., attractive, clean, appropriate hairstyle), gestures and body orientation (i.e., leaning toward another, open body position, gestures), movement (i.e., relaxed and calm movements), face and eyes (i.e., mutual gaze, smiling), voice (i.e., short pauses, positive vocal inflections), space (i.e., stands closer to a person, leans forward while seated), touch (i.e., friendly handshake, touch on hand), environment (i.e., warm, secure, pleasant), scent (i.e., pleasant, scents of one's own culture), and time (i.e., promptness, spending time with another).

CIVILITY SUMMARY

Overall, remember that civility and nonverbal communication involve the following:

- Judging another's nonverbal behavior based on our own cultural display rules may cause us to make misinterpretations about nonverbal civility.
- Behaviors understood as civil for Americans vary in terms of the various co-cultures that exist within the United States.
- Nonverbal immediacy behaviors reflect ethical and civil communication because they communicate respect, responsibility, and caring.

REVIEW QUESTIONS

1. Define *nonverbal communication*. What is the relationship between verbal communication and nonverbal communication?
2. Why should we interpret nonverbal communication with care?
3. Why is knowledge of nonverbal communication important in your everyday life?
4. What are the functions of nonverbal communication?
5. Describe the four categories of nonverbal communication and the types of behaviors included within them.
6. Why is road rage considered an example of uncivil nonverbal communication?
7. How can we improve our ability to engage in civil nonverbal communication by using immediacy behaviors?
8. How does culture influence nonverbal communication?
9. How can nonverbal communication affect your career?
10. How do gender stereotypes and expectations influence the interpretation of nonverbal communication?

5 Civil Listening and Responding with Confirmation

THE OPRAH WINFREY NETWORK (OWN) made its debut during the first week of January 2011. Winfrey said that she wanted to create a cable network that included programs that weren't mean spirited. A *New York Times* television writer affirmed that Winfrey had succeeded when she described OWN as a network where pessimism, scorn, and ridicule are nowhere to be found.[1] Oprah and her OWN have been lauded for their attempt to foster civility in cable television and in our culture in general. One AOL television news reporter wrote of Oprah's push toward civility, "I hope it spreads—to other cable channels, to the guy walking down the street dropping F bombs while shouting into his cell phone, and also to the dark halls of the worldwide Web."[2]

Winfrey is known not only for attempts to foster civility but also for her ability to listen. During a press conference to announce the launch of OWN, Winfrey commented that her greatest strength is paying attention. In addition to listening and empathizing with

> **CHAPTER OBJECTIVES**
>
> After reading this chapter, you will be able to:
>
> **5.1** Define *listening*.
> **5.2** Explain the relationship among listening, civility, and ethics.
> **5.3** Describe the stages in the listening process and identify the types of listening.
> **5.4** Apply strategies to improve your ability to engage in civil listening.
> **5.5** Communicate confirming listening response styles.
> **5.6** Explain the association between listening and confirming responses with culture, workplace (your career), and gender contexts.

interview guests, Winfrey says that she listens to herself and learns from her mistakes.[3] In fact, the secret to Winfrey's success is her ability to listen.[4]

WHY IT MATTERS

Oprah Winfrey's ability to listen and empathize with her guests encourages them to reveal their feelings and honestly discuss their problems. Do people feel comfortable discussing their problems with you because of the way you listen and respond? Listening and responding to others in a civil and ethical manner communicate that we *confirm* who they are or acknowledge and respect them and their thoughts and feelings; we refer to this type of listening as **civil listening**, or **confirming listening**. Michael Josephson, founder and president of the Josephson Institute of Ethics, states, "The virtue of respectfulness is demonstrated by being courteous [and] being civil . . . an important but often neglected aspect of respectfulness is listening to what others say."[5]

What can we do to help people cope with their problems? Is there a way we can communicate with others that will facilitate their recovery from disease? How can we contribute to a stable marriage and relational satisfaction? One answer to these questions is the same: When we listen and make confirming responses, we can help others and enhance our relationships.

Speakers feel acknowledged, honored, and confirmed when we listen to them with care and attention. This happens when we are fully emotionally present with others, withhold judgment, and avoid distractions.[6] Similarly, receiving confirming responses can help people cope more successfully with problems, manage upset feelings, and maintain both a positive sense of self and a positive outlook on life.[7] Receiving confirming responses has also been correlated with and, in some cases, found to directly result in improved resistance to and recovery from disease and infection, enhanced psychological adjustment, and reduced mortality.[8]

Listening and responding with confirmation also enhance relationships. Researchers have discovered that husbands who listen to their wives tend to have happy and stable marriages, whereas husbands who fail to listen to their wives may find themselves headed for divorce. Conflicts that involve various family members can also be resolved with effective listening.[9] In addition, confirming responses are related to relational satisfaction.[10] Listening and confirming responses are relationally significant because they can communicate commitment, compassion, interest, and love.

In this chapter, you will learn about the definition of and characteristics associated with listening and why listening and responding with confirmation are important to your everyday life. You will read about how listening relates to civility and ethics and about the stages and types of listening. You will also learn how to improve your ability to engage in civil listening and to respond with confirmation while you listen to others. In addition, you'll read about listening and confirming responses in culture, workplace (your career), and gender contexts.

---

civil listening Also known as *confirming listening*, a listening style that communicates our belief in the quality of all people.

confirming listening Also called *civil listening*, a listening style that communicates our belief in the quality of all people.

DEFINITION OF LISTENING

Think back to your days in elementary school. Did your teachers provide you with instruction in reading, writing, and speaking? You probably read many childhood storybooks, practiced handwriting, and learned vocabulary words and how to pronounce them. However, did your teachers ever instruct you about listening? We engage in listening more than we read, write, and speak, yet rarely are we taught how to listen well to others.[11]

Listening is a complex skill that does not have a widely accepted definition. Even the number of components associated with the listening process engenders disagreement.[12] However, a common definition posits that listening involves six stages that don't

TECH CHECK

Listening Preference Profile

What type of listening style do you possess? Do you tend to focus on relationships and emotional cues, or do you concentrate on the content and accuracy of a message? Do you focus on direct and concise messages, or do you concentrate on a message's logic and organization? These questions relate to four types of listening styles: people oriented, content oriented, time oriented, and action oriented. You can take the Listening Preference Profile to find your typical listening style. Ask yourself how this style affects your interpersonal relationships and think about what you can do to improve your listening scores and consequently improve your communication with others.

---

listening A complex skill that does not have a widely accepted definition. However, a common definition posits that listening entails six stages that don't necessarily have to be enacted in order: hearing, understanding, remembering, interpreting, evaluating, and responding.

necessarily have to be enacted in order: hearing, understanding, remembering, interpreting, evaluating, and responding.[13]

In general, college students spend approximately 24 percent of "communication time" engaged in listening, compared with 20 percent of the time speaking, 8 percent of the time reading, and 9 percent of the time writing.[14] In addition, students are spending more time listening to mediated communication channels and on the Internet.[15] College students listen to the radio 4 percent of the time; listen to music 8 percent of the time; watch TV 8 percent of the time; and talk and listen on the phone 7 percent of the time.[16] In terms of the Internet, college students spend their communication time writing and reading email (5 percent) and in using the Internet (13 percent). In fact, "lurking," a negative term used for people in public online spaces who don't participate actively, may be a form of listening and tracking other's contributions.[17] Because we can engage in a wide variety of listening, we should consider improving our ability to listen, not only to help ourselves in our everyday life but also to help others.

LISTENING, CIVILITY, AND ETHICS

Listening can be described as "an inherently civil act."[18] However, many of us engage in types of listening that can be characterized as uncivil. This form of listening is disconfirming.

Uncivil Listening: Disconfirming Others

disconfirming listening A type of uncivil listening that does not acknowledge and respect a speaker's verbal and nonverbal messages. Specific types of disconfirming listening are defensive listening, pseudolistening, confrontational listening, and literal listening.

Disconfirming listening communicates disrespect, a lack of restraint, and/or a lack of responsibility. This type of listening includes:

- **Defensive listening**—Interpreting messages as criticism and personal attacks.
- **Pseudolistening**—Pretending to listen even though we focus on our own thoughts and miss the speaker's message.
- **Confrontational listening**—Listening carefully for flaws in a message to refute them or attack the speaker in response.

Psuedolistening is a disconfirming type of listening that occurs when we pretend to listen even though we focus on our own thoughts.

- **Literal listening**—Listening to the content of a message and ignoring the "feeling" of the message. Literal listening occurs when we overlook nonverbal communication and the emotional tone of a message. For example, when we happily reply, "Good to hear it!" after someone sighs and hesitantly says, "I feel okay," we respond on the basis of literal listening.

Civil Listening: Confirming Others

As mentioned earlier in this chapter, civil listening is a confirming listening style that communicates our belief in the equality of all people. Civil listening is ethical because it means that we treat people as equals even if we dislike their opinions and because it requires that we respect others and what they say.[19] In fact, thinking and acting in an ethical manner emerge as a result of a commitment to civil listening.[20] Civil listening is also beneficial because sometimes people just want to be confirmed—that is, feel acknowledged and respected. A civil response from a conversation partner can be interpreted as an act of confirmation. However, civil listening isn't easy because it means that we must be open to what others have to say and acknowledge the possibility that they may be right, and we may be wrong. If we listen to others with an open mind—that is, without searching for flaws in what they say and accepting the possibility that they are correct—we place our ego at risk (i.e., instead of changing their minds, we might change ours). This occurs because who we think we are is tied to our beliefs, whether they concern a political party affiliation, an opinion about abortion, or a belief in a god. Such important beliefs are at risk when we engage in civil listening. But if we expect others to listen civilly to us and give us an opportunity to persuade them to our way of thinking, we must also listen civilly to them and give them an opportunity to convert us to their way of thinking.

Civil listening is not only risky, it is time-consuming. It may be that people who already think they are too busy won't spare the time to attempt civil listening. However difficult it may be to patiently attend to others' communication, we may find that others will patiently listen to us in return.[21]

Engaging in the following strategies can help us improve our ability to engage in civil listening:[22]

- *Planning our listening*—We can make a conscious effort to make listening, instead of refutation, our goal. We can say to ourselves that we will make time to listen or that this is a time *just* to listen.
- *Demonstrating that we are listening*—We can take the task of listening seriously by engaging in nonverbal immediacy behaviors such as making eye contact and nodding. We can also communicate our commitment to listening by using vocal cues (e.g., "uh-huh," "hmmm") and verbal cues (e.g., saying "Go on" and "I see").
- *Becoming fully involved with a speaker*—We can give direction and shape to what someone says and to what someone communicates without words. Later in this chapter, you will learn that you can prompt and question your listening partner, express your reassurance and concern, and paraphrase your partner's verbal and nonverbal communication to engage in civil listening that is confirming.

ASK THE ETHICIST: Do I Have to Listen?

Question Why should I listen to people who have different opinions from mine? Why can't I just say "I don't want to listen" and walk away?

Answer You don't have to listen. And you do have the right to walk away. But it's probably a good idea to think about the implications of refusing to listen or walking away.

Listening is important because it shows that we value the other person. In fact, the feeling of being truly listened to is so close to the feeling of being loved that most people cannot tell the difference.[23] Others may interpret your refusal to listen as an indication that you have a low opinion of them.

Listening to both sides of an argument is also an important part of the democratic process we value in the United States (though, perhaps, we practice it less frequently than we should). Americans are described as people who look for sources that validate their opinions. These sources may consist of political blogs, television news shows, or specific books. Unfortunately, this is a type of anti-intellectualism and is a departure from how Americans formerly learned about politics. At the turn of the twentieth century, people would pack lecture halls to hear those they didn't agree with because they wanted to know what the other side was saying. Still today, if you don't listen to opinions contrary to your own, you are unlikely to learn anything.[24]

When you think about walking away from people who hold different opinions than you do, it is important to think about the meaning of an exit. Generally, we don't feel good if someone says to us "I don't want to hear any more" and walks away from us. It signals a disregard for our thoughts and a disregard for the relationship. Walking out is a powerful message, but it is limited in its long-term effect. It closes the door to further communication. Walking out also confuses listening with agreement. When we stay to listen, we do not imply that we concur with all that a speaker has to say. When we listen, we sacrifice our visceral desire to run and substitute a desire to try to understand the other.

By tuning out or walking out on others, we indicate that the others are not worthy of our consideration. That seems uncivil.

STAGES AND TYPES OF LISTENING

"You're not hearing me!" How often have you been the target of this accusation? People sometimes say this to communicate the perception that their conversation partner is not listening to them. In reality, hearing is just the first of six stages in the listening process. The stages and types of listening are illustrated in Figure 5.1. The entire process includes:

- Hearing
- Understanding
- Remembering
- Interpreting
- Evaluating
- Responding

Various types of listening are associated with particular stages in the listening process, such as:

- Appreciative listening
- Comprehensive listening
- Empathic listening
- Critical listening
- Active listening

The stages and types of listening are illustrated in Figure 5.1.

Stages and Types of Listening

> **Stage 1:** Hearing (during which appreciative listening may occur)
> Obstacles include:
> • Noise (and multi-tasking)
> • Selectivity

> **Stage 2:** Understanding (during which comprehensive listening can occur)
> Obstacles include:
> • Thinking we know what someone means before s/he is finished speaking

> **Stage 3:** Remembering
> Obstacles include:
> • Thinking about what we're going to say next
> • Thinking about what others are thinking of us

> **Stage 4:** Interpreting (during which empathic listening may occur)
> Obstacles include:
> • The tendency to engage in literal listening

> **Stage 5:** Evaluating (during which critical listening may occur)
> Obstacles include:
> • Failing to suspend or delay judgment before we form an opinion

> **Stage 6:** Responding (which involves active listening; verbal and nonverbal responses to others)
> Obstacles include:
> • Passive Listening

hearing The reception and processing of sounds.

appreciative listening A type of listening in which we engage when we want to enjoy and appreciate the messages we listen to.

FIGURE 5.1 Stages and Types of Listening
Researchers have identified six discrete stages that make up the listening process.

Multi-tasking impairs our ability to receive verbal and nonverbal communication from the environment.

Stage 1: Hearing and Appreciative Listening

Hearing is necessary for all listening that includes vocal communication; however, it is not a sufficient condition for effective listening. Since hearing involves the reception and processing of sounds, the ability to select and concentrate on the stimuli to which you choose to attend is important.[25] Hearing is often the key component in **appreciative listening**, when we focus on appreciating and enjoying the messages we listen to. Appreciative listening can occur when no one else is present, such as when we listen to music or the sounds of nature. Appreciative listening can also occur in the presence of others, such as when we listen to someone read poetry aloud or when we focus on a conversation partner's nonverbal communication as she or he acts out a story while speaking.

Various obstacles can make it difficult to receive stimuli from the environment and listen to others. These obstacles include noise and selectivity.

Noise Recall from Chapter 1 that noise is anything that can interfere with the listening process. For example, semantic noise might interfere with our ability to listen. If a stranger walks up to us and says, "Yo, dude!" or "Hey, girl!" as a conversation starter, we may focus on our intrapersonal communication (e.g., "What a jerk!") if we dislike such forms of address. Psychological noise such as feeling tired, hungry, or preoccupied with another matter can also interfere with the listening process. Moreover, our very physiology creates noise that interferes with the listening process. People can understand extremely rapid speech, up to 600 words per minute. Because most people speak at about 100 to 150 words per minute, however, we can concentrate on our own thoughts while someone is speaking.[26]

A CASE STUDY IN ETHICS

Cochlear Implants

Ethical communication reflects trustworthiness, responsibility, respect, fairness, caring, and concern for the community. Keep the components of ethical communication in mind as you read the following case study and answer the discussion questions.

N.B. "Deaf" with a capital "D" indicates membership in Deaf culture; "deaf" with a small "d" indicates an auditory condition.

Can people listen if they are physically unable to engage in hearing, the first stage of the listening process? Deaf people do listen—with their eyes! As much as a hearing person listens to spoken language, a deaf person's eyes listen to a visual language. American Sign Language (ASL) is a visual–spatial language that uses nonmanual markers (NMMs)—facial features that convey meaning and grammatical information.[27] However, not everyone believes that deaf people can listen without hearing. Peter and Nita Artinian, both Deaf, have a young deaf daughter, Heather. Peter's hearing brother, Chris, and his hearing wife, Mari, have a deaf son. Within the extended family of both Deaf and hearing individuals, a battle rages regarding whether to surgically implant the children with cochlear devices. A cochlear implant can help deaf or hard-of-hearing individuals perceive sounds. Success cannot be guaranteed after the device is implanted underneath the skin behind the ear, and long periods of adjustment and therapy are expected after implantation. Effective recognition of sound and use of intelligible speech are not guaranteed, and a hearing aid will be ineffective because of the nerve damage that results from implantation. However, many hearing parents and doctors perceive the cochlear implant to be a modern miracle and a cure for deafness. Members of the Artinian family have argued both sides of the cochlear implant debate.

Peter fears that the implants will destroy Deaf culture and obliterate his culture's language, ASL. His concern has been echoed by various Deaf advocates, who compare the more powerful hearing culture and its support of implantation with other powerful groups that have engaged in cultural genocide and attempted to eradicate cultures by suppressing their language. Peter's mother has argued that Heather will suffer as an outsider in a hearing world, but Peter has countered that implanting Heather will cause her to miss out on the Deaf life that he embraces. Peter's argument is similar to those of other Deaf culture advocates, who believe that they are not afflicted with a disability. Members of Deaf culture contend that the idea of "curing" a Deaf individual is similar to "curing" a black person by changing her or him into someone who is white. Peter has also reminded his mother that Heather changed her mind about the implant and signed, "I'm not ready to have a cochlear implant yet. I'm too afraid." However, his mother has lectured Peter that he should "forget Deaf" and that first he is a father who should do what's right for his child. Furthermore, she has asserted that the decision to implant should not be Heather's but her parents'.

Peter's hearing brother, Chris, and his hearing wife, Mari, implanted their deaf son when he was one year old. Their child can speak and has been mainstreamed into a public school. Mari's Deaf mother has described the type of hearing that implanted people experience as "robotic hearing at best." She has argued against implantation and laments that her grandson has only a rudimentary knowledge of ASL. Mari's mother is afraid that she and her husband, who is also Deaf, will lose the ability to communicate with their grandson.[28]

Discussion Questions

1. Is it ethical to make use of cochlear implants if the devices have the potential to eliminate a culture's language and eventually the culture itself?
2. Is it ethical for a dominant culture to prescribe what is considered a "disability" and to "fix" persons who are considered disabled?
3. Is it ethical to implant a child with a cochlear device against her or his wishes?
4. Is it ethical to deny an implant to a child because family members fear losing their culture?

Multitasking can also act as noise and interfere with the listening process. One characteristic of the "Millennial Generation," people born between 1982 and 2002, is that they often multitask by juggling a text messaging conversation, listening to a song on an iTunes playlist, surfing the Web, and reading a classic book for homework—all at once.[29] However, neurological research has found that when it comes to media and information content, we listen poorly to multiple sources. For example, students who access websites, text others, and talk to classmates during a professor's lecture have a difficult time switching from one task to another and fail to ignore irrelevant information. Multitaskers also get distracted constantly, and their memory becomes disorganized. Additional research has found a relationship between students who multitask in class and poor analytic reasoning and writing ability.[30]

Selective Listening. Another problem related to receiving verbal and nonverbal stimuli is **selective listening**, which involves attending to some parts of a message and ignoring others. It's not possible to select and attend to all stimuli from the environment; in our fast-paced and technologically oriented society, we are bombarded with information. We therefore sometimes fail to perceive parts of messages that don't interest us, that make us uncomfortable, or that conflict with our opinions. We may also isolate parts of messages that are of interest to us, that make us happy, or with which we agree. For example, do you know someone who was told "Let's still be friends" during a breakup? Perhaps this friend, still in love with a relational partner, sublimated the "I don't think we should see each other anymore" part of the message and happily concluded that the relationship had a chance of survival because the partner wanted to stay friends.

> **selective listening** A type of disconfirming listening during which we attend to some parts of a message and ignore others.

Stage 2: Understanding and Comprehensive Listening

Understanding refers to listening comprehension. **Comprehensive listening** is crucial when we want to learn, understand, and recall information. A typical application of this stage in the listening process occurs when we need to follow directions and make decisions. Listening to an instructor give a lecture or a friend tell a story is an example of comprehensive listening.

Understanding is also particularly important when you listen to information in a lecture or presentation. To understand what we hear, we must recognize the meanings of words and be able to use sound cues to form tentative images. However, complete understanding between people is impossible because meanings are personal and unique (and sometimes we purposefully use abstract words, which can cause misunderstandings).[31]

One problem that can get in the way of understanding is thinking that we know what a speaker means before she or he is finished speaking in a conversation. A similar problem is believing that we understand the main point of a presentation before the speaker comes to the conclusion of the speech. In a conversation, this belief may cause us to interrupt in order to interject our own point of view. During a speech, this may cause our mind to wander. In such cases, we may misunderstand the sender's message.[32]

> **comprehensive listening** A type of listening in which we engage when we want to learn, understand, and recall information.

Stage 3: Remembering

Have you ever met someone for the first time and after a few minutes of conversation realized that you've already forgotten her or his name? This often occurs because we're too busy thinking about what we're going to say next and/or what others may be thinking about us. Memory involves the ability to store information and retrieve it when necessary.[33] Research illustrates that there are various types of memory and that we use memory in different ways when we listen. Short-term listening is associated with interpersonal skills in a variety of contexts, such as making positive impressions in job interviews. Specifically, respondents with good short-term memory ask more questions during an interview than do those with poor short-term memory, and they tend to be perceived as having excellent listening skills.[34] Short-term memory is also involved in remembering people's names after we have just met them. You will soon read about a technique that can

Empathic listening occurs when we want to understand and experience the feelings of a conversation partner.

empathic listening A listening style during which we listen to understand and experience the feelings of a conversation partner. We can engage in empathic listening by paraphrasing for feelings.

evaluative listening A type of listening in which we engage when we want to judge the soundness of a message.

critical listening Also known as *critical thinking*, a listening style in which we analyze and evaluate messages by delaying or suspending judgment before forming an opinion. Critical listening also includes separating fact from inference, assessing the source(s) of the information, and focusing on the form of reasoning.

help you improve your short-term memory and avoid the embarrassment associated with not remembering someone's name.

Stage 4: Interpreting and Empathic Listening

Interpreting entails considering meaning from a speaker's point of view. This requires you to perceive a situation from the speaker's perspective and to pay attention to the emotional meaning of the message. Interpreting also involves making sure that conversation partners know they are being understood. This stage in the listening process therefore requires social sensitivity, which is based on taking into account nonverbal as well as verbal messages. One obstacle to effective interpreting is the tendency to engage in literal listening, which you learned earlier in this chapter is an uncivil listening style in which we focus solely on words and disregard nonverbal behavior. However, effective interpretation includes listening to not only what a speaker says but to what he or she doesn't say. Interpretation also involves **empathic listening** in order to understand and experience the feelings of a conversation partner. Later in this chapter, you will learn about the difference between empathy and sympathy and how to engage in empathic listening by using a feelings paraphrase.

Stage 5: Evaluating and Critical Listening

We are all influenced by our own past experiences, values, predispositions, and attitudes; these unique experiences, characteristics, and attributes affect how we listen to others in terms of evaluation. An evaluation is a judgment. The deliberate process of evaluation occurs when we listen to messages designed to persuade us and when we engage in decision making. Effective listeners understand that they are influenced by a variety of factors that may not influence others, and they attempt to delay evaluating ideas until they understand a speaker's message. In other words, effective listeners try to be as objective as possible prior to making evaluations.[35]

We use **evaluative listening** when we want to judge the soundness of a message. Our ability to evaluate messages is influenced by our capacity to engage in critical thinking. Sometimes labeled **critical listening**, this type of listening refers to activities involved in analyzing and evaluating messages. To successfully evaluate a message, we must suspend or at least delay judgment before we form an opinion. Recall the last time you listened to some negative gossip. Did you immediately believe that the message was truthful? We should critically analyze the messages we listen to before we accept their validity.

Stage 6: Responding and Active Listening

Active listening involves verbal and nonverbal responses to others that let them know we are paying attention and taking responsibility for understanding their meanings. At its most basic, active listening requires us to be attentive to others and to expend mental and emotional energy to understand and respond in a civil and ethical manner. Many people don't realize that effective active listening requires time and effort. On the other hand, **passive listening** is practiced by those who believe that it's a speaker's

active listening A type of listening that features verbal and nonverbal responses to others that let them know we are paying attention and taking responsibility for understanding their meanings.

passive listening A type of listening that assumes that it's the responsibility of a speaker to ensure that the listener understands. Because passive listeners merely absorb information, they believe that any misunderstanding is the fault of the speaker.

responsibility to ensure that the listener understands. Passive listeners tend to equate hearing with listening and assume that all they must do is soak up communication directed toward them. Because passive listeners merely absorb information, they believe that any misunderstanding is the fault of the speaker. Clearly, this is far from the truth.

IMPROVING OUR ABILITY TO ENGAGE IN CIVIL AND EFFECTIVE LISTENING

We can improve our ability to listen civilly and ethically during all six stages of the listening process: hearing; understanding; remembering; interpreting; evaluating; and responding. We can improve the ability to listen civilly and ethically by reducing distractions and recognizing our propensity to listen selectively, focusing on understanding and becoming aware of interrupting behavior, using a five-second strategy to remember names, experiencing empathy with others and observing nonverbal behaviors, using critical thinking skills, and communicating confirming responses. These strategies are illustrated in Figure 5.2.

Stage 1: Improving the Ability to Hear Messages and Engage in Appreciative Listening

We can improve our ability to receive messages by reducing or eliminating distractions and by recognizing our propensity to engage in selective listening. These strategies can also improve our ability to engage in appreciative listening. For example, we can mentally prepare ourselves to listen by blocking distracting thoughts that might interfere with the listening process. We may want to engage in self-talk to tell ourselves that we must give the speaker our full attention; we can return to our thoughts once the conversation ends. In terms of multitasking, we can avoid the harmful effects of doing too many things at once by giving our full attention to a speaker, whether we are in a conversation or listening to a professor's lecture. We can also acknowledge that we may often miss parts of a message. In addition, we can counteract the tendency to selectively listen by planning to respond with a paraphrase of what we believe the speaker means.

Stage 1: Hearing
We can improve our ability to **receive** messages and engage in **appreciative listening** by:
• Reducing distractions
• Recognizing our propensity to listen selectively

Stage 2: Understanding
We can improve our ability to **understand** messages and engage in **comprehensive listening** by:
• Focusing on understanding
• Becoming aware of interrupting behavior

Stage 3: Remembering
We can improve our ability to **remember** messages by:
• Using a five second strategy to remember names

Stage 4: Interpreting
We can improve our ability to **interpret** messages and engage in **empathic listening** by:
• Experiencing empathy with others
• Observing nonverbal behaviors

Stage 5: Evaluating
We can improve our ability to **evaluate** messages and engage in **critical listening** by:
• Using critical thinking skills (separate fact from inference, assess evidence, focus on reasoning)

Stage 6: Responding
We can improve our ability to **respond** to messages and engage in **active listening** by:
• Using confirming responses that validate others with expressions of affection, respect, and concern

FIGURE 5.2 Improving Our Ability to Engage in Civil Listening
We can improve our listening skills by focusing on the important elements of each listening stage.

Stage 2: Improving the Ability to Understand Messages and Engage in Comprehensive Listening

There are a number of ways you can improve the ability to understand a message you are listening to. These techniques include focusing on understanding and becoming aware of your interrupting behavior. One way to improve your ability to understand messages is to catch yourself when you think "I know what she or he's going to say" or "What a stupid comment!" Even if you consider yourself to be an expert about a topic, there is always a possibility that you will learn something new when someone speaks. You can also improve your ability to engage in comprehensive listening by listening for main ideas while focusing on supporting details. In addition, you can improve your ability to understand messages by monitoring your behavior and by analyzing the types of conversations during which you are most likely to interrupt. Ask yourself if you interrupt conversations when you speak to particular people or when you talk about specific topics. The first step in decreasing the frequency of your interruptions is to increase your awareness of your interrupting behavior.[36]

Stage 3: Improving the Ability to Remember Messages

A memory improvement technique that lasts a mere five seconds can help you remember people's names. Have you ever attended a party, met someone new, and realized once your conversation ended that you had forgotten her or his name? It is important to remember others' names because this confirms our conversational partners. The five-second strategy for remembering names involves:[37]

- *First second: Focus on the moment of introduction*—Refrain from rehearsing what you plan to say or worrying about the impression you'll make.
- *Second second: Listen for the name*—Listen for every letter in the person's name, especially the first initial.
- *Third second: Repeat the name aloud and visualize the name*—Repeat the name to make sure you get it right and then imagine the first initial etched on the person's forehead. A visual image can help you remember someone's name.
- *Fourth second: Think of someone you know who has the same name*—This once again creates a visual image to help you remember the person's name.
- *Fifth second: Use the name during and at the end of the conversation*—This will personalize the conversation and reinforce your memory.

Stage 4: Improving the Ability to Interpret Messages and Engage in Empathic Listening

empathy Attempting to understand the thoughts and feelings of others and also vicariously experience the emotions of others.

sympathy Feeling sorrow for another person or persons.

To improve our ability to interpret others' messages, we need to learn how to engage in empathy. Empathy is a key element in interpreting messages that allows us to go beyond someone's literal meaning and consider feelings and indirect messages.[38] **Empathy** occurs when we not only attempt to understand the thoughts and feelings of others but also vicariously experience the emotions of others.[39] Empathy isn't the same as sympathy. **Sympathy** refers to feeling sorrow *for* another person rather than feeling *with* that person. For example, suppose a friend tearfully tells you that a beloved pet has been put to sleep. You can attempt to empathize with your friend by imagining yourself dealing with the death of your own four-legged companion. You can also imagine that you are the friend who is coping with the loss of a pet. Engaging in perspective taking can help you empathize with others. You can also improve your ability to empathize by observing a speaker's nonverbal behavior for insight into how the speaker may be feeling.

Stage 5: Improving the Ability to Evaluate Messages and Engage in Critical Listening

We can use critical thinking skills to enhance our ability to evaluate the messages we listen to and engage in critical listening. Specifically, we can use our critical thinking skills to do the following:

- *Separate fact from inference*—A fact is independently verifiable and typically based on sense data, while an inference is an interpretation of a fact. The statement "She didn't speak to him all night" is a fact, but the statement "She deliberately ignored him at the party" is an inference.
- *Assess the source(s) of information*—Suppose a student warns you not to enroll in a class taught by Professor X. Ask yourself about the credibility of the source; did this student enroll in a class taught by Professor X, or is she or he merely repeating gossip? If the student enrolled in one of Professor X's classes, is she or he telling you not to enroll as a result of receiving a (deserved) poor grade?
- *Focus on the form of reasoning*—Have you listened to a stereotype in the form of "All _____s [insert group] are _____ [insert adjective]?" This comment may be based on an experience with one or two people. This is an error in induction—that is, making a general conclusion based on a limited number of specific instances.

Stage 6: Improving the Ability to Respond to Messages and Engage in Active Listening

Consider a situation in which a speaker discloses a problem and a listener fails to respond. It's not that the listener doesn't want to respond; the problem is that she or he doesn't know how to react. Perhaps you've been in a similar situation. As a speaker, how might you feel when you don't receive a response from the person who is listening to you? As a listener, how might you feel when you can't think of something to say? Responding, the last component of the listening process, communicates our attention and interest in a speaker and our own reactions to what we listen to. In the following section, you will improve your ability to engage in active listening by learning about and communicating confirming responses that:

- Indicate you are listening to a conversation partner. Using prompts and asking questions can reinforce your attention.
- Reassure your conversation partner and express concern.
- Interpret what you hear. Paraphrasing what a conversation partner says verbally and what the partner may communicate nonverbally helps you interpret the meaning of the message.

CONFIRMING LISTENING RESPONSE STYLES

As mentioned earlier in this chapter, civil listening confirms others because it communicates our belief in the quality of all people. Civil (confirming) listening and confirming responses are two sides of the same coin. **Confirming responses** can be defined as civil verbal and nonverbal behaviors that express affection, respect, and concern. People who make use of a variety of confirming listening response styles are perceived as sensitive, concerned, and involved.[40] Prompting and questioning, reassuring and expressing concern, and paraphrasing thoughts and feelings are civil and ethical confirming responses which demonstrate that we have listened to others.

confirming responses Civil verbal and nonverbal communication that expresses affection, respect, and concern.

Prompting and Questioning

"Go on."
"I'm listening."
"What happened next?"

These comments are examples of prompting and questioning, skills that invite conversation partners to continue speaking and offer additional information. When used in a positive way, these skills reflect active listening and are ethical because they let others know that we are paying attention and taking responsibility for understanding their meanings.

Prompting and questioning, reassuring and expressing concern, and paraphrasing thoughts and feelings are civil and ethical confirming responses that demonstrate that we are listening to others.

Prompting
Prompts include silence, sounds, or words that let a speaker know that we not only are listening but also desire the speaker to continue. Prompts can be placed on a continuum that ranges from complete silence to vocalizations such as "Mmm" and "uh-huh" to words ("yeah") and complete sentences ("I see" and "Go on"). One problem with prompting is that they may be communicated in an uncivil and insincere manner and can mask the fact that a listener isn't paying attention. For example, maybe you've been involved in a phone conversation during which you hear your listener respond with "Mmm" and "uh-huh" but you also hear the clicking and clacking of a computer keyboard in use. Defensiveness is a common result of such an experience because the listener disconfirms us by suggesting that what we have to say is not as important as using the computer. Therefore, it is best to give a speaker our full attention and to use prompts in conjunction with other types of confirming responses.

Questioning
Asking questions enables us to obtain additional information and/or guide a speaker to a certain conclusion that we have in mind. **Open-ended questions** such as "What should I do about my relationship?" can encourage meaningful and thorough answers. Responses to open-ended questions tend to be descriptive and provide us with insight into what a conversation partner thinks and feels. In contrast, **closed-ended questions** such as "Should I end my relationships?" often evoke one-word responses and may not provide us with additional information we can use to keep a conversation going. However, both types of questions enable us to civilly and ethically communicate our respect of another because they illustrate that we are involved in a conversation and are interested in what a person has to say.

There are a number of suggestions and caveats to consider in questioning others. We should probably avoid asking too many questions at one time, which can send a speaker on a wild goose chase; both the speaker and listener can lose sight of the real topic. Asking too many questions may also lead a conversation partner to believe that she or he is being given the "third degree." We should also avoid questions that communicate criticism and/or reflect a hidden agenda or an underlying motive. Leading and loaded questions are especially problematic because they are uncivil and unethical. A **leading question** is a type of closed-ended question that suggests the "correct" answer and/or attempts to guide a respondent's answer. Leading questions also communicate judgment and criticism. "You mean you *finally* broke up with her/him?" is an example of a leading question. Rather than seeking to clarify or support, this question suggests that that the breakup should have occurred

prompts Silence, sounds ("Mmm" and "Uh-huh"), or words ("Go on" and "I'm listening") that let a speaker know that you are listening and you want the speaker to continue.

open-ended questions Questions that require more than a "yes or no" answer. Responses to open-ended questions tend to be descriptive and provide us with insight into what a conversation partner thinks and feels.

closed-ended questions Questions that often evoke one-word responses and may not provide us with additional information we can use to keep a conversation going.

leading questions Questions that suggest a "correct" answer and/or attempt to guide a respondent's answer.

loaded questions Closed-ended questions that typically provide only two alternatives and which presuppose something that has not been proven or accepted.

long ago. A **loaded question** is a type of closed-ended question that typically provides only two alternatives and presupposes something that has not been proven or accepted. For example, "Do you want to go out with that person or me?" is a loaded question because there may be other alternatives (e.g., you might want to go out with someone else or with no one at all). This question also presupposes that you want to go out with either person when that actually may not be true. Leading and loaded questions can cause a conversation partner to become defensive, believing that her or she is a target of manipulation.

Reassuring and Expressing Concern

"I've been in a similar situation, so I know what you're going through."

"I'm concerned about you, but you're resourceful, and I know you'll work things out."

These comments are expressions of concern and reassurance. Reassurance and responses that express concern communicate that we care about our conversation partner, sympathize with a speaker, and/or empathize with her or his feelings. These responses are civil and ethical because they communicate caring as well as respect. We can express our concern by suggesting that we understand a conversation partner's thoughts and feelings because we have been in a similar situation. This type of response is called **relational feedback**. It is a brief description of a situation that parallels the speaker's and points to a connection between the speaker's experience and your own.[41] We can also express concern and reassurance by empathizing with a speaker.

relational feedback A confirming response that involves a brief description of a situation that parallels a speaker's and points to a connection between the speaker's experience and your own.

Unfortunately, your partner may not perceive your messages as helpful, even if you communicate concern and reassurance in a manner that confirms others. By responding with "I know exactly what you mean," you might steer the conversation away from the speaker's problems to a lengthy description of your own experience in a similar situation. In this instance, you will not be perceived as helpful and may be considered unethical. When you engage in relational feedback, therefore, your comments about your personal experience should be brief. Additional problems associated with the expression of concern and reassurance include the perception of a lack of interest or understanding on the part of a listener. Perhaps you've expressed a problem and felt that the listener was not truly interested when she or he responded with "I know you can handle this" or "Oh, you'll be all right." Similarly, overusing reassurance may mistakenly communicate that you believe that a speaker should not feel as she or he does. Expressions of concern and reassurance are best used in conjunction with other types of confirming responses, such as prompting, questioning, and paraphrasing.

Overusing reassurance may mistakenly communicate that we believe that a speaker should not feel as she or he does.

Paraphrasing Thoughts and Feelings

"It seems to me that you may be reacting to more than just one situation. Does this make sense to you?"

"I bet you're feeling confused. Am I right?"

paraphrase A type of confirming response in which you reword the speaker's message in terms of your understanding of its meaning.

These sentences illustrate a paraphrase. A **paraphrase** rewords a speaker's message in terms of your understanding of its meaning. Paraphrasing does not entail parroting back a speaker's entire message but instead requires you to interpret the meaning of a speaker's message and to communicate that meaning in your own words. Because you can never be certain of what a speaker means or how a speaker feels, paraphrasing is a way to check whether you have correctly understood a speaker's message. Even if a speaker informs you that your paraphrase is incorrect, she or he has learned that you are listening attentively and will feel confirmed because you are sincerely trying to understand her or his thoughts and/or feelings. Moreover, responding with a paraphrase is civil and ethical because it communicates caring and respect for others' ability to solve their own problems. Paraphrasing includes:

- Rephrasing the speaker's comments to communicate your understanding of what the speaker means
- Communicating the paraphrase in a tentative manner so you don't appear to have a corner on the truth or that you know what the speaker means or feels better than she or he does
- Asking for feedback or ending a paraphrase with a rising inflection to obtain speaker feedback about the clarity of your understanding
- Delivering the paraphrase in a nonjudgmental manner, avoiding words that are evaluative (e.g., *good*, *bad*, *right*, *wrong*) and nonverbal behaviors that communicate that you disapprove of the speaker and/or the speaker's comments (e.g., shaking your head back and forth, rolling your eyes)

content paraphrase A confirming response in which you reword the speaker's message in terms of your understanding of the speaker's thoughts. Content paraphrasing can be used when you listen to a lot of information, when you are given complex directions and/or instructions, and when the information is technical and laden with unfamiliar jargon.

There are numerous ways to begin a paraphrase; suggestions regarding how to begin a paraphrase are listed in Table 5.1.

Table 5.1 Ways to Begin a Paraphrase

There are many ways to begin a paraphrase of another's communication. Always try to communicate in a style that is natural for you; there's no need to sound like someone else. Use the suggestions below to begin your paraphrases, or use them to generate additional methods to initiate your paraphrases.

What I hear you saying . . .	I'm getting that you . . .
As I see it . . .	Could it be that . . .
Maybe you feel . . .	I wonder if . . .
Is it conceivable that . . .	Maybe I've got it all wrong, but . . .
I'm not sure if I'm with you but . . .	Would you buy this idea as your own . . .
Maybe this is a long-shot, but . . .	Correct me if I'm wrong, but . . .
Is it possible that . . .	I'm not sure if I'm with you; do you mean . . .
I'm not certain I understand; do you mean . . .	It seems that you . . .
Does it sound reasonable that you . . .	Let me see if I understand you; you . . .
Could this be going on; you . . .	I get the impression that . . .
Let me see if I am with you; you . . .	I somehow sense that maybe you feel . . .
I guess that you're . . .	Is there any chance that you . . .

Source: G. M. Gazda, R. P. Walters, and W. C. Childers, *Human Relations Development: A Manual for the Health Sciences*. Boston: Allyn & Bacon, 1975.

Confirming Listening Response Styles   105

feelings paraphrase A confirming response in which you reword the speaker's message in terms of your understanding of the speaker's emotions. Paraphrasing for feelings requires you to monitor the speaker's nonverbal communication for clues about the speaker's emotions.

There are two types of paraphrases: one that focuses on the literal content of a communication and one that focuses on a speaker's feelings, even if the feelings aren't expressed verbally. It is likely that you'll use both types of paraphrasing while attempting to understand another's thoughts and feelings.

Paraphrasing for Content   You can use a **content paraphrase** when you listen to a lot of information, when you are given complex directions and/or instructions, and when the information is technical and laden with unfamiliar jargon. You can also use content paraphrases to comprehend other meanings that may not be communicated in an overt manner and to buy time to allow yourself to calm down in a heated discussion or argument. For example, suppose you are listening to someone tell a story about trying to get into a class that had already reached the maximum enrollment. The speaker describes how the uncooperative advisor insisted that she or he take a night class that had not yet filled. You can respond to the speaker by focusing on interpretations that the speaker does not state verbally, such as "It sounds like the advisor was trying to control you" or "I hear you saying that the advisor didn't respect you or what you wanted" or "It seems to me that the advisor wasn't fair; is that what you're thinking?" You can also use a content paraphrase during a heated discussion. Paraphrasing can slow down a conversation because it forces the participants to listen well and think about how to respond before actually doing so. Specifically, paraphrasing confirms a conversation partner because you tentatively summarize the meaning of her or his communication in your own words and check to see if your interpretation is correct *before* you respond with your own viewpoints.

Paraphrasing for Feelings   **Feelings paraphrasing** requires you to monitor a speaker's nonverbal communication for clues about what the speaker might be feeling. If you were to use a feeling paraphrase to respond to the speaker who wasn't allowed to enroll in a class, you could say, "You sound really frustrated and upset. Am I right?" It may be tempting to react to this example of a paraphrase with the idea that it overstates the obvious. However, paraphrasing for feelings communicates that you confirm another person's emotions. Paraphrasing for feelings works especially well when emotions run high. When someone is allowed to express intense emotions and feel that his or her emotions are acknowledged, respected, and understood, the person is able to calm down and respond in a rational manner. Paraphrasing for feelings is a powerful way to confirm others and demonstrate that we respect them, their thoughts, and their feelings.

It's important to be realistic about the use of confirming communication and the outcomes associated with their use. Engaging in a content paraphrase with a powerful or irrational conversation partner may not lead to a desired result. For example, "Don't put words in my mouth!" might be the angry response to your communication of a content paraphrase. Silence may be best in situations such as these because nothing you can say or do will convince a powerful or irrational partner of your confirming motivation. Knowing that communication skills won't always "work" can help you plan for and anticipate situations that would otherwise be unexpected.

A content paraphrase can be used when we listen to a lot of information, when we are given complex directions and/or instructions, and when the information is technical and laden with unfamiliar jargon.

TRENDS IN TECHNOLOGY AND SOCIAL MEDIA

Supportive Communication

Imagine dealing with a significant problem and wanting to discuss it with someone else. If none of your friends or family members are available to speak with you, what do you do? You might decide to go online not only to seek support but to express it. You might join a support group to help cope with your problem.

Common online support groups are available for medical conditions, sexual orientation, addictions, eating disorders, shyness, and loneliness.[42] People are attracted to online support groups because they offer anonymity; people tend to disclose more about their problems online than face-to face because they may believe that they won't be as readily judged. Online support seekers also use the Internet to find others who share their problems and concerns and perceive these support networks as valuable. The attraction of online support is particularly significant for people who contend with uncommon problems and may not be able to locate and associate with face-to-face support groups in their physical vicinity.

People also express computer-mediated comfort and support via email messages, social networking sites, and online memorials. Most people use email to maintain ties with friends and family. One study that researched college students' authentic supportive emails (rather than self-reported descriptions of email messages) found that messages are primarily sent by family members, friends, and romantic partners. The problems addressed in emails include deaths of loved ones, loneliness, romantic difficulties, physical illness, problems with friends and roommates, and academic challenges. Both women and men send email messages that include advice and concern for a recipient's emotional state. However, women tend to be more satisfied with the use of email as a medium for social support than are men.[43]

Social networking and online memorial sites provide an opportunity to share condolences and support those in mourning. Memorializing on the social networking site MySpace enables mourners to publicize their grief, communicate praise for the deceased, petition the deceased for help (e.g., for help and guidance in particular situations), and share a narrative of the deceased's life.[44] Mourners use Facebook to commiserate no matter the geographic distance or time of day and to avoid the social awkwardness that sometimes accompanies not knowing what to say to family and friends of the deceased.[45]

People also use Twitter to communicate grief and mourning. One study of the communication of grief after the death of pop singer Michael Jackson found that many people used Twitter to express their acceptance of Jackson's passing and share their immediate reactions to his death. People also used Twitter to direct other people to other social networking sites that paid tribute to Jackson and on which memorials were created. Twitter also publicized rituals such as "Michael Mondays," during which followers tweeted about Jackson, which in turn kept his memory alive and connected users with other Jackson fans.[46]

Young people who use social networking sites to grieve and memorialize the deceased are changing the way we mourn. Those who use social networking sites to mourn report that they value and appreciate online support over traditional support groups.[47]

Discussion Questions

1. Can you think of a type of online support group that might be able to help you with a problem you're experiencing currently?

2. Do you send messages of social support via email? Do you receive messages of social support via email? Do you prefer email or face-to-face messages when sending and receiving communication that expresses social support? Explain your answer.

3. Have you used a social networking site such as Facebook to post a comment about and/or mourn someone who recently died? Do you agree with the respondents in the social networking study who believe that online support is more valuable than traditional forms of support?

LISTENING, CONFIRMING RESPONSES, AND CONTEXTS

Listening and responding with confirmation are important in your everyday life as they relate to culture, your career, and gender. Perhaps you listen to people from various cultures and engage in listening with managers and coworkers at your place of employment. You may even sometimes wonder why someone you know doesn't listen and respond in the same way you do. (It may be due to the influence of gender.) Knowing how culture, the workplace, and gender influence listening can help you improve your ability to engage in civil listening and respond with confirmation.

Listening, Confirming Responses, and Culture

Your perception of civil listening and confirming responses is affected by the culture(s) and co-culture(s) to which you belong. The same holds true regarding how others perceive your ability to listen and respond with confirmation. Because the United States is an individualist/low-context culture that values direct expression of thoughts and feelings, it makes sense that U.S. communication scholars have concentrated their research on speaking rather than listening.[48] The limited research about cross-cultural listening has found that not only does our culture affect how we construct reality (e.g., whether the individual is more important than the group and vice versa), culture also influences our listening behavior. For example, it is easier for members of some cultures to "feel with" other people while listening to them speak. "Sympathetic listening" focuses on being in harmony with another person and rejects the idea of individuals as separate beings. This type of listening is characteristic of Blackfoot Indians and other groups of Native Americans. In these collectivist cultures, individuals are not differentiated from one another, and members are attuned to the natural world (including other humans). On the other hand, a different type of listening focuses on the distinction between a speaker and a listener, and it suggests that the gap between the two can be bridged with effective communication. "Rational listening" is based on the development of individualism in Western culture and is characteristic of individualistic/low-context cultures such as the dominant culture in the United States.[49]

Additional research illustrates that knowledge of cross-cultural listening differences can affect the ability to conduct international business. Richard Lewis, author of *When Cultures Collide: Managing Successfully Across Cultures*, writes that listening styles are not uniform across cultures. Specifically, French people tend to listen for information, Germans typically listen for information and technical details, and people in many Arab countries tend to listen for knowledge. Managers who successfully tailor their communication in terms of the presentation of information or the presentation of procedural knowledge can facilitate business negotiations in other cultures.[50] Knowledge of such cross-cultural listening styles can enable you to adapt your communication so that your messages will be received effectively.

Listening is critical for success in the workplace.

Listening, Confirming Responses, and Your Career

Effective listening is critical for success in the workplace. Workers report that they spend the majority of their communication time within organizations engaging in listening.[51] Employers frequently cite listening as one of the most desired abilities.[52] In fact, listening is considered to be such an important organizational skill that 60 percent of Fortune 500 companies provide listening instruction to their employees.[53] The necessity of effective listening is recognized by organizations associated with the health care profession, the military, companies involved in marketing, and organizations associated with sales.[54]

Although most employees believe that the ability to listen well is a crucial aspect of effective management, employees tend to be dissatisfied with their supervisors' listening behavior. Researchers have discovered that managers who listen to employees contribute to employee satisfaction and productivity. Supervisors who listen effectively to their employees also increase employee commitment and self-confidence, and they positively influence how employees perceive a company's core values.[55] Listening also enhances upward mobility, and "if you are interested in advancing in your career, there is no more important skill to practice and develop than listening."[56] Employees who are skilled at listening learn how members of a company interpret their environment and create shared meaning; this means that such employees can communicate appropriately across various situations, such as negotiating a contract or hosting a business professional from a different culture.[57] Employees who listen well typically hold high-level positions within organizations,[58] and the ability to listen and respond with confirmation is related to an employee's chances of promotion.[59] Unfortunately, employees often derail their careers and miss opportunities, not because of a shortfall in professional or technical expertise but because of problems on the job that stem from a shortcoming of "soft skills" such as listening, self-awareness, empathy, and likeability.[60]

Listening, Confirming Responses, and Gender

Do women and men listen and offer confirmation in a similar manner? Research reveals that gender influences the listening behavior of women and men and affects how we respond when others communicate about their problems.

Women's dissatisfaction with how men listen may be due to differences in communication style.

Listening and Communication Style Women tend to be dissatisfied with the way that men typically listen. In a study of approximately 4,500 women, 77 percent of the respondents reported that they weren't satisfied with their male partners' amount and style of listening. In the same study, 69 percent of the respondents said that men don't listen to or ask questions about their partner's opinions or activities, and 41 percent of the respondents thought that men exhibit nonverbal cues that indicate they don't listen when women speak.[61] Women's dissatisfaction with how men listen may be due to differences in communication style. For example, women tend to ask more questions than men, and women typically communicate using more prompts, such as "uh-huh" and "mmmm," to indicate that they are listening than do men. Furthermore, whereas women use "yeah" to indicate that they are paying attention and to encourage the speaker to continue, men tend to use "yeah" when they agree with what a speaker says. The result is that women perceive that men don't listen to them when they speak.[62]

Troubles Talk According to sociolinguist Deborah Tannen, ethnographic research involving case studies has found that when women talk about their problems, their underlying message is to request acknowledgment and validation. Therefore, women engage in "troubles talk," or relational feedback, as a way to connect with others and to demonstrate empathy, connection, and relational concern. Tannen believes that women become frustrated when men respond to their problems with advice and instructions rather than engaging in troubles talk or relational feedback to demonstrate empathy and understanding. Similarly, men may become angry when women attempt to comfort them with a similar disclosure of their own. Men may perceive that women attempt to put themselves in a one-up position by minimizing the problem when women communicate a similar problem that they have experienced.[63]

Not all researchers agree with Tannen's findings that learned gender expectations significantly influence how men and women communicate confirmation and support. Empirical evidence demonstrates that gender differences in the communication of support are small in magnitude, and most gender-related studies of social behavior use research designs that assess differences but ignore similarities.[64] Overall, the empirical research about the influence of gender on communication fails to support the conclusion that men and women differ significantly in their communication of and reactions to confirming messages.[65] We should therefore be wary of claims that gender significantly affects the way men and women communicate.

CHAPTER SUMMARY

Now that you have read this chapter you can:

5.1 Define *listening*.

Listening is a complex skill that involves six stages: hearing, understanding, remembering, interpreting, evaluating, and responding. Speakers feel acknowledged, honored, and confirmed when we listen to them with care and attention.

5.2 Explain the relationship among listening, civility, and ethics.

Although listening is described as an inherently civil act, we engage in uncivil listening when we disconfirm others by listening defensively, using pseudolistening, engaging in confrontational listening, and listening only for literal information. Civil listening is a confirming listening style that communicates our belief in the quality of all people. In addition, thinking and acting in an ethical manner emerge as a result of the commitment to civil listening. To improve our ability to listen civilly, we can plan our listening, demonstrate that we are listening, and become fully involved with a speaker.

5.3 Describe the stages in the listening process and identify the types of listening.

Six stages are associated with the listening process. Stage 1 is hearing, which involves the reception and processing of sounds. Hearing is often the key component in appreciative listening, when we focus on appreciating and enjoying the messages we listen to. Stage 2 is understanding, which refers to listening comprehension; comprehensive listening is crucial when we want to learn, understand, and recall information. Stage 3 is remembering, which involves the ability to store information and retrieve it when necessary. Stage 4 is interpreting, or considering meaning from a speaker's point of view. Interpretation also involves empathic listening, which we use to understand and experience the feelings of a conversation partner. Stage 5 is evaluative listening, during which we judge the soundness of a message. Evaluative listening is associated with critical listening, during which we analyze messages we listen to. Stage 6 is responding, which involves verbal and nonverbal responses to others that let them know we are paying attention and taking responsibility for understanding their meanings.

5.4 Apply strategies to improve your ability to engage in civil listening.

You can improve your ability to listen civilly and ethically during all six stages of the listening process: hearing, understanding, remembering, interpreting, evaluating, and responding. Reducing distractions and recognizing your propensity to listen selectively; focusing on understanding and becoming aware of interrupting behavior; using a five-second strategy to remember names; experiencing empathy with others and observing nonverbal behaviors; using critical thinking skills; and communicating confirming responses will help you improve your ability to listen civilly and ethically.

5.5 Communicate confirming listening response styles.

Confirming listening responses can be defined as civil verbal and nonverbal behaviors that communicate affection, respect, and concern. Prompts include silence, sounds, or words that let a speaker know that we not only are listening but also want the speaker to continue. Asking questions enables us to obtain additional information and/or guide a speaker to a certain conclusion that we have in mind. Relational feedback is a brief description of a situation that parallels the speaker's and points to a connection between the speaker's experience and our own. We use a paraphrase to reword a speaker's message in terms of our understanding of its meaning.

5.6 Explain the association between listening and confirming responses with culture, workplace (your career), and gender contexts.

Knowing that culture affects how we perceive listening and confirming responses allows us to understand why it might be more difficult for members of individualist cultures to engage in sympathetic listening than for members of collectivist cultures. In addition, employers frequently cite listening as one of the most desired abilities in employees, and employees who listen well typically hold high-level positions within organizations. Men and women tend to reply to the communication of problems with different types of confirming responses. This can cause misinterpretations as we may expect someone of the opposite gender to respond similarly to the way we do.

CIVILITY SUMMARY

Overall, remember that civility, listening, and confirming communication involve the following:

- Civil listening is a confirming listening style that communicates our belief in the equality of all people.
- Civil listening isn't easy because we must be open to what others have to say and acknowledge the possibility that they may be right, and we may be wrong.
- If we expect others to listen civilly to us and give us an opportunity to persuade them to our way of thinking, we must also listen civilly to them and give them an opportunity to convert us to their way of thinking.

REVIEW QUESTIONS

1. What is the definition of listening?
2. What are the relationships among listening, civility, and ethics?
3. What are the stages in the listening process? What are some of the listening challenges involved in each of the stages?
4. How can you improve your ability to listen in a civil manner at every stage in the listening process?
5. What are some active listening response styles that enable you to confirm a speaker in a civil manner? What are some of the problematic outcomes that may result when you use any of these styles, and how can you avoid them?
6. How does the culture context affect the listening process?
7. What can supervisors do to improve how they listen to employees? What are the positive outcomes of effective listening in the workplace?
8. Do you believe that men and women are more similar than different in their expression of confirming communication? Explain your answer.

PART II CIVIL INTERPERSONAL COMMUNICATION

6 Interpersonal Relationships and Civil Communication

ACTOR KATE HUDSON, who has starred in films such as *How to Lose a Guy in 10 Days*, *Bride Wars*, and *Something Borrowed*, is devoted to her family. Daughter of celebrities Goldie Hawn and Bill Hudson, she considers actor Kurt Russell, her mother's partner of almost 30 years, her dad. Hudson says that she has wonderful family relationships not only with her parents but with her brother, sisters, and half-brothers, who all live in close proximity.[1] When she was 21 years old, Hudson married Chris Robinson, former lead singer of the Black Crowes. The union produced son Ryder in 2004, and Hudson was joyous when she said that the addition of her son to the union created a family.[2]

Although Hudson was committed to keeping her family intact, she and Robinson divorced in 2007. However, they are on good terms and remain close. In fact, Hudson has been seen cheering at Ryder's baseball games with Robinson, his new wife

CHAPTER OBJECTIVES

After reading this chapter, you will be able to:

6.1 Define and describe the types of interpersonal relationships.

6.2 Explain how civility and civil communication affect interpersonal relationships.

6.3 Identify two theoretical perspectives that can explain and predict interpersonal relationships.

6.4 Explain the difference between content and relational communication.

6.5 Use metacommunication to improve your civil communication.

Allison, and their one-year-old daughter, Cheyenne. Speaking about her marriage with Robinson, Hudson has said that she has no regrets because the union produced Ryder, and she still has a deep love for her ex-husband.[3] In July 2011, Hudson and fiancé Matt Bellamy had a baby boy they named Bing. Hudson explained that they chose their baby's name because it reflected family relations: Bellamy's mother's maiden name was Bingham, and Kurt Russell's dad is named Bing.[4] Although engaged to Bellamy, Hudson doesn't think marriage is necessary and attributes her focus on healthy relationships to her large, unconventional family.[5]

WHY IT MATTERS

Do you describe your family as "conventional" or "unconventional"? Do you and others you know speak civilly about present and former family members? Have you used uncivil communication when describing family members, and have family members used uncivil words to describe you?

Interpersonal relationships are important because they can prevent loneliness and positively affect our mental and physical health. Scholars contend that people have a fundamental need for relationships and we find it difficult to function without them.[6] Human beings are born with the need to create and maintain interpersonal relationships, and we form relationships with friends, coworkers, and family members to help us feel that we're not alone.[7] As children, our friends and family members help us develop social skills such as role-taking, regulating emotional expression, and managing conflict, which in turn can influence relationship formation and prevent loneliness.[8] In addition, people who have many strong interpersonal relationships are twice as likely to survive after a heart attack as people who do not have strong social relationships.[9] One investigation that reviewed more than 60 studies about relationships and health demonstrated that just as cigarette smoking, high blood pressure, and obesity are risk factors for early death, so is a lack of positive interpersonal relationships.[10] Anxiety and stress, alcoholism, and drug use are also related to a lack of interpersonal relationships.[11] In all, our friends and family members help us cope with problematic situations by providing us with comfort and empathy.[12] In fact, having friends and family members we can turn to for social support can predict our overall happiness.[13] It appears that the benefits of positive interpersonal relationships may be known to the Millennial generation (young adults born since the early 1980s) because unlike members of earlier generations, they believe that marriage, time with children, relationships with coworkers, and friendships are central to their future.[14]

In this chapter, you will read about the definition and types of interpersonal relationships—specifically relationships that involve family members and friends. You'll learn about the association between interpersonal relationships and civility and read about two theories that can explain and predict interpersonal relationships. You will also read about how the use of metacommuncation can improve relationships, and you will learn about the association between interpersonal relationships and culture, workplace, and gender contexts.

DEFINITION AND TYPES OF INTERPERSONAL RELATIONSHIPS

Think about the various relationships you have with family members, friends, instructors, coworkers, and/or acquaintances as you read the following definition of a relationship; does it accurately characterize any of *your* relationships? And how does this definition fit Kate Hudson and her family?

Definition and Types of Interpersonal Relationships

relationship A voluntary commitment that is constantly in process and marked by continuing, significant interdependence between specific individuals.

A **relationship** can be defined as a voluntary commitment that is constantly in process and marked by continuing, significant interdependence between specific individuals.[15] A relationship is "voluntary" because we can choose to end our association with another person, and it is "constantly in process" because relationships change. Even family relationships are voluntary in that we can choose to eliminate any communication and association with blood relations. The relational commitment we have with others is interdependent because we rely and depend on our relationship partners just as they rely and depend on us. Just as we learned that communication can be viewed on a continuum from personal to impersonal, our relationships can also be viewed on a continuum that ranges from personal to impersonal.

Impersonal and Personal Relationships

impersonal relationships Relationships in which we communicate with others based primarily on their social or occupational roles (e.g., nurturer, server, disciplinarian, cashier).

personal relationships Relationships in which we communicate with others based primarily on their uniqueness.

In **impersonal relationships**, we communicate with others based primarily on their social or occupational roles (e.g., server, disciplinarian, cashier). In our **personal relationships**, we communicate with others based primarily on their uniqueness. Uniqueness means that we recognize that the person with whom we're communicating is unlike all other persons we know. Of course, people in our relationships may have similar eye color, political views, or past histories, but no two people are completely alike. Even when people have the same biological raw material (e.g., identical twins), they experience the world differently.[16]

Sometimes it may be difficult to categorize a relationship as personal or impersonal. As illustrated in Figure 6.1, we can better understand our relationships by comparing them across both time (the duration or frequency of the relationship) and the types of communication that take place. For example, we may eat at a favorite restaurant and converse with our favorite server each week ("time"). Although we will speak to our server impersonally in terms of the role she occupies (i.e., we'll ask about the specials and order a meal), we may have learned enough about her over time to talk about personal topics

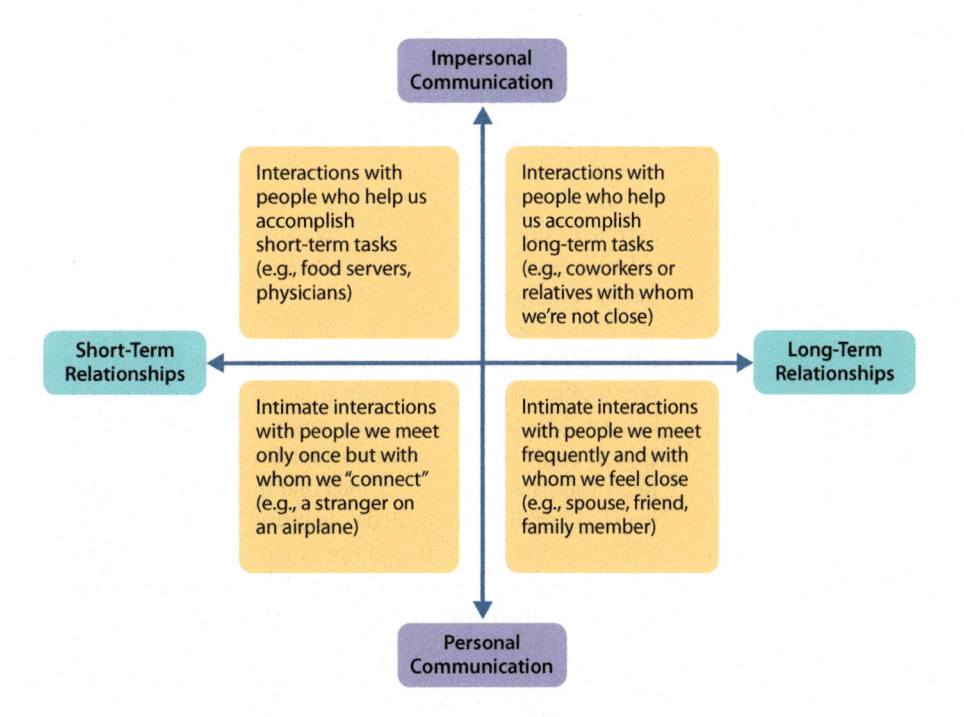

FIGURE 6.1 Time, Communication, and Relationships

Can you categorize the people you meet and know into these four categories? Can you identify a time when an impersonal or short-term relationship may have "advanced" to a personal, long-term relationship?

	Impersonal Communication	
Short-Term Relationships	Interactions with people who help us accomplish short-term tasks (e.g., food servers, physicians)	Interactions with people who help us accomplish long-term tasks (e.g., coworkers or relatives with whom we're not close)	**Long-Term Relationships**
	Intimate interactions with people we meet only once but with whom we "connect" (e.g., a stranger on an airplane)	Intimate interactions with people we meet frequently and with whom we feel close (e.g., spouse, friend, family member)	
	Personal Communication	

> ## ASK THE ETHICIST: Is It Okay to Be Impersonal with Others?
>
> **Question** Is it okay to be impersonal with others? I'm not sure I like it when people treat me as though I am the role I'm occupying at the moment.
>
> **Answer** Impersonal communication that is both civil and ethical is possible. But it's important to understand the difference between impersonal communication and dehumanized communication.
>
> When we communicate impersonally, we often do so recognizing that we cannot create and sustain intimate relationships with everyone we meet. So when we communicate impersonally, we largely focus on some kind of task that we accomplish in conjunction with the other person, and we limit any communication that isn't related to that task. For example, when you are greeted by the proprietor of a shop with "How are you today?" you recognize the question as simply a greeting ritual, and you respond accordingly, with "Fine, thanks" or something similar. In impersonal communication, we remember that the other is an individual with unique thoughts, feelings, and needs, even though our communication may be based on her or his social or occupational role (e.g., shop owner). Although we coordinate a task with the other, we may communicate pleasantries and talk about common knowledge, such as the winning sports team or lousy weather, so we don't treat the other as simply the role he or she is occupying. In impersonal communication as well as personal communication, we can demonstrate respect, restraint, and responsibility, and our civil communication ensures that neither party feels diminished by the interaction.
>
> Contrast this with dehumanized communication, when we act as though one person fulfilling a role can be easily substituted for by any other. Here we ignore the fact the other person is an individual with thoughts, feelings, and needs, and instead we treat that person as though he or she is simply there to accomplish the task at hand. This kind of dehumanizing goes both ways, as when someone taking your food order simply thinks of you as "the Cobb salad on Table 5." When we disrespect others by denying their humanity and failing to see them as unique individuals, we're communicating uncivilly.

not clearly associated with the role of server, such as her children or other unique topics related to the server's interests (both impersonal and personal communication).

Family Relationships

We can see from the opening example of Kate Hudson that the term *family* can be defined in many ways, and a widely agreed-upon definition doesn't exist. In the broadest sense of the word, we can define **family** as "networks of people who share their lives over long periods of time bound by marriage, blood, or commitment, legal or otherwise, who consider themselves as family and who share a significant history and anticipated futures of functioning in a family relationship."[17] Who do you consider to be members of your family? Perhaps you include a biological, adoptive, and/or step (grand)mother and/or (grand)father; assorted aunts, uncles, and cousins; the person with whom you or a parent has chosen to cohabit; and maybe your pets. There are various types of families, such as stepfamilies; gay, lesbian, bisexual, and transgender (GLBT) families; families that are childfree by choice; single-parent families; and families where grandparents raise grandchildren.[18] Recent statistics support the idea that there's more than one definition of *family*. Approximately 12 million unmarried cohabiting couples reside in the United States in more than 6 million households.[19] In addition, there are about 13.7 million single parents raising 21.8 million children.[20] For the first time in 2010, the national census recognized same-sex couples and their children as family units. As of this writing, the 2010 census national statistics about the number of GLBT parents are not available. Statistics compiled in 1994 from PFLAG (Parents, Families and Friends of Lesbians and Gays) estimate that 6 to 14 million

family A group of people with a past history, a present reality, and a future expectation of interconnected, mutually influencing relationships.

Definition and Types of Interpersonal Relationships   115

children have a gay or lesbian parent. Because families come in all shapes and sizes, modern definitions tend to focus less on typical family roles (e.g., mother, father) and more on how a family functions.

The Influence of Family Relationships   Our beliefs, attitudes, and values are molded by our family, and our relationships with family members are the most influential relationships in our lives.[21] The family in which we are raised also strongly influences our relationships throughout our lifetime. Early patterns of attachment with our parents affect the attachments we form as adults. For example, children who are allowed to be both affectionate and independent with their mothers are likely to be comfortable with intimacy and trust in adulthood.[22] As adults, initial levels of network support actually predict subsequent levels of love, satisfaction, and commitment approximately a year and a half after the initial levels are identified.[23] Many of our friends can be considered a "voluntaristic family." Because we depend on these friends for companionship and social support, for many people these relationships may be even more important than family based on blood ties.[24]

The television show *Modern Family* supports the idea that there is more than one definition of "family." Jay Pritchett is married to a young Columbian woman and is helping to raise her pre-teen son. Jay's daughter Claire is a married stay-at-home mom in a traditional family, while his son Mitchell and partner Cameron have adopted a Vietnamese baby.

Family Communication   Research has shown that communication in a family differs from communication in other contexts in several ways. For example, family conflict is frequent and more difficult to escape than conflict in other contexts, especially in light of the close physical proximity and experiences shared by family members. In addition, because family members are interdependent, communication between two members of a family may affect other members.[25] For example, try to recall a situation when a member of your family was in a bad mood, communicated in an uncivil manner, and began an argument. Perhaps someone in your family said, "I was in a good mood until XXX came home!" and subsequently he or she began to communicate uncivilly. Families also establish rules that affect communication. **Family rules** concern the "shoulds" and "oughts" that are the expected behaviors everyone in the family is aware of, and they range on a continuum from explicit to implicit.[26] Explicit family rules define the degree of freedom of expression in the family—that is, what we can talk about, when and where we can talk about it, and to whom we can talk. Explicit family rules may be communicated with the sentence, "We should/shouldn't discuss such subjects/use those words in our family!" Similarly, family stories illustrate implicit rules that affect communication. Instead of articulated rules, shared stories communicate the family's history, expectations, and identity; they instruct, warn, and communicate issues that matter to a specific family.[27] Stories about births and deaths, immigration and foreign travel, and triumphs and tragedies can communicate implicit rules about the importance to the family of helping others, what it means to live a moral life, and how to deal with adversity. These implicit rules also influence how we communicate with others.

family rules Rules that concern "shoulds" and "oughts" and that range on a continuum from explicit to implicit.

Friendships

Think about the people you consider your friends. **Friends** are people who like each other, enjoy each other's company, and establish voluntary relationships.[28] Why do you believe these people are your "friends" as opposed to "acquaintances"? You may be thinking that your friends like the same things you do (e.g., sports, music), share the same values, and are

friends People who like each other, enjoy each other's company, and establish voluntary relationships.

TECH CHECK: Friendship Inventory

We expect our friends to accept us, to be dependable and reliable, and to trust us. Do you believe that your friendship network is strong and mutually beneficial and that you can reach out to a strong network of friends if you need help? On the other hand, do you believe that your friendship network is inconsistent and/or unreliable?

there for you when you need them. These qualities characterize relationships among friends. In fact, friendships tend to be based on similarity, need fulfillment, and support:[29]

- **Similarity**—We tend to be attracted to people with whom we have something in common, such as similar beliefs, interests, experiences, and backgrounds. Of course, it's possible to have friends whose personalities differ from ours. This most often occurs when the differences fulfill our needs.
- **Need fulfillment**—A timid person may choose a friend who is extremely extroverted because they complement each other. On the other hand, a sports enthusiast may choose a fellow sports enthusiast as a friend because they "fit" together—that is, each provides something that the other person needs, someone to listen to and enjoy stories about sports.
- **Support**—We expect our friends to "be there" for us. We count on friends to accept us, even with our flaws, and to accept us as we change over time.

We expect to invest time, energy, and effort into our friendships, and our friendships enable us to feel close to others. Whether we are female or male, old or young, homosexual or heterosexual, we expect our friends to accept us, to be dependable and reliable, and to trust us.[30]

Communication in Friendship Relationships As in the relationships we have with members of our family, we sometimes find ourselves in conflict with one or more of our friends. Managing conflict in our relationships with friends often depends on our knowledge of what topics or issues seem to trigger conflict. You may have a friend with whom you avoid talking about politics because such conversations routinely become heated, but you enjoy talking about politics with a different friend. You know to avoid talking about her or his ex-partner because you hold differing opinions about the ex and the reasons for the breakup. Our knowledge of which topics tend to promote conflict episodes with our friends can help us create **friendship rules** that prescribe effective and appropriate communication in these relationships. The following are some examples of typical friendship rules:[31]

- Respect privacy. (A conflict may follow if we push our friend to disregard a personal boundary and share information considered to be personal.)
- Keep confidences. (A conflict may arise if we betray a friend's trust by sharing a secret.)
- Avoid public criticism. (A conflict may occur and our friend may lose face if we criticize our friend in front of others.)
- Sustain equity. (A conflict may develop if we fail to "give and take" in equal proportions, especially concerning debts and favors.)

friendship rules Rules that prescribe effective and appropriate communication in our relationships with friends.

"Keeping confidences" is an example of a friendship rule.

Interpersonal Relationships and Culture

Research demonstrates that perceptions of friendship differ from culture to culture and among co-cultures in the United States.

TRENDS IN TECHNOLOGY AND SOCIAL MEDIA

Facebook and Friendship

Do you have Internet friends on Facebook, My Space, LinkedIn, or on some other social networking site? Among adults 18 and over, Facebook is the social networking site of choice, with almost three-fourths of young adults "friending" others and sharing information on this site.[32] At the end of September 2012, Facebook had over 1 billion monthly active users and 584 million daily active users.[33] To acquire friends on Facebook, you merely send a "friend request" and wait for the target to confirm you as a "friend." But what is friendship, and what are "friends" in the age of Facebook?[34] Have we simply reduced friendship to a Wall post or a distraction?

Communication scholars have found that the meanings of *Internet friends* and *friendship* are personally subjective, ranging from a personal and positive acquaintance to an indiscriminate addition designed to increase the sheer number of "friends" listed on one's profile.[35] These types of friends and friendships are described in terms of strong and weak ties. **Strong ties** are friends who are confidants, people with whom we share multiple interests, and people we can call on in an emergency. **Weak ties** are friends who are distant acquaintances, people we know only in a particular context, and people toward whom we feel little responsibility. Studies illustrate that both strong and weak ties are sustained on social networking sites and that even a sparsely connected network of weak ties has advantages, such as providing access to a variety of experiences and ideas.[36] Research conducted in 2011 indicates that social networking sites include **dormant ties**, or ties that were once very important and active in a social network but are now dormant because of job changes or mobility.[37] In addition, while Facebook makes it easy to collect virtual friends who we don't know well (weak ties), it also has the ability to extend these virtual friendships to those for whom we feel responsible and whom we trust (strong ties).[38]

And what about the concern that users spend more time online with Facebook friends than they do face-to-face with friends? A number of studies illustrate that the majority of Facebook friends are those whom users have met and with whom they've interacted in person.[39] According to a PEW Internet and American Life Project report, the primary motivation for social networking site users is to stay in touch with current friends and family members and to reconnect with friends with whom they've lost contact.[40] In fact, most of our Facebook friends are:[41]

- People we know from high school (22 percent)
- Extended family members (12 percent)
- Coworkers (10 percent)
- College friends (9 percent)
- Members of our immediate family (8 percent)
- People we know from voluntary groups (7 percent)
- Neighbors (2 percent)

Overall, people who communicate via social networking sites are less likely to be socially isolated than those who do not, and "people on Facebook typically have a larger number of strong ties; this means that rather than undermine intimacy, Facebook supports it."[42]

Discussion Questions

1. What do you think accounts for the popularity of Facebook and other social networking sites? Do you know of any friends or acquaintances who don't use social networking sites to share information and keep up with others?

2. According to research conducted by the PEW Internet and American Life Project report, the majority of our Facebook friends are people we knew in high school. Is this true of your Facebook friends?

3. Approximately how much time do you spend on social networking sites each day? Do you think your time on social networking sites takes away from time you could spend communicating with friends on a face-to-face basis?

---

strong ties Friends who are confidants, people with whom we share multiple interests, and people who can be called on in an emergency.

For example, friendships are perceived as mostly voluntary and spontaneous in individualist cultures. European-American friendships are typically based on shared experiences, activities, and events. European Americans tend to have friends with whom they go to the movies, other friends with whom they play sports, and still other friends with whom they just "hang out."[43] However, people in collectivist cultures perceive friendships to be less spontaneous and to involve more long-term commitment and obligation. Specifically, people in the Chinese culture typically make few short-term acquaintances, and friendships are based on social connections. Although connections are important in the United States and are typically made through networking in one's area of employment, connections in China underlie the purposeful cultivation of friendships. Family relationships also differ from culture to culture. Decision making in collectivist cultures such as Japan, Korea, and China is highly dependent on family members. Families typically decide on their children's university, profession, and marital partner.[44]

There are also differences among ethnic groups within the United States in terms of relationships. Latinas/Latinos tend to believe that support is most important in their relationships, and Asian Americans emphasize positive and caring exchanges or ideas. African Americans typically believe that respect and acceptance are most important in their relationships, and European Americans perceive recognizing individual needs as an important relational characteristic.[45] Despite the many similarities between homosexual and heterosexual relationships, close friends may be more important for gay people than for straight people because of strained relationships with their families.[46]

Interpersonal Relationships and Gender

In terms of friendship, both women and men value close friends and the ideals on which friendships are built. Women and men value "symmetrical reciprocity," which relates to loyalty, mutual regard, support, and trustworthiness. Violations of these ideals are detrimental to all friendships.[47] However, how these ideals are expressed tends to differ in male and female same-sex friendships. Research illustrates that self-disclosure and intimate communication create closeness in friendships between women. Communication between women friends often centers around their relationship because the friendship itself is considered important, interesting, and worthy of discussion. By contrast, male same-sex friends communicate closeness and intimacy in the form of activity rather than talk. Men typically create and experience friendships while engaging in actions that cultivate a sense of camaraderie and companionship, such as watching or playing sports or working on handicrafts or fix-it projects. However, this doesn't mean that men tend to be less supportive or express less concern for their relationship partners than women.[48] Overall, recent research demonstrates that gender-based differences in interpersonal relationship characteristics, such as the expression of intimacy and support, tend to be inconsistent and relatively small.[49]

Gendered relationships within the family can also influence our relationships throughout our lifetime. For example, children who are allowed to be both affectionate and independent with their mothers are likely to be comfortable with intimacy and trust in adulthood. Children who learn to be overly dependent on their mothers may seek extreme levels of closeness and may be terrified of abandonment as adults.[50] In addition, research illustrates that satisfaction and commitment in a relationship will increase or decrease over time, as perceptions of support from one's social network (e.g., friends, family) increases or decreases. In fact, initial levels of network support actually predict subsequent levels of relational satisfaction and commitment approximately a year and a half after the initial levels are identified. This finding is especially true for women, whose perceptions of approval from family members and friends are important in predicting the eventual survival of a dating relationship.[51]

Close friends may be more important for gays than for straights because of strained relationships with their families.

weak ties Friends who are distance acquaintances, people we know in a particular context, and people toward whom we feel little responsibility.

dormant ties Social ties that were once potentially very important and active in someone's social network but for various reasons, such as moving or changing jobs, have become dormant.

INTERPERSONAL RELATIONSHIPS AND CIVILITY

According to an Associated Press–Ipsos poll, 70 percent of those questioned believe that Americans are ruder in the twenty-first century than they were 20 or 30 years ago, and 69 percent of the respondents blamed the increase in rudeness on celebrities, athletes, and public figures who behave rudely and are poor role models. Similarly, 73 percent of those questioned pointed to TV shows and movies that include rude behavior as the cause for the increase in incivility. However, 93 percent of the respondents placed the blame on parents who fail to teach civility to their children.[52]

Although parents may believe that their children learn rude and disrespectful communication from their friends, many children learn uncivil behaviors at home, without their parents' realization. Parents don't recognize that interrupting and talking over their children's messages communicates disrespect and that children learn to model their disrespectful behavior.[53] Children are also disrespected when they're on the receiving end of messages that indirectly disconfirm them, such as being ignored.[54] In addition, children watch and mimic their parents shout obscenities at drivers whose skills aren't up to par, engage in sideline rage during athletic activities, and bicker and fight whether the children are present or not.

At one time, it was taken for granted that parents would teach their children to use good manners and civil behavior. However, parents who came of age during the "cultural shifts" of the 1960s and 1970s have tended to de-emphasize the importance of manners. Similarly, parents who came of age in the 1980s, or the "me decade," may have encouraged incivility in their children by modeling a "me-first" mentality. Moreover, today's harried single parents may feel too busy getting food on the table to teach a child to say "please" and "thank you."[55] Although some school districts have attempted to encourage "character education" in students, education experts maintain that instilling respect for others is a process that must begin early in life, in the home. In fact, in one survey of the more than 2 million U.S. American families that have chosen to home school their children, it was found that parents want to avoid exposing their children to the ill manners and incivility found in public schools.[56] Some experts believe that children should learn within the family to respect others and communicate in a respectful manner. One way that parents can teach their children civil behavior is by setting aside their own interests for "the greater good." For example, parents who openly bicker in front of their children teach the lesson of thinking only of themselves, whereas postponing an argument until the children are no longer in earshot (and resolving it in a civil manner) is a choice made for the sake of civility. Parents should make a conscious effort to disagree with an attitude of mutual respect so children can learn that adults *can* demonstrate respect and love even when they aren't in agreement. And teaching respectful behavior means that parents must be civil when they communicate with rude shopkeepers, bad drivers, and intrusive telephone salespersons. Parents should also teach their children about civil communication by not saying behind people's backs what they wouldn't say face-to-face. Children who see their parents set aside their own concerns for the greater good are more likely to do the same when they reach adulthood.[57]

Although parents may believe that their children learn rude and disrespectful communication from their friends, often parents teach these behaviors at home without realizing it.

Interpersonal Relationships and Your Career

Americans are spending 10 percent more time on the job than they did 50 years ago, and workplace relationships can contribute to job satisfaction or dissatisfaction.[58] Coworkers are the most important source of support, both personally and practically, in public and private organizations.[59] Coworkers tend to share common experiences with us, such as working in the same department and working for the same supervisor. In addition, we may spend more time with our coworkers than we spend with friends outside the workplace. The workplace environment itself facilitates the creation of friendships.[60]

Many employees contend that uncivil communication is a part of their workplace environment. In one workplace incivility study of more than 800 employees in the United States, one in five employees claimed that they had been the target of a coworker's uncivil communication at least once per week. Two-thirds of those studied said they had witnessed uncivil communication among other employees at least once a month, and 10 percent said they witnessed incivility among colleagues every day.[61] The study found that 60 percent of workplace incivility occurs in workplace relationships between superiors and subordinates. Those with more power communicate uncivilly by keeping subordinates waiting, interrupting conversations, speaking in condescending tones, and using demeaning language. Among equals, incivility takes many forms, including sabotaging coworkers' efforts, "blind-forwarding" coworkers' potentially damaging email, and gossiping. When uncivil behavior is aimed at employees of higher status, it typically takes the form of ignoring or forgetting specific details of a superior's requests and spreading gossip about high-status employees.[62] To reduce incivility in the workplace, some public and private organizations have a code of ethics that includes well-defined ways employees are expected to communicate with each other. These communication expectations may include treating people with dignity and respect, communicating honestly, and being willing to listen to others' opinions. These behaviors contribute to a civil work environment and facilitate the creation of workplace friendships.[63]

THEORETICAL PERSPECTIVES ABOUT INTERPERSONAL RELATIONSHIPS

When you engage in communication in a personal relationship, you most likely are able to explain and predict your relational partner's behavior because of your past history with the person and your awareness of the unique ways he or she thinks and feels. However, is it possible to explain and predict the behavior of people we don't know as it pertains to relationship development? Can we also explain how relationships are formed and predict when and how relationships may be created? Communication researchers have developed various theories that explain and predict human behavior related to relationship formation.[64] Two theories are particularly useful in explaining how and predicting whether we will form relationships with others: attraction theory and uncertainty reduction theory. Think about one of your close relationships as you read about these theories and consider whether they can explain the behavior of that relational partner and why and how the relationship developed.

interpersonal attraction A motivational state that brings people together by causing them to think, feel, and act in a positive manner toward each other.

attraction theory A theory which predicts that we are attracted to and may initiate relationships with people we believe are physically attractive, who are similar to us, and who are in physical proximity to us.

Attraction Theory

Most relationships begin with **interpersonal attraction**, the motivational state that brings people together by causing them to think, feel, and act in a positive manner toward each other. As illustrated in Figure 6.2, **attraction theory** states that interpersonal attraction is based on physical attraction, similarity, and proximity.

Theoretical Perspectives About Interpersonal Relationships

physical attraction A component of attraction theory that is based on the extent to which we view another person's physical self as attractive.

Physical Attraction **Physical attraction** is based on the extent to which we view another person's physical self as attractive. The focus of physical attraction may include factors such as someone's size, height, skin tone, or clothing. In terms of physical attraction, heterosexual women and men tend to judge the opposite sex differently regarding what is considered attractive. While both men and women are attracted to physical attributes, more than 50 studies illustrate that women value personality, intelligence, kindness, sensitivity, and a sense of humor as more important than physical attractiveness. On the other hand, men value physical attractiveness more in a potential friend or romantic partner.[65] Although we typically think of physical attractiveness as it relates to intimate relationship formation, research illustrates that we also are attracted to good-looking people when we engage in relationship formation with friends and at work.[66] Compared to face-to-face communication, one study of computer-mediated communication (CMC) using a text-based format found that conversation partners tend to ask questions that are more direct and engage in self-disclosure, which in turn enhances interpersonal attraction. Visual-based CMC also promotes direct questions and self-disclosure, but the physical appearance of a partner overshadows the mediated effects of direct questioning and self-disclosure so that physical appearance has more of an influence on overall attraction.[67]

Similarity Do "birds of a feather flock together," or do opposites attract? Overall, we're likely to be attracted to and form relationships with people who are similar to ourselves. Friends who are similar to us provide us with social validation and help us feel good about who we are. We therefore may be attracted to people whose childhood experiences, values, interests, and personalities are similar to our own.[68] On the other hand, if we perceive the differences to be complementary or beneficial to us, we are also attracted to people who are different from us.

Complementary differences are attractive because these differences are perceived as positive. Therefore, someone who engages in thoughtful planning may be attracted to someone who acts in a spontaneous manner, and someone who is shy may be attracted to someone who is an extrovert. Therefore, we may be attracted to someone as a friend if she or he has differences that complement us. However, in general we are more attracted to people who are more similar to us than we are to those who are different.[69]

proximity A component of attraction theory that is based on the idea that we are more likely to be attracted to people who are in closer proximity to us than to those who are not.

Proximity Research illustrates that we are more likely to be attracted to people who are in closer **proximity** to us than those who are not.[70] For example, we are more likely to talk to and form relationships with classmates who sit on either side of us and roommates or neighbors who live right next door. However, social networking sites such as Facebook and MySpace, chat rooms, and instant messaging and email enable us to develop and deepen friendships with anyone, no matter how geographically close or distant they are.[71] Interestingly, "digital proximity," or how reachable a friend is online, is related to online friendship formation and relationship strength.[72] Even MMORGs (massively multiplayer online role-playing games) promote the creation of virtual

FIGURE 6.2 Attraction Theory Attraction theory states that interpersonal attraction is based on physical attraction, similarity, and proximity.

Physical Attraction – the focus of physical attraction may include size, height, skin tone, and clothing

Similarity – we are attracted to people who are similar to us or whose differences complement us

Proximity – we are more likely to be attracted to people who are in closer proximity to us than those who are not

friendships. For example, in a study of MMORGs such as World of Warcraft, City of Heroes, Ultima Online, EverQuest II, Lineage II, RuneScape, Guild Wars, and Blade Mistress, approximately three-quarters of players surveyed reported that they had made good friends within the game. In addition, one-quarter of those surveyed said that they play MMORGs with family members and real-life friends.[73] Attraction theory explains and predicts that if you and another person are physically attracted to each other; you share similar interests, values, or experiences (or perceive that the differences between you are positive); and you live somewhat close to each other, it's likely that you and the other person will develop a relationship.

Uncertainly Reduction Theory

Uncertainty reduction theory, developed by Berger and Calabrese, is another theory that explains and predicts how interpersonal relationships are developed. The theory says that sharing information allows us to explain and predict human behavior. Uncertainty reduction theory postulates that reducing uncertainty (or increasing predictability) about their own and others' behavior is a primary concern when strangers meet.[74] Think about the last time you were introduced to and began a conversation with a classmate. It is likely that you asked questions such as "What's your major?" "What classes are you taking this semester?" and "Where's your hometown?" The answers to these questions will provide you with **social information**, or various types of interpersonal information communicated by people during interaction. You ask questions to seek social information and to reduce your uncertainty about the new acquaintance and predict her or his behavior. Furthermore, if you and your classmate respond to each other with nonverbal immediacy behaviors such as making eye contact, nodding your head, and smiling, these are signs that initial high levels of uncertainty have been reduced. If you and your new acquaintance continue to communicate, personal disclosures may occur, and the number of questions asked will decrease. In long-term relationships in which many disclosures have occurred, we no longer need to obtain new information and can usually predict the answers to questions such as "What do you think of immigration reform?" and "Which political party is to blame for the country's current economic trouble?"[75]

As illustrated in Figure 6.3, communicators attempt to obtain three types of social information from conversation partners in order to create interpersonal relationships:[76]

- **Social information based on demographic data**—This type of social information includes biographical material (e.g., age, birthday, occupation) and sociological material (e.g., goes to concerts, attends a religious congregation, works out).
- **Social information based on personal beliefs**—This type of information typically is not discussed in initial interactions because disclosing this information may be risky. Questions that focus on this type of data include those that concern a person's beliefs, opinions, and attitudes. Think about your roommate, partner, or someone you know well. What are some strong beliefs that person holds? How did you learn about this information, and does this knowledge help you explain and predict her or his behavior?

uncertainty reduction theory A theory which suggests that sharing information allows us to explain and predict human behavior. Uncertainty reduction theory postulates that when strangers meet, their primary concern is to reduce uncertainty or increase predictability about the behavior of both themselves and others in the interaction.

social information Various types of interpersonal information communicated by people during interaction. We ask questions to seek social information and to reduce our uncertainty about new acquaintances and to predict their behavior.

FIGURE 6.3 Berger and Calabrese's Uncertainty Reduction Theory

Uncertainty reduction theory illustrates that sharing information allows us to explain and predict human behavior.

To reduce uncertainty, we can obtain:

Explanations for another's behavior based on personal knowledge and history

Information about personal beliefs, attitudes, and opinions

Demographic data (biographical and sociological information)

- **Social information based on explanations for another's behavior**—This type of social information is difficult to obtain because it is based on knowing someone extremely well and obtaining various types of information over the years. Knowledge of this information makes life predictable. For example, in a long-term friendship, you may know how your friend will react to the question "Do you want to go swimming?" based on your knowledge of a near-drowning experience that friend experienced as a child.

Exactly how do we obtain knowledge about demographic data, personal beliefs, or data that explains another's behavior? Uncertainty reduction theory suggests three categories of information-seeking behaviors that we use to reduce our uncertainty about others:[77]

Watching an individual converse with others is an unobtrusive way of gathering information about someone and illustrates the passive social information-seeking strategy to reduce uncertainty.

- **Passive social information seeking**—We engage in passive social information seeking when we observe others unobtrusively without communicating with them. Examples of this type of information seeking include watching someone conversing with others and obtaining information by accessing a person's Facebook site. In fact, strangers, acquaintances, friends, and romantic partners use Facebook to reduce uncertainty about others.[78] Although we may obtain only demographic data when we use this strategy, our feelings of uncertainty may lessen and our feelings of similarity and liking may increase in relation to the person we are learning about.

- **Active social information seeking**—While active social information seeking is not as unobtrusive as passive social information seeking, this strategy also doesn't involve direct contact with the person with whom we want to reduce uncertainty. Active social information seeking involves asking others about the person we're interested in and actually creating environments in which we can observe the person. For example, you may ask your roommate, who shares a class with the person of interest, to invite her or him to your apartment so you can observe the person interacting with your roommate.

- **Interactive social information seeking**—This information-seeking strategy involves direct face-to-face contact with the person of interest. Interactive social information seeking involves asking questions, engaging in self-disclosure, and using nonverbal immediacy behaviors effectively and appropriately to enable the person of interest to feel at ease with us.

To summarize, attraction theory explains and predicts that relationship formation is likely to occur if you and another person:

- Are physically attracted to each other
- Are similar
- Live or work in close proximity to one another

Uncertainty reduction theory explains and predicts that relationship formation may occur when you reduce the uncertainty in the relationship by acquiring:

- Demographic data about someone
- Information about the person's beliefs
- Knowledge about the person based on her or his history

Once again, think about a close relationship in which you are involved. Can you explain the behavior of your relationship partner and creation of the relationship in terms of attraction theory and/or uncertainty reduction theory? If asked for advice or your opinion about relationship formation, can you help another person explain and predict someone's behavior and whether a relationship will occur by considering attraction theory and/or uncertainty reduction theory?

RELATIONAL COMMUNICATION

relational communication
Communication in which people engaged in conversation not only interact about the content of communication but also about their association.

Whether or not we're primarily engaged in a personal or impersonal relationship, **relational communication** demonstrates that we not only interact about the content of communication but also interact about our association with a conversation partner. Without our realizing it and without explicit mention, a single message can communicate information about a topic and about a relationship. Relational communication includes the subject of an interaction and the implicit information about the participants' relationship. These messages are described as occurring at the content and relational levels of communication.[79]

Content and Relational Levels of Communication

content-level meaning The content of the words and sentences that are communicated.

relational-level meaning The unspoken meaning of a message that can be ascertained, in part, from nonverbal communication.

The **content-level meaning** of a message refers simply to the content of the words and sentences that are communicated. The **relational-level meaning** of a message concerns the unspoken meaning that can be ascertained, in part, from nonverbal communication. The way something is said (interpreted by a speaker's eye contact, facial expression, and/or gestures) is an example of nonverbal behavior that influences meaning at the relational level of communication.

In addition, the interpretation of relational messages can be influenced by the past experience and personal associations that we bring to a conversation. For example, suppose a sibling says, "Please get off of the computer." The meaning on the content level is obvious: Our sibling wants us to get off the computer. But what about the meaning at the relational level, where relationships are defined and negotiated? If our sibling communicates this message with a smile and a calm tone of voice and places a hand on our shoulder, he or she may be communicating that our relationship is based on respect and affection. Similarly, we are more likely to construe the relational meaning as positive if our sibling has made previous requests that we spend time away from the computer so he or she can engage in an activity with us. On the other hand, if our sibling communicates this message with a frown and an angry tone of voice and crosses her or his arms, our sibling may be communicating that the relationship is based on control and a power differential. In addition, we are more likely to construe the relational meaning as being negative if our sibling has previously demanded that we cease engaging in particular activities. Even though people typically interpret relational meanings based on nonverbal communication and past experiences, we should remember that our perceptions of others' nonverbal messages and intentions may be incorrect.[80] For instance, the sharp tone of voice our sibling uses to tell us to get off the computer may have nothing to do with us and may just reflect a hard day at school or fatigue. It may even be that a relational meaning interpreted as control (e.g., "Drive carefully!" or "Put on your jacket") may be an expression of affection and an attempt to establish connection.

Relational-Level Messages

Have you ever found yourself feeling angry with a conversation partner and not knowing exactly why? Maybe you've been in arguments and realized you didn't understand what you were actually arguing about. It may be that the reason for your anger and the disagreement rests on the relational level of meaning.

Texting or talking on a cell phone while ignoring a face-to-face conversation partner may be interpreted as a relational-level message of disrespect.

affection In terms of relational communication, the force to become close with a relational partner.

control The force to gain dominance. Control can be communicated at the relational level of meaning.

respect In terms of relational communication, acknowledging others by listening well and validating their points of view.

metacommunication "Communication about communication" or "communication about relationships." We can metacommunicate about both the content of a message and the underlying relational message.

What exactly about a relationship is communicated at the relational level? Every relationship and every conversation can be considered a blend of affection (or "connection") and control. **Affection**, the force to become close with a relational partner, and **control**, the force to gain dominance, are communicated at the relational level. In addition to affection and control, respect is sometimes included as a relational message. As you learned in earlier chapters, **respect** concerns acknowledging others by listening well and validating their point of view (without necessarily agreeing with it). When others do not take us seriously, we may perceive ourselves as targets of disrespectful behavior, and this can be a source of relational conflict. In fact, respect can be a predictor of relational success or failure. Think about the role that respect plays in your relationships. Have you experienced relational conflict because you thought your partner hadn't taken you seriously? Have you ended relationships or conversations because you thought you were being disrespected?

Even though our strongest reactions to messages tend to occur at the relational level, we typically aren't aware of the multitude of relational messages that confront us each day. Sometimes we're unaware of relational messages because they match our expectations about the amount and type of affection and control in our relationships. However, conflicts can arise at the relational level when we or someone with whom we're close feels uncomfortable about relational meanings.[81] For example, do you become upset when a roommate or family member tells you to put out the dog, pick up the mess, or turn off the light? You don't become upset at the particular request (whether or not it deals with the dog, the mess, or the light); however, you become upset because that particular someone feels entitled to tell you what to do. As a result, you may say, "Don't tell me what to do!" and begin to fight not about the request itself but about whether this person has the power to control your actions.

People react more strongly and emotionally to relational meanings than to meanings on the content level of communication, even with the knowledge that interpretations of nonverbal communication and others' motivations may be incorrect.[82] Let's return to the example of a sibling asking you to get off the computer. Based on your sibling's nonverbal communication, you may interpret the relational message as one in which your sibling is trying to spend more time with you. Since you want to be sure that your sibling understands that your relationship is based upon love and affection, you may respond with happiness and a click on the mouse to get off the computer. On the other hand, based on your sibling's nonverbal communication, you may interpret the relational message as one in which your sibling is trying to control you. Since you want to be sure that your sibling understands that your relationship is based on an equal distribution of power (in other words, your sibling can't boss you around), you may respond with anger and a refusal to get off the computer. In either case, it is not the content of the message but the unstated relational meaning of the message that communicates about the relationship and determines whether you decide to get off the computer.

IMPROVING OUR ABILITY TO COMMUNICATE CIVILLY AND EFFECTIVELY WITH METACOMMUNICATION

One way to improve our interpretations of content and relational meaning is to use a communication skill known as **metacommunication**, which has been defined both as "communication about communication" and "communication about relationships." Metacommunication is civil because it is based on restraint, respect, and responsibility.

Specifically, instead of instinctively responding to our immediate interpretation of a message or the interpretation of our relationship, we exhibit *restraint* by using metacommunication. Similarly, we demonstrate that we *respect* our conversation partners by asking them about their meanings of messages, and we demonstrate *responsibility* by acknowledging that our interpretations may be incorrect. Our use of metacommunication is also ethical because it illustrates that we can be trusted to base our communication on restraint, respect, and responsibility; we are fair and caring; and in the long run, we use metacommunication for the common good of the community. We can metacommunicate about both the content of a message and the underlying relational message.

Metacommunication at the Content Level of Meaning

At the content level, metacommunication can clarify how the actual meaning of a message is to be interpreted. Have you ever uttered sentences such as "This is important," "I didn't mean it," or "I'm sorry I said that"? Have you ever asked questions such as "Are you kidding?" or "Do you understand what I'm saying?" or "Want to hear

---

A CASE STUDY IN ETHICS

Cell Phone Subterfuge

You have read that ethical communication reflects trustworthiness, responsibility, respect, fairness, caring, and concern for the community. Keep the components of ethical communication in mind as you read the following case study and answer the discussion questions.

James E. Katz, professor of Communication at Rutgers University, contends that some people use cell phones to indirectly communicate with people who surround them. For example, some people stage fake phone calls as explanations for their behavior, such as scolding a pretend child for invading a wallet when they find themselves without cash in a checkout line. Others pretend to be talking on their cell phone when they are actually trying to get a good angle to take a photo on it. Still others create fake phone calls for reasons of safety. Loudly saying "I'll meet you in a few minutes!" may be helpful when you think you're being followed.

Some people, with the help of other cell phone users, use their cell phones to lie. "Cell phone alibi clubs" are flourishing in many parts of the world as a way to help callers make excuses and hide their whereabouts. People pay a fee to join a club and are subsequently linked to thousands of members to whom they can send text messages en masse that ask for help. When a potential collaborator indicates her or his willingness to phone a "victim," the caller and collaborator create a lie, and the collaborator phones with the excuse. Similar to alibi clubs, companies offer audio recordings that can be played in the background of such phone calls. Sounds such as honking horns, a dentist's drill, and ambulance sirens can be used to make a phone call sound realistic.

Although fake cell phone calls, cell phone alibi clubs, and background audio recordings may reflect questionable ethics, some individuals find nothing wrong with their use. Harry Kargman, founder of a company that sells audio background sounds, says that using background sounds is "not necessarily malicious or nefarious." Michelle Logan, founder of an alibi club based in San Diego, says that such clubs allow us to spare others' feelings with "white lies."[83]

Discussion Questions

1. Do you think it's ethical to stage fake phone calls?
2. Is it ethical to use alibi clubs and/or background audio recordings?
3. Do you agree with Michelle Logan that alibi clubs spare others' feelings?

something funny?" If so, you are metacommunicating at the level of content.

Metacommunication at the Relational Level of Meaning

Recall that metacommunication on the relational level is often communicated through nonverbal behavior and may occur in response to past conversations and events. Similarly, metacommunication on the relational level can clarify our perception of how we and our relationship are perceived in terms of affection, control, and respect. Let's return to the example of your sibling asking you to get off the computer. If you respond to the request with "Do you want me to spend time with you?" you are metacommunicating about a relational-level interpretation of affection. If you respond to the request with "Stop ordering me around!" you are metacommunicating about a relational-level interpretation of control. In addition to affection and control, our verbal communication can also indicate where we see ourselves and our relationship in terms of respect. For example, content-level metacommunication about a political viewpoint, such as saying, "I can understand why you say that, but I disagree with your opinion" communicates our respect for others on the relational level. Nonverbally, metacommunication can communicate our affection and respect with focused eye contact, head nods, and vocalizations that suggest understanding and acknowledgment (e.g., "uh-huh"). However, even the best attempt at metacommunication may be perceived as insulting if it's accompanied by a sarcastic tone of voice, rolling eyes, or laughter.

Using verbal metacommunication and nonverbal communication such as focused eye contact and head nods communicate respect at the relational level of communication.

CHAPTER SUMMARY

Now that you have read this chapter you can:

6.1 Define and describe the types of interpersonal relationships.

In impersonal relationships, we communicate with others based primarily on their social or occupational roles (e.g., server, disciplinarian, cashier). In our personal relationships, we communicate with others based primarily on their uniqueness. Our relationships can be viewed on a continuum that ranges from personal to impersonal. Interpersonal relationships occur among family members and between friends and coworkers.

6.2 Explain how civility and civil communication affect interpersonal relationships.

Although parents may believe that their children learn rude and disrespectful communication from their friends, uncivil behaviors are taught to children at home, without their parents' realization. While some school districts have attempted to encourage "character education" in students, education experts maintain that instilling respect for others is a process that must begin early in life in the home. Children who see their parents set aside their own concerns for the greater good are more likely to do the same when they reach adulthood.

6.3 Identify two theoretical perspectives that can explain and predict interpersonal relationships.

Attraction theory states that interpersonal attraction is based on physical attraction, similarity, and proximity. Physical attraction is based on the extent to which we view another person's physical self as attractive. Similarity is a quality that illustrates that we tend to be attracted to people who validate who we are and what we believe. Proximity is based on the idea that we are more likely to be attracted to people who are in closer proximity to us than those who are not. Uncertainty reduction theory states that sharing information allows us to explain and predict human behavior and relationships. We ask questions to seek social information and to reduce our uncertainty about new acquaintances and predict their behavior. The three types of social information that communicators attempt to obtain from conversation partners are demographic data, personal beliefs, and information that explains another's behavior. We use three categories of information-seeking behaviors to reduce our uncertainty about others: passive social information seeking, active social information seeking, and interactive social information seeking.

6.4 Explain the difference between content and relational communication.

Relational communication demonstrates that we not only interact about the content of communication but also interact about our association with a conversation partner. The relational-level meaning of a message concerns the unspoken meaning that can be ascertained, in part, from nonverbal communication. At the relational level of meaning, we communicate the interpretation of our relationship based on affection, control, and respect.

6.5 Use metacommunication to improve your civil communication.

Metacommunication is a skill that has been defined both as "communication about communication" and "communication about relationships." We can metacommunicate about both the content of a message and the underlying relational message.

CIVILITY SUMMARY

Overall, remember that civility and interpersonal relationships involve the following:

- Parents can teach their children civil behavior by setting aside their own interests for "the greater good," such as postponing an argument until the children are no longer in earshot; communicating respectfully to rude shopkeepers, bad drivers, and intrusive telephone salespersons; and not saying behind people's backs what they wouldn't say face-to-face.
- To reduce incivility in the workplace, some public and private organizations have codes of ethics that include well-defined ways employees are expected to communicate with each other. These communication expectations may include treating people with dignity and respect, communicating honestly, and being willing to listen to others' opinions.
- Metacommunication is civil because it is based on restraint, respect, and responsibility.

REVIEW QUESTIONS

1. What is the difference between impersonal and personal relationships? Why is it important to understand the difference?
2. How can we characterize family and friendship relationships? How are they similar, and how are they different? Describe communication in family and friendship relationships.
3. What is the role of the family in terms of teaching children about civil communication?
4. Describe and explain attraction theory and uncertainty reduction theory. Explain how they relate to interpersonal relationships in your life.
5. What is relational communication? How can metacommunication help your interpretations of messages and your relationships?
6. Why is it important to understand the association between interpersonal relationships and the culture, workplace (your career), and gender contexts?

7 Intimate Relationships, Romantic Relationships, and Civil Communication

CHAPTER OBJECTIVES

After reading this chapter, you will be able to:

7.1 Compare and contrast the definitions of intimate and romantic relationships.

7.2 Explain how communication plays a role in relational development and satisfaction.

7.3 Describe how communication through intentional self-disclosure can influence the creation and development of intimate relationships.

7.4 Describe relationship development stage models and use the associated communication skills and strategies to develop, maintain, or terminate your relationships.

7.5 Use the dialectical tensions model to evaluate the changes in your relationships as circumstances change.

7.6 Explain the relationship between intimate relationships, romantic relationships, and civility.

WHEN PARTNERS IN AN intimate relationship decide to end their association, their talk frequently consists of insults, accusations, and recrimination (in other words, uncivil communication). However, relationships don't have to end in this manner. In June 2011, Jack White, the former lead singer of the band The White Stripes, and his wife, model and singer Karen Elson, announced that they had decided to divorce. Instead of sending a press release that implied blame or a plea for privacy, the couple released a statement about a party to celebrate their six-year wedding anniversary and their impending divorce. The couple stated that they intended to honor their time together with a divorce party designed to confirm their friendship and celebrate the past and future with friends and family members.[1] Invitations to the party asked guests to celebrate a new anniversary and breaking the bonds of marriage. The public announcement of the un-nuptial celebration also included the statements that they would continue to be trusted friends and that they appreciated the time they had shared together and the time they would share together in the future.[2]

White has ended other relationships in a similar manner. He continued to work with his first wife, Meg White, after their divorce, and Meg was maid of honor when Jack and Karen married in 2005.[3] He also refuses to speak negatively about former girlfriends, such as actor Renee Zellweger and socialite Heidi Davis.[4] One marriage and family therapist summarized the White–Elson divorce as an example of respect—not only for each other but for others who know and care about them.[5]

WHY IT MATTERS

Intimate relationships are important because, like interpersonal relationships in general, they affect physical and mental health. For example, cross-cultural studies demonstrate that cardiovascular disease is more common and is more likely to be fatal among people who have few close friends, who experience high levels of family conflict, and who are separated or divorced.[6] In addition, studies conducted over the past 40 years show that significant relationships that experience disruptions are the *cause* of disruptions in the immune system.[7] For example, immunosuppression (i.e., low resistance to disease) is related to separation from family and peers, family conflict, divorce, and bereavement.[8] On the other hand, married people tend to be healthier and live longer than people who are single, separated, or divorced.[9] In terms of psychological health, divorced people have higher suicide rates than those who are married.[10] In fact, marital happiness is the most important predictor of happiness in life—more so than money, occupation, or education.[11] Married people are also less likely to experience depression than are people who are not married.[12] However, marital unhappiness is related to both depression and poor physical health.[13] It's important to remember that a paucity of intimate relationships doesn't necessarily doom you to experience physical and psychological problems. However, the communication in and quality of your relationships is related to the quality of your life.

Do you know of people who seemed happy in their intimate or romantic relationships, but their relationships ended nonetheless? What causes people to create, maintain, or terminate intimate or romantic relationships? How can we avoid talking about former or current relationship partners in an uncivil manner? These are just some of the questions we answer in this chapter. Specifically, you will learn about why it's important to study intimate relationships and the definitions of intimate and romantic relationships. You will learn about communication in intimate and romantic relationships and consider social penetration theory, a theoretical perspective about intimate relationships that concerns self-disclosure. You will also learn about relationship stages and the opposing relational dialectics that can occur at any stage in a relationship. In addition, you will learn about skills that will help you improve your ability to initiate, maintain, and terminate your intimate relationships and strategies that can help you cope with relational dialectics. In addition, you will read about the association between intimate and romantic relationships and civility. Finally, you will learn about the association between intimate and romantic relationships and the culture, workplace (your career), and gender contexts and how this knowledge can improve your intimate relationships.

DEFINITION OF INTIMATE AND ROMANTIC RELATIONSHIPS

Suppose there is someone with whom you enjoy spending time. Perhaps you have a close relationship based on sharing emotions, socializing with friends, physical closeness, sharing ideas, and/or engaging in activities together. The relationship you have with this special person can be described as intimate. Even if you don't believe that you are presently in an intimate relationship, it's likely that at some point in your life, you will find yourself in an intimate relationship. Intimate relationships need not be romantic, and you may actually have a current relationship with a friend, coworker, or family member that can be characterized as intimate.

Intimate Relationships

When you think about the meaning of intimate relationships, do you picture a loving couple who enjoy romance? While romantic relationships are most often intimate, not all intimate relationships are romantic. *Intimacy* centers on feelings of closeness that develop from personal disclosures between communication partners.[14] In fact, intimacy is considered a defining component of any close relationship.[15] Overall, **intimate relationships** can be characterized by five qualities. While some intimate relationships can be described by just one of these qualities, others may be a combination of many:[16]

- **Emotional qualities**—In this type of intimate relationship, you believe that your partner listens to you when you need someone to talk to, and you can communicate your feelings without your partner feeling defensive.
- **Social qualities**—In this type of intimate relationship, you and your partner enjoy spending time with others and have a number of friends in common.
- **Sexual qualities**—In this type of intimate relationship, you are satisfied with your sex life, and sexual expression is viewed as an essential part of your relationship.
- **Intellectual qualities**—In this type of intimate relationship, you feel equal to your partner intellectually, and you believe that she or he respects your ideas.
- **Recreational qualities**—In this type of intimate relationship, you and your partner share many interests and find time to do fun things together.

It's realistic to assume that some if not most of our relationships are more impersonal than personal and therefore can't be defined as intimate. Even personal relationships with some family members may not be considered intimate. On the other hand, you and a friend may have an intimate relationship based on sharing important feelings and seeing films together (emotional and recreational qualities associated with intimacy). You may also have an intimate relationship with a roommate with whom you exchange important ideas and socialize with the many friends you have in common (intellectual and social qualities associated with intimacy). What is important to remember is that not all of our relationships will be intimate and that we can have intimate relationships with people for whom we don't have romantic feelings.

Romantic Relationships

What do you picture when you consider the word *romance*? Perhaps you envision dinners by candlelight, long walks on a deserted beach, or physical closeness. Regardless of what picture comes to mind, your imaginary scene includes someone in addition to yourself. You probably not only see this real or hypothetical partner as someone with whom you share an intimate relationship but as someone with whom you share a romantic relationship. **Romantic relationships** are based on intimacy but also go beyond intimacy to include passion and commitment. These three components comprise Sternberg's "the triangle of love."[17]

- **Intimacy**—Intimacy centers on feelings of closeness that develop from personal disclosures between communication partners. Intimacy typically remains stable

---

intimate relationships
Relationships that can be characterized by one or more of five qualities: sharing emotions, socializing with friends, physical closeness, sharing ideas, and/or engaging in activities together.

romantic relationships
Relationships based on intimacy, passion, and commitment.

over the course of a relationship and accounts for the comfort that romantic partners feel in each other's company.

- **Passion**—Passion is most important during the early stages of romantic relationship development. Passion typically refers to the fireworks or sparks between people who are attracted to each other. In addition to sexual feelings, passion can entail an ardent desire for another based on emotional, intellectual, or spiritual attraction.
- **Commitment**—Commitment refers to the decision to maintain and sustain a relationship based on love. Commitment tends to be the strongest predictor of relational satisfaction and is the most stable characteristic in the triangle of love. Commitment is the intention to stay together, despite the difficult times that are an inevitable part of any romantic relationship.

Intimate Relationships, Romantic Relationships, and Gender

How do friendships turn into romantic relationships? It may occur when physical attraction is paired with sexual attraction. You can be physically attracted to someone of your own or the opposite sex because you admire her or his physical attributes without being sexually attracted to the individual. However, **sexual attraction** occurs when we desire to engage in sexual activity with someone and this desire is heightened while in the company of the individual.[18] In a study of more than 300 American university students, more than one-half of the students surveyed said they had engaged in sexual activity with a nonromantic opposite-sex friend—in other words, they had had "friends with benefits."[19] Even though sexual activity has been found to change platonic relationships to intimate relationships, more than half of the students surveyed in the study reported that the nature of their relationship had not changed after engaging in sexual activity.[20]

In addition to resulting from sexual attraction, intimacy often results from self-disclosure. Research suggests that while men and women express closeness in different ways, intimacy that grows from engaging in activities is just as valid as intimacy that grows from self-disclosure and relationship talk. This means that while women may more often think that intimate relationships are created and shared on the basis of emotional qualities, men may believe that intimate relationships are created and shared in terms of recreational qualities. For example, diversionary tactics to relieve men's stress and enhance feelings of closeness are typically more effective for a man than is talking about a problem. On the other hand, women typically believe that talking about a problem enhances feelings of closeness more than engaging in a shared activity or using diversionary tactics. However, we have been socialized to perceive friendships and intimate relationships on the basis of a feminine standard that misrepresents and devalues how men typically express intimacy.[21] This means that intimate relationships based on recreational qualities are just as effective as intimate relationships based on sharing emotions.

Intimate Relationships, Romantic Relationships, and Culture

Cultural issues play an important role in relationships and relational communication. In terms of romantic relationships, Americans tend to emphasize passion and intimacy. Americans of European ancestry date for companionship and romance, but dating relationships aren't viewed as necessarily leading to an engagement and marriage. Although family members may have some influence on whether a dating couple decides to marry, the people involved in the dating relationship make the ultimate decision to

sexual attraction A desire to engage in sexual activity with someone; this desire is heightened while in the company of the individual.

Gays and lesbians typically measure success in intimate relationships in terms of equality, happiness, and satisfaction. Heterosexuals, on the other hand, measure success in terms of commitment, marriage, and endurance.

marry. On the other hand, collectivist cultures perceive that acceptance by family members takes precedence over passion and intimacy and that commitment is more important than romantic love. Dating is also perceived differently in diverse cultures. For example, dating a person more than twice in Spanish culture may mean that an engagement and marriage will ensue. In India, marriages tend to be arranged by parents, and in Algeria, the selection of a spouse may require the acceptance of the entire extended family.[22]

Regarding American co-cultures and intimate relationships, researchers conclude that relationships between members of different ethnic groups are similar to relationships between partners who belong to the same ethnic group. This is because inter- and intra-ethnic relationship partners provide similar reasons for the development of intimate relationships:

- Personal liking
- Perceived common interests and goals
- Similar levels of relational intimacy, commitment, and satisfaction[23]

For immigrants in the United States, intercultural relationships are more likely to occur as they become more accustomed to their new culture. In other words, the more immigrants adopt Western worldviews, values, and beliefs, the more likely they are to engage in relationships with native-born Americans. However, family attitudes about intercultural dating and marriage and the diversity of parents' friends will either encourage or discourage such relationships.[24] In addition, perceptions of success and competence of a relationship may be different for gays and lesbians than for heterosexuals. For example, gays and lesbians typically measure success in terms of equality, happiness, and satisfaction, while heterosexuals measure success in terms of commitment, marriage, and endurance.[25]

Intimate Relationships, Romantic Relationships, and Your Career

Many people think that good places to meet a potential relationship partner are a school, a house of worship, and a place of employment. Indeed, the workplace is a common place to meet intimate relationship partners, with research indicating that up to 80 percent of U.S. employees have experienced a romantic workplace relationship.[26] In one survey of 1,000 employees, 19 percent responded that they would welcome the opportunity to engage in a workplace relationship.[27] There are also benefits associated with workplace relationships. People involved in workplace romances among peers are perceived as approachable and friendly and are rarely judged as less productive or somehow hampered by their relationship. In addition, one benefit of workplace romances is a high degree of work satisfaction.[28] However, workplace romances also have drawbacks.

One problem associated with workplace romances is that the partners and the relationship itself tend to be the focus of rumor and gossip.[29] A failed workplace romance can be extremely difficult for the partners because they may be forced to continue to work together, even in the face of hard feelings about the breakup. In addition, because trust may decrease, productivity and teamwork can be affected negatively when a peer works with a coworker involved in a romance with an individual of higher organizational status.[30] Negative consequences of workplace romances may be even more difficult for female employees than for male employees. For example, when a subordinate female employee becomes romantically involved with a male superior, other employees may judge the female to be using the relationship to advance her career. On the other hand, males in workplace romances are not judged as harshly as females.[31] Because workplace romances can be detrimental to relational partners as well as many others in an organization, some businesses have explicit rules prohibiting such relationships.[32] Therefore, you may want to warn someone about the hazards of workplace romances if you recommend looking for a mate at a place of employment.

COMMUNICATION IN INTIMATE AND ROMANTIC RELATIONSHIPS

Think about an intimate or romantic relationship in which you or someone else was involved, or an intimate or romantic relationship on a television show or film with which you're familiar. Did the relationship partners communicate differently at the beginning of the relationship than they did at the end? Communication describes and influences the development of intimate and romantic relationships. Recall that we strive to reduce uncertainty about a (potential) relationship partner by obtaining information: the person's demographics (e.g., age, occupation, likes), beliefs and opinions, and other information that may help explain and predict his or her behavior. This means that at the beginning of an intimate or romantic relationship, you may seek to acquire information by talking about the ways a partner communicates intimacy (e.g., buying cards and presents, going out to a special dinner, completing a household chore). Regarding romantic relationships, there is typically a large amount of explicit talk during courtship and early marriage, as a couple gets to know each other. However, unspoken understandings may become the rule as a relationship matures. Research has found that couples make use of an implicit style of communication as they become increasingly stable and homogeneous.[33] A partner may know without asking the best way to express love and/or appreciation for a relationship partner (whether it's via cards and presents, dinner, chore completion, or other personal contact). However, we may expect periods of explicit talk if an intimate or romantic relationship becomes unstable and/or undergoes redefinition. For example, if we believe our relationship is under threat (e.g., our mate may be attracted to someone else), we may feel compelled to ask what we can do to show love and appreciation and to strengthen the relationship.[34]

Not only does communication describe and influence the development of intimate and romantic relationships, it also affects perceptions of relational satisfaction. Stable and satisfied couples exhibit five times more positive than negative interaction behaviors.[35] Furthermore, listening and confirming communication are related to marital satisfaction. Spouses who receive confirming communication from their partners are more likely to provide high levels of confirming communication in return. Moreover, married partners who empathize with their spouse's feelings express higher levels of marital satisfaction than do couples who fail to communicate understanding and empathy.[36] On the other hand, problems in communication may relate to marital difficulties. Research reveals that the communication of intimacy and displays of affection decrease very quickly after marriage; however, the number of negative interactions stays the same. In addition, some married couples are too busy to invest the time needed to "work" on their marriage, and when they find the time to talk to each other, the conversation tends to focus on business (e.g., instrumental tasks) rather than pleasure (e.g., companionate talk).[37]

SELF-DISCLOSURE AND SOCIAL PENETRATION THEORY

Perhaps among your circle of friends, you've heard the question "Why does she (he) stay with him (her)?" Maybe you've been asked what caused your relationship with another person to become intimate. You have read about attraction theory and uncertainty reduction theory, two theories that can explain and predict how relationships are created. Self-disclosure and social penetration theory can explain and predict how relationships develop and change over time.

Self-Disclosure

Self-disclosure refers to the deliberate communication of personal information to another person.[38] Although researchers don't always agree about the definition of self-disclosure, its deliberate nature most often distinguishes self-disclosure from other forms of verbal and nonverbal communication that reveal something about the self. For example, you might wear jewelry or tattoos that may or may not be intended to hint at a personality trait unknown to others. On the other hand, self-disclosure is defined as deliberately divulging something personal about ourselves that others do not know. While personal self-disclosure, such as "I had a rough day at school," allows others to better understand how we think and feel, relational self-disclosure, such as "I like spending time with you," tells partners about how well they are getting along and informs them about the state of their relationship. Both types of self-disclosure influence how our relationships develop and are maintained.[39] In fact, self-disclosure is considered a defining characteristic of relationship development and feelings of intimacy.[40]

The process of self-disclosure unfolds over time; this process includes who discloses, what is divulged, how partners influence each other regarding whether or not to disclose, and when and where the disclosure occurs. The process can occur within a single conversation or across days, weeks, months, or years.[41] In addition, although self-disclosure is recognized as necessary for achieving relational closeness, sharing personal information by itself may not create intimacy. Instead, it is the emotional and behavioral response of the disclosure recipient and the discloser's reactions to the recipient's response that create intimacy. For example, you may tell a relational partner about the time your appendix burst and how you were rushed to the hospital. You talk about the pain, your fear, and how long it took to recover. Your partner may respond with confirming communication such as questioning, prompting, reassurance, and paraphrasing. You then believe that the recipient understands you, cares about you, and validates your thoughts and feelings; feeling understood, cared for, and validated creates intimacy in a relationship.[42]

Social Penetration Theory

Social penetration theory, developed by psychologists Irwin Altman and Dalmas Taylor, states that relationships develop and change in terms of the type and depth of the

---

self-disclosure The deliberate communication of personal information to another person. In terms of social penetration theory, self-disclosure includes the breadth of information we share with others and the depth of information that we choose to self-disclose.

social penetration theory A theory that explains how relationships develop and change in terms of the self-disclosure that occurs between relational partners.

We develop intimate relationships with others when we self-disclose a wide breadth of topics in an in-depth manner.

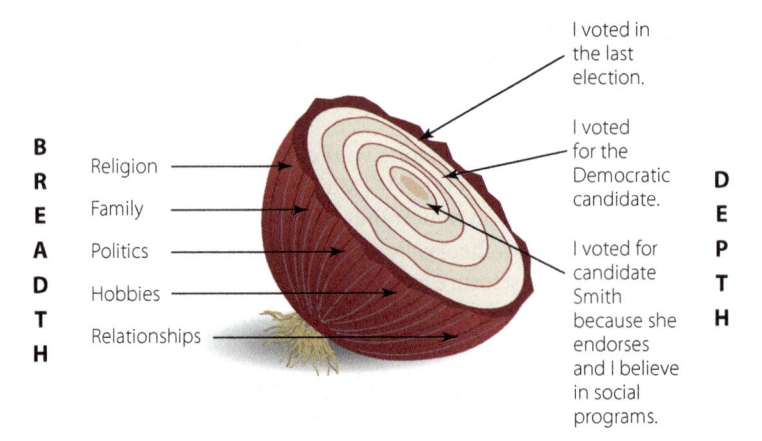

FIGURE 7.1 Social Penetration Theory

Altman and Taylor use the onion analogy to describe the breadth and depth of disclosures we make to our relational partners.

self-disclosure between relational partners. Social penetration occurs when our self-disclosure moves from shallow, superficial topics, such as our favorite breed of dog or where we spent our last vacation, to topics that are deeper and more intimate, such as our worldview or fears. The intimacy of our relationships is characterized not only by the depth of topics about which we self-disclose but also by the breadth or variety of topics about which we self-disclose.[43] For example, we may limit our conversations with a casual work acquaintance to work-related topics, but we begin to discuss topics related to our personal life as we become more intimate friends.

Figure 7.1 illustrates how this theory compares developing relationships with a peeled onion wedge. Specifically, social penetration theory suggests that we have various layers of information about ourselves. Our onion wedge illustrates the breadth, or variety, of topics about which we and our relational partners can converse. On the left side of the onion wedge, we see that we can disclose about various topics, such as religion, family, politics, hobbies, and relationships. Notice that the arrows that point away from these topics circle the onion; this is to show that breadth of self-disclosure is important for social penetration to take place. When our onion is peeled away, we see layers that illustrate the depths at which we self-disclose intimate information. We develop intimate relationships with others when we self-disclose a wide breadth of topics in an in-depth manner. In other words, we allow others to penetrate through the outside onion layers of superficial topics (e.g., "Have you seen any good movies lately?"), to middle layers of topics that are not readily known to others (e.g., "Who did you vote for in the last presidential election?"), and finally to the onion's core of deeply personal topics (e.g., "Do you believe in God?"). Depth of self-disclosure is illustrated on the right side of Figure 7.1 in terms of statements about politics. Note that the arrows that point away from these statements reach different inner layers of the onion. "I voted in the last election" may be considered a somewhat superficial disclosure; therefore, the arrow stops at an outer layer of the onion. "I voted for the Democratic candidate" is a more personal disclosure, and therefore the arrow stops at the middle layer of the onion. "I voted for candidate Smith because she endorses and I believe in social programs" is an in-depth personal disclosure; therefore, the arrow stops close to the onion's core.

Self-Disclosure and Relational Intimacy Engaging in self-disclosure doesn't guarantee relational intimacy. Disclosing a disturbing secret to an intimate partner may even contribute to the demise of the relationship. Because of the risk, we should ask ourselves the following questions before deciding to engage in self-disclosure:

- Am I planning to disclose an appropriate amount of information? (We don't want to overwhelm a potential partner with a wide breadth of material.)
- Am I planning to disclose an appropriate type of information? (We don't want to frighten off a potential partner with intimate and in-depth details of our personal life.)
- Will I be embarrassed if my disclosure is communicated to others? (We should make sure that the risks associated with disclosing to an untrustworthy partner are risks we can live with.)
- Can I effectively and appropriately deal with my disclosure if it's not reciprocated? (We should realize that although disclosure usually begets disclosure, this isn't always the case.)
- Will my disclosure place an unfair burden on my partner? (We don't want to unfairly ask a partner to keep a secret or self-disclose only for our sense of relief from guilt.)

Social penetration theory has been criticized as being overly simplistic and linear. For example, the theory ignores the tendency of relational partners to self-disclose to create a sense of intimacy with their partners at certain times and to refrain from self-disclosure to create a sense of autonomy at other times. In addition, social penetration theory ignores the ways that people nonverbally self-disclose about themselves, such as playing sports (which can disclose courage) or running errands for others (which can disclose loyalty and altruism).[44] Finally, some researchers suggest that the importance of self-disclosure in scientific research doesn't reflect the reality of everyday relationships. Current studies suggest that self-disclosure comprises only a small portion of communication between relational partners and that intimacy is reinforced by relational communication which is unremarkable and mundane. This means that "everyday talk" may be just as important in maintaining relational intimacy as self-disclosure.[45]

STAGE MODELS

Theories such as attraction theory, uncertainty reduction theory, and social penetration theory explain and predict the reasons why people create, maintain, and possibly dissolve their various relationships. We can also study relationships by looking at models that describe and illustrate relational development. A common type of relational development model is a **stage model**, which suggests that relationships follow a trajectory and can be classified in terms of particular phases of integration, maintenance, or termination.

stage models Models that illustrate relationships in terms of following a trajectory. Stage models also classify relationships in terms of particular stages that illustrate integrating, maintenance, or termination.

Knapp and Vangelisti's Staircase Model of Relationship Development

A well-known stage model is Mark Knapp and Anita Vangelisti's "staircase model," or "ten-stage model" of relationship development.[46] As noted in Figure 7.2, Knapp and Vangelisti's model illustrates the 10 broad phases of coming together and coming apart. The staircase model can describe relationships among close friends, business partners, or romantic relationships. It also can describe relationships that end after only a few stages and relationships that never move beyond the early stages.

The stages of coming together are:

- Initiating (casual interaction, with the goal of establishing a relationship)

- Experimenting (small talk about a variety of subjects that can help you discover whether the relationship is worth pursuing)
- Intensifying (an increase in the breadth and depth of self-disclosure)
- Integrating (when relational partners and others view the pair as a couple)
- Bonding (a public ritual that formalizes the exclusive nature of the relationship)

The stages of coming apart are:

- Differentiating (relationship partners attempting to regain their unique identities)
- Circumscribing (constriction of the breadth and depth of self-disclosure)
- Stagnating (relationship partners closing themselves off from each other)
- Avoiding (partners physically distancing themselves from each other)
- Terminating (the end of the relationships)

There are drawbacks associated with the staircase model and other stage models of relationship development. One criticism is that stage models treat relationship development as an invariant succession of stages and that the earlier stages must occur before the later stages can happen. However, not all relationships develop and deteriorate in a step-by-step manner; for example, some partners marry during the intensifying and integrating stages, and other partners may leave a relationship during the stages related to relationship maintenance. The model also doesn't illustrate the idea that one partner may believe the relationship reflects a particular stage (e.g., "differentiating"), while the other partner believes that the relationship reflects another (e.g., "avoiding"). In addition, stage models don't include the opposing forces or tensions that occur in all relationships, no matter what the stage. However, these opposing forces are reflected in the model of dialectical tensions, which we will discuss later in this chapter.

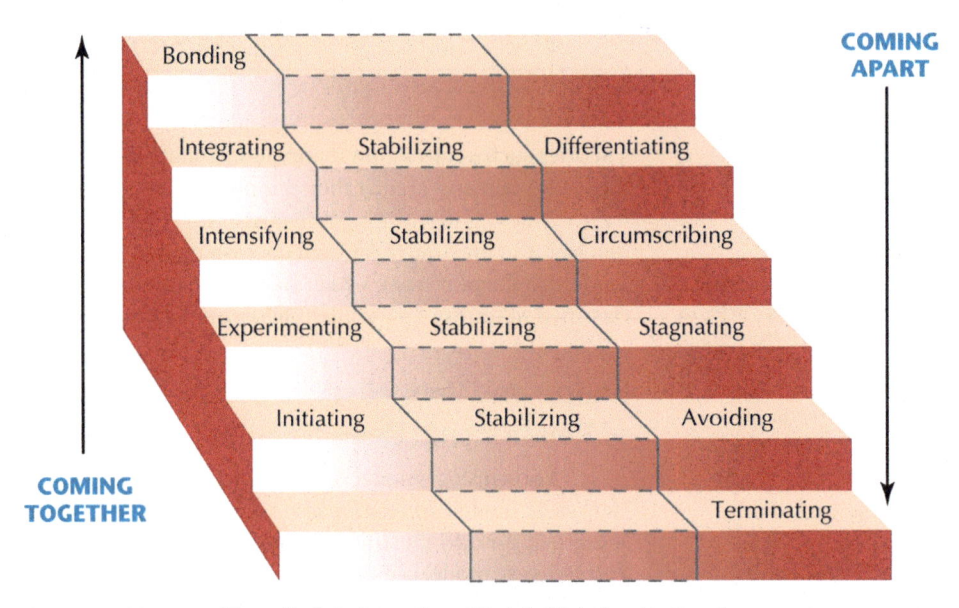

FIGURE 7.2 Knapp and Vangelisti's Staircase Stage Model of Relationship Development
Knapp and Vangelisti's research reveals 10 broad stages that can be used to describe a relationship's development and deterioration.

Source: Knapp, Mark L. and Vangelisti, L. *Interpersonal Communication and Human Relationships*, 5th ed. Published by Allyn & Bacon, Boston, MA. Copyright © 2005 by Pearson Education. Reprinted by permission of the publisher.

Improving Our Ability to Communicate Civilly and Effectively in Stages of Relationship Development

A number of strategies or clusters of skills characterize communication associated with each phase of a relationship. Rather than focus on skills associated with each stage of the Knapp and Vangelisti staircase model, we will concentrate more generally on skills we can use to initiate, maintain, and terminate an intimate relationship.

Initiation Strategies and Skills

Initiation strategies refer to the ways we approach and initiate contact with a potential relationship partner to whom we are attracted. Recall that attraction theory predicts that we are drawn to and may initiate relationships with people we believe are physically attractive, who are in physical proximity to us, and who are similar to us. But exactly *how* can we approach a nice-looking person who lives close by and appears to share similar attitudes?

Asking questions that will engage others, such as those that focus on the environment and the people with whom we speak, is a skill that can help us when we approach others and initiate conversations. However, asking questions may prove unsuccessful when we try to communicate interest in initiating a relationship. Communicating about the environment, the other person's family, and recent activities may be excellent ways to start a conversation, but they may fail to indicate that we are looking for more than a conversation partner. To compensate for this problem, some people rely on "pickup lines" that suggest a desire to initiate a relationship. A **pickup line** is a rehearsed question or comment designed to make the communicator appear attractive to a potential relationship partner. Unfortunately, there is no guarantee that a potential partner will perceive a pickup line as creative or humorous; in fact, a pickup line can actually backfire and be perceived as rude or offensive.

Experts warn that "canned come-ons" should be the last resort for attempting to initiate a relationship because they may communicate insincerity and can be used to attract anyone. Pickup lines fail to communicate a potential partner's uniqueness and what special individual features a communicator finds attractive.

Pickup lines can prevent a relationship from getting off the ground; a direct approach may have a better chance of success in initiating a relationship. A direct approach is sincere, honest, and gets straight to the point. An example of a direct approach to initiating a relationship is, "Hi, my name is _____ and I've seen you at _____. I'd like to get to know you better." Another direct approach entails a sincere compliment about a person's smile or clothing. In addition, approaching a stranger and saying, "Hi, how are you?" may be more effective than resorting to using a pickup line.[47] However, even a direct approach to relationship initiation can be interpreted as a pickup line or can cause an unexpected response.

Maintenance Strategies and Skills

The next phase in the relationship life cycle concerns maintenance strategies. What do you do to sustain your relationships and keep from taking your partners for granted? It may help to think of relationships as gardens in which trees and flowers are maintained with care and attention. Just like the contents of a garden, a relationship will deteriorate and perhaps die if we don't take actions to prolong its health. **Maintenance strategies** sustain the meaning of a relationship held by the

---

initiation strategies The ways we approach and initiate contact with a potential relationship partner to whom we are attracted.

pickup line A rehearsed question or comment designed to make the communicator appear attractive to a potential relationship partner.

maintenance strategies Behaviors used to sustain the meaning of a relationship held by the relational partners. Maintenance behaviors have been conceptualized as both nonstrategic and strategic actions that can prevent deterioration of the relationship.

There is no guarantee pickup lines will be perceived as creative or humorous, and pickup lines can actually backfire and be interpreted as rude or offensive.

TECH CHECK: Relational Maintenance Strategies

Do you think you communicate in a manner that helps maintain relationships over time, whether they involve family, friends, or romantic partners? If no, which of the five relationship maintenance strategies areas is the best place for you to begin improving your ability to maintain relationships? If yes, which of the five relationship maintenance areas include the strategies you typically use? With which specific strategy or strategies do you excel? Which strategy or strategies can use improvement?

relational partners. Maintenance behaviors have been conceptualized as both nonstrategic and strategic actions that prevent relational deterioration. We use nonstrategic maintenance behaviors in everyday talk that is ordinary, mundane, and perhaps trivial. However, everyday talk is important because it provides relational partners with an image of their relationship and an idea of its future. When we tell jokes, discuss what should be prepared for dinner, and talk about other people's relationships, clothing, or personality characteristics, we communicate as a couple about our shared worldview, attitudes, and understanding of our relationship. Relationships are sustained by the realization that partners share priorities and values.[48]

Strategic behaviors also contribute to relationship maintenance, both online and in face-to-face contexts.[49] We can use five strategies to maintain our relationships:[50]

- **Positivity**—We can attempt to make interactions pleasant by being cheerful, doing favors, and avoiding criticizing our partner. We can also engage in behaviors such as expressing appreciation for a partner.
- **Openness**—We can engage in direct discussions about our relationship, give and seek advice, and demonstrate empathy.
- **Assurances**—We can support, comfort, and communicate feelings for our relationship partner.
- **Social networks**—We can rely on and accept our relationship partner's friends and family members.
- **Sharing tasks**—We can help equally with chores and other tasks that must be done.

appreciation A relationship maintenance tactic of communicating that we feel grateful and that we are thankful for our relational partner and the relationship itself.

One way to communicate the maintenance strategy of positivity is by expressing appreciation for our relationship partners. **Appreciation** communicates that we feel grateful and that we are thankful for our relational partner and the relationship itself. Expressing appreciation is civil because it demonstrates that we respect our partner and what she or he does for us. The communication of appreciation is also civil because it illustrates that we can be trusted to acknowledge the good that others do for us, that we are fair and caring, and that in the long run, we communicate appreciation for the common good of the community. The expression of appreciation is ethical when we exhibit respect, restraint, and appreciation in a responsible manner (e.g., we don't "overdo it" or use appreciation to ingratiate ourselves to another). We can communicate appreciation for a relational partner by using a simple three-step method:[51]

- Describe our partner's specific actions that we believe contribute to our well-being.
- Describe the particular need(s) the partner fulfills.
- Describe how we feel when our needs are fulfilled (we can actually say the words "I appreciate...").

Using a mobile device for short and frequent calls that reaffirm a feeling of connectedness via everyday talk can foster high levels of love and commitment between relationship partners.

TRENDS IN
TECHNOLOGY AND SOCIAL MEDIA

The Internet, Social Media, and Relationship Initiation and Maintenance

To what extent do relational partners use the Internet and social media to initiate and maintain their relationships? A number of studies illustrate that creating and maintaining relationships is a primary motive for communicating via the Internet.[52]

The process of relational initiation that begins online is similar in many ways to relationships that begin in face-to-face settings. However, Internet communication can be described as **hyperpersonal**, or more sociable, personal, and intimate than what is found in face-to-face interaction. It is easy to start a relationship online because Internet users aren't biased by physical appearance or constricted by geographic limitations. People encounter others' messages in newsgroups and chat rooms and interact based on knowing they already have something in common. For example, a study of MMORPGs (massively multiplayer online role-playing games) such as World of Warcraft, City of Heroes, Ultima Online, EverQuest 2, Lineage II, RuneScape, Guild Wars, and Blade Mistress has found that approximately 50 percent of participants were mutually attracted to another player. The study concluded that "MMORPGs offer a safe environment for players to become emotionally involved with others."[53]

In terms of relational maintenance, the Internet contributes to "media multiplexity" in that people who communicate frequently use multiple media to do so. In other words, the more people see each other face-to-face, text, and talk on the phone, the more they use the Internet and vice versa. For example, partners in intimate relationships report that they use instant messaging (IM) with greatest regularity to maintain their relationships, followed by face-to-face communication, email, and phone calls. The use of IM not only creates another channel for the everyday talk that functions to maintain relationships, it also allows relationship partners to use the maintenance strategies of positivity, openness, assurances, social networks, and sharing tasks to communicate the interpretation of their relationship.[54] Similarly, using a mobile device for short and frequent calls that reaffirm a feeling of connectedness via everyday talk can foster high levels of love and commitment between relationship partners. While texting has been found to be a dominant modality for communication among college students, research reveals that voice calls are more suitable than texting in affecting relationships.

Compared to voice calls, a limited amount of information may be sent via texting, and voice-based messages may be preferred over text messages in terms of relationship maintenance.[55] Overall, the Internet and social media are part of a communication system in which people use many means to create and maintain relationships.[56]

Discussion Questions

1. How many of your relationships do you maintain by posting comments on social networking sites?

2. Do you frequent newsgroups or chat rooms? Have you established any online relationships based on the commonalities you share with newsgroup and/or chat room users?

3. Do you agree with the statement "MMORPGs offer a safe environment for players to become emotionally involved with others"? Why or why not?

4. Various studies conclude that technology and social media are used to create and maintain relationships. Do you know of any examples in which technology and social media was used to terminate relationships? Do you believe it is effective and appropriate to terminate relationships by means of social media versus a face-to-face context?

"Forgetting" to attend events is an uncivil and unethical manipulation tactic used to terminate relationships.

hyperpersonal communication Internet communication that is more sociable, personal, and intimate than what is found in face-to-face interaction.

termination strategies Strategies used to end a relationship. Such strategies include manipulation, withdrawal/avoidance, and positive-tone strategies.

These three steps do not have to occur in any particular sequence, and sometimes we can express our appreciation about behaviors of others, even those that are mundane or routine, with a simple "I appreciate you for . . ." or "Thank you for . . ."

By expressing appreciation on a regular basis, we strengthen our relationships over time. Positivity has also been related to satisfaction with a relational partner and the relationship itself. Using a strategy of positivity and the skill of expressing appreciation to maintain a relationship is rewarding to both partners.[57]

Termination Strategies and Skills Have you ever been on the receiving end of a termination message? Has a partner looked you in the eyes and communicated directly that she or he wanted to end the relationship, or did your partner drop hints and otherwise communicate the intention to break up in an indirect manner? There are three types of **termination strategies**: manipulation, withdrawal/avoidance, and positive-tone strategies.

One of the most painful cognitive and emotional outcomes of a breakup is the doubt and confusion it creates; therefore, relational partners seek explanations about a termination. However, communicating termination strategies at the end of a relationship in a direct and forthright manner is easier said than done. Most people communicate termination talk in indirect and general terms. Partners often believe that it's kinder to allow a relationship to drift apart than to be direct. In reality, we don't truly spare our partner's feelings by avoiding contact and refusing to tell her or him in a direct manner that the relationship is over and why it is ending.[58] Sometimes we even act unethically by deliberately provoking a partner into initiating a breakup![59] Research shows that people are more apt to use manipulation strategies or withdrawal/avoidance strategies than positive-tone strategies in a direct manner:[60]

- **Manipulation**—Manipulation tactics entail intentionally provoking a relational partner to initiate a breakup. We may purposefully leave an email on our computer screen that demonstrates an intimate relationship with someone else, or we may fail to keep our promises and commitments by not showing up at prearranged times or intentionally "forgetting" to attend important events. Manipulation occurs when we fail to take responsibility for our desire to terminate a relationship and intentionally act in a dishonest manner to get our partner to take action. We should avoid this termination strategy as it is uncivil and unethical.

- **Withdrawal/avoidance**—The withdrawal/avoidance strategy uses indirect tactics, such as reducing the frequency and/or intimacy of contact with a partner, to achieve relationship termination. Telling a partner that we're too busy doing other things to spend time together and failing to return phone calls are two tactics associated with the withdrawal/avoidance strategy. Another withdrawal/avoidance tactic is changing the relationship status indicator on Facebook to "single" or "it's complicated."[61] "Defriending" friends on Facebook is also considered a unilateral relationship termination tactic (i.e., defriending can be accomplished without a Facebook friend's acceptance and/or knowledge).[62] Withdrawal/avoidance tactics may not be clearly unethical, but they lack the directness and clarity of positive-tone strategies.

- **Positive tone**—The positive-tone strategy uses direct communication that indicates a desire for termination yet demonstrates respect for a relational partner. Skills associated with the positive-tone strategy include owning our thoughts and feelings, using descriptive language, and using metacommunication. Positive-tone tactics honor what was once a meaningful and intimate partnership with another individual and communicate the desire to end on a positive note. An example of a positive-tone termination message is "I've thought about this for a long time, and I've made a difficult decision. We had a lot of good experiences together, and I'll always remember the fun times. However, I am at a point where I want us to see each other exclusively, but you've repeatedly told me that you want to go out with others. I no longer want to experience hurt and disappointment each time I hear you tell me how much I mean to you, knowing that you continue to date other people. In the long run, it will be better for me if we stop seeing each other."

DIALECTICAL TENSIONS MODEL

Whereas stage models of relational development describe relationship development and deterioration in terms of particular phases, other models reflect the idea that relationships are ongoing and that relational meaning ebbs and flows, based on a partner's perceptions of the relationship and her or his relationship partner. Communication scholar Leslie Baxter has developed a model of **dialectical tensions** which shows that relationships oscillate between opposing ends of a continuum, as various factors push or pull the relationship partners together or apart. Dialectical tensions suggest that relationships evolve and change over time because partners constantly reassess and redefine their needs. The dialectical tensions model illustrates the various tensions that partners may experience during a decline in their relationship and offers an alternative to automatically moving toward disintegration.

dialectical tensions A model that illustrates that relationships oscillate between opposing ends of a continuum. Dialectical tensions suggest that relationships evolve and change over time because partners constantly reassess and redefine their needs.

Baxter's Model of Dialectical Tensions in Relationships

Figure 7.3 illustrates three dialectics in the Baxter model that function as examples of the normal push and pull in relational life: autonomy/connection, novelty/predictability, and openness/closedness.[63] Note that these dialectics occur at different points in a relationship; they describe a tug-of-war that pulls a relational partner in two different directions at once.

FIGURE 7.3 Dialectical Tensions

Baxter's research identified three dialectics, or tensions, that many couple experience in the course of their relationship.

ASK THE ETHICIST: "To Lie or Not to Lie; That Is the Question"

Question How should I respond if my friend asks me about someone he or she has just met and I don't think much of that person?

Answer That's a difficult situation to be in and illustrates the openness/closedness dialectic. On the one hand, you want to be honest with your friend (openness). On the other, you don't want your words to come back to haunt you in the future if the relationship becomes serious. And if you don't say anything (closedness), how will you respond if in the future your friend comes to you for support and understanding after breaking up?

One thing is certain: If you don't say anything at the beginning, it is best to avoid saying anything later if the relationship turns sour. Claiming that you knew the other person was no good when you didn't say anything early on is likely to make your friend feel worse.

Remember that when a person asks you a question like this, you don't have to respond immediately with your explicit opinion. For example, you can ask your friend to describe what is attractive about the other person or ask your friend how he or she envisions the relationship developing.

If you decide to disclose that you don't like the other person, it is more helpful to do so in a specific way (e.g., "It bothers me that he/she forgets to call you") rather than general (e.g., "He/she gives me the creeps"). Stressing your desire for the other to be happy and satisfied is also important. If your friend winds up in a serious relationship, be prepared to be civil. That's the ethical thing to do.

---

autonomy/connection dialectic A dialectic that reflects the tension between wanting to be independent and wanting to feel connected.

Autonomy/Connection The **autonomy/connection dialectic** reflects the tension between wanting to be independent and wanting to feel connected to your relational partner. Sometimes we want to spend time with a relational partner and enjoy the same activities that our partner likes; at other times, we want to be alone and prefer to emphasize our individuality. At times you may want to be with your partner and to emphasize your similarity, make an effort to enjoy a sports event, play, or game of pool. At times you may want to be alone and focus on the activities that you enjoy and your partner doesn't, such as shopping, tinkering with the car, or playing computer games. These examples show the natural human needs for both autonomy and connection, and partners constantly attempt to preserve their individual uniqueness while also sustaining their mutual relational bond.

novelty/predictability dialectic A dialectic that concerns the tension between wanting predictability and routine in a relationship and the desire for novelty and newness.

Novelty/Predictability The **novelty/predictability dialectic** concerns the tension between wanting predictability and routine in a relationship and desiring novelty and newness. At times we prefer routine and stability in our relationships. For instance, it may be comforting to know that we don't have to worry about our romantic partner not showing up for a regularly planned evening out. However, too much predictability in our relationships can cause boredom, and then we seek to infuse our relationships with novelty. For example, we may enjoy the combination of excitement and anxiety brought about by a new relational partner who may or may not show up for a last-minute outing. These scenarios illustrate our need for the comfort we find in relational security and stability and the excitement we experience in relational spontaneity and unpredictability.

openness/closedness dialectic A dialectic that reflects the tension between wanting to self-disclose and engage in open communication and our desire for privacy.

Openness/Closedness The **openness/closedness dialectic** reflects the tension between wanting to self-disclose and engage in open communication and desiring privacy. At times we want to become close to others by revealing our emotions; at other times we want to protect ourselves by withholding information that can leave us vulnerable. Suppose you consider divulging to a relational partner that you were involved in an argument with someone at work. The argument left you feeling angry and frustrated. You decide to disclose because you believe that your partner will give you sympathy and communicate understanding. At other times you may consider keeping such information to yourself because you believe your partner will give you advice and criticize you for engaging in an argument at the workplace. Therefore, you decide to keep this information private so as not to listen to the advice and criticism.

Improving Our Ability to Communicate Civilly and Effectively When Contending with Relational Dialectics

Dialectics are a natural part of all healthy relationships, and relational partners can use at least four methods to deal with the tension caused by conflicting needs:[64]

- **Neutralization**—When relational partners give up some of what they want, their desires can be partially met; that is, they can negotiate between the two extremes of a dialectic continuum. For example, although college students who live on campus or in an apartment may want to be autonomous from their parents, they may realize that, however bothersome, they can tolerate one or two calls per week from Mom and Dad. From the opposite perspective, although parents of college students may want to know every detail about their offspring's life, they may realize that an email or a text message every now or then is sufficient to remain connected with their child. In this example, neither college students nor their parents are completely meeting their needs for autonomy or connection, but they have compromised so that their needs are partially met.

- **Selection**—Placing emphasis on one dialectic need and ignoring or neglecting the opposite dialectic need for a certain period of time. For example, we may deliberately ignore the need for autonomy during a 24/7 week-long family reunion, and we may just as deliberately ignore the need for connection and concentrate on some "alone time" for a few days after the reunion ends.

- **Separation**—Giving priority to a specific dialectical need in certain circumstances and placing emphasis on the opposing dialectical need in others. For example, we may desire a day-to-day routine that affords stability and a sense of security in our lives (predictability), but during an overseas trip, we may engage in spur-of-the-moment adventures, such as waking up without a plan for the day, taking walks without a map, and hopping a train to a last-minute destination (novelty).

- **Reframing**—Engaging in perspective taking redefines opposing dialectics as no longer threatening a relationship. For example, suppose a female believes that her male partner is rejecting her when he comes home from work and stares at the TV or goes into the computer room and shuts the door. She wants to talk to him about his day and share her experiences; he wants to relax without communicating. The female partner may believe that his lack of communication and need to be alone is a quest for autonomy in the face of her attempts at connection. However, suppose she reads about the influence of gender and brain differences on communication. She learns that males typically perceive communication as a means to an end rather than an end in

Instead of perceiving that a partner is ignoring you when he or she plays computer games, you can reframe the perception of the situation and interpret your partner's behavior as merely a way to unwind after a hard day at work.

itself. She reads that communication isn't as pleasurable for men as it is for women and that men often perceive communication as work. The female partner also learns that communication entails more brain power for men than for women because women's brains are hard-wired to facilitate communication.[65] Armed with this knowledge, she engages in perspective taking and reinterprets her partner's behavior. Because she now redefines the dialectic, she realizes that her partner isn't rejecting her by not talking after a long day at the office; his silence is an attempt to relax and rejuvenate in his home, a place where he isn't forced to "work" (i.e., talk). The dialectic of autonomy (e.g., the male partner's lack of communication and need to be alone) will continue to be present in the relationship but will no longer be seen in *opposition to* or in *conflict with* the need for connection.

> Experts can predict an impending divorce with 94 percent accuracy when a couple uses disconfirming messages as a communication style, has negative recollections of their relational history, and exhibits high amounts physiological stress.

disconfirming communication
Communication that does not validate others. We communicate disconfirmation when we ignore people, fail to acknowledge their thoughts and feelings, and refuse to accept their opinions and emotions.

INTIMATE RELATIONSHIPS, ROMANTIC RELATIONSHIPS, AND CIVILITY

You learned earlier in this chapter that satisfied couples listen to each other and communicate confirmation. On the other hand, couples who feel less satisfied with their relationship communicate with each other more often by using disconfirming communication. **Disconfirming communication** does not validate others, is disrespectful, and is therefore uncivil. Think about an intimate or romantic relationship in which you're involved or one with which you're familiar. How would you describe the communication that characterizes the relationship? Recall that confirming communication includes the ability to listen well; the skills of responding with questions and prompts, reassurance and confirmation; and the use of paraphrasing to understand another person's thoughts and feelings. Does this type of communication describe you and your partner (or the partners you know in an intimate relationship)? On the other hand, do you and your partner (or those partners in the intimate relationship of which you are aware) typically include insults, sarcasm, and blame in your communication? Does the communication also include silence and a refusal to engage in conversation? If so, the relationship may be headed for a breakup.

We communicate disconfirmation when we ignore people, fail to acknowledge their thoughts and feelings, and refuse to accept their opinions and emotions. Research demonstrates that feeling validated by one's spouse results in marital satisfaction and a positive perception of the marital relationship. However, disconfirming marital communication decreases the extent to which a spouse feels understood and validated by her or his partner.[66]

Sociologist John M. Gottman has identified four types of disconfirming messages that not only contribute to marital dissatisfaction but also predict divorce.[67] Taken as a whole, these disconfirming messages communicate disrespect, a lack of restraint, and the shirking of responsibility—in other words, uncivil communication:

- **Criticism**—Whereas complaints are aimed at specific actions and behaviors, criticism involves negative words about a partner's personality or character. Criticism is common in most relationships but can usher in the other three types of disconfirming messages if pervasive.
- **Contempt**—Contempt is based on long-simmering negative thoughts about a partner and is evident in sarcasm, name-calling, hostile humor, and mockery.

A CASE STUDY IN ETHICS

The Secret Lover Collection

Ethical communication reflects trustworthiness, responsibility, respect, fairness, caring, and concern for the community. Keep the components of ethical communication in mind as you read the following case study and answer the discussion questions. Try to remember the last time you scanned the mind-boggling variety of missives that line the greeting card shelves in your local store. There are cards for every holiday, cards for special occasions, and cards that express sentiments for no particular reason. But have you noticed cards especially designed for persons involved in an extra-relational affair? The "Secret Lover Collection" includes 24 different cards with illustrations of hearts, flowers, and star-crossed lovers. The collection includes sentiments such as "I just love breathing you in," "I never expected to fall in love with you," "The holidays won't feel right without you by my side," and "I can't go on like this anymore."

Cathy Gallagher, a former advertising executive and the creator of the cards, is tired of listening to people express outrage over the Secret Lover Collection. "The conservatives and the talk shows are just going crazy, like nobody ever had affairs before my cards were out there," she notes. "Well, they did. People make choices. I want to do this without judgment."[68] Gallagher hints that disdain for her cards smacks of hypocrisy. She asks if hotels check couples for a marriage license when they rent a room. Do florists and jewelers ask about the relationship between the recipient and the individual making the purchase? If greeting cards are supposed to be available for all purposes, then why not for an affair?

"A lot of people don't set out to have affairs, but it kind of happens," she maintains. "There are generic cards that say 'I love you' but nothing that explains the emotions specific to their relationship." Gallagher is also somewhat surprised at all the finger-wagging. "Affairs have been going on since the beginning of time. This is just facilitating communication between lovers. This isn't for one-night stands. There's an emotional intensity that I'm helping them express."[69]

Discussion Questions

1. Is it ethical to help lovers in emotionally intense affairs "facilitate communication"?
2. Do you agree with Gallagher that greeting cards are supposed to help people express feelings, no matter what the situation?
3. Is it hypocritical to judge a greeting card designer for "encouraging" extramarital affairs without judging hotel clerks, florists, and jewelers who fail to "discourage" such affairs?

Nonverbally, contempt is communicated by eye-rolling, sneering, and "tsking." Contempt is considered the most poisonous disconfirming message because it communicates disgust with a partner.

- **Defensiveness**—Defensiveness occurs when we believe that our self-concept is under attack. Communicating defensively is a way to blame a partner (e.g., "You're the problem, not me!") and typically escalates a conflict.
- **Stonewalling**—Also labeled "withdrawal," stonewalling occurs when a partner physically and/or mentally disengages from a situation. A stonewaller fails to give verbal and nonverbal feedback during a conversation and may act as if she or he doesn't care what a partner has to say. Stonewalling typically occurs when the other three disconfirming responses become overwhelming and it is perceived as a way out.

Gottman can predict the occurrence of future divorce with 94 percent accuracy by assessing whether couples use these four types of disconfirming messages, how partners recall their relational history, and their physiological stress.[70] Once again, think about the intimate relationship in which you're involved or one with which you're familiar. To what extent does disconfirming communication such as criticism, contempt, defensiveness, and stonewalling describe the relationship? How can the communication skills that you've learned so far help diminish the disconfirming communication in your or another couple's relationship?

CHAPTER SUMMARY

Now that you have read this chapter you can:

7.1 Compare and contrast the definitions of intimate and romantic relationships.

Intimate relationships can be characterized by at least one of five qualities: emotional qualities, social qualities, sexual qualities, intellectual qualities, and recreational qualities. While romantic relationships are most often intimate, not all intimate relationships are romantic. Romantic relationships are based on intimacy and also passion and commitment.

7.2 Explain how communication plays a role in relational development and satisfaction.

At the beginning of an intimate or romantic relationship, we communicate to share information that will help to establish the relationship. Communication also plays a role later on in the life of a relationship when it can play a role in relational satisfaction. Couples who exchange positive interactions are more satisfied; couples who engage in negative communication have more marital difficulties.

7.3 Describe how communication through intentional self-disclosure can influence the creation and development of intimate relationships.

Self-disclosure refers to the deliberate communication of personal information to another person. While personal self-disclosure, such as "I had a rough day at school," allows others to better understand how we think and feel, relational self-disclosure, such as "I like spending time with you," tells partners about how well they are getting along and informs them about the state of their relationship. Both types of self-disclosure influence how our relationships develop and are maintained. Social penetration theory states that relationships develop and change in terms of the type and depth of the self-disclosure between relational partners. The intimacy of our relationships is characterized not only by the depth of topics about which we self-disclose but also by the breadth or variety of topics about which we self-disclose.

7.4 Describe relationship development stage models and use the associated communication skills and strategies to develop, maintain, or terminate your relationships.

A common type of relational development model is the stage model, which suggests that relationships follow a trajectory and can be classified in terms of particular phases of integration, maintenance, or termination. A well-known stage model is the staircase model of relationship development, which illustrates the 10 broad phases of coming together and coming apart. Communication skills associated with this model include asking questions to engage others and using "pickup lines" with care to initiate a relationship, expressing appreciation to maintain a relationship, and using a positive-tone strategy based on direct communication that indicates a desire for termination yet demonstrates respect for a relational partner.

7.5 Use the dialectical tensions model to evaluate the changes in your relationships as circumstances change.

The dialectical tensions model illustrates that relationships evolve and change over time because partners constantly reassess and redefine their needs. Three dialectics function as examples of the normal push and pull in relational life: autonomy/connection, novelty/predictability, and openness/closedness. Communication strategies you can use to deal with dialectical tensions include neutralization (giving up some of what relational partners want so their desires can be partially met), selection (placing emphasis on one dialectic need and ignoring or neglecting the opposite dialectic need for a certain period of time), separation (giving priority to a specific dialectical need in certain circumstances and placing emphasis on the opposing dialectical need in others), and reframing (engaging in perspective taking to redefine opposing dialectics as no longer threatening a relationship).

7.6 Explain the relationship between intimate relationships, romantic relationships, and civility.

Disconfirming communication, such as criticism, contempt, defensiveness, and stonewalling (withdrawal), is associated with marital dissatisfaction and divorce. Taken as a whole, disconfirming messages communicate disrespect, a lack of restraint, and the shirking of responsibility—in other words, uncivil communication.

CIVILITY SUMMARY

Overall, remember that civility, intimate relationships, and romantic relationships involve the following:

- Expressing appreciation is civil because it demonstrates that we respect our partner and what she or he does for us. The communication of appreciation is also civil because it illustrates that we can be trusted to acknowledge the good that others do for us, that we are fair and caring, and that in the long run, we communicate appreciation for the common good of the community.

- Manipulation tactics intentionally provoke a relational partner to initiate a breakup. We should therefore avoid this termination strategy as it is uncivil and unethical.

- Disconfirming communication does not validate others, is disrespectful, and is therefore uncivil.

REVIEW QUESTIONS

1. Why is it important to study intimate relationships? Is our quality of life doomed to be poor if we have only a few intimate relationships?

2. What are the qualities on which intimate relationships are based? Why aren't all intimate relationships considered to be romantic relationships?

3. How does communication influence the development of intimate and romantic relationships?

4. What are self-disclosure and social penetration, and how do they influence the creation and development of intimate relationships?

5. What models are used to study relationship formation, maintenance, and termination?

6. Describe and explain the communication strategies and skills that can be used to initiate, maintain, and terminate intimate relationships.

7. Describe and explain the communication strategies and skills that can be used to contend with relational dialectics.

8. What is disconfirming communication, and why is it uncivil?

9. How can knowing how culture, the workplace, and gender influence intimate and romantic relationships help you improve your communication with people with whom you share intimate and romantic relationships?

8 Civil Communication in Conflicts

WHEN KANSAS TEENAGER Emma Sullivan visited her state capitol on a field trip, she wasn't impressed with what Governor Brownback had to say. She tweeted her opinion to her 60 followers, writing "Just made mean comments at gov brownback and told him he sucked, in person #heblowsalot." Despite the fact that Sullivan had not met Governor Brownback nor spoken with him personally, within days Sullivan had amassed more than 12,000 followers and created a public conflict that led to a public apology, although not the one originally demanded.[1]

How did one tweet become such a big issue? The tweet, Sullivan says, was part of a conversation she and a friend were having about what they would say to Brownback were they to actually meet him, and it was intended for her audience of friends. However, the governor's office monitors both Twitter and Facebook for comments about the governor. Staff members felt the comment was offensive and informed the organizers of the

> **CHAPTER OBJECTIVES**
>
> *After reading this chapter, you will be able to:*
>
> **8.1** Define *interpersonal conflict* and illustrate examples of conflict situations.
>
> **8.2** Describe three theoretical approaches to conflict and apply them to help resolve conflict situations.
>
> **8.3** Explain some causes of conflict and how some conflict can be avoided.
>
> **8.4** Explain why it is possible to experience conflict and yet remain civil and identify the communication options you have to manage a conflict situation.
>
> **8.5** Apply the S-TLC system of communication to your own conflict situations.
>
> **8.6** Identify some strategies to keep conflict from escalating to violence.
>
> **8.7** Explain the options you have in communicating forgiveness and/or apologies to another person.

field trip, who in turn contacted Sullivan's high school. She was called into the principal's office and instructed to write a letter of apology. Sullivan refused, citing her freedom of speech, and her parents supported her decision. Eventually, the governor issued a statement of apology to Sullivan, stating that "My staff over-reacted to this tweet, and for that I apologize. Freedom of speech is among our most treasured freedoms."[2] While Sullivan would have liked a more personal apology, others were disappointed that she got off so easily. As one writer put it, "If you were my daughter, you'd be writing that letter apologizing to Kansas Gov. Sam Brownback for the smart-alecky, potty-mouthed tweet you wrote after meeting with him on a school field trip. Also, that smartphone? The one you posed with, proudly displaying the tweet.... turned off until you learn to use it responsibly."[3]

WHY IT MATTERS

Do you think Sullivan chose the best way to express her opinion about Governor Brownback? Should she have apologized? Did the governor's staff overreact? Should a conflict be played out on such a large scale?

Many people find it difficult to think of conflict and civility as being linked. One reason is that people generally have very negative perceptions of conflict. They use words like *war*, *battle*, and *volcano eruption* to describe conflict, and they may describe the feeling of being in conflict as being "tossed around in a windstorm."[4] In fact, people have such overwhelmingly negative views of conflict that when they are able to resolve a conflict civilly and productively, they tend not to call it a conflict at all.[5]

Conflicts help create and build interpersonal relationships by allowing people to identify and maintain appropriate boundaries.[6] Despite the fact that conflicts strain our relationships, conflicts occur wherever people have to negotiate important relationships with one another—in friendships, love relationships, work relationships, and so on.[7] Conflict is simply a fact of life; even when we try to avoid it, we rarely can.

While it may seem almost impossible for us to think of conflict and civility as being linked, when we act with respect, restraint, and responsibility, and when we are sincere in our desire to resolve an issue, we are addressing conflict civilly. This includes taking the time to listen to others, to control our desires to hurt each other, and to communicate in ways that acknowledge our contribution to the conflict. In addition, we are fair in the way we approach the conflict by not attributing all the blame to the other person, caring about the way the other wants to resolve the conflict, and maintaining respect for the other during the course of the conflict.

As we encounter conflict, it is often difficult to remain civil and act ethically toward the other person, as both Emma Sullivan and Governor Brownback discovered. In this chapter, you will learn about the ways in which conflicts occur in relationships, the most effective means of confronting those conflicts, and some guidelines for maintaining civil and ethical communication with the other person or persons in the conflict.

interpersonal conflict A problematic situation with the following four unique characteristics: the conflicting parties are interdependent; the conflicting parties perceive that they seek incompatible goals or outcomes or that they favor incompatible means to the same ends; the perceived incompatibility has the potential to adversely affect the relationship if not addressed; and there is a sense of urgency about the need to resolve the difference.

DEFINITION OF CONFLICT

There are many terms that people use when they refer to conflict. Some call it a *confrontation*; others may call it a *quarrel*. To some, it is a *disagreement* or a *difference of opinion*, to others an *opportunity for bargaining* or *negotiation*. In this chapter, we focus on a specific kind of conflict: conflict that occurs between people in close relationships, or interpersonal conflict.

Interpersonal conflict is a problematic situation where:

- The conflicting parties are interdependent.
- The parties have the perception that they seek incompatible goals or outcomes or that they favor incompatible means to the same ends.

- The perceived incompatibility has the potential to adversely affect the relationship if it is not addressed.
- There is a sense of urgency about the need to resolve the difference.[8]

Situation

A **conflict situation** is determined by the people who play out particular roles, the specific context where it takes place, the particular point in time when the interchange occurs, and the expectations for behavior implied within it. For example, when you attend a class at your college, you are involved in a situation. You have a particular role (student), the situation occurs in a particular place at a particular time (the classroom at the appointed hour), and there are expectations regarding how you should behave (come to class on time and prepared, don't interrupt the teacher, and so on).

Problematic situations arise when partners perceive that they seek different outcomes, or they favor different means to the same ends. A conflict situation is generally viewed as:

- Two or more competing responses to a single event (e.g., you and I have different ideas concerning the way we should respond to an unexpected bill)
- Differences between individuals (e.g., we don't see eye to eye on how to complete a group project)
- Perceptions that important relational rules have been violated (e.g., having a guest overnight without first consulting your roommate)

Definitions of *conflict* often assume that conflict begins when someone says something about the issue to the person perceived as causing it.[9] However, a conflict may exist when people are not arguing or even talking to each other. Long before we decide to say something to another person, we might see that we are experiencing a conflict with that person. For example, one study found that when people experienced negative emotions, they became more evasive and equivocal in their communication with the person associated with those emotions.[10] People who are not speaking to each other, purposively avoiding contact, giving each other the silent treatment, using nonverbal displays to indicate conflict, or sending mixed messages to each other may be in a conflict situation.

Interdependence

Interdependence occurs when those involved in a relationship characterize it as important and worth the effort to maintain. *Interpersonal conflicts occur with people who are important to us*, such as friends, coworkers, or family members. When the other person isn't someone with whom we have to communicate often, we don't have the same sense of obligation to resolve the problem. However, this doesn't give us permission to act irresponsibly; treating people civilly and ethically generally decreases the probability of conflict.

Incompatible Goals or Means

Incompatible goals occur when two parties are seeking different outcomes; for example, they each want to buy a different car but can afford only to buy one. **Incompatible means** occur when two parties agree on the same goal but differ in how they should

---

Conflicts involve people who are important to us and issues that don't go away just because they are ignored.

conflict situation A setting in which conflict occurs, which seems familiar to the participants and which helps to provide clues for managing the conflict that is occurring.

problematic situations Situations that occur when partners perceive that they seek different outcomes or favor different means to the same ends.

interdependence A relationship that is characterized by all involved in it as one that is important and worth the effort to maintain.

incompatible goals Goals that seek different outcomes; for example, we want to buy two different cars but can afford only one.

incompatible means Means that try to achieve the same goal but differ in how to do so; for example, we agree on the same car but on not whether to finance it or pay cash.

attain it; for example, they agree on the same car but not on whether to finance it or pay cash. Incompatible goals and means can create the perception that the other is frustrating our attempts to achieve something or that the other person threatens our interests.[11] Whether or not our perceptions of the conflict situation are accurate, *until we are able to confirm or change those perceptions, we act as though our perceptions are real.* Our perceptions drive our view of reality, but sometimes they drive us inaccurately.

Emotional Residues

emotional residues Lingering emotional responses to the memory of a conflict.

Emotional residues, the feelings we experience in the aftermath of a conflict, are like carpet stains—they are noticeable, make us feel uncomfortable and dissatisfied with the relationship, and lead us to desire change. If we dominate our partners and always win arguments, our partners may feel unhappy and look for more satisfying relationships elsewhere.

Sense of Urgency

sense of urgency A point in a conflict situation at which at least one person in the conflict feels it must be addressed because things cannot continue as they are.

The definition of *conflict* that we've been using emphasizes that the issue or problem underlying a perceived conflict generally has reached a point where there is a **sense of urgency** to resolve the conflict. At least one person in the conflict feels it must be addressed because things cannot continue as they are.

THEORETICAL PERSPECTIVES ON CONFLICT BEHAVIOR

Communication researchers have proposed a number of theories to explain and predict conflicts and conflict behaviors. In this chapter, we look at three of them: social exchange theory, which assumes that people engage in conflict to increase their relationship rewards; styles theory, which assumes that people act in predictable ways when faced with a conflict; and phase theory, which assumes that conflicts unfold in fairly predictable stages.

Social Exchange Theory

social exchange theory A theory developed by psychologists John Thibaut and Harold H. Kelley, in which perceived rewards and costs determine whether people develop, maintain, or terminate their relationships.

rewards Features of a relationship that are considered positive.

costs Features of a relationship that are considered negative.

A question people frequently ask themselves when facing a conflict is whether addressing the conflict is worth the trouble. This question describes the heart of **social exchange theory**, developed by psychologists John Thibaut and Harold H. Kelley, in which perceived rewards and costs determine whether people develop, maintain, or terminate their relationships.[12] **Rewards** refer to features of a relationship that are considered positive, and **costs** relate to features of a relationship that are considered negative. Relationship rewards can take the form of good feelings, need fulfillment, economic stability, and social status. Relationship costs can take the form of anxiety, insecurity, and the investment of too much time and too much energy. Although the preferred ratio between rewards and costs varies from person to person and from time to time, social exchange theorists contend that people conduct a cost–benefit analysis when determining whether they should invest in a relationship, given what they get out of it. One investment people make is addressing conflict because it takes time and emotional energy to confront another person.

From a social exchange point of view, conflict arises when one person in a relationship thinks that the outcomes are too low and perceives that the other may resist any attempt to raise the outcomes. Let's look at a roommate situation to understand this theory better. If you really like having your best friend as a roommate, but you've come to discover that he or she has a number of habits that really bother you and make it difficult for you to study, you will probably want to talk to your roommate about it. You'll know that although there is a cost associated with engaging in the conflict, the rewards outweigh the cost. You won't build up a great resentment toward your roommate by swallowing your resentments. You will most likely see this as a reward because it is hard to maintain a friendship with someone if you are harboring resentments toward the other person. You'll be able to study in your room rather than having to go to the library (another reward). Even though it is likely that your roommate is unable or unwilling to meet all of your demands, creating a cost associated with engaging in conflict, the potential rewards still offset those costs.

The dynamics of the relationship and the conflict may change, though, if you and your roommate don't see your relationship in the same way. If you consider your roommate your best friend, but your roommate doesn't think of you the same way, your roommate has more power in the relationship. In that case, the cost of engaging in conflict (i.e., the potential loss of friendship with your roommate) may be higher than the potential reward of studying in your room or simply ignoring the things that your roommate does that bother you.

Overall, social exchange theory leads to two insights about conflict behavior. First, the theory recognizes that people are often quite purposeful about the way they "do" conflict, calculating the costs of various options and weighing those costs against the potential rewards the options might bring. Second, social exchange theory illustrates that people in conflicts choose actions based not only on their particular outcomes but also on their cost for the relationship. People may deliberately avoid a conflict because the current costs of initiating one are too high. Conversely, they may engage in a conflict because the costs of not doing so are too high.

Although some people initially react to social exchange theory negatively, thinking it is wrong to use an economic model to explain relationships, social exchange theory does make sense. We don't like believing that we put more into a relationship than we receive. If we have hope of staying in the relationship, we work to increase our rewards relative to our costs. On the other hand, if the costs continue to rise without some increase in rewards, people tend to cycle out of the relationship—as they see conflict as creating too high a "cost" with respect to the "reward" they might receive; they do not communicate their concerns and eventually do not communicate at all.

styles theory A theory which suggests that people have preferred means of dealing with conflict situations and generally use those preferred means whenever possible.

Styles Theory

Styles theory contends that people have their own preferred means of dealing with conflict situations and generally use those preferred means whenever possible. This theory has intuitive and lasting appeal, as it provides a means for people to easily assess their own behavior and to see a connection between theory and action. It also claims that people tend to respond to conflict situations based on their conflict style, or their preferred mode of dealing with conflicts.

Five Styles of Conflict

M. Afzalur Rahim identified five styles of conflict based on how much concern a person has for others versus how much concern a person has for himself or herself. One can have little concern for either oneself or others, or a high concern for both of them, or some other combination in between. As illustrated in

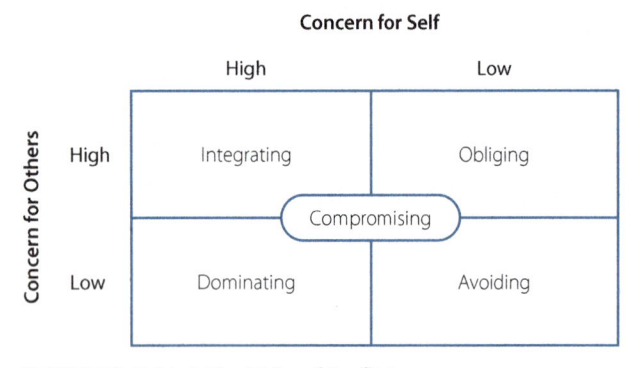

FIGURE 8.1 Rahim's Five Styles of Conflict
Rahim argued that people choose different styles of conflict depending on the degree of concern they have for others and the degree of concern they have for themselves.

Source: Conflict Styles: A Measure of Handling Interpersonal Conflict. M. Afzalur Rahim. *The Academy of Management Journal*. Vol 26, No. 2 (June 1983), pp. 368–376. Academy of Management. http://www.jstor.org/stable/255985. Accessed 30/01/2012 20:15

	Concern for Self	
	High	Low
Concern for Others High	Integrating	Obliging
	Compromising	
Concern for Others Low	Dominating	Avoiding

Theoretical Perspectives on Conflict Behavior 155

Figure 8.1, these two basic dimensions underlying the five styles are labeled as "concern for self" (or one's personal goal) and "concern for others" (or the relationship).[13] The five conflict styles differ in the way they focus on one's own or the other's outcomes:

- **Avoiding**—**Avoiding** can be physical, as in not making contact with the other person in the conflict, or communicative, as in refusing to talk about the conflict or changing the subject. People are more likely to use an avoiding style when they are unconcerned about the conflict issue and the other person. For example, if a problem arises between you and your roommate just before the end of the school year, and you don't expect to room together again, you probably will avoid dealing with the conflict because it won't be worth the energy it takes to address it.

- **Obliging**—**Obliging** means giving in to the other person's requests without asking for much in return. People often accommodate when they believe the relationship is more important than the conflict issue at hand. In the early stages of a roommate relationship, you might accommodate the wishes of your roommate because you are still getting to know each other and don't want to create an uncomfortable atmosphere in your living situation.

- **Dominating**—**Dominating** occurs when people believe that getting their way with respect to the conflict issue is more important than the relationship they have with the other person. In a roommate situation, you might stand your ground and tell your roommate you don't want to share your small living space with overnight guests. The relationship between you and your roommate is less important to you than having a living space that is occupied by people who are not paying the rent.

- **Compromising**—**Compromising** is the art of finding a middle ground between what you want and what the other person wants in the situation. In many ways, a compromise represents a loss for both people, as each person has to give up a little of what he or she wants in order to get along with each other in the present. If you share a dorm room with a roommate, for example, coordinating sleep and study times can be difficult if you are on different schedules. You may have to give up some of your desires in order to live comfortably with the other person.

- **Integrating**—People **integrating** in a conflict are committed to treating both their relationship with the other person and the issue at hand as equally important. For example, if you and a friend have a long relationship, and something important comes between you, trying to compromise, accommodate, or avoid the conflict is likely to hurt your relationship. Collaborating requires that you work to find a solution that suits both of you equally well, with neither party giving up something important to get along with one another.

Whether or not people consistently engage in a particular style or choose among them depending on the situation, it is clear that the style chosen to address a conflict greatly impacts the way in which a conflict is resolved. Some researchers argue that the conflict style chosen has more influence on the outcome of the conflict than does the issue involved in the conflict.[14]

Styles Theory and Culture
Styles theory has generated a great deal of research that examines the different uses of conflict management styles by members of different cultures, organizational members, and men and women. Individualist cultures, for example, teach their members to manage conflicts by asserting individual interests and by moving quickly toward tangible outcomes or goals and that effective conflict resolution involves dealing openly with a problem and working together on possible solutions. In other words, individualist cultures most often use dominating, compromising, and integrating styles.

---

avoiding A conflict strategy that circumvents the conflict by physical means, as in not making contact with the other person in the conflict, or communicative means, as in refusing to talk about the conflict or changing the subject.

Obliging A conflict strategy that involves giving in to the other person's requests without asking for much in return.

dominating A conflict strategy that people use when they believe that getting their way with respect to the conflict issue is more important than the relationship they have with the other person.

compromising A conflict strategy that focuses on finding a middle ground between what you want and what the other person wants in the situation.

integrating A conflict strategy that puts equal importance on the issue to be resolved and the relationship with the other person in the conflict, resulting in an outcome that satisfies both parties.

> ### TECH CHECK — Conflict Management Styles
>
> How do you typically contend with conflict? Do you tend to withdraw, attempt to accommodate the other person's desires, force your preferred outcome on your conversation partner, give up a little of what you want (and your partner does the same), or work together to find a win–win resolution that satisfies you and the other person? Complete the Conflict Management Styles assessment to discover which style you typically exhibit during conflict situations. When you are finished, ask yourself whether you are usually satisfied with the results of your conflict situations and whether you should attempt a different conflict styles approach.

By contrast, collectivist cultures teach members to emphasize cultural values and to restrain their emotions during conflict. In addition, effective conflict resolution in collectivist cultures requires the subtle negotiation of identity-related issues such as pride, honor, dignity, and shame before possible solutions can be addressed.[15] Obliging and avoiding are more likely to be used by collectivist cultures. For example, members of the Chinese culture tend to be less direct and confrontational than Americans, and Americans use direct solution-oriented styles more than members of the Taiwanese culture do. People from the Netherlands and Canada (both individualist cultures) are taught that it's appropriate to openly confront and accuse others during conflict, but people from Spain and Japan (both collectivist cultures) are not. Similarly, Arabs and Mexicans tend to use the avoiding style more than do Americans, and Americans typically use the dominating style more than do people in Arab and Mexican cultures.[16]

It is interesting to note that the avoiding conflict style is considered a "lose–lose" orientation to conflict in individualist cultures (and is described as such in this chapter). When we view the avoiding style as reflecting a low concern for self and others, however, we ignore the important role that avoiding can play in maintaining identify for self and others in collectivist cultures.[17]

Styles Theory and the Workplace

Research on conflict styles used in the workplace has found that superiors tend to use forcing or dominating strategies based on their power in conflicts with subordinates. Subordinates tend to avoid, compromise, or smooth over problems in conflict communication with their superiors.[18]

Incivility in the workplace can be both the cause of a conflict (e.g., a person perceives a conflict when he or she is treated uncivilly) or the result of a conflict (e.g., a person perceives a conflict and responds with incivility). Importantly, recent research has demonstrated a link between the use of certain conflict styles and the tendency for people to respond in a civil or uncivil manner. When a conflict is addressed using a dominating style, people are more likely to respond in an uncivil manner. On the other hand, when a conflict is addressed using a integrating style, people are more likely to respond in a civil manner.[19]

Styles Theory and Gender

Many writers contend that women and men engage in different types of conflict behavior because of socialization, in particular, because socialization teaches women to be more sensitive to and aware of existing problems in a relationship.[20] Feminine socialization, they argue, teaches women to respond to conflicts by talking about the topic under dispute and attempting to resolve it. Because masculine socialization places little emphasis on how to talk about problems, men may communicate that an issue is unimportant or simply not respond when conflict eventually erupts. Men may also exit a conflict situation if they feel they can't control it and will ultimately "suffer defeat."

However, these views are not uniformly supported by empirical and observational studies. While some studies do find these differences,[21] a review of conflict-related gender research revealed that approximately 1 percent of conflict behavior differences can be explained by gender. This means that women and men act similarly in conflict situations about 99 percent of the time.[22]

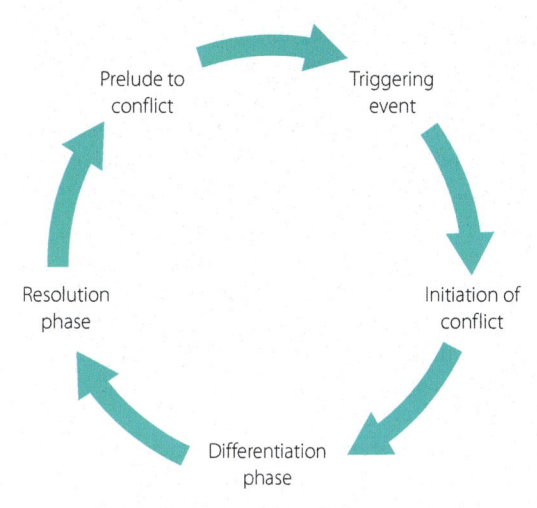

Theoretical Perspectives on Conflict Behavior   157

FIGURE 8.2 A Phase View of Conflict

Abigail and Cahn's research in conflict reveals that couples in conflict tend to follow a five-step process as they work through a conflict event.

Source: Ruth Anna Abigail and Dudley D. Cahn, *Managing Conflict Through Communication*, 4th ed. Boston: Pearson, 2011, 22.

Although women and men may exhibit some differences in conflict communication, these differences are inconsistent. The influence of the situation, the individuals involved in the conflict, and factors that relate to the relationship between the couple in conflict are more influential than gender in shaping conflict behavior. In addition, the small differences that exist in gender-related conflict behaviors diminish with age.[23] Overall, women and men are more similar in their use of conflict styles than they are different in conflict situations.

Phase Theory

You may have noticed that your conflicts are often alike in the way they are played out: You have a complaint about another person, you point it out to that person, the other responds, the two of you go back and forth for a while, and then you find a way to work things out. **Phase theory** starts with this assumption: *Conflict unfolds in fairly predictable ways over a period of time and progresses through recognizable phases of interaction.*

Phase theory is useful for a number of reasons. Although it may seem overly simplistic in its depiction of conflict, it does suggest that conflicts have a cyclic pattern: Conflicts arise, are dealt with in some way, and then die out, only to set the stage for the next conflict. In addition, phase theory emphasizes the process of conflict, viewing conflict as *dynamic, changeable, and moving toward some end*. Phase theory focuses on conflict as interaction over time, as something that unfolds as people interact with one another. Further, phase theory points out that conflicts have triggering events, actions seen by participants as initiating the conflict and bringing it to their attention. Finally, phase theory assumes that the way in which people engage in a conflict in the present will have an effect on the way they engage in conflict in the future. Figure 8.2 illustrates the five phases that a *successfully* resolved conflict moves through, with each phase affecting the next.[24]

phase theory A theory which assumes that conflict unfolds in fairly predictable ways over a period of time and progresses through recognizable stages of interaction.

prelude to conflict All the factors and events that lead up to a conflict.

Prelude to Conflict The **prelude to conflict** consists of all the existing circumstances that make conflict possible between those involved. The prelude includes:

- Who is in the conflict situation (e.g., how many are involved, their age, their sex)
- The relationship between those in the conflict (e.g., whether they are friends, coworkers, etc.) and their conflict history (i.e., how they have engaged in conflict in the past)
- Other interested parties to the conflict (i.e., who has a stake in how the conflict is resolved)
- The physical and social environment of the conflict situation

In the prelude to conflict, the potential for conflict exists because of the people involved and the other social and physical factors that define the situation. Like the first block in a line of dominoes, these variables affect the course of conflict.

triggering event A behavior that at least one person in a conflict points to as the "beginning" of the problem.

Triggering Event The **triggering event** is a behavior that at least one person in the conflict points to as the "beginning" of the problem. Those involved in the conflict don't always point to the same behavior as the trigger for the conflict. Triggering events include saying something upsetting, doing something offensive, breaking a relationship rule, and not doing something that others expect one to do. For example, you may have experienced some long-term dissatisfaction with the way your roommate leaves clothes and objects all over the house. On a particular day, you trip over a pair of shoes and narrowly avoid hurting yourself. For you, the trigger of your conflict is the roommate's messiness. You finally say something to the other person, and in doing so, you trigger a conflict about the other's perception of you as "controlling." For that person, a conflict exists in which the trigger is your attempt to influence her or his behavior. While you both are experiencing one conflict episode, the behavior that each of you sees as the trigger to it is different.

Initiation Phase The **initiation phase**, or response, occurs when the conflict is brought into the open. This happens when at least one person makes known to the other that a conflict exists, such as reacting to another's upsetting comment, pointing out the offensive nature of the other's behavior, calling attention to the breaking of a relationship rule, or reminding the other to do something he or she is not doing.

Differentiation Phase The **differentiation phase** occurs when the participants talk to one another about the conflict, presenting both sides of the story, moving back and forth, and escalating and deescalating. The differentiation phase can last anywhere from a few minutes to days or even weeks. It is in this stage that the conflict becomes quite obvious to others. This phase serves a useful purpose of allowing both parties to explain how they see the conflict and what they want to happen as a result of the conflict.

Resolution Phase The **resolution phase** occurs when those involved agree to some outcome to the conflict. A successful conflict resolution occurs when the parties have made a decision to end the disagreement, and they are both satisfied with the outcome. Sometimes, those involved may decide that the issue is settled for the time being while recognizing that it may arise again in the future.

initiation phase The stage of conflict in which at least one person makes known to the other the presence of a felt conflict.

differentiation phase The phase of conflict in which the participants work out the problem using constructive or destructive strategies and tactics, presenting both sides of the story, moving back and forth, and escalating and deescalating.

resolution phase The stage when those involved in a conflict agree to some outcome.

CAUSES OF CONFLICT

If conflict begins with some kind of triggering event, what behaviors constitute those triggers? We need to remember that triggers are a matter of perception and that those involved in the conflict won't necessarily see the same behavior as a triggering event. Keeping that in mind, we see that the triggering events are different in organizations and groups than in friendship and intimate relationships.

Conflict in Organizations and Groups

When you think about the numbers of hours each week that you spend at the workplace, it's not surprising that conflicts occur. Sources of interpersonal conflict in an organization may include:

- **Unequal power distribution**—For example, if your coworker is promoted to supervisor and now has authority over you, you may experience an increased level of conflict until the two of you get used to the new arrangement.
- **Unclear role expectations**—Conflict often arises in organizations because people aren't sure what to do, especially in situations they haven't handled previously. For example, if a nonprofit organization decides it's going to conduct a regular assessment of an outreach program, there may be some confusion about who is responsible for gathering and analyzing the data.
- **Insufficient information**—Have you ever heard a decision announced in an organization and said to yourself, "I have no idea what that person is talking about."

Causes of Conflict

Ambiguity may trigger conflict for those affected by a decision. In addition, people may not have enough information to make an important decision, and this may cause conflict for them as well.

- **Differences in beliefs, attitudes, values, and rules for behavior**—If you're a person who has a strong work ethic, and you're willing to put in overtime to get a job done, you may be very frustrated by the actions of a colleague who leaves at the end of day whether the job is finished or not.[25]

Conflict in Relationships

Failure to reap our expected rewards from a relationship can often act as a triggering event that is the prelude to a conflict situation. Researchers have identified seven types of rewards that people expect to receive in order to be satisfied in long-term romantic relationships: love, status, helping, information, gifts, money, and shared time together.[26] Some of these rewards are also applicable to family, friendship, and workplace relationships. When people perceive that they are not receiving the rewards they expect from their relationships, there is potential for conflict.

Love We expect that those who love us will behave in loving ways toward us. **Love** includes nonverbal expressions of intimacy, passion, and commitment in romantic relationships. In friendships and family, love includes nonverbal expressions of positive regard, warmth, and comfort.

When we feel unloved, we often initiate conflict to restore a sense of connection in the relationship. For example, a child or even an adult who feels neglected may behave negatively in order to get some kind of attention from another person. In a group, a person might withdraw from interaction if he or she feels as though his or her contributions are not appreciated. And most of us can identify people in organizations who have shut down emotionally because they don't get a sense of appreciation from coworkers.

Think about the people with whom you interact regularly; can you recall the last time you expressed your appreciation for them? The next time you interact with someone important to you, you may want to use the three-step method for expressing **appreciation**: describe the specific actions that you believe contribute to your well-being, describe the particular need(s) that the partner fulfills, and describe how you feel when your needs are fulfilled.

Status We give **status** to our relational partners when we use confirming communication, verbal and nonverbal expressions of high or low prestige or esteem. This may include comments such as "Wow, I really like the way you put together your paper together" or "We couldn't have completed this job without your help." Recall that disconfirming

---

love A relationship reward with nonverbal expressions of intimacy, passion, and commitment in romantic relationships and nonverbal expressions of positive regard, warmth, and comfort in friendships.

appreciation A relationship maintenance tactic which communicates that we feel grateful and that we are thankful for our relational partner and the relationship itself.

status A relationship reward that involves verbal and nonverbal expressions of high or low prestige or esteem.

Jeff Ireland, general manager of the Miami Dolphins, failed to communicate perceptions of esteem or prestige for wide receiver Dez Bryant when instead of focusing on Bryant's abilities or interests, he asked in a pre-draft interview if the player's mother had ever been a prostitute.

communication—criticism and contempt—can destroy intimate relationships. Criticism reflects a lack of esteem for the other, and contempt attacks prestige. Hearing or seeing evidence that another does not think highly of us can trigger conflict.

Helping Helping involves doing for others actions that demonstrate affection indirectly. These actions can include picking up after another person, washing a car, running an errand, or typing a paper. When one person in the relationship feels as though he or she helps the other quite a bit, and does not perceive help in return, it can trigger conflict. For example, if you frequently loan your clothes to a roommate who returns them unwashed or who doesn't offer any kind of help in return, you may become resentful. In addition, if one person in a relationship gives a great deal of service to someone outside the relationship that causes less service to the relationship, conflict will be triggered. This is often the case, for example, in second marriages, where spouses may still attend to needs of an ex-spouse while neglecting the needs of the current spouse.

> **helping** A relationship reward that involves receiving assistance from a partner on a difficult task.

Information Information may include advice, opinions, instructions, or enlightenment through self-disclosure. For example, if you go to a trusted friend and ask what you should do about some situation, you will feel let down if that person refuses to offer any advice. When you engage in self-disclosure with a friend but perceive that your friend is disclosing very little, you may feel as though you are lacking a reward in a relationship. And if one relational partner is acting withdrawn but refuses to disclose why he or she is upset, the other partner may think there is a potential conflict because of the lack of information. A lack of information creates ambiguity for us, and many people initiate conflict to decrease the uncertainty they are feeling.

> **information** A relationship reward in the form of advice, opinions, instructions, or enlightenment given through self-disclosure.

Gifts People often see spontaneous or unplanned gifts as a token of affection and a reflection of the love of the other (not because of the cost but because of the thoughtfulness). For them, a lack of gifts can trigger conflict. Moreover, it becomes a conflict that is hard to solve. If I tell you I want you to give me presents, and you do, I might think that you are doing it only because I asked. However, if I ask and you fail to give me presents, I will be even more upset.

> **gifts** A relationship reward in the form of spontaneous or planned offerings of material items.

Money The financial contribution each person makes to a relationship is made in the form of **money**, whether in a friendship or a more intimate relationship such as marriage. If your friend is always short on cash when you go to lunch, and you never seem to get the lunch money back, it can trigger a conflict. If you feel you have worked very hard in your job, but you find that you are not advancing or that others make the same amount of money for doing less work, it can lead to conflict.

> **money** A relationship reward in the form of the financial contributions each person makes to a relationship.

Time Shared time spent together, or lack of time spent together, can be a cause of conflict in a friendship, a family, or an intimate relationship. We expect those who are important to us, and to whom we have reason to believe we are important, to spend time with us before spending time with others. When we do not have enough time with others, we may initiate conflict to determine why time isn't being spent together.

> **shared time** A relationship reward in the form of time spent exclusively with loved ones where you are not distracted by work or people external to the relationship.

OPTIONS IN CONFLICT MANAGEMENT

Everyday language reflects the variety of ways in which we regard conflict: We talk about handling conflict, dealing with it, avoiding it, or resolving it. **Conflict management** is the communication behavior a person employs based on his or her analysis of a conflict situation.[27] Conflict management involves using alternative ways to deal with conflict,

> **conflict management** The behavior a person employs based on his or her analysis of a conflict situation.

A CASE STUDY IN ETHICS

Parents, Pixels, and Political Parties

Ethical communication reflects trustworthiness, responsibility, respect, fairness, caring, and concern for the community. Keep the components of ethical communication in mind as you read the following case study and answer the discussion questions.

Ted Gambordella, a Republican, is incensed that his only son, Teddy, a junior in high school, is a Democrat. Ted is so exasperated with his son's choice of political party that he refuses to fund Teddy's college education unless he becomes a Republican. Teddy accepts his father's refusal to help him through college and maintains that he won't switch parties just to get his father's money. Instead, Teddy started a website, www.onemillionreasonswhy.com, to raise college funds. He hopes that supporters will purchase pixels, the dots on computer screens, as advertising space. The pixels cost $1.00 each, and buyers are required to purchase a minimum of 100 pixels. Teddy has sold 10,200 pixels but must sell many more to pay for his college education.

Teddy says that it would be easier to persuade his dad to change his mind about Republican politics than to change his own party affiliation. Although new to politics, Teddy attends Dallas Young Democrats meetings and says that it's "cool" to talk to people who see the world as he does. Jeff Barrows, the sponsor of the Young Democrats club, said that Teddy is the type of person who will work toward a solution if one lies within reach, as evidenced by his online entrepreneurial spirit.

Teddy's mother, Debra, also a Republican, doesn't want to get involved in the father–son conflict and says that she supports both her son and her husband. Debra asserts that Teddy is rebelling by becoming a Democrat, which is better than drinking or doing drugs. Ted echoes similar sentiments and suggests that he's proud of Teddy's initiative, even though he disagrees with his son's political affiliation. Ted asserts that he was liberal in college but now listens to Rush Limbaugh and donates money to the Republican Party. Ted believes that Democrats are too extreme, but he hopes that Teddy's site promotes some intelligent political discussions. Ted also harbors the hope that Teddy will come around to a more mature way of thinking about politics, the way he did.[28]

Discussion Questions

1. What do you think is causing this conflict?
2. Do you believe that Ted Gambordella is engaging in ethical conflict management? Is Teddy Gambordella responding to his father's conflict behavior in an ethical manner?
3. Is it ethical for Debra Gambordella to stay out of the conflict?
4. Do you think this conflict is being handled in a civil manner? What might you do differently if you were involved in such a conflict?

---

including resolving it, bringing it under control for the time being, and avoiding it. Effective conflict management occurs when our communication behavior is both ethical and civil, and it produces desirable results for all the parties concerned.

Understanding conflict management in this way means that you have communicative choices to make when in a conflict situation. When conflicts arise, they arise because of the way both people act with respect to one another. We make our conflicts together; it is rare that a conflict is entirely the fault of one person in the relationship. You can choose among various options to deal with conflicts. You may avoid or confront conflicts. You may react peacefully or violently. You may treat others with respect and civility or verbally abuse others. You may simply give in or insist on having everything your way.

One way of understanding communication in conflict is to look at the focus people put on the participants in the conflict. When faced with a conflict, people generally respond in one of three ways: They can respond in other-centered, self-centered, or relationship-centered ways. These orientations encompass behaviors such as nonassertiveness,

Singer Pink spoke about a fight during which her husband owned his thoughts by saying, "Baby, when you call me names, it hurts my feelings. Please try to stop." Pink responded with, "Wow, thank you for telling me how you feel," and says she now fights fair.[29]

other-centered approach An orientation in conflict that leads us to choose strategies based on how well they will serve the needs and desires of the other person.

self-oriented approach An orientation in conflict that leads us to choose strategies based on how well they will serve our needs and desires.

relationship-oriented approach An orientation in conflict that leads us to choose strategies based on how well they will serve the relationship with the other person.

aggressiveness (both passive and overt), and assertiveness, which are often used in conflict situations.

The Other-Oriented, Nonassertive Approach

The **other-centered orientation** is "all about you." A person who takes an other-oriented approach, for example, will be nonassertive by choosing avoidance or obliging as his or her communication option. In both cases, people taking this approach choose to lose or give up on what they would like to have as an outcome to the conflict situation. When a person avoids the conflict, both sides essentially lose because no effort is made to move toward resolution. People who avoid conflicts often say things like "We don't have a conflict" or "Whatever."

When a person obliges he or she lets the other person determine the outcome of the conflict. As noted earlier, the meaning and use of obliging is culturally bound. In the United States, accommodating sometimes is a matter of not caring enough about an issue or not caring enough about one's relationship with another to engage in a conflict. People who choose an obliging approach say things like "I'll go with your decision" or "Let's just try to get along."

The Self-Oriented, Aggressive Approach

The **self-centered orientation** is "all about me." A person who takes a self-oriented approach may be covertly passive aggressive or overtly aggressive. His or her objective is to win either openly or without another's involvement. People who engage in passive aggressiveness give the appearance of being agreeable but then go ahead and do whatever they want in response to the situation. Behaviors such as backstabbing and sabotage are common with passive aggressiveness, and people who engage in this behavior may purposely "forget" things, engage in joking about the issue but then deny that it means anything, utilize strategic stupidity (e.g., "I can't ever remember how to send a fax"), or cry on demand.

Overtly aggressive behaviors include both verbal and nonverbal displays. Verbally, people may engage in competitive messages such as "You should. . . ," "It's not my fault," "Why are you so upset over nothing?" or "I suppose you want me to fix everything." Nonverbally, people may force their way on another by glaring, pointing fingers, pushing, shoving, hitting, or using weapons to achieve the outcome they desire.

The Relationship-Oriented, Assertive Approach

The **relationship-oriented approach** is "all about us." The civil way to engage in conflict is to take a relationship-oriented approach, an assertive approach that chooses integrating or compromise as a communication option. When we take this approach, we emphasize that both the relationship and the issue are important to us. When we compromise, we acknowledge that we are both going to win and lose in the situation; we try to find a place to meet in the middle. Examples of compromising messages are "What do each of us want the most?" and "Let's do it your way this time, and next time we'll do it my way." integrating is often the ideal way to resolve a conflict, although realistically it requires an investment of time and energy. In collaborating, we look for ways where both parties can win. Integrative messages include "I understand," "I did that? I'm sorry," and "How can we solve this?"

Identifying Your Options

Let's look at one example that can illustrate the various ways people can respond to a conflict. Suppose you decided to celebrate your birthday by getting together with your close friends at a nice restaurant. Your best friend doesn't show up and doesn't call. You see him or her a day later, and your friend says nothing about missing your birthday. What can you do?

You may take an other-centered, nonassertive approach and do very little. You might start avoiding your friend, or you might not bother to say hello when you see him or her, giving attention to neither the relationship nor the issue. Or you could decide that you don't want to upset your friend by bringing up the issue and simply accommodate

---

TRENDS IN TECHNOLOGY AND SOCIAL MEDIA

What's the Best Way to Do a Conflict?

When you have a conflict with someone, how do you tell that person about it? Most communication scholars will tell you that it is better to talk to the other person via face-to-face (FTF) communication than in some kind of computer-mediated communication (CMC) setting (e.g., texting, a social networking site). That way, you can look at the other person and see how he or she is responding to your issue. But is this the way you'll get the best response from the other person?

Perhaps not. One study found that men and women respond more positively to partners who use CMC to talk about conflict and less positively when partners choose to use FTF communication about a conflict.[30] It may be that CMC allows a person more thinking time to respond. Or perhaps it's because you can read a conflict message, blow up in private, and then respond.

Is there a similar effect when groups engage in conflict? For example, some studies have found that people express conflict more readily online than in FTF groups, perhaps because of the relative anonymity associated with an online group. However, the differences may be due to the amount of time groups spend communicating. Typically, people exchange many more messages in FTF groups than they do in CMC groups.

In a study comparing CMC and FTF groups, researchers provided additional time to CMC groups to convey messages so their overall message exchange was equivalent to the FTF groups. The CMC and FTF groups exhibited similar amounts of conflict regarding goals and choices during the initial and later stages of message exchange. The researchers concluded that when given enough time for equivalent message exchange, FTF and CMC groups develop in a similar manner.[31]

Additional research concerning CMC and FTF conflict has been conducted to determine whether participants in the CMC context use more positive or negative conflict management messages. Positive conflict management occurs when we express logical statements, share information and alternatives, and prevent the group from rushing to agreement too early. Negative conflict management occurs when we state preferences without a logical argument, suppress differences of opinion, and encourage early agreement without determining whether group members are really on board with the decision. Study results indicate that FTF communication produces higher levels of positive conflict management when group members are focused on problem-solving tasks that require cooperation.[32]

Discussion Questions

1 How do you react if someone brings up a conflict via CMC rather than in person? Is it easier for you to resolve the conflict, or is it harder?

2 What kind of conflict would you rather talk about FTF? Using CMC?

3 If you are a member of an online group, describe how conflict is handled in your group. Do you think it gets resolved more quickly than in FTF groups of which you are a member?

4 In your experience, do you think people use more positive conflict messages in online or FTF groups?

A study of MMORPG games found that people who tend to be aggressive are likely to manifest problematic Internet use (PIU), a syndrome comprised of behavioral, cognitive, and emotional symptoms that cause difficulties in life offline.[33]

(treating the relationship as more important than the issue) by thinking that he or she must have had a good reason for missing your party.

If you take a self-centered approach, you might become passive aggressive, or act in ways that look cooperative but really are not. These may include purposely missing a celebration your friend is holding while apologizing for your absence. Or you may become more aggressive by hostilely questioning your friend about why he or she missed your birthday. You may even resort to verbal abuse or physical aggression. This approach does little or nothing to resolve the conflict you have with your friend.

Finally, you can take an assertive approach that balances both your needs and the needs of your friend while giving equal attention to the relationship and the issue. You could ask your friend out to coffee and ask why he or she didn't come to your party, while explaining that you were hurt by his or her absence. You might find out why he or she wasn't there, and you may be able to resolve the negative feelings you have about the incident. At the very least, you'll have a better sense of the quality of the relationship you have with someone you consider to be a best friend.

From the very beginning of a conflict, we can make choices about how we will act with respect to the other. These choices are driven by our desire to be civil and ethical—or not. Taking a relationship-oriented approach to resolving a conflict is most likely to produce a win–win outcome as well as help you act in a civil and ethical manner.

IMPROVING OUR ABILITY TO COMMUNICATE IN CONFLICT SITUATIONS

One of the greatest challenges people in conflict situations face is figuring out what to say and when to say it. Conflict can overwhelm us emotionally and can short-circuit our ability to say things in a way the other person understands. Knowing a system for resolving conflict, knowing how to send effective messages, and remembering to address every conflict situation with civility can make the process a little less stressful.

The S-TLC Conflict Resolution System

S-TLC A conflict resolution process that has four steps: Stop, Think, Listen, and Communicate.

One conflict resolution system is called **S-TLC**, which stands for Stop, Think, Listen, and Communicate.[34] By following these four steps, you can often resolve interpersonal conflicts using basic communication skills:

Step 1: Stop When you realize that a conflict exists, begin by telling yourself to stop. Don't overreact to the other person. Remember that you have a choice about how to respond. Behaviors that help you stop include taking a breath and letting it out slowly, drinking a glass of water or some other beverage, and sitting down and asking the other person to sit as well.

Step 2: Think Before you act, ask yourself what is going on. Is the conflict really about you, or is someone just blowing off some steam? Remind yourself not to take the conflict too personally but to wait and hear the other person out.

Step 3: Listen Most people tend to justify themselves the moment they hear criticism rather than really listen to what the other person is saying. The ability to truly hear what the other person is saying is as important as what we say in a conflict.

Step 4: Communicate Decide what approach to the conflict you will take and then speak. You can try to avoid the conflict, accommodate the other person, compromise, compete, or collaborate. The important point is that you need to decide what you will do rather than simply react to the other person.

Civility and Effective Conflict Messages

Once you decide to communicate in a conflict situation, it's important to do so in a way that keeps the conflict from getting out of control. One way to communicate effectively in conflict situations is to be sure you understand your partner's perspective. You can do this by paraphrasing your partner's comments.

Another way to communicate effectively is to frame a conflict message in a way that helps the other person understand what you are thinking. The way you state problems in a conflict situation affects the other person's response. For instance, you should own your thoughts and feelings instead of placing blame. An interesting research finding indicates that as a conflict progresses, people tend to dig in and simply repeat what they have said previously or use a smaller vocabulary in describing their problems. Although elaborating on the problem and finding additional ways to express themselves may serve to clarify their perspective so that the other can understand, people essentially do the opposite. In addition, their communication becomes more difficult to follow because they use fewer words that overtly connect sentence parts with each other. They wind up expecting the other to fill in the blanks, and the other person may not be able to do it.[35]

Sometimes the most effective way to communicate our perspective in a conflict situation is to address it directly. There are six **confrontation steps** to move through as you manage a conflict with another person:

1. Prepare yourself: Identify your problem/needs/issues.
2. Notify your partner: Tell the person, "We need to talk."
3. Confront your partner: Talk to the other person about your problem. Be sure to use personalized communication and **I-statements.**
4. Consider your partner's point of view: Listen, empathize, and respond with understanding.
5. Resolve the problem: Make a mutually satisfying agreement.
6. Follow up on the solution: Set a time limit for reevaluation.[36]

Not all conflicts can be resolved by following just six easy steps, but it helps to know what to do and what not to do when confronting someone with whom you disagree. Also, keep in mind that when you find yourself stopped at one step, you can backtrack one or more steps to allow for a more thorough discussion before attempting to move forward.

confrontation steps Actions taken to move through a conflict: preparation, arranging a time to talk, confrontation, considering the other's point of view, resolving the problem, and setting a time to follow up.

I-statements Language we can use to personalize a conflict by owning up to our feelings rather than making them the responsibility of the other person.

AVOIDING VIOLENCE IN CONFLICTS

Every interpersonal conflict carries with it the seeds of abuse. Physical aggression is often linked to initial verbal aggression, and it starts early in life. Men who are exposed to family-of-origin violence are more likely to be verbally aggressive, domineering, and negative with their dating partners, showing potential for physical aggression.[37] Verbal aggression is also a part of a pattern of escalation that frequently leads to episodes of physical violence in dysfunctional marriage couples.[38]

Violence in interpersonal conflict has received a significant amount of attention from social scientists in communication and other disciplines.[39] **Interpersonal violence** is not difficult to recognize; it occurs when a partner imposes his or her will on another through verbal or physical intimidation. The term *violence* refers to medium to severe acts, such as physical abuse and verbal abuse.[40] Abusive behavior ranges from less intense acts, such as a verbal attack, to more intense acts, such as a physical attack. People may plan their attacks, or they may act spontaneously with violence or abuse.[41]

Both verbal and physical aggression take a toll on those who experience it. A study of health workers found that incidents of verbal aggression caused at least as much stress on the job as incidents of physical aggression.[42] Another study demonstrated that students are less likely to attend college classes taught by verbally aggressive professors.[43]

Physical aggression is experienced at all ages, beginning with young children. For example, a study of sixth-grade schoolchildren found that they see physical aggression as a natural response to certain kinds of verbal aggression, particularly those associated with attacks on physical characteristics, ethnicity, or race.[44] In addition, a recent study revealed that as many as 35 percent of high school students experience a physical altercation in a year's time.[45]

In many cases, people see violent behavior as necessary and appropriate; indeed, sometimes it is the only acceptable solution to them.[46] However, we usually have choices in conflict situations. We can choose to leave a room to calm down, focus on facts instead of demeaning a person, and describe what we feel like doing (e.g., "I'm so angry I want to punch a hole in the wall!") without actually doing it. Although conflict is inevitable, it need not, and should not, harm our relationships with others, get out of control, or turn violent.

interpersonal violence A partner's imposing his or her will on another through verbal or physical intimidation.

IMPROVING OUR ABILITY TO COME TOGETHER AFTER CONFLICT

Think about a conflict with someone close to you and how it affected your relationship. Did the relationship end after the conflict, or did the relationship continue? What do you think influenced the decision to terminate or maintain the relationship? When we manage our conflicts well, addressing them in a timely manner and working out mutually beneficial solutions, our relationships generally return to "normal," whatever that means for us. There are times, though, when things get out of hand. We say things we don't mean to say. We hear things that really hurt our feelings. Participants in such conflicts are emotionally affected by the intensity of the conflict. If in the heat of the moment you've told me you think I'm a rotten human being, I'm going to remember that for a while and wonder why you would say such a thing.

Researchers refer to these kinds of conflicts as **relational transgressions**, where those involved have broken important rules of the relationship.[47] Rules involve "shoulds" and "oughts," and they range on a continuum from explicit to implicit.[48] These might include avoiding calling each other names, lying to the other, or failing to provide help when it is requested. When relational transgressions occur, we can ask for and communicate forgiveness and engage in reconciliation behaviors if we want our relationship with the other person to continue. For some, this is the natural outcome to an emotionally charged conflict; for others, it is a difficult thing to accomplish.[49]

relational transgression A conflict where those involved have broken important rules of the relationship.

Understanding Forgiveness and Reconciliation

Researchers in the field of forgiveness agree that forgiveness and reconciliation are not the same.[50] **Forgiveness** is an intrapersonal communication process that consists of self-talk that focuses on letting go of feelings of revenge and desires to retaliate. When we forgive, we think differently about the transgression so that it does not define us or dictate how we act in the future. **Reconciliation** is an interpersonal communication process in which we talk about the conflict and take actions to restore a relationship or create a new one. We can convince ourselves that we ought to forgive and do so without actually reconciling. Sometimes, we reconcile without completely forgiving. Ideally, we try to do both.

Forgiveness and reconciliation are the opposites of unforgiveness and revenge. **Unforgiveness** is an intrapersonal communication process that consists of self-talk that focuses on feelings of revenge and desires to retaliate.[51] Our self-talk may include rehearsals of what we would like to do if we have a chance to hurt the other person in the way that we feel we have been hurt. This self-talk is fueled by our tendency to see the hurts we have received as far more harmful as the hurts we have inflicted.[52] **Revenge** is behavior we take with the goal of getting even with the other person by harming that person in the same way we believe we have been harmed.

One man's inability to forgive a mistake that destroys his family drives the storyline in *Star Trek*.

forgiveness An intrapersonal communication process that consists of self-talk that focuses on letting go of feelings of revenge and desires to retaliate.

reconciliation An interpersonal communication process in which we talk about a conflict and take actions to restore a relationship or create a new one.

unforgiveness An intrapersonal communication process that consists of self-talk that focuses on feelings of revenge and desires to retaliate.

revenge Behavior we take with the goal of getting even with the other person by harming that person in the same way we believe we have been harmed.

Communicating Forgiveness and Reconciliation

We typically communicate forgiveness by engaging in self-talk and by verbally and nonverbally communicating with our relationship partner. When you have been involved in a relational transgression and believe that you have been wronged, you have five communication strategies available to you to communicate forgiveness and reconciliation: closing, cloaking, coping, civility, and (re)creating (see Figure 8.3). These strategies are based on the combination of your willingness to forgive and the behaviors you engage in that may or may not help to reestablish your relationship with the other person.

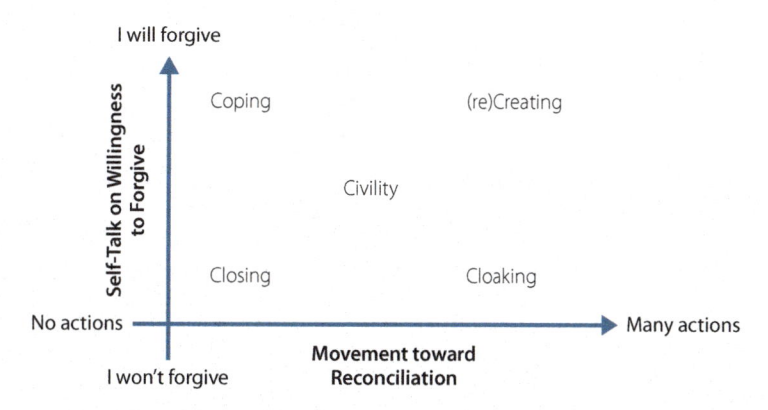

FIGURE 8.3 Strategies for Communicating Forgiveness and Reconciliation

The communication strategies we engage in after a relational transgression depend on our willingness to forgive or take actions to reestablish a relationship with the other person.

closing A forgiveness strategy that consists of telling yourself that you don't want to forgive the other person and refusing to engage in reconciliation behaviors that will restore the relationship.

Closing
Closing is a strategy that consists of telling yourself that you don't want to forgive the other person and refusing to engage in reconciliation behaviors that will restore the relationship. Unless the other person is willing to pursue you and beg for your forgiveness, it's likely that the relationship will end. In Jane Austen's *Pride and Prejudice*, for example, Elizabeth holds a grudge against Mr. Darcy because he makes disparaging comments about her and her family, but she eventually marries him because he convinces her that he's not the person she thought he was.

cloaking A forgiveness strategy that consists of telling yourself that you don't want to forgive the other person but engaging in minimal interaction with the other.

Cloaking
Cloaking occurs when you tell yourself that you don't want to forgive the other person but engage in minimal interaction with the other. In this case, you have a need to disguise your lack of forgiveness for the sake of everyone around you. Your interaction with the other is imposed on you by circumstances beyond your control. You don't have a desire to forgive the other person, but you don't have a way to completely avoid that person, either. Over time, you may be able to work around the relational transgression or even communicate about it implicitly. For example, suppose a coworker took credit for an idea of yours. If you were to make a snide remark about the idea in a meeting, and the coworker were to credit you for the idea, you might move toward forgiveness and reconciliation even though you never explicitly engage in communication about the transgression. In this case, you may be able to rebuild the relationship. On the other hand, if you don't forgive but still interact with the other person, you are likely to be resentful. It is possible that your communication with the other will be uncomfortable and limited.

coping A forgiveness strategy that consists of telling yourself that you want to forgive the other but do not want to continue a relationship with that person.

Coping
A **coping** strategy occurs when you tell yourself that you want to forgive the other but do not want to continue a relationship with that person. This is a good option when you believe that the other person is likely to hurt you again. In this case, your self-talk focuses on thinking differently about the transgression so that you don't see it as having irreparably hurt you. If you were very much in love with another person, and that person decided the relationship couldn't continue and didn't want to see you again, you might use self-talk for focus on the good things that came from the relationship rather than the hurt of it ending. Research on the processes of forgiveness has demonstrated that this kind of self-talk about the transgression is likely to result in better psychological and physical health.[53]

civility A forgiveness strategy that involves respecting the other by restraining from a focus on the transgression and communicating responsibly, using neutral language.

Civility
Civility is a middle-ground strategy. It is used when you are able create some self-talk that leads to forgiveness, and you can make some movement toward reconciliation. Recall that civility is based on the ideas of restraint, respect, and responsibility. The strategy of civility means that you respect the other by refraining from a focus on the transgression, and you communicate responsibly, using neutral language. For example, you may have a sibling who continues to say insulting things to you. In the past, you've reacted and blown up in response. However, you could try to use self-talk to convince yourself that your sibling's insulting behavior is a reflection on your sibling rather than you, and you could decide to respond civilly, regardless of your sibling's behavior.

(Re-)Creating
When our most intimate and important relationships are rocked by a relational transgression, (re-)creating is the strategy that has the best chance of restoring the relationship. We use a **(re-)creating** strategy when we engage in self-talk that helps us think differently about the transgression at the same time that we do things that communicate reconciliation to the other, such as asking the other person to spend time together, making dinner for that person, and so on. People who are able to use the (re-)creating strategy understand that it's not an all-or-nothing, handle-only-once communication strategy. To restore a relationship, people need to communicate about the transgression and agree on its meaning for their relationship.

(re-)creating A forgiveness strategy that consists of self-talk that helps us reframe the transgression at the same time that we do things that communicate reconciliation to the other.

Asking for Forgiveness with Apologies

Although there is scant research about asking for forgiveness, research findings are consistent concerning the importance of apologies in rebuilding relationships after a transgression. An **apology** is a statement that includes an admission of guilt, an expression of remorse, and a promise not to engage in damaging behavior again. The primary reason people refuse to forgive is that they have not received an apology or a sufficient explanation of the other's behavior.[54] And, since people often refuse to forgive when the other has not offered an apology or explanation, they also might believe that by withholding forgiveness, they can prevent the transgressor from hurting them again.[55] In addition, a person's perception of an apology will affect whether it is accepted. When a person is offended, being offered an apology that is too elaborate for the offense or too simple may result in a lack of forgiveness.[56] If someone bumps into you, causing you to spill your cola down a white shirt, but simply says "Sorry," you're unlikely to see that as an acceptable apology. Similarly, if a friend is very late for an important date and begins a detailed story about the events that led up to being tardy, you're likely to become suspicious and not see it as an appropriate apology.

What is the best way to apologize? Apologies first require that you understand and admit that you have behaved in a hurtful way toward another and that an apology is necessary. Once you have done that, it's important that your apology contain these aspects:[57]

- An explicit expression of remorse (e.g., "I'm sorry.")
- A *specific* statement of why you feel remorse (e.g., "I'm sorry *for putting a dent in your car*," as opposed to, "I'm sorry for *what happened*.") and being sorry for the

Many people claim that the reason they don't forgive others is because they have not received an apology.

apology A statement that includes an admission of guilt, an expression of remorse, and a promise not to engage in damaging behavior again.

ASK THE ETHICIST — What's So Bad About Revenge?

Question What's so bad about hating someone or even planning to get revenge? Don't some people deserve it?

Answer There's a Chinese proverb that says, "One who pursues revenge should dig two graves." Hating someone and plotting revenge may seem to feel good. We can become enamored with the idea of getting even and achieving a sense of justice. Unfortunately, while we may think that what *we* do balances the scales, it rarely does from the *other person's* point of view. Suppose, for example, you find out that the person you just broke up with has been gossiping about you to some of your mutual friends. He or she may even have lied about the nature of your relationship. In such situations, our first reactions are often anger and hate. After that, we often consider how we can get even with the other person. Will it accomplish anything to tell people that you hate the other person? If you take revenge, will it actually create balance, or will it prompt the other to try something even more extreme? It is likely to lead to more destructiveness.

Civility is based on respect, restraint, and responsibility; it means setting aside your own desires for the sake of getting along with others. In the preceding example, instead of seeking revenge, you make a point to talk things over with your former dating partner after you have calmed down, communicating forgiveness and engaging in reconciliation behaviors. That's the ethical—and civil—thing to do.

right thing (e.g., "I'm sorry *I called you a liar*," as opposed to, "I'm sorry *you feel that way*.")

- A comment that accepts responsibility for your actions (e.g., "It's my fault.")
- A truthful explanation for the offensive behavior without an excuse for the offense or shirking of responsibility (e.g., "I'm sorry. *I wasn't looking where I was going*," vs. "I'm sorry I bumped into you, *but I had to answer my cell phone quickly*.")
- A promise of future good behavior, which indicates that the offensive behavior is not reflective of the offender's true character, and therefore the victim can trust the behavior will not recur (e.g., "I'll be more careful in the future.")
- An offer of restitution (e.g., "I'll pay to have it cleaned.")

Understanding how to conduct a conflict properly and how to make amends when needed are important skills for your life. The more you practice these skills, the more you will find them easier to adopt and the more success you will experience in your relationships.

CHAPTER SUMMARY

Now that you have read this chapter you can:

8.1 Define *interpersonal conflict* and illustrate examples of conflict situations.

You know that an interpersonal conflict has four characteristics. The people in an interpersonal conflict are interdependent, they perceive that their goals or activities are incompatible, they believe that the incompatibility has the potential to hurt their relationship, and they feel a sense of urgency about resolving the issue.

8.2 Describe three theoretical approaches to conflict and apply them to help resolve conflict situations.

Three theoretical approaches to conflict discussed in this chapter are social exchange theory, which assumes people look at both rewards and costs in relationships; styles theory, which assumes that people gravitate to preferred means of behavior when faced with a conflict; and phase theory, which assumes that conflicts unfold in fairly predictable ways.

8.3 Explain some causes of conflict and how some conflict can be avoided.

When faced with a conflict, you can identify a triggering event, describe the initiation and differentiation phases, and explain how you resolved the conflict.

8.4 Explain why it is possible to experience conflict and yet remain civil and identify the communication options you have to manage a conflict situation.

While it may seem almost impossible for us to think of conflict and civility as being linked, when we act with respect, restraint, and responsibility and are sincere in our desire to resolve an issue, we are addressing conflict civilly.

You know that you can take one of four approaches to resolving a conflict: You can be passive and let the other person take the lead; you can be passive aggressive and pretend to cooperate while in reality failing to do so; you can be aggressive and force your desires on the other person; or you can be assertive and balance your needs with the needs of the other person.

8.5 Apply the S-TLC system of communication to your own conflict situations.

You know that when you are faced with a conflict situation, the best thing to do is stop (not react), listen to what the other person has to say, think about your options, and then communicate your point of view.

8.6 Identify some strategies to keep conflict from escalating to violence.

Verbal aggression often can lead to physical violence; both can take a toll on those involved. Instead of resorting aggression and violence, we can choose to calm down, focus on the facts, and describe our feelings.

8.7 Explain the options you have in communicating forgiveness and/or apologies to another person.

You understand that forgiveness is the process of letting go of negative feelings toward the person who hurt you, and it does not necessarily mean that you continue the relationship. You can engage in closing (not forgiving and making no movement toward reconciliation), coping (forgiving but making no movement toward reconciliation), cloaking (not forgiving but continuing to interact with the person who hurt you), civility (allowing the possibility of both forgiveness and reconciliation), or (re-)creating (being willing to do the work of both forgiving and reconciling with the person who hurt you).

You understand that an effective apology includes an admission of guilt, an expression of remorse, and a promise not to engage in the offensive behavior again.

CIVILITY SUMMARY

Overall, remember that civil communication in conflicts involve the following:

- Effective conflict management occurs when our communication behavior is both ethical and civil, and it produces desirable results for all the parties concerned.
- The civil way to engage in conflict is to take a relationship-oriented approach, an assertive approach that chooses collaboration or compromise as a communication option.
- People have such overwhelmingly negative views of conflict that when they are able to resolve a conflict civilly and productively, they tend not to call it a conflict at all.
- In the workplace, when a conflict is addressed using a dominating style, people are more likely to respond in an uncivil manner. On the other hand, when a conflict is addressed using a collaborating style, people are more likely to respond in a civil manner.
- In terms of forgiveness, the strategy of civility means that you respect the other by refraining from a focus on the transgression, and you communicate responsibly, using neutral language.

REVIEW QUESTIONS

1. What are the four major characteristics that define interpersonal conflict?
2. How is interpersonal conflict different from an argument or someone just letting off steam?
3. How are conflict management skills and civility related to one another?
4. What are two theoretical approaches to conflict? How do they differ in their explanation of conflict and conflict behavior?
5. What are the five styles of conflict?
6. What are the five stages of a conflict? Do all the people in the conflict perceive them as starting and ending in the same way?
7. What are your communication options in a conflict?
8. What does S-TLC stand for? Why is the order important?
9. What is forgiveness? How is it different from reconciliation?
10. What are the five options you have for forgiveness and reconciliation after you've been hurt by another person?
11. What are the components of an effective apology?

PART III CIVIL SMALL GROUP COMMUNICATION

9 Civil Communication in Groups

CHAPTER OBJECTIVES

After reading this chapter, you will:

9.1 Describe the relationship between group communication, civility, and ethics.

9.2 Distinguish between the different kinds of groups in which you take part.

9.3 Explain the stages of development in a group.

9.4 Analyze the climate of a group by describing its norms, communication patterns, roles, and diversity and explain the importance of cohesiveness in a group.

9.5 Describe the types of power, the qualities that make a leader, the roles of followers, and how leaders emerge in groups.

NO ONE DISPUTES that Harry Potter is an integral part of Western culture. From muggles to wizards, butterbeer to chocolate frogs, and ordinary life to one full of magic, Harry Potter's world has captivated millions. The sixth book in the series, *Harry Potter and the Half-Blood Prince*, sold 6.9 million copies in the first 24 hours, setting a new U.S. sales record.[1] But it's not just the magic and the conflict between good and evil that make Harry Potter so riveting. An essential ingredient of the Harry Potter stories is the relationships among the members of the Gryffindor house, one of the four student groupings at Hogwarts

School of Magic. As Gryffindor's leader, Harry creates vision and cohesion for the members. Theirs is not a perfect group by any means, but despite conflicts among them, Harry, Hermione, and Ron form a core in the group that is inseparable. Whether she intended it or not, J. K. Rowling created a series of stories that demonstrates the way a group can form, grow, and perform despite—or perhaps because of—the different attributes of each of the members. The series demonstrates the joy that can be found in group interaction when the skills of the group are challenged by the task at hand *and* the group members are able to meet that challenge. In fact, when groups experience **flow**, or being absorbed in a task while feeling competent to meet it, they experience more enjoyment than to individuals experiencing a sense of flow without sharing it with others.[2]

WHY IT MATTERS

As Harry and his friends found, much of our lives is spent in groups. Our families constitute the first group we encounter. As we enter school, we are grouped by grade and onto sports teams. We may align ourselves with others by participating in other activities such as debate and science clubs or musical activities such as marching band. We form friendship groups, some of which endure throughout school and others that endure for a lifetime.

Everyone functions in groups, and groups are the key to our productivity and satisfaction. Organizations depend on groups to create, produce, distribute, and sell their products or services. Within organizations, we may form relationships that carry over into our personal lives in friendship. Can you think of a friend you met at work? Groups of friends, families, and other groups such as our faith associations are often places of refuge when our lives threaten to overwhelm us. What groups have helped you to cope when you have felt challenged by your life? From humankind's earliest days, we have come together to make life easier for one another.

The saying "two heads are better than one" is generally true in situations that require problem solving or task accomplishment. Research has generally demonstrated that groups outperform individuals in both the quantity and quality of their performance,[3] although it depends on how the tasks are distributed within the team. If the group members simply combine their tasks together without integration, the group performance is no better than if the group members are working by themselves.[4] For example, if you are assigned to a group that is tasked with presenting the content of a book to your class, your group will perform better if everyone reads the entire book and works on the presentation together rather than simply taking turns describing each member's section of the book. When the output of a group that has simply divided the work without integration is compared to the output of a highly talented individual, the group performance is slightly lower than the individual's. If the group composition includes some low-performing members and the task is complex, it might be better to hand off the task to a high-performing individual.[5] In addition, when creativity is needed, groups are not the best choice. Group members attempting to solve a problem creatively will produce fewer ideas than the same number of people working individually.[6]

With the right members and combination of skills, groups are often capable of accomplishing more than individuals can accomplish by themselves. Unfortunately, we do not always experience groups in such a positive light. Can you think of an activity that involved family members, a project that involved classmates, or a task that involved coworkers during which one or more group members didn't do their fair share? Most of us have had the experience of working on a group project where a member contributed little while reaping the same reward as everyone else on the team. For some people, this experience results in **grouphate**—a negative attitude toward working in groups. However, there is a direct relationship between the amount of someone's training in group behavior and the attitude that person has toward group work. When people feel equipped to deal with group behavior, they develop

flow Being absorbed in a task while feeling competent to meet it.

grouphate A negative attitude toward working in groups.

positive attitudes toward working in groups.[7] Because you will spend much of your life in groups, understanding the way in which groups operate and the most effective ways to communicate within them is a skill that will serve you well.

This chapter examines the nature of groups and explores the ways they develop. It explores group climate through understanding norms, roles, and the ways people respond to one another. You'll learn about leadership and the way it operates in groups. In addition, this chapter focuses on strategies you can employ to make your group experiences more satisfying.

GROUP COMMUNICATION AND CIVILITY

Have you ever been part of a group that you were required to join? Perhaps it was a group project in school. It might have been roommates that were assigned to you when you entered college. Or it could be people that you had to work with in your job. There is often a difference in our ability to be civil when our membership is voluntary and when it is involuntary. When the groups we participate in are voluntary, it is relatively easy to remain civil with the other group members. We join the group for the purpose of enjoying the company of the various group members, and we know we can leave at any time. However, when we join groups involuntarily, issues of civility are more likely to arise.

Many of us are members of involuntary groups in which we hold long-term membership; families and jobs are two such involuntary groups. While our previous experience with others may improve our group skills, it may also have the opposite effect: We may have become so familiar with the other members that we can anticipate what they will say about certain topics. If you're in such a group and hear a particular idea come up, you might think, "I really hope Mary (or John) doesn't go off on that again." You may even begin to shut down and stop listening before the conversation even starts. Aesop, a writer who lived around 600 B.C.E., wrote various tales meant to teach different truths. One of his proverbs was "Familiarity breeds contempt." When we know people well enough to know their faults, and when we must interact with them frequently but have little or no relationship beyond a particular setting, we may fail to offer them civil respect.

Listening to others with respect, showing restraint when we feel as though we are hearing a particular idea for the umpteenth time, and communicating responsibly with others are vital skills in effective group communication. The successful development of groups and teams depends on members being able to communicate with one another civilly and effectively.[8] You need to allow others to lead the discussion when they have more knowledge than you do. You need to realize that you don't have all the answers and that you don't *have* to have all the answers, but you take time to tell your fellow group members that you value their skills, talents, and expertise. When we are able to do these things, groups develop positively and are productive.

TRENDS IN TECHNOLOGY AND SOCIAL MEDIA

Flaming and Group Communication

Do you think Frank's comment in the following exchange is a compliment or a put-down?

> Brent: I think the in-service went really well.
> Frank: The in-service ALWAYS goes well.
> Brent: What's THAT supposed to mean?!?!

Without hearing his tone of voice and seeing his facial expression, it's difficult to interpret Frank's comment, but Brent's reply suggests that he perceives Frank's message to be a hostile attack, or "flame."[9]

Flaming, common in computer-mediated communication (CMC), is characterized by intense and/or negative language, swearing, or communication that is intended and perceived as hostile. One explanation of flaming is that it results from the reduced availability of nonverbal cues available online and a "computer subculture" (e.g., hackers and computer enthusiasts) that rejects established values and norms of civility.

Reduced cues don't seem to be the only reason for flaming. The reduced cues explanation cannot account for flaming because it is not found universally across every newsgroup, bulletin board, and network. Group norms and social contexts contribute to levels of flaming. In other words, flaming occurs if it is considered to be an expected social norm of the group in which it happens.

One study of four university-related Usenet social newsgroups found that behavioral norms, cultural identification, and views about religion and national conflicts influenced the type and amount of flaming. Messages among the four newsgroups illustrated a significant difference in levels of flaming, and more than 76 percent of the flames occurred when the interaction concerned political, religious, or cultural topics. This research suggests that the history of interaction among group members and the cultural, religious, and political backgrounds of computer users affect the level of flaming in newsgroups.

Flaming is also related to computer users' individual motives and gender. People flame to satisfy needs or to achieve personal goals. Specifically, users flame to pass time, to escape, and to have control and dominance over others. High levels of assertiveness and sensation seeking predict flaming, and males engage in flaming more than females.[10]

Let's return to the example of Brent and Frank. Brent may know he's been flamed because he is familiar with the norms and social context of his group and with Frank's motives and personality. This example illustrates that "computer-mediated communication is looking more and more like any other medium of communication where the tone and emotional content is affected by social and interaction context, rather than the medium itself."[11]

Discussion Questions

1. How do you respond to someone you think is flaming you?
2. What have you noticed about the reactions others have to a flaming message in your online groups?
3. What topics are most likely to create a desire in you to flame another person?

WHAT CHARACTERIZES GROUPS?

flaming Intense and/or negative language, swearing, and communication that is intended and perceived as hostile.

group A human communication system composed of three or more individuals, interacting for the achievement of some common goal(s), who influence and are influenced by each other.

A **group** is composed of three or more people who are able to influence one another through interaction. A group is more than people gathered in the same place; to be a group, members must have a common goal and work toward that goal as a unit.[12] In addition, members have a sense of identity with the group and understand the expectations of membership. Group members expect to have important personal needs (e.g., social, financial) met by their membership in the group. Finally, a group must consist of more than two people because of the different dynamics that occur when three people are together as opposed to two.[13]

There are many different kinds of groups, including family, support (e.g., Shopaholics Anonymous), project or task, learning (e.g., a study group), activity (e.g., Little League), neighborhood (e.g., a homeowner's association), service (e.g., Odd Fellows, music or arts), and many more. Given the increasingly digital nature of our world, we may belong to several virtual groups, such as MMORPGs (massively multiplayer online role-playing games; a genre of role-play video games) or virtual communities, where we interact with others we have never met.

After examining how groups and teams differ, we'll move on to group goals and then look at three types of groups: task-oriented, relationship-oriented, and virtual groups.

Distinguishing Groups from Teams

How are groups different from teams? When comparing the concepts of groups and teams outside an organizational context, people generally see groups as more loosely organized and more oriented toward personal satisfaction, while teams are more tightly organized and oriented toward task accomplishment.[14]

In the context of an organization, though, the distinction between groups and teams becomes more pronounced. The most important differences between groups and teams have to do with the composition of the group or team, the way members work on tasks, and the accountability each member has in terms of the group's or team's goal.[15] Leaders who create teams are generally mindful of the skills each member brings to the team. There is a deliberate attempt to balance the strengths and weaknesses of the members so that tasks can be accomplished with efficiency and speed. Ideally, a team is created to encompass more skills than any one person alone could have. In many groups, on the other hand, members are interchangeable. While a member who leaves will be missed, that member is more easily replaced than a team member would be.

The way in which a task is accomplished also distinguishes between groups and teams. Generally, group tasks are performed alongside one another but do not necessarily require cooperation or input from other members for their completion. Group members may share information, but such sharing is informal. You might think of the tasks a group accomplishes as being comparable to an assembly line. Each person does a job that contributes to the whole, but there is not a great need to collaborate to get things done. A team, on the other hand, is a group of people sharing information to create something together that accomplishes the goal of the team. Members may exchange tasks or help one another out in different areas.

Personal satisfaction and a sense of belonging are important factors in sustaining group membership.

Teams work on a common task and are accountable as a whole for its accomplishment.

In addition to differences in membership and task structure, team and group members are accountable for their work in different ways. While group members may be individually accountable for accomplishing tasks assigned to them, team members are accountable together. Consider how a sports team is judged: One member may have amazing skills, but if the team loses a game, those skills are overshadowed by the team's defeat. In a work team, a person who excels at the expense of others or fails to share information because of a desire to stand out creates a liability. On the other hand, in a work group, a person who performs consistently better than his or her peers might have more opportunities for advancement.

In a way, all teams are groups and share the important characteristics of shared goals, identification, expectations for behavior, and so on with groups. But not all groups are teams. Since teams start off as groups, we will simply use the term *group* in the remainder of this chapter and the next as we discuss the different dynamics of group behavior and problem solving.

Identifying the Goal of a Group

As discussed earlier, a distinguishing factor of a group is that the members perceive that they have a goal in common with the other members and that they work with the other members to achieve that goal. How do we identify a group's goal?

A **goal** is an outcome that a person or group wants to achieve. It can be tangible, such as creating a new project management system, or intangible, such as providing companionship for the members of the group. Groups that we are assigned to, such as school project groups or work groups, often have the goal provided for them. If your employer tells you and three other people to investigate a problem in the organization, your goal is to find a solution to the problem. That's a tangible goal. On the other hand, if several people in your living area meet each Friday to study and then spend some time relaxing afterward, it is harder to identify your group's goal. Is it getting better grades? Sharing time together? Intangible group goals are harder to identify, but that does not mean they don't exist. When goals are intangible, people are likely to point to the identity of the group (e.g., the Friday Night Club) as the goal that the group is working to achieve.

goal An outcome that a person or group wants to achieve.

Short-Term, Task-Oriented Groups

Short-term, task-oriented groups come together for a limited period to accomplish a particular tangible goal and then disband when the goal has been achieved. Class project groups, ad hoc task force groups, and study groups are among the groups that comprise this type.

In your college career, you have undoubtedly completed classroom projects that required group work. When you participate in a short-term group, completing the task is your primary focus. Often, that focus allows you to avoid "process work" such as creating working habits and defining expectations of other members. The external time constraint associated with the school calendar, the instructor's expectations, and the defined scope of the assignment also help group members avoid having to engage in process discussions. While you may finish a group project and end your participation with others, it is possible that you will find yourself with some of the group members in a future class on a future group assignment.

short-term, task-oriented group A group that forms for a limited period to accomplish a particular goal and then disbands when the goal has been achieved.

Long-Term, Relationship-Oriented Groups

long-term groups Groups that members enter and remain with for indefinite time periods.

Long-term groups, as the name implies, are composed of members who join and remain with the groups for indefinite periods. Typically, their existence is not task dependent but is relationship dependent. People join such groups for a variety of reasons. Some join to fulfill a need for community or to avoid loneliness. Others join groups because they are attracted to the members of the group that they perceive to be similar to and/or physically attractive. People also join groups because they are attracted to the group's activities, goals, or identity. Families, while considered long-term groups, typically have less flexibility in whether their members remain.

An example of a long-term, relationship-oriented group might be one that focuses on a hobby. People join such groups because they like to meet with others to talk about their hobbies. They also join to get new ideas about engaging in their hobbies. For example, members of a quilt guild benefit by seeing the work that others are doing, exchanging supplies for different kinds of projects, and arranging classes for members to take together.

virtual groups Groups composed of members who do not meet face-to-face but who interact with each other via the Internet or telephone conferences.

Virtual Groups

Virtual groups are composed of members who do not meet face-to-face but who interact with each other via the Internet or telephone conferences. A virtual group may be a work group that is geographically dispersed but whose members are dependent on one another to accomplish a task. A virtual group also may be composed of people who come together to discuss topics, share ideas, or play a game, as in newsgroups, Yahoo hobby groups, and MMORPGs. Virtual groups may function as communities where people feel a connection to one another through shared stories and experiences.[16]

Are you a member of an online group? A face-to-face or location-based group? What differences do you see between them? One obvious difference is that a face-to-face group depends on people being able to interact with each other personally; they depend on members being close to the location of the group. If you join a community sports team, for example, you are part of a location-based community. You can't play softball by yourself.

Online communities are based on common interests but aren't limited by time and distance. For example, Yahoo has groups for almost any interest you can name. Facebook has a wide variety of groups, including a contingent that would like to have a "dislike" option in addition to the "like" button in response to Wall posts.

Whether a group is location based or online, there are expectations for how members should behave. Location-based groups typically don't have overly explicit rules for behavior. As a new member of a community softball team, for example, you will likely be told about practice times, gear you need to provide, uniforms, and other general information. You may not immediately realize that your lack of participation in the after-game pizza party is bothering others unless someone mentions it to you. In that respect, expectations in location-based groups tend to be ambiguous; frequently, you discover them only if you fail to meet them.

Online groups, on the other hand, have very specific rules for interaction and conditions for membership. You are expected to read and agree to them before you are allowed to participate in the group. For example, online communities have rules about the way in which people should talk to one another through their postings. If a person breaks a rule about posting behavior, the moderator of the group will quickly notify that person. A

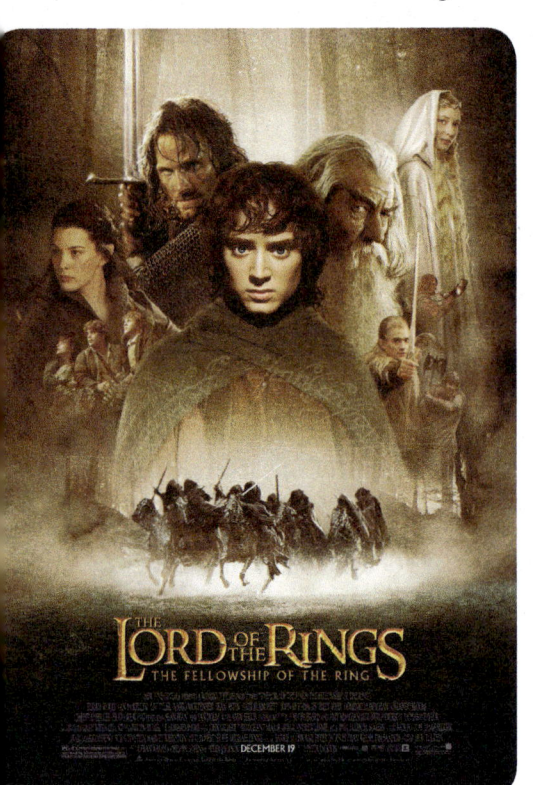

When eight companions join Frodo in his quest to return the One Ring to Mount Doom to destroy it, they find themselves not only working toward the quest but also working through different expectations of the way in which the quest should be completed.

Hobbies often form the basis for long-term, relationship-oriented groups.

person who persists in breaking the rules will be asked to leave the group.[17]

Group Work and Productivity

The use of short-term groups has increasingly become the norm in the workplace. Two factors help to gauge the usefulness of groups as they relate to productivity: the group size and the behaviors of group members. Research indicates that the larger the group, the less effective it will be. A study of more than 300 work groups found that the most effective groups, in terms of managing expectations of one another and productivity, had three or four members. Once groups reach seven or more members, group development and productivity decrease.[18]

Group work is also a factor in productivity. Typically, researchers have assumed that groups that work together cohesively are more productive than groups that do not. But the relationship is not as clear-cut as previously thought. A recent study found that two types of behaviors affect group performance. One behavior is performance monitoring, or observing how another group member is producing. The second is backing up behavior, in which group members help identify the mistake of another member and take steps both to correct the mistake and train the member not to repeat it. Backing up behavior is especially important when groups are in their early stages because members are learning other skills and training one another to do a task. Backing up behavior is less important as a group develops skills. The study suggests that group training in organizations will do little to improve performance unless it focuses on helping people decide *when* to engage in group work behaviors rather than *whether* to engage in them.[19]

HOW GROUPS DEVELOP

At some time in your life, you may have played on a community sports team, such as Little League, or belonged to a group such as a scouting troop or a band. When groups come together, they generally experience clearly identifiable phases of development. Bruce Tuckman, in his classic work on small group formation, has identified five phases that he called *forming, storming, norming, performing, and terminating* and that subsequent research has confirmed.[20] You have probably experienced these phases in the various groups you have belonged to. Think about these phases as they relate to one of the groups to which you belong. Do the phases accurately describe the development of your group? Can you recall a specific group meeting or situation that illustrates movement from one phase to the next?

Forming

forming The first phase of group development in which members come together to create a group.

In the **forming** phase, members come together to create a group. The unfamiliarity with who is in the group and what the various members bring to it creates some conflicts related to expectations. If you feel you have a particular talent to contribute to a group, and you find that someone else is planning to contribute from that same area, you might feel uneasy about your place in the group. As members become acquainted, test personal boundaries, and try to determine what their roles in the group will be, the group's structure is very tentative.

While group formation isn't quite as risky as skydiving, people are often intimidated by the process of entering a group and becoming a part of it.

Recent research has examined the way newcomers enter virtual groups. Newcomers to online groups have a particular challenge in that online groups tend to be decentralized and anonymously text based.[21] That is, online groups rarely have a set leader, and most interaction is based on written exchange rather than spoken communication. An examination of more than 100 online groups revealed that the most effective way for members to enter online groups is by asking for information and by demonstrating that they have already participated in the group through the reading of archived posts or perusal of the online site. Less effective is to claim to identify with other group members (as one might do in a face-to-face group), most likely because it is harder to establish identification with others in a text-based situation. In other words, you will have a better chance of joining an online group, such as a support group for new parents, when you prove that you're familiar with the group, its website, and the topics discussed rather than claiming that you're similar to most of the current members.

When the forming stage is accomplished successfully, members become more attracted to the group and develop a sense of loyalty to it; they then also have a good idea of how the group is structured.[22]

Storming

storming The second phase of group development, which occurs as people begin to feel some identification with the group but don't really feel a sense of unity around its purpose.

The next phase, **storming**, occurs as people begin to feel some identification with the group but don't feel a sense of unity around the group's purpose. In many ways, group members are struggling with the idea of belonging and the desire to remain independent. In the storming phase, group members may use conflict quite purposefully to help create a sense of their role in the group and to influence how the group will function. In a new group, the forming stage encompasses information gathering about other members. In the storming phase, you might challenge another member's ability to assume leadership if you expected to be the leader, or argue with that person about the best way to lead the group. Successful management of this stage will increase trust among group members and create a greater sense of their purpose.

Norming

norming The third phase of group development, in which the group begins to fall into regular patterns of behavior that allow members to plan effectively for the work they will do.

norm An expectation for behavior that all members of a group should observe.

role A collection of behaviors that a particular person is expected to have in a group.

As a group works through the conflicts of the storming phase and begins to fall into routines, it reaches the **norming** phase. Also called the "trust and structure stage," this phase allows group members to plan effectively for the work they will do. In order to be effective and to survive, long-term groups must come to agreement about the way they will relate to one another. These agreements are known as **norms**, or expectations of all members in the groups with respect to behavior, and **roles**, which are a collection of behaviors that a particular person is expected to have in a group. Norms for a student government group might include attending all meetings, being prepared, not criticizing ideas until they are fully presented, being supportive of the group, and so on. Roles would include various member tasks, such as taking minutes, setting the agenda, representing the group to your school's administration, and so on.

Spurred on by the need to quickly accomplish a specific task or activity, the team members begin to accept both their own individual roles as well as the responsibilities of fellow participants. A sense of unity emerges as members begin to understand what is expected of them and perform satisfactorily within those expectations. As unity emerges, an outsider is more able to observe who fills what role and what the norms of the group are. Some individuals may assert themselves more regularly and be recognized as leaders. Unlike the conflict of the storming phase, in the norming phase, conflict is about solidifying a member's position in the group. That is, where conflict was previously focused on "What is my role?" conflict now is focused on "This is the way I see my role and will act in it." When groups begin to settle into the norming stage, they waste less time engaging in conflict over what they should do and spend more time focusing on the most effective way to accomplish the tasks they have decided on.

Performing

Finally, the development process culminates in the members' awareness that they are focusing on the real work that they have come together to accomplish—the presenting problem. In this **performing** phase, conflict focuses individuals on accomplishing team goals and reaching consensus. At this point, people know what they need to do and how they need to do it. If they run into difficulties, they have a clear sense of where to go to solve the problem.[23]

performing The fourth phase of group development, which occurs when members are aware that they are focusing on the presenting problem.

Terminating

The final phase of group development is **termination**. The group itself may end, the particular task may end, or some members may depart or be replaced by newcomers to the group. In the termination stage, members may be anxious about the group ending but typically express appreciation for the leader of the group.

Although the empirical research on Tuckman's model has not been extensive, it supports the model's argument that groups come together, test their boundaries, create expectations, perform to meet those expectations, and then come to an end. Think about these phases as they relate to one of the groups to which you belong. Do the phases accurately describe the development of your group? Can you recall a specific group meeting or situation that illustrated movement from one phase to the next? How can knowledge of these phrases help make your communication more effective and appropriate the next time you become a member of a new group or in the group to which you currently belong?

termination The final phase of group development, in which the group itself may end, the particular task may end, or some members may depart or be replaced by newcomers to the group.

CREATING GROUP CLIMATE

Think about the last time you attended a group for the first time. Did the people seem friendly or unfriendly? Did you feel welcome or unwelcome? Did you want to return? The feelings you experienced when you first came to the group were a reflection of the group's climate. The **climate** of a group—that is, the psychological atmosphere that surrounds its members—has a big impact on whether people will remember it as a beneficial or negative experience. Four factors that affect group climate are the norms that develop in the group, the way in which people speak to one another, the roles people assume in groups, and the cohesiveness that develops in a group. Let's look at each of these factors.

climate The psychological atmosphere of a group.

Group Norms

As you read earlier, norms are the rules or standard of expectations for all members in a groups with respect to behavior. Some group norms are assumed but never discussed, such as arriving on time, ensuring that one's work is ready when there is a

A CASE STUDY IN ETHICS

The Politics of Exclusion

Ethical communication reflects trustworthiness, responsibility, respect, fairness, caring, and concern for the community. Keep the components of ethical communication in mind as you read the following case study and answer the discussion questions.

In a recent case argued before the U.S. Supreme Court (*Christian Legal Society v. Martinez*), a religious group tried to establish its right to be recognized as a legitimate campus group while excluding people who do not endorse its core values, including the condemnation of homosexuality. The Christian Legal Society (CLS) is a national group founded in 1961, with chapters in a number of universities. Meetings are devoted to Bible study and discussion of ways in which chapter members can apply their faith as practicing attorneys.

A CLS chapter at the University of California's Hastings Law School started as an open group but moved to membership requirements in 2004. At that time, it started requiring members to sign a statement of faith and would not allow anyone with a sexually immoral lifestyle (which the group defined as engaging in homosexual behavior) into the chapter. The university withdrew official recognition for the chapter (which largely impacts funding), citing its policy that membership in endorsed campus groups could not be based on religious belief or sexual orientation. It did, however, allow the group to continue to meet on campus.

The Supreme Court affirmed the right of the university to deny recognition to a campus group that has exclusionary policies. The Supreme Court "upheld the university's open-access policy and said other law schools have similar policies" and ruled that "the university need not provide a religious-based exception to its policy that groups must open membership to all students who want to join."[24]

Discussion Questions

1. Do you think college and university clubs have a right to limit their membership? To what extent?
2. Do you think the university has a right to refuse to recognize a club whose values are different from the university's? Which values should be recognized?
3. Does it matter that the university withdrew its recognition for the CLS when it still allowed the club to meet on campus?

---

deadline, or participating in social events planned by the group that may be unrelated to the group's purpose. Norms of this sort become apparent when a group member violates them. Other group norms may be purposely generated, as in a business task group that takes time to deliberately establish expectations before undertaking the task before it.

Norms affect group climate not only because of the expectations they create (which may or may not be positive) but also in the way group members respond or fail to respond to behavior that is deviant from the norms that have been established. For example, a work group may expect that its members will contribute money for gifts to members experiencing significant events such as marriage, childbirth, or college graduation. Failing to do so might result in a chillier climate for the person who skips the opportunity to contribute, but that person might not be told directly about his or her violation of the norm. Norms that are not explicitly identified and not discussed when they are broken can be problematic for group members. On the other hand, if group members explicitly create a norm that expects civil communication among group members but creates no mechanism to correct uncivil behavior, the norm won't be in place very long.

But why do people follow the norms established by the group? They do so because either they accept the norms as legitimate expectations or they fear that not following the norm will result in a **sanction**, or punishment for failing to follow the group norm. Not

sanction A punishment for failing to follow a group norm.

Creating Group Climate

everyone in a group will be subject to the same sanction, though. Research indicates that higher-status members can get away with more norm violations without sanctions than can lower-status members. This may be due to group members viewing a violation differently when a high-status member commits it versus a lower-status member committing the violation. It also may be because lower-status members are intimidated by higher-status members, so they don't enforce a sanction even when they see a behavior as deviant from the norm.[25]

For example, if you are part of a work group in which one member performs at a higher level than anyone else, that person will probably not be viewed as negatively if he or she arrives late to a meeting as someone who does not perform at such a high level. However, when higher-status members *are* sanctioned, they typically receive greater punishments for a norm violation than do those of lower status.[26] Group members might not say anything to a high-performing member if that member is late one or two times, but if that member fails to produce his or her share of the work, the norm violation will be seen as even more negative than if one of the other group members failed to produce work in a timely manner.

When norms are clear and the sanctions for violating them are fairly applied, they affect group climate in a positive way. Group members experience a lower level of uncertainty and are able to focus on the task at hand. However, when norms are unclear and/or the sanctions for breaking them are unevenly applied, norms have the potential to negatively affect group climate.

When groups have established norms and clarified expectations for performance, they generally find it enjoyable to work together.

Responding to One Another

As we have made a point of saying throughout this textbook, the way we speak to one another can build or destroy relationships. In previous chapters, you learned about confirming messages that help build relationships and communicate worth to the other person. These messages are most helpful in building a positive group climate.

In group discussions, however, people are particularly susceptible to a lack of restraint and to creating harmful responses such as those that include shift response, competitive interrupting, and ambushing.[27] These behaviors are examples of uncivil communication that illustrate disrespect for other group members through the refusal to listen and validate the comments of other group members.

shift response A situation that occurs when a person turns a conversation to himself or herself rather than follow the expected course of the conversation.

talkover A situation that occurs when more than one person speaks at the same time in a group.

Shift Response A **shift response** occurs when a person turns the conversation to himself or herself rather than follow the expected course of the conversation. It is a competitive move that people use when they want the attention for themselves. A shift response is different from a confirming message. Whereas a confirming message is meant to indicate that you are listening and want to hear what the other person has to say, a shift response essentially cuts off the other's communication. Shift responses are especially prevalent in groups where **talkovers** (more than one person speaking at the same time) happen as a matter of course as people help others express something. Talkovers can be helpful when one person starts an idea and gets stuck, and another picks up the thread of the idea before the first person has actually finished in order to encourage the first person to complete his or her thought. The difference, though, is that a shift response shuts down a person rather than allow her or him to finish an idea. Consider the following examples:

Shift Response

Cameron: I hate it when Professor Small dumps extra reading on us at the last minute. It really makes me disorganized.

Whitney: I hate the pop quizzes much more.

Confirming Response

Cameron: I hate it when Professor Small dumps extra reading on us at the last minute. It really makes me disorganized.

Whitney: It sounds like you're frustrated. How do you plan to get the reading done?

Competitive Interrupting Another kind of uncivil communication behavior that can negatively affect group climate is **competitive interrupting**. Competitive interrupting is similar to a shift response but differs because people using a shift response generally follow the rule that only one person should talk at a time. When a person engages in competitive interrupting, he or she isn't waiting for the other person to finish. Competitive interrupters start in with their own idea before the speaker has finished his or her idea.[28] Sometimes interruptions are okay. For example, we use them to acknowledge what the other person is saying ("Uh-huh") or to express support ("Right!"). On the other hand, people using competitive interruption shift the attention to themselves. Competitive interrupters don't have the patience or desire to hear what other people say. They simply want to be heard.

competitive interrupting A kind of uncivil communication in which a listener doesn't allow others to finish, but starts in on his or her own idea before the speaker has finished his or her idea.

Ambushing A final communication behavior that can affect group communication climate is **ambushing**, or waiting to pounce the moment someone stops speaking. If you are busy thinking about what you are going to say, especially to prove the other person wrong, you are unlikely to be listening to the idea he or she is presenting. Ambushing is particularly unhelpful in task groups that are trying to generate ideas for problem solving.

ambushing Waiting to pounce the moment someone stops speaking.

Roles Members Play

A third factor that can affect the climate of a group's communication involves the various roles people play in the group. As we defined it previously, a *role* is a collection of behaviors that a particular person is expected to play in a group. Roles are created when people interact with one another, and they can be formal or informal:

formal role A role that arises out of a person's assigned position in a group.

- A **formal role** arises out of a person's assigned position in a group. In a group, for example, there may be an assigned leader or convener for the group. In addition, people have different positional roles such as secretary, treasurer, historian, and so on. In addition to indicating a person's place in the group, formal roles have particular expectations associated with them and may even have documented job descriptions.

informal roles Roles that arise from the way in which people actually interact with one another.

- **Informal roles** in groups arise from the way people actually interact with one another. In any group, those working together come to know which member can find an obscure reference, who can finesse the arrangements for a social event, and who can break the tension when people become agitated. Such talents are not necessarily attached to formal roles.

Table 9.1 describes many of the types of formal and informal roles that people play in groups.
As people act informally in groups and organizations, they may choose one or more of the three types of informal roles:

task roles Informal group roles that include giving and receiving information, helping information flow, and clarifying ideas.

maintenance roles Informal group roles that include supporting and encouraging others, helping relieve tensions in the group, and monitoring the feelings of the group.

disruptive roles Informal roles in groups that include such things as demanding the center of attention, clowning around, and being cynical about all the tasks the group takes on.

- **Task roles** include giving and receiving information, helping information flow, clarifying ideas, and keeping track of what the group has done.
- **Maintenance roles** include supporting and encouraging others, helping relieve tensions in the group, and monitoring the feelings of the group. The communication associated with maintenance roles is civil, as it is typically based on respect, restraint, and responsibility. For example, comments used to maintain the group may include "That's a great idea. Let's be sure we spend enough time discussing it" or "Let's be sure to let each person finish his or her thought before moving on to the next person."
- **Disruptive roles** are often the source of conflicts in groups and organizations, and they include such things as demanding the center of attention, clowning around, and being cynical about all the tasks the group takes on.

People may experience role conflict when they don't feel as though the role they have been assigned fits them or when they aren't treated in the way they believe the role deserves. Role conflicts can divert a group from its purpose, so outlining the expectations people have of one another is an important part of the group process.

Cohesiveness: Balancing Fit and Diversity

The final factor that affects group climate is the level of cohesiveness members feel that the group has. **Cohesiveness** can be defined as a set of factors that act to keep group members together and committed to the group. Typically, a cohesive group has a stable membership (i.e., few people are added to or leave the group). Smaller groups have higher cohesiveness than larger groups. And groups whose members are satisfied tend to be more cohesive than groups whose members are not.

cohesiveness A set of factors that act to keep group members together and committed to the group.

One of the difficulties in creating cohesiveness is that group members often try to sidestep the real work of creating it by focusing on member "fit," or similarity, within the group. Often, groups believe that if they ensure the fit of the members, cohesiveness will naturally occur because the members will be able to assume that they are all approaching the problem the same way. Cohesiveness arises out of honest communication; fit often focuses on superficial characteristics that may or may not impact the group. Some retail establishments, for example, have a particular style they look for in potential employees, sometimes at the cost of discovering whether a potential employee has the appropriate work ethic for the company. Similarly, some groups focus on things that may have nothing to do with the group's purpose, expecting that if people share characteristics such as socioeconomic background, ethnicity, gender, or education, the group will get along much better than if people are different from one another.

Diversity in groups includes factors beyond ethnic and gender diversity and includes things such as differences in the way people process information and personality differences. When groups must add members, they may feel a need to maintain or increase their cohesiveness, or they may feel a need to create a greater diversity in their membership. The push to maintain cohesiveness is known as **reinforcing fit**, and the push toward diversity is known as **extending fit**.[29] It's very difficult to achieve both simultaneously. There can be both advantages and disadvantages on both sides.

reinforcing fit The result of groups choosing members that will maximize the cohesiveness of the group.

extending fit The result of a group emphasizing diversity over cohesiveness in group membership.

Cohesive groups are more productive and generally more fulfilling for the people who fit with the group's identity. But often, group members think they are seeking out others who fit the group identity and goals when really they are simply looking for people who are just like them. The advantage of creating diversity in a group is that the group will be more creative. At the same time, the group may suffer from internal conflict between people who just don't see things eye-to-eye.[30]

Table 9.1 Roles People Play in Groups

At times the informal roles that group members play may have more influence on the workings of the group than do the formally assigned roles.

Formal Roles

Role	Definition
Chair	• Sometimes responsible for the selection of group members • Generally influences the selection of members into formal roles • Sets the agenda for the group • Convenes the group
Secretary-recorder	• Serves a group memory function • Takes minutes of meetings • Keeps group's records and history
Parliamentarian	The person who insures that members of the group follow the rules they have adopted to guide discussion, most frequently Robert's Rules of Order.
Treasurer	• May collect dues when the group requires them • Helps create and maintain a budget for the group • Disperses funds from the group as needed

Informal Roles

Task Roles	Definition
Initiator-contributor	• Offers lots of ideas and suggestions • Proposes solutions and new directions
Information seeker	• Requests clarification • Solicits evidence • Asks for suggestions and ideas from others
Opinion seeker	• Requests viewpoints from others • Looks for agreement and disagreement
Information giver	• Acts as a resource person for group • Provides relevant and significant information based on research, expertise, or personal experience
Clarifier-elaborator	• Draws together ideas of others • Shows relationships between facts and ideas • Promotes teamwork and coordination
Orienter	• Keeps group on track • Guides discussion • Reminds group of goal • Regulates group activities
Evaluator-critic	• Challenges the prevailing point of view for the sake of argument to test and critically evaluate the strength of ideas, solutions, or decisions
Energizer	• Prods the group to action • Stimulates group discussion
Procedural technician	• Distributes materials • Sets up meeting space • Performs other routine tasks that allow the group to function

Maintenance Roles	Definition
Supporter-encourager	• Bolsters the spirits and goodwill of the group • Provides warmth, praise, and acceptance of others • Includes reticent members in discussion
Harmonizer-tension reliever	• Maintains the peace • Reduces tension through humor and by reconciling differences between members
Gatekeeper-expediter	• Controls channels of communication and flow of information • Encourages evenness of participation • Promotes open discussion
Feeling expresser	• Monitors feelings and moods in the group • Suggests discussion breaks when the mood turns ugly or when energy levels flag
Compromiser	• Looks for middle ground among various positions to bring the group to agreement

Disruptive Roles	Definition
Recognition seeker	• Seeks recognition and attention by monopolizing conversation • Prevents others from expressing their opinions fully • Wants the spotlight
Self-confessor	• Uses the group as audience to self-disclosure not relevant to the issue under discussion
Isolate	• Deserts the group • Withdraws from participation • Acts indifferent, aloof, and uninvolved • Resists efforts to be involved with decision making
Clown	• Engages in horseplay and thrives on practical jokes and comic routines • Diverts members' attention away from serious discussion of ideas and issues • Steps beyond the boundaries of mere tension reliever
Blocker	• Thwarts progress of the group • Does not cooperate • Opposes much of what the group attempts to accomplish • Incessantly reintroduces dead issues • Makes negative remarks to members
Aggressor	• Tries to dominate the group • Competes with members • Abuses those who disagree • Picks quarrels with members • Interrupts to interject own opinions into discussion
Zealot	• Tries to convert members to a pet cause or idea • Exhibits fanaticism
Cynic	• Displays a sour outlook • Engages in fault-finding • Focuses on negatives • Predicts failure

Source: Adapted from Kenneth D. Benne and Paul Sheats, "Functional Roles of Group Members," Journal of Social Issues 4 (1948), 41–49.

> ### ASK THE ETHICIST: Is Diversity a Matter of Ethics?
>
> **Question** I understand the importance of creating diversity in work groups and not excluding people from different kinds of organizations, but what's so important about creating diversity in groups that are a community for me? Why is that an ethical issue?
>
> **Answer** It's not seeking out similar people that is unethical. However, when there is too much conformity in a group, the group tends to make poor decisions, as evidenced by many decades of research on group dynamics. Beyond the quality of the decision, though, there is a more insidious effect when everyone thinks the same and acts the same in a group. Remember your high school days, when most people had a group? Generally those groups were homogenous—group members were more similar to one another than different from one another. In such a case, the group often fails to see beyond its own perspective. Group members begin to take their point of view for granted, not even considering that there may be other ways to see the world. In taking their views for granted, groups begin to invoke privilege over others, creating perceptions of in-group and out-group members and of superiority and inferiority between groups. That seems unethical.

POWER AND LEADERSHIP IN GROUPS

What do you think of when you hear the word *leader*? Do you think of a person who can get other people to follow his or her direction? What enables a leader to do that? Before we can talk about leadership, we need to discuss the types of power that a leader may use.

Power in Groups

What is power? Is it something that people simply have? Is it something they can acquire? **Power** has typically been viewed as a resource available to people in groups that allows them to influence others to behave as the power holder wishes. John R. P. French and Bertram Raven identified six types of power that a leader may use:[31]

power A resource available to people in groups that allows them to influence others.

- **Reward**—The power holder has the ability to provide desired outcomes in exchange for compliance by the power target.
- **Coercion**—The power holder has the ability to punish the power target if she or he does not comply with the power holder's wishes.
- **Legitimacy**—The power holder has power over the target because of internalized values that the target adheres to; those values dictate that the power holder has a right to compel target's behavior and that the target has an obligation to cooperate.
- **Expertise**—The power holder has power over the target because the holder is more knowledgeable about the situation and is better able to determine what should be done and by whom.
- **Reference**—The power holder has power over the target because the target admires or identifies with the holder and wants to maintain the relationship they have.
- **Information**—The power holder has power over the target because the holder knows more about this particular situation than the target does. Information power is limited to a particular situation.

In subsequent research, Raven noted that the bases of power were slightly more complex than he and French had originally conceived. For example, reward and coercive power can be viewed personally or impersonally. That is, the power holder may provide a reward directly from his or her own resources, or she or he may arrange for the reward to be received from organizational resources. Likewise, coercion can be personal (i.e., the power holder directly punishes the power target) or impersonal (i.e., the power holder uses the resources of the group to punish the power target). Both expert and reference power can be positive or negative, or, as the saying goes, "If you can't be a good example, then be a horrible warning." Finally, legitimate power can be based on a sense of obligation, such as family relationships, as well as internalized values.[32]

Power functions because of dependency; that is, the power user has power over the target of power because the target is, in some way, dependent on the power user to achieve his or her goals. If the target does not value the rewards that are offered, is not afraid of the punishments that are threatened, does not accept the legitimacy of the power holder's position or her or his expertise, rejects the information holder offers, and has no desire to maintain the relationship with holder, then the power holder has no power over the power target.

Leadership in Groups

leadership A communicative process that encompasses the ability to engage in mutual influence with others in the group in order to move toward the accomplishment of the task at hand.

The study of **leadership** in groups has a long and rich history and has embraced a number of definitions. At first, researchers believed that leadership qualities were due to *traits* a person possessed (or didn't possess), such as charisma and knowledge of the relevant task. They found, however, that simply having such traits was insufficient to actually result in a person being an effective leader.[33] After that, researchers focused on the behaviors that leaders performed, or the *functions* of leadership in a group. These functions—task functions and process functions—are similar to two roles, task and maintenance, that were discussed previously. From this point of view, a group could have many leaders because leadership was a behavior rather than a static role.[34]

Then attention turned to the communication *style* leaders used in an effort to see if one means of leading (e.g., being directive or nondirective) was superior to another.[35] Next, it was argued that effective leadership was dependent on the *situation*—the kind of followers one had and the kind of task that needed to be accomplished.[36] Other researchers linked the idea of leadership with *power*, claiming that leadership was best identified by answering these questions: Who defines whom? Whose decisions are followed? Who opposes significant change (because change usually redistributes power)? Who talks the most (or is listened to the most)? Who can take his or her point of view for granted?[37] See Table 9.2 for a summary of the various approaches to defining leadership.

In the twenty-first century, researchers agree that leadership is largely a matter of social influence. Not only do leaders influence their followers; followers influence the leader. From this point of view, leaders cannot exist without followers, and leadership is created through the communication of a vision for the group through mutual influence between leaders and followers rather than by one-sided use of the bases of power. When groups are led through social influence, group members are likely to feel more satisfied with their group experience.[38] This kind of leadership is also called *transformational leadership*. A **transformational leader** is a person who is supportive of his or her followers and recognizes them as individuals. Transformational leaders set high expectations for their followers while providing support for their followers to meet those expectations. In addition, transformational leaders are able to voice a shared vision of the future rather than imposing a vision on their followers.[39]

transformational leader A person who is supportive of his or her followers and recognizes them as individuals.

Table 9.2 Summary of Historical Approaches to Leadership

The roles and positions of the group leader have evolved as researchers have studied group dynamics and learned how groups can be made to function more effectively.

Approach to Leadership	Definitions
Traits	Leaders are people who have particular attributes, such as: • Intelligence • Social skills • Charisma • Persuasive skills
Functional	Leadership is a set of behaviors that must be performed for a group to be effective. Leadership behaviors are focused on: • The task (e.g., helping to set an agenda, proposing new ideas, seeking information from others) • The process (e.g., managing conflict, monitoring communication levels so no one person dominates)
Styles	Leaders tend to adopt one of three ways of acting toward the group: • Authoritarian (giving orders and operating from a control perspective) • Democratic (consulting with the group, getting input before making decisions) • Laissez-faire (a non-involved approach that sometimes is not leadership at all)
Situational	Leaders need to adapt to the needs of group members, the task, and the amount of stress in the situation: • Autocratic approaches work when the task is very structured and the situation is stressful (e.g., cleaning up after a natural disaster) • Generally, a democratic style works best.
Power	Leaders are those who wield power in the group. You can identify leaders by noting: • Who is listened to the most • Who can take his or her point of view for granted • Whose decisions are followed
Social influence/ transformational leadership	Leadership is a matter of social influence: • Leaders create a vision for group members, whose identification with the vision leads them to higher productivity • In turn, group members (or followers) impact leader behavior and perceptions of leadership behavior

Source: Adapted from J. R. Clinton, *A Short History of Leadership Theory*. Altadena, CA: Barnabas Publishers, 1992.

The Importance of Following

While being a follower is sometimes seen negatively, effective following is just as important as effective leading. A leader can't exist without followers and vice versa. In fact, many studies point to the conclusion that follower attitudes and attributes have a large impact on perceptions of leadership and on leadership behavior. Followers who are extraverted and motivated, for example, see their leaders as more transformational in their behavior than do followers with low job satisfaction, who view their leaders more negatively.[40] The study of **followership** focuses on the behaviors a follower takes with respect to his or her leader, such as taking or refusing responsibility, communicating or failing to express opinions, and approaching problem solving proactively or reactively.[41] Followership behaviors can be classified into three general approaches:

- **Passive followers** are focused on taking orders and following directions. They value the expertise of the leader over their own, and they emphasize loyalty to the leader as one of their main expectations.
- **Active followers** offer opinions when given the opportunity but also emphasize loyalty to the leader. They are generally responsive to their leaders but do not initiate behavior on their own.
- **Proactive followers** see themselves as partners of their leaders. They see their role as helping to advance the leader's and organization's mission, and they challenge their leaders if they feel the leaders are making bad decisions.[42]

The art of following is as important as leading—and it is generally underrated. Good followers are able to assume responsibility; in fact, some argue that this is the most important aspect of being a good follower.[43] In addition, good followers serve the leader by helping the leader conserve energy and by defending the leader publicly; challenging the leader when he or she demonstrates arrogance and/or abuse; participating in transformation of oneself and of the leader and processes; and leaving when the time is right.

For groups and organizations to be effective, it is imperative that both followers and leaders focus on the purpose of the group or the organization. Too often, groups or organizations fall into a pattern of focusing on the leader instead of the purpose; such a focus can devastate the group or organization if the leader proves too fallible or must leave suddenly.[44] In other words, a group that depends on the leader alone to make things happen will not be as effective as a group in which both its leader and its members are committed to the goals and purposes the group is intended to achieve.

Despite advances in thinking about followership, however, a survey of senior-level executives revealed their bias toward leadership as a top-down kind of behavior rather than the mutual influencing model that proponents of followership promote. Even though many more of us are destined to be followers than leaders, it will take some time before people really believe that following is as important as leading.[45]

followership The behaviors of a follower with respect to his or her leader, such as taking or refusing responsibility, communicating or failing to express opinions, and approaching problem solving proactively or reactively.

passive followers Followers focused on taking orders and following directions.

active followers Followers who offer opinions when given the opportunity but also emphasize loyalty to the leader.

proactive followers Followers who see themselves as partners of their leaders.

Without followers, there is really no leader in a group.

Leadership Emergence in Groups

As with research concerning the definition of leadership, a number of studies have been devoted to understanding how people become leaders in groups where everyone starts on the same footing. Overall, studies indicate that the person who best presents both an ability to create task efficiency while maintaining sensitivity to the social dimension of the group is most likely to emerge as leader.[46] But the process of getting there is rather interesting.

Groups go through a process of elimination when they are determining who will be the leader. Quiet people are eliminated first, while talkative people are seen as potential leaders. However, a person who talks too much or expresses strong opinions will be eliminated from leadership consideration. In addition, bossy people or people who are irritating to the group get the axe. In the end, someone who evidences good listening and the task and social considerations mentioned earlier will most likely wind up as the leader of the group.[47]

There are a number of "thou shalt nots" for people who aspire to leadership in groups. These including being late and missing important meetings, coming unprepared, evidencing apathy, dominating the conversation, being a poor listener, expressing rigid viewpoints, bullying others, and/or using abusive language. Think about these "thou shalt nots" as they relate to your experience in groups. Do you know group members who exhibit one or more of these behaviors? If so, were they perceived as leaders? Do *you* exhibit one or more of these behaviors? (If so, are you perceived as a leader?)

How Do Men and Women Respond Differently to Group Situations?

Gender differences in group behavior arise in both leadership emergence and in how men and women view competition within a group situation.

Despite a great deal of evidence that indicates men and women function equally well as leaders, women are often overlooked for group leadership and find themselves at the receiving end of more negative attitudes than male leaders receive.[48] However, both men and women can find themselves being penalized when they succeed in areas that are not considered appropriate for their gender. Men who succeed at a job that is typically female gendered, such as an administrative assistant, are seen as ineffectual and are generally less respected than women doing the same job. Women, on the other hand, tend to be interpersonally disliked when they are successful at a male-gendered job, such as law enforcement. However, both men and women who succeed in jobs that are seen as inconsistent for their gender are seen as less preferable as supervisors than people operating in gender-consistent positions.[49]

CHAPTER SUMMARY

Now that you have read this chapter you can:

9.1 Describe the relationship between group communication, civility, and ethics.

You realize that some of your most important relationships are created in groups and that groups are able to accomplish tasks that individuals alone cannot.

You understand that long-term groups are especially demanding in terms of the ability to be civil. Long-term groups may not survive high levels of incivility. Further, you can describe the ethical issues that revolve around including or excluding people from groups.

9.2 Distinguish between the different kinds of groups in which you take part.

A small group is more than an aggregate of people; it is three or more people acting together to achieve goals and sharing a sense of identity about their group membership. People often use the terms *group* and *team* interchangeably. You understand that much of your life is spent in small groups, and the satisfaction that can be derived from them is often higher than satisfaction you may derive from working alone.

You are able to list the different kinds of groups in which you take part and can classify them according to whether they are long-term groups such as a support group; short-term, project-oriented groups such as class projects; or virtual groups such as online communities devoted to hobbies.

9.3 Explain the stages of development in a group.

You understand that effective groups typically develop in four stages and terminate in a fifth stage. They come together for the forming stage, they spend some time storming about what should be done, they settle down into a norming phase where they agree on expectations, and they spend a great deal of time in the performing stage, where they are accomplishing their goals. Finally, groups reach a termination phase, where they disband or some members are replaced by others.

9.4 Analyze the climate of a group by describing its norms, communication patterns, roles, and diversity and explain the importance of cohesiveness in a group.

You understand that the climate of a group is determined by its communication patterns, roles, and diversity. You are aware that using a shift response where you transfer attention from the speaker to yourself negatively affects the group climate. You also know that competitive interrupting (i.e., ignoring the give and take of conversation) and ambushing (i.e., simply waiting to say what you want without listening to the other group members) are both detrimental to group climate.

You are now able to explain how roles operate in groups. You know that roles are both formal, with specific job descriptions, and informal, where they are played by different people at different times. Formal roles may include the facilitator, the recorder, the treasurer, and so on. Informal roles may be task oriented, moving the group toward its goals; maintenance oriented, helping the group have good relationships; or disruptive, creating problems in the group dynamics.

It is important to distinguish the kind of fit you are looking for rather than simply search out people who are just like yourself. You also understand how important it is to get different viewpoints by seeking out people different from yourself to be group members.

9.5 Describe the types of power, the qualities that make a leader, the roles of followers, and how leaders emerge in groups.

You can explain that leadership is a two-way influence process between leaders and followers. You understand that there are no leaders without followers and vice versa, and that being a follower is not necessarily a negative thing. You also understand how leaders emerge in groups where there is no formal appointment. Those who emerge as leaders are the ones who speak up but not too much, who evidence respect for others as well as listening skills, and who are able to balance task and social demands in the group.

You know now that in the most productive groups, both leaders and followers focus on the purpose of the group rather than on the leader or its members. Good followers know how to both support and challenge the group leader as appropriate.

CIVILITY SUMMARY

Overall, remember that civil communication in groups involves the following:

- When the groups we participate in are voluntary, it is relatively easy to remain civil with the other group members. However, when we join groups involuntarily, issues of civility are more likely to arise, and we may have to work harder at being civil.

- When we know people well enough to know their faults, and when we must interact with them frequently but have little or no relationship beyond a particular setting, we may fail to offer them the civil respect we should.

- The successful development of groups and teams depends on members being able to communicate with one another civilly and effectively.

- If group members explicitly create a norm that expects civil communication among group members but creates no mechanism to correct uncivil behavior, the norm won't be in place for very long.

- Maintenance roles include supporting and encouraging others, helping relieve tensions in the group, and monitoring the feelings of the group. The communication associated with maintenance roles is civil, as it is typically based on respect, restraint, and responsibility.

REVIEW QUESTIONS

1. What is the nature of a group? What are its essential ingredients?
2. Why is group work so important for us?
3. What is the relationship between small-group communication and civility?
4. What are the different types of groups that people may be a part of?
5. What are the stages of group development?
6. What is climate in small-group communication? What determines group climate?
7. How does the way we communicate with one another affect the climate of a group?
8. How do the roles that people play affect the climate of a group?
9. How does the tendency to reinforce fit in a group or encourage diversity in a group affect group climate?
10. What is power? What forms the basis for power?
11. What is group leadership? How do people become leaders in groups?
12. Why is it important to understand followers as well as leaders?

10 Group Processes and Civil Communication

WHAT DO THE following lawmakers have in common?

- California Lieutenant Governor Abel Maldonado (Democrat)
- New York City Mayor Michael Bloomberg (Independent)
- Former Florida Governor Charlie Crist (Republican)

The commonalties shared among these lawmakers go beyond public service performed as former and current elected officials. These and other lawmakers have joined a group called "No Labels," created to focus on core issues such as better jobs, national security, and the environment.[1] The goal of No Labels is to put categories aside and unite Republicans, Democrats, and Independents to build a citizen's movement that works across party lines to find practical solutions to national problems. The group collects views and opinions through social media and other forms of technology to represent one voice—the citizens of the United States.[2] No Labels founder Nancy Jacobson insists that

CHAPTER OBJECTIVES

After reading this chapter, you will be able to:

10.1 Describe the relationship between civility, ethics, and group communication processes.

10.2 Identify the communication and decision-making patterns in a group of which you are a member.

10.3 Explain the central task of a group.

10.4 Analyze a problem using the steps in group problem solving and explain the link between creativity and problem solving.

10.5 Compare vertical thinking and lateral thinking, apply standard problem techniques, and construct a mind map for a problem.

10.6 Identify the three barriers to effective decision making in groups.

10.7 Address different types of conflict in groups.

10.8 Plan and run a meeting.

the group isn't a new political party and doesn't have an issues platform. Instead, the 150,000-member movement was formed to promote a bipartisan approach to politics and to create a space where compromise and working across party lines are considered acceptable.[3]

Although Jacobson asserts that No Labels is a "lobbyist group for bipartisanship" rather than a civility project, the group expects members of Congress to adopt a code of conduct that includes:[4]

- Being civil in public discourse and behavior and standing against incivility wherever it is encountered. Members of Congress should use respectful language and should call others out, including members of one's own party, when they fail to communicate civility.
- Treating those who hold differing opinions with respect.
- Taking evidence seriously by communicating and acting on the basis of facts and evidence, even when evidence cuts against preferred positions.

WHY IT MATTERS

A quote that has sometimes been attributed to Albert Einstein asserts that "insanity is doing the same thing over and over and expecting different results." Too often, politics have been characterized by polarized, uncivil discourse. The No Labels group is working to change the way political discourse occurs, and by doing so, it may bring about different results. The same can occur in terms of group problem solving. Without an understanding of the various ways decisions can be made, we are likely to resort to our accustomed ways of doing so and expecting that the results will be appropriate to the situation. Having a variety of problem-solving methods in your repertoire is more likely to create productive and satisfying results. For example, you have undoubtedly attended meetings that were painful to experience because they lacked purpose or because the leader was not able to keep the group on topic. Having the knowledge required to run a meeting efficiently will help ensure that you are not one of the painful memories others experience.

While you most likely will not find yourself in a situation that calls for you to cross party lines to solve a national problem, you will probably work with groups and teams that engage in problem solving and solution finding. In this chapter, you'll learn about the different ways groups communicate, make decisions, and solve problems. You'll also read about different problem-solving techniques and barriers to effective problem solving. In addition, you'll learn about some ways to address conflicts in groups. Finally, you'll learn how to run a meeting effectively when you are the leader of a group.

GROUP PROBLEM SOLVING, CIVILITY, AND ETHICS

Codes of ethics specify what type of civil behavior is expected of employees and members of professional organizations. While such codes of ethics are direct and explicit, implicit codes of ethics may govern decision-making groups. For example, group leaders may implicitly trust that members will represent their projects accurately to others (trustworthiness); clients may take for granted that a consultant will put client needs ahead of the needs of the consulting firm (fairness); and students in an academic group may assume that all group members will complete their tasks to finish an assignment (responsibility).[5]

Many problem-solving groups have expectations for members that are not explicit. These expectations are summarized in Table 10.1.[6]

The implicit standards for ethical behavior that concern focusing on ideas when in conflict and demonstrating tolerance are based on civility; both standards are founded on the ideas of respect, restraint, and responsibility. For a group to behave civilly during a

Table 10.1 Expectations for Members of Problem-Solving Groups

Even when the expectations for a group are not explicitly defined, when group members use civil and ethical behaviors at a meeting, it is likely to be a productive meeting.

Expectation	Behavior
Doing your best	Group members have expectations that each member will perform to his or her highest ability.
Working for the group good	Groups assume that each member has an ethical responsibility to put the group good ahead of individual good.
Engaging others rationally	Groups members should be able to search for truth by using reasoning and logic in their discussions.
Playing fair	Group members should not engage in power struggles because they can subvert the group good and jeopardize group goals.
Listening well	Group members should be committed to using good listening skills.
Preparing for group meetings	Groups believe that members will "do their homework" and engage in advance planning to create the most advantageous group outcomes.
Avoiding personal attacks and engaging in conflict that concerns ideas	Group members assume that a person's ideas should be examined without attacking the member who originates the idea.
Using objectivity	Group members should separate fact from opinion and engage in perspective taking to understand others' viewpoints.
Displaying tolerance	Group members should understand that other members may not be as facile in communication skills as others.
Thinking critically	Group members must be willing to engage in close scrutiny of evidence and arguments to ensure their correctness.

conflict, group members must be able to question and examine evidence and arguments in an in-depth and thorough manner. At the same time, group members should avoid insulting the people who formulate such arguments. To make this assumed standard explicit, members of a new group may want to state directly that they want to examine a particular argument without offending the person who presented the argument. The commitment to tolerance requires forbearance when faced with offensive and crude behavior and communication that does not include offensive and crude responses. Group members who haven't been trained in small group discussion and communication skills may not realize that their communication is uncivil. Responding in kind is less effective than modeling civil communication and good group discussion skills so that other members can learn to engage in civil communication.[7]

COMMUNICATION AND DECISION MAKING IN GROUPS

This section covers topics that will help you apply your knowledge of small group communication more effectively. A good way to start is with an examination of a historically significant series of studies on patterns of communication in groups and how they affect task completion. Following that, we'll examine the ways in which people can come to decisions in groups.

A CASE STUDY IN ETHICS

Are You Decision Fatigued?

Recently, a group of researchers examined the decisions an Israeli parole board made to determine the factors that affect whether a prisoner will be released on bail or remanded back to jail. Surprisingly, the determining factor wasn't the nature of the crime, the original sentence levied on the prisoner, how much time the prisoner had already served, or even the prisoner's conduct in jail. The determining factor in granting parole was the time of day at which the prisoner appeared before the board. Those appearing in the morning had a better chance of being paroled than those appearing later in the day.[8] Researchers refer to this effect as "decision fatigue."

Decision fatigue, which occurs in decision-making groups, presents challenges to those who are committed to acting civilly. Here's why:

> The more choices you make throughout the day, the harder each one becomes for your brain, and eventually it looks for shortcuts, usually in either of two very different ways. One shortcut is to become reckless, to act impulsively instead of expending the energy to first think through the consequences.... The other shortcut is the ultimate energy saver: do nothing. Instead of agonizing over decisions, avoid any choice.[9]

Acting civilly and acting ethically require that we make decisions about our behavior—we must choose to be respectful, restrained, and responsible. But as the day wears on and those decisions are added to all the other decisions we have to make in a day (e.g., what to eat for breakfast, what route to take to work), it becomes harder and harder to exercise the willpower we may need in the face of uncivil behavior from another. Roy F. Baumeister, a leading researcher in this area, offers some hope for us, though.[10] He concludes from his research that self-control is often a matter of structuring one's day so that fewer decisions need to be made. People with good self-control avoid temptations and set up their lives to minimize the need to make decisions. For example, rather than having to decide whether to exercise each day, people can conserve their willpower by agreeing to meet a friend daily to do so. We can also improve our ability to act civilly by making it a habit rather than something we need to decide to do.

Discussion Questions

1. Do you agree that it is harder to be civil and ethical as the day goes on? Why or why not?
2. How can you structure your life to reduce the number of decisions you have to make each day?
3. Can acting civilly and ethically become an ingrained habit so that it doesn't require a decision to act in that manner?

Patterns of Communication

Some of the earliest experimental research on communication focused on group problem solving. Specifically, Alex Bavelas and his colleagues at Massachusetts Institute of Technology were interested in how the flow of messages between group members arranged into different communication networks affected the way a group functioned and its performance level.[11] A **communication network** is a pattern of interaction between group members that dictates who an individual may exchange information with.

To ensure that group members adhered to their assigned pattern, the experiments were designed so that group members were physically separated from one another and could only communicate with their assigned partners. Bavelas's research group examined

communication network A pattern of interaction between group members that dictates who an individual may exchange information with.

Communication and Decision Making in Groups

The Circle   The Wheel   The Chain

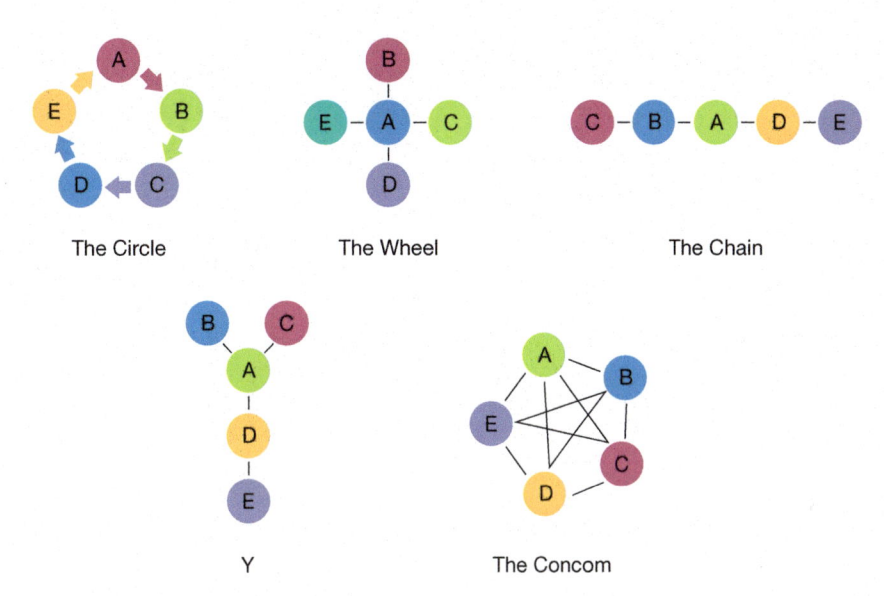

Y   The Concom

FIGURE 10.1 Five-Person Network Patterns

Think about these patterns of communication in various decision-making groups you belong to and determine which of these patterns most closely resembles what goes on in your group.

Source: Figure adapted from Alex Bavelas, "Communication Patterns in Task-Oriented Groups," *Journal of the Acoustical Society of America* 22 (1950): 725–730.

the effects of five different communication networks: circle, chain, Y, wheel, and all channels. These are shown in Figure 10.1.

The first four patterns are centralized, meaning that communication is restricted and that one person generally handles more communication than the rest of the group members. In the *circle pattern*, group members may only communicate with the individuals on either side of them. If B needs information from D, B must send a message through C, or through A and E, and then wait for A or C to relay the answer back. The *chain pattern* is one in which the person in position A (the leader) only receives communication from B or D. If C or E has a question that must be answered by C, each of them must relay that question through B or D in order to receive an answer.

In the *Y pattern*, Person A is the pathway for all communication flowing out to B and C and down to E by way of D. Depending on the number of messages that must be generated, this pattern can become very stressful for Person A. The *wheel pattern*, a variation of the Y pattern, poses the same difficulties for Person A. The *all-channel pattern* places no restriction on the way messages can flow in the group.

In Bavelas's research, while the circle, chain, Y, and wheel patterns had a significant effect on the productivity of the group, they did so in different ways, depending on the complexity of the task facing the group. When tasks were simple, a centralized pattern worked better. It minimized the amount of unnecessary communication about the task and allowed group members to complete it quickly. However, when the task was complex, when the information the members had about the task was ambiguous, or when information was not evenly distributed among the group members, the all-channel pattern worked much better.

For example, suppose you have to work on a group project with four other people. You all have a copy of the assignment, and it is fairly straightforward. Each person in the group is to research an aspect of a problem, and the separate sections are to be joined into a larger paper. Does it make sense for every member of the group to email multiple versions of his or her portion of the paper to everyone, or should one person serve as the collector/collator and then send a final combined copy out to the members? On the other

TRENDS IN TECHNOLOGY AND SOCIAL MEDIA

Twitter and Group Communication

Do you tweet? Twitter is a social networking site that "serves as a quick relay service for sharing ideas, thoughts and concerns with others who have similar interests, both locally and at great distance."[12] Whether you decide to update friends about your day, communicate to members of a work team about the next phase in an ongoing project, or contact conference attendees about a place to meet, Twitter can be used to facilitate communication among members of a group.

For example, Twitter is used at colleges to engage students in course content with live discussion threads that promote team building.[13] Twitter can be used to build a job-search network and create a professional presence in the Twittersphere.[14] Twitter has also been described as a new informal communication medium that can be used at work to facilitate collaboration. In this context, Twitter may build common ground, enhance information sharing, and maintain connections among colleagues.[15]

A new service called GroupTweet can turn a "standard Twitter account into a group communication hub where members can post updates to everyone in the group using direct messages. When the group account receives a direct message from a group member, GroupTweet converts it into a tweet that all followers can see."[16] For example, suppose a delegation from your club or organization is attending a conference. To easily communicate with each other during the conference, you can create a Twitter account and give it a name (e.g., MyCommGrp). The next step is to register the account on GroupTweet and ask everyone in the delegation to sign up for a Twitter account and follow MyCommGrp (and you, as MyCommGrp, will follow them back). Whenever someone in the delegation sends a direct message to MyCommGrp (e.g., "There's a welcome reception in Room A at 7:00"), everyone in the group will get it.[17]

Journalist David Carr sums up Twitter as "lightweight, endlessly useful," and a tool that "gets better as more people use it. Brands are using it, institutions are using it, and it is becoming a place where a lot of important conversations are being held."[18]

Discussion Questions

1. Do you use Twitter? What do you like about it? What are its limitations?
2. Have you tried the GroupTweet function? What do you use it for?
3. What other functions do you think Twitter can serve?

---

hand, suppose your instructor has given only a portion of the assignment to each person in the group. None of you knows what the final product should look like unless you put your various pieces of information together to reason out what is expected. In this case, going through a single person would overburden that one person and result in frustration for people who were hearing about only part of the task.

Research on communication networks largely disappeared in the 1970s because researchers kept coming to the same conclusions about the effects of communication patterns on the flow of information.[19] However, new research arose that looked at networks of communication based on relationships, and with the rise of social network sites such as Facebook and Twitter, communication networks continue to generate interest for communication scholars.[20]

Decision-Making Patterns in Groups

The decision-making pattern that a group adopts will affect the way in which the team goes about problem solving. There are three common ways for groups to make decisions

- **The leader makes a decision.** This type of decision making is similar to the chain communication network discussed previously, and it works well for minor decisions, such as where a group should meet or who to ask to type up a report. This type of decision making is also appropriate when the leader or designated decision maker has information that the group members do not have. It's best to engage in this type of decision making when you are confident that your group will accept and support your decision.[21] For example, if you are a manager responsible for scheduling different shifts, you may have to announce a sudden change because of one worker's serious illness. Your group is likely to accept the decision when it hears the reason behind it. On the other hand, imagine that you are a member of group that typically plans the annual end-of-the-year party. Your coworkers eagerly look forward to this celebration each year, and your team is well known for designing the most creative events. This year, your leader makes the decision to cancel the party because of budget constraints. Because the group considers the party an important event, the leader's decision is not likely to be readily supported by the group. Simply announcing such a decision may result in you and other group members becoming angry and distrustful of the leader. It would be better if the leader engaged in the second type of decision making—that is, consulting with the group prior to making the final decision.

- **The leader consults with the group but uses her or his authority to make a final decision (the consultative method).** This type of decision making, similar to the Y or wheel communication pattern, works well when the leader doesn't have all the important information. Members are likely to accept and support the eventual decision because they have a chance to provide input into it. In addition, the type of decision making is effective when time is short and/or group members can't agree on a decision but a decision must be made. This type of decision making is considered appropriate for major decisions. To return to the example of the end-of-year party, the leader of your organization calls a meeting to discuss how the budget may affect the end-of-year party. Some group members believe that money should be appropriated from other accounts to fund the party, while others assert that the party is a waste of money and should be canceled. Still other group members suggest that that party be scaled down and that employees sign up to bring food and drink. If the leader considers the group members' suggestions before she or he makes the final decision, this example illustrates the consultative method.[22]

- **The group makes a decision by voting or by reaching consensus.** A group **consensus** occurs when members come to a decision that is acceptable to the group; however, it doesn't mean that the decision is the best one of all or that it is everyone's first choice. Consensus is essentially an "I can live with that" approach to reaching a decision and requires all-channel communication. When leaders turn a decision over to the group and ask the group to come to consensus, they are committed to taking the time to hear all the points of view on the decision. Reaching consensus is often a lengthy process because it requires that people agree to the decision.

    A vote is sometimes used in place of reaching consensus, particularly when time is limited but the leader wants the group to make the decision. However, many votes are split, and even a large majority doesn't guarantee that the results of the vote illustrate agreement by consensus.[23] In the case of the end-of-year party, the team members and all employees could be asked to vote on a solution. The end result might be a split vote and no consensus.

When groups and leaders join together to address problems, they can access different methods of problem solving. In the next section, we'll explore both step-by-step and holistic problem-solving methods that can help group members reach consensus.

consensus The agreement that results when members come to a decision that is acceptable to the group; however, it doesn't mean that the decision is the best one of all or that it is everyone's first choice.

INTRODUCTION TO GROUP PROCESSES

Think about a decision you've had to make. How did you do it? Did you consider all your options on your own, or did you ask various friends and relatives what they thought you should do? Whether we seek out the advice of people one by one or sit together in a group to share information, we generally approach problem solving with the help of others.

The central function that groups serve, whether in education, business, or one's personal sphere, is to accomplish some task that is, more often than not, associated with problem solving. Groups are typically composed of members who bring a variety of skills to the situation. That variety makes it more probable that the group will generate diverse solutions to the problem.

In the first group where we hold membership, our families, we are often focused on solving problems as we address issues of behaviors, expectations, and relationship management. At an interpersonal level, problem solving might revolve around helping people learn more skills, such as a quilting group arranging classes for its members. Alcoholics Anonymous and other kinds of support groups are oriented toward helping people deal with their addictions. When you are assigned to a group as a part of your studies at your college or university, your problem-solving efforts are focused on getting yourself and the other members organized sufficiently to produce a paper or project that earns the grade you seek. Businesses and organizations routinely use focus groups, standing committees, and work groups to accomplish their tasks.

Group Problem Solving and Your Career

Almost any career you choose will require the skills needed to engage in problem solving. Certain careers, such as engineering and computer security, focus on the ability to solve problems and create solutions. However, in just about all jobs, certain groups of employees work together to ensure that things run smoothly. For example, managers in professional occupations, construction, and fast food work together to solve problems. In addition, engineers typically work in groups to solve problems. They usually focus their energies on creating something new or making something better. Each member is a specialist and has a particular role to play within the problem-solving group. Other careers than require problem solving in teams include animation for video games or films, health care, and research.[24] It may be impossible for you to think of a career that doesn't include some measure of teamwork or require the ability to solve problems. Educators, financial specialists, law enforcement professionals, and most occupations other than those that can be described as a "one-(wo)man shop" will necessitate the ability to work with others to solve problems.

Watch the Video "The Politics of Sociology" at MyCommunicationLab

PROBLEM-SOLVING: THE HEART OF GROUP PROCESSES

When people come together to make a decision, it's not a good idea to simply throw out ideas and hope one of them will work. Groups that engage in specific problem-solving steps more frequently generate workable solutions than those that do not.[25] The following section looks at the steps a group can take to solve a problem.

Steps in Problem Solving

Until recently, advice concerning the way in which individuals or groups should proceed in problem solving has been largely unchanged since John Dewey described Reflective Thinking model in the early twentieth century.[26]

Problem-Solving: The Heart of Group Processes

Dewey's Reflective Thinking Model As you see in Table 10.2, Dewey's Reflective Thinking model includes six steps: defining the problem (which includes determining the type of question the problem involves), analyzing the causes of the problem (what gave rise to it), identifying criteria for an acceptable solution (what can and can't be done to address the situation, what resources are available), generating possible solutions, selecting the best solution, and implementing the solution while setting up a time to evaluate its effectiveness. Dewey also provided specific advice for how to accomplish all six steps.

Using Dewey's Reflective Thinking model is a logical and methodical way to go about solving a problem. However, working through each step require some time, which is not always available in this fast-paced world. In addition, groups can often get bogged down in defining and identifying causes of a problem rather than looking for ways to address the problem.

Scripts More recently, writers have tried to expand the options available to people faced with the challenge of solving a problem. Murnighan and Mowen, who examined high-stakes decisions that people in organizations make, created a method they refer to as SCRIPTS, which stands for "*s*earch for the threats and opportunities in the decision, find the *c*ause of the situation, evaluate the *r*isks of the situation, apply *i*ntuition and emotion, take different *p*erspectives, consider the *t*ime frame for making the decision, and then *s*olve the problem."[27] Let's look at each of these steps in more detail:

1. **Search for signals of threats and opportunities.** The search step involves more than simply examining the problem. This step is more proactive than reactive. It requires that group members be alert to early signs of problems and take steps to address them while they are manageable. In the SCRIPTS method, groups need to think ahead to decide what kind of error would be more costly—missing an

Since our group membership so frequently calls on us to be involved in problem-solving, it is important to understand the various means that can be used to accomplish it.

Table 10.2 Comparing Dewey's Reflective Thinking with Murnighan and Mowen's SCRIPTS

Using the SCRIPTS method can help decision makers make good decisions when they lack the resources or time to follow every step in the Reflective Thinking model.

John Dewey's Reflective Thinking Model	Keith Murnighan and John C. Mowen's SCRIPTS Technique
1. Define the problem: • Questions of fact • Questions of value • Questions of policy	1. Search: Search for signals of threats and opportunities.
2. Analyze the causes of the problem.	2. Cause: Find the causes.
3. Identify criteria for an acceptable solution.	3. Risks: Evaluate the risks.
4. Generate potential solutions.	4. Intuition: Apply intuition and emotion.
5. Select the best solution.	5. Perspectives: Take different perspectives. 6. Time: Consider the time frame.
6. Implement the solution.	7. Solve.

opportunity or making a blunder that costs time and money. If you are proactive, you can deal with many problems while they are still relatively small.

2. **Find the causes.** In the cause step, the group tries to determine the root causes of the problem and to link them to solutions. This method encourages groups to go beyond identifying a simple cause and effect and to think more broadly about the multiple causes that might be behind a problem. As the various causes are identified, solutions are generated.

3. **Evaluate the risks.** A group next moves to the evaluation of risks. What are the possible hazards associated with the various solutions that have been generated? The most important thing for groups to do in this step is to ensure that they do not miss opportunities for effective solutions or act too quickly and create untoward consequences.

4. **Apply intuition.** The next step, intuition, is where the SCRIPTS method begins to deviate significantly from Dewey's Reflective Thinking model. In this step, a group must balance rationality with intuition or gut feelings. Intuition involves having faith in what you think is a good idea and how you feel about your ideas. Intuition is a part of our personalities; some of us listen to our "inner voices" more than other people do. Sometimes, an assessment of all the data available simply leads to indecision. In this case, it is important to examine the "feel" of the possible decision. For example, imagine that you are on a committee to determine whether a new youth activity center should be built in your community. You've examined the data, and the advantages and disadvantages seem equally matched. At this point, Murnighan and Mowen would tell you to act on your instincts—what you feel is the best thing to do rather than to depend on the data alone. If the group is still at odds, though, over what different members believe their intuition is telling them, the group should have predetermined rules that will guide how they break the stalemate. The group may decide to take a vote and go with the decision of the majority, to continue discussion until they come to consensus, or turn the decision over to someone in leadership above them.

5. **Take different perspectives.** Following the application of intuition, groups must try to see the problem and solution from different perspectives. Too often, the way we view a problem is based solely on our own experiences, and we fail to take other ways of seeing into account. For example, if you have led a fairly sheltered life and have not ever found yourself challenged by joblessness or potential homelessness, you might be inclined to see such events as a matter of personal failing, whereas a person with different life experiences might perceive it as the result of a series of unfortunate events. In proposing solutions, you might be focused on strategies that address individual needs, whereas someone with different perspectives may look at larger issues that have affected the problem, such as outsourcing of jobs or lack of affordable housing. Groups addressing a problem need to be especially careful to look at the problem from as many different angles as possible.

6. **Consider the time frame.** Considering the time frame is the next step in the SCRIPTS method. This is more than simply considering the urgency of the problem. It also requires that a group think in terms of how those affected by the problem will perceive the timing of the solution. For example, at the time of this book's publication, British Petroleum is advertising how committed it is to environmental issues in the wake of the Gulf of Mexico oil spill in 2010. Many viewers dismiss the commercials as "bogus propaganda," noting that some fishing spots and bays are still closed because of oil contamination.[28] The best solutions will fit with the expected timing of those affected by it.

7. **Solve.** The final step is to solve a problem. In this step, a group should calculate the maximum risk associated with making a decision and compare it to its overall probability of success. If the probability of success is higher than the risk, the group should act; if not, it should wait out the problem or seek different solutions.

Creativity and Problem Solving

Researchers have known for a long time that groups have the capacity to be more creative collectively than their individual members can be separately.[29] **Creativity** is a process of making sense of some problem in a new way.[30] Creativity, or thinking outside the box, encompasses a desire to take new perspectives, create value in new ways, listen to others, support and respect others when new ideas are presented, and be open to doing things differently.[31] These practices have much in common with those of civility. Tayloe Harding connects creativity and civility when he claims that:

> Providing tools to our students to help them think and act creatively is essential for the advancement of a civil society. . . . A focused effort to help tomorrow's leaders learn not just facts, but also the skills to advance society by, for example, producing more sustainably productive, healthy, and safe neighborhoods and communities, must be a greater part of our daily endeavor as twenty-first-century educators.[32]

It is simply not enough to learn about problem solving in groups without carefully considering the role that creativity plays in generating more viable solutions. But creativity must be connected to an ethical system because the historical record demonstrates the evil people can commit when they are creative without respect to the consequences of their ideas (e.g., the medical "experiments" conducted in concentration camps by Nazi doctors).

Creativity is important to group problem solving for a variety of reasons. Perhaps the most important reason is a self-serving one: You are more likely to enjoy your experiences in small groups when you respond to the situation with creativity. The use of creative methods in problem solving is also associated with higher levels of health: People who have more chances to utilize creative problem solving in their jobs are physically younger than their years suggest.[33]

Within groups, the pressures to stifle creativity can be intensified. Group processes that can result in stifled creativity include:

- **Individual differences in communication style.** When there are differences in how vocal and how quiet members are, the quieter members may self-censor because they are intimidated by more dominant members.
- **A defensive communication climate.** If there is a strong sense of competition in the group, members are more likely to focus on their own needs than on the group process and/or a creative outcome.
- **Cultural norms.** If our way of looking at the world is one that discourages creativity, we might look at those who are trying to encourage creativity in a group as nonconformists or strangely behaving others.

creativity The process of making sense of some problem in a new way.

The use of creative methods in group problem-solving is enjoyable and is associated with high levels of health.

- **Pressure to conform.** When a group overemphasizes norms at the expense of thinking in new ways, it becomes difficult for members to share alternative perspectives. The fear of being ostracized, particularly where group membership is prized, will discourage group members from offering ideas that seem outside the box.[34]

Given all the forces that work against creativity, can we still learn to be creative? Generally speaking, the answer is yes, although it is quite easy for the training to fade if it is not supported by other influential people (e.g., teachers, supervisors) or if the training is too domain specific. For example, if you are trained to solve a particular kind of puzzle (spatial, verbal, or mathematical), it is unlikely that your training in one type of puzzle will carry over to the other kind.[35] On the other hand, few of us are called upon to solve spatial, verbal, and mathematical problems. Creativity training is most effective when people receive training that can be applied across a number of problem-generating situations.[36] Training has also been shown to be effective for small group brainstorming, with those trained generating a larger number of ideas overall and more creative ideas than groups that were not trained.[37] Most important to becoming more creative is the decision to do so; as Robert Sternberg says, "Deciding for creativity does not guarantee that creativity will emerge, but without the decision, it certainly will not."[38]

IMPROVING OUR ABILITY TO ENGAGE IN CIVIL AND EFFECTIVE PROBLEM SOLVING

To achieve effective solutions to group problems, we often have to think of them differently. One way to do this is to start asking questions that we don't normally ask. For example, we can approach "what if" in silly ways: "How would I respond if the other person were the president of the United States?" "How would I respond if the other were a gorilla?" "What would I do if I knew I had only 10 days to live?" The point is to ask questions that may not even be related to the problem in order to think about it differently.

Second, we can imagine how others might handle the problem. How would your sister, brother, mother, father, aunt, uncle, or friend handle it? How would the other person handle it? Finally, we can imagine we're the problem itself: How would you want to be handled if you were actually the problem? Although a little silly, these methods can lead us to new ways of thinking.

Vertical and Lateral Thinking

To take the idea of thinking differently further, Edward de Bono has identified two ways of thinking differently: vertical and lateral.[39] **Vertical thinking** involves moving through a series of steps, making sure that one is completed before the next one is started. Dewey's Reflective Thinking model and the SCRIPTS process are both predominantly vertical means of problem solving. Each of these processes assumes that we move through the steps sequentially and complete each step before we move on to the next. The potential danger in vertical thinking is that, if we believe we have drawn all the right conclusions as we go along, the final conclusion seems to be more or less inevitable. One way to ensure that we truly test all our assumptions is to engage in lateral thinking as well as vertical thinking.

Lateral thinking "is concerned with restructuring . . . patterns (insights) and provoking new ones (creativity)."[40] If we utilized a lateral thinking approach to brainstorming, we would consider every group member's contribution, regardless of how ridiculous it might seem. Whereas in vertical thinking we search for the "right" pattern, in lateral thinking we search for all the patterns we can see. Lateral thinking does not require that

vertical thinking A problem-solving technique that involves moving through a series of steps, making sure that one is completed before the next one is started.

lateral thinking A problem-solving technique that is concerned with restructuring patterns (insights) and provoking new ones (creativity); it is a nonlinear problem solving approach.

Improving Our Ability to Engage in Civil and Effective Problem Solving

we be right; it only requires that we consider a number of different options. Sometimes a bad idea causes someone to think of a much better one or causes someone to see ways to combine bad and good ideas into a superior one.

Standard Problem-Solving Techniques

Some of the techniques proposed by de Bono have become standard in communication textbooks. Several are discussed here: brainstorming, reverse brainstorming, fractionation, and six hats.

brainstorming A problem solving technique in which group members quickly contribute as many ideas as they can think of without judging whether the idea is good or bad.

Brainstorming **Brainstorming** is a method of getting a large number of ideas out in front of group members in a short period of time. When groups brainstorm, it is important to suspend any judgment of the ideas presented. Members are encouraged to present ideas as quickly as possible, with one member of the group acting as a recorder. When all the ideas have been presented, the group begins to categorize them and decide which ones are feasible.

reversal A problem solving technique that entails working backward from the goal or end result.

Reverse Brainstorming Another idea-generating process is the opposite of brainstorming and is known as reverse brainstorming, or reversal.[41] **Reversal** entails working backward from the goal or end result. What would it take to get there? For example, if you are trying to increase customer satisfaction with a process or a product, you might want to start by thinking of all the ways you could make customers dissatisfied with it. Thinking this way helps us see some of the factors causing the problem that we might not have seen before.

fractionation The process of breaking down a problem into smaller pieces and then dealing with each piece, one at a time.

Fractionation Another process, known as **fractionation**, is a process of breaking down a problem into its smallest pieces and then dealing with each piece, one at a time. For example, if you are writing a group project with others, you need to break it down into all the pieces that have to be done—research, combining the research, putting ideas in the right order, getting the paper typed, proofreading, and so on. By breaking down the project into these smaller pieces, the task looks less overwhelming than it does when you look at it as a whole. As an old saying goes, "How do you eat an elephant? One bite at a time."

six hats approach A problem-solving technique that requires one to ask questions from different vantage points.

The Six Hats Method The **six hats method** is another problem-solving approach that is especially useful in small groups. In this approach, you ask questions from six different vantage points. An important part of the process is that each person in the group has a chance to think from the perspective of each hat. There are six hats, each with its own perspective:

- **White hat.** Calls for information known or needed. Using the white hat perspective, you would list everything you know about the conflict—who is involved, why they are involved, what the issues are, when the conflict started, etc.
- **Red hat.** Signifies feelings, hunches, and intuition. Using the red hat perspective, you would list the feelings you have about the conflict. What do you think is going on that might not be evident?
- **Yellow hat.** Symbolizes values and beliefs. From this perspective, you want to think about whether the solution you're seeking is consistent with the person you believe yourself to be. Is it something that can work for you? Is it something you can live with? Is it something you can be proud of?
- **Black hat.** Stands for a contrarian judgment, the devil's advocate, or a pessimist. From this perspective, you focus on why something may not work or how it could go wrong. When everything is going well, what might you be overlooking that could go wrong?

- **Green hat.** Focuses on creativity: unforeseen possibilities, imaginative alternatives, and new ideas. The green hat asks for different ways of looking at the problem. This is the lateral thinking approach.
- **Blue hat.** Takes a macro approach to managing the thinking process. Using a blue hat perspective is a way of keeping yourself honest in the whole process. Have you really thought of all the angles? Are there other ways of achieving the same goal? Is the goal worthwhile?

The Six Hats method of problem-solving has each group member asking questions in terms of six perspectives or "hats."

While the hats appear here as a list, you are free to begin with any one of them: There's not a right or wrong way to start. You can also go back and forth among the various hats.

Essentially, lateral thinking is a way of turning problems on their sides or upside down in order to think about them and see them in a new way. Such thinking can be helpful in moving us toward resolution of a conflict we are facing.

Mind Mapping

Some methods in creative thinking are visual in nature, "right-brain" approaches to analysis using colors and images instead of logical relationships between words. One of the foremost is called mind mapping. Similar to brainstorming and fractionation, **mind mapping** uses ideas to generate others. By looking at ideas together and linking them, you can often think of a better way to deal with a problem than you would have otherwise. This method has become a great tool for encouraging creativity, brainstorming, and learning. Mind mapping is a process that was popularized by Tony Buzan;[42] it was actually first created to help people take notes more effectively. Since that time, several computer programs have been created to help people make mind maps.

Unlike outlining, which presumes a linear relationship between elements of a problem, and which also requires that we know how those elements are related before we start, mind mapping does not require a starting point. In a way, mind mapping is a visual means of brainstorming, except that many of the relationships between the ideas are created as you are generating the mind map. Mind mapping can be done individually or within a group. Some of the best results are generated when each person in the group creates a mind map of the problem and then the group members compare the various maps.

Mind mapping has several rules:

- Start with a large piece of unlined paper and something to write with. You can make your map smaller and without color, but colors help you start to see relationships between concepts.
- Place a central image or graphic representation of a problem in the center of the page. Write down what you think the problem is about.
- Use only one or two words as labels to represent key ideas. If you can't think of a word, draw a picture.
- Write quickly and don't restrict your thinking. It's important to get everything on paper. Don't censor yourself.
- Once you have your thoughts down, start making connections. Identify ideas that are related.
- Draw colored lines between concepts that seem to be related. Use those colors to help make sense of the problem.[43]

mind mapping A problem-solving technique for making your ideas visible.

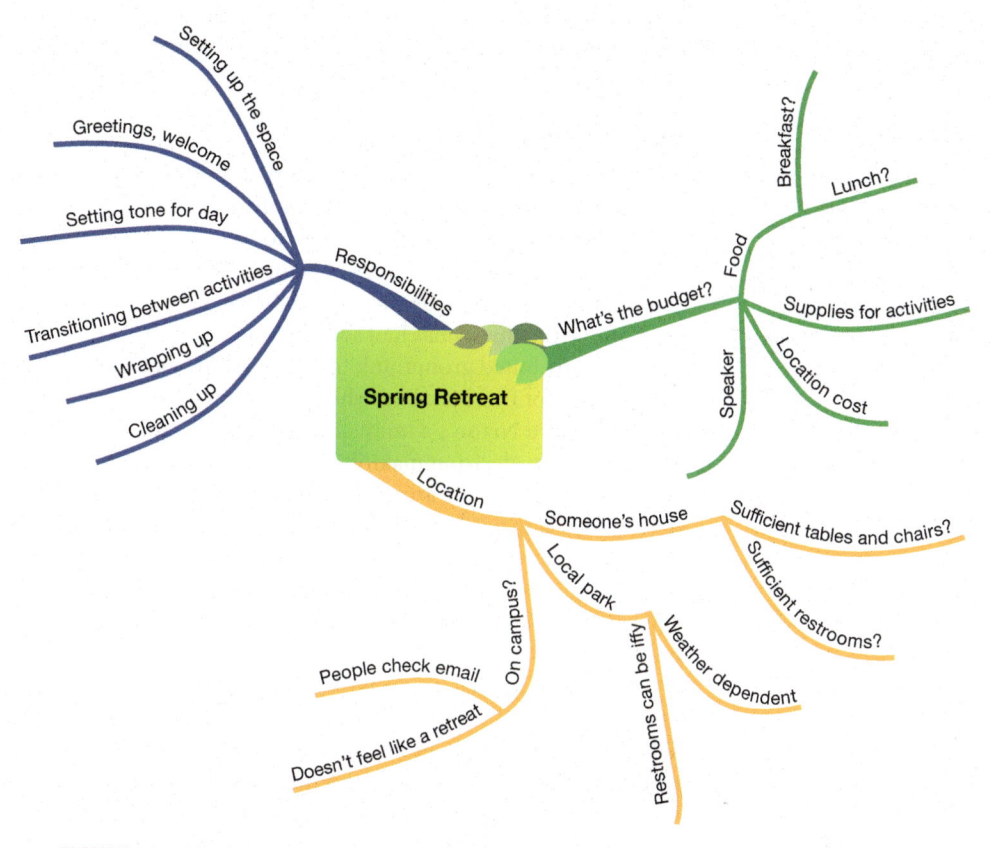

FIGURE 10.2 Mind Map

A group can use a mind map to plan a team building retreat.

Source: Map created by Ruth Anna Abigail using iMindMap software.

- At this point, it helps to ask a few questions:
  - What were you thinking when you started? Is it still the same?
  - When you see the whole picture, how is your thinking affected?
  - What unexpected ideas or relationships among them emerged?
  - Are there any parts out of balance?
  - Do you need to fill in anything else?[44]

Figure 10.2 shows a finished mind map used to plan a staff development retreat. This diagram helps the group members keep track of all the things they need to consider as they plan the day.

The mind-mapping technique can show how many issues are really present in a problem and how they affect each other. It can also be used like a diary, for self-analysis, to prepare for teaching and presentations, and for management of tasks.

BARRIERS TO EFFECTIVE PROBLEM SOLVING

The first part of this chapter provides a number of ways to achieve effective problem solving in groups. This section provides a cautionary tale of what can happen when groups fail to explore all the possibilities inherent in a problem and instead ignore dissenting voices in the problem-solving process. Groupthink, the Abilene paradox, and the Lucifer effect can contribute to ineffective group problem solving.

Groupthink

groupthink A barrier to problem solving that occurs when people are so committed to the group and its integrity as a cohesive unit that they fail to engage in conflict when they should.

Explore the Concept "Enhancing Groups" at **MyCommunicationLab**

Irving Janis coined the term **groupthink** to describe situations that occur when people are so committed to the group and its integrity as a cohesive unit that they fail to engage in necessary conflict over the problem to be solved.[45] When a group is highly cohesive and wants to maintain an image of being cohesive, members of the group censure themselves and do not speak up even when they believe the group is headed toward a bad decision. While the theory has had some detractors,[46] the greater weight of evidence supports it.[47] Janis attributed groupthink to the decisions made by political groups responsible for the bombing of Pearl Harbor, where warnings were ignored, and the Watergate scandal during Richard Nixon's administration. Groupthink has also been identified as a key factor in the faulty decision making in Ronald Reagan's administration that led to the United States agreeing to trade arms for the Iran hostages held between November 1979 and January 1981,[48] and has been linked to the Space Shuttle *Challenger* explosion in 1986.[49] Recently, researchers have asserted that the invasion of Iraq during George W. Bush's administration can also be attributed to groupthink.[50] Groupthink also occurs at the smaller group level, where members may decide on a course of action that doesn't work out for the group.

Irving argues that groupthink can be identified by the presence of these symptoms. First, group members believe that the group is more powerful and moral than people outside the group. Second, group members ignore or explain away any information that could challenge their thinking about the situation, and they stereotype anyone who is opposed to the course of action they have chosen. Finally, group members engage in self-censorship by not sharing any ideas that deviate from the consensus the group has reached. When members are silent, others in the group interpret that silence as agreement. Some members may also pressure potential deviants to conform to the group decision by accusing them of disloyalty when disagreement arises. Other members may function as gatekeepers to ensure that contrary information doesn't reach the group.

The results of groupthink can be disastrous. When groups get caught up in groupthink, they fail to define their goal and determine the best array of options. Such groups may ignore the potential risks of the choice they have made, and they may also filter information against their predetermined decision.

So how do groups avoid getting caught up in groupthink? The most effective way is to make sure that someone is always wearing the "black hat" (i.e., playing the devil's advocate) during discussions about information, potential courses of action, and the costs and benefits of taking a course of action. If at least one person is openly challenging the assumptions of the group, the group is much less likely to engage in groupthink.

The Abilene Paradox

Abilene paradox A barrier to problem solving that occurs because people fail to voice their opinions about the decision being made.

Unlike the phenomenon of groupthink, which is the result of mismanaged conflict, Jerry Harvey believes that the **Abilene paradox** results from mismanaged agreement.[51] That is, while people believe they are in disagreement with others over the decision being made, they in fact do agree with others that the decision is wrong, but no one voices that opinion.

Harvey came up with the idea of the Abilene paradox as a result of a disastrous family outing. He and his wife were visiting her parents. It was hot, and the thought of cooking wasn't appealing. When Harvey's father-in-law suggested that they drive to Abilene for dinner, everyone seemed to agree that it was a good idea. They set off on the 60-mile

Barriers to Effective Problem Solving

A 60-mile car ride without air conditioning and an unsatisfactory meal prompted researcher Jerry Harvey to describe the "Abilene Paradox," which occurs when group members fail to voice a dissenting opinion.

trip in a car without air conditioning to eat at a diner that left them unsatisfied. When they returned, they began to quarrel and then realized that no one had actually wanted to go. The father-in-law claimed to have been throwing out a random suggestion; the others went along because they believed everyone else was in agreement.

The Abilene paradox occurs because people experience anxiety over choosing a particular course of action, fear being separated from the group, have negative fantasies about what might happen if they do speak up, and are unwilling to take the consequences of what might happen if they do. In Harvey's case, the family members didn't know what was the best option for dinner, and they wanted to stay together and so agreed to the Abilene trip because they believed others wanted to go. They also were afraid of having other family members angry with them if they disagreed with the idea of driving to Abilene. The paradox can be recognized from these conditions:

- Those involved agree privately about the nature of the problem but don't say anything. Everyone in the family thought the trip to Abilene was a bad idea, but no one actually said so.
- Those involved also agree privately on what the solution would be but don't realize they are in agreement. No one in the family recognized that others didn't want to go to Abilene.
- With nothing said, the group goes along with what they think is consensus and may wind up doing something they don't want to do. Only when someone speaks out do others voice their opinions.

The Abilene paradox may actually be a variation of groupthink, but there are some important distinctions. In groupthink, the members have a sense of superiority about

---

ASK THE ETHICIST — Why Should I Speak Up?

Question Sometimes it seems that other group members get peeved when I point out that a group is off track in its discussion. When am I obligated to speak up? What if people don't like me when I do?

Answer Unfortunately, people who point out the obvious are sometimes seen as "rocking the boat." They disturb the comfortable feeling the group has that everything is going well and as planned. When a person calls attention to the fact that the discussion is off the agenda, or the group is dangerously close to groupthink, the rest of the group has a tendency to close ranks against the person speaking up and to ostracize him or her. That doesn't make it very appealing to speak up.

On the other hand, what happens if you see a group going off track, or engaging in groupthink, and you don't speak up? If the consequences for the group aren't long term, it might not matter to you. But what if the group winds up making a bad decision that has long-term effects? What if speaking up might prevent such an outcome? The desires to be liked and to fit in are part of everyone's makeup, but they shouldn't prevent us from choosing an ethical course of behavior in a group setting.

their group and a kind of "us versus them" mentality when faced with a decision. In the Abilene paradox, group members are driven more by fear of separation from the group. So, when a group member holds back comments in a groupthink situation, it is largely because he or she doesn't want to destroy the group's illusion of cohesiveness and superiority. When a group member holds back comments in an Abilene paradox, it is largely because he or she fears being kicked out of the group.

The Lucifer Effect

Lucifer effect A barrier to problem solving that is applied to situations where groups commit great harms due to the release of situational constraints that would otherwise keep them from behaving in such a manner.

The **Lucifer effect** is a term coined by Philip Zimbardo, whose recent book of the same name explicates a number of situations where groups commit great harms even though they start with good intentions. Zimbardo argues that the release of situational constraints allow people to behave in ways that would otherwise be unthinkable.[52] Among the situations Zimbardo identifies reflecting the Lucifer effect are the Milgram obedience experiments, where, in the guise of a learning experiment, ordinary people administered potentially lethal shocks to victims they could not see. We include it here as an example of conflict in groups because, largely, the Lucifer effect occurs where group members' desire to avoid conflict results in a failure to resolve issues.

What leads to the Lucifer effect, and how can it be combated? The effect occurs when the right combination of circumstances in a group causes group members to act in ways contrary to their personal beliefs and values. In essence, the circumstances of the situation become more powerful than the people in the situation. These circumstances include the rules that govern the situation, the roles that people play, and the ways in which roles relate to one another. Let's look at each of these factors.

We have previously discussed the importance of rules, which tell people what to expect and how to act in particular situations. When people are in a group or an organization for a long time, rules may come to have "an arbitrary life of their own and the force of legal authority even when they are no longer relevant, are vague, or change with the whims of the enforcers."[53] For example, say that you are in a group or an organization that, when you question why something is done a particular way, you are told that is just the way it is or that is the way we always do it. When rules are unquestioned, and people obey them without thinking, the circumstances for the Lucifer effect begin to appear.

A second aspect of the situation that leads to the Lucifer effect is the role that a person enacts in the situation. When a person cannot separate himself or herself from the role that is expected, there can be negative outcomes. For example, if you are in a subordinate role in a group or an organization, you may not feel it is your place to bring up negative aspects of a decision being made. Your decision not to engage in a conflict in this case may lead to serious consequences.

The final aspect of the situation that leads to the Lucifer effect is the way in which roles relate to one another. You can't be a subordinate unless someone is over you and vice versa. When the roles that people play become entwined to the point that they no longer think about what they are doing or what others expect of them, the Lucifer effect becomes possible.

Essentially, the Lucifer effect is a condition that occurs when people do not stop and think about what is happening and engage in conflict when they realize they are veering off into dangerous territory. The Lucifer effect is a reminder of the importance of engaging in a moderate amount of task conflict and a sufficient amount of process conflict to ensure that we know what we are doing and where we are going in a group. As Zimbardo notes:

> We all want to believe in our inner power, our sense of personal agency, to resist situational forces.... For some that belief is valid.... For many, that belief in

personal power to resist powerful situational and systemic forces is little more than a reassuring illusion of invulnerability. Paradoxically, maintaining that illusion only serves to make one more vulnerable to manipulation by failing to be sufficiently vigilant against attempts of undesired influence subtly practiced on them.[54]

Clearly, some negative and even potentially dangerous consequences can arise when people don't properly manage the conflict they encounter in their groups. The next section provides some advice to equip you to handle conflict effectively and efficiently.

HANDLING CONFLICT IN GROUPS

Group members depend on one another to complete a task or to achieve the psychological benefits they expect from being in the group. Personality clashes may fuel conflicts. Differences in goal seeking concerning the task may lead to conflict, or differences about the way to achieve the task may lead to conflict. Both have the potential to affect working relationships between team members.

As explained in Chapter 8, group conflicts may not necessarily be overt, apparent, or open. Frequently, before group members actually talk about a conflict, they are aware of the undercurrents and are already trying to predict the way the conflict will unfold so they can respond to it appropriately. For example, you may be working on a class project and notice that one of your group members has been talking less in the group and has demonstrated different nonverbal behavior than you previously observed. You are aware that a conflict is probably going to occur before the group member says anything.

Conflicts in groups, while sharing the same basic characteristics as interpersonal conflict (e.g., a problematic situation, interdependent people) are best understood by examining the issue that drives the conflict. Most conflicts in groups can be broadly categorized into four types: instrumental/task-oriented conflict, relationship-oriented conflict, identity-oriented conflict, and process-oriented conflict.[55]

instrumental/task-oriented conflict The assumption that a moderate amount of conflict, as opposed to very low or very high levels, results in cognitive flexibility, creative thinking, and problem-solving abilities.

You may be aware that a group conflict is about to take place when you notice that some group members aren't speaking and are engaging in nonverbal behaviors that you hadn't previously observed during other meetings.

Instrumental/Task-Oriented Conflict

While a group sets instrumental goals in the form of mission statements, policies, handbooks, or the requirements of an assignment, group members may have their own ideas of how best to go about getting a job done. **Instrumental/task-oriented conflict** occurs among members of a group over how to get a job done. Even where the goals, tasks, positions, and goals are prescribed, there is usually some ambiguity associated with getting the job done. You probably have experienced this when completing a class project in a group. While you have much of the information you need to complete the task, often you will find that other group members don't interpret the assignment the same way. This type of conflict may not be a problem in the long run. A moderate amount of instrumental/task-related conflict, while it may take precious time to resolve, may result in greater efficiencies and productivity in the long run.[56] If you take the time to clarify the outcome the group is seeking, you are likely to produce a better group project. Under some conditions, though, task conflict does decrease group member satisfaction and feelings of well-being. When groups continue to engage in conflict over the best way to accomplish a task, even when they have accomplished the task well, feelings of satisfaction and well-being are affected.[57] Under these conditions, group members get worn out by the conflict.

Relationship-Oriented Conflict

Relationships in groups are formal and informal. **Relationship-oriented conflict** is tied to concepts such as power, trust, supportiveness, competition, and rules that govern types of interpersonal relationships. It occurs when people are unsure of or do not agree with the rules of interaction in the group. Under the best circumstances, relational conflict may be a stimulus for critical thinking, disclosure, examination of motives, and an opportunity to understand another's viewpoint. Under most circumstances, though, relationship conflict is the prime culprit for stress among group members and loss of productivity within the group. If you find that you are more focused on why another group member is rubbing you the wrong way than you are on the project you are trying to complete, your contribution to the group is going to be negatively affected.[58] As with persistent conflict over a task, relationship conflict negatively affects feelings of satisfaction and well-being.[59]

relationship-oriented conflict A type of group conflict that occurs when people are unsure of or do not agree with the rules of interaction in the group.

Identity-Oriented Conflict

Identity goals concern a person's desire for status, prestige, and authority as he or she finds a place in the group. **Identity-oriented conflict** occurs when others treat a person contrary to the way that person sees himself or herself. If you have typically been an A student who has consistently performed well in group projects, you might expect others to defer to your expertise when you are working in a group. If someone you perceive as less capable tries to take over the lead for the group, you may find yourself in an identity conflict.

identity-oriented conflict A type of group conflict that occurs when others treat a person contrary to the way that person sees himself or herself.

Process-Oriented Conflict

The last type of conflict groups experience is centered on processes and procedures. **Process-oriented conflict** has to do with disagreements over the working style that is typical of a group. In other words, process conflict concerns the ways the group should manage communication and conflict. Some people prefer to achieve group goals in a more open, consensual, and fair way, addressing disagreement immediately and not progressing on a task until everyone in the group has reached consensus. Others may prefer to defer to a leader rather than put every disagreement out for discussion. Still others seem more chaotic, with no clear plan or set of expectations. Process conflict can be managed by clarifying expectations for a group before the group proceeds very far with its assigned task.

process-oriented conflict Disagreements over the working style that is typical of a group.

As there are different types of conflict in groups, problems can arise when some important issues in one type of conflict are neglected in favor of less important issues of another type of conflict. For example, suppose you are in a community group that has volunteered to raise money for improvements to the local library. Based on information available to you, you've set a particular dollar amount as a goal and have some ideas about the way the money should be raised, although nothing has yet been established. Some positive effects of process conflict could be establishing rules about how you will gather information, generate ideas, test your assumptions about those ideas, and handle disagreements in the group. When people fail to clarify differences over process issues, they may begin to experience negative emotions about them and personalize process issues into relationship issues.

Generally speaking, once process issues have been addressed in a proactive manner, task conflicts should take precedence over other types of issues if a group is to survive and prosper. Typically, writers in the field of group conflict have asserted that, while relationship- and process-oriented conflict can be expected to have negative effects on group performance and satisfaction, task-oriented conflict should result in higher productivity in the long run. From this point of view, task-oriented conflict helps groups avoid moving too quickly and assuming they have consensus when they do not.[60] Moderate levels of task-oriented conflict alone (without relationship- or process-oriented conflict) lead to the best productivity.[61]

It is apparent that if conflict in groups is to have any beneficial effect, it must be managed at its early stages, using strategies appropriate to the type of conflict experienced. Conflict that is not managed quickly is a source of stress that can also make members feel helpless.[62]

Watch the **Video** "Helping Annie" at **MyCommunicationLab**

IMPROVING OUR ABILITY TO CREATE CIVIL AND EFFECTIVE GROUP MEETINGS

When you meet in groups to address problems and generate solutions, it is helpful to have an understanding of how to run an effective meeting. Interestingly, while there is no shortage of advice on how to run a meeting, very little scholarly research has been conducted to determine whether these techniques are really the most effective. A survey of more than 600 executives reported that more than half were extremely bothered when:[63]

- The effectiveness of a meeting was not demonstrable.
- Meetings went too long.
- Members drifted off the subject.
- Members made emotional outbursts.
- Members weren't prepared or didn't participate.
- Members were too wordy when speaking.
- Members failed to listen to one another.

The following sections explore guidelines for running effective meetings, the roles that members play in meetings, and the effects of culture and gender on communication behavior in meetings. Knowledge of these topics will help you avoid the problems listed above and will help you be a more effective member of a group.

Questions and Guidelines Related to Running Meetings

If you are considering whether to call a meeting, asking yourself certain questions and following specific guidelines can help you achieve meeting effectiveness. These questions and guidelines include:

When meetings are run well, members experience higher satisfaction.

- Asking whether a meeting should be called or whether you can simply gather the information you need from a number of individuals. Often, people conduct meetings to have people share information that not all the members need to hear. If only you need an update from people you are working with, but they don't really need to hear updates from one another, you don't need a meeting.

- Determining the purpose of the meeting. If a meeting is necessary, determine its purpose by deciding what you want to accomplish by having the meeting. For example, if people need to hear updates from others, be sure that as much of the information as possible is sent out prior to the meeting so that people can raise questions and receive answers rather than simply hearing a number of different reports. Is there a particular problem that needs to be solved, or is there a task that needs to be accomplished? Once you have clarity on what you already know and what you want to accomplish, you can decide on the next step you need to take, such as gathering more information or moving toward a decision.

- Deciding who needs to attend the meeting. Although you may be tempted to invite a large number of people, accomplishing a task or planning a project is best suited for a group of five to seven people. Resist inviting people who don't have a stake in the task. On the other hand, routine meetings will typically have a higher number of attendees than will one-time meetings.

- Deciding time and place. Determine the time and location of the meeting and make sure that everyone is aware of those details. Be sure to have set opening and closing times. As the convener of the meeting, you should create an agenda that covers all the different items the meeting must address. Sometimes it helps to have a particular amount of time assigned to different items so that everything will be discussed or accomplished before the meeting ends. Your agenda should be sent out no later than 24 hours in advance of the meeting. A sample agenda is shown in Figure 10.3.

In addition, determine whether you will need audiovisual equipment for the meeting and arrange for it if necessary. Prepare handouts and make sufficient copies for everyone; alternatively, you can email the handouts to participants. In addition, arrange for someone to keep notes of the meeting discussion. During the meeting, be sure to stay close to your agenda and try to keep discussion on the topic at hand. Determine action items, distribute them among group members, and specify times for those items to be accomplished.

Within 24 hours of your meeting, be sure to distribute the minutes and remind members of the commitments they made to take particular actions and the time by which those actions should be accomplished. An easy way to remember how to conduct a meeting is in Shirley Fine Lee's acronym RA!RA! which stands for "assigned meeting *r*oles, a written *a*genda, keeping *r*ecords, and assignment of *a*ctions."[64]

Roles Members Play in Meetings

You have read about roles, or the behaviors that people engage in when they are involved in groups. Roles can be formal or informal, and they can be task oriented, maintenance oriented, or disruptive in nature. Formal roles in a meeting include the convener, who sets the agenda and determines who should be invited to the meeting. Meetings should have a recorder who takes minutes and prepares them for distribution by the leader. Formal meetings will also include a parliamentarian, to ensure that people take turns to speak and that people speak to the issue under discussion. A group's historian is responsible for keeping the minutes of the group organized and accessible for members to consult when needed. A treasurer is necessary if the group collects dues or raises funds through sales or events.

Date of the Meeting:		Location:	
Starting Time:		Ending Time:	
Invited Attendees:			
Voting Members:	Representing:		Term End:
Ellen Wilde	Marketing		2015
Ex-Officio Members			
Non-voting:	Representing:		Term End:
Mark Dismal	Accounting		No end date
Agenda:			Time Allocated:
1. Introductions			5 minutes
2. Approval of minutes from last meeting			5 minutes
3. Old Business			20 minutes
Topic	Action Item	Person Responsible	Follow Up Date
4. New Business			20 minutes
Topic	Action Item	Person Responsible	Follow Up Date
5. Items to Share, Assignments			10 minutes
6. Adjournment			

FIGURE 10.3 Agenda

This figure shows an example of an agenda. At the beginning of a meeting, it has many blank entries, and team members can use it as a guide to keep track of the decisions that are made—such as who will be responsible for taking action and when the task must be completed.

Culture and Meeting Behavior

When researchers first began to examine the effects of culture on group member behavior, they looked at the obvious factors of ethnicity and race in addition to other factors such as age and gender. Demographic variables were assumed to have an effect on group member behavior because it was assumed that they would prompt others to respond to them in stereotyped ways. For example, researchers assumed that group members might act differently toward someone considerably older than themselves and might treat information provided by that person differently than they would information provided by their peers. Demographic variables are easily measured and demonstrate an effect on behavior when the group being studied is of a short-term, temporary duration. Much of our knowledge about group behavior has been derived from settings in which strangers (quite often college students) come together to accomplish some task under controlled conditions and then depart. But when researchers turned their attention to groups that stay together, the picture began to change.[65]

Recently, researchers have begun to distinguish between surface-level diversity (e.g., age, gender) and deep-level diversity, which includes values, attitudes, beliefs, personality factors, work habits, experiences, and so on.[66] Their findings have indicated that while surface-level diversity variables may impact initial interactions between group members, as time goes on, members are more impacted by deep-level diversity issues. Over time, the more members perceive that they resemble each other with respect to values, beliefs, work habits, and so on, the less impact those variables have on group member behavior.[67]

Problems arise, however, when perceptions of similarity don't develop. If you have been in a group for a long time, you may be very aware of the differences between you and others. For example, it may be a source of great frustration to you that as an optimist, you find that your work and performance depend on working closely with a pessimist. People are unlikely to change their core personality characteristics. In this case, the need for civility and ethical communication becomes paramount. We can appreciate our differences without insisting that others change so that the group purpose can be achieved.

Gender and Meeting Behavior

Although gender is considered to be a surface-level variable, effects due to it are apparent in both short-term and long-term groups. Men and women behave differently in meetings, but the differences depend on the composition of the group—all male, all female, or mixed. In mixed groups, men talk more, assume leadership positions, and receive more positive and less negative feedback than women. Men interrupt women more frequently than they do other men, while women interrupt men and other women equally.[68] In addition, in mixed groups, men use humor more frequently and more successfully than women. That difference was so pronounced in early research studies that some writers concluded that women in general lacked a sense of humor.[69]

When women are observed in all female groups, their behavior is different than when in mixed groups. In all-female groups, women use much more humor than do men in all-male groups. They laugh much more than men do in their same-sex groups. In addition, women use humor in different ways. Women use humor to build group cohesion; their humor tends to emphasize the connectedness of the group members. Men more typically use humor to create and reinforce hierarchy.[70] For example, a woman might tell a story about herself that illustrates a mistake she made in order to create a sense of identity among other group members who may fear making such a mistake. A man might tell a story about a success he experienced that others are not likely to equal.

A final area where differences are observed has to do with leadership in the group. Women prefer norms that emphasize equality over hierarchy. That preference is demonstrated by what happens to group leadership over time in groups that have equal numbers of men and women or that are composed primarily of females. In those groups, even if the group had a designated leader at the beginning, over time leadership spread out equally among the group members. Male-dominated groups, on the other hand, tend to maintain hierarchy, with leadership clearly designated in one position.[71]

Women use more humor and laugh more when in groups with other women than they do in mixed groups when men are present.

✓
Study and **Review** materials for this chapter are at **MyCommunicationLab**

CHAPTER SUMMARY

Now that you have read this chapter you can:

10.1 Describe the relationship between civility, ethics, and group communication processes.

Acting civilly and ethically in a group situation may be difficult when you have had to make a number of decisions previously. You are now aware of the impact of decision fatigue on your behavior and the way it might impede your ability to act in a civil and ethical manner.

10.2 Identify the communication and decision-making patterns in a group of which you are a member.

Communication networks can be centralized or decentralized. Centralized communication networks require people to send their messages by way of one or two people, while decentralized networks allow group members to communicate freely about the task at hand. When the task is simple, a centralized network is more efficient, but when the task is complex, a decentralized network will work better.

In addition, groups can operate in one of three decision-making patterns. Sometimes, a leader will simply make a decision and announce it. This pattern is necessary when time is short and a decision must be made immediately. At other times, a leader will consult the group members and solicit information before making a decision. This pattern helps to raise group member commitment to the decision. Finally, a leader may simply join the group and allow each person to have an equal voice by taking a vote or working until the group reaches consensus. Consensus means that everyone in the group can commit themselves to the decision but not necessarily that everyone agrees that the decision is the best one that could be made.

10.3 Explain the central task of a group.

You can explain that groups are typically to bring together the skills of a variety of people to solve problems that would be difficult to grapple with as an individual.

10.4 Analyze a problem using the steps in group problem solving and explain the link between creativity and problem solving.

You can analyze a problem using the steps in group problem solving. You can use the Dewey's Reflective

Listen to the **Audio Chapter Summary** at **MyCommunicationLab**

Thinking model: defining the problem, analyzing the causes of the problem, identifying criteria for a solution, generating solutions, selecting the best solution, and implementing the solution. You can also address a problem by using the SCRIPTS technique, which consists of searching for threats and opportunities, finding the causes, evaluating the risks, applying intuition, taking different perspectives, considering the time frame, and solving the problem. Creative thinking is something that most people can do, and addressing problems in a variety of ways is more likely to lead to a good solution than engaging in familiar ways of thinking about the problem.

10.5 Compare vertical thinking and lateral thinking, apply standard problem techniques, and construct a mind map for a problem.

There are times when vertical thinking, or working from cause to effect, is useful. In addition, breaking familiar patterns and provoking new insights through lateral thinking can be useful.

You can use five standard techniques for solving problems: brainstorming, reverse brainstorming, fractionation, and the six hats method, which emphasizes different ways of looking at the problem in order to engage in problem solving.

Mind mapping is a visual brainstorming technique that looks for all the different pieces of a problem and the way in which they are connected.

10.6 Identify the three barriers to effective decision making in groups.

Failure to engage in good decision making in a group can result in negative outcomes. Groupthink is the result of groups suppressing conflict and disagreement in order to maintain the illusion of unanimity. The Abilene paradox results in people saying what they think others want to hear rather than what they really think. The Lucifer effect can arise when the circumstances of a group lead people to behave in ways contrary to their true values and beliefs.

10.7 Address different types of conflict in groups.

Conflict in groups typically falls into one (or more) of four categories. Instrumental/task-oriented conflict relates to how the group will get a task done. Relationship-oriented conflict refers to violations in the rules of interaction for that group. Identity-oriented conflict refers to disagreements over the status, prestige, and authority of the group members. Process-oriented conflict refers to disagreements over the group's working style.

10.8 Plan and run a meeting.

You need to first determine whether a meeting is even needed, decide what you want to accomplish, and then choose who needs to be there. It is important to apprise a group of the location and time of the meeting, and it's important to distribute an agenda ahead of time. Staying with the agenda is important, and so is following up with minutes and reminders of commitments that members have made.

CIVILITY SUMMARY

Overall, remember that group processes and civil communication involve the following:

- Implicit standards for ethical behavior, such as those that instruct us to demonstrate tolerance and to focus on ideas when in conflict, are based on civility.
- Group members who aren't trained in small group discussion and communication skills may not realize that their communication is uncivil. Responding in kind is less effective than modeling civil communication and good group discussion skills so that other members may learn and eventually engage in civil communication on their own.
- Providing tools to students to help them think and act creatively is essential for the advancement of a civil society.

REVIEW QUESTIONS

1. What is the relationship between civility, ethics, and group communication processes?
2. Describe the communication networks that groups can use to process information.
3. Compare and contrast Dewey's Reflective Thinking model with the SCRIPTS method of problem solving.
4. Describe the link between creativity and problem solving.
5. Demonstrate the difference between vertical thinking and lateral thinking by applying Dewey's Reflective Thinking model or SCRIPTS and the fractionation, reversal, and six hats methods to a problem of your choice.
6. Describe groupthink, the Abilene paradox, and the Lucifer effect and show how one of them might occur in a group of which you are a member.
7. What is the difference between instrumental, relationship-, identity-, and process-oriented conflicts?
8. What are the steps in planning a meeting?

Study and **Review** the **Flashcards** at **MyCommunicationLab**

PART IV CIVIL PUBLIC SPEAKING

11 Preparing Civil Public Speeches

CHAPTER OBJECTIVES

After reading this chapter, you will be able to:

11.1 Analyze your audience effectively and engage audiences in civil communication.

11.2 Determine your general purpose for a speech, apply brainstorming techniques for generating ideas about your topic, and create a thesis based on your general and specific speech purposes.

11.3 Choose an effective organizational strategy for a speech.

11.4 Use standard outlining conventions to construct a formal speech outline.

11.5 Craft effective introductions and conclusions, as well as use good transitions in your speech.

11.6 Plan, gather, and use supporting material appropriately for your speech.

HAVE YOU EVER attended an event where the speaker failed to engage the audience? Perhaps you felt embarrassed for the speaker, hoping he or she could just get through the presentation as quickly as possible. On the other hand, have you been to an event where you were so engaged with what the speaker had to say that you did not notice how quickly the time went by? In the first instance, you probably were grateful that you were not the speaker, and it even may have reinforced ideas you have about public speaking being an activity you would like to avoid. In the second instance, you probably admired the speaker's performance and may even have wondered if you were capable of performing similarly.

Consider this example, which illustrates what can happen when public speakers fail to engage their audiences. On February 13, 2011, *Elle Magazine* hosted its annual Style Awards ceremony at the Grand Connaught Rooms in London, England. A variety of celebrities gathered to find out who would win the coveted style icon award. The recipient was Emma Watson, known best for her role as Hermione Granger in the *Harry Potter* movies, who had asked to be introduced by fashion designer Vivienne Westwood if she won the award. Unfortunately, Westwood not only did not know who Watson was, but she apparently made no effort to find out prior to appearing onstage to present the award. Westwood spent most of her time onstage rambling about why she did not know Watson and that she did not watch television or go to the movies. A speech which should have been designated to introduce and honor Watson and explain why she was chosen to win the award instead had a self-serving focus on the presenter. Watson smiled graciously and gave Westwood a hug after receiving her award.[1]

WHY IT MATTERS

Westwood could have avoided this embarrassing situation if she had taken the necessary steps to address her listeners in a civil way by showing greater sensitivity to their needs and to the occasion itself. First, Westwood should have understood that few topics sell themselves. Even the most interested, motivated audience needs to be convinced that their attendance at a lecture or speech is not wasted time. Second, as Westwood was introducing someone who had won an award relevant to her profession, she should have had some idea why the award was given. Most importantly, though, Westwood failed to communicate civilly and ethically. Her rambling did not reflect restraint. Her lack of preparation made her look irresponsible. And her disregard for Watson and the award showed a lack of respect. In this instance, Westwood failed to present herself as a trustworthy communicator, which points to a lack of ethics.

In this chapter, you will learn how to prepare civil public speeches. You will learn how to engage your audience with civility by determining the general purpose of your speech, selecting your topic and generating ideas, moving from information to speech, and organizing your information. You will also read about introductions, transitions, and conclusions, as well as gathering and using supporting material and writing a speech outline.

Listen to the **Audio Chapter** at **MyCommunicationLab**

Explore the **Concept** "Audience Analysis" at **MyCommunicationLab**

Maslow's Hierarchy of Needs
A theory of psychology proposed by Abraham Maslow in 1943. Maslow's hierarchy identifies several basic needs of all human beings: self-actualization, esteem, love/belonging, safety, and physiological needs.

ENGAGING YOUR AUDIENCE WITH CIVILITY

Preparing civil public speeches first necessitates that you effectively engage your audience. You must always think about how your listeners will process your message and how they will react and respond. In addition, you will want your audience to take an active interest in your subject. You also want your audience to think that they need to know more about your subject, and you create hunger by appealing to their needs. Abraham Maslow's research on human motivations led him to create **Maslow's Hierarchy of Needs**, illustrated in Figure 11.1. Maslow determined that people will work first to satisfy their basic physiological needs and then safety needs, belonging needs, esteem needs, and self-actualization needs. Once people meet their lower-level needs, they are motivated to meet the higher-level needs.

A speech can appeal to any level of needs. A policy maker might appeal to physiological needs by arguing for measures providing communities with greater access to clean water. The president, on the other hand, might give a speech appealing to safety needs by promising greater national security through a stronger national defense. A member of a fraternity or sorority might give a speech appealing to students' need for belonging, while that same speech might also emphasize self-actualization needs through the organization's achievement and its members having earned the respect of others. Speakers also may appeal to listeners' needs for self-actualization by asking them to

FIGURE 11.1 Maslow's Hierarchy of Needs

As you consider which of the audience needs you are appealing to, consider the speaking strategy that will meet those needs.

consider how an issue conforms or does not conform to their sense of morality. Not too long ago, both politicians and protest leaders asked the American public to consider the morality of waging war in Iraq.

A successful speech targets specific needs, if possible. For instance, if you want to tell your audience about basic features of tae kwon do, which needs would you appeal to? Tae kwon do involves kicks, blocks, and punches, so you could appeal to physical health, which is a basic physiological need. On the other hand, you could talk about the need to defend yourself so as not to be a victim of crime, evoking fear and appealing to the safety need. You could also talk about how tae kwon do teaches discipline and goal-setting, which lead to a sense of accomplishment. In this instance, you would be appealing to the need for respect. Here's an example of what you might write:

> Think back for a moment to a time when you accomplished something that meant a lot to you. Maybe you won a trophy for an athletic event, earned a high grade in a difficult class, or summoned up enough courage to say "hello" to that good-looking person standing on the other side of the room. Your accomplishment may appear to be insignificant to others, although it may be important to you. Perhaps your accomplishment involved finally cleaning out that stuffed-to-the-gills closet or finally losing those last five pounds. Although these examples are all different, they share at least one thing in common: the sense of self-respect you feel when you set and meet a goal.
>
> What if I told you that it is possible to participate in a specific activity that can improve your physical and mental health, foster positive thinking, *and* boost your self-respect by setting and achieving goals? This particular activity helps create inner confidence that can be applied to various situations and experience. This activity is tae kwon do. According to *The Sport Journal*, published by the United States Sports Academy, tae kwon do increases self-esteem and confidence. The tae kwon do Information.org website states that the activity promotes self-respect and happiness and can help you cope during difficult times. In all, you will achieve a feeling of accomplishment on an ongoing basis, when you participate in tae kwon do.

You can use a similar process with your audience. Whether your ultimate goal is to impart knowledge or influence an attitude or a behavior, you must first convince your audience that you know something they want or need to know. The only way to do this effectively is to understand what your audience believes, what they want, and so forth. Therefore, you should find out as much as you can about your audience by using Maslow's Hierarchy of Needs in combination with a psychographic and demographic analysis.

Considering Your Audience's Psychographics

A civil speaker has the responsibility to respect the audience. A key factor in this respect means that you must consider your listeners' feelings, or **psychographics**, and how you can make yourself and your subject even more important and relevant to your listeners. In analyzing your audience, consider the psychographic variables or factors related to their attitudes, beliefs, and values. The audience's **attitudes** reflect their general tendency to view you and/or your topic favorably, unfavorably, or neutrally. Their **beliefs**, on the other hand, reflect a specific instance of something the listeners see as true or untrue. The

psychographics Relates to how a speaker and a subject can become even more important and relevant in relationship to the audience's attitudes, beliefs, and values.

attitude An audience's tendency to view a speaker and a topic favorably or unfavorably.

belief What listeners accept as true or untrue.

audience's **values** represent their core feelings related to the inherent worth of a concept or an idea.[2] In fact, some would argue that a person's values help shape his or her beliefs and attitudes because values represent underlying standards of desirable behavior justifying those beliefs and attitudes. A speaker and the audience may share values but differ in their beliefs; both speaker and the audience may value a just society but may disagree over how to achieve it. A speaker, for instance, might express his or her belief that the death penalty helps achieve a just society, while his or her audience might believe that the death penalty actually works against this goal. Considering these aspects of psychographics can help you speak effectively and civilly to your audience.

Attitudes You can ask yourself the following questions to gain insight into your audience's attitudes:

- *Does your audience support your position on the issue?* A politician giving a speech supporting higher wages for manual laborers to a group of steel workers in Pittsburgh will likely receive a very positive response.

- *Are listeners neutral or apathetic toward your stance or perspective on the issue or subject?* In many instances, listeners not yet have formulated opinions or may not even care about your subject. Such circumstances necessitate that you find ways to help listeners identify with your subject. A speech on campus, for example, encouraging students to join a fraternity or sorority will first need to connect with students' need for group identity and belonging.

- *Do listeners oppose your position? Is the audience divided on the issue?* A speech supporting tax vouchers for private schools, for instance, necessitates first knowing the audience's attitude toward public education. Your audience might support public education, yet your speech will attempt to persuade them to support tax incentives that help people send their children to private schools. An effective speech given by a CEO about the corporation being bought by another organization requires that the speaker know her or his employees' attitudes about corporate takeovers. The audience may support a takeover to prevent their corporation from declaring bankruptcy but will most likely be concerned about budget cuts and layoffs. The CEO will want to talk about the benefits of the takeover but will need to also acknowledge the concerns of the audience in such an instance, such as by acknowledging audience opinions first and then presenting your side.

Beliefs The following questions can help you learn about what your audience perceives as true or not true:

- *What are your audience members' beliefs underlying the issue about which you will speak? Does the audience share your beliefs?* A presidential candidate speaking at his or her party's convention, for example, can assume that the audience shares the candidate's belief related to the role of government. A Republican candidate speaking at the Republican convention will likely share with the audience a belief in a more limited role of government in society.

- *Do various audience members hold different beliefs or see the reality of the situation differently?* An informative speech to retirees helping them understand health care

To target audience needs in a speech about Tae Kwon Do, a speaker can appeal to physiological needs (health), safety needs (self-defense), and self-esteem needs (accomplishment and self-respect).

value A strong feeling of the audience related to the inherent worth of a concept or an idea.

options may be met with a number of different beliefs. Some listeners, for example, may believe health care is a human right, while others might see it as a market-driven commodity or service.

Values The following questions will help you discover the values that your audience possesses:

- *How does the audience view the inherent worth of your idea or ideas?* A speech proposing to bulldoze an old housing development so that a company can erect a new shopping mall might be met with resistance if an audience of community members deems it immoral to force people out of their homes for this purpose. On the other hand, an audience of community members might see building a shopping mall as beneficial if it helps stimulate the local economy. In either case, members of the audience value *community*, but they value it from opposing points of view.

- *What do listeners view as desirable or ideal standards of behavior?* A speech defending a political or business leader against allegations of impropriety might be met with resistance from listeners if they expect leaders always to conduct themselves ethically and morally. Moreover, the audience may already believe the charges against the person are true, thereby making the job of communicating his or her innocence even more difficult. Regardless, though, audiences adhere to and place value on what they view as desirable or ideal standards of behavior.

Often, speechmakers focus on values more than attitudes or beliefs because larger numbers of people are likely to share certain values. President Obama's speech at the memorial service for the six people killed in a shopping mall in Arizona in 2011, for example, demonstrates an attempt to appeal to the value Americans place on community and, in essence, democratic ideals. Obama said that "the loss of these wonderful people should make every one of us strive to be better in our private lives—to be better friends and neighbors, co-workers and parents." Obama went onto say that "only a more civil and honest public discourse can help us face up to our challenges as a nation."[3] By emphasizing the importance of strong communal bonds and civility, he appealed to the values, beliefs, and attitudes that most of his audience members were likely to hold.

Considering Your Audience's Demographics

Once you have determined how your audience feels about you and your topic, you are ready to consider what other factors may come into play as you try to determine how your audience will react to you and your speech. Civil public speaking necessitates that you analyze demographic characteristics. **Demographic characteristics** are factors that help you know as much as you can about your audience before you craft your speech; they may include such factors as cultural difference, age, and sex or gender. When you consider demographic characteristics, you demonstrate that you intend to engage listeners with civility because doing so suggests that you respect audience members' different biases, backgrounds, and beliefs. Consider the following questions associated with age, sex/gender, group membership, cultural diversity, and number of people in your efforts to analyze your audience:

Age

- What is the predominant age of your audience? How can you speak to the interests and concerns of the main ages of your audience? How can you avoid making references with which your audience will fail to identify? For example, will an audience

demographic characteristics Characteristics such as the size of the audience, group composition, cultural differences, age, and gender.

of mostly persons over the age of 55 or 60 identify readily with references to popular music from the early 21st century?

Sex/Gender

- How can sex affect the way you approach your topic? What topics, for example, may be more appropriate for audiences that are predominantly female? Male?
- How might you avoid the use of gender-biased language or the universal *he*? You will probably alienate members of your audience if you continually refer to people in general using the pronoun *he* when those persons could be male or female.

Group Composition

- What interests do the audience members share?
- Do audience members share certain opinions or perspectives? If so, what are those perspectives? For example, a political candidate giving a speech at his or her party's convention can assume that the listeners' opinions are likely to be comparable to his or her own.

Cultural Diversity

- Do your listeners represent different races or ethnicities?
- Is your audience made up of a dominant cultural group?
- Do you realize that your own experiences and biases may cause you to stereotype members of the audience? Do you know that your experiences and biases may not be shared by your audience and are therefore willing to "let go" of your stereotypes?
- Does your audience share a common religion and socioeconomic background? Since these factors are difficult if not impossible to ascertain without specifically asking audience members, be sure that you don't assume that you and your audience share religious beliefs or the same socioeconomic background (e.g., avoid saying, "As Christians/Jews/Muslims/etc., we all believe that…").

Size of the Audience

- Is your audience large or small? You may be able to be more intimate with a small audience.
- What topics are appropriate or inappropriate, based on the number of people to whom you are speaking? For example, a speaker describing his or her past abusive relationship will likely make an audience of several hundred people feel uncomfortable. Such topics are probably more appropriate for much smaller groups.

These five demographic characteristics, together with the psychographic profile of your audience, represent important considerations, but your analysis should not end here. You can also try to find out whether your audience is positive, negative, or neutral toward you and/or the topic. Some audience members may be sympathetic, while others may be negative or even hostile toward the subject you have chosen. Still other listeners might find themselves neutral or perhaps indifferent. If so, it is your job as the speaker to encourage them to care about the subject of your speech. Very few listeners, however, will

To predict how your audience may react to your speech, you can focus on audience demographic characteristics such as age, sex and gender, group composition, cultural diversity, and size of the audience.

Engaging Your Audience with Civility   227

voluntary audience Listeners who freely choose to listen to a speaker and a speech.

captive audience Listeners who have little choice but to listen to a speech.

time The duration of a speech as well as the interval in which it occurs in the context of other events.

occasion The circumstances and events surrounding the moment of the speech as well as the tone of that moment (e.g., sorrowful, cheerful).

respond neutrally to a speech on, for instance, abortion because most people have very strong opinions on this issue. The following section explains in greater detail the types of audiences encountered in public speaking situations.

Types of Audiences

In general, you will encounter two different types of audiences. A **voluntary audience** is, as the name suggests, a group of people who choose to listen to you speak. No one is taking attendance to make sure they are there. They have come because they want to learn something from you. A **captive audience**, on the other hand, has little choice but to listen to you. Workers attending a mandatory meeting are a captive audience. People attending an important ritual such as a graduation ceremony are a captive audience. They have not really come to hear the speaker. They have come to see a family member march across the stage and receive a diploma. A group of your fellow students in a class on public speaking is essentially a captive audience—and an artificial one at that. Besides their common enrollment in the class, most students share few beliefs and attitudes with their classmates. In order to engage these listeners with civility, it is also important to acknowledge, in some way, that a captive audience has not chosen to hear your speech.

A voluntary audience is already motivated to listen to you but generally has high expectations concerning your message, which you will need to ascertain. On the other hand, you need to work harder to gain the attention of a captive audience. Audience members may sometimes even feel resentment about having to listen to you. You will soon read that your introduction is of utmost importance in gaining a captive audience's attention and justifying your presence. Most importantly, though, determining what the audience wants can help you tailor your speech to meet their expectations in an ethical and civil way.

The Occasion

To engage an audience, a speaker must show respect for the occasion. Simply put, the occasion is determined by the circumstances surrounding it. On September 11, 2001, a stunned nation watched as terrorists flew two airplanes into the Twin Towers in New York, and the towers burned and fell as a result. At the same time, hijackers flew a plane into the Pentagon, and passengers on United Flight 93 fought hijackers even as the plane plummeted to the ground. President George Bush and his administration recognized that the **time** and the **occasion** called for a speech to unite the nation and offer hope to its shocked and grieving citizens. Bush reassured the nation by saying:

President George W. Bush presented a speech that recognized the importance of the occasion when he attempted to unite the nation and offer hope to its shocked and grieving citizens after 9/11.

Today, our fellow citizens, our way of life, our very freedom came under attack in a series of deliberate and deadly terrorist acts.... These acts of mass murder were intended to frighten our nation into chaos and retreat. But they have failed. Our country is strong. A great people has been moved to defend a great nation. Terrorist attacks can shake the foundations of our biggest buildings, but they cannot touch the foundation of America. These acts shatter steel, but they cannot dent the steel of American resolve. America was targeted for attack because we're the brightest beacon for freedom and opportunity in the world. And no one will keep that light from shining. Today, our nation saw evil—the very worst of human nature—and we responded with the best of America. With the daring of our rescue workers, with the caring for strangers and neighbors who came to give blood and help in any way they could.... This is a day when all Americans from every walk of life unite in our resolve for justice and peace. America has stood down enemies before, and we will do so this time. None of us will ever forget this day, yet we go forward to defend freedom and all that is good and just in our world.[4]

place The physical environment where a speech occurs.

Place is another important aspect of the occasion. All speeches occupy a physical space; for example, the room in which you will speak is such a space. Is the room large or small? Will audience members become distracted by outside noise from a hallway? How will you adjust to the room so that you can give the best possible speech? You know, for example, that you will need to adjust your volume, or relative loudness of your voice, if

A CASE STUDY IN ETHICS

"Discouraging Jeerers"

On two recent occasions, college students heckled guest speakers at publicized campus events addressing the ongoing conflict between Jewish and Islamic people in the Middle East. In one instance, Israeli Prime Minister Ehud Olmert had been asked to give a 20-minute speech on the University of Chicago campus. However, it took Olmert around an 90 minutes to deliver his remarks because jeering students and protesters continually interrupted him. Hecklers acted out in response to the Israeli government's hard-line stance toward Palestinian people living on the West Bank and the Gaza Strip. About one week later, Geert Wilders, an openly anti-Islamic Dutch lawmaker, gave a speech at Temple University, but the question-and-answer period ended abruptly when he, too, encountered heckling from the audience. In this instance, students were expressing their discontent with university's sponsorship of someone with anti-Islamic tendencies.

Officials from the University of Chicago wrote a letter to students, faculty, and staff, admonishing the protesters' behavior during Prime Minister Olmert's speech. The hecklers, in response, disagreed, and their leader argued that Olmert was suspected of war crimes and that they were defending justice and human rights by confronting him. Temple University, on the other hand, issued a statement before Wilders's speech, indicating that it respected the rights of student organizations to invite individuals holding a wide variety of views and ideas. The statement, although possibly intended to discourage jeering or heckling, apparently failed to achieve that purpose.[5]

Discussion Questions

1. Do you believe that these audiences should have behaved in a more civil manner for these speech occasions?

2. It is acceptable to heckle speakers that the audience regards as war criminals or intolerant bigots?

3. Is there a civil alternative other than heckling that audiences can use to express their dissatisfaction with a speaker and/or a speaker's position on controversial issues?

audience expectations What listeners anticipate the speaker will tell them and what they will learn or gain from the speech.

you're speaking in a smaller room. In the Chapter 12, you will learn about volume as a factor in delivering your speeches with civility.

Finally, **audience expectations** surround any occasion for speaking and are critical for understanding how you can engage listeners with civility. Barack Obama's listeners expect him, as president, to come across as competent, intelligent, confident, and articulate. This does not mean that his speeches should be boring or that he does not use humor appropriately; however, it means that Obama must respect the occasion and recognize that people necessarily perceive him in a certain way. Furthermore, every occasion is unique. There are obvious differences between a memorial service, a fundraising speech, and a speech on the Senate floor, but more subtle differences also apply to the circumstances of each individual event.

PLANNING YOUR SPEECH TOPIC

Writing an effective speech requires much planning and preparation. Even highly engaging speakers who appear to speak "off-the-cuff" most likely plan the basics of their speech prior to delivering it. Determining the general purpose of the speech, selecting your topic, determining the specific purpose of the speech, and formulating the thesis statement are crucial steps in the planning and preparation of an effective speech.

Determining the General Purpose of a Speech

Whatever situation you find yourself in with respect to public speaking, the general purpose of the speech you are delivering is found in the speaking situation itself. You would not want to persuade an audience to protest against higher taxes if you were called upon to speak at a graduation, nor would you explain the advantages and disadvantages of becoming a vegan at a funeral. We must take into account the audience we are addressing, the occasion of the speech, our knowledge and credibility, and a number of other variables before we determine our purpose and topic.

There are three general speech purposes: to inform, to persuade, and to inspire. Keep in mind, too, that civility and ethical obligations surround any purpose of any speech. If you establish an informative purpose for a speech, then it becomes unethical to shift into persuading your audience. For example, how would you feel if you decided to attend a speech that was designed to provide you with information about the services provided by the Humane Society, and the speaker shifted the topic to persuading you that you should donate money to the organization? It is always important to respect audiences, and beginning with an informative purpose and then moving to persuasion results in deception.

informative speech A speech that provides the audience with new information, raises awareness of some issue, or communicates additional information about a topic that the audience already knows about.

Speeches to Inform An **informative speech** is one where the speaker seeks to provide the audience with new information, raise awareness of some issue, or communicate additional information about a topic that the audience already knows about. Occasions where an informative speech is appropriate include:

- A forum discussion, where several people present different aspects of a general topic
- A presentation concerning the advantages and disadvantages of different business systems
- A classroom where you are asked to report on a particular topic
- A meeting of a civic organization or another type of professional organization

- A meeting of hobbyists (e.g., a doll club) where you provide information related to the hobby

Important considerations to keep in mind when preparing an informational speech include:

- Are you providing new information to your listeners?
- Have you investigated the level of information your audience already has?
- Is your information presented at the appropriate level (neither too simple nor too complex for the audience)?

Speeches to Persuade The aim of a **persuasive speech** is to create or instill, change, or reinforce the attitudes, beliefs, values, or behaviors of the audience. Occasions where a persuasive speech is appropriate include:

- Political rallies
- Meetings where you are presenting a particular point of view
- Fundraising gatherings for social or environmental causes
- Sales meetings

Important considerations to keep in mind when preparing the persuasive speech include:

- Will the audience think you are a believable source on this topic?
- Are you asking for a reasonable amount of change?
- Have you presented a fair representation of the topic?

persuasive speech A speech that seeks to change the attitudes, beliefs, values, or behaviors of an audience.

Speeches to Inspire An inspirational speech is a speech you give to an audience that already agrees with you. The purpose is to create an even greater commitment to values, beliefs, attitudes, or behaviors that the audience already endorses. An inspirational speech directs the audience toward a particular action that is consistent with the existing attitudes and beliefs of the audience. Inspirational speeches are appropriate for:

- Religious services
- Graduation ceremonies
- Professional retreats
- Other ritualistic events

In addition, speeches to inspire often involve entertaining the audience. Many people, though, think an entertaining speech is simply a string of gags and jokes designed to make the audience laugh. But that's only half of the story. An effective entertaining speech is designed to make the audience laugh while it makes a point about something. You probably will not be prompting action on the part of your audience as much as you will be providing an alternative view of something they see daily.

President Barack Obama used humor by referencing the film *The Lion King* when making the point to the White House press corps that he was born an American citizen.

For example, each year the U.S. president presents a humorous speech to a gathering of the White House press corps and is roasted in turn at the White House Correspondents' Dinner. During the 2011 White House Correspondents' Dinner, President Obama roasted himself regarding "birthers" and their beliefs that the president was born in Africa and therefore is not an American citizen. After saying, "Tonight for the first time I am releasing my official birth video," the president showed a clip of the Disney movie *The Lion King*, which takes place in Africa. As soaring music played in the background and the lion cub Simba was held high in the air by Rafiki, advisor to Simba's father, the king, the president's birthday was time-stamped on the lower-right side of the screen.[6] This portion of the roast made the audience laugh but also made a point about the "birthers" and their refusal to give up the claim that the president was not born a U.S. citizen.

In writing an entertaining speech, it is important to respect the bounds of taste for the audience we are addressing. Avoiding scatological humor as well as humor that dehumanizes another person is also important.

Selecting Your Topic and Generating Ideas

Once you have established the general purpose for a speech, you must select your topic. Often the topic about which you are speaking will be defined by the audience or the occasion, but at other times the speaker may establish the speaking topic. Typically instructors encourage students to select the topics they will speak about for their classroom speeches. Speech instructors generally say that students can choose topics from two broad categories for classroom speeches: subjects they already know a great deal about or subjects they desire to know more about.

Choosing a Topic Based on Personal Experience
You may choose to speak about a topic that is familiar to you. If so, you can rely on your own knowledge and experience for basic information (although, as you will read at the end of this chapter, you may still need to research some additional information). Your instructor might give you an assignment that asks you to give an informative speech. In considering your topic, you decide to present a speech about volunteering since you have experience as a volunteer. You will then give your audience information that will enable them to choose a volunteer opportunity that best suits them. However, abiding by your informative purpose, you will avoid convincing them that they should engage in volunteer activities. Telling an audience that they "should" or "must" think a certain way or follow a course of action is associated with persuasive, rather than informative, speeches.

Speakers can choose topics based on personal experience. A person speaking about disabilities, for example, may suffer from a disability him or herself.

Choosing a Topic Based on Research
The Internet provides a wealth of ideas that can be used as possible speech topics. Later in this chapter, you will read how to evaluate Internet sources, but for now, understand that a reliable Internet source includes a sponsoring organization (e.g., the Red Cross, CNN), the author of the source, and the date the information was compiled and/or written. In addition, as you undoubtedly know, many people have Facebook and Twitter accounts and actively use those accounts to maintain ties with friends and family members. However, you can also use Facebook and Twitter as well as other social networking sites to help select an interesting current topic. You can read friends' Facebook Wall posts, for example, to get some ideas for topics that may be of interest to your audience. Major organizations (e.g., companies, government agencies, universities and colleges) typically have Facebook pages that you can access for additional information. In addition, you can scan Twitter feeds from the major news

Table 11.1	Brainstorming for Student Volunteering	
Sources for Volunteer Opportunities	**Jobs of Volunteers**	**Kinds of Volunteering Opportunities**
Office of Student Volunteerism	Peer-Led Team Learning (PLTL)	Tutor
Student Success Center	Orientation Team Member (OTM)	Community service
Student Employment Office	Supplemental Instruction (SI)	Volunteering at orientations
Office of Undergraduate Education	Alternative Spring Break (ASB) leader	
Student Success Center		

networks to ascertain up-to-the-minute issues. Remember that you can use resources you have grown accustomed to visiting every day to help prepare a speech.

Generating Ideas An effective way to begin investigating a topic is to brainstorm everything you might say in a speech. **Brainstorming** involves generating ideas by free associating words and ideas. To help with this free association, you can try clustering—or choosing one key idea and grouping similar ideas around it—as a technique if the topic is very familiar to you; otherwise, you can conduct an Internet search to help get started. With regard to the volunteerism topic, you could start with a sheet of paper, create a table, and divide your topic into broad categories. Then you could list the specific topics that fall under each category; Table 11.1 shows how this might look.

> **brainstorming** A technique for generating ideas that involves freely associating words and ideas.

You will most likely strike certain items from this list as you begin to narrow in on a topic that interests you. Clearly you cannot address *everything* about student volunteer opportunities in a seven- or eight-minute speech. Of course, you may *not* know very much about your subject, based on experience or prior knowledge. In that case, conducting an Internet search is an effective way to obtain additional information. Using a popular Internet search engine such as Yahoo or Google, you could enter a search string such as *volunteer opportunities*. The results should provide you with a series of hits to help you begin brainstorming the topic (see Figure 11.2).

The initial search string ("volunteer opportunities") gives you a place to begin, but you will probably want to experiment with several possible search strings to assist in narrowing the topic (e.g., "volunteer opportunities for students," "volunteer opportunities associated with UT Dallas").

It's a good idea to begin thinking about your topic as soon as you know the assignment. It is also a good idea to pay close attention to class discussions and reports in the media on important subjects and make sure you write down in your notes ideas for topics when those ideas occur to you. Again, remember that preparation for the speech begins when your instructor first makes the assignment. Deciding on a topic early on gives you more time to prepare an excellent speech.

Creating a Specific Speech Purpose

After choosing your topic, you need to narrow your topic by creating a specific speech purpose from your general purpose. Due to time constraints, however, you may not be able to say everything you might wish to say. You may not accomplish anything with the audience if you attempt to state everything you know about your subject. Therefore, you can use the generation of a specific purpose statement as a way to help define your topic before you seek out specific evidence and other supporting material.

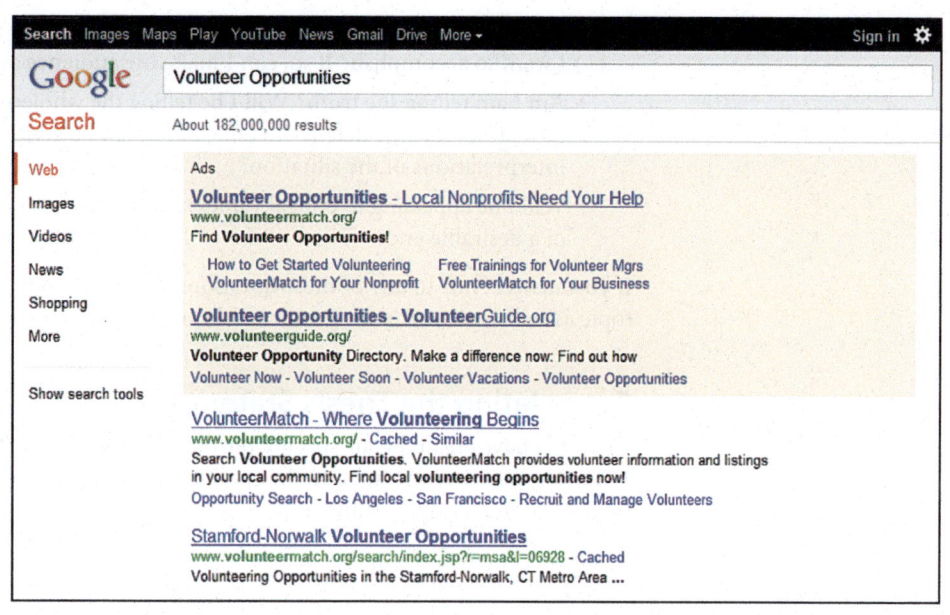

FIGURE 11.2 Google Search in Brainstorming "Volunteer Opportunities for College Students"

Google and the Google logo are registered trademarks of Google Inc., used with permission.

Your first search will yield a list similar to this one. You can refine your search by including additional details for the type of opportunity you are looking for.

specific purpose statement
A statement that limits a topic by precisely identifying what the speaker intends to accomplish.

In a **specific purpose statement**, you limit your topic by specifying what you intend to accomplish in your speech. In other words, what will your audience know, be able to do, believe, understand, value, and/or want to do at the end of your speech? While the specific purpose becomes more of a note to yourself, the thesis statement, which we discuss later in this section, is a note to your audience that tells them what you want them to take away from your speech.

Here are some examples of specific purpose statements:

- At the end of my speech, my audience will know that various on-campus offices offer a variety of volunteer opportunities for UT Dallas students.
- At the end of my speech, my audience will be persuaded that outsourcing harms the employment prospects of recent college graduates.
- At the end of my speech, my audience will be inspired by the work that UNICEF has accomplished in helping the world's children.

It is important to be realistic in your specific purpose statement. For an informative speech, you may be able to increase your audience's understanding of how something works, but you cannot guarantee that they will actually be able to apply this knowledge. For example, a speaker can probably explain the mechanics of a car engine, but that does *not* mean he or she can actually enable audience members to be auto mechanics. Think about what you are realistically able to accomplish through your speech and then plan accordingly.

Before proceeding with crafting your speech, make sure that your purpose is ethical as well as feasible. Furthermore, it should reflect civility in showing respect, restraint, and consideration for your audience. Subject your topic to four civil and ethical tests:

- Do I have good intentions toward my audience? Do I have their best interests at heart? Does my speech reflect my intentions?

- On balance, will my speech result in good effects? Are there disadvantages to what I want to accomplish? If so, can I make the audience aware of them?
- Am I am telling the truth? Will I be telling the whole story? Can the speech I give be truthful if some details are omitted? Will I be giving equal time to alternative interpretations of the situation?
- Will I be appealing to ethical values? Am I advocating questionable means because of a desirable end?

If you answer "no" to any of these questions, you might reconsider your approach to the topic as well as rethink your general and specific speech purposes.

Formulating the Thesis Statement

After you have created your specific purpose statement and it has passed the civil and ethical tests, you are ready to build the speech. The following example continues with the topic of volunteer opportunities:

> *General purpose:* To inform
> *Specific purpose:* At the end of my speech, my audience will know about student volunteer opportunities associated with the University of Texas at Dallas.

As a speaker, ask yourself why you have chosen this particular topic. You intend to inform your audience, but why should they know about this topic? Why is it important? How does the topic affect their lives? How do the points chosen for elaboration fit together? The thesis statement attempts to answer all these questions. A **thesis statement** is one sentence that summarizes the central or controlling idea of a speech. You will articulate your thesis in the opening or introduction so that your audience understands your overall point. Whereas the specific purpose is a note to yourself, the thesis statement is a note to your audience, telling them what you want them to take away from your speech.

thesis statement One sentence that summarizes the central or controlling idea of a speech.

Consider the examples that follow as thesis statements that suggest the specific purpose and tell the audience where you expect to lead them in the speech:

> *Thesis statement (informative speech):* Various on-campus offices offer a variety of volunteer opportunities for UT Dallas students.
> *Thesis statement (persuasive speech):* We should participate in volunteer opportunities associated with UT Dallas.
> *Thesis statement (inspirational speech):* Volunteering is an ethical way to help ourselves and others because it enables us to solve problems, strengthen communities, and transform our own lives.

These examples illustrate the point that the thesis statement tells the audience the central idea that you want them to take away from the speech.

ORGANIZING YOUR INFORMATION

As you gather information for a speech, you need to think about the way you want to organize it, and as the last section of this chapter discusses, you need to outline your speech according to your organizational strategy. While it is possible simply to guess which organization might be best, following a standard form for structuring your speech will help ensure that it flows smoothly. Four common approaches to organizing an informative speech are topical, chronological, spatial, and familiar to unfamiliar. Persuasive speeches, on the other hand, are often organized around the speaker's argument or thesis, with the main ideas offering support for that point. However, persuasive speeches can also prove the speaker's point by showing advantages and disadvantages to the proposed action. Inspirational speakers might rely on narrative, or story-telling, for relating their message to audiences, but again, persuasive and informative speakers might also relate narratives in supporting a main idea.

Topical Organization

A topical organization is based on categories. Using our example of the student volunteerism speech, the categories you could pull from the various ideas you generated previously could be based on the offices that sponsor volunteer activities and events. You could also create categories related to time and commitment, such as "What student volunteer opportunities are day-long events?" and "Which student volunteer opportunities last a week or longer?" Topical organization generally uses categories that are familiar to the audience. However, if you think the familiarity of your categories might "turn off" your audience ("Here we go again, same old stuff"), try inventing some unique categories to keep their attention.

A speech about fun activities on a Friday night in your home town could be divided in this way:

A. Activities that require little money
B. Moderate-cost activities
C. More expensive activities

Because your audience is likely interested in the cost of things to do in your hometown, you can frame your discussions around free activities, cheap activities, and costly activities. You simply use the categories to keep people interested.

Chronological Organization

A chronological organization is based on the time when events occurred. If you are describing an event, you start at the beginning and explain how occurrences transpired in order until the end. Starting in the middle and creating flashbacks may work in the movies, but it generally isn't a good idea in speeches. You would also use a chronological pattern if you were explaining a historical development, such as the evolution of a type of machinery. A chronological order might look like this if you were describing the history of the sewing machine:

A. First working prototype
B. First patents
C. Mechanical decorative stitches
D. Computerized sewing
E. Sewing machines more expensive than cars

You will notice that the chronological pattern necessitates that the speaker first address the origin of the sewing machine before discussing computerized sewing so that the audience understands the sequence of events. Discussing computerized sewing before first working prototype and first patents, for instance, would leave listeners feeling unsure of how one event led to another in the evolution of the sewing machine.

Spatial Organization

Sometimes it makes sense to organize a topic in terms of space. For example, if you were describing sites in southern California for a first-time visitor, you might explain how different areas of amusement parks are laid out in relation to one another. You would not tell someone, for example, to first go to one area of a park for one ride and then head over to another part of the park for a different ride.

A topic that might lend itself to spatial organization could involve sightseeing in southern California. Note, though, that the following outline uses spatial organization for the major topics and topical organization for the second level:

- A. Things to do in the San Diego area:
    1. Sea World
    2. San Diego Zoo
    3. Naval shipyards
    4. Historical Del Coronado Hotel
- B. Things to do in Orange County:
    1. Beach resorts (Laguna and Newport)
    2. Amusement parks (Disneyland, Knott's Berry Farm)
- C. Things to do in the Los Angeles area:
    1. La Brea Tar Pits
    2. Los Angeles Dodgers or Los Angeles Angels of Anaheim game
    3. Hollywood

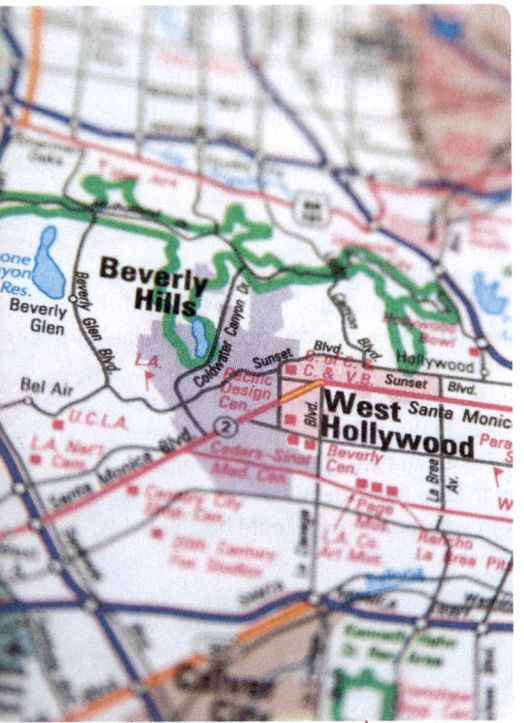

Sight-seeing in southern California is a topic that lends itself to spatial organization.

Familiar to Unfamiliar Organization

When you are trying to explain a process with which the audience is not acquainted, it might help to compare it to something they already understand. This method of organizing involves moving from the familiar to the unfamiliar. You discuss what the audience already knows and then, using that knowledge, you explain what they do not understand. For example:

- I. Body
    - A. Crafting a speech is much like writing an essay:
        1. Both have a general purpose, specific purpose, and thesis.
        2. Both should be logically organized.
        3. Both should utilize transitions to smooth the flow of ideas.
        4. Both need an introduction that stimulates interest.
        5. Both need a conclusion that leaves the listener or reader knowing what was most important.
    - B. Speeches are different from essays for several reasons:
        1. They utilize more repetition.
        2. They should use simpler language.
        3. They use more sentences of varied length.

Comparing Advantages and Disadvantages

As a way to organize the speech, comparing advantages and disadvantages is more frequently used by speakers who intend to persuade their audiences than by speakers who intend to inform their audiences. Persuasive speakers organize their speeches around an argument (i.e., the thesis) they wish to prove. In doing so, they assert their main point or thesis, and then they present their case, based on the main ideas of the speech. Persuasive speakers, though, can also show the advantages of a proposed action by pointing to a problem or need and then explaining how their proposal can bring about necessary and beneficial change.

Consider this example, using the thesis related to outsourcing and employment:

Thesis: We should stop outsourcing jobs overseas so that recent college graduates can find employment.

I. Body
   A. Recent college graduates find it difficult to obtain employment.
      1. There are few jobs for which college graduates can apply.
      2. The outlook for future graduates will not improve.
   B. Outsourced jobs prevent recent college graduates from finding employment in the U.S.
      1. Many jobs formerly found in the U.S. are now found abroad.
      2. Corporations can pay foreign workers lower wages than workers in the U.S.
   C. Keeping jobs in the U.S. will be beneficial for recent college graduates.
      1. College graduates will more easily find employment.
      2. College graduates will be able to invest in their economic future.

This example illustrates how a speaker can persuade the audience by showing them how stopping the outsourcing of jobs results in positive benefits for recent college graduates. Although the example appeals to the listeners' pocketbooks, it is important to note that the speech connects with the audience's American values of patriotism and future orientation.

Narration or Story-Telling

A speaker giving an inspirational speech will likely relate stories or narratives to illustrate his or her ideas. This account, for example, from New York City firefighter Dennis Smith could help support an inspirational speech on the sacrifices of first-responders during the 9/11 tragedy:

> When we got there, the air was just dense. It was like oatmeal. And so I stayed there for 57 consecutive days. I'm a well-trained firefighter. I worked in the busiest firehouse in the world for many years. And there aren't many people who have been in as many burning buildings as I have been in. So I worked…
>
> The 343 firefighters lost in the World Trade Center became objects of reverence. Because everyone recognized that they went into the building when everyone else was running out. The very famous photo of the man running up the stairs when everyone else is running down is very much in the minds of the people who remember 9/11. I also remember clearly the sacrifice 23 NYC police officers and 37 Port Authority police officers.[7]

In this case, the inspirational speaker could organize his or her speech around powerful narratives of first responders who witnessed the tragedy as well as those who lost their lives. Smith's story is also useful because of his use of vivid description (e.g., "the air was like oatmeal"), which aids the audience in visualizing the effects of this tragedy. Adopting such an organizational strategy will ultimately support a general purpose to inspire, and it will also support the specific purpose of inspiring the audience to recognize the sacrifices of first responders during the 9/11 tragedy.

Being listener oriented when choosing your method of organization is another organizational strategy. How is your audience likely to respond best to your topic? What will make the most sense to your listeners? What will keep their interest highest throughout the speech? Answering these questions will help you decide on the best method of organization. Making deliberate choices for structuring and organizing your speech in relationship to the occasion and audience will help you fulfill your general and specific speech purposes.

TRENDS IN TECHNOLOGY AND SOCIAL MEDIA

YouTube and Public Speaking

In some ways, it seems as though YouTube has always been a part of our media experience. In reality, it came into being in 2005. It was started by three former employees of PayPal, who created the domain name in order to create a space where people could share and view videos.[8] Reports indicate that by 2012, every minute, more than 60 hours of videos were being uploaded to the site.[9]

Since that time, YouTube has become a place where you can view everything from "how to" videos to commercial movies. And in many ways, YouTube has changed the way we think about public speaking. Search for "public speaking how to" on YouTube, and you'll get more than 200,000 results. Want tips on how to control your public speaking anxiety? There are more than 2,500 videos. You can view examples of great speeches, and you can view examples of not-so-great speeches. And whereas public speaking once required an audience, it now requires just a video camera and a way to upload the result.

An article by Megan O'Neill in *SocialTimes* argues that one of the ways YouTube has changed the world is that it has given people a place to speak out and spark change through what they broadcast. YouTube allows people to raise awareness of issues that might have gone unnoticed in the past. O'Neill points to the story of Neda Agha-Soltan, an Iranian woman:

. . .who was killed in protests over the Iranian election of 2009. The world had no idea what was going on in Iran until a video of Neda being killed was uploaded to YouTube. It spread like wildfire and soon the entire world jumped into action, doing what they could to stop the troubles in Iran and show their support.[10]

It would be difficult to argue that YouTube has not changed the world. But as with other social media, there are few checks and balances on information that is conveyed via YouTube. Given its open social nature, people may upload information that is not true, and there may be no way to refute it adequately.

Discussion Questions

1. Have you used YouTube to speak out on a subject? If not, have you thought about doing so?
2. Can you think of a topic that you first heard about on YouTube? Did you follow up with research from another source?
3. What are the challenges associated with YouTube as a substitute for speaking in organized public venues? What are the advantages?

WRITING A SPEECH OUTLINE

So far, this chapter has addressed planning your speech's content, ways of gathering information, and choosing the best organizational strategy. Once you have chosen the best strategy for organizing a speech, you are ready to outline your speech. A good practice is to create the body of the speech first before writing the outline itself.

Creating a formal outline is an important part of speech preparation. It helps ensure that you are thinking about the way major points or main ideas relate to one another. This is the standard format for an outline:

I. Introduction
II. Body of the speech
    A. First major point or main idea
        1. Support
        2. Support
            1. Secondary support
            2. Secondary support

  B. Second major point or main idea
    1. Support
    2. Support
  C. Third major point or main idea
III. Conclusion

Follow these six rules for using standard outline format:

1. The rule of parallel structure dictates that you have at least two points on the same level—so if you have an A, you have a B; if you have a 1, you have a 2, and so on. Although it may seem like an arbitrary rule, the reason for parallel structure is that it is impossible to divide something into fewer than two parts.

2. The major points that you choose to include in your outline should encompass your entire thesis statement.

3. Each major point should address only one idea or theme.

4. Limit your major points to no more than five and subdivide each one into no more than five subpoints.

5. The major points in your speech should be equally important, should be related to one another, and should be phrased using parallel grammatical construction.

6. Use words and phrases so that you can easily glance down at the outline and continue giving the speech without stopping to interpret sentences or longer statements.

  Many people reject the notion of writing an outline. They consider doing so a waste of time or they do not really understand how to write one. Writing outlines is a discipline, and like all disciplines, it seems difficult and awkward at first. The payoff is that as you gain skills at outlining, writing becomes more efficient and fun.

Creating the Body of the Speech First

Despite what you might think, with speech writing, it is not always best to begin at the beginning. Formulating an interesting opening line bogs down even the most experienced speakers. Oftentimes, speakers waste time just staring at the paper while trying to think of a good opening sentence.

  Because you already have written your thesis statement, you know what end you are trying to achieve through the presentation of your main points. For the student volunteerism speech, you need to explain each category of volunteer opportunities. Beginning with an explanation or description of each volunteer category helps orient the audience to the overall subject. Then you need to tell the audience what each category offers, as related to helping others and personal rewards. Here's what you might write:

Three offices on the UT Dallas campus offer volunteer opportunities to students:

- The Office of Student Volunteerism
- The Office of Undergraduate Education
- The Student Success Center
- What each office offers in terms of student volunteer opportunities:
- The Office of Student Volunteerism promotes the "Viva Volunteer" day event and the week-long Alternative Spring Break.
- The Office of Undergraduate Education seeks Orientation Team Mentors to work at Freshman Orientation sessions and success camps.
- The Student Success Center includes student volunteers who provide Supplemental Instruction and Peer-Led Team Learning sessions.

Creating a Formal Outline

A formal outline includes complete sentences placed in an outline format. You will read in Chapter 12 about presentation or speaking outlines, which include words and phrases to jog your memory. You use a presentation outline when you practice your speech before presenting it. You create a formal outline while writing and organizing a speech. The formal outline for your student volunteerism speech might look something like this:

> Remember that an introduction should capture the audience's attention, appeal to audience needs and arouse audience interest, and state the thesis and establish credibility. It should also clearly state the thesis or overall point and preview the organization of the speech.

> The first main idea for the speech helps orient the audience to the Office of Student Volunteerism.

> The speaker elaborates on each supporting point of the outline so that listeners gain a complete sense of the subject—in this case, the importance of volunteerism.

I. Introduction
II. Body of the speech
  A. The Office of Student Volunteerism, or OSV, is a "one-stop shop" for volunteer opportunities.
    1. The OSV sponsors the "Viva Volunteer" day-long event in conjunction with the international "Make a Difference Day."
       a. The OSV website lists approximately 30 agencies, 32 projects, and 349 participants associated with the Viva Volunteer event.
       b. Some of the agencies helped by Viva Volunteer participants include the Richardson and Plano Animal Shelters, the Dallas Children's Theater, Goodwill Industries, Foster Kids Charity, and the Neighborhood Services Council.
       c. Student Erin Hoffer, who volunteered at the Plano Community Garden, asserted how satisfying it is to "feed the hungry, educate the ignorant, and give back with service."
    2. The OSV also sponsors the week-long "Alternative Spring Break," or ASB, a program during which students participate in various community service projects, learn about social events, and develop leadership skills.
       a. Each ASB opportunity is designed for a specific social issue, and participants perform approximately 40 hours of community service during an ASB trip.
       b. You may want to volunteer for a current ASB trip such as building a Habitat for Humanity house in Jackson, Mississippi; helping wild animals recover at the Peace River Refuge and Ranch in Silver Springs, Florida; assisting the National Coalition for the Homeless by serving meals at soup kitchens in Washington, DC; or working with Oklahoma State Parks, helping the Three Forks Nature Center staff restore the natural beauty of Sequoyah State Park in Hulbert, Oklahoma.
       c. Katie Walser, a historical studies major who volunteered on a sustainability project in Elm Mott, Texas, said that her ASB experience was vastly different from her life as a college student and that she wants to give her time to "spread the wealth."
  B. The Office of Undergraduate Education offers a variety of volunteer opportunities.
    1. Each year, the Office of Undergraduate Education presents the "Freshman Year Experience," which includes two-day freshmen orientation sessions.
       a. You may want to volunteer to become an orientation team mentor, or OTM, to assist new students with the transition to university life.
       b. The Freshman Experience website explains that students become an OTM not only to mentor new students but to work as a team to connect with a group and hold a high-profile leadership position at UT Dallas.
    2. The Office of Undergraduate Education also uses the Freshmen Year Experience to offer student success camps.
       a. OTMs organize the various success camps prior to the beginning of each semester.
       b. Senior Cayman Nava, a computer science major and three-time OTM, says, "It's a hard transition from high school to college, and this experience helps a lot."

> The speaker provides a source that explains what happens when a student becomes an OTM. He or she should keep in mind that all the main ideas require adequate support from sources.

    c. Freshmen camp members not only report making friends with other freshmen but with their OTMS as well.
  C. The Student Success Center has volunteer opportunities that assist students in achieving academic goals in a variety of subject areas via a variety of services.
    1. According to the Supplemental Instruction website, this program provides academic support to students in what are labeled "historically difficult classes."
      a. Examples of such classes include freshman-level chemistry and history, sophomore-level psychology and economics, and junior-level biology.
      b. During each session, the SI leader reviews the topics and information covered in class during that week and provides guidance and encouragement to students who attend the sessions.
    2. Peer-Led Team Learning, or PLTL, is an expansion of Supplemental Instruction in which every student's active participation is required for the group to succeed; therefore, student attendance is mandatory.
      a. The PLTL website explains that PLTL leaders are second-year students who have been previously successful in a course; are recommended by their professors; and are excellent interpersonal communicators.
      b. Nujeen Zibari, a sophomore biology major and PLTL leader for calculus, contends, "It's been a real gift to be able to work with these students."
III. Conclusion

> *The speaker provides sufficient information so that the listeners can make an informed decision and so that the speaker can fulfill the speech purpose.*

> *A good speech concludes effectively by signaling the close, summarizing the main ideas, and making a final appeal.*

FORMULATING THE INTRODUCTION, TRANSITIONS, AND CONCLUSION

After creating your outline, it's time to think about the best way to open and close your speech. In addition, you'll want to think about creating transitions from one point to the next. Good transitions as well as a strong opening and closing enable your audience to easily follow your speech. These features also help you engage listeners with civility by acknowledging their need to follow what you are saying without experiencing frustration.

Introduction

The introduction of your speech achieves several purposes. Most importantly, it should gain the audience's attention. What are you about to tell the audience that is unique? What can you add to their knowledge? Furthermore, the introduction demonstrates the importance of your topic and the reason you have chosen to talk about it. Why should the audience listen to you? What matters about the things you will say?

Capturing Your Audience's Attention You can use several methods to capture your audience's attention, such as:

- *Referring to the occasion.* Doing so helps you, as the speaker, engage with your listeners. By referring to the occasion, you establish what you already share in common with the audience: the time of the event taking place in the context of other events. A person giving a eulogy at a funeral, for instance, might refer to the occasion of mourning the person's death to connect immediately with listeners.

- *Mentioning something familiar to your audience.* Mentioning something familiar helps them engage what you will say in your speech. This technique is especially useful when addressing more complex topics in which many listeners may lack familiarity. An informative speech with a specific purpose of helping people understand different diet plans might begin with the question "How many of you have tried a variety of methods to lose weight but enjoyed little success?"

- *Asking a question, telling a story, presenting a quotation, or using humor.* You can begin your speech, for example, with a joke that relates to the overall theme of your speech and the occasion. Telling a joke, however, will likely undermine your credibility if listeners fail to understand it or see its relevance.

It is often tempting for beginning speakers to stand up and say, "Hi. My speech is on. . ." or "Today I'm going to give a speech on . . ." These kinds of openings are known as **sledgehammer introductions**. Everyone knows you intend to give a speech. You are there because the occasion calls for a speech. You run the risk of sounding like a kindergarten child getting up for "Show and Tell" when you don't take the trouble to think of a creative way to introduce your topic.

sledgehammer introduction A lackluster opening that needlessly states the intent of the speaker and the speech.

Adapting to Your Audience

Adapting to or appealing to the needs of the audience suggests why the audience should listen to you. In other words, this portion of the introduction actually motivates the audience to listen and tells them why they should care about the topic. Earlier in this chapter, you read about various ways to adapt to a specific audience. Maslow's Hierarchy of Needs, audience psychographics, and audience demographics are tools you can use to adapt to your audience and heighten their interest in your topic. For example, suppose you decide to deliver a speech about Social Security to classmates in your communication course. Your audience is composed of ethnically diverse women and men in their late teens and early 20s, and you believe your audience values self-sufficiency and independence. Rather than focus on Maslow's safe and security needs, you decide to capture audience interest by focusing on esteem needs. In this portion of the introduction, you might say:

> Some, if not most, of you in this audience may not spend even a fleeting thought on the necessity of contributing to Social Security. As college students, we are too busy taking classes, finding time for a social life, and concerned about eventually finding that first "real" job. However, since we soon may find ourselves with a college degree and on our own at last, it's important for us to become and remain self-sufficient and independent as long as possible. Buying into Social Security is one way for us to maintain independence well into our retirement years. Imagine for a moment how you might feel if you constantly had to ask your children or relatives for loans. What would your friends think of you if you worked all your life but saved nothing for the future? What would you do if you discovered you could no longer stay in your house or apartment or didn't have enough money to buy groceries?

Notice that this portion of the introduction about Social Security uses words and phrases that not only help adapt your topic to the audience, but also help adapt by suggesting that you, the speaker, are similar to audience members. Words and phrases such as "we," "us," and "as college students" enable the audience to identify with you and feel that you understand who they are and what they believe is important.

Establishing Your Credibility

So far, you've learned that effective introductions attract audience attention and arouse their interest in your speech. But there is still something missing. You need to show your audience that you are the one with the proper information concerning their saving needs. You would want to add some information that helps establish your credibility. **Credibility** refers to your ability to make the

credibility A speaker's ability to earn the audience's trust.

audience believe you—or, more importantly, your ability to earn their *trust*. You can establish credibility by mentioning your personal experience or familiarity with the topic and using example and statistics. You can also "borrow" credibility by quoting a source who is an expert on the topic. For example, in a speech about the economic situation in Italy, the speaker could use a source like this one:

> According to Domenico Lombardi, a senior fellow at the Brookings Institution, the Italian economy cannot generate enough resources to pay for its debt.[11]

Stating the Thesis and Previewing Your Topic After gaining the audience's attention, your introduction should state your thesis (not necessarily word for word, but as close as possible) and preview the main points/ideas that you will be covering. Here is a possible introduction for student volunteer opportunities:

Capture your audience's attention.

> Former President Bill Clinton remarked, "Volunteering is an act of heroism on a grand scale. And it matters profoundly. It does more than help people beat the odds; it changes the odds." Have you ever thought about volunteering to help the lives of others? Whether it's spending one day helping various local agencies; one week in the service of others out-of-state; or one semester helping students succeed in college, UT Dallas has a volunteer opportunity to fit into every student's hectic life.

Adapt to your audience.

> You may be thinking, "Not Me!" As UT Dallas undergraduates, I know that we enroll in difficult and time-consuming classes. We also try to maintain an active social life while juggling certain family obligations, and we participate in organizations and activities associated with our future careers. However, volunteer service can provide benefits for others *and* for you. Even spending one day in the service of others can be rewarding. According to the Corporation for National and Community Service, volunteerism enables us to solve problems, strengthen communities, improve lives, connect to others, and transform our own lives. In addition, the World Volunteer website illustrates that volunteering gives us the opportunity to learn or develop a new skill, provides us with a sense of achievement, and can boost our career options. I know firsthand the benefits of volunteering because last semester I was an FYL—or First-Year Leader. The Freshman Experience website states that FYLs are an integral part of the freshman-year experience because they are "mentors, friends and sources of information." The 39 other FYLs and I taught one discussion section each of the Freshman Seminar class, and we made lesson plans, assigned grades, and helped freshmen navigate that tricky first semester of college.

Establish your credibility.

State the thesis and preview your topic.

> You still may be thinking that you're too busy or have too many other responsibilities to participate in a volunteer activity. However, it's likely that one or more of your UT Dallas classes will require a service learning assignment in which you must volunteer for community service. You will save yourself time and effort (and may impress your professor) if you are already engaged in a volunteer opportunity. The good news is that you can sign up for volunteer experiences right here on campus because various on-campus offices offer a variety of volunteer opportunities for UT Dallas students. Three on-campus offices that sponsor volunteer activities are the Office of Student Volunteerism, which promotes the "Viva Volunteer" day event and the week-long Alternative Spring Break; the Office of Undergraduate Education, which seeks Orientation Team Mentors to work at freshman orientation sessions and success camps; and the Student Success Center, for which you can volunteer to provide students with Supplemental Instruction and Peer-Led Team Learning sessions.

Transitions

After writing your introduction, turn your attention to the transitions in your speech or the statements that tie together the various points of your speech. If a finished speech were the human body, the outline would be the skeleton of the speech, and the transitions would be the muscles that cause the skeleton to move. Transitions are the links between the different ideas in a speech. A good transition contains elements of the point just made as well as the next point. Techniques for transitioning effectively include internal previews, internal summaries, and transitional words and phrases.

Internal Previews An internal preview is a concise version of what the speaker will explore, discuss, and/or elaborate on in the speech. It helps the audience follow along from one main idea to the next. For example, you can use an internal preview to move from the introduction to the body of the speech. Consider this excerpt from a sample outline for our speech on student volunteerism:

> Introduction
> **A.** The Office of Student Volunteerism, or OSV, is a "one-stop shop" for volunteer opportunities.
> **1.** The OSV sponsors the "Viva Volunteer" day-long event in conjunction with the international "Make a Difference Day."
> **2.** The OSV also sponsors the week-long "Alternative Spring Break," or ASB, a program during which students participate in various community service projects, learn about social events, and develop leadership skills.
> *Transition:* In addition to the OSV, the Office of Undergraduate Education also offers a variety of volunteer opportunities.

Here, the internal preview forecasts the volunteer opportunities associated with a different campus office, and the audience can then expect to hear about additional volunteer activities and events.

Internal Summaries An internal summary brings together the central points and themes previously discussed in the speech, and it signals closure to those points. An internal summary does not conclude the entire speech but rather reviews a portion of it. An internal summary in the speech on student volunteerism might look something like this:

> So far, we have discussed volunteer opportunities associated with the Office of Student Volunteerism, such as working during "Viva Volunteer" day and participating in the "Alternative Spring Break." In addition, we've learned about the volunteer activities associated with the Office of Undergraduate Education, such as becoming an OTM at freshman orientation and success camps. The Office of Student Success also offers students some volunteer opportunities, specifically tutoring others in the Supplemental Instruction and Peer-Led Team Learning programs.

An internal summary helps the audience reflect on your discussion up to that point in the speech; you can then proceed to your last area of discussion—in this case, student volunteer opportunities offered by the Student Success Center. The internal summary offers a reminder of the previous ideas and also signals a point of completion.

Transitional Words and Phrases Another type of transition is the use of words and phrases that help connect one idea to the next. Some transitional words and phrases are slightly more subtle than others. For example, the construction *not only . . . but also* represents a very common subtle transition, as in "Not only does the Office of Student

Volunteerism promote volunteer events and activities, but also students volunteer with the Office of Undergraduate Education to work at freshman orientation sessions and success camps." Such a statement helps you link two previously separate ideas in a speech.

Some transitional words and phrases are more explicit; some examples are *furthermore*, *moreover*, *in addition*, *first*, *second*, and *third*. These transitional devices suggest that another idea will follow the preceding one and will build on it.

Other transition words and phrases point to opposing viewpoints or qualify points. The conjunction *however* is one such transition, and other examples are *nonetheless*, *on the other hand*, and *in another sense*. In the student volunteerism speech, for instance, a transition showing that you are moving from one point of view to a different one might go something like "In addition to the OSV, the Office of Undergraduate Education also offers a variety of volunteer opportunities."

You can illustrate transitional words and phrases by using nonverbal communication when connecting one speech idea to the next.

Conclusion

An effective opening and good transitions are critical components of any speech. Closing a speech is just as important as opening it. Your conclusions should neither end too abruptly ("stop on a dime") nor trail off with no finality. Communication professor David Zarefsky explains that your conclusion should accomplish at least three goals. It should signal that the end is coming, summarize the main ideas, and make a final appeal to the audience.[12]

Signaling That the End is Coming In signaling the close, you make sure the listeners know the speech is ending. You do not want to simply end the speech without warning them that you are about to close. You can signal the end of the speech by saying *in conclusion*, *in short*, *in summary*, *all in all*, or *in closing*. Simply saying *thank you* without offering any indication that the speech is coming to an end is a common mistake of inexperienced speakers. On the other hand, you should avoid "false endings," or misleading signals that suggest the ending is near. For example, a speaker using the transition word *finally* indicates to the audience that the speech is almost over, but if he or she continues to summarize the main ideas, the speaker is not really closing the speech just yet. You can also nonverbally tell your audience that a speech is coming to a close by pausing, changing your tone of voice, taking a step, or slowing your rate of speech.[13]

Summarizing the Main Ideas Summarizing the main ideas helps remind the audience of the major points or areas of discussion. Remember, though, that a summary does not repeat those ideas verbatim but reiterates key points, highlighting, for instance, key words or phrases from the speech.[14]

Making a Final Appeal to the Audience Finally, a conclusion should make a final appeal to the audience. Making a final appeal helps the audience understand the response you are seeking from them. The final appeal is your last chance to remind listeners of what you want them to think or the action you want them to take after hearing your speech. Be mindful that in an informative speech, you refrain from suggesting that the audience hold a certain opinion or engage in a course of action. While this type of appeal is appropriate for a persuasive speech, it is not appropriate for an informative speech.[15] (You may be accused of behaving uncivilly and unethically if an audience expects to be informed but instead finds that it is the target of persuasion.)

In preparing your conclusion, you should apply certain strategies for effectively closing your speech. First, you should prepare the conclusion only after constructing the body of the speech. Second, make sure you explicitly link the conclusion to the body of the speech so that your audience will know how it relates. Third, you should make the conclusion relatively brief so that it does not detract from the speech itself. Finally, and as previously mentioned, an effective conclusion tells the audience, one last time, what you want them to act on or to believe.

In revisiting the student volunteerism speech example once more, consider how effectively the speaker concludes this speech:

Signal that the end is coming.

In conclusion, pioneer anthropologist Margaret Mead stated, "Never doubt that a small group of committed people can change the world. Indeed, it is the only thing that ever has." You can do your part to change the world and provide benefits for others as well as yourself by volunteering for the Viva Volunteer day event or Alternative Spring Break with the Office of Student Volunteerism; becoming a OTM at Office of Undergraduate Education Freshman Orientation sessions and success camps; and working as an SI or PLTL leader in the Student Success Center. The Corporation for National and Community Service cites that approximately 64.3 million people volunteered through or for an organization at least once in 2011, a national volunteer rate that reached a five-year high. You can continue this trend by signing up here on the UT Dallas campus to be a volunteer today.

Summarize the main ideas.

Make a final appeal to the audience.

GATHERING AND USING SUPPORTING MATERIAL

Civil communication, including civil public speeches, necessitates that a person engage in ethical communication. Ethical communication requires appropriate and effective use of supporting material. At this stage of your life or career, you probably do not yet possess the requisite credentials for making a point without citing an authority for support. Therefore, this section addresses how you can use source material in your speeches to engage in civil, ethical communication with an audience. To use support, you first gather and select information; then you arrange those materials according to the purpose and structure of your speech.

Planning Your Supporting Material

Before beginning the process of gathering and selecting information, you should review your thesis and main ideas to determine what you need to learn about your topic. After you make these determinations, you can create a research plan that helps you identify the various kinds of information you need to support each of your points as well as the types of research (e.g., news articles, articles from journals, interviews) necessary for your topic.

Gathering and Selecting Information

It is important to remember that different topics require different kinds of research. In any case, your topic will require *research*, which you can locate using a variety of resources, including the World Wide Web and your local library. You may also obtain information by interviewing an expert on your topic.

Research Using the World Wide Web You undoubtedly know that you can obtain a great deal of information on the World Wide Web. Not everything you find there, though, is credible or reliable. Therefore, you should answer a number of questions before choosing to use a website as a source:

- Who authored or wrote the page? You should *not* use a source in which no identifying information has been provided (e.g., sponsoring organization or author's name).
- If sources are listed, what are those sources? What are those authors' credentials? You should try to determine the author's affiliation as well as his or her educational background, employment history, and/or accomplishments. Sometimes this information, just like with print sources, is provided for you on the page.
- What organization published the page? Take a look at the domain name (e.g., whitehouse.gov) for an indication about what company, government agency, or nonprofit organization publishes the page.
- Does the domain name end in .edu, .gov, .org, as opposed to .net or .com? Domain names with .edu, .gov, and .org tend to be more credible.
- When was the page produced and updated? This information is usually provided at the bottom of the page.

Library Research The library remains the best place to find credible information, despite the ubiquity of the World Wide Web and the Internet. (You should remember that Web research is a good addition to, but not substitute for, library research.) Each library is unique in its own way, but certain resources are common to most libraries. A computerized library catalog, for example, provides information on all the books and other materials located in that particular library. Each work has been recorded according to subject, author, and title, but in most cases, you can also search using keywords to find material that may be suitable for your topic. Many libraries subscribe to various databases that are also computerized and provide collections of very credible material from a wide variety of sources. LexisNexis and JSTOR, for example, contain multiple articles from news services, magazines, scholarly journals, conference papers, books, and/or law journals. Another benefit of using a library is that you have access to a professional librarian who can help you in your search.

Interviewing Interviewing an expert on your topic may be an excellent way to obtain credible and reliable information. It also helps stimulate your own thinking while saving you time researching on the Internet or locating sources in a library. Furthermore, interviewing helps clarify ideas by making them more understandable through questions and answers. Consider this sample interview questionnaire for someone who is a student volunteer:

Sample Interview Questionnaire

1. Why do you volunteer?
2. What are the most rewarding aspects of volunteering?
3. For which programs and agencies have your volunteered, and what have you accomplished in your capacity as a volunteer?
4. How has volunteering affected your life as a college student?
5. How might your volunteer experience affect your life in the future?

Using Supporting Material

After obtaining supporting material, you need to determine how you will use it in your speech. You can use supporting material for several purposes. For instance, it can help you define less familiar terms. In the student volunteerism speech, audience members might need for you to define and characterize the acronym FYL and what it represents (First-Year Leader). You could do this by quoting the definition found on the UT Dallas Freshman Experience website. Supporting material also helps make a speech interesting in that you can use it to open the speech or capture the audience's attention. Most importantly, though, supporting material helps you prove your point. In pointing out that volunteering is rewarding for others and for yourself, you can quote a volunteer and highlight the benefits he or she has experienced as a volunteer (e.g., "According to student Erin Hoffer, who volunteered at the Plano Community Garden, it is satisfying to 'feed the hungry, educate the ignorant, and give back with service.'").

As indicated earlier, there are several types of supporting material:

- *Statistics*—Numerical facts and data (e.g., "Hispanics made up 7 percent of voters in the 2010 congressional elections.")[16]
- *Definitions*—A word or phrase that explains the meaning of a term (e.g., "The word *paradigm* is defined as a "philosophical or theoretical framework of a scientific school or discipline within which theories, laws, and generalizations and the experiments performed in support of them are formulated.")[17]
- *Examples*—Specific cases that demonstrate a general idea (e.g., "South Padre Island in Texas is a good destination for experiencing the warm waters in the Gulf of Mexico.")
- *Analogies*—Comparisons that help the audience relate the more familiar to the less familiar (e.g., "Sorbet is like ice cream in that is cold, sweet, and tasty; however, it doesn't contain milk or cream.")
- *Anecdotes*—Brief stories, often based on personal experience, that help illustrate a point (e.g., "The material taught in statistics courses can sometimes appear to be incomprehensible. I enrolled in my first statistics course during my junior year of college. On the first day, my professor used words such as *mean, mode, standard deviation*, and *ANOVA*, and she wrote symbols on the white board that I'd never seen before. I became so confused and lost that I thought I had stumbled into a foreign language class!")
- *Quotation or testimony*—Direct or paraphrased remarks that can make your content more memorable for the audience and help support specific points in the speech (e.g., "Mark Zuckerberg, co-creator and CEO of Facebook, believes that 'by giving people the power to share, we're making the world more transparent.'")[18]

Regardless of the type of support you use, you should always make sure to use your material ethically. Avoiding bias, for instance, is important in establishing and maintaining credibility with an audience. In other words, you need to avoid presenting evidence from sources that advance clearly slanted agendas. A speech on foreign policy will seem this way if several of your pieces of evidence come from *National Review*, a publication with a very right-wing political agenda. Similarly, listeners may perceive a speech arguing against the death penalty as biased if most of the support comes from *The New Republic*, a publication with a very left-wing political agenda.

In choosing material from sources, you might decide, for example, to use a direct quotation from one of your articles. Your point might reference the importance of volunteering on your campus, but in making that point, you should use an unbiased source. Citing an article from *The Investigator* magazine, for example, is probably better than citing a direct quotation from promotional literature from an organization that seeks volunteers. The promotional literature will be slanted toward volunteering for that particular organization.

ASK THE ETHICIST: Sharing Resources

Question I understand that it is important to cite all the sources I use in writing a paper. But what is the big deal about including citations in a presentation? Can't I just have them available if someone wants to know where I got my information?

Answer One of the difficulties in oral communication, as opposed to written communication, is that the act of communicating is located in a particular time and place. Unless someone disagrees with what you have to say, that person is unlikely to ask you for your references. But when you state something without attributing it to the source of the information, people are very likely to think the words or ideas are your own, when they are not. The ethical thing is to take extra care and provide information that makes it clear which ideas are yours and which ones are not.

No matter what kind of support you choose, you must always use supporting material in a way that engages the audience with civility. Avoiding bias and preparing original work as a speaker (i.e., avoiding plagiarism) are two ways to make your communication civil when giving public speeches.

CHAPTER SUMMARY

Now that you have read this chapter you can:

11.1 Analyze your audience effectively and engage audiences in civil communication.

To analyze audiences effectively, you first identify the needs of your listeners and target those specific needs. Second, you analyze for demographic characteristics, including cultural diversity, gender, age, group membership, and number of people. Third, you consider the audience's attitudes, beliefs, and values and recognize whether the audience members are voluntary or captive listeners. Finally, any situation for public speaking requires that you respect the occasion.

11.2 Determine your general purpose for a speech, apply brainstorming techniques for generating ideas about your topic, and create a thesis based on your general and specific speech purposes.

Speakers can engage at least three different general purposes: speaking to inform, to persuade, and to inspire. An informative speech provides an audience with new information, raises awareness of some issue, or creates positive or negative feeling toward the subject. A persuasive speech is given to change the attitudes, beliefs, and/or values of an audience and call them to take specific action. A speech to inspire creates greater commitment to values, beliefs, attitudes, and behaviors; such speeches include speeches of introduction and speeches of tribute as well as eulogies. Brainstorming is a good strategy for generating ideas for your speech. You can engage in brainstorming by freely associating any words and ideas that come to mind about your topic. A specific speech purpose limits the topic by specifying what you will accomplish in the speech. You base your thesis statement on your specific speech purpose, and you create your thesis statement by telling listeners where you expect to lead them in the speech. The thesis statement says to the audience that the main ideas and information you provide will support one overarching claim.

11.3 Choose an effective organizational strategy for a speech.

You will outline your speech according to your organizational strategy, and you will base that organizational strategy on the general speech purpose you are trying to fulfill. If you are giving an informative speech, for example, you will likely choose a topical, chronological, spatial, or familiar to unfamiliar pattern of organization. Persuasive speakers normally organize their speeches according to their argument or thesis while inspirational speakers typically make use of narrative or story-telling.

11.4 Use standard outlining conventions to construct a formal speech outline.

In writing an outline, you brainstorm your topic and then create the formal speech outline. You can use six rules for standard notation to help construct the outline.

11.5 Craft effective introductions and conclusions, as well as use good transitions in your speech.

An introduction should, first and foremost, capture the audience's attention. It should also demonstrate the importance of the topic, establish the purpose, and preview the topic to give the audience an idea of what to expect. You can construct effective transitions through the use of internal previews, internal summaries, and transitional words and phrases. Finally, a good conclusion should signal that the ending is near, summarize the main ideas, and make a final appeal to the audience.

11.6 Plan, gather, and use supporting material appropriately for your speech.

Gathering good supporting materials involves first conducting research using the World Wide Web or the library and/or by interviewing experts on your subject. To use material effectively, you need to know the differences between different types of support (e.g., statistics, examples, anecdotes) and use that support ethically in civil communication with audiences.

CIVILITY SUMMARY

Overall, remember that preparing civil public speeches involves the following:

- Civility and ethical obligations surround the purpose of any speech. If you establish an informative purpose for the speech, then it is unethical to shift into persuading your audience.
- A civil speaker has the responsibility to respect the audience. A key factor in this respect means that you must consider your listeners' feelings, or psychographics. When you consider demographic characteristics, you demonstrate that you intend to engage listeners with civility because doing so suggests that you respect audience members' different biases, backgrounds, and beliefs.
- Good transitions as well as a strong opening and closing enable your audience to easily follow your speech. These features also help you engage listeners with civility by acknowledging their need to follow what you are saying without experiencing frustration.
- No matter what kind of support you choose, you must always use supporting material in a way that engages the audience with civility. Avoiding bias and preparing original work as a speaker (i.e., avoiding plagiarism) are ways you can achieve civil communication when giving public speeches.

REVIEW QUESTIONS

1. How can you show your audience that you have something worthwhile to say and that your topic is important?
2. What are the components of the *occasion* in public speaking situations?
3. What is the difference between an informative purpose and a persuasive purpose?
4. What are the characteristics of an effective speech introduction?
5. What are the characteristics of an effective speech conclusion?
6. How can you find good supporting materials for a speech?
7. What are the rules for constructing an effective speech outline?

12 Delivering Public Speeches with Civility

ON SEPTEMBER 18, 2007, computer science professor Randy Pausch gave the "Last Lecture: Really Achieving Your Childhood Dreams" as part of the "Journeys" lecture series at Carnegie Mellon University, in which faculty members "share their reflections on their journeys—the everyday actions, decisions, challenges, and joys that make a life."[1] The occasion of his "Last Lecture" was particularly noteworthy because Pausch, himself, was suffering from terminal pancreatic cancer and died from the disease almost one year later. Although "achieving childhood dreams" represented a major focus of the lecture, the predominant theme of Pausch's speech actually related to how people should treat one another. Pausch told his audience that "everybody has a good side" and that, to succeed in life, they should "show gratitude," "work hard," and "focus on others," not themselves. His speech also stressed that people should interact civilly with each other in all facets of their lives.[2]

CHAPTER OBJECTIVES

After reading this chapter, you will be able to:

12.1 Understand what it means to deliver public speeches with civility.

12.2 Know strategies for controlling anxiety about speaking publically.

12.3 Choose an appropriate method of delivery for your audience and purpose.

12.4 Understand techniques for effective delivery in your speeches.

12.5 Know how to create and use presentation aids effectively.

12.6 Effectively practice speeches to improve delivery.

WHY IT MATTERS

Pausch's lecture not only related themes of civility but also exemplified civil delivery. **Delivery** refers to the presentation of a speech and includes mannerisms or gestures, tone of voice, volume, eye contact with listeners, rate, posture, and pronunciation, as well as enunciation of words. In addition, delivery relates to a speaker's physical appearance, the clothes he or she wears, his or her personal grooming, and the speaker's presentation aids. A speaker engages in civil delivery when he or she shows respect for the audience, addresses his or her topic in a responsible manner, and demonstrates restraint through the appropriate expression of emotion.

The chapter addresses how you can deliver your speeches with civility by taking into account all these concerns; it begins with how you can control your anxiety and nervousness about speaking so that you can effectively present your message to the audience. This chapter also provides some clear advice on creating visual aids from available software.

delivery The presentation of a speech, including use of gestures and body language, tone of voice, eye contact, volume, and rate.

DELIVERY, CIVILITY, AND ETHICS

Sometimes, it is easiest to point to an opposite in order to define a concept. While civil delivery may be a little hard to identify, uncivil delivery is not. The accompanying Case Study in Ethics helps illustrate uncivil delivery.

Expressing emotions appropriately helps you interact civilly with an audience. Phil Davison, the subject of the case study you just read, failed to communicate civilly with his audience, especially in terms of conveying emotions. Davison communicated anger, even rage, to his listeners, making them feel as though he resented them. Davison did

A CASE STUDY IN ETHICS

Uncivil Delivery

In 2010, Phil Davison ran as a Republican candidate for the office of treasurer in Stark County, Ohio. While campaigning for that office, Davison gave a short speech to approximately 100 people. He shouted throughout the speech, saying things like "Politics is not touch football!" and "I will not apologize for my tone tonight!" He also continually paced back and forth and occasionally hit the lectern with his fist.

Davison's campaign had focused a great deal on his anger about the way the current treasurer had managed the office, and Davison's intention was to show his belief in the issues. However, Davison's gestures and mannerisms as well as his tone of voice suggested hostility and anger toward the audience. A blogger in the audience during the speech wrote notes about Davison's delivery that "went viral." Even though Davison said that he did not intend to alienate his listeners, his delivery shows how a speaker can offend listeners—in this case, by screaming and yelling at them. Davison did not win the nomination, and he wished the nominee good luck.

At an interview the next day, Davison said that he knew it might have been a little too much but it captured how he felt. He also said that if his words affected someone in a positive way then it was beneficial to deliver the speech in that manner.[3]

Discussion Questions

1. How might you advise Davison to gain his audience's attention in a more civil way?
2. Besides his shouting, how did Davison's delivery possibly alienate his audience?
3. How could Davison's tone have been more civil and engaging?
4. Do you agree with Davison that his speech (or offending an audience) was "worth it" if it motivated even one person to become involved in his or her community?

not intend to send this message, and he did indeed feel anger about the situation in the Stark County Treasurer's Office. However, Davison's emotional outbursts only alienated his listeners.

Delivering a speech effectively is critically important to engaging your audience civilly. You can respect your audience by understanding that it is composed of people who will react to your message on both emotional and intellectual levels. Therefore, your visual presentation, as reflected in your gestures, eye contact, voice, and facial expressions, influences whether listeners will view your speech favorably. You can exhibit restraint by refraining from communicating intense emotions such as extreme anger and frustration as you deliver your speech. Finally, you can demonstrate responsibility toward your "community" (in this case, your audience) by practicing your speech prior to your presentation. This will facilitate engagement by preventing the audience from being distracted by delivery problems that may occur during the speech.

CONTROLLING ANXIETY

You have probably listened to a speaker who appeared to be nervous. Did the person's nervousness prevent him or her from communicating effectively with you? How could the speaker have overcome feelings of anxiety so that he or she could present a good speech? The first step in answering these questions lies in understanding communication apprehension.

Understanding Communication Apprehension

communication apprehension Nervousness or fear that interferes with a person's ability to communicate with another.

Communication apprehension is nervousness or fear that interferes with a person's ability to communicate with another. When a person becomes nervous about a speaking situation, a physiological change occurs when his or her body begins to produce adrenaline.[4] Adrenaline can cause a person to experience a pounding heart, dry mouth, butterflies in the stomach, shaking hands and legs, and/or blushing.[5] The symptoms can also become obvious to the audience, thereby making it difficult for the speaker to communicate his or her message effectively.

Nervousness associated with speaking in front of groups is normal and may stem from a variety of factors. For example, a speaker may be apprehensive because he or she has failed to prepare adequately. On the other hand, a speaker may fear the unknown, not being aware of the audience's expectations or what they may think of the speaker. A speaker may also experience anxiety and apprehension because he or she feels self-conscious in front of other people.

TECH CHECK

Report of Public Speaking Anxiety

James McCroskey conducted extensive research about why many people experience communication anxiety. He concluded that some people are "wired" for more communication anxiety than others, based on their genetic tendencies.

A high score on this profile does not necessarily mean that you cannot give an effec-tive speech; rather, it may indicate that you have to work harder with the strategies to combat anxiety than a person who has less apprehension.

Some apprehension can be a good thing because it helps make you alert for the speaking situation and helps to ensure that you perform well. Too much apprehension, however, can become paralyzing and hurt your ability to communicate effectively. Therefore, as a speaker, you need strategies for managing communication apprehension.

Techniques for Handling Nervousness

Using specific strategies can help you manage communication apprehension. These strategies include practicing the speech, preparing both physically and mentally, acting confident, and beginning with a strong opening.

Practicing the Speech It may seem obvious that practicing your speech is an effective technique for overcoming speech anxiety and nervousness, but beginning speakers sometimes forget this very important piece of advice. Throughout this chapter, we discuss how you can use practice time to your benefit.

In practicing your speech, you can replicate the situation you will face during the actual speech. For example, you should adhere to the same time constraints as the final speech. If your instructor has asked you to give a seven-minute informative speech, time yourself and make sure your speech stays within that seven-minute limit. In addition, you can practice the speech in front of an audience. Ask your friend or roommate to sit and listen to the speech as you present it. Your practice "audience" can give you some helpful advice upon hearing it, and you can gauge the reaction of actual listeners instead of guessing how people *might* react and respond to your message. (Additional advice about practicing a speech is provided at the end of this chapter.)

Some speech anxiety may help make you alert and perform well.

Preparing Physically and Mentally Speaking is a physical activity, and adequately preparing your body will help you do your best, including getting adequate sleep the night before your speech and making sure you eat well. Many speakers find that they can help actively prepare their bodies for what is to come by taking the time to do deep breathing, body stretches, or gentle exercises before the speech. Since speaking affects both the body and the mind, many speakers may also find it helpful to meditate or take a short walk to help clear their minds of the thoughts that may be troubling them before they begin to speak. In terms of eating right, it's best to avoid drinking carbonated beverages prior to a speech. Such beverages may cause an unforeseen burp to interfere with the presentation and therefore promote additional speech anxiety!

Acting Confident Remembering to *appear* confident (even if you don't feel confident) while you practice will help you overcome anxiety and replicate the feeling of confidence during the speech. Your audience can't see the butterflies in your stomach or your pounding heart, so don't draw attention to these physiological sensations. Acting confident involves maintaining eye contact with the audience, and speaking clearly and loudly enough to be heard, using appropriate gestures. Be mindful, though, that acting confident does not mean coming across as overconfident or even arrogant. Overconfidence and arrogance may interfere with your ability to engage your audiences with civility. Rather, work toward conveying to your audience that you believe in and value what you are saying. In addition, visualizing yourself succeeding can help bolster your confidence. Before the speech, imagine yourself in front of the audience and that they will receive your

TRENDS IN TECHNOLOGY AND SOCIAL MEDIA

Virtual Reality Therapy (VRT) and Communication Apprehension

In 2002, researchers Sandra Harris, Robert Kemmerling, and Max North published a study investigating the effectiveness of VRT in helping university students overcome anxiety about public speaking.[6] The researchers contend that "individuals with public speaking anxiety most often experience a variety of symptoms in a public speaking situation, including palpitations, sweating, gastrointestinal discomfort, diarrhea, muscle tension, and confusion."[7] They go on to explain VRT as an emerging treatment for reducing speech anxiety.

Eight students participated in this study. Each student respondent completed a personal inventory relating their confidence as speakers, and they self-reported their attitudes toward speaking in general.[8] The researchers also measured the students' heart rates before, during, and after the experiment.[9]

The students completed four 12- to 15-minute sessions of individual treatment. During these treatments, each student wore a head-mounted display that projected an auditorium scene in virtual reality.[10] In the first session, a student stood at a virtual podium with a microphone while the researchers measured his or her pulse. The researchers then asked the student to prepare a two-minute speech to give during a session that would take place two weeks later.[11]

After two weeks, the students returned for a second session. They were asked to recite the Pledge of Allegiance while standing at the microphone in the virtual auditorium. The researchers used applause to encourage the students to speak, and they manipulated the situation by slowly filling the auditorium with audience members.[12] Once again, they measured the students' heart rates. The third and fourth sessions required students to present the two-minute speech while the researchers manipulated the scenario by including "members of the audience speaking to each other (i.e., not paying attention to the speaker); members of the audience laughing; members continuously asking the speaker to speak louder; and audience applause, consistently used at the end of the speech."[13]

Harris, Kemmerling, and North found that the VRT sessions appeared to help students reduce speech anxiety based on their self-report inventories and physiological measurement of heart rate.[14] The students said that simulating a speaking situation helped them overcome their fears, but they also reported that practicing the speech was key and that "doing it over and over limits the anxiety."[15]

The students' comments suggest that, although VRT helps simulate the situation in a realistic way, the value in it lies in facilitating or encouraging them to practice. Practice becomes a very important part of overcoming apprehension and anxiety about speaking publically.

Discussion Questions

1. Do you think VRT holds promise as a means for helping students overcome speech anxiety?

2. Do you think real-life (versus virtual) practice in front of no audience members, some audience members, and a full audience can produce the same results as the VRT study?

3. What can you do in terms of practice scenarios and the number of times you practice to replicate the results obtained in the VRT study?

4. How might using VRT help you engage your audiences with civility?

---

message favorably. Just as a basketball player at a free throw line will likely have more success by visualizing the ball going through the hoop, you will likely have more success by visualizing yourself as a confident, engaging, and effective speaker.

METHODS OF DELIVERY

Overcoming communication apprehension represents a major factor in engaging audiences with civility. Another issue in delivery, however, is deciding the most effective method for presenting your speech: speaking from a manuscript, speaking from an outline, speaking from memory, speaking with little preparation, or speaking extemporaneously. (See Table 12.1 on page 257 for a summary of the delivery methods.)

Speaking from a Manuscript

You may have observed a politician or another speaker speaking from a teleprompter or manuscript that contains the text of his or her speech. Although the speaker "reads" the text word-for-word, he or she should not ignore aspects of civil delivery in communicating with an audience in order to be effective. In other words, the speaker should maintain eye contact with the audience while reading the text. (The next section of this chapter addresses the importance of good eye contact with audiences.) During special occasions, such as a presidential address to Congress or a eulogy, the speaker will often present from a manuscript because it is important that he or she not stray from the specific wording of a speech.

Speakers who use a teleprompter "read" the text word-for-word yet maintain effective eye contact with their audience.

Speaking from Notes or an Outline

Earlier you learned about outlining as a technique for preparing a speech. Sometimes, though, speakers also use notes or an outline for presenting their messages. While speaking, a speaker will glance down at the notes to remember what to say next. Most teachers recommend that students do *not* use a whole-sentence outline but instead prepare a presentation outline, using only enough words and phrases to help trigger the memory. Later in this chapter, you will learn about speaking from a presentation outline.

Speaking from Memory

A memorized speech may be appropriate for a special occasion speech. The ancient Greeks and Romans valued this form of delivery, and school children have studied famous orations and recited those orations from memory. Politicians and orators may also write out their speeches and present long memorized orations. Memorizing speeches poses several problems that can make it an ineffective method. First, the speaker might not be able to adequately adapt to the audience by taking their feedback into account. In addition, the speech may come across as stiff or stilted, and the audience may lose interest if the speech sounds memorized. Finally, perhaps the most pressing problem relates to the chance that a speaker might forget a line and stumble, even losing the whole flow of the speech.

Speaking with Little or No Preparation

When a speaker gives a speech with little or no prior preparation, it is known as an **impromptu speech**. Impromptu speeches are spontaneous. This method of delivery is often appropriate for informal talks or comments about someone else's speech. Impromptu speaking may also help teach a speaker to think quickly and organize thoughts at a moment's notice. This delivery method forces a speaker to use the little available time to focus on a small number of main ideas and to organize and convey those ideas as simply and clearly as possible. Impromptu speaking may also allow you to take cues from previous speakers, so you can refer to how their messages relate to your own.

impromptu speech A speech given with little or no prior preparation.

Speaking Extemporaneously

Extemporaneous speeches are similar to impromptu speeches in that both require spontaneity. Extemporaneous speeches, however, are more planned in that the speaker has enough time to prepare in advance what he or she will say. These speeches, for example, are common in competitive forensics, both at the high school and college levels. In such situations, speakers select a topic and prepare for 30 minutes. They then give a 7- to

extemporaneous speech A speech given after some preparation but whose wording is composed at the time of delivery.

Table 12.1 Pros and Cons of the Types of Delivery

Choose the type of speech delivery that best meets the needs of your speaking situation.

Type of Delivery	Pros	Cons
Speaking from a manuscript	Encourages the speaker's use of precise, stylistically effective wording. Allows the delivery of sensitive messages that must not vary from the script.	May hinder the speaker's ability to make eye contact. May cause the speaker to get lost in the manuscript. Inhibits spontaneity; the speaker cannot always respond to audience nonverbal feedback.
Speaking from a presentation outline	Aids in the speaker's ability to make eye contact. Allows the speaker to respond and adapt to audience nonverbal feedback.	May be a difficult mode of delivery for apprehensive speakers who feel secure using a full-sentence manuscript.
Speaking from memory	Encourages use of precise, stylistically effective wording. Promotes a high degree of eye contact with an audience.	May seem stiff or stilted. May make it difficult to adapt to the audience and take into account audience feedback. May hurt delivery due to faulty memory.
Speaking with little preparation (impromptu)	Helps the speaker learn to think quickly and organize thoughts at a moment's notice.	May limit the speaker's message because it usually contains only a small number of main ideas. May limit the effectiveness because there is little or no time to prepare or practice the speech beforehand.
Speaking extemporaneously	Allows the speaker to organize thoughts in advance, prepare notes, and briefly rehearse the speech. Allows the speaker to maintain a conversational tone and good eye contact because the exact wording is not established beforehand.	Many speakers believe extemporaneous speaking combines the best aspects of all delivery types.

8-minute speech to an audience. Extemporaneous speeches are also the most commonly required method in communication courses, but in that case, the speaker is encouraged (or required) to do extensive preparation, including researching supporting evidence, preparing an outline or notes, preparing presentation aids, and rehearsing the speech.

TECHNIQUES FOR EFFECTIVE DELIVERY

Regardless of the method of delivery, you, as a speaker, need to remember how vocal quality, use of gestures and body language, and appropriate eye contact can positively or negatively affect your speech.

Effective Vocal Delivery

Any vocal pattern, no matter how pleasing initially, can become monotonous. Therefore, it is important to create variety in your vocal pattern so that your audience does not grow tired and bored with your speech. Effective vocal delivery includes a number of aspects, including volume, verbal and pregnant pauses, enunciation and pronunciation, and rate.

Volume **Volume** refers to the relative loudness of a voice. Speaking loudly, at least at first, is probably fine until you can determine your listeners' reactions. They will let you know, through nonverbal cues, whether they can hear you without difficulty. Speaking more loudly at first can also convey confidence.[16] Speaking too softly can also present problems: If your volume is too low, listeners simply will not be able to hear you. Again, you must gauge whether audiences can hear you effectively by paying attention to their feedback. In some circumstances, you might receive that feedback quite directly, with someone in the room speaking up and telling you they cannot hear you. After you've determined that your volume is appropriate, you can vary the volume of your voice to convey meaning; for example, you can raise your volume at certain times to emphasize key ideas or themes. When you practice your speech, use the volume that you will need to use in the actual speech.

Techniques for effective delivery, such as using gestures appropriately and varying your volume, can help you give a strong speech.

volume The relative loudness of a person's voice.

verbal pause Also known as a vocal pause, a noise such as a stammer that a speaker makes to fill moments of silence, usually while he or she is trying to gather thoughts.

Verbal Pauses **Verbal pauses**, also known as vocal pauses, are distracting and take away from the overall effectiveness of a speech. Verbal pauses include stammers such as "uh" and "uhm" that speakers make in moments of silence and usually while attempting to gather their thoughts. This repetition, however, usually results from nervousness, and most instructors will tell you to practice being silent when you pause.

On the other hand, you can strategically use pauses during a speech for emphasis or to give your audience time to process what you have just said. You can mark your notes, outline, or manuscript with slash marks so that you know when to take a pause; then you can rehearse the speech out loud, pausing when you come to those slash marks.

enunciation Articulating words clearly.

Enunciation and Pronunciation **Enunciation** refers to a person's ability to articulate words clearly. Sometimes speakers slur words instead of saying each word distinctly. For example, they might say "wanna" instead of "want to" or "Whatcha doin'?" instead of "What are you doing?" However, a speaker who enunciates every word with "em-pha-sis-on-each-syll-a-ble" may come across to listeners as arrogant, or the speech may seem monotonous. Speakers who enunciate clearly are practicing civility as they respect the audience's need to understand the words being spoken.

pronunciation Saying words correctly.

On the other hand, **pronunciation** refers to whether a speaker says words correctly. When they study foreign languages, for example, students are taught to pronounce words correctly so that others can understand them when they speak. Mispronouncing words in a speech will not only cause the audience to possibly misunderstand you, but it might also diminish your credibility. Again, be sure to practice your speech with correct pronunciation.

rate The speed at which a speaker speaks.

Rate **Rate** is the speed at which a speaker speaks. Both speaking too fast and speaking too slowly can be problematic. Audiences may find it difficult to follow someone who speaks too fast, while a speaker who speaks too slowly may irritate listeners. Practicing a speech is a good method for finding the appropriate rate of speech.

One way to improve your vocal delivery is to read aloud selections of poetry, particularly selections that solicit emphasis and feeling. Choose a poem and practice reading the selection aloud. As you read, you can use the following techniques to improve your vocal delivery:

- Vary your volume, rate, and pitch.
- Find the appropriate places for pauses.
- Identify (by highlighting or underlining) the key words and/or phrases you think should be given emphasis.

Good Use of Gestures and Nonverbal Communication

Appropriately using hand gestures can benefit a speech; misuse of hand gestures and poor posture can hinder your overall effectiveness. This section addresses ways you can avoid engaging in distracting hand gestures that may prevent your audience from receiving the impact of your message.

You can use gestures effectively in a variety of ways while avoiding mannerisms that distract audiences from your message. Gestures, for example, can emphasize action. When you say a verb, you can use your hands for emphasis. In addition, use of gestures can support the visual impact of a speech, and pausing briefly after a gesture can be a good technique. On the other hand, you should refrain from using the same hand motions over and over again and keep your hands free by placing your notes on the lectern. Avoid the temptation to hold a pen, pencil, or laser pointer while giving a speech. Similarly, avoid putting your hand in your pocket and playing with change, your car keys, jewelry, or your hair. You may have seen a speaker who seems unable to control his or her hands or arms. Sometimes speakers move their hands in a nervous fashion or even wave their arms about, but doing so detracts from what a speaker is trying to say. Table 12.2 lists several distracting gestures that can hurt the overall effectiveness of a speech and how to overcome them.

Furthermore, it is important to maintain proper posture while giving a speech. Most instructors advise students to maintain a relaxed and natural stance in front of audiences. Avoid standing too stiffly and never moving at all. Remember, though, that your stance should not become *too* relaxed; for example, leaning on a lectern, sitting on a desk, crossing your legs, and slouching are inappropriate ways to present yourself to listeners.

So what *should* you do with gestures while speaking? A speaker can use hand gestures effectively for emphasis, and good use of gestures can add a great deal to a speech. Former President Bill Clinton, for example, very effectively uses his hands when emphasizing a significant point. He tends to raise his closed left hand when stressing something important.

You can also use gestures for highlighting transitions. For example, in discussing possible alternatives for solving a problem, you might say, "On the one hand, we could adopt this solution" and hold up your left hand; then you can say, "On the other hand, we should consider another possibility" and motion with your right hand.

Appropriate Eye Contact and Visual Delivery

Speech instructors often emphasize the importance of maintaining eye contact with an audience. Eye contact is important because you want your audience to feel as though you are talking *to* them and certainly not *at* them. Moreover, making good eye contact helps you, as a speaker, engage your audiences with civility. Effective eye contact with all audience members suggests respect and that you intend for them to benefit from your message.

Former President Bill Clinton tends to use his hands when emphasizing an important point.

Table 12.2 Avoiding Distracting Gestures
Effective gestures can help to convey your message, and distracting gestures interfere with your ability to deliver your message.

Distracting Gesture	Description	More Effective Gesture
Dancing feet	Moving feet nervously in an up-and-down motion or shifting back and forth on the balls of the feet.	Move your feet naturally as you turn to face different parts of the audience, display your presentation aids, or shift your position.
Turning body away from the audience	Turning your body to the side and focusing your attention away from the listeners or turning around completely with your back to the audience.	Face your audience, turning as needed to make eye contact with everyone in the room.
Playing with loose change in pocket	Putting your hand in your pocket and playing with change or car keys so that the audience hears the jingle.	Coordinate your hand gestures with your spoken message in a natural and spontaneous way. Deliberate hand gestures can be helpful in several ways, such as to indicate size, emphasize key information, signal a transition, or point to information in your presentation aids. However, avoid pantomiming or playing charades as forced, unnatural gestures are distracting to an audience.
Playing with hair or touching the head	Touching or rubbing your head or playing with your hair while speaking.	
Waving arms	Waving arms in an exaggerated manner with no management of the movement.	
Praying hands	Clasping your hands across your upper stomach as if you are praying.	
Folding arms in front	Folding arms in front of your body, suggesting a closed stance and creating psychological distance from listeners.	

At various points, making eye contact with people seated in different parts of the room can help you communicate with your listeners in a civil way. For example, speakers, at times, tend to focus on the people seated directly in front of them and don't acknowledge those seated to the right and left. In addition, students giving speeches in class often look only at the instructor. This tendency is not surprising, given that the instructor is the person assigning them a grade, so they feel compelled to make sure he or she understands the message.

Some speakers fail to look at the audience at all. They sometimes focus their attention entirely on the notes, outline, or manuscript they have on a lectern in front of them without ever looking up at their listeners, or they look too frequently at the projection screen when using digital slides. Some speakers have been known to face to the side—even turn their backs to the audience—when motioning to a screen, thereby turning themselves away from listeners. All these behaviors are ineffective techniques that are uncivil toward the audience. If you are able to find a friend to listen as you practice, be sure to practice using effective eye contact as you speak.

Proper Attire

Like eye contact, your attire can affect whether you successfully deliver a speech. Dressing appropriately shows sensitivity to the occasion. Wearing casual clothing, for example, to speak at a formal occasion suggests poor visual presentation and lack of respect for the event and the audience. Furthermore, dressing appropriately to meet audience expectations can help you practice civil delivery. Listeners, for instance, expect the president to dress in a suit and tie when he gives a speech. On the other hand, Steve Jobs, the founder of Apple, could stand before audiences dressed a little more casually because people did not really expect him to be dressed more formally. Your instructor will define the

Speakers should express their emotions appropriately to connect with their audience.

requirements for you related to dress, but undoubtedly, he or she will forbid, for example, shorts, T-shirts, and ball caps as attire for speeches.

Your choice of attire may also complement your topic. If you are demonstrating a cooking technique, for example, a chef's hat and apron would help set the stage for your audience.

Communicating Emotions

At the beginning of this chapter, you read about Randy Pausch's "Last Lecture." Pausch's lecture is an example of appropriate and civil delivery in that he showed his audience respect and attempted to demonstrate the principles he was putting forth in the speech. For example, he smiled and laughed during the speech, and he made good eye contact with all members of his audience. In addition, he used humor effectively and even spoke of his own cancer with a degree of levity. Early in the speech, Pausch claimed that he was actually in very good physical condition, and he dropped to the floor and began doing pushups.[17]

As illustrated in Pausch's "Last Lecture," effective visual presentation and good delivery help you connect with your audience. You want your audience to feel at ease with you as a speaker, and you should express your emotions appropriately and engage the audience with civility to achieve that goal. The most direct way to express emotions appropriately is through facial expressions. Research says that seven facial expressions of emotion exist across cultures: sadness, anger, disgust, fear, interest, surprise, and happiness.[18] An awareness of your facial expressions can help you connect with your audience; these expressions say something to them about your attitude toward the subject of your speech as well as toward them. Stern looks, for example, will most likely give the audience an uneasy feeling and inhibit your ability to communicate effectively; a friendly smile may help to put both you and your audience at ease. Being aware of how loudly you speak and your tone of voice can also help you communicate your emotions in an effective manner.

In another sense, speakers can mask their emotions. They can replace an expression with another that does not accurately reflect the person's feelings.[19] Honesty is a very important aspect of giving a speech—not just with regard to what you say but also how you communicate nonverbally. Effective nonverbal communication helps you address your audience in an authentic—and civil—way.

PLANNING, PREPARING, AND USING PRESENTATION AIDS

Using presentation aids effectively can help support your speech by making your main ideas even more concrete. This section addresses the purpose of presentation aids, when to use such aids, and the use of presentation software.

The Purpose of Presentation Aids

In using presentation aids, you need to remember to give the speech, not the visual aids. In other words, visual aids, such as PowerPoint slides, do not communicate the point of your presentation to audiences; rather, you use these aids to support the message you are conveying to your listeners. We live in an increasingly visual and verbal culture in which both elements interact to make meaning. Furthermore, visual aids can make a speech more compelling for an audience, aid them in comprehension and retention, and enhance your credibility.

You can use visual aids to

- Help your audience understand your ideas
- Emphasize important ideas
- Help your audience follow your argument
- Help listeners remember your presentation

PowerPoint, however, can sometimes encourage bad habits and poor speaking. *Small Business Computing.com* writer Angela R. Garber first coined the phrase "Death by PowerPoint" in 2001.[20] Garber and other critics of PowerPoint say that it becomes a convenient prop for bad speakers and just reduces complicated messages to simple bullet points. Critics assert that PowerPoint elevates style over substance. A presentation that uses PowerPoint can bore audiences because it may present information in a long and drawn-out manner that causes listeners to lose interest. Garber also advises speakers to guard against presentational or visual aids failing. For example, a projector for showing electronic slides may not be available.[21] Or the computer that stores your PowerPoint file may fail, or you might accidentally leave your thumb drive at home. You need to be prepared to give your speech effectively under such circumstances.

Despite the concerns and issues just mentioned, PowerPoint and other visual aids can be beneficial in helping you communicate a message. But before you use PowerPoint or any other visual aid, it is important to know when to use such aids as well as how to use those aids effectively and appropriately.

A speaker can use visual aids to emphasize important ideas and help listeners remember those ideas.

When to Use Presentation Aids

Knowing your general purpose is the first step in understanding whether to use presentation aids. Recall from Chapter 11 the general purposes for speaking: to inform, to persuade, and to inspire. A speech with an informative purpose, such as teaching your audience a process, would likely benefit from presentation aids. You might offer a demonstration of the process so that your listeners gain a good sense of it. A persuasive speech proposing one solution to a problem over other options might require use of PowerPoint or Prezi slides so that your audience can clearly understand and remember the options you are addressing. However, you would probably *not* use presentation aids in giving an inspirational speech because such aids would not do much to bolster your claims or substantiate your message.

Consider the following questions in making decisions about whether to use visual aids for your speech:

- Does the audience expect the use of visual aids?
- Will visual aids help me communicate my message more clearly?
- Will visual aids help motivate the audience to listen to the speech?
- Will visual aids enhance my speech without being too distracting?

If you answer "yes" to any of these questions, you should decide on the best visual aid for your speech and use the aid when you practice your speech. You must always consider the audience, the occasion, and your speech purpose in designing and using visual aids.

Using Presentation Software

Today, the most common presentation aids are computer-generated slides from software programs. PowerPoint is a common software application for presentations, and many people now also create highly visual presentations using Prezi. Prezi is most appropriate for presentations about very intricate subjects; however, it may be too complex for a first classroom speech. If you use any presentation software, you need to use it effectively and also avoid the pitfalls of using this technology.

The following guidelines can help you effectively integrate and use computer-generated slides in a speech:

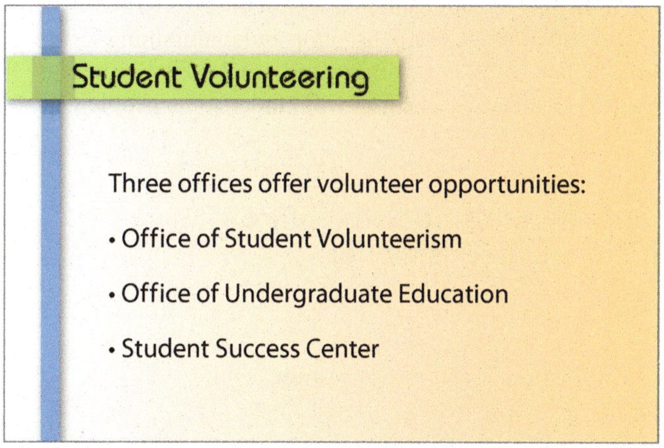

- *Keep the visual aids simple.* Most speech instructors agree that slides as visual aids should be simple, clear, and direct. Many people go overboard with PowerPoint. Sometimes speakers design slides with far too much text and too many graphics. When you do this, your audience will focus their attention on reading the slide rather than listening to you. Using a limited number of fonts is also important for keeping the slides simple. A good rule of thumb is to use no more than two types of fonts for an entire presentation. You can use one font for the title or major headings and one font for the subtitles or other text.

- *Use a mix of text and graphics in creating your slides.* It is important to give your slides a little variety. Your slides should incorporate both text and graphics. Slides that display only text with no other graphics or pictures may seem boring to listeners.

- *"Unpack" your slides while giving the speech.* "Unpacking" a slide means that you gesture to the slide with your hand (e.g., specific bullet points) while you present the speech. However, avoid turning your body to the side or away from the audience in doing so. Speakers often unpack a slide when they wish to emphasize a particular point they are making in the speech. Unpacking also helps guide the audience through the speech and helps them see how the visual aids support the speaker's point.

- *Do not read directly from your slides.* You are giving the speech, not the slides. Reading directly from the slides will seem as though you are reading to your audience.

- *Create slides that are large enough for your audience to see.* Although the point may seem obvious, sometimes speakers simply do not create visuals aids (e.g., computer-generated slides) that audience members can easily see. A speaker should also keep the size of the room in mind when creating slides and use fonts that are large enough to be readily seen.

You read in Chapter 11 that a good introduction previews the speech structure for the audience. In addition, a speaker using slides can provide a forecast or overview slide that identifies the main ideas of the speech. Figure 12.1 illustrates how speakers can overview the speech structure in this way.

Slide A

Student Volunteering

Three offices offer volunteer opportunities:
- Office of Student Volunteerism
- Office of Undergraduate Education
- Student Success Center

Slide B

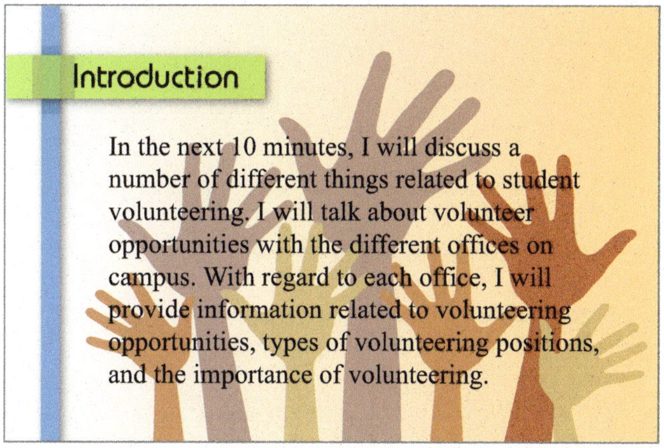

Introduction

In the next 10 minutes, I will discuss a number of different things related to student volunteering. I will talk about volunteer opportunities with the different offices on campus. With regard to each office, I will provide information related to volunteering opportunities, types of volunteering positions, and the importance of volunteering.

FIGURE 12.1 Effective and Ineffective Preview Slides

Slide A includes a manageable amount of information that previews the overall message of the speech. Slide B contains too much information, and the background and font are too distracting for the audience to read.

The first slide in Figure 12.1 identifies the main areas of the speech, and the audience learns exactly what to expect from the speaker. Furthermore, this slide enables listeners to follow the structure more easily.

The second slide in Figure 12.1 shows an ineffective forecast or preview slide. This slide is ineffective for several reasons. First, listeners must work too hard to identify the speaker's main ideas from the text. Bulleted lists help listeners to very quickly see and process the main ideas and make the content more accessible for the audience. Furthermore, the background makes it difficult to distinguish the text in the foreground. Finally, the text font and its small size also make the slide difficult to read.

Consider the examples of effective and ineffective slides in Figure 12.2 that display the supporting information for the first main point in the speech. The first slide in Figure 12.2 is effective because it displays an appropriate amount of text. An audience can easily scan the slide for the information while still listening and maintaining focus on the speaker. The second slide in Figure 12.2, on the other hand, is less effective because it contains far too much text, and the small size of the font will hinder some people's

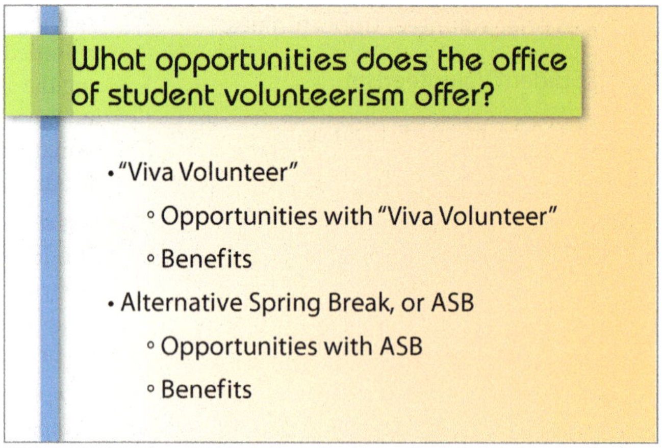

Slide A

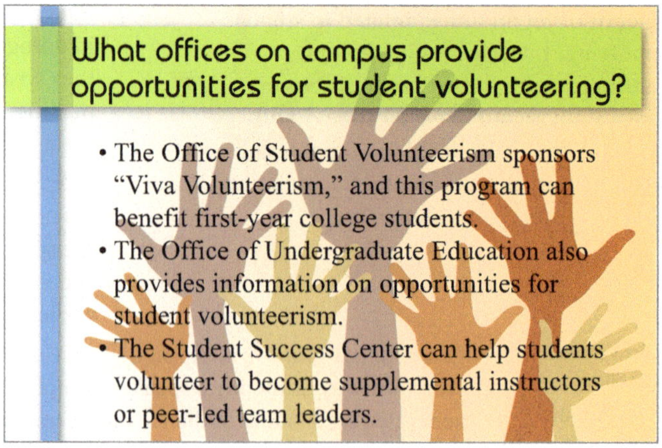

Slide B

FIGURE 12.2 Effective and Ineffective Slides Showing the Support for the First Main Point

Slide A includes a manageable amount of information that describes the supporting material the speaker plans to offer for the first main point. Slide B contains too much information, and the font is too distracting for the audience to read.

ASK THE ETHICIST: Should Two Different Speakers Use the Same Visual Aids?

Question My friend and I are taking the same public speaking class with different instructors. Both of us have to give the same kind of speech, so we thought about collaborating on our speeches. We are required to use visual aids in the speech and want to make one set together for both of us to use. Another friend said she doesn't think this is a good idea. Why not?

Answer It is true that much of your work after you graduate from your college program will be completed in groups whose members collaborate with one another. In organizations, it is expected to be the case, and people are evaluated based on their efforts together. In a public speaking class, however, you are evaluated on your individual performance. If you are evaluated on collaborative work, that work is completed with others in your class, not people outside your class. The problem is that it confuses the issue of who creates what, and when instructors evaluate your performance, that's an issue that needs to be clear. By all means, share information with your friend, and work together to create ideas, but be sure that the presentation and visual aids are your own creation. That's the most ethical way to approach it.

---

ability to read it effectively. What other problems do you see with this slide as a presentation aid?

It's important not to overload your slides with text. Doing so will result in the audience spending unnecessary time and effort trying to read your slides rather than listening attentively to your speech. Long before the advent of PowerPoint, speakers were encouraged to follow the "6 × 6 Rule."[22] This rule says that no more than six words should appear across a slide, and no more than six words should go down a slide, not counting the header.[23] The 6 × 6 Rule logically results in 36 words per slide, which is probably still too many. A better guideline is to use no more than 25 words per slide.[24]

Figure 12.3 shows the difference between effectively and ineffectively constructed conclusion slides. Notice that the first slide uses a question for a heading to help signal the conclusion, which lets the audience know the end is coming. In this speech, the speaker would also summarize the main ideas. The three bullet points on this slide highlight the speaker's summary, although it does not contain every single statement the speaker would make in giving the synopsis.

The second slide, on the other hand, provides too much text. It provides the speaker's entire conclusion as a paragraph, so the audience will likely spend time reading it rather than listening to the speaker give the conclusion. Again, visual aids should quite literally serve as aids; in other words, you use electronic slides and other aids to support the message of your speech. Your visuals do not—and should not—communicate the message for you.

Conveying Information on Slides

It is common for speakers to use graphs and charts to display statistical data to provide supporting evidence for the audience. Presenting this information can help speakers make their point. However, presenting this information ineffectively can hurt a speech. Speakers should avoid what many refer to as "data dump," or crowding a presentation—especially charts and graphs—with too much information.

Consider the example in Figure 12.4, which returns to our sample speech from Chapter 11. It clearly lists the various participating agencies for the Office of Volunteer

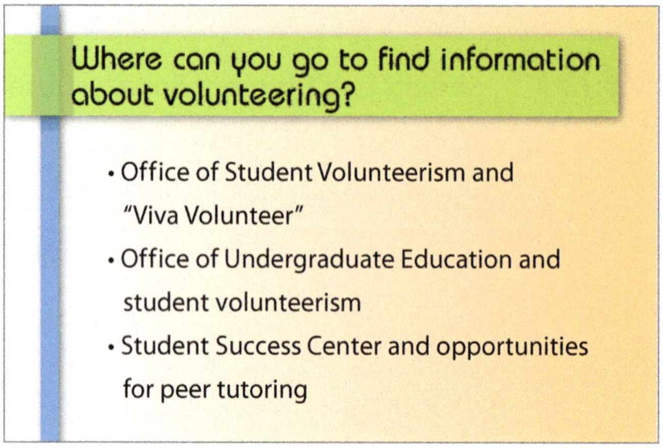

FIGURE 12.3 Effective and Ineffective Conclusion Slides
Slide A includes a manageable amount of information that displays the concluding points of the speech. Slide B contains too much information, and the font is too distracting for the audience to read.

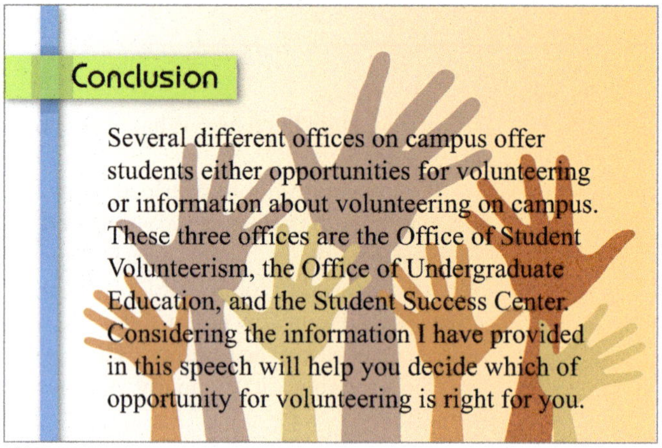

Services in a legible format. Although the speaker also lists the agencies as part of the speech, the chart helps the listener remember the list and potentially find one of the agencies appealing for his or her own volunteer activity.

Similarly, a speaker can use information in graphs effectively and ineffectively, as illustrated in Figure 12.5. In this case, the speaker intends to refer to the practice of job outsourcing in various industries. A bar chart clearly displays the relevant information: the total number of jobs outsourced in a year and the percentage of jobs outsourced in each sector. As the speaker discusses each of these sectors, he or she can refer the listeners to the slide.

In using charts and graphs, remember to make the text and numbers legible. The audience should be able to read everything on the slide, and the speaker can explain the areas of the chart or graph that he or she wants the audience to understand. In addition, avoid clutter and strive for simplicity and clarify. As previously mentioned, you need to create visuals that are large enough for your listeners to see clearly.

Agencies Participating in the "Viva Volunteer" Event:
- Plano Animal Shelter
- Dallas Children's Theater
- Goodwill Industries
- Foster Kids Charity
- Neighborhood Services Council

FIGURE 12.4 An Effectively Constructed Chart: Office of Student Volunteerism's Participating Agencies
This chart presents information in an effective way with the right amount of space between each agency on the list.

Total number of U.S. jobs outsourced in 2011
2,273,392

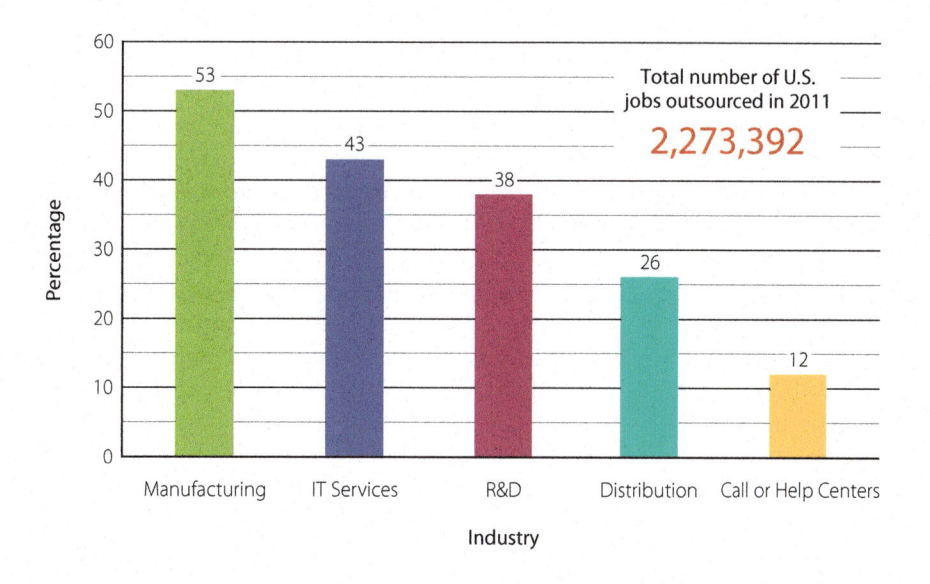

Industry	Percentage
Manufacturing	53
IT Services	43
R&D	38
Distribution	26
Call or Help Centers	12

FIGURE 12.5 An Effective Graph: Job Outsourcing in the United States, 2011
This graph is effective because it displays information in a clear and understandable way.
Source: "Job Outsourcing Statistics," *Statistic Brain*, www.statisticbrain.com/outsourcing-statistics-by-country/.

PRACTICING YOUR SPEECH

Earlier in this chapter, you read about strategies to manage your anxiety and address communication apprehension. Managing communication apprehension requires *practice*. However, you also need to practice the speech for other reasons. This section provides some additional guidance to help you practice your speech in a strategic way while being mindful of civil engagement with audiences.

Using a Speech or Presentation Outline

In order to speak from an outline, you need to create a speech or presentation outline that will serve as notes to help you remember the main ideas for the speech. In Chapter 11, you read about preparing a full-sentence outline when you begin to compose your speech; however, using that outline as you actually present your speech would be too distracting. To create a presentation outline, you can begin with the formal outline and then reduce it to short phrases or words to help trigger your memory. In other words, you would *not* use whole sentences or paragraphs in a presentation outline to give a speech. To get used to using your presentation outline, you should practice with the outline several times before the actual speech occasion.

Follow these guidelines for converting your original outline to a speech or presentation outline:

- *Follow the same structure as the original outline.* You should match the structure you used for that outline in creating the speech or presentation outline. Furthermore, you should use the same symbols, notations, and pattern of indentation as in the original outline.
- *Use key words.* Do not use the complete sentences from the formal outline in the presentation outline. Using full sentences will most likely cause you to read directly from your outline. Key words, however, will help you remember your main ideas. One exception to this rule is to include the exact words of any quotations you intend to use.
- *Make the speech outline legible.* Make sure you can read your speech outline and easily determine what your notations mean. You might use large letters or all capital letters in some instances. Sloppy writing or scribble, for obvious reasons, can cause problems for you when presenting your speech.
- *Use delivery cues.* Make notations on the outline to tell yourself *how* you want to say something. Use brackets, underline words, and/or mark words and phrases with a highlighter or write them in different colors to note transitions, pauses, and/or specific citations and quotations. Such notations represent **delivery cues**, or directions for delivering or giving a speech.

delivery cues Notations on a presentation outline that tell a speaker *how* to say something. Brackets, underlined words, and/or words and phrases marked with a highlighter or written in different colors to note transitions, pauses, and/or specific citations and quotations are examples of delivery cues.

Consider the following presentation outline:

I. Introduction
   A. Attention-getter: Quote from Bill Clinton:

   "Volunteering is an act of heroism on a grand scale. And it matters profoundly. It does more than help people beat the odds; it changes the odds."

   B. Thesis statement
   C. Preview of 3 main points: (OSV, ASB, and Undergrad Ed)

[PAUSE]

[TRANSITION]

II. Body of the Speech
   A. Office of Student Volunteerism
      1. OSV sponsorship of "Viva Volunteer" Day
         a. OSV website information
         b. Agencies helped by Viva Volunteer participants

[Display Chart]

         c. Student Erin Hoffer quotation: "feed the hungry, educate the ignorant, and give back with service."

2. "Alternative Spring Break"
    a. 40 hours of community service
    b. Volunteering opportunities
    c. Katie Walser and ASB experience

[TRANSITION]

B. Office of Undergraduate Education and volunteer opportunities
    1. "Freshman Year Experience"
        a. Orientation Team Mentor
        b. Freshman Year Experience website explains OTM
    2. "Freshmen Year Experience" and student success camps
        a. OTMs organize various success camps
        b. Experience beneficial [cite senior Cayman Nava, computer science major and 3-time OTM]
        c. Benefits of OTM

[TRANSITION]

C. Student Success Center and volunteer opportunities
    1. Historically difficult courses website [cite Supplemental Instruction website]
        a. Examples: chemistry, history, sophomore-level psych and econ, and junior-level biology
        b. During each session, SI leader reviews topics and information covered
    2. Peer-Led Team Learning is an expansion of Supplemental Instruction
        a. PLTL volunteers [cite PLTL website]
        b. Benefit of working as PLTL [quotation from Nujeen Zibari: "It's been a real gift to be able to work with these students."]

[TRANSITION]

III. Conclusion
    A. Review of 3 Main Points [PAUSE]
    B. Closure: Quote from Margaret Mead:

"Never doubt that a small group of committed people can change the world. Indeed, it is the only thing that ever has."

    C. Final remarks

Practicing a speech is the best way to achieve an effective delivery.

Practicing with Presentation Aids

If you plan to use presentation aids, you need to practice with those aids. PowerPoint slides, for example, require "unpacking"; in other words, you need to practice motioning to the slides when stressing certain key points. Practicing with your presentation aids also helps you become more comfortable with them. The more comfortable you feel with your presentation aids before you give the speech, the more effectively you will use those aids when the time comes.

Simulating the Situation

If possible, simulate the occasion of the speech. You might even re-create the layout of your classroom and ask a few friends to act as audience members. You will also need to time the speech to make sure you are abiding by such constraints. Practicing the speech will help you determine whether it is too long or too short.

Practicing Delivery

Practice represents the best way to achieve effective and civil delivery; references to practice are made throughout this chapter. You can even video or audio record your speech during a practice session; doing so will tell you a great deal about flaws in your delivery. For example, you might hear several verbal or vocal pauses in certain key parts of the speech. If you are planning to use presentation aids as a part of your speech, your practice sessions should include practice on displaying and referring to your aids as you speak. Identifying delivery glitches in advance can help you overcome problems and improve the overall presentation of the speech.

CHAPTER SUMMARY

Now that you have read this chapter you can:

12.1 Understand what it means to deliver public speeches with civility.

Civil speakers relate effectively to their audience on both emotional and intellectual levels and take responsibility for their spoken messages.

12.2 Know strategies for controlling anxiety about speaking publically.

Feeling anxiety about public speaking is normal, but speakers must learn to control their nerves. Practice is the most important technique for controlling anxiety. You can also prepare both physically and mentally, act confident, and begin with a strong opening.

12.3 Choose an appropriate method of delivery for your audience and purpose.

Modes or methods of delivery include speaking from a manuscript, speaking from an outline, speaking from memory, speaking with little preparation, and speaking extemporaneously. Choosing an appropriate method depends on your audience and purpose as well as the occasion.

12.4 Understand techniques for effective delivery in your speeches.

Vocal quality, gestures, body language, and eye contact can affect your speech in positive or negative ways. It is important to maintain an appropriate volume for the audience as well as avoid verbal and pregnant pauses in your delivery. Your rate of speaking, pronunciation, and enunciation and even the way you dress can determine whether you effectively engage your audience with civility. You want your audience to feel at ease with you as a speaker. Expressing emotions by appropriately using facial expressions, vocal volume, and vocal tone can help you achieve this goal. Respecting your listeners is also important as they will react and respond on both emotional and intellectual levels.

12.5 Know how to create and use presentation aids effectively.

Presentation aids help you give a speech; these aids do *not* give the speech for you. Guard against presentation aids failing or not being available. Ask certain key questions before deciding to use presentation aids and be sure to design those aids in an effective way.

12.6 Effectively practice speeches to improve delivery.

It takes practice to manage your communication apprehension and give a competent speech. Prepare a delivery outline and use it during your practice sessions. Practice using your presentation aids as you speak. Try to simulate the speaking situation to make your practice sessions as realistic as possible. And finally, practice the delivery style that you will use in your actual speech.

CIVILITY SUMMARY

Overall, remember that delivering public speeches with civility involves the following:

- You can respect your audience by understanding that it is composed of people who will react to your message on both emotional and intellectual levels.
- You can exhibit restraint by refraining from communicating intense emotions such as extreme anger and frustration as you deliver your speech.
- You can demonstrate responsibility toward your "community" (in this case, your audience) by practicing your speech prior to your presentation. This will facilitate engagement by preventing the audience from being distracted by delivery problems that may occur during the speech.

REVIEW QUESTIONS

1. What factors may contribute to communication apprehension?
2. What is the best way to control anxiety about speaking publically?
3. How can you act confident in front of an audience?
4. When might you want to speak from a manuscript?
5. What is the difference between enunciation and pronunciation?
6. How can speakers use gestures effectively?
7. What are the benefits of using presentation aids?

13 Giving Civil Informative and Special Occasion Speeches

CHAPTER OBJECTIVES

After reading this chapter, you will be able to:

13.1 Understand the difference between informative and persuasive speaking.

13.2 Choose an appropriate informative speech purpose.

13.3 Apply strategies for giving interesting and civil informative speeches.

13.4 Compose an effective informative speech.

13.5 Apply strategies for giving effective special occasion speeches.

13.6 Understand how civility relates to both informative speaking and speaking for special occasions.

ON OCTOBER 25, 2009, First Lady Michelle Obama spoke at an event celebrating National Breast Cancer Awareness Month.[1] Mrs. Obama's speech literally helped *raise awareness* about this issue by providing information on breast cancer. Her speech, however, did *not* actually ask the audience to take action, nor did it seek to change anyone's mind. Rather, the First Lady sought to elevate the consciousness of her audience by giving information. Although those attending the event were already committed to the breast cancer cause, Mrs. Obama sought to speak to others who possibly lacked awareness of the issue.

In the speech, Mrs. Obama said that because of the increase in donations for breast cancer research, "the number of women getting regular mammograms has dramatically increased, and the five-year survival rate when breast cancer is diagnosed in time is 98 percent—and that's compared to 74 percent in the early '80s."[2] However, she also cited significant statistics about consequences of this disease, explaining that "40,000 women a year still die from this disease. That's one woman every 13 minutes who's dying from this disease today."[3]

By providing information, Mrs. Obama also raised awareness of the high cost of treatment, even for people with insurance coverage. She explained that some breast cancer patients still paid an average of more than $6,200 in one year. Treatment cost some insured patients as much as $10,000 or $20,000 while 5 percent paid more than $30,000.[4]

WHY IT MATTERS

In this day of information overload, we are often bombarded with facts and figures that speakers fail to adapt so that listeners can really understand them. Michelle Obama cited facts and figures but put them into context (e.g., "one woman every 13 minutes who's dying from this disease"). She also talked about the high cost of treatment even for those who are insured, and again she presented those figures in a way the average person could understand. She treated the issue with sensitivity, and she engaged her audience with civility. For example, she expressed her gratitude for the sacrifices, contributions, and efforts made thus far by individuals already committed to the issue.[5] She also said that she looked forward to working with individuals already engaged in raising breast cancer awareness.

In this chapter, you will learn how to effectively give informative speeches that provide the audience with new information or raise awareness of some issue—such as breast cancer. You will discover means of motivating an audience when that audience may have little or no interest in what you have to say. You will encounter the different ways to organize information and learn how to use supporting material in an informative speech. You will also learn that giving an informative speech differs from giving a persuasive one in that you are focused on helping the audience understand something more fully or to a greater degree than before. Finally, you'll be introduced to three different special occasion speeches you are likely to give in your lifetime.

WHAT IS INFORMATION?

Can you picture yourself presenting an informative speech sometime in your future? What types of informative speeches might you present as they relate to your current or future occupation? A salesperson may need to present information regarding how to use a unique product; a doctor may have to give a speech at a community forum about medical self-care; a computer programmer may need to explain new software to her or his team; and a military officer may need to brief new recruits. The point is that knowing how to construct and deliver an informative speech will be useful to you in terms of your career and in other facets of your life (e.g., volunteering at a house of worship, coaching an intramural team).

Can you picture yourself presenting a special occasion speech sometime in your future? You may be asked to toast a bride and groom at their wedding or to deliver a eulogy at a funeral. In terms of your current or future occupation, you may present a speech to nominate a coworker for committee membership or announce that you are leaving your job. Knowing how to construct and deliver a special occasion speech will be useful to you in various facets of your life, including your career.

As an informative speaker, you will present information in a neutral way without taking a side. Take a moment to consider these topics:

- High school abstinence-only sex education programs
- Legalization of marijuana
- Gay marriage

You might think that none of the topics listed here will make a good informative speech topic. You have likely linked topics about abstinence, marijuana, and gay marriage to persuasion—as something that should or should not occur, or as a consequence, or as a result that is either good or bad. For example, the following persuasive speech specific purpose statements might relate to these topics:

- To persuade my audience that we *should* use abstinence-only sex education programs to teach high school students about sex
- To persuade my audience that legalizing marijuana will result in *harmful* consequences that will affect the majority of Americans
- To persuade my audience that voting to approve gay marriage will *justly* provide all U.S. citizens equal rights

Notice the words *should*, *harmful*, and *justly*. These words tell you that the speeches associated with the three topics will be persuasive. This is because (as you will read in Chapter 14) the goals of persuasive speaking include creating an audience attitude or opinion, changing an attitude or opinion held by the audience, reinforcing an audience attitude or opinion, and motivating an audience to action (e.g., voting for the approval of gay marriage in an upcoming election). Words that take a stand (e.g., *should*, *ought*, or *must*) and words that are evaluative (e.g., *harmful*, *justly*) are used to create, reinforce, and change attitudes and also to promote a behavioral response.

Now take a look at the following informative speech specific purpose statements related to the same three topics:

- To inform my audience about the three types of abstinence-only sex education programs typically taught in high schools
- To inform my audience about how legalized marijuana is used to treat medical ailments
- To inform my audience about strategies political groups have used to influence the passage of gay marriage referendums in certain states

Do you see that words such as *should*, *ought*, and *must* are not included in these specific purpose statements? In addition, evaluative words that suggest something is good or bad or right or wrong are not included in informative speech specific purpose statements. This is because the purpose of informative speeches is to provide the audience with neutral information rather than to persuade the audience.

Informative speeches can be used to raise awareness about important topics such as environmental issues.

INFORMATIVE SPEECH PURPOSES

Generally, speech instructors say that informative speeches adhere to three different informative speech purposes. One purpose concerns providing the audience with knowledge about a topic about which they are unaware. Another purpose concerns providing listeners who already know something about a topic with new and/or additional

Informative Speech Purposes

information about that topic. Still another informative speech purpose involves providing the audience with information so they can make a decision. Informative speakers will address audiences to raise awareness, provide new information, or set an agenda.

Raising Awareness

In certain speaking situations, you might attempt to raise your listeners' awareness of some issue. Often an audience may lack knowledge about an object, a process, an event, or an idea. You can raise audience awareness by providing the audience with information that the audience members do not possess. Conducting an audience analysis can help you determine whether your audience may lack knowledge about:

- Fiber-optic cable (an object)
- How implanted computer chips enable quadriplegics to move artificial limbs (a process)
- The Joplin tornadoes (an event)
- Postmodernism (an idea)

Consider your audience's demographic characteristics, such as age, gender, group composition, and cultural diversity. These characteristics may provide you with clues about whether the audience has prior knowledge about your topic. For example, suppose you decide to present an informative speech about the Joplin tornadoes. You conduct a demographic audience analysis and find that the predominant age of your university audience is 20 years (age), you have more females than males in the class (sex), most of the audience is geographically heterogeneous because many students come from cities other than the one in which your university is located (group composition), and the audience is made up of people from a variety of cultural backgrounds (cultural diversity). Because many members of your audience come from various cities and some from other states, they may not be aware of the three savage tornadoes that have hit Joplin, Missouri, since 1971 (an area of the United States with which they may not be familiar). Therefore, you decide that you will raise awareness about the Joplin tornadoes in an informative speech that introduces the audience to the topic.

When your audience already has knowledge about the topic, you can present "advanced information" (such as a speech about Asperger's Syndrome that focuses on Albert Einstein and other famous scientists who may have had Asperger's) rather than focus on basic facts.

Providing New Information

Audiences usually know something about most subjects *in general*. For example, most people know that autism is a type of communication disorder, but they probably do not know all the particulars. Listeners may need new and/or additional information so that they can update their common knowledge. For example, suppose you decide to present an informative speech about Asperger's syndrome, a communication disorder on the autism spectrum, to your community college audience. You conduct a demographic audience analysis and find that the predominant age of your audience is 18 years (age), you have an equal number of males and females (sex), most of the audience members live with their parents and attended public schools in the local school district (group composition), and the audience has a varied cultural background (cultural diversity). Because you are also a product of the local public school system, you know that most audience members attended school with classmates who have been diagnosed with Asperger's syndrome. In addition, members of your audience may have had closer contact with someone with Asperger's syndrome (e.g., a friend, a sibling). An audience member himself or herself may be an "aspy." Based on your audience analysis, you decide that the majority of your audience has a general knowledge of Asperger's syndrome. You can therefore focus on and present the most recent and in-depth information about Asperger's syndrome without having to concentrate on too much background information.

Making a Decision

Informative speakers can do more than simply provide new or additional information for audiences. It may be that listeners need information so that they can make an informed decision; speakers can therefore define a series of options for an audience so that they can eventually choose one option. The speaker, however, is *not* calling the audience to action or asking them to change their minds. If a speaker were asking listeners to act or change their minds, then the speaker would be engaged in a persuasive purpose rather than an informative one.

THE PROCESS OF INFORMING AUDIENCES

Can you recall listening to a speech you would describe as "boring"? What is it that makes a speech "boring"? Of course, delivery often plays a role (as you know if you've ever endured listening to a speaker with a monotonous voice). However, you may also decide that certain topics are "boring." The good news is that any speaker can make any potentially "boring" topic interesting to an audience. Speeches may also seem boring if they're unclear, disorganized, lack support, and fail to engage the audience. Any speaker can employ several strategies for giving an interesting—and civil—informative speech. These strategies include motivating the audience, making the information accessible, using clear language, using an effective organizational pattern, using appropriate supporting material, and engaging the audience.

Motivating the Audience

In giving an informative speech, you must be able to motivate the audience to listen to you and to learn from the speech. A speech on health care options, for example, could connect with listeners' safety needs in that you could appeal to their sense of security related to health. Connecting with the audience's needs also coincides with an overall goal of civility in giving speeches because audiences will appreciate that you have attempted to identify with them and their needs. A good opening with an effective attention getter also encourages an audience to want to listen to you.

Suppose you decide to present a speech about three types of insurance: major medical, dental insurance, and short-term disability. You realize that this topic may seem boring to college students, so you must create an introduction that will cause your audience

A speaker can motivate audience members to listen by appealing to their needs, such as when a professional appeals to listeners' safety and security needs.

to become interested in the topic. To motivate your audience to listen to your information about dental insurance, you might say:

> All of us have them, but most of us take them for granted. We use them to tear, gnash, and crunch. We try to clean them and take precautions so they'll last us a lifetime. You've probably guessed by now that I'm talking about your teeth. Because we tend to take dental health for granted, you may think that you need to limit your health care insurance coverage to trips to your primary care physician and the hospital emergency room. You may believe that you don't need insurance to cover work done on your teeth. However, dental insurance can help make regular visits to the dentist more affordable. Regular dental visits, which typically include a checkup and cleaning, may be expensive, but dental insurance can save you thousands of dollars later on should you need emergency treatment. Dental insurance can also cover unexpected conditions that require you to undergo a root canal, receive a cap or crown, or get treatment for periodontal gum disease.
>
> And don't make the mistake of thinking that these or other medical conditions won't happen to you! We're college students who are young, active, and in good health. So who needs to worry about "unexpected conditions?" We do! Do you ride a bike? Have you ever thought that you might suffer a spill and chip a tooth? Does your diet primarily consist of pizza, chips, and noodles? Have you ever thought that the slight twinge you feel every now and then in your molar might turn into a painful toothache brought on by a severe cavity? Dental insurance can provide you with the financial cushion you'll need to help you cope with a chipped tooth or unexpected cavities.

Making the Information Accessible

> *Specific purpose statement:* Today I'm going to speak to you about the Olympics.
> *Thesis statement:* The Chautauqua movement assemblies were very popular.

What's problematic about the specific purpose statement and thesis statement above? The specific purpose statement about the Olympics is very broad, and the thesis statement about the Chautauqua movement uses abstract language that hinders understanding. Both statements may cause audience members to lose interest in your speech. However, we can "make information accessible" by presenting information so that listeners can easily follow your message. Two strategies for making the information more accessible are limiting the amount of information presented and connecting the unfamiliar to the familiar.

Limit the Amount of Information Presented
Your audience will be able to absorb only some of the information from your speech. Cognitive psychologists say that in general, people can remember only seven plus or minus two pieces of information in any given interval. In other words, giving too much information may leave your audience feeling overwhelmed and unable to grasp your overall message. In an informative speech about the Olympics, for example, you wouldn't try to speak about every sport included in the competition. This would definitely result in information overload. Instead, you might speak about the three most dangerous sports, the most unusual sports, the most ancient sports, and so on.

Connect Unfamiliar Information to the Familiar
When you speak on topics with which the audience will likely have little or no familiarity, you need to find a way to link

unfamiliar information to the familiar. You can make a general comparison, or you can use a *metaphor* (a comparison where the speaker does not explicitly state the similarity between two different things which share at least one characteristic in common) or *simile* (a comparison where the speaker explicitly states a similarity between two different things) as strategies to accomplish this goal. Metaphors and similes are explained in depth later in this chapter. For now, we will use a general comparison to illustrate how a speaker can connect the unfamiliar with the familiar. For example, a speaker could use a comparison

---

TRENDS IN TECHNOLOGY AND SOCIAL MEDIA

Taking Words Out of Context

How many times have you accessed YouTube or another video file-sharing site and seen only a portion of a film, live action event, or presentation? Knowing what came before or after the portion posted on the site will most likely give you additional insight about the portions available to the public. Occasionally, knowing the before and after context can even change the overall meaning of a video posted on the Web.

During the 2012 presidential campaign, the Obama and Romney camps both used social media to take their opponents' words out of context. The Republican National Committee, for example, posted a Web video criticizing President Obama for "forgetting about the recession." In a speech, Obama stated:

> So it was a house of cards, and it collapsed in the most destructive, worst crisis that we've seen since the Great Depression. And sometimes people forget the magnitude of it, you know? And you saw some of that I think in the video that was shown. Sometimes I forget. In the last six months of 2008, while we were campaigning, nearly 3 million of our neighbors lost their jobs; 800,000 lost their jobs in the month that I took office.[6]

The RNC video, however, eliminated the portion of the speech in the posting that comes after the sentence "Sometimes I forget." But that deleted information shows that Obama truly doesn't forget the magnitude of the economic collapse. *The Washington Post* "Fact Checker" columnist Glenn Kessler wrote, "When the full remarks are viewed in context, the RNC really appears to be straining to claim that Obama says he forgets about the recession."[7]

On the other hand, the Obama camp also took some of Mitt Romney's words out of context. At one point during the presidential campaign, a woman told Romney that she commuted five hours to work because her company left Iowa. She asked Romney how he might keep jobs in Iowa, and he said that businesses sometimes invent more efficient ways to compete and that "our productivity equals our income."[8] In a CNN interview, Obama advisor David Axelrod accused Romney of lecturing the Iowa woman about the economy in general and her specific financial struggles with his "productivity equals income" comment.[9] Furthermore, a post on former Obama economic advisor Jared Bernstein's blog claimed that Romney knew more about the "economy of Wall St., not Main St." "Fact Checker" columnist Glenn Kessler scolded the Obama campaign when he wrote, "What appears to have begun as a commentary on business efficiency has, via the Obama campaign, turned into a failure to understand that American incomes have been dropping.... It's clear the woman who asked the question was not talking about her 'financial struggles.' She wanted to know how businesses could be enticed to stay in Iowa."[10]

Posting portions of a speech out of context is an uncivil act; it can distort the interpretation of the entire speech and can negatively affect the people who make the comments. It does not appear, though, as if quoting out of context in social media will end anytime soon.

Discussion Questions

1. Can we truly speak freely if we know that our remarks may be posted on a social networking site and taken out of context?

2. Have you had your words taken out of context and posted on a social networking site? How does taking something out of context reflect uncivil behavior?

3. Do you think the investigations of "fact checkers" such as Glenn Kessler go far enough in exposing political comments that are taken out of context?

to explain the popularity of the Chautauqua movement, which comprised a series of lecture and performance-based assemblies held in various locations in the nineteenth century. Specifically, a speaker could say:

> Just as modern amusement parks are packed with tourists in the heat of summer, hordes of listeners streamed to Chautauqua tent assemblies under the sweltering sun.

Using Clear Language

Using clear language is necessary for most audiences. **Obfuscation**, however, tends to alienate listeners. Obfuscation means the speaker has used obscure or confusing references, leaving the audience feeling a little bewildered. Twentieth-century British Prime Minister Winston Churchill was a great statesman and orator, known for his preference for plain, clear language. One of Churchill's most famous speeches occurred during World War II, when he exclaimed that as British citizens, "we shall fight on the beaches, we shall fight in the fields and in the streets, we shall fight in the hills." Churchill illustrated the power of clear language when he stated, "What if I had said, instead of 'We shall fight on the beaches,' 'Hostilities will be engaged with our adversary on the coastal perimeter?'"[11]

> **obfuscation** Use of obscure or confusing references that leave the audience feeling bewildered.

COMPOSING AN INFORMATIVE SPEECH

You must also take into account a number of factors in composing your informative speech. For example, it is important to choose an appropriate strategy for communicating information. You also need to use good supporting material so that your audience can fully understand the information you are providing. Using effective visual aids goes along with using good supporting material. Such aids help listeners visualize more abstract and complex concepts.

Choosing a Strategy for Communicating Information

You need to choose an appropriate strategy to help your audience understand the information in your speech. Depending on the situation, you will communicate information by using definition, description, explanation, and/or demonstration.

Definition Informative speakers often must define unfamiliar concepts, terms, and ideas for their audience. For example, a software engineer giving an informative presentation to a group of managers will probably need to define several unfamiliar terms, as many in management are not technical specialists. Similarly, if you give an informative speech on specialized topic from your field of study (e.g., physics, mechanical engineering, architecture, graphic art), you will need to define terms for your classmates, many of whom are probably not that familiar with your academic discipline.

Description Sometimes informative speakers need to use description to paint a vivid mental picture. Speakers use description to relate objects, events, places, or processes more clearly for listeners. In the workplace, a technician, for example, might describe in precise detail the characteristics of a new product design for his or her colleagues. Doing so helps them "see" the design.

When you use description, you begin by explicitly stating the idea. Then you explain why you want to describe it. You also emphasize significant details and omit less significant

A process demonstration can help the audience follow steps to achieve a desired result.

or irrelevant ones. The technician from the previous paragraph might first describe the product design in general and then relate the important features and aspects of the design.

Explanation Some informative speeches explain how the listener can do something or follow a process. These speeches can fulfill some instructional goal for the audience. For example, an audience might learn how to upload an attachment using Yahoo or Hotmail, or they might better understand how to invest their money wisely for retirement. Clearly, in one informative speech for class, you cannot show listeners how to conduct complex experiments in nuclear physics. But you can help them understand how to successfully complete certain tasks.

Informative speeches that explain also serve to clarify complicated concepts for the audience. Explaining a concept involves relating its relevant features. For instance, in explaining *annuity*, a financial advisor will identify the time value of money, interest rate, and future value as important aspects of the concept. The advisor will then, most likely, cite contrasting examples of the concept, perhaps explaining the distinction between fixed and variable annuities.

Demonstration Demonstration, to some degree, is closely related to explanation in that the speaker actually shows the audience how to do something. In fact, speakers often combine explanation and demonstration, first telling the audience in words how to do something and then showing them how to do it. Topics for a demonstration speech can range from to showing listeners how to make a pie to how to use the latest iPad.

Speakers demonstrating a process often use a chronological organization for their speech. In other words, they show the audience how to follow steps in order to achieve the desired result.

Using Appropriate Supporting Material

As you probably already know, you need to obtain good information to support your informative speech. To locate good information, you can use a number of methods for gathering information, such as using the World Wide Web for research, conducting library research, and interviewing.

As you already know, you must provide sources to support the major points in a speech; this helps establish your credibility. Your audience will be more willing to trust you if you cite authorities that back up what you are saying. Good supporting material, therefore, is very important for any informative speech.

Using Visual Aids for Informative Speeches

Informative speeches benefit from effective visual aids that help the audience understand the content. Good visual aids can help the listeners visualize the subject you are addressing, and in some cases, they are central to the presentation. For example, suppose an architect must present to a potential client the different architectural styles for building design. He or she may present pictures of the Victorian style, Adam style, and the Adirondack style. Seeing these pictures will help bring the

Good visual aids can help the audience visualize your subject.

information to life for listeners by making it more concrete. If the architect/speaker were to describe only in words Victorian style, Adam style, and Adirondack style, it would be more difficult for the audience to actually comprehend the appearance of those styles.

Informative speeches explaining complex and abstract processes (e.g., packet switching, information networks) also need good visual aids. Flowcharts, for example, can help an audience visualize a process more clearly. When informative speeches include a great deal of statistical and numerical data, graphs and charts can be helpful for the audience. Again, the combination of hearing the message verbally and seeing the information presented visually can help listeners both comprehend and retain the information from a speech. Graphic presentation aids can augment your informative speech and help you communicate more effectively with your audience.

SPECIAL OCCASION SPEECHES

What do the following types of speeches have in common?

- Speeches that introduce an upcoming speaker
- Toasts
- Speeches to present or accept an award

All three of these speeches are examples of special occasion speeches. Such speeches may present information about a person, place, or thing. In addition, such speeches may attempt to persuade you that a person, place, or thing is worthy of appreciation. Neither of these, however, is the primary purpose of special occasion speeches. Special occasion speeches "aim to fit the special needs of a special occasion."[12] Special occasion speeches are typically inspirational and pay tribute to the topic of the speech.

Types of Special Occasion Speeches

Special occasion speeches include eulogies, testimonials, dedications, speeches that nominate others (e.g., to become members of a committee or club or to run for office), after-dinner speeches, welcoming speeches, and retirement speeches. Inaugural addresses, commencement addresses, and keynote addresses are additional examples of special occasion speeches. The following sections describe three types of special occasion speeches that you may be asked to present sometime in the near future: speeches of introduction, speeches to present or accept an award, and toasts.

Special occasion speeches are typically inspirational and pay tribute to the topic of the speech.

Speeches of Introduction As the label implies, a speech of introduction is used to introduce a speaker to an audience. Although sometimes categorized as a type of informative speech, a speech of introduction that focuses on why the upcoming speaker is praiseworthy can be categorized as a special occasion speech. The main focus of such a speech should be the upcoming speaker rather than the speaker who is making the introduction. Therefore, the person making the introduction attempts to create enthusiasm for the speaker and helps establish the speaker's credibility for audience.

Speeches to Present or Accept an Award Speeches to present or accept an award occur when someone is receiving some form of public recognition. If you present an award, you can conduct an audience analysis to see if the listeners know about the purpose of the award. You may need to include a short explanation of the award in addition to why the award recipient deserves the recognition.

If you are accepting an award for which others were nominated, a civil communication gesture is to mention the names of those who hoped to receive it and praise their accomplishments.

Toasts Toasts typically celebrate one or more people during a special occasion, such as a wedding or birthday party. Toasts typically follow a protocol that includes standing and raising a glass of any type of beverage and speaking flattering words about the occasion. After the speech has ended, the toast continues when the speaker and audience raise their glasses higher and some may "clink" their glasses with others. Guests take a swallow of their beverage and sit down at the conclusion of the toast.

Strategies for Giving Special Occasion Speeches

Special occasion speeches are written and delivered to mark the "specialness" of a person or an occasion. Special occasion speeches are usually inspirational and praise a person, place, or thing. Audience members come to appreciate and value the topic of a special occasion speech when a speaker uses language creatively and delivers the speech in an effective manner.

Using Language Creatively The creative use of language includes integrating metaphors, similes, and anaphora into a speech:

- Earlier in this chapter, you learned that a **metaphor** is an implicit comparison between two different things that share at least one characteristic in common. You can create a metaphor by borrowing language associated with the first person, place, or thing and applying it to the second person, place, or thing. An example of a metaphor is "My true love's 'junk-mobile' was a royal carriage that took us to places I read about in fairy-tales." This metaphor compares a beat-up car to a royal carriage. Comparisons can also be across types of people, places, or things. For example, a person can be compared to an animal, a process to a person, and so on.

- You also read earlier in this chapter that a **simile** is a comparison between two different things that also share at least one attribute. However, unlike a metaphor, a simile is an explicit comparison because it always includes the word *like* or *as*. An example of a simile is "My Siamese cat is like a whirling-dervish when she streaks from room-to-room and literally bounces off the furniture."

- **Anaphora** occurs when the first word or group of words that occur at the beginning of a sentence are repeated in the next clause of the same sentence and/or are repeated in subsequent sentences. An example of anaphora is "Sometimes I wish I could move to the sea. Sometimes I wish I could win the lottery. And sometimes I wish I could appreciate what I already have without yearning for something different."

Delivering a Speech Effectively and Civilly Effective delivery in a special occasion speech varies according to the type of special occasion speech presented. For speeches of introduction, speeches to present or accept an award, and toasts, it is critical to be brief. With the exception of an acceptance speech, the focus of these speeches is on someone

---

metaphor A comparison where the speaker does not explicitly state the similarity between two things that share at least one characteristic in common.

simile A comparison where comparison where the speaker explicitly states a similarity between two different things.

anaphora Repetition of the first word or group of words from the beginning of a sentence in the next clause of the same sentence and/or are in subsequent sentences.

other than the current speaker. A brief speech will help the audience concentrate on the upcoming speaker, award winner, or person who deserves tribute. Longer special occasion speeches may call for the use of a manuscript of the entire speech. Unlike speaking notes in an outline form, manuscript delivery enables you to deliver a speech as written; this is especially important when the speech includes the creative use of language. Eye contact, pauses, and changes in pitch are nonverbal ways to enhance the reception of a special occasion speech. You may want to mark on your manuscript, for example, the places where you want to pause and change your tone of voice.

A CASE STUDY IN ETHICS

"You're Not Special!"

In his Wellesley High School class of 2012 commencement address, English teacher David McCullough, Jr., told the graduating seniors, "You've been pampered, cosseted, doted upon, helmeted, bubble-wrapped…nudged, cajoled, wheedled and implored. You've been feted and fawned over and called 'sweetie pie.'…But do not get the idea you're anything special. Because you're not."[13] McCullough scolded students for appreciating accolades more than achievement.[14] He did, however, temper his speech with humor about the graduates' ceremonial robes and quips he linked to noted scholars ("You've learned, too, I hope, as Sophocles assured us, that wisdom is the chief element of happiness; second is ice cream…just an fyi").[15] He concluded by saying:

> Exercise free will and creative, independent thought not for the satisfactions they will bring you, but for the good they will do others, the rest of the 6.8 billion—and those who will follow them …. The sweetest joys of life, then, come only with the recognition that you're not special. Because everyone is. Congratulations. Good luck. Make for yourselves, please, for your sake and for ours, extraordinary lives.[16]

McCullough wasn't prepared for the attention he received after he delivered his speech. He said that media outlets from *around the world* wanted an interview and that his speech was analyzed and criticized by bloggers, talk-show hosts, and tweeters.[17]

Although the response to McCullough's speech was overwhelmingly positive, others thought his words had no place in a commencement address. Katie Roiphe, a professor of journalism at New York University, wrote that while the world typically loves a challenging graduation speech that lacks the warmth and inspiration usually found in such addresses, McCullough's speech may have gone too far. She stated that although McCullough attempted to end on a high note by inspiring graduates to live worthwhile lives, the heart of the presentation was the critique of the overly nurtured "Millennial Generation." Other critics said that telling graduates how "unspecial" they are just before they discover the world outside high school is just mean.[18]

Discussion Questions

1. What do you think of the message behind McCullough's words? Consider both the content and his method of delivery.

2. Do you think McCullough adapted to the occasion and to the audience?

3. Can you think of other types of special occasion speeches that had a mixed reception?

INFORMATIVE SPEECHES, SPECIAL OCCASION SPEECHES, AND CIVILITY: AVOIDING PLAGIARISM

University of Alberta Medical School Dean Philip Baker gave a stirring speech at the 2011 convocation banquet. Graduating medical students and their families heard stories about his child who was ill, his wife's medical issues, and a patient's personal problems. One medical student described the speech as "phenomenal" and as reflecting very well on the evening. However, when students later conducted an online search of the speech, they discovered that Baker had used surgeon Atul Gawande's 2010 Stanford University medical school convocation speech as his own.[19]

Medical student Jonathan Zaozirny, who was in the audience during Baker's speech, said, "The speech that we just received from the dean was word-for-word… and it was a bit of a shock."[20] Zaozirny further commented that Baker never mentioned that he was referencing a speech written by someone else and suggested that an apology from Baker was called for.[21] Baker eventually did apologize—to the students, to Dr. Awande, and to his colleagues at the University of Alberta. Nonetheless, Baker was accused of tarnishing the reputation of the faculty of medicine and the integrity of the graduating class, the medical school, and the university.[22] Shortly after Baker issued the apology, he was asked to step down as dean of the medical school. In his resignation statement, Baker wrote that he never intended to detract from the accomplishments of the graduating medical students and that he hoped his resignation would bring closure to the incident.[23]

Plagiarism occurs when we present another person's ideas as our own. We plagiarize not only when we copy others on a word-for-word basis but when we paraphrase the ideas of others without attributing the source. Plagiarism is something that writers as well as speakers should avoid because it is an uncivil and unethical practice. Recall that *civility* reflects a choice we make to consider others' thoughts and feelings and that *civil communication* refers to the choice we make to communicate on the basis of respect, restraint, and responsibility. Plagiarizing another's words and/or ideas is disrespectful because it disconfirms the true author of a message. Plagiarism is also an irresponsible act in that it disregards how stealing words and ideas may affect the community. In the case of Philip Baker, the use of Atul Gawande's words as his own was irresponsible because Baker disregarded how his plagiarism could affect the student, medical school faculty, and university communities. Even student Jonathan Zaozirny asserted that Baker had a responsibility to his audience to write and present an original speech.[24]

Plagiarism is not only uncivil, it is also unethical. Recall that ethics is a system of standards that defines what behaviors are right and good and allows us to decide among behavioral options. Ethical principles include trustworthiness, responsibility, respect, fairness, caring, and concern for the community. Baker's act of plagiarism demonstrated that he was not trustworthy, responsible, or respectful and that he had little concern for the community.

We can avoid plagiarism by being aware of the various forms that plagiarism can take and by making sure that we attribute ideas that aren't our own to their original source.

Forms of Plagiarism

Does plagiarism occur only when you present an entire speech written by another as if it were your own? Is it plagiarism when you take ideas from more than one source and tweak passages to include your own research and words? What if you use just a few limited ideas from someone else and paraphrase them without citing the source? These examples illustrate three forms of plagiarism: global plagiarism, patchwork plagiarism, and incremental plagiarism.

plagiarism Presenting another person's ideas as our own.

ASK THE ETHICIST: Paying for Online Research

Question I am an extremely overworked college student who must balance academics, employment, and family. Why shouldn't I pay an online company to gather research information for me if it will give me more time to engage in activities that are work and family related and are beneficial to others?

Answer It's tempting to delegate what we see as mundane tasks when we feel as though we have too much to do. Gathering information is sometimes viewed as a tedious prerequisite to the "real" task of presenting information to others. The ethical dilemma here is clear-cut: You are presenting someone else's work as your own. Your instructors, unless they specify otherwise, expect you to gather your own information. And you don't know if the person conducting the research has biased the information in one way or another to reflect his or her beliefs. You're taking for granted that the person conducting the research for you is doing so ethically—keeping the context of quotes accurate, correctly citing the source of information, and so on. You have no real way to judge whether the researcher acting on your behalf has acted ethically.

In addition to the ethical dilemma, you are losing an important opportunity to increase your skills. Conducting research becomes easier each time you do it. In addition, you learn to evaluate information and judge whether it is reliable. You can't do that if someone else is gathering the information for you. You lose the opportunity to see different points of view and understand how people come to those points of view. And when your understanding of others and how they think about things is limited, you are more likely to stereotype different positions on a particular topic. That seems uncivil.

Global Plagiarism Global plagiarism occurs when someone takes an entire speech from another source and passes it off as her or his own. This type of plagiarism is blatant and rarely, if ever, can be deflected by an "I didn't know it was plagiarism" excuse. Former Medical School Dean Philip Baker was guilty of this type of plagiarism when he presented Dr. Atul Gawande's speech without referencing him as the author.

Patchwork Plagiarism Patchwork plagiarism occurs when someone takes material from two or three sources and passes it off as her or his own. Even if you conduct research and include original thoughts in your speech, it is still plagiarism if you don't attribute authorship of the thoughts of others. An example of patchwork plagiarism may have occurred when Arizona State University history professor Matthew Whitaker presented a speech about the historical roots of Senate Bill 1070 (Arizona's controversial immigration law). In the presentation, Whitaker used the exact words of a *Washington Post* article and a blog post from an anti-war website. Jonathan Bailey, director of a copyright and plagiarism consulting business, investigated Whitaker's speech after it was posted on YouTube. Bailey found that about 30 percent of Whitaker's speech was taken from other sources and that he could just about "read along" from the newspaper article as Whitaker delivered the presentation. Although Whitaker added his own words at the ends of sentences in a few instances and skipped a number of sentences that appeared in the newspaper article, he failed to cite the source of his information. Whitaker did, however, eventually cite the blog's author after he quoted some of the material. In the end, Whitaker denied plagiarizing and defended his actions by saying that he intended to mention the two sources. However, Whitaker explained that due to the emotional intensity of occasion for the speech, he made reference to only one name and forgot the other.[25] Whitaker's actions led to an Arizona State University investigation of charges of plagiarism in Whitaker's speech and published articles. While the investigative committee concluded

In doing library research, it is important to remember that source citation is necessary when using direct quotations and when summarizing someone else's ideas.

that Whitaker had not committed "systematic or substantial plagiarism," the committee asserted that there were "reasons for concern about occasional carelessness in the use of materials and sources and some less-than-optimal detail in attribution."[26] Professor Whitaker's actions also negatively affected his community. Specifically, one history professor resigned in protest over the committee's decision, and Whitaker's case resulted in contentious debate among the faculty about what "crosses the line" in terms of plagiarism.[27]

Incremental Plagiarism Incremental plagiarism occurs when speakers don't cite the sources for "increments," or specific parts, of a speech. Often the increments that are presented without citation are quotations and paraphrases. While it is obvious that a verbatim increment such as a direct quotation requires a source citation, it is just as important to cite a source when you use your own words to summarize others' ideas. An example of incremental plagiarism occurred when Australian Labor Minister Anthony Albanese presented a speech to the National Press Club of Australia. Albanese said to his audience:

> In Australia we have serious challenges to solve, and we need serious people to solve them. Unfortunately, [Opposition Leader] Tony Abbott is not the least bit interested in fixing anything. He is only interested in two things—making Australians afraid of it and telling them who's to blame for it.[28]

Immediately after his presentation, Albanese was accused of stealing the lines from the 1995 film *The American President*, starring actor Michael Douglas. In the film, Douglas's character responds to criticisms made by political opponent Bob Rumson:

> We have serious problems to solve, and we need serious people to solve them. And whatever your particular problem is, I promise you, Bob Rumson is not the least bit interested in solving it. He is interested in two things and two things only—making you afraid of it and telling you who's to blame for it.[29]

Albanese said that he hadn't seen *The American President* and that his staff had compiled the speech. Although he described the incident as more than a simple "cut and paste," he said he would counsel rather than fire the staff members who wrote this portion of the speech. Opposition Leader Tony Abbott responded to the situation by joking about the lack of originality on the part of the Labor-led government: "What it shows is that this government has no ideas of its own for the improvement of Australia."[30]

Attributing Ideas to an Original Source

Once you are aware of the different types of plagiarism, you can take a number of steps to avoid plagiarism of any form. Overall, it's important to credit the source whenever you borrow an idea from someone else or from a source that may not have an author. This is true whether you quote word-for-word or paraphrase an idea from a particular source. You can civilly and ethically credit a source during a speech presentation by remembering to state:

- The first and last names of the source
- The source's credentials (if you are quoting or paraphrasing a person)
- The document, website, speech, or other place from which you obtain the material

For example, Philip Baker could have said:

> In surgeon **[credentials]** Atul Gawande's **[first and last name]** 2010 Stanford University medical school convocation **[speech from which the material is obtained]**...

We can also attribute information to a source by beginning or ending a sentence or clause with the words *according to*:

> According to the editorial "Civility Challenge: A New Conversation" in the February 1, 2013, edition of *The Dallas Morning News*... **[newspaper from which the material is obtained]**

Note that the example above does not list the author or authors of the editorial; this is because the newspaper does not include the name(s) of the author(s). However, enough information is presented in the citation to enable the audience to realize that the source is credible; if desired, they could find a copy of the source.

If you are ever in doubt about whether to use a citation, err on the side of caution and attribute the material to a source. Remember that it's not necessary to include every piece of source information when you attribute material during a speech. Can you imagine what audience members would think if they were subjected to source citations like this:

> According to the *BBC news website*, located at http://news.bbc.co.uk/2/hi/health/2988647.stm, copyright date Wednesday, April 30, 2003, which I accessed on Sunday, February 17, 2013..."?

This citation is well suited for the bibliography or reference section placed at the end of a formal outline, but it includes too much detail for a source citation delivered during a speech presentation. Instead, you could say:

> The April 2003 BBC news website **[website from which the material is obtained]** includes statistics that illustrate...

The following are additional measures you can take to avoid plagiarism and attribute ideas to an original source:

- *Give yourself plenty of time to prepare a speech.* This holds true no matter what type of speech you are presenting (informative, special occasion, or persuasive). Don't wait until the last minute to prepare, or it might be tempting to "lift" an entire speech or parts of a speech from other sources.
- *Mark your research notes to remind yourself of quotes and paraphrases.* It is helpful to identify the sources of the material you have gathered for your speeches so you know to cite the sources when you write your speaking outline or manuscript.
- *Remember that plagiarism of any sort is uncivil and unethical.* Various online tools and software packages are available to detect plagiarism, and it's likely that you'll be caught if you use the ideas of others without crediting your sources. Remind yourself that not only will plagiarism negatively affect members of your community, it will also negatively affect you. After reading about the three examples of plagiarism, would you use the words *trustworthy* or *respectful* to describe former Medical School Dean Philip Baker, Arizona State University history professor Matthew Whitaker, and Australia Labor Minister Anthony Albanese? Probably not. Consider how others might describe *you* if you were caught plagiarizing material in a speech.

SAMPLE STUDENT SPEECH

HIV Home Testing

The speech presented in this section illustrates the concepts you have read about in this chapter. Reading this student's speech will help you use various techniques for composing an effective informative speech.

In preparing this speech, the student identified the general purpose and the specific purpose and also composed a thesis. In this speech, the student's general purpose is to inform, and the specific purpose is to provide new information for the audience about the OraQuick at-home AIDS test. The student's actual specific purpose statement might be:

Specific purpose statement: At the end of my speech, my audience will understand the benefits, drawbacks, and future implications of the OraQuick at-home AIDS test.

The thesis for this speech might look like this:

Thesis: The OraQuick Advance Rapid HIV—1/2 Antibody Test offers a number of benefits and a few drawbacks.

As you read this student's speech, pay particular attention to the way the student gains the audience's attention, organizes the message, and uses evidence for support. Take note of how the speaker connects with the audience and strives to fulfill the informative purpose.

What do you see as the occasion for this speech?

Many listeners likely relate to this story or anecdote because they are interested in information about HIV home testing. The speaker also shows sensitivity toward the audience by showing that he or she empathizes with their concerns and fears about HIV. In doing so, the speaker has connected with the audience and treated them with civility.

The speaker could use a visual aid here—such as graph—to illustrate the predicted yearly rise in the number of persons infected with AIDS and HIV worldwide.

The introduction also emphasizes the importance of the issue. In doing so, the speaker, once again, has shown the audience that he or she identifies with their concerns.

Has the speaker transitioned effectively between the opening and the body of the speech? Why or why not?

The introduction forecasts the mains ideas of the speech. Forecasting the main ideas makes it easier for listeners to follow the speech structure.

"I wish I had a crystal ball to conjure out the answers." Nicolas Sheon, HIV InSite Prevention editor, expressed this on August 24, 2000, in two different scenarios. The first scenario was fear. I had unprotected sex for the first time. I'm so scared to go get a test. Recently, I had mild fever and diarrhea. What are the odds that I'm HIV positive? The second scenario is anxious waiting. I want to propose to my girlfriend, whom I have not had sex with yet. However, I know I haven't always played it safe. So I decided to go to the clinic today for an HIV test. And as I wait for the results, I cannot stop thinking, "What if I'm HIV positive?" While even a crystal ball cannot combat the fear of going to get an HIV test or the anxiety of waiting for the results, a new testing device will quickly and anonymously reveal these answers.

Today there is the OraQuick Advance Rapid HIV-1/2 Antibody Test, or simply OraQuick. The *Sunday Oregonian* of October 23, 2005, asserts that the widespread use of this technology will be the largest revolution in HIV treatment in the United States since scientists developed high-quality antiretroviral drugs in the late 1990s. According to the Federal Document Clearinghouse congressional testimony of June 23, 2005, there are approximately 40 million people living with AIDS around the world today. The *Science Letter* of July 12, 2005, contends that as many as 300,000 HIV-infected people in the United States alone may be unaware that they are, in fact, infected, and thus unaware that they could spread the infection. Widespread use of the OraQuick technology will result in testing of more individuals, early treatment, and prevention of further spread of a truly deadly disease.

To better understand the widespread use of this technology, we will first discuss the development of at-home HIV testing kits and OraQuick; next, we'll look at how it works and its benefits; and finally we'll discuss a few drawbacks as well as future implications associated with the nationalization of this extremely valuable product. The concept of at-home HIV testing kits has been around for more than a decade, but since the first model was released in 1987, issues such as misdiagnosis and lack of counseling prevented the idea

Informative Speeches, Special Occasion Speeches, and Civility: Avoiding Plagiarism

from taking off. Currently, according to the Food and Drug Administration at www.fda.gov, as of October 25, 2005, there are more than a dozen different HIV testing kits being advertised on the market, mostly via the Internet, and all without the approval of the FDA. Unapproved HIV testing kits do not come with a guarantee of accuracy or delivery of dependable results. Proper training to interpret these results is not provided with the kits, and they have complicated procedures, yielding inconsistent results.

> *The speaker can pause briefly here to allow the audience to process, or digest, what has just been said.*

Incorrect outcomes can have grave consequences in terms of mental anguish, access to proper medical treatment, and future transmission of the disease. However, new developments in at-home testing technology have been able to overcome these obstacles with the development of OraQuick. According to the *Business Wire* of June 15, 2005, OraSure Technologies created the very first at-home HIV testing kit that uses oral fluids instead of blood, with over 99 percent accuracy. This product is currently sold only to clinics, physicians' offices, and community-based organizations. But a federal advisory board plans to make an initial decision concerning the widespread marketing of OraQuick on November 4, 2005. The *Morning Call* magazine of November 4, 2005, reports OraSure Chief Executive Officer Doug Michels was happy with the hearing, and the panel suggestions and looked forward to meeting the FDA official in the next 30 days to determine the next move. Fortunately, and for now, it has immense support from health officials, AIDS advocates, and the general public. After it gets approval, OraQuick will be sold over the counter, easily accessible to the general public.

> *The speaker has used a variety of sources to support the speech. Doing so helps the speaker further establish credibility with the audience.*

To better understand why medical experts chose this product for widespread and personal use, we must understand how it works and its benefits. This technology is easier to use than a pregnancy test. The use of the product is as simple as swab the inside of your mouth, put the swab in the fluid, and 20 minutes later you'll have the results. In a more descriptive fashion, according to the associated Press of October 26, 2005, to take the test, the person swabs the inside of their mouth between the cheek and the cells, picking up not saliva but only cells that line the mouth. The user then inserts the swab into a vial of fluid that is provided with the kit. 20 minutes later an indicator will light up if the test detects the presence of HIV antibodies, meaning it will let the individual know whether or not he or she carries the virus that causes AIDS.

> *The speaker uses the word* understand *to emphasize the informative purpose. The speaker also helps the audience understand the OraQuick test by comparing it to a home pregnancy test—something with which listeners likely have greater familiarity.*

Because of the product's simplicity and accuracy, OraSure has sold over 3 million of the tests since 2002 to doctors, clinics, and hospitals, for about $12 to $17 each. According to the *Philadelphia Inquirer* of November 4, 2005, the company has not yet decided what to charge its consumers. While the testing procedure for OraQuick does have a few drawbacks, its benefits extol the importance of the widespread use of this technology. Initially, this test is extremely easy to use. Because you can test at home, and you don't need to draw blood, OraSure is the easiest available technology on the market.

> *The speaker uses explanation to relate how listeners can use the home HIV test.*
>
> *Should the speaker have cited a source for this statement? Why or why not?*

Additionally, the test guarantees patients' privacy. According to the *Sunday Oregonian* of October 23, 2005, unlike with HIV tests at clinics, with OraQuick, patients' names are not registered; they can take the test anonymously, without even having to go to a doctor's clinic. Furthermore, getting an answer in less than 20 minutes with over 99 percent accuracy, according to www.oraquicktest.com, also promotes the use of the product. The *PR Newswire* of October 13, 2005, notes that every year about 8,000 people who test positive for HIV at health clinics never return to pick up their results; widespread availability of at-home HIV testing kits would likely alleviate this situation.

> *The speaker uses the word* additionally *as a transition.*

Unfortunately, however, there are drawbacks associated with OraQuick. But its future implications give it a promising future. The most eminent controversy associated with this product is ear of suicide attempts and lack of professional help. This fear was substantiated when a man from San Francisco committed suicide after using an at-home testing kit and

> *The speaker presents benefits and drawbacks equally so that listeners have ample information about this product.*

getting a positive result, states the previously mentioned *New York Times* of October 26, 2005. However, recent advances in treating AIDS have turned the disease into a chronic one, and many experts now believe that easy testing is key to bringing it under control, according to the *UPI* magazine of October 14, 2005.

Second, individuals who test positive might not get professional help, resulting in lack of treatment. Another negative aspect, according to the *Morning Call* magazine of October 13, 2005, is that OraQuick might just not take off due to lack of trust. The *Philadelphia Inquirer* of November 4, 2005, reports that risks include misinterpretation of results and potential adverse outcomes for test takers, such as panic after getting a positive result without counseling, and the inability of health workers to reach people for follow-up. Other issues are cost and availability of the tests to those who need them the most, according to the FDA website.

> The speaker transitions between the previous main idea and the next one.

While it does have drawbacks, OraQuick's future implications give it a promising future. The death toll due to AIDS is very large, not only in the United States but abroad as well. At the federal meeting of November 4, Sue Jones of OraSure told the panel that the company intends to develop packaging and education materials in several languages to walk people through taking the test and explain what the results mean. This would enable the product to be used around the globe. In fact, the *African News* of November 7 asserts that a South African mining company was able to double the number of employees tested last year simply by using OraQuick, as employees often refused the voluntary tests out of fear of dirty needles. If patients are identified at an early stage, the disease will still be deadly. But with the right treatment, the patient might have a chance at a considerably longer and much less painful life.

> The speaker consistently cites sources to support the speech.

According to Gene Capello, executive director of AIDS Institute, a Washington, DC–based national public policy organization, on CNN of October 13, 2005, the current environment is better suited for at-home HIV testing kits simply because there's treatment available today that can allow an HIV-positive person to live a relatively normal life, taking away the prior stigma of HIV being a death sentence. In addition, it may help reduce the number of AIDS cases. According to the *Guardian* of October 13, 2005, wider access through testing could help identify more positive cases and improve prevention methods.

Dr. Freya Spielberger, a researcher in the Center for AIDS in Washington, DC, said that having a rapid, over-the-counter, accurate testing device is the most powerful strategy we have to bring down the number of HIV infection cases. According to the *New Scientist* of November 12, 2005, women are not discouraged from doing home breast exams just because finding a lump might make them nervous. Hence, HIV test kits shouldn't be disapproved because of fear of depression if its positive effects outweigh the negative ones. Last but not least, if approved, this test could encourage the development of similar at-home testing kits for diseases such as syphilis, hepatitis C, and influenza, according to Doug Michels, OraSure's CEO. Finally, as for combating the most controversial drawback, Dr. Joseph Inungu, an expert witness from Central Michigan University, states that psychologically, a positive test does not seem to increase a risk of suicide.

> The speaker once again compares the OraQuick test with something familiar to many audience members.

> The conclusion summarizes the main ideas of the speech and reiterates the informative purpose.

Today we discussed the development of the at-home HIV testing kit OraQuick; next, we explained how it works and its benefits; finally, we discussed a few drawbacks as well as implications associated with a product that might be a steppingstone toward controlling the spread of the HIV virus. While looking at a crystal ball cannot possibly give us a magic cure for AIDS, nationalization of a new technology such as OraQuick might just be an effective choice for prevention.

CHAPTER SUMMARY

Now that you have read this chapter you can:

13.1 Understand the difference between informative and persuasive speaking.

Persuasion requires intent. It is an interactive process and one that is never coercive. Informative speaking, on the other hand, does not call audience members to action or seek to change their minds. An informative speaker will attempt to set an agenda, provide new information, or create positive or negative feeling.

13.2 Choose an appropriate informative speech purpose.

Your informative speech purpose may vary, depending on the occasion and the audience. Purposes for informative speaking include raising awareness of an issue, providing new information, and setting an agenda.

13.3 Apply strategies for giving interesting and civil informative speeches.

Giving an informative speech requires you to use strategies to motivate and engage the audience, make the information accessible, and use clear language.

13.4 Compose an effective informative speech.

Composing an effective speech requires that you use an effective organizational pattern, choose, appropriate supporting material and visual aids, and engage the audience.

13.5 Apply strategies for giving effective special occasion speeches.

Special occasion speeches benefit from the use of metaphor, simile, and anaphora. In addition, special occasion speakers should be mindful of effective delivery techniques, such as maintaining good eye contact and pausing at appropriate times.

13.6 Understand how civility relates to both informative speaking and speaking for special occasions.

Plagiarism is both uncivil and unethical. Representing someone else's as your own without proper attribution will rob you of your credibility and leave your audience feeling as though you lack respect for them. It is important to remember to cite sources appropriately for your informative speeches. With regard to civility and special occasion speeches, remember to respect the occasion and, again, the audience.

CIVILITY SUMMARY

Overall, remember that giving civil informative and special occasion speeches involves the following:

- Referencing portions of a speech out of context is an uncivil act; it can distort the interpretation of the entire speech and can negatively affect the people who gave the speech.
- If you are accepting an award for which others were nominated, a civil communication gesture is to mention the names of those who hoped to receive it and praise their accomplishments.
- You can civilly and ethically credit a source during a speech presentation by remembering to state the first and last names of the source, the source's credentials (if you are quoting or paraphrasing a person), and the document, website, speech, and so on from which you obtain your speech information.
- Various online tools and software packages are available to detect plagiarism, and it's likely that you'll be caught if you use the ideas of others without crediting your sources. Remind yourself that not only will plagiarism negatively affect members of your community; it also will negatively affect you.

REVIEW QUESTIONS

1. What are the three purposes of informative speeches?
2. What are the strategies for giving effective and civil informative speeches?
3. Why is it important to limit the information you provide for audiences?
4. What does it mean to connect the unfamiliar to the familiar?
5. How can you motivate an audience to listen to and learn from your informative speech?
6. What are the organizational patterns for effective informative speeches?
7. What are some types of visual aids you can use for informative speaking situations?
8. What is a special occasion speech?

14 Giving Persuasive Speeches with Civility

CHAPTER OBJECTIVES

After reading this chapter, you will be able to:

14.1 Understand the nature of persuasion.
14.2 Choose an appropriate persuasive speech purpose.
14.3 Describe the process and nature of persuasive arguments.
14.4 Compose an effective persuasive speech.
14.5 Avoid logical fallacy in giving persuasive speeches.
14.6 Explain invitational rhetoric.

IN JANUARY 2010, U.S. Secretary of State Hillary Rodham Clinton spoke at the Newseum in Washington, DC. Her speech established the country's stand on Internet freedom. Secretary Clinton emphasized the importance of information networks in bringing people together and illustrated how vital networks had become after a major earthquake in Haiti the previous week. She also condemned other governments—specifically the governments of China, Tunisia, Uzbekistan, Vietnam, and Egypt—for taking actions to suppress Internet freedom. Not only did she intend to persuade audiences of the correctness of the U.S. position, Clinton also sought to convince listeners that governments should halt online censorship as well as stop restricting access to the Internet.

WHY IT MATTERS

While Clinton's speech embraced themes of civility, it also demonstrated a civil approach to persuasive speaking. Secretary Clinton, for example, first thanked the person who introduced her before proceeding with her message, and she acknowledged the speech occasion by describing the Newseum as a "monument to some of our most precious freedoms."[1] In addition, while her speech held condemnation for governments that suppress Internet freedom, that criticism came after a strong argument about the importance of open networks, made especially timely by recent events. Her speech also demonstrated both a sensitivity to and engagement with her audience.

What are the means by which a speaker can demonstrate sufficient knowledge about a topic and construct an argument that others will find compelling? And how can a speaker do this in a civil and ethical manner? This chapter addresses how you can give persuasive speeches with civility. It will help you understand the process of persuasion and the different means by which people can be persuaded. You will learn how to build an argument that takes into account your audience's beliefs and values without engaging in logical fallacies. You will also learn how to compose persuasive speeches effectively and how to civilly engage your audience.

WHAT IS PERSUASION?

persuasion The process by which speakers engage audiences to move them to action or to change their minds.

What does it mean to persuade an audience? A simple definition of **persuasion** is the process of attempting to influence others to engage in action. Persuasion, however, involves more than attempts at influencing behavior. When we engage in persuasive communication, our goals may be to:

- Create an attitude not previously held by an audience
- Strengthen an attitude already held by an audience
- Change an attitude held by an audience
- Encourage the audience to act in a certain way

intent The speaker's desire for the audience to listen to and accept his or her message.

In all these cases, persuasive speaking requires **intent**; in other words, the speaker creates a message that he or she wants the receiver or listener to accept.

Contrast the success of Secretary Clinton's speech with one presented by Julia Gillard, the prime minister of Australia. Her attempt to persuade others to follow Australia's lead in creating economic growth failed to convince her audience. Indeed, many were offended and found her presentation uncivil.

Rhetoric and Argumentation

rhetoric Methods or strategies speakers and writers employ to persuade audiences.

coercion Social influence involving force or threat of force.

argumentation The process of forming reasons to support conclusions.

The Greek philosopher Aristotle wrote about **rhetoric**, which, for many, refers to the methods speakers and writers use to persuade audiences. In fact, Aristotle described rhetoric as a speaker's ability to "see the available means of persuasion."[2] However, in seeking or seeing those means, a speaker should remember that persuasion is not coercive. For example, threatening violence to others unless they hand over money is not persuasion. It is **coercion** because it allows the other no reasonable choice in response. On the other hand, appealing to others' sense of altruism while requesting a monetary donation is an example of persuasion as an interactive process that is also ethical and civil.

Persuasion relies on **argumentation**, the process of forming reasons to support conclusions. Making persuasive arguments, however, means that speakers advance positions with strong support. It does not mean that a person engages in shouting matches with someone else or behaves in a verbally hostile way toward another person. Rather, persuasive arguments rely on the use of persuasive appeals to compel the audience to change their minds or move them to action.

A CASE STUDY IN ETHICS

Uncivil Persuasion

In June 2012, the leaders of the G20 nations met in Cabo San Lucas, Mexico, for a summit. At that summit, Australian Prime Minister Julia Gillard gave a speech in which she intended to persuade the other leaders that their countries should follow "Australia's way" in stimulating economic growth:

> Take note of the Australian way. A credible commitment to fiscally responsible growth is the only way forward. Australia has shown this is the way.[3]

Her speech urged increased financial integration across the Eurozone as well as more responsible fiscal policy to facilitate economic growth. It was also Gillard's first address to the G20.[4] She went on to say:

> I hope Australia's own strong economy can be a sign of confidence to other countries. While we acknowledge that every country faces its own unique circumstances, we do believe there are some lessons for the world in the Australian way.[5]

Her remarks, however, alienated several other world leaders, and Jose Manuel Barroso, president of the European Commission, was particularly offended by her "lecture."[6] In fact, even an Australian delegation of business professionals who attended the summit were shocked, with one labeling her remarks as "rude."[7] The leaders felt as though Gillard was wrong to tell them that Australia's way was best. Many attendees of the G20 summit viewed Gillard's attempt at persuasion as arrogant and disrespectful.

Discussion Questions

1. How could Prime Minister Gillard have framed her comments differently, given her audience of G20 leaders and representatives?
2. Why did the other leaders perceive Gillard's comments as "arrogant" and "rude," as well as label her speech a "lecture"? Could she have communicated her thoughts in a more civil manner? Explain.
3. Did the other G20 leaders have a right to be offended? Why or why not?

---

logical appeal A speaker's use of logical reasoning to persuade an audience of his or her position.

emotional appeal A speaker's attempts to arouse emotion in listeners to compel them to believe his or her claim or argument.

ethos appeal An appeal through the speaker's character to convince the audience of his or her claim.

The Persuasive Appeals

In *On Rhetoric*, Aristotle explains three different kinds of persuasive appeals. A **logical appeal**, or *logos* appeal, refers to the speaker's use of reasoning and argument to persuade an audience of his or her position. An environmental scientist, for example, uses the logos appeal when speaking about the causes of global warming and the impacts of global warming on the human race. In an **emotional appeal**, or *pathos* appeal, on the other hand, a speaker attempts to arouse emotion in listeners (e.g., compassion, fear, anger) to compel them to believe his or her argument. Television commercials that solicit donations for starving people in developing countries use the pathos appeal when they show pictures of malnourished children living in abject poverty. The appeal through the speaker's character, or the **ethos appeal**, also helps convince an audience of the speaker's claim. A speaker's credentials represent a very direct way of establishing credibility; if he

> **Table 14.1 Types of Persuasive Appeals**
> Aristotle's three types of appeal can help today's speakers decide what will be most effective argument for their audience and their speaking purpose.
>
> | Type of Appeal | Example |
> |---|---|
> | **Logos:** Logical appeal | The U.S. government should reduce entitlement spending because it increases the deficit and therefore seriously affects the domestic economy. |
> | **Pathos:** Emotional appeal | Sending financial assistance to the Sudan helps feed thousands of starving children. |
> | **Ethos:** Appeal through character and credibility | Based on my 20 years of research on thermodynamics, I can confirm that these theories are valid. |

consciousness raising A process of engaging listeners to become more aware of commitments they have taken for granted.

or she is a medical doctor, for instance, then the audience knows the person is qualified to speak about the effects of high cholesterol. Moreover, a speaker conveys honesty and trustworthiness to his or her audience and treats listeners with civility in using the ethos appeal. Table 14.1 provides additional examples of these appeals.

PERSUASIVE SPEECH PURPOSES

Different speaking situations call on speakers to choose different persuasive purposes. A speaker may attempt to strengthen the audience's commitment for a cause such as gun control or universal health care coverage. On the other hand, a speaker may try to weaken an audience's commitment. Many political advertisements are designed to raise doubts about one candidate while promoting a different one. Some speakers seek to convert the audience over to their side. Speakers also sometimes attempt to induce their audiences to act. Effective speakers analyze the speaking situation and the audience they intend to address and then choose a persuasive purpose. In choosing a persuasive purpose, they anticipate how they can accomplish that purpose and engage audiences with civility.

To Strengthen Commitment

Although many people think of persuasion as changing someone's mind completely, speakers often attempt to strengthen an audience's commitment to a belief. Political candidates, for example, giving speeches at their party's convention are attempting to achieve this goal. The audience of delegates at the Republican or Democratic National Convention already agrees—at least in general—with the candidate's ideas. The candidate does not need to alter audience members' beliefs related to any one particular issue, but instead tries to generate an increased commitment for his or her (and the political party's) positions.

Furthermore, a candidate's political speech also functions to raise consciousness. By engaging in **consciousness raising**, a candidate encourages listeners to be more aware of commitments they have previously made. The speaker, therefore, is motivating listeners to identify intentionally with values

Aristotle wrote about rhetoric, philosophy, drama, and poetry in Athens between 384 and 322 B.C.E.

and strengthen their convictions in these values. In a similar sense, a convention speech may also seek to create a sense of urgency. A candidate's speech, for instance, typically needs to convince other political party members that their support legitimately matters. In these situations, a speaker usually emphasizes the importance of the issue, that it will be decided soon, and that the audience's actions could make a difference.

To Weaken Commitment

A persuasive speaker may sometimes face a **hostile audience**, which means that listeners are strongly opposed to his or her position. Rather than try to change their minds completely, the speaker attempts to make listeners less certain of their position or perhaps willing to consider other points of view. In order to achieve this goal of weakening the audience's commitment to a position, the speaker can challenge or refute the other side's position. On the other hand, the speaker can also find exceptions or distinctions that weaken the opposition. A speaker opposed to gay marriage, for example, might offer up the possibility of civil unions as a viable alternative to homosexual marriage.

To Convert the Audience

Speakers who try to convert listeners basically want them to change their minds about something. They want to convince the listeners to accept something they previously rejected or held in disdain. For example, at the end of the Vietnam War, then President Richard Nixon gave a national address in which he asked Americans to support an invasion of Cambodia. President Nixon knew that at the time of the speech, most Americans had grown weary of U.S. involvement in Vietnam and wanted troop withdrawal from Southeast Asia. Nixon's speech, however, attempted to convince the audience that invading Cambodia was necessary for bringing an end to the war. In other words, he was trying to convert most Americans by asking them to change their minds about continuing military action in the region.

To Induce a Specific Action

In many instances, persuasive speakers want the audience to actually take a specific action, not just change their mind about something. Commercial advertising is one example of this kind of persuasion in that advertisers want the public to buy a particular product. Other kinds of advertising may be aimed at encouraging people to act in ways that are healthier for themselves or for the world around them. They are geared toward creating prosocial behavior.

Advertising encourages the audience to take a specific action.

hostile audience Listeners who are strongly opposed to the speaker's position.

THE PROCESS OF PERSUADING AUDIENCES

When you give a persuasive speech, you need to consider the type of claim or proposition you will advance, the desired outcome, and the directness of your approach. All these factors help determine whether your persuasive speech is successful. Furthermore, you should always consider whether your message is ethical and civil. Are you asking the audience to do something that will bring about a greater good? Are you asking them to invest time and money in something that will benefit them or benefit society? Are you giving this speech with sincere intentions?

The Nature of Persuasive Arguments: The Toulmin Model

Consider this argument:

> The Buick Regal is the best midsize luxury sedan in its class. According to *Consumer Reports*, the Regal has better reliability ratings than any other sedan in its class, consistently scoring 9.9 of 10.
>
> *U.S. News and World Report* notes that consumers see "reliability" as the most valued quality in an automobile. The 2012 Buick Regal was rated a bit lower for reliability, but it is usually ranked highest in this category. Although the Acura Integra scored slightly higher for reliability than the Regal for 2012, the Regal has scored highest in reliability over the past 10 years.

We can describe the parts of this argument using the Toulmin Model. The **Toulmin Model**, named after former University of Chicago English professor Stephen Toulmin, sometimes referred to as the Toulmin "Method," contains three basic parts as well as three additional components that help us define the nature of arguments.[8] It is best to understand the Toulmin Model as a "model" in the literal sense; that is, the Toulmin Model is less a formula for creating arguments than a way to help you think about how your arguments convey something to an audience.

The Toulmin Model says that every argument has at least three parts: a **claim**, or the basic argument itself, the **grounds** or evidence supporting it, and a **warrant**. A warrant is an underlying assumption that represents the chain of reasoning linking a claim with the evidence or grounds.

Warrants perform an important function in any argument. The example in Table 14.2 gives a basic claim for the argument "The Buick Regal is the best midsize luxury sedan in its class." The evidence supports the idea that the Regal performs better in reliability than any other car in its class. Here, the arguer is making an assumption related to *reliability* and the Regal as the best midsize luxury sedan. The warrant, therefore, is that "reliability is a major factor in determining the quality of midsize luxury sedans."

In addition, as illustrated in Table 14.3, arguments *can* have backing, qualifier, and rebuttal or refutation of the other position or objections that the audience might raise. **Backing** is additional support or evidence for the warrant or unstated assumption, and the **qualifier** is the speaker's exceptions to the claim. Words or phrases such as *usually*,

Toulmin Model A model for argumentation named after former University of Chicago English professor Stephen Toulmin. It is used to describe a basic structure of all arguments that includes the components of the claim, the warrant, and the support or evidence.

claim The central argument of a speech.

grounds Evidence supporting a claim.

warrant An unstated underlying assumption that connects a claim to the evidence supporting it.

backing Additional evidence or support for a warrant.

qualifier An exception to a speaker's claim, signaled by words such as *usually* or *often*.

Table 14.2 Sample Claim, Evidence, and Warrant

You can be sure you are presenting a logical persuasive speech by considering all three elements of Stephen Toulmin's model as you prepare your argument.

Element	Example
Claim	The Buick Regal is the best midsize luxury sedan in its class.
Evidence/grounds	*Consumer Reports* says that the Regal has better reliability ratings than any other midsize luxury sedan on the road today, consistently scoring 9.9 of 10.
Warrant	Reliability is a major factor in determining the quality of midsize luxury sedans.

Table 14.3 Sample Backing, Qualifier, and Rebuttal
A complex argument may need additional information to be an effective argument.

Element	Example
Backing	*U.S. News and World Report* notes that consumers see "reliability" as the most valued quality in an automobile.
Qualifier	The 2012 Buick Regal was rated a bit lower for reliability, but it is usually ranked highest in this category.
Rebuttal/refutation	Although the Acura Integra scored slightly higher for reliability than the Regal for 2012, the Regal has scored highest in reliability over the past 10 years.

rebuttal A speaker's refutation of a competing claim.

often, *in most instances*, and *except under certain circumstances* signal qualification. A **rebuttal** is a refutation for a competing claim. Offering rebuttal is important because it shows the audience that the speaker has indeed considered the other side; offering an answer for an other position helps bolster the speaker's credibility.

Types of Claims

When speakers engage in persuading audiences, they advance claims that are typically included in specific purpose statements. As the basic argument of a speech, a claim can reflect fact, value, or policy.

claim of fact An assertion that a condition exists, did exist, or will exist.

Fact **Claims of fact** state whether a condition exists, did exist, or will exist. Some facts are simple, such as these:

> The American colonies declared their independence from Great Britain in 1776.
> The current population of the United States is approximately 313 million people.
> The president of France is Francois Hollande.

Facts, however, can be more complex than these. Facts usually support claims as evidence, but we do disagree over some facts. Archeologists, for example, might disagree about how to categorize a particular artifact, while historians might debate the causes of some event. For example, consider this claim:

> Japanese economic expansionism was the primary cause of World War II.

This claim is supported by historical evidence that Japan was expanding its empire in East Asia and the Pacific. Other historians, however, might cite other causes as "primary," such as Germany's invasion of many European nations.

claim of value An assertion that something is preferable or not preferable.

Value Moral and aesthetic judgments are **claims of value**. Value claims assert that something is good or bad, better or worse, or right or wrong. The following are examples of this type of claim:

> *The Dark Knight* is a better movie than *Iron Man*. [aesthetic judgment]
> Capital punishment is morally unjustifiable. [moral judgment]

In addition, speakers often use value statements to support other claims. For example, a person arguing for abolishing capital punishment may, in support of the claim, state that the death penalty is cruel and unusual punishment. The speaker may perceive—and probably correctly—that listeners embrace constitutional principles even though some may have reservations about abolishing the death penalty.

Policy **Claims of policy** assert whether a course of action should be taken. The words *should*, *ought to*, or *must* usually signal these kinds of propositions. Consider these examples:

> The American government should provide health care for all citizens.
> Our university ought to extend the add–drop period.

Claims of policy are closely connected to morality judgments or political philosophy, but such claims should be grounded in feasibility; in other words, they should be doable.

claim of policy An assertion that an action should or should not be taken to address a given set of circumstances.

Persuasion as an Interactive Process: The Elaboration Likelihood Model

Persuasion alters perceptions by changing knowledge, beliefs, or interests. Persuasion also results from speakers and listeners cooperating jointly to develop meaning and understanding. We can better understand the process of persuasion in terms of the **elaboration likelihood model**.

The elaboration likelihood model is a framework for categorizing and understanding the basic processes that underlie effective persuasion. The model tells us that *elaboration* refers to the extent to which we think about issues and logical arguments included in a message. The *elaboration likelihood*—that is, the ability to focus on reasoning and evidence rather than a speaker's delivery or emotional appeals—is likely to be high when an audience can engage in critical thinking and apply arguments and information to their current lives or to associations and experiences in their memory. However, not all audiences are motivated to and have the ability to conduct in-depth analyses of a speaker's reasoning and evidence. Sometimes audience members are persuaded more by emotion and appeals to the senses than by logic.[9]

elaboration likelihood model A framework in which speakers or listeners cooperate jointly to develop meaning and understanding.

The elaboration likelihood model emphasizes two routes that can lead to successful persuasive communication:[10]

- The *central route* occurs when an audience carefully considers the merit of the argument(s) and information presented.
- The *peripheral route* occurs when an audience focuses on a persuasive cue (e.g., the attractiveness or likeability of the speaker).

Whereas the central route concerns the quality of arguments in a persuasive attempt, the peripheral route focuses on the senses that are associated with the topic of persuasion. In other words, the central route is based on logical appeals, and the peripheral route is based on emotional appeals and/or ethos appeals. For example, suppose you intend to persuade an audience to donate to the Red Cross. If you focus on how the donation will provide shelter for a certain percentage of the population displaced by a natural disaster, you are attempting to persuade by taking the central route. On the other hand, if you focus on how the donation will give you a sense of well-being and self-satisfaction, you are attempting to persuade by taking the peripheral route.

Speakers need not focus solely on the central route or the peripheral route when they attempt to persuade an audience. Instead, persuasive attempts are more effective when they include logical appeals *and* appeals to the senses because the likelihood of elaboration varies among different listeners and among topics for any given person. Remember that a relatively high likelihood of elaboration means that a listener will be persuaded by deliberate and active thinking about the speaker's topic and message. However, a person with a relatively low likelihood of elaboration will focus more on factors that don't require a lot of thought, such as a speaker's delivery. Regardless of the approach, an effective speaker will frame the message in a civil way.

Directness of Approach

Persuasive speakers can engage in two different approaches to persuasion: direct and indirect.

Direct Persuasion

Direct persuasion means the speaker will state his or her purpose in very explicit way. In most cases, a speaker chooses this approach with an audience supportive of the message or an audience in which support is likely to be mixed. Both appeals based on argumentation (logic and reasoning) and appeals geared to the senses and emotions can be used in direct persuasion. For example, consider the following speech introduction:

> You can't stop it. You can't hide from it. You can plan, pray, and do everything in your power to minimize its effects. But it's likely that it will kill you. What am I talking about? Aging. Why would an audience of college students want to listen to a speech about aging? Because every day, even at our age, we lose brain cells, and our culture tells us that the inevitable and natural march of time is something we should somehow reverse. According to Dr. Caleb Finch, the William F. Kieschnick Chair in the Neurobiology of Aging at the University of Southern California, the brain loses 5 to 10 percent of its weight between the ages of 20 and 90. In addition, I'm sure you've seen quite a few TV commercials and print ads that promise certain cosmetics and cosmetic surgery can restore youthful beauty. We need not assume that our brain function will automatically decrease as we age; we also need not assume that normal signs of aging make us look ugly. Knowing how to "exercise our brain" and how our society manipulates our perception of aging will help every one of us age well.

The first few sentences of this introduction are attention-getters that could relate to a variety of topics (e.g., certain type of diseases, F5 tornadoes). But the answer to the rhetorical question lets us know that this speech is about aging. In addition, the thesis, which is located immediately after the audience adaptation and credibility portions of this introduction, is also direct: "Knowing how to 'exercise our brain' and how our society manipulates our perception of aging will help every one of us age well."

Indirect Persuasion

In **indirect persuasion**, the speaker deemphasizes his or her purpose or thesis in some way. Like direct persuasion, logical and emotional appeals can be used in indirect persuasion. This approach can be used when you believe your audience may oppose your viewpoints. However, indirect persuasion is risky in that an audience may feel they've been tricked into listening if a speaker is not upfront about the topic. Because an audience may believe that indirect persuasion may be uncivil, an indirect approach should be used with care. Consider the following example:

> I want to see my grandchildren. It may seem odd to make this statement, especially since I don't have children, but I sometimes dream about my future grandchildren and the milestones their lives. I want to see them during their early years, when they learn to walk and talk. I imagine waving to them as they go to school and angering their parents when I give them sugary sweets as after-school snacks. I want to see them during their teenage years, when they begin to question the world around them and make independent decisions. I see us talking about current events, the latest model of cars, and, of course, boyfriends and girlfriends. I want to see them during their adult years, when they graduate from college and get their first "real" job. I visualize them

---

direct persuasion An approach in which a speaker states the purpose in a very explicit way. In most cases, a speaker chooses this approach with an audience supportive of the message or with an audience in which support is likely to be mixed.

indirect persuasion An approach in which a speaker deemphasizes the purpose and/or thesis of the speech in some way.

TRENDS IN TECHNOLOGY AND SOCIAL MEDIA

Twitter and the Political Process

Janet Johnson, Ph.D., a nationally known researcher who studies Twitter and its use in the political process, shared this experience:

> In Fall 2011, the Republican Party had 15 debates from September until December to help decide who would eventually become the GOP 2012 presidential candidate. The major news outlets on both cable and broadcast television stations took turns televising the debates. Since the rise in social media, most news networks used Twitter to interact with the audience at home. During one of these debates on CNBC on November 9, 2011, I was at home, on my couch, live tweeting the debate. To my surprise, CNBC ran one of my tweets on their ticker feed at the bottom of the television screen. My tweet read, "Herman Cain please don't answer with 999 again." When I first saw my tweet, I instantly felt I was a part of the political process.

The amount of interaction and participation through electronic venues (e.g., Twitter) is increasing. According to The Pew Internet & American Life Project, about 15 percent of online adults use Twitter and 8 percent of them use it on a typical day.[11] Since smart phones make accessing Twitter easier, it is not surprising that one in five smart phone owners tweets.[12]

Of course, political campaigns are taking advantage of these trends. When Barack Obama announced his 2008 choice for vice president, Senator Joe Biden, he used social media, and "as a result of Obama's methods, candidates learned that they could respond to their opponents and discuss their issues directly with the electorate."[13] This new access to the electorate through Twitter helped revolutionize a new way to campaign and communicate.[14] Even Congress is adopting Twitter as a way to inform and give access to constituents. In fact, research shows that members of Congress use Twitter for informational posts.[15] Politicians need to keep creating content on these social media venues to do the following:

1. Keep the constituents informed about policy
2. Help cultivate public opinion
3. Move constituents to action

Obama used Twitter to organize and mobilize his constituents during his campaign, and he has continued to do so during his presidency. Specifically, "President Obama is using Twitter and other social media tools to deliver his policy messages, to rally support for his initiatives and to continue connecting people to broader communities of change."[16] Technology has also allowed Obama to take advantage of the Internet's ability to gather like-minded people.[17]

In future elections, more digital natives will be able to vote, and their ideal mode of communication will become more mobile and instant. Twitter is redefining the campaign landscape that makes politicians more accessible to the masses. The days of a candidate relying solely on one-way communication venues such as print, radio, and television to motivate American citizens to vote are over. In Twitter's very short existence, the social media tool "has changed the ways in which people communicate, breaking down walls and opening up new avenues for users and followers alike."[18]

Discussion Questions

1. Do you think electronic venues and social networking sites are changing the way we understand persuasion? Why or why not?
2. Do you agree with the last statement, that the social media tool "has changed the ways in which people communicate, breaking down walls and opening up new avenues for users and followers alike"? Why or why not?

getting married and creating their own lives, which, of course, will include me every now and then. So I want to see my grandchildren. However, all of us in this room may be prevented from ever seeing our grandchildren.

What is this speech about? You may believe it has something to do with grandchildren or perhaps factors that may prevent us from seeing our grandchildren, such as geography, splintered families, and so on. How would you feel if, as an audience member, you finally realized the speech is about stopping nuclear proliferation? Would you feel tricked into listening because the opening focuses on something that most of us can relate to (family ties)? Or would you want to listen because you know that a nuclear war may prevent you from seeing your grandchildren? Would you resent the speaker for presenting an "anti-nuke" speech with an opening that focuses on grandchildren rather than an introduction more directly aligned with the topic of nuclear proliferation?

Persuasive Outcomes

Persuasive speaking requires intent, which also means that persuasive speakers desire certain outcomes from audiences. Achieving a desired outcome involves changing listeners' minds or moving them to action.

Changing Listeners' Minds Persuasive speakers sometimes wish to change the minds of their listeners about a fact, value, or policy. In attempting to change their minds, a speaker may work toward strengthening commitment for a cause he or she already supports. The speaker, however, may also try to weaken listener opposition to that same cause or issue. In the workplace, for example, you may find yourself one day needing to convince management that employees at your company need an across-the-board salary increase. Management, however, may be very opposed to giving across-the-board pay increases because, according to them, the company simply cannot afford to do so. The speaking situation calls for you to change management's mind, so you can point to a future increase in revenue. Or it may be that you can identify a number of unnecessary expenditures that the company can eliminate so that it can commit those funds to pay raises. You may also argue that there is an unknown cost in not giving raises, as people may leave the company. Unless employees are incompetent or stealing from the company, it is generally more cost-effective to retain present employees than to replace them with new people who must be trained.

Moving the Audience to Action Sometimes, persuasive speakers want their audiences to actually act on what they are saying. Secretary Clinton's speech, referenced at the beginning of this chapter, calls for repressive governments to cease autocratic control over the Internet as well as adopt policies that protect Internet freedom. She was also speaking, at least in part, to a necessarily hostile audience, and later in this chapter, you will learn how to more effectively address listeners who do not agree with your position.

COMPOSING A PERSUASIVE SPEECH

Now that you understand the basic nature of persuasion, you can compose your own persuasive speech. To compose a persuasive speech, you must define your persuasive speech purpose, structure your message effectively, and select strong evidence to support your proposition or claim. If you engage in fallacious reasoning, you will likely lose credibility with your audience.

Establishing Credibility

Earlier in this chapter, you read about appealing through ethos and how that relates to establishing credibility. Establishing your credibility as a speaker, as you know, is critically important for persuading audiences. Listeners must see you as believable before you can begin to persuade them. In order to see you as believable, the audience must view you as competent, as possessing character, and as charismatic.

Competence Simply put, listeners should see you as someone who knows what he or she is doing. A software engineer, for example, must come across as competent if he or she is to persuade managers that they should commit resources to a particular product design. Similarly, a legislator speaking before Congress must seem competent to garner votes from the other members of the House or Senate.

Character Audience members should perceive that you have character, that you are an ethical person who is communicating your message in an honest and ethical—and civil—way. Providing listeners with inaccurate information, for example, will only negatively affect their view of you.

Charisma You have learned that good speakers come across as interested and enthusiastic about their message. Neither you nor your speech will excite listeners if you come across as not charismatic. Exhibiting charisma does not mean, though, that you display behavior that seems contrived or forced. However, you need to compel listeners to consider what you have to say.

Adapting to an Audience

Perhaps the most important aspect of giving a persuasive speech is adapting to your audience. You need to address the audience in such a way that you find common ground with listeners, but they may not respond favorably to your message. Therefore, anticipating counterarguments and organizing according to anticipated response is important for your persuasive speech purpose.

Finding Common Ground Even if your audience is hostile toward you or your position, you may be able to establish common ground with them. You can begin by discussing issues and themes on which you agree. For example, a Republican candidate for office speaking to the United Auto Workers union might first assert his or her respect for the union's work and the important role unions play in the U.S. economy before arguing that unions should receive fewer concessions from corporate management and the government. Similarly, a Democratic candidate for office speaking to a group of business leaders might first state his or her support for business before advocating for higher taxes. In both instances, the candidates attempt to engage audiences with civility and respect by finding common ground.

Organizing According to Anticipated Response Persuasive speakers structure speeches so that they can lead their audience to agree with them. If you were giving a speech asking listeners to support new environmental regulations governing toxic chemical waste, you would most likely ask them if they wanted such waste disposed of near their own homes. The audience would likely respond that they do *not* want waste disposal near where they live. Then you would ask them to support new regulations so that no one must suffer the negative effects of toxic chemical dumping.

Of course, if the audience already agrees with you, you can arrange your speech so that it reinforces existing attitudes, values, and beliefs. You can then devote more time to persuading them to take action. On the other hand, if listeners disagree, in principle, with your stand, you need to spend more time at the beginning of the speech convincing them. As with any other speech, remember to engage your audience with civility and to respect their point of view, regardless of whether they agree with you.

Structuring the Message

The way you organize a persuasive speech can affect the way listeners respond to your message. Effective persuasive speakers organize their message based on the needs, attitudes, beliefs, behaviors, and background of the audience. In doing so, most persuasive speeches are organized according to one of the following common structures: problem–solution, comparative advantage, refutational, and Monroe's motivated sequence, which is a variation on the problem–solution organizational scheme.

The following examples show how a speaker can adapt the same argument to these four different structures. The speaker in this case is Jane, a member of a university's information technology (IT) department, and she plans to give a speech to persuade upper administration that the university needs a new learning management system (LMS), given that the current LMS is outdated and failing to adequately meet the needs of students and faculty.

problem–solution organization An organizational strategy in which the speaker defines the present condition, or status quo, as unsatisfactory and then argues for a way to bring about needed change.

Problem–Solution Speakers who adopt the **problem–solution organization** claim that current circumstances, or the status quo, need to be changed for the betterment of all those involved. A speaker who follows this organizational scheme must first prove the existence of a problem. In arguing that a problem exists, a speaker may establish the cause of the problem. Establishing cause helps listeners comprehend the scope of the problem and its consequences. Then he or she must argue for a particular solution to rectify the existing situation. In arguing for a solution, a speaker needs to convince the audience of the plausibility and feasibility of the solution; in other words, the speaker should prove that the solution is workable.

Now, consider how Jane, a member of the IT department, might use this strategy in attempting to persuade the administration that the university should purchase and implement a new LMS:

> *Claim:* Our university must purchase and implement a new learning management system, given that our current system does not adequately meet the needs of our students and faculty.
>> *First main point:* The current learning management system is difficult to use, and both students and faculty frequently lose data.
>> *Second main point:* The university administration should commit the financial resources to purchasing a new learning management system.

In this example, Jane will probably devote some effort to clearly establishing the problems associated with the LMS by describing the consequences of the problem to both faculty and students. Then, Jane will likely state the proposed solution (purchasing the new system), explain that the university has the financial resources to purchase a new system, and indicate why this purchase is justified.

comparative advantage organization An organizational strategy in which the speaker shows how one option is more effective than other alternatives.

Comparative Advantage In a **comparative advantage organization**, the speaker attempts to show that if the audience adopts his or her stance, they will gain something better. A speaker who adopts this organizational strategy assumes that the audience already comprehends the gravity of the problem. If you choose this organizational scheme, you will spend most of your time showing the audience that your position is superior to available alternatives.

It is important to establish credibility by identifying all possible alternatives when using the comparative advantage organization. Identifying all alternatives means you address the alternatives with which your audience is familiar as well as those with which they lack familiarity. Failing to address all possible alternatives may leave your listeners feeling as though you are not well informed on the issue. And if your audience believes you to be ill informed, they may be skeptical of your comparative advantage as a result.

Jane could adopt this organizational strategy in the following way:

Claim: Our university should purchase and implement Learning Management System X as opposed to Learning Management System Y or Z.
First main point: Learning Management System X offers the end user more options and features than Learning Management System Y or Learning Management System Z.
Second main point: Learning Management System X costs less than Learning Management System Y or Learning Management System Z.

Effective persuasive speakers structure their message based on the needs and backgrounds of their listeners.

refutational organization An organizational strategy in which the speaker responds to and counters the opposite position on an issue.

Refutational A speaker who uses the **refutational organization** first presents arguments opposed to his or her own position and then follows those with arguments supporting his or her position. A speaker will likely choose this organizational scheme if the opposing side has advanced weak arguments in support of its position.

A speaker who uses the refutational organization should present the opposing position, describing the other side's stance fully and explaining the support for their argument. He or she should address the opposition's objections for the audience. If the speaker does not do so, listeners will probably consider the other side's position as he or she speaks. The speaker will respond to the other side's position and, in doing so, will be advancing the claim.

The following example assumes that the university has ruled out Learning Management System X as a possible option. Jane, however, refutes the reasons the university administration has used for dismissing it, and in doing so, she makes a case for choosing X:

Claim: Learning Management System X actually represents an effective option for our university.
First main point: The university administration claims that Learning Management System X is too expensive and does not offer faculty and staff enough features and options.
Second main point: Although its short-term costs may be higher, Learning Management System X will actually cost less in the long term.
Third main point: Learning Management System X provides benefits that the university administration has overlooked.

Monroe's motivated sequence An organizational strategy developed by Alan H. Monroe that organizes a speaker's message according to the audience's motivations.

Monroe's Motivated Sequence **Monroe's motivated sequence**, first articulated by Alan H. Monroe, shows how a speaker can organize his or her message according to the audience's motivation.[19] The motivated sequence has five steps: attention, need, satisfaction, visualization, and action (see Table 14.4). It is a variation of the problem–solution organization.

Table 14.4 Monroe's Motivated Sequence

Using Monroe's organization for a persuasive speech may help you move the audience to action. In this table, examples from a speech about a university learning management system illustrate the technique.

Step	Description	Example
Attention step	Serves as the introduction of the speech and gains the audience's attention.	Many of you may remember that last fall semester, Dr. Jones was teaching an entry-level mechanical engineering course to approximately 100 students. He uploaded all activities, quizzes, major exams, and assignment descriptions to the current learning management system. Dr. Jones also stored all of his students' written work on this system. In November, though, the system crashed, and both he and his students lost everything. Furthermore, Dr. Jones was not alone. Other faculty and students across campus lost their information. To make matters worse, this wasn't the first time the system had crashed and caused major difficulties.
Need step	Seeks to convince the audience that a change in the current situation is necessary; defines the current problem.	The current university learning management system is faulty. Not only do faculty and students consistently lose data, the system is costly to operate and maintain. Furthermore, the system is outdated, and it lacks a user-friendly design and does not provide very many features and options for faculty and students.
Satisfaction step	Provides the audience with the means to fulfill the motivation and explains how the solution will work.	The university should form a committee to evaluate options for replacing the existing learning management system. The administration should also commit significant financial resources to providing the students and faculty with the best learning management system.
Visualization step	Paints a mental picture of the solution.	Today, we have seen the magnitude of this problem and how it affects students and faculty from all colleges and schools at this university. The administration must take action to rectify this situation for the betterment of this institution.
Action step	Asks the listeners to take specific steps to bring about a solution to the current problem.	Please let the president of our university know that we need to take action to replace the learning management system.

The last column of Table 14.4 shows how Jane might use Monroe's motivated sequence in persuading the administration that the university needs a new LMS. In using this organizational scheme, Jane first gains the audience's attention by telling a relatable story that captures, in a very concrete way, the seriousness of this problem. Then she clearly states the nature of the problem and its consequences. The satisfaction step articulates what action should be taken to rectify the problem, and the visualization step provides a mental picture of the solution. Finally, the action step asks the audience to do something specific to bring about the change.

PERSUASIVE SPEAKING AND INCIVILITY: LOGICAL FALLACIES

You probably hear logical fallacies all the time—statements like "That person is so stupid, her argument couldn't possibly make sense" or "The government must create new jobs. An automobile factory in Michigan has recently laid off over half its workers." Such statements are assertions based on erroneous or fallacious reasoning. In the first example, calling the person stupid fails to address the substance of the argument. Furthermore, the one case of many factory employees in Michigan losing their jobs does not, in and of itself, justify a nationwide effort to create jobs.

Persuasive claims must meet standards of sound logic and good sense. Many times, though, speakers advance arguments that do not meet such standards. Fallacious arguments can cause a speaker to lose credibility; furthermore, audiences may perceive the speaker as uncivil because critical listeners may perceive that the speaker is attempting to dupe or deceive them with illogical reasoning.

Definition and Types of Fallacies

A strong argument will likely compel an audience more than a flimsily constructed claim. One way claims can be weakened is through fallacious reasoning. Some of the most common kinds of fallacious reasoning are ad hominem, generalizing, slippery slope, post hoc fallacy, and red herring.

ad hominem A logical fallacy in which a speaker attacks the character of the opposition rather than address the substance of the other side's position.

Ad Hominem
Ad hominem attacks are very common in today's culture. *Ad hominem* literally means "to the man." You have probably heard a politician criticize an opponent as a "bleeding-heart liberal" or as an "elitist pro-business supporter" in an effort to discredit the other side's stand. Neither of these criticisms, however, addresses the substance of the opponent's argument. The speaker is really only engaging in name-calling.

generalizing Reaching a conclusion by making sweeping and broad claims.

overstatement An argument that is an unqualified generalization.

Generalizing
Generalizing means reaching a conclusion by making sweeping and broad claims. Errors in generalizing include overstatement and hasty generalization.

Overstatement happens when an argument is an unqualified generalization. It refers to all members of a category or class, but the evidence supports an assertion about only some of the class. Words like *all*, *every*, *always*, and *never* tend to signal overstatement. A person who says, for example, that "all corporations pollute the environment" is engaging in overstatement. While some corporations *do* pollute the environment, not *all* corporations are guilty of doing so.

hasty generalization A logical fallacy that draws a conclusion from insufficient evidence.

Hasty generalizations, on the other hand, draw conclusions from insufficient evidence. Consider this example:

> Corporations pollute the environment. Just last week, a company in the northeastern United States was caught dumping toxic waste into a major river.

The arguer's claim, "Corporations pollute the environment," is supported by the evidence of one company's activities dumping toxic waste into a major river. This evidence, however, is too limited because the sample size (one corporation) is too small to provide a basis for this generalization.

slippery slope A logical fallacy that suggests a domino effect on a given issue. A speaker contends that if a particular course of action is taken or that if something is permitted to occur, a series of terrible consequences will take place as a result.

Slippery Slope
Slippery slope suggests a domino effect on a given issue. The speaker suggests that if one course of action is pursued or if something is allowed to happen, then a series of terrible consequences will occur. This kind of argument assumes that these consequences will result but does not take into account evidence, historical examples, or the reasonableness of people. It also presents a final consequence that no one would find desirable.

In the workplace, someone proposing a new product design might argue that the company's failure to adopt that design will result in loss of profits. Then the person could pursue that argument even further, contending that loss of profits associated with this one product will cause the company to go bankrupt. The arguer, however, does not consider a number of factors, including that the company produces other products that make money and that management would not normally stake the company's success or failure on one product design.

Post Hoc Fallacy **Post hoc, ergo propter hoc** is Latin that, translated literally, means "after this, therefore because of it." This argument confuses causation and chronology or correlation; in other words, it suggests that just because something negative followed an event, that event, therefore, caused that something negative to happen. For example, someone might say, "Since the president was elected, the economy has taken a turn for the worse. We should vote for his opponent in the upcoming election." This person has engaged in the post hoc fallacy because he or she has assumed that the election of the current president caused an economic downturn. He or she is not really proving with evidence that the president's election caused the downturn. Rather, the arguer is erroneously asserting that the president is to blame because the downturn occurred shortly after the last election.

post hoc, ergo propter hoc A logical fallacy that confuses causation and chronology. The speaker wrongly asserts that just because something negative followed an event, that event, therefore, caused that something negative to happen.

Red Herring A **red herring** introduces some irrelevant point or issue in a debate. An employee, for example, who contends that a company's new CEO lacks qualifications because his brother was once convicted of a white-collar crime has engaged in this fallacy. The fact that the new CEO's brother went to prison has nothing to do with whether the CEO is capable of handling the position.

red herring A logical fallacy that introduces some irrelevant point or issues into a debate.

Avoiding Logical Fallacy

By avoiding logical fallacy, you can persuade your audiences through thoughtful, ethical, and civil persuasion. Table 14.5 provides examples of the logical fallacies discussed in this chapter—fallacies that are common and fallacies that can weaken the claim of your speech.

Again, avoiding logical fallacy helps you engage your audiences with civility. Making logical arguments shows respect for your listeners' intelligence and will therefore encourage them to accept your message.

Table 14.5 Examples of Logical Fallacies
If your audience recognizes your reasoning as fallacious, they may discount everything you have said in your speech.

Fallacy	Example	Corrective Measure
Ad hominem	That scientist's ideas on creationism are just wrong. He's a religious nut.	Attack the idea instead of the person.
Generalizing	All pit bulls are extremely aggressive animals.	Recognize that there often are exceptions to commonly held generalizations.
Slippery slope	Stricter laws regulating hand gun ownership will result in loss of Second Amendment rights, which will, in turn, lead to the government creating a police state.	Make sure that each step of the argument follows logically from the one before.
Post hoc, ergo propter hoc	Crime in this neighborhood was low until those people moved into the corner house. They must be the cause of the recent criminal activity.	Check the logic that connects the claim and the warrant to be sure it actually supports the claim.
Red herring	The senator's mother enjoys betting on horse races. Therefore, the senator lacks the moral fiber to serve in the U.S. Congress.	Check the logic that connects the claim and warrant to be sure it actually supports the claim.

ASK THE ETHICIST: Using Fear Appeals and Personal Attacks

Question I want to give a speech on the need to eliminate our general studies program. Politicians use negative ads in which fear appeals and personal attacks are used to sway voters, so why shouldn't I say that continuing to make us learn this stuff will only result in increased numbers of people being unable to make a living quoting Shakespeare and winding up on welfare and food stamps?

Answer Alas, poor Shakespeare, we knew him well. He often gets blamed for unemployment. Seriously, though, there are a couple reasons fear appeals are a bad idea. From a research perspective, it's hard to know how much fear will actually be persuasive—too little and people don't pay attention, too much, and they tune it out because it's overwhelming. From an ethical perspective, moving people to make a decision in a negative manner (e.g., deciding in order to avoid something they fear) is less virtuous than presenting a variety of options and giving reasons you support a particular one. A person acting on the emotions aroused through a fear appeal makes a less informed decision, and urging someone to make an uninformed decision is not ethical. Remember also that civil communication comprises respect, restraint, and responsibility. A persuader who resorts to fear appeals doesn't respect the ability of his or her audience to make an informed decision. In addition, the use of fear appeals does not reflect either restraint or responsibility on the part of the persuader. That seems uncivil.

PERSUASIVE SPEAKING AND CIVILITY: INVITATIONAL RHETORIC

> To invite my audience to explore, and to explore myself, the issues involved in the federal mandate to require all citizens to obtain health insurance.
> To invite my audience to consider some of the positive outcomes of stricter immigration laws.

Do these two specific purpose statements reflect speeches to inform, speeches to persuade, or both? The answer is that these specific purpose statements do something other than inform and persuade: They issue an invitation for a speaker and an audience to explore ideas and issues, clarify viewpoints, and express personal beliefs and values. In other words, the two specific purpose statements reflect invitational rhetoric.

Earlier in this chapter, you read that Aristotle defined rhetoric as persuasion. In 1995, Sonja Foss and Cindy Griffin offered a theory of "invitational rhetoric" and challenged the communication discipline to rethink the definition of rhetoric and, by extension, persuasion. Foss and Griffin wrote that rhetoric does not *always* involve attempts to change others and does not *only* concern persuasion. The authors contended that defining rhetoric as "persuasion" limits our understanding of the complexities involved in persuading others. For example, some people hold beliefs about political and social issues that are so strong that attempting to change them is unrealistic.

In addition, sometimes trying to change the behavior of others is inappropriate because we do not have enough information about them to suggest the best course of action. Rather than define rhetoric as persuasive attempts to change others' opinions and behaviors, Foss and Griffin said that rhetoric is an invitation for speakers and listeners to understand each other and create a relationship based on equality.[20] **Invitational rhetoric**

invitational rhetoric (invitational speaking) Rhetoric in which a speaker enters into a public dialogue with an audience.

(or **invitational speaking**) occurs when speakers enter into a public dialogue with an audience. A **public dialogue** refers to a civil and ethical exchange that includes sharing perspectives and facts, asking questions, and participating in thought-provoking discussions.[21] This means that invitational speaking includes a speaker's right to be heard and his or her responsibility to listen to others. Unlike traditional persuasion, in which a speaker's goal is to convince an audience about an opinion and/or a course of action, invitational rhetoric is about sharing perspectives and inviting others to understand various viewpoints. Therefore, the goal of invitational rhetoric is neither to share information nor to convince an audience to change beliefs and engage in certain actions (although providing information and persuading audience members may occur). Instead, an invitational speaker's goal is to explore different viewpoints about an issue so that the speaker and audience will have a deeper understanding of and be able to analyze the issue in a more complete way.[22]

Invitational speakers relate stories, share personal opinions, and accept different viewpoints.[23] They avoid using phrases such as "you should" and "the best position is." Instead, invitational speeches use phrases that communicate equality and respect, such as "I believe this because" and "Although you may not agree, I think that." In addition, an invitational speaker engages the audience in an end-of-speech discussion so that their viewpoints, concerns, and suggestions are respectfully acknowledged and discussed. Audience members are encouraged to participate even when they hold positions at odds with the speaker. While facilitating the discussion, an invitational speaker will use phrases such as "Why do you believe as you do?" and "Why do you prefer that solution?" The key to a successful invitational discussion is to promote the exploration of an issue by encouraging audience members to articulate their views and by responding to their opinions in a respectful manner.[24]

Three conditions are needed for the invitational rhetoric process to be effective: safety, value, and freedom. *Safety* refers to an audience believing that their ideas and feelings won't be trivialized or denigrated by the speaker or other members of the audience. The condition of safety can be accomplished when a speaker communicates that audience members' beliefs and attitudes are worthy of exploration and will not be ridiculed or dismissed, even if the beliefs and attitudes are at odds with his or her own. *Value* concerns the idea that speakers recognize that audience opinions have merit, even if a speaker disagrees with those opinions. Value occurs when speakers engage in perspective taking and paraphrasing, and it is based on respect. *Freedom* refers to knowing that audience members can think for themselves and that speakers need not decide what others should think or how they should act. Freedom is accomplished when everyone involved in an invitational discussion asks questions, initiates ideas, and communicates their views.[25]

Invitational rhetoric is not the only appropriate form of rhetoric, and it shouldn't be used in all situations. In addition, some communication situations include the use of both components of invitational rhetoric and traditional persuasion.[26] However, "the invitational components contribute to an outcome that consists of respecting the audience and reaching an understanding—one grounded in civility even if the understanding is in the final form of mutual disagreement."[27]

Invitational rhetoric means that a speaker has entered into a public dialogue with an audience.

public dialogue A civil and ethical exchange that includes sharing perspectives and facts, asking questions, and participating in thought-provoking discussions.

SAMPLE STUDENT SPEECH

Mandatory Minimums

The following speech illustrates the concepts you have read about in this chapter. Reading this student's speech will help you use the different techniques for composing an effective persuasive speech.

In preparing this speech, the student identified the general purpose and the specific purpose and also composed a thesis. In this speech, the student's general purpose is to persuade, and the specific purpose is to convince the audience that mandatory minimum sentences are negative and impose unfairly harsh punishments for minor offences. The student's actual specific purpose statement might be:

> *Specific purpose statement:* At the end of my speech, my audience will support abolishing mandatory minimums.

The thesis for this speech, on the other hand, might look like this:

> *Thesis:* Mandatory minimums impose harsh, unfair punishments for the most minor offences and therefore should be abolished.

As you read this student's speech, pay particular attention to the way the student gains the audience's attention, organizes the message, and uses evidence for support. As you read, notice the ways the speaker connects with the audience and strives to fulfill the persuasive purpose:

> The speaker uses a relevant story or anecdote to gain the audience's attention. The story also works as an emotional appeal because it elicits sympathy from the audience for the speaker's cause.

Things were going well for Weldon Angelos, a 22-year-old up-and-coming record producer in Salt Lake City. But as the *New York Times* of January 11, 2006, explains, Angelos's life came crashing down around him in 2003, when a federal jury convicted him of selling marijuana on three separate occasions. According to the sentencing decision filed in the U.S. District Court in Utah, on November 16, 2004, Angelos carried a gun with him when he made two of these sales. Though he didn't use, or even display, the gun, its very presence at the drug deals forced the judge to sentence him under federal mandatory minimum laws to 55 years in prison. The sentencing decision noted that if Angelos had provided weapons to a terrorist organization, hijacked an aircraft, committed second-degree murder, and raped a 10-year-old child, he would have received a lower combined sentence than he got for selling about $1,000 worth of marijuana.

> Could the speaker have transitioned more effectively between the opening story about Angelos and this part of the speech? Why or why not?
>
> The speaker forecasts the structure of the speech by identifying the main ideas. The speaker is treating listeners with civility by helping them follow the speech.

According to a November 23, 2004, slate.com article, there are more than 100 federal mandatory minimum sentencing provisions, which require judges to sentence perpetrators of specific crimes to fixed minimum terms. Despite the fact that *The New Criminologists* of November 20, 2005 tells us that rates of violent crime have been declining steadily for over 10 years, the Center for Policy Alternatives website, copyright 2006, states that since they were enacted, mandatory minimums have increased prison costs by over $4 billion, so in order to fight these laws that make a mockery of our constitutional prohibition against cruel and unusual punishment, we must first examine the dangers of mandatory minimums. Next, we will explore the steps that the Supreme Court and Congress can take to eliminate these unfair laws, before examining how the world will look once mandatory minimums are done away with. When that's all done, we'll finally discuss what each of us can do to eliminate these unfair sentencing policies.

> The speech follows a problem–solution organizational pattern. This part of the speech explains why the present condition, or status quo, is unsatisfactory.

Initially, the problems with mandatory minimums can be divided in two ways. First, they impose overly harsh sentences, and next they prevent any chance of rehabilitating criminals because mandatory minimums lay out blanket sentences for all defendants who commit a particular crime. They pay no attention to the factors involved in an individual defendant's actions, which traditional judge or jury sentencing can take into account. The

Persuasive Speaking and Civility: Invitational Rhetoric

The speaker provides multiple citations to support the claim. Providing citations for the speaker's evidence helps him or her establish credibility.

Does the story of Nicole Richardson function as a persuasive appeal? Why or why not?

This statement reflects the speaker's use of transition. The speaker is connecting the previous discussion to a new main idea or area of discussion.

The speaker transitions between the major parts of the speech.

The speaker is presenting solutions to the problems associated with mandatory minimums.

The reference to Angelos connects back to the introduction and helps the audience understand how taking this action can help solve the problems associated with mandatory minimums.

How does this part of the speech illustrate the use of logical appeal?

With regard to delivery, the speaker can pause here before beginning the last part of the speech.

How might you revise this transition to make it more effective?

St. Petersburg Times of May 17, 2005, reports that defendants sentenced under mandatory minimum laws often receive 10, 15, or 20 years or more in prison for nonviolent, first-time offenses. According to the website of the Drug Policy Alliance, copyright 2006, 18-year-old Nicole Richardson learned about these unfair laws firsthand, when her boyfriend sold drugs to an undercover agent. Nicole had nothing to do with the sale, but when she answered her telephone and gave another undercover agent the phone number where her boyfriend could be reached, she was charged with involvement in a drug dealing conspiracy, and she received a 10-year mandatory minimum sentence.

Even in cases where defendants commit more serious crimes than handing out a phone number, the Eighth Amendment to our Constitution mandates a sentence that is proportionate to the offense rather than predetermined justice. Mandatory minimums also are problematic because they prevent any chance of rehabilitating criminals. A 2004 report from the Justice Policy Institute notes that rehabilitation programs work better than imprisonment, recidivism, and substance abuse, and they are much less expensive option than incarceration. For example, Maryland's use of treatment programs has lowered its annual cost per offender from $20,000 to only $4,000. Despite this, when a defendant is facing a mandatory minimum, the judge in the case cannot choose to send him or her to a rehab program, even if the judge feels that the defendant and society would be better served by doing so.

Now that we have examined the dangers of mandatory minimums, we will explore the steps that the Supreme Court and Congress can take to eliminate these unfair policies. Initially, the Supreme Court must produce clear precedent on the issue of mandatory minimums. The *Desert Morning News* of January 11, 2006, reports that lawyers for Weldon Angelos are considering appealing his case directly to the Supreme Court. In his ruling, Utah District Court Judge Paul Cassell noted that he believed that Angelos's sentence was cruel and unusual but that he couldn't ignore the mandatory minimum law because the Supreme Court has failed to produce clear precedent on this issue. The justices must accept this case and use the opportunity to clearly explain what constitutes cruel and unusual punishment.

Next, Congress must eliminate mandatory minimums and let judges do their jobs. The trial process is designed to ensure that judges know the circumstances of a defendant's case before making a decision, a factor that mandatory minimum statutes ignore completely. And according to a June 23, 2005, press release from Families Against Mandatory Minimums, prosecutors can even appeal sentences if they believe judges are being too lenient. Thus if Congress were to eliminate mandatory minimums, judges would be able to hand out fairer sentences tailored to defendants, and the appellate system would ensure that those sentences were appropriate.

Now that we have examined the steps that the Supreme Court and Congress can take to eliminate mandatory minimums, we will explore what the world will look like once mandatory minimums are eliminated. The most important thing that will occur is that our justice system will become inherently more fair because each defendant will have the circumstances of his or her case explored by a judge individually rather than just receiving a blanket sentence laid down for all defendants. Even more importantly perhaps, though, is the idea that the judiciary will become more independent of Congress. If Congress no longer lays out the exact sentences that judges must give defendants, the judiciary will be able to make independent decisions and won't suffer so much interference from Congress. Thus, if mandatory minimums no longer exist in the United States, defendants will be able to receive individualized sentences that are more fair than the blanket sentences they are receiving now, and our judiciary will be more independent.

After examining all of these things, it is imperative that we explore the steps that each of us can take to discuss how mandatory minimums can be eliminated. First and foremost,

The speaker is telling the audience what actions they can take to bring about needed change to the status quo.

The closing of the speech alludes to the introduction by making mention of the Angelos case. The speaker is reminding listeners that the Angelos case illustrates why mandatory minimums should be abolished.

What is the occasion for this speech?

we must fundamentally alter the way we view criminals. It isn't easy to have sympathy for people who break the law, but locking them up for decades does nothing to make our country a safer place. The first step to ensuring that criminals can be rehabilitated, instead of discarded, is to eliminate mandatory minimum laws. Use the website mandatorymadness.org to let your representatives know that they should vote against proposed mandatory minimum bills. Also, research your political candidates' positions on the justice system and let them know at the ballot box just how detestable mandatory minimums are. Members of Congress enact these laws to garner favor with voters, so the best way to combat them is to let our representatives know that we do not approve. Because of mandatory minimum laws, 22-year-old Weldon Angelos is facing what amounts to a life sentence for selling pot.

After examining the dangers of mandatory minimums, the steps that the Supreme Court and Congress can take to eliminate them, what the U.S. justice system will look like once they're gone, and what each of us can do to make this better future come about, hopefully, we are a little bit closer to restoring some justice to our justice system.

CHAPTER SUMMARY

Now that you have read this chapter you can:

14.1 Understand the nature of persuasion.

Persuasion requires intent. It is also an interactive process and one that is never coercive. Persuasion and coercion represent two diametrically opposed concepts.

14.2 Choose an appropriate persuasive speech purpose.

You should choose the appropriate speech purpose, based on the situation for speaking (e.g., the occasion, the audience). You will persuade your audience in an effort to strengthen their commitment, to weaken their commitment, to convert them, or to induce a specific action.

14.3 Describe the process and nature of persuasive arguments.

The Toulmin Model helps you structure an effective argument by breaking it down into its component parts: your claim (or central theme), the evidence you present, and the warrant that links your claim to the evidence. Your claim can be one of fact, value, or policy. You can use a direct or indirect approach to reach your desired outcome.

14.4 Compose an effective persuasive speech.

To compose a persuasive speech, you must consider your audience and purpose—as in any other speech—and you must also structure your message effectively for that audience. Use of persuasive appeals, the Toulmin Model, or Monroe's motivated sequence can help you achieve your speech goals. You can also assert four different persuasive speech purposes: strengthening a commitment, weakening a commitment, conversion, or inducing a specific action.

You want your audience to perceive you as credible because their ability to see you as such is critical for you to be able to persuade them. To establish credibility, you convey competence, character, and charisma.

Adapting to an audience for a persuasive speech means that you find common ground with listeners, organize according to anticipated response, and anticipate potential hostility.

14.5 Avoid logical fallacy in giving persuasive speeches.

Engaging in logical fallacy diminishes your credibility, and if you use fallacious reasoning, listeners may feel as though you lack respect for them. Ad hominem, generalizing, slippery slope, post hoc, and red herring are common logical fallacies that effective persuasive speakers avoid.

14.6 Explain invitational rhetoric.

Invitational rhetoric occurs when a speaker enters into a public dialogue with an audience. When a speaker enters into a public dialogue, her or she treats the audience with civility.

CIVILITY SUMMARY

Overall, remember that giving persuasive speeches with civility involves the following:

- Persuasive speakers should always consider whether their message is ethical and civil. Ask yourself, "Am I asking the audience to do something that will bring about a greater good? Am I asking them to invest time and money in something that will benefit them or benefit society? Am I giving this speech with sincere intentions?"
- Indirect persuasion is risky in that an audience may feel they've been tricked into listening if a speaker is not upfront about the topic. Because an audience may believe that indirect persuasion may be uncivil, an indirect approach should be used with care.
- You can engage audiences with civility and respect by finding common ground, even if your audience is hostile toward you or your position. This can be accomplished by discussing issues and themes on which you both agree.
- Fallacious arguments can cause an audience to perceive a speaker as uncivil because more critical listeners may believe that the speaker is attempting to deceive them with illogical reasoning.
- Invitational rhetoric contributes to an outcome that consists of respecting the audience and reaching an understanding—one grounded in civility even if the understanding is in the final form of mutual disagreement.

REVIEW QUESTIONS

1. Define *persuasion*.
2. What are the different kinds of claims?
3. What is the difference between direct persuasion and indirect persuasion?
4. What models can help you structure your message for a persuasive speech?
5. What are the steps in Monroe's motivated sequence?
6. What does it mean to engage in a slippery slope fallacy?
7. How can you adapt to an audience for a persuasive speech?
8. How can you establish credibility for a persuasive speech?
9. What are the three conditions for effective invitational rhetoric?

NOTES

Chapter 1

[1] "MTV Awards: West Disrupts Swift's Speech; Tribute to MJ," *CNN.com*. March 25, 2009. www.cnn.com/2009/SHOWBIZ/TV09/14/mtv.music.vieo.awards/index.html (accessed September, 9, 2009). See also Kyle Anderson, "The All-American Rejects Thought Kanye West Was 'Rude' at the VMAs," MTV Newsroom. September 14, 2009. http://newsroom.mtv.com/2009/09/14/all-american-rejects-kanye-west-vma/ (accessed September 14, 2009).

[2] David Zax, "Choosing Civility in a Rude Culture," *Smithsonian*, December 1, 2008. www.smithsonianmag.com/arts-culture/Choosing-Civility-in-a-Rude-Culture.html?c=y&page=1 (accessed November 25, 2010).

[3] "Obama Appeals for Return to 'Civility,'" *Politico*, February 5, 2010. www.politico.com/news/stories/2010/32568.html (accessed March 1, 2011). See also "Remarks by the President at University of Michigan Spring Commencement," Whitehouse.gov, May 1, 2010. www.whitehouse.gov/the-press-ofice/remarks-president-university-michigan-spring-commencent (accessed March 2, 2011).

[4] Helene Cooper and Jeff Zeleny, "Obama Calls for a New Era of Civility in U.S. Politics," *The New York Times*, January 12, 2011. www.nytimes.com/2011/01/13/us/13obama.html (accessed March 1, 2011).

[5] Daniel M. Shea and Barbara Steadman, *Nastiness, Name-Calling and Negativity: The Allegheny College Survey of Civility and Compromise in American Politics*. Meadville, PA: Allegheny College, 2010.

[6] *Civility in America: A Nationwide Study*, June 23, 2010. www.webershandwick.com/resources/ws.flash/WS_Civility_Study_Social_Media_Exec_Summary_6_10.pdf (accessed June 25, 2010).

[7] *Civility in America 2011*, June 20, 2011. www.webershandwick.com/resources/ws/flash/CivilityinAmerica2011.pdf (accessed June 27, 2011).

[8] Pier M. Forni, *Choosing Civility*. New York: St. Martin's Griffin, 2002.

[9] Stephen L. Carter, *Civility: Manners, Morals, and the Etiquette of Democracy*. New York, NY: Harper Perennial, 1999.

[10] Forni.

[11] Forni, 9.

[12] Carter. See also Forni.

[13] Chris Mayo, "The Binds That Tie: Civility and Social Difference," *Educational Theory* 52 (2002): 169–186.

[14] Colleen Flaherty, "Professor's Civility Requirement Sets off Debate on Free Speech," *Inside Higher Ed*, November 19, 2012. www.insidehighered.com/news/2012/11/19/professors-civility-requirement-sets-debate-free-speech#.UKpcsFlQ0Ho.email (accessed November 19, 2012).

[15] Richard Boyd, "The Value of Civility?" *Urban Studies* 43 (2006): 863–878.

[16] Mayo.

[17] Zax.

[18] Boyd.

[19] Emrys Westacott, *The Virtue of Our Vices: A Modest Defense of Gossip, Rudeness, and Other Bad Habits*. Princeton, NJ: Princeton University Press, 2012.

[20] Carter, 110.

[21] Forni.

[22] Forni.

[23] Michael Josephson, *Making Ethical Decisions*. Los Angeles: Josephson Institute of Ethics, 2002.

[24] Thomas Shanks, "Everyday Ethics," *Issues in Ethics* 8 (1997). www.scu.edu/ethics/publications/iie/v8b1.everydayethics.html (accessed July 11, 2009).

[25] Forni.

[26] Boyd.

[27] "NCA Credo for Ethical Communication, *National Communication Association*. http://natcom.org/Default.aspx?id=134 (accessed September 10, 2011).

[28] Richard L. Johannesen, *Ethics in Human Communication*, 5th ed. Long Grove, IL: Waveland Press, 2002.

[29] Rod L. Troester and Cathy S. Mester, *Civility in Business and Professional Communication*. New York: Peter Lang, 2007.

[30] "NCA's Mission," *National Communication Association*. http://www.natcom.org/Default.aspx?id=46 (accessed September 12, 2011).

[31] "NCA Credo."

[32] Kristin M. Hall, "Gay Couple Asked to Reverse Shirt at Dollywood," *Yahoo! News*, July 27, 2011. http://news.yahoo.com/gay-couple-asked-reverse-shirt-dollywood-200120079htm (accessed July 28, 2011). See also Jeremy Kinser, "Did Dollywood Discriminate Against a Lesbian Couple?" *The Advocate*, July 20, 2011. www.advocate.com/News/Daily_News/2011/07/17/Did_Dollywood_Discriminate_Against_a_Lesbian_Couple_/ (accessed August 31, 2011).

[33] Hall. See also Alex Murashko, "Dolly Parton's Dollywood Charged with Gay Discrimination," *The Christian Post*, July 23, 2011. www.christianpost.com/news/dolly-partons-dollywood-charged-with-gay-discrimination-52751/ (accessed August 31, 20110).

[34] Harriette Cole, "Reclaiming Civility," *The Root*, November 9, 2010. www.theroot.com/views/reclaiming-civility (accessed November 24, 2010).

[35] Troester and Mester.

[36] Ibid.

[37] Troester and Mester, 16.

[38] "Updated: Change in Internet Access by Age Group, 2000–2010," *PEW Internet and American Life Project*, September 10, 2010. www.pewinternet.org/Infographics/2010/Internet-acess-by-age-group-over-time-Update.aspx (accessed December 30, 2010).

[39] Aaron Smith, "Mobile Access 2010," *PEW Internet and American Life Project*, July 7, 2010. http://pewinternet.org/Reports/2010/Mobile-Access-2010.aspx (accessed July 7, 2010). See also Amanda Lenhart, "Cell Phones and American Adults," *PEW Internet and American Life Project*, September 2, 2010. http://pewinternet.org/Reports/2010/Cell-Phones-and-American-Adults.aspx (accessed December 16, 2010).

[40] Mary Madden and Kathryn Zickuhr, "65% of Online Adults Use Social Networking Sites," *PEW Internet and American Life Project*, August 26, 2011. http://pewinternet.org/Reports/2011/Social-Networking-Sites.aspx (accessed August 26, 2011).

[41] Nancy K. Baym, *Personal Connections in the Digital Age [Digital Media and Society Series]*. Boston, MA: Polity Press, 2010.

[42] John T. Cacioppo and William Patrick, *Loneliness: Human Nature and the Need for Social Connection*. New York: W.W. Norton, 2009.

[43] Kaveri Subrahmanyam and Gloria Lin, "Adolescents on the Net: Internet Use and Well-Being," *Adolescence* 43 (2007): 659–677.

[44] Suvena Sethi, Andrew J. Campbell, and Louise A. Ellis, "The Use of Computerized Self-Help Packages to Treat Adolescent Depression and Anxiety," *Journal of Technology and Human Services* 18

(2010): 144–160; Sum R. Shima, Mark Mathews, Ian Hughes, and Andrew J. Campbell, "Internet Use and Loneliness in Older Adults," *Cyberpsychology and Behavior* 11 (2008): 208–211.

[45] Subrahmanyam and Lin. See also John T. Cacioppo and Louise C. Hawkley, "Perceived Social Isolation and Cognition," *Trends in Cognitive Sciences* 13 (2009): 447–454.

[46] Andrew Keen, *The Cult of the Amateur: How Today's Internet Is Killing Our Culture*. New York, NY: Doubleday/Currency, 2007; Cass Sunstein, "The Daily We: Is the Internet Really a Blessing for Democracy?" *Boston Review*, Summer 2001. http://bostonreview.net/BR26.3/sunstein.php (accessed January 30, 2010).

[47] Matthew A. Gentzkow and Jesse M. Shapiro, "Ideological Segregation Online and Offline," Chicago Booth Initiative on Global Markets Working Paper No. 55, April 13, 2010. http://ssrn.com/abstract=1588920 (accessed December 30, 2010).

[48] Baym, 2.

[49] Baym. See also Marco C. Yzer and Brian G. Southwell, "New Communication Technologies, Old Questions," *American Behavioral Scientist* 52 (2008): 8–20.

[50] Baym, 153.

[51] Westacott.

[52] Drew Olanoff, "Facebook Announces Monthly Active Users Were at 1.01 Billion as of September 30th, an Increase of 26% Year-over-Year," *Tech Crunch*, October 23, 2012. http://techcrunch.com/2012/10/23/facebook-announces-monthly-active-users-were-at-1-01-billion-as-of-september-30th/ (accessed November 12, 2012).

[53] Ingrid Lunden, "Twitter May Have 500M+ Users but Only 170M Are Active, 75% on Twitter's Own Clients," *Tech Crunch*, July 31, 2012. http://techcrunch.com/2012/07/31/twitter-may-have-500m-users-but-only-170m-are-active-75-on-twitters-own-clients/ (accessed November 12, 2012).

[54] J. Gill Alastair and Jon Oberlander, "Perception of E-Mail Personality at Zero-Acquaintance: Extraversion Takes Care of Itself; Neuroticism Is a Worry," *Proceedings of the 25th Annual Conference of the Cognitive Science Society*. Boston: 2003: 456–461.

[55] Joan E. Aitken, *Human Communication on the Internet*. Boston: Allyn & Bacon, 2004.

[56] J. M. Kayany, "Contexts of Uninhibited Online Behavior: Flaming in Social Newsgroups on Usenet," *Journal of the American Society for Information Science* 49 (1998):1135–1141.

[57] Baym. See also Abdul K. Sinno, Rafic Sinno, and John Stewart, "Social Media, Where Interpersonal Communication Meets Mass Communication," in John Stewart (ed.), *Bridges Not Walls: A Book about Interpersonal Communication*, 11th ed. New York: McGraw Hill, 2012, 61–71.

[58] Troester and Mester, 17.

[59] Craig Storti, *Figuring Foreigners Out: A Practical Guide*. Boston, MA: Intercultural Press, 1999.

[60] "Obama's Bow to Japanese Emperor Sparks Criticism." Star-Telegram.com, November 17, 2009. www.star-telegram.como/238/1770402.html (accessed November 18, 2009). See also S. Griffith, "Outrage in Washington over Obama's Japan Bow," *Yahoo! News*, November 16, 2009. http://news.yahoo.com/s/afp/20091116/pl_afp/japanusdiplomacyasiasobama (accessed November 28, 2009).

[61] Christine M Pearson, L. M. Andersson, and J. W. Wegner, "When Workers Flout Convention: A Study of Workplace Incivility," *Human Relations* 54 (2001): 1387–1419.

[62] Christine Pearson and Christine Porath, *The Cost of Bad Behavior: How Incivility Is Damaging Your Business and What to Do About It*. New York: Portfolio, 2009.

[63] L. M. Cortina, V. Magley, J. Williams, and R. Langout, "Incivility in the Workplace: Incidence and Impact," *Journal of Occupational Health Psychology* 6 (2001): 64–80.

[64] Deborah Tannen, *The Argument Culture: Stopping America's War of Words*. New York: Ballantine Books, 1998.

Chapter 2

[1] "Blown Call Ends Perfect Game Bid," *The Dallas Morning News*, June 3, 2010, C3.

[2] Ben Walker, "Selig Won't Overturn Call That Cost Perfect Game," Msnbc.com, June 3, 2010. http://nbcsports.msnbc.com/id/37479309/ns/sports-baseball/ (accessed June 6, 2010).

[3] Hampton Stevens, "Armando Galarraga's More Perfect Game," *The Atlantic*, June 2010. www.theatlantic.com/culture/archive/2010/06/armando-galarragas-more-perfect-game/57627 (accessed June 6, 2010).

[4] Ronald B. Adler and George Rodman, "Perceiving the Self," in Kathleen M. Galvin and Pamela J. Cooper (eds.), *Making Connections: Readings in Relational Communication*, 4th ed. Cary, NC: Roxbury, 2006, 75–79.

[5] Kenneth N. Cissna and Rob Anderson, "Communication and the Ground of Dialogue," in Rob Anderson, Kenneth N. Cissna, and Ronald C. Arnett (eds.), *The Reach of Dialogue: Confirmation, Voice, and Community*. New York, NY: Hampton Press, 1994, 930.

[6] Jennifer D. Campbell, "Self-Esteem and Clarity of the Self-Concept," *Journal of Personality and Social Psychology* 59 (1990): 538.

[7] "Symptoms of Low Self-Esteem." *JobBank USA*, 2004. www.jobbankusa.com/lowse.html (accessed June 6, 2010).

[8] Vincent R. Ruggiero, "Bad Attitude: Confronting Views That Hinder Students' Learning," *American Educator* 21 (Summer 2000): 1–10.

[9] P. M. Forni, *Choosing Civility*. New York: St. Martin's Griffin, 2002, 168.

[10] Roy F. Baumeister, "The Lowdown on High-Esteem: Thinking You're Hot Stuff Isn't the Promised Cure-All," *Los Angeles Times*, January 24, 2005. www.latimes.com/news/opinion/commentary/la-oe-baumeister25jan,0,1298447.story?coll=la-news-comment.opinions (accessed February 6, 2005).

[11] Amber DeBono, Dikla Shmueli, and Mark Muraven, "Rude and Inappropriate: The Role of Self-Control in Following Social Norms," *Personality and Social Psychology Bulletin* 37, no. 1 (2011): 136–146.

[12] Ibid.

[13] Forni, 24.

[14] Richard L. Marsh, Gabriel I. Cook, and Jason L. Hicks, "Gender and Orientation Stereotypes Bias Source-Monitoring Attributions," *Memory* 14 (2006): 148–160.

[15] Richard Brislin, *Understanding Culture's Influence on Behavior*. Fort Worth, TX: Harcourt Brace, 1993.

[16] Ellen Summerfield, *Survival Kit for Multicultural Living*. Boston, MA: Intercultural Press, 1997.

[17] Brislin.

[18] Adam N. Joinson, "'Looking at,' 'Looking up' or 'Keeping up with' people? Motives and Uses of Facebook." *Proceedings of the Twenty-Sixth Annual SIGCHI Conference on Human Factors in Computing Systems*. New York: Association for Computing Machinery, 2008, 1027–1036. See also Nina Haferkamp, Sabrina C. Eimler, Anna-Margarita Papadakis, and Jana Vanessa Kruch, "Men Are from Mars, Women Are from Venus? Examining Gender Differences in Self-Presentation on Social Networking Sites," *Cyberpsychology, Behavior, and Social Networking* 15, no. 2 (2012): 91–98; and Stokes, Trevor "Social Networking Continues Gender Stereotypes,"

[18] *International Business Times*, December 19, 2011. www.ibtimes.com/articles/269513/20111219/social-networking-continus-gender-stereotypes.htm (accessed December 24, 2011).

[19] Herbjorn Nysveen, Per E. Pedersen, and Helge Thorbjonsen, "Explaining Intention to use Mobile Chat Services: Moderating Effects of Gender," *Journal of Consumer Marketing* 22, no. 5 (2005): 247–256.

[20] Julia T. Wood, "She Says/He Says: Communication, Caring, and Conflict in Heterosexual Relationships," in Julia T. Wood (ed.), *Gendered Relationships*. New York: Mayfield, 1996, 149–162. See also Deborah Tannen, *You Just Don't Understand: Women and Men in Conversation*. New York: Ballantine, 1990.

[21] Adam D. Galinsky, Joe C. Magee, M. Ena Inesi, and Deborah H. Gruenfeld, "Power and Perspectives Not Taken," *Psychological Science* 17 (2006): 1068–1074.

[22] David L. Bradford and Allan R. Cohen, *Managing for Excellence: The Guide to Developing High Performance in Contemporary Organizations*. New York: Wiley, 1984.

[23] Kelly G. Shaver, *An Introduction to Attribution Processes*. Mahwah, NJ: Lawrence Erlbaum Associates, 1983.

[24] Joseph B. Walther and Natalya N. Bazarova, "Misattribution in Virtual Groups: The Effects of Member Distribution of Self-Serving Bias and Partner Blame," *Human Communication Research*, 33 (2009): 1–26.

[25] Tom Hays and Larry Neumeister, "Bernard Madoff Gets Maximum 150 Years in Prison," *Yahoo! News*, June 19, 2009. http://news.yahoo.com/s/ap/20090629/ap_on_bi_ge/us_madoff_scandal (accessed July 3, 2009). See also Monica Gagnier, "The Rise and Fall of Bernard L. Madoff," *BusinessWeek*, December 12, 2008. www.businessweek.com/blogs/recession_in_america/archives/2008/12/the_rise_and_fa.html (accessed July 3, 2009); and Eileen Ambrose, "Making Sure Your Financial Advisor Is No Madoff," *The Baltimore Sun*, July 5, 2009. www.baltimoresun.com/business/money/bal-bz.ml.ambrose05jul05,0,7154065.story (accessed July 5, 2009).

[26] Julie Creswell and Landon Thomas, Jr., "The Talented Mr. Madoff," *The New York Times*, January 24, 2009. www.nytimes.com/2009/01/25/business/25bernie.html (accessed July 3, 2009).

[27] Nicky Hayes, *Foundations of Psychology*, 3rd ed. Belmont, CA: Cengage, 2000.

[28] Ronald E. Riggio, *The Charisma Quotient*. New York: Dodd, Mead, and Co., 1987.

[29] Craig Storti, *Figuring Foreigners Out: A Practical Guide*. Boston, MA: Intercultural Press, 1999.

[30] Myron W. Lustig and Jolene Koester, *Intercultural Competence: Interpersonal Communication Across Cultures*, 4th ed. Boston: Allyn & Bacon, 2003.

[31] Judith N. Martin and Thomas K. Nakayama, *Experiencing Intercultural Communication: An Introduction*, 2nd ed. New York: McGraw-Hill, 2005.

[32] Peter A. Andersen, *Nonverbal Communication: Forms and Functions*. Palo Alto, CA: Mayfield, 1999.

[33] Lustig and Koester.

[34] Harry C. Triandis, Christopher McCusker, and Harry C. Hui, "Multimethod Probes of Individualism and Collectivism," *Journal of Personality and Social Psychology* 59, no. 5 (1990): 1006–1020.

[35] Lustig and Koester.

[36] Triandis, McCusker, and Hui.

[37] Lustig and Koester.

[38] Eun-Yun Kim, *The Yin and Yang of American Culture*. Boston: Intercultural Press, 2001.

[39] Peter Kollock and Jodi O'Brien, "A Perspective for Understanding Self and Social Interaction," in Jodi O'Brien and Peter Kollock (eds.), *The Production of Reality: Essays and Readings on Social Interaction*, 3rd ed. Thousand Oaks, CA: Pine Forge Press/Sage, 2001, 35–59.

[40] Storti.

[41] Mark P. Orbe, *Constructing Co-Cultural Theory: An Explication of Culture, Power and Communication*. Thousand Oaks, CA: Sage, 1998.

[42] Jeffrey S. Burks, Richard E. Nisbett, and Oscar Ybarra, "Cultural Styles, Relational Schemas, and Prejudice Against Out-Groups," *Journal of Personality and Social Psychology* 79 (2000): 174–189.

[43] Simine Vazire and Samuel D. Gosling, "e-Perceptions: Personality Impressions Based on Personal Websites," *Journal of Personality and Social Psychology* 87 (2004): 123–132.

[44] Joseph P. Mazer, Richard E. Murphy, and Cheri J. Simonds, "I'll See You on 'Facebook': The Effects of Computer-Mediated Teacher Self-Disclosure on Student Motivation, Affective Learning, and Classroom Climate," *Communication Education* 56 (2007): 1–17

[45] Tom Tong, Stephanie, Brandon Van Der Heide, Lindsey Langwell, and Joseph B. Walther, "Too Much of a Good Thing? The Relationship Between Number of Friends and Interpersonal Impressions on Facebook," *Journal of Computer-Mediated Communication* 13 (2008), 531–549.

[46] Shanyang Zhao, Sherri Grasmuck, and Jason Martin, "Identity Construction on Facebook: Digital Empowerment in Anchored Relationships," *Computers in Human Behavior* 12 (2008): 1816–1836.

[47] Judith Rosenbaum, *Self-Presentation as a Balancing Act: A Qualitative Exploration of Impression Management Goals and Behaviors on Facebook*. Presented at the 97th annual convention of the National Communication Association, New Orleans, LA, 2011.

[48] Amy L. Gonzales, and Jeffrey T. Hancock, "Mirror, Mirror on my Facebook Wall: Effects of Exposure to Facebook on Self-Esteem," *Cyberpsychology, Behavior, and Social Networking* 14, nos. 1–2 (2011): 79–83.

[49] Laura Robinson, "The Cyberself: The Selfing Project Goes Online, Symbolic Interaction in the Digital Age," *New Media & Society* 9, no. 1 (2007): 93–110.

[50] Robert Rosenthal and Lenore Jacobson, "Pygmalion in the Classroom," in Jodi A. O'Brien and Peter Kollock (eds.), *The Production of Reality: Essays and Readings on Social Interaction*, 3rd ed. Thousand Oaks, CA: Pine Forge Press/Sage Publications, 2001, 35–60.

[51] Donald Hamachek, "Dynamics of Self-Understanding and Self-Knowledge: Acquisition, Advantages, and Relation to Emotional Intelligence," *Journal of Humanistic Counseling, Education, and Development* 38 (2000): 230–243.

[52] John J. Seta, Catherine E. Seta, and Todd McElroy, "Better Than Better-Than-Average (or Not): Elevated and Depressed Self-Evaluations Following Unfavorable Social Comparisons," *Self and Identity* 5 (2006): 51–72.

[53] Stephen Bochner, "Cross-Cultural Differences in the Self Concept: A Test of Hofstede's Individualism/Collectivism Distinction," *Journal of Cross-Cultural Psychology* 25 (1994): 273–283.

[54] Hazel Rose Markus and Shinobu Kitayama, "Culture and the Self: Implications for Cognition, Emotion, and Motivation," *Psychological Review* 98 (1991): 224–253. See also Judith N. Martin and Thomas K. Nakayama, *Experiencing Intercultural Communication: An Introduction*, 2nd ed. New York: McGraw-Hill, 2005.

[55] Marc Adams, Shelley Craig, and Alexander Pangborn, *It's Not About You: Understanding Coming Out and Self-Acceptance*. Seattle: Window Books, 2010. See also William F. Skinner, "The Prevalence of Victimization and Its Effect on Mental Well-Being among Lesbian and Gay People," *Journal of Homosexuality* 30 (1996): 93–121.

[56] Albert Bandura, *Self-Efficacy: The Exercise of Control*. New York: Freeman, 1997.

[57] Ingeborg Wender, "Relation of Technology, Science, Self-Concept, Interest, and Gender," *Journal of Technology Studies* 30 (2004): 43–51.

[58] Ibid.

[59] Andrew Reilly and Nancy A. Rudd, "Social Anxiety as Predictor of Personal Aesthetic Among Women," *Clothing and Textiles Research Journal* 27, no. 3 (2009): 227–240.

[60] Janet T. Spence and Robert L. Helmreich, *Masculinity and Femininity: Their Psychological Dimension and Antecedents*. Austin, TX: University of Texas Press, 1978.

[61] Zaheer Hussain and Mark D. Griffiths, "Gender Swapping and Socializing in Cyberspace: An Exploratory Study," *CyberPsychology and Behavior* 11 (2008): 47–53.

[62] R. Foels and Thomas J. Tomcho, "Gender, Interdependent Self-Construals, and Collective Self-Esteem: Women and Men Are Mostly the Same," *Self and Identity* 4 (2005): 213–225.

[63] Scott Parks, "Work Together and No One Loses," *Dallas Morning News*, May 12, 2003, 2B, 13B.

Chapter 3

[1] David Brooks, "Media Fails by Politicizing Mental Illness," *The Dallas Morning News*, January 12, 2011, 17A.

[2] Froma Harrop, "Arizona Shooting Was a Political Attack," *The Dallas Morning News*, January 11, 2011, 13A.

[3] Paul Krugman, "Climate of Hate," *The New York Times*, January 9, 2011. www.nytimes.com/2011/01/10/opinion/10krugman.html?_r=1&ref=paulkrugman (accessed January 11, 2011).

[4] Harrop.

[5] Mark DeMoss, "Don't Expect Civility," *Politico*, January 17, 2011. http://dyn.politico.com/news/stories/0111/47677.html (accessed January 30, 2011).

[6] Charles K. Ogden and Ivor A. Richards, *The Meaning of Meaning*. New York: Harcourt Brace, 1923.

[7] Ayub Kahn, "Muslim Student Delivers 'Jihad' Speech at Harvard Graduation," *IslamOnline.net*, June 7, 2002. www.islamonline.net/english/News/2002-06/07/article18.shtml (accessed March 4, 2003). See also Rubin Navarette, "Students Need a Free Speech Lesson: Calls to Censor Commencement Speaker Are Disquieting," *The Dallas Morning News*, June 7, 2002. www.dallasnews.com (accessed June 15, 2002).

[8] "Jihad," *Online Etymology Dictionary*, © Douglas Harper, 2010. www.etymonline.com (accessed December 29, 2001).

[9] "App," Netlingo.com. www.netlingo.com/dictionary/a.php (accessed December 28, 2009).

[10] Tom Dalzell, "The Power of Slang. Do You Speak American? Words That Shouldn't Be? Sez Who?" www.pbs.org/speak/words/sezwho/slang/ (accessed January 5, 2005). See also K. Mack, "Dictionary Editors Tackle the Tough Word Questions," *Dallas Morning News*, July 22, 2000, 4C.

[11] Lustig and Koester.

[12] Victor Godinez, "Video Games take Command of War Epics as Movies Retreat from Recent Conflicts," *The Dallas Morning News*. December 22, 2009, 1A, 2A. See also Marc Ambinder, "The Story Behind 'Medal of Honor,'" *The Atlantic*, October 13, 2010. www.theatlantic.com/entertainment/archive/2010/10/the-story-behind-medal-of-honor/64441/ (accessed June 11, 2011).

[13] Peter Ives, "In Defense of Jargon," *Bad Subjects: Political Education for Everyday Life*, March 1997. http://bad.eserver.org/issues/1997/31/ives.html (accessed January 28, 2011).

[14] Beverley Fehr, *Friendship Processes*. Thousand Oaks, CA: Sage, 1996.

[15] Mary Ann Fitzpatrick and Anthony Mulac, "Relating to Spouse and Stranger: Gender-Preferential Language Use," In Pamela J. Kalbfleisch and Michael J. Cody (eds.), *Gender, Power, and Communication*. Mahwah, NJ: Lawrence Erlbaum Associates, 1997, 213–231.

[16] David Crystal, *Language and the Internet*. Cambridge, UK: Cambridge University Press, 2002. See also Neil Randall, "Lingo Online: The Language of the Keyboard Generation," *msn.ca*, June 11, 2002. www.arts.uwaterloo.ca/~nrandall/LingoOnline-finalreport.pdf (accessed November 20, 2006).

[17] "'Unfriend'—A Feeling of Removal in 2009?" *The Dallas Morning News*, November 18, 2009, 8A.

[18] Deborah Tannen, *You Just Don't Understand: Women and Men in Conversation*. New York: Ballantine Books, 1990.

[19] Rosalind Barnett and Caryl Rivers, "Men Are from Earth, and So Are Women. It's Faulty Research That Sets Them Apart," *Chronicle of Higher Education* 51, no. 2 (2004): B11.

[20] Fitzpatrick and Mulac.

[21] W. Barnett Pearce, "A Coordinated Management of Meaning: A Rules-Based Theory of Interpersonal Communication," In George Miller (ed.), *Explorations in Human Communication*. Thousand Oaks, CA: Sage, 1976, 17–36. See also W. Barnett Pearce and Vernon E. Cronen, *Communication, Action, and Meaning: The Creation of Social Realities*. New York: Praeger, 1980.

[22] Pearce and Cronen. See also W. Barnett Pearce and Karen A. Pearce, "Taking a Communication Perspective on Dialogue," In Rob Anderson, Leslie A. Baxter, and Kenneth M. Cissna (eds.), *Dialogue: Theorizing Difference in Communication Studies*. Thousand Oaks, CA: Sage, 2003, 39–56.

[23] Alex Stone, "Finding the Right Word Odor," *Discover*, September 2005. www.discover.com/issues/sep-05/rd/finding-the-right-word-odor/ (accessed August 17, 2005).

[24] "'Pink Slime' Label Stuck Like Filler," *The Dallas Morning News*, May 22, 2012, 3A.

[25] M. E. Young, "Fighting Words: The Other Battle," *Dallas Morning News*, April 7, 2003, 1A, 10A.

[26] William Lutz, *The New Doublespeak: No One Knows What Anybody Is Saying Anymore*. New York: Perennial, 1997. See also William Lutz, *Doublespeak: From Revenue Enhancement to Terminal Living—How Government, Business, Advertisers and Others Use Language to Deceive You*. New York: HarperCollins, 1990.

[27] "Food Security in the United States," Briefing Room, *USDA Economic Research Service*. U.S. Department of Agriculture, November 15, 2006. www.ers.usda.gov/briefing/FoodSecurity/ (accessed November 20, 2006).

[28] Brian Ross and Richard Esposito, "CIA's Harsh Interrogation Techniques Described," *ABC News*, November 18, 2005. http://abcnews.go.com/WNT/Investigation/story?id=1322866 (accessed May 22, 2009).

[29] "Just Make It Sound Nicer," *Newsweek*, April 20, 2009, 9.

[30] R. B. Moore, "Racist Stereotyping in the English Language," In *Voices: A Selection of Multicultural Readings*. Belmont, CA: Wadsworth, 1995, 9–17.

[31] P. Butler, "A Mix of Colors: Country's Swirling Demographics Put New Twist on Meaning of 'Minority,'" *Dallas Morning News*, June 3, 2001, 1J, 6J.

[32] P. Pringle, "California Looks to Find Identity in Changing Face," *Dallas Morning News*, December 24, 2000, 1A.

[33] Larry A. Samovar and Richard E. Porter, *Communication Between Cultures*, 5th ed. Belmont, CA: Wadsworth, 2004. See also William B. Gudykunst and Y. Y. Kim, *Communicating with Strangers*, 4th ed. New York: McGraw-Hill, 2003.

[34] William B. Gudykunst, *Bridging Differences: Effective Intergroup Communication*, 4th ed. Thousand Oaks, CA: Sage. See also Larry A. Samovar, Richard E. Porter, and Edwin R. McDaniel, *Communication Between Cultures*, 7th ed. Boston: Wadsworth, 2009.

[35] Myron W. Lustig and Jolene Koester, *Intercultural Competence*, 6th ed. Boston: Allyn & Bacon, 2009.

[36] Gudykunst. See also Samovar et al.

[37] Lustig and Koester.

[38] Mary Fong, "The Crossroads of Language and Culture," in Larry A. Samovar and Richard E. Porter (eds.), *Intercultural Communication: A Reader*, 9th ed. Belmont, CA: Wadsworth, 2000, 211–216.

[39] J. L. Lunsford, "ValuJet Unauthorized as Hazardous Carrier," *Dallas Morning News*, May 16, 1996, 1A.

[40] Edward C. Stewart and Milton J. Bennett, *American Cultural Patterns: A Cross-Cultural Perspective*, rev. ed. Boston: Intercultural Press, 1991.

[41] "Free Inquiry Statement of Purpose," Council for Secular Humanism, www.secularhumanism.org/index.php?section=fi&page=purpose (accessed January 7, 2010).

[42] "Clear Wording Urged to Avoid Airline Crashes," *Dallas Morning News*, February 22, 1990, 3A.

[43] Clarence Page, "They were Victims of our 9/11 Paranoia," *Houston Chronicle*, September 24, 2002. http://www.chron.com/opinion/editorials/article/Page-They-were-victims-of-our-9-11-paranoia-2105157.php (accessed March 26, 2013).

[44] David M. Jabusch and Stephen W. Littlejohn, *Elements of Speech Communication*, 3rd. ed. New York: Rowan and Littlefield, 2004.

[45] Ibid.

[46] "Cheney Curses Leahy on Senate Floor," *msnbc.com*, June 24, 2004. www.msnbc.com/id/528948/ns/politics/chency-curses-leahy-senate-floor/# (accessed June 4, 2001).

[47] Michael Sheridan, "Vice President Biden Caught on Mic; Calls Health Care Bill a 'Big f—ing Deal,'" *New York Daily News*, March 23, 2010. http://articles.nydailynews.com/2010-03-23/news/27059874_1_ing-deal-health-care-mic (accessed June 4, 2011).

[48] "Profanity," *The Free Dictionary*. www.thefreedictionary.com/profanity (accessed February 15, 2001).

[49] "Rudeness Survey Stirs Up Public Debate About the Decline of Civility in the U.S.," *The Public Agenda: The Inside Source for Public Opinion and Policy Analysis*, Summer 2002, 1, 5.

[50] M. Gross, "Watch Your Mouth! Americans See Profanity Getting Worse," *AP/Ipsos Poll*, March 28, 2006. www.ipsos-na.com/news/pressrelease.cfm?id=3031 (accessed March 29, 2006). See also "Who Gives a @#$% About Profanity? Poll Says 75% of Women and 60% of Men Don't Like Swearwords," CNN.com, March 28, 2006. www.cnn.com/2006/US/03/28/profanity.ap/index.html (accessed March 29, 2006).

[51] Ruth A. Abigail, and Dudley D. Cahn, *Managing Conflict Through Communication*, 4th ed. Boston: Allyn & Bacon, 2010.

[52] Natalie Angier, "Almost Before We Spoke, We Swore," *New York Times*, September 20, 2005. www.nytimes.com/2005/09/20/science/20curs.html (accessed February 4, 2011). See also "Mass. Town OKs $20 Fines for Swearing in Public," *Associated Press*, June 11, 2012. www.rr.com/news/topic/article/rr/55255121/69848184/Mass_town_OKs_fines_for_swearing_in_public?empid=RRWMHero# (accessed June 12, 2012).

[53] "The Best Party on Campus," University of Iowa College Republicans, April 2011. http://hawkeyegop.org/2011/04/18/conservative-coming-out-week/ (accessed June 11, 2001).

[54] "1940 Statement of Principles on Academic Freedom and Tenure," American Association of University Professors. www.aaup.org/AAUP/pubsres/policydocs/contents/1940statement.htm (accessed June 11, 2011).

[55] Nina Earnest, "Professor Receives Slew of Backlash After F-word Email," *The Daily Iowan*, April 22, 2011. www.dailyiowan.com/2011/04/22/Metro/23036.html (accessed June 11, 2011).

[56] Scott Jaschik, "When Students Drop the F-Bomb," *Inside Higher Ed*, May 19, 2010. www.insidehighered.com/news/2010/05/19/swear (accessed May 19, 2010).

[57] David Moltz, "Taking on Habits That Suck," *Inside Higher Ed*, May 24, 2010. www.insidehighered.com/news/2010/05/24/onondaga (accessed May 25, 2010).

[58] Park.

[59] James V. O'Connor, *Cuss Control: The Complete Book on How to Curb Your Cursing*. New York: Three Rivers Press, 2000.

[60] Stephen L. Carter, *Civility: Manners, Morals, and the Etiquette of Democracy*. New York: HarperPerennial, 1998.

Chapter 4

[1] "Slideshow: Celebrity Sightings," *Associated Press*, December 14, 2007. http://today.msnbc.msn.com/id/22261200/ns/today-entertainment/ (accessed February 1, 2011).

[2] "Depp Dubbed Best Autograph; Diaz Voted Worst," *Access Hollywood*, May 12, 2006. www.accesshollywood.com/depp-dubbed-best-autograph-diaz-voted-worst_article_249 (accessed February 1, 2011).

[3] "Johnny Depp Seems Nice," *The Blemish*, October 7, 2010 from http://theblemish.com/2010/10/johnny-depp-seems-nice/ (accessed February 1, 2011).

[4] "Charities," *Johnny Depp Web*. www.johnnydppweb.com/info/charities/ (accessed February 1, 2011).

[5] Ibid.

[6] Judee K. Burgoon and Gregory D. Hoobler, "Nonverbal Signals," in Mark L. Knapp and Gerald R. Miller (eds.), *Handbook of Interpersonal Communication*, 3rd ed. Thousand Oaks, CA: Sage, 2002, 240–299.

[7] M. Argyle, F. Alkema, and R. Gilmour, "The Communication of Friendly and Hostile Attitudes by Verbal and Nonverbal Signals," *European Journal of Social Psychology* 1 (1971): 385–402.

[8] Mark L. Knapp and Judith A. Hall, *Nonverbal Behavior in Human Interaction*, 5th ed. Belmont, CA: Wadsworth, 2002. See also T. Brosnahan, *Turkey: A Travel Survival Kit*, 2nd ed. Oakland, CA: Lonely Planet, 1988.

[9] Peter Bull and G. Connelly, "Body Movements and Emphasis in Speech," *Journal of Nonverbal Behavior* 9 (1986): 169–187.

[10] Andrew F. Wood and Matthew J. Smith, *Online Communication: Linking Technology, Identity, and Culture*, 2nd ed. Mahwah, NJ: Lawrence Erlbaum, 2005. See also Kirk W. Duthler, "The Politeness of Requests Made via Email and Voicemail: Support for the Hyperpersonal Model," *Journal of Computer-Mediated Communication* 11 (2006): 6. http://jcmc.indiana.edu/vol11/issue2/duthler.html (accessed May 30, 2007).

[11] Jeremy N. Bailenson, Nick Yee, Scott Brave, Dan Merget, and David Koslow, "Virtual Interpersonal Touch: Expressing and Recognizing Emotions Through Haptic Devices," *Human–Computer Interaction* 22 (2007): 325–353.

[12] Myron W. Lustig, and Jolene Koester, *Intercultural Competence: Interpersonal Communication Across Cultures*, 4th ed. Boston: Allyn & Bacon, 2003.

[13] Ibid.

[14] Holley S. Hodgins and Richard Koestner, "The Origins of Nonverbal Sensitivity," *Personality and Social Psychology Bulletin* 19 (1993):

[14] 466–473. See also Anna-Marie Dew and Colleen Ward, "The Effects of Ethnicity and Culturally Congruent and Incongruent Nonverbal Behaviors on Interpersonal Attraction," *Journal of Applied Social Psychology* 23 (1993): 1376–1389.

[15] Mark P. Orbe and Tina M. Harris, *Interracial Communication: Theory into Practice*. Belmont, CA: Wadsworth, 2001.

[16] Smiljana Antonijevic, "From Text to Gesture Online: A Microethnographic Analysis of Nonverbal Communication in the Second Life Virtual Environment," *Information, Communication, and Society* 11 (2008): 221–238. See also Nick Yee, Jeremy Bailenson, Mark Urbanek, Francis Chang, and Dan Merget, "The Unbearable Likeness of Being Digital: The Persistence of Nonverbal Social Norms in Online Virtual Environments," *CyberPsychology and Behavior* 10 (2007): 115–121.

[17] Frances H. Rauscher, Robert M. Krauss, and Y. Chen, "Gesture, Speech, and Lexical Access: The Role of Lexical Movements in Speech Production," *Psychological Science* 4 (1996): 226–231. See also Robert M. Krauss and Uri Hadar, "The Role of Speech-Related Arm/Hand Gestures in Word Retrieval," In Lynn S. Messing and Ruth Campbell (eds.), *Gesture, Speech, and Sign*. Oxford, UK: Oxford University Press, 1999, 94–116; and Sharon Begley, "Living Hand to Mouth: New Research Shows that Gestures Often Help Speakers Access Words from Their Memory Banks," *Newsweek*, November 2, 1998, 69.

[18] Knapp and Hall. See also "Study: Human Posture Can Communicate Fear," CNN.com, October 19, 2004. www.cnn.com/2004/TECH/science/11/19/med.us.fearcontagi.ap/index/html (accessed October 22, 2004).

[19] Katinka Dijkstra, Michael P. Kaschak, and Rolf A. Zwann, "Body Posture Facilitates Retrieval of Autobiographical Memories," *Cognition* 102 (2007): 139–149.

[20] Knapp and Hall.

[21] Virginia P. Richmond and James C. McCroskey, *Nonverbal Behavior in Interpersonal Relations*, 5th ed. Boston: Allyn & Bacon, 2004.

[22] Meredith Levinson, "How to Be a Mind Reader," *CIO Magazine*, December 2004. http://www.cio.com/article/103250/How_to_Be_a_Mind_Reader_The_Art_of_Deciphering_Body_Language (accessed March 4, 2005). See also Paul Ekman, *Emotions Revealed*. New York: Times Books, 2003.

[23] Mary Duenwald, "The Physiology of ... Facial Expressions," *Discover*, January 2005. http://209.85.165.104/search?q=cache:2VOxYamRQpoJ:discovermagazine.com/2005/jan/physiology-of-facial-expressions+Duenwald%2BPhysiology%2Bfacial%2Bexpressions%2BDiscover&hl=en&ct=clnk&cd=1&gl=us (accessed March 8, 2005).

[24] Roland Neumann and Fritz Strack, "'Mood Contagion': The Automatic Transfer of Mood Between Persons," *Journal of Personality and Social Psychology* 79 (2000): 211–223. See also "Irate Caller ID: For Empathy, Press 4," *USC Trojan Family Magazine*, Autumn 2004, 21.

[25] Dennis R. Preston, "Language Prejudice: Language Myth #17," *Do You Speak American?* PBS.org, 2005. http://209.85.165.104/search?q=cache:qgs6Rdol-HgJ:www.pbs.org/speak/speech/prejudice/attitudes/+Speak%2BAmerican%2BLanguage%2BMyth%2B17&hl=en&ct=clnk&cd=1&gl=us (accessed February 25, 2005).

[26] Knapp and Hall. See also Daniel S. Hamermesh and Jeff E. Biddle, "Beauty and the Labor Market," *American Economic Review* 84 (1994): 1174–1194; and K. M. Thomas, "Court Appearance: A Defendant's Grooming, Clothes, and Behavior Can Help Win or Lose a Case," *Dallas Morning News*, December 10, 1996, 1C, 4C.

[27] M. Navarro, "Hip Huggers," *Dallas Morning News*, December 30, 2004, 5E. See also Danielle Almeida, "Where Have All the Children Gone? A Visual Semiotic Account of Advertisements for Fashion Dolls," *Visual Communication* 8 (2009): 481–501.

[28] Amanda Reid, Vince Lancuba, and Bridget Morrow, "Clothing Style and Formation of First Impressions," *Perceptual and Motor Skills* 84 (1997): 237–238.

[29] "For Students: Elementary Dress Code," Mesquite Independent School District. www.mesquiteisd.org/students/policies/elemdress.asp (accessed June 14, 2011).

[30] Karel Holloway, "Long Hair Gets Mesquite Pre-kindergartner in Trouble," *The Dallas Morning News*, December 14, 2009. http://mesquiteblog.dallasnews.com/archives/2009/12/long-hair-gets-mesquite-prekin.html (accessed June 14, 2011).

[31] Karel Holloway, "Pre-K Student, Mesquite ISD Tangled Up in Dress Code Fight Over Hair," *The Dallas Morning News*, December 16, 2009. www.dallasnews.com/news/education/headlines/20091215-Pre-K-student-Mesquite-ISD-3563.ece (accessed June 14, 2011). See also Jeff Carlton, "Taylor Pugh: 4-Year-Old Texas Boy Suspended for Long Locks," *The Huffington Post*, December 17, 2009. www.huffingtonpost.com/2009/12/17/taylor-pugh-4yearold-texa_n_395550.html (accessed June 14, 2011).

[32] Debbie Denmon, "Pre-Schooler's Parents Claim Mesquite ISD Is Setting Double Standard on Hair," *WFAA-TV*, January 12, 2010. www.wfaa.com/news/local/Pre-schoolers-parents-claim-Mesquite-ISD-is-setting-double-standard-on-hair-81268667.html# (accessed June 14, 2011).

[33] Karel Holloway, "Parents Reject Mesquite ISD's Compromise on Boy's Long Hair," *Texas Cable News*, January 12, 2010. www.txcn.com/sharedcontent/dws/news/localnews/stories/011210dnmetmeshair.6c3b6e7c.html# (accessed June 14, 2011).

[34] Ibid.

[35] Froma Harrop, "The Casualization of America," *Dallas Morning News*, February 12, 2010. www.dallasnews.com/sharedcontent/dws/dn/opinion/viewpoints/stories/DN-harrop_13edi.State.Edition1.2a06ace.html (accessed February 17, 2010).

[36] T. Robberson, "What a Headscarf Means: A Symbol of Piety, a Terroristic Threat, or a Call to Arms?" *Dallas Morning News*, June 20, 2004, 1H, 6H.

[37] "Sarkozy: Burqas Anti-Woman," *The Dallas Morning News*, June 23, 2009, 6A.

[38] Ali Akbar Dareini and Brian Murphy, "Dress Code Getting Even Stricter: Hair, Jewelry Now Targets of Morality Squads," *The Dallas Morning News*, June 26, 2011, 16A.

[39] Knapp and Hall.

[40] Craig Storti, *Figuring Foreigners Out: A Practical Guide*. Boston: Intercultural Press, 1999.

[41] B. Marvel, "The Distance. Communication Is Not All About Words: How We Position Ourselves Speaks Volumes," *Dallas Morning News*, August 7, 2004, 1E, 3E.

[42] Edward T. Hall, *The Hidden Dimension*. New York: Doubleday, 1969.

[43] Richmond and McCrosky.

[44] Sei Jin Ko, Charles M. Judd, and Diederik A. Stapel, "Stereotyping Based on Voice in the Presence of Individuating Information: Vocal Femininity Affects Perceived Competence but Not Warmth," *Personality and Social Psychology Bulletin* 35 (2009): 198–211.

[45] Cliff Nass, "Technology Spotlight: Machine Voices," *Do You Speak American?* 2005. www.pbs.org/speak/ahead/technology/voiceinterface/ (accessed January 25, 2006).

[46] Judith A. Hall and Gregory B. Friedman, "Status, Gender, and Nonverbal Behavior: A Study of Structured Interactions Between Employees of a Company," *Personality and Social Psychology Bulletin* 25, no. 9 (1999): 1082–1091. See also Deborah S. Stier and Judith A. Hall, "Gender

47. Virginia P. Richmond, James C. McCroskey, and Mark L. Hickson, *Nonverbal Behavior in Interpersonal Relations*, 7th ed. Boston: Allyn & Bacon, 2011. See also Mark L. Knapp and Judith A. Hall, *Nonverbal Behavior in Human Interaction*, 7th ed. Belmont, CA: Wadsworth, 2009.

[Preceding note text]: Differences in Touch: An Empirical and Theoretical Review," *Journal of Personality and Social Psychology* 47, no. 2, (1984): 440–459.

48. Peter A. Andersen, "The Evolution of Biological Sex Differences in Communication," in Daniel J. Canary and Kathryn Dindia (eds.), *Sex Differences and Similarities in Communication*, 2nd ed. Mahwah, NJ: Lawrence Erlbaum Associates, 2006, 117–135. See also Judith A. Hall, "Gender Effects in Encoding Nonverbal Cues," *Psychological Bulletin* 85 (1978): 845–857; and L. P. Stewart, P. J. Cooper, and A. D. Stewart (with S. A. Friedley), *Communication and Gender*, 4th ed. Boston: Allyn & Bacon, 2003.

49. Barbara Bate and Judy Bowker, *Communication and the Sexes*, 2nd ed. Long Grove, IL: Waveland Press, 1997. See also Clifford Nass, "Machine Voices," *Do You Speak American?* 2005. www.pbs.org/speak/ahead/technology/voiceinterface/ (accessed January 5, 2005); and Leslie R. Brody and Judith A. Hall, "Gender, Emotion, and Expression," in Michael Lewis and Jeannette M. Haviland-Jones (eds.), *Handbook of Emotions*. New York: Guilford, 2000, 338–349.

50. Cynthia Berryman-Fink, "Preventing Sexual Harassment Through Male–Female Communication Training," in Gary L. Kreps (ed.), *Sexual Harassment: Communication Implications*. Cresskill, NJ: Hampton Press, 1993, 267–280. See also N. M. Henley and S. Harmon, "The Nonverbal Semantics of Power and Gender: A Perceptual Study," in Steve L. Ellyson and John F. Dovidio (eds.), *Power, Dominance, and Nonverbal Behavior*. London: Springer-Verlag, 1985, 151–164; and Nancy Henley and Jo Freeman, "The Sexual Politics of Interpersonal Behavior," in Jo Freeman (ed.), *Women: A Feminist Perspective*. New York: McGraw-Hill, 1994, 78–90.

51. Michael Gross, "AP/Ipsos Poll: The Decline of American Civilization, or at Least Its Manners," Ipsos, October 14, 2005. www.ipsos-na.com/news/pressrelease.cfm??id=2827 (accessed October 4, 2005). See also "The Decline of Manners in the U.S.," CNN.com, October 14, 2005. www.cnn.com/2005/US/10/14/poll.rude.ap/indeex.html (accessed October 14, 2005).

52. Daniel J. Canary and Melissa A. Tafoya, *Road Rage as a Communicative Event*. Presented at the National Communication Association conference, Boston, 2005.

53. Tara E. Galovski and Edward D. Blanchard, "Road Rage: A Domain for Psychological Intervention?" *Aggression and Violent Behavior* 9 (2004): 105–127.

54. Carrie Lock, "Deception Detection: Psychologists Try to Learn How to Spot a Liar," *Science News Online*, July 31, 2004. www.sciencenews.org/articles/20040731/bob8.asp (accessed December 24, 2004). See also T. R. Levine and Steven A. McCornack, "Behavioral Adaptation, Confidence, and Heuristic-Based Explanations of the Probing Effect," *Human Communication Research* 27 (2001): 471–502.

55. Aldert Vrij, "Why Professionals Fail to Catch Liars and How They Can Improve," *Legal and Criminological Psychology* 9 (2004): 159–181. See also S. Mann, A. Vrij, and R. Bull, "Suspects, Lies, and Videotape: An Analysis of Authentic High-Stakes Liars," *Law and Human Behavior* 26 (2002): 137–149; and A. Vrij, K. Edward, and R. Bull, "People's Insight into Their Own Behaviour and Speech Content While Lying," *British Journal of Psychology* 92 (2001): 373–389.

56. Mark C. Knapp, *Lying and Deception in Human Interaction*. Boston: Pearson Education, 2008. See also Xiaoqing Hu, Hao Chen, and Genyue Fu, "A Repeated Lie Becomes a Truth? The Effect of Intentional Control and Training on Deception," *Frontiers in Psychology* 3 (2012): 1–7.

57. Diane M. Christophel, "The Relationships Among Teacher Immediacy Behaviors, Student Motivation, and Learning," *Communication Education* 39 (1990): 323–340. See also James C. McCroskey, Aino Sallinen, Joan M. Fayer, Virginia P. Richmond, and Robert A. Barraclough, "Nonverbal Immediacy and Cognitive Learning: A Cross-Cultural Investigation," *Communication Education* 45 (1996): 200–211; James C. McCroskey, Virginia P. Richmond, Aino Sallinen, Jaon M. Fayer, and Robert A. Barraclough, "A Cross-Cultural and Multi-Behavioral Analysis of the Relationship Between Nonverbal Immediacy and Teacher Evaluation," *Communication Education* 44 (1995): 281, 291; and James C. McCroskey and Virginia P. Richmond, "Increasing Teacher Influence Through Immediacy," in Virginia P. Richmond and James C. McCroskey (eds.), *Power in the Classroom: Communication, Control, and Concern*. Mahwah, NJ: Lawrence Erlbaum, 1992, 101–119.

58. Pamela J. Cooper and Cheri J. Simonds, *Communication for the Classroom Teacher*, 8th ed. Boston: Allyn & Bacon, 2006. See also Marjorie A. Jaasma and Randall J. Koper, "The Relationship of Student-Faculty Out-of-Class Communication to Instructor Immediacy and Trust and to Student Motivation," *Communication Education* 48 (1999): 41–47.

59. John A. MacArthur and Kristen Bostedo-Conway, *Exploring the Relationship between Student-Instructor Interaction on Twitter and Student Perceptions of Teacher Behavior*. Paper presented at the National Communication Association, New Orleans, 2011.

60. Richmond and McCrosky.

61. Virgina P. Richmond and James C. McCroskey, "The Impact of Supervisor and Subordinate Immediacy on Relational and Organizational Outcomes," *Communication Monographs* 67 (2000): 85–95.

62. Ibid.

63. Jason J. Teven, James C. McCroskey, and Virginia P. Richmond, "Communication Correlates of Perceived Machiavellianism of Supervisors: Communication Orientations and Outcomes," *Communication Quarterly* 54 (2006): 127–142.

Chapter 5

1. Alessandra Stanley, "The TV Watch: A No Cynicism Zone on Oprah's Network," *The New York Times*, January 2, 2011. http://artsbeat.blogs.nytimes.com/2011/01/02/the-tv-watch-a-no-cynicism-zone-on-oprahs-network/?src=twt&twt=artsbeat (accessed January 8, 2011).

2. Bernie Goldberg, "Opinion: Can Oprah Help Restore Civility?" *AOL News*, January 4, 2011. www.aolnews.com/2011/01/04/opinion-can-oprahs-own-network-help-restore-civility (accessed January 8, 2011).

3. Carina A. MacKenzie, "Oprah Winfrey on OWN: 'I Am Not in Love with Myself; I Am a Woman on Purpose,'" *Zap2it*, January 6, 2011. http://blog.zap2it.com/frominsidethebox/2011/01/oprah-winfrey-on-own-i-am-not-in-love-with-myself-i-am-a-woman-on-purpose.html (accessed January 8, 2011).

4. Nancy Colasurdo, "The Lost Art of Listening," *Fox Business*, September 20, 2010. www.foxbusiness.com/personal-finance/2010/09/20/lost-art-listening (accessed January 8, 2011).

5. Michael Josephson, "Listening: A Vital Dimension of Respect," *Character Counts*, September 9, 2009. http://charactercounts.org/michael/2009/09listening_a_vital_dimension_of_1.html (accessed September 9, 2009).

6. Harriette G. Lerner, "How to Be a Good Listener," in Karen M. Galvin and Pamela J. Cooper (eds.), *Making Connections: Readings in Relational Communication*, 3rd ed. New York: Oxford University Press, 2003, 130–131.

[7] Brant R. Burleson, "Comforting Messages: Features, Functions, and Outcomes," in John A. Daly and Mary Wiemann (eds.), *Strategic Interpersonal Communication*. Thousand Oaks, CA: Sage, 1994.

[8] Terrence L. Albrecht, Brant R. Burleson, and Donald Goldsmith, "Supportive Communication," in *Handbook of Interpersonal Communication*, 2nd ed. Thousand Oaks, CA: Sage, 2002, 419–449.

[9] John M. Gottman, James A. Coan, Sybil Carrere, and Catherine Swanson, "Predicting Marital Happiness and Stability from Newlywed Interactions," *Journal of Marriage and the Family* 60 (1998): 5–22. See also John M. Gottman, *Why Marriages Succeed or Fail*. New York: Simon & Schuster, 1994.

[10] Albrecht, Burleson, and Goldsmith. See also Wendy Samter, "Unsupportive Relationships: Deficiencies in the Support-Giving Skills of the Lonely Person's Friends," in Brant R. Burleson, Terence L. Albrecht, and Irwin G. Sarason (eds.), *The Communication of Social Support: Messages, Interactions, Relationships, and Community*. Thousand Oaks, CA: Sage, 1994, 195–214.

[11] Judi Brownell, *Listening: Attitudes, Principles, and Skills*, 2nd ed. Boston: Allyn & Bacon, 2002. See also "Listen and Make the Connection," *International Listening Association*, July 4, 2006. www.listen.org/Templates/try_new.htm (accessed July 31, 2006); and Gary Goldstein and Peter Fernald, "Humanistic Education in a Capstone Course," *College Teaching* 57, no. 1 (Winter 2009): 27–36.

[12] Jan Flynn, Tuula-Ritta Valikoski, and Jennie Grau, "Listening in the Business Context: Reviewing the State of Research," *The International Journal of Listening* 22 (2008): 141–151.

[13] Brownell.

[14] Kathryn Dindia and Bonnie L. Kennedy, *Communication in Everyday Life: A Descriptive Study Using Mobile Electronic Data Collection*. Paper presented at the National Communication Association convention, Chicago, 2004.

[15] Ibid. See also Laura A. Janusik and Andrew D. Wolvin, "24 Hours in a Day: A Listening Update to the Time Studies," *The International Journal of Listening* 23 (2009): 104–120.

[16] Dindia and Kennedy.

[17] Kate Crawford, "Following You: Disciplines of Listening in Social Media," *Journal of Media and Cultural Studies* 23, no. 4 (2009): 525–535.

[18] Paula T. Bartholome, "The Civility of Listening," *Listening Professional* 2, no. 1 (Summer 2003): 9.

[19] Josephson.

[20] Elizabeth Jean Nelson, "Response: Compassionate Listening and the 'Ethics for the New Millennium,'" *The International Journal of Listening* 24 (2010): 181–184.

[21] Stephen L. Carter, *Civility: Manners, Morals, and Etiquette of Democracy*. New York: Harper Perennial, 1999.

[22] Peter M. Forni, *Choosing Civility*. New York: St. Martin's Griffin, 2002.

[23] David Augsburger, *Caring Enough to Hear and Be Heard*. Ventura, CA: Regal Books, 1982.

[24] Susan Jacoby, "Talking to Ourselves," *Los Angeles Times*, April 20, 2008, M1, M10–11.

[25] Helene Gilbert, "Do Deaf People Listen?" in Shelley D. Lane (ed.), *Interpersonal Communication: Competence and Contexts*, 2nd ed. Boston: Pearson, 2010, 209.

[26] Andrew Wolvin and Carolyn Coakley, "A Survey of the Status of Listening Training in Some Fortune 500 Corporations," *Communication Education* 40 (1991): 152–164.

[27] Brownell.

[28] "Sound and Fury," PBS.org, 2003. www.pbs.org/wnet/soundandfury/film/video.html (accessed July 29, 2006). See also J. Desai, "Falling on Deaf Ears," *Science and Spirit Magazine*, 2002. www.science-spirit.org/article_detail.php?article_ed=467&pager=2 (accessed July 13, 2004).

[29] Scott Carlson, "The Net Generation Goes to College," *The Chronicle of Higher Education*, October 7, 2005. http://chronicle.com/article/The-Net-Generation-Goes-to/12307 (accessed December 17, 2009). See also Andrea McAlister, "Teaching the Millennial Generation," *American Music Teacher* 59, no. 1 (2009): 13–15.

[30] Clifford Nass, "Interview," *Digital Nation: Life on the Virtual Frontier*, PBS.org, February 2, 2010. www.pbs.org/wgbh/pages/frontline/digitalnation/interviews/nass.html (accessed February 4, 2010). See also Maggie Jackson, "Judgment of Molly's Gaze and Taylor's Watch," in Mark Bauerlein (ed.), *The Digital Divide*. New York: Jeremy P. Tarcher/Penguin, 2011, 271–294.

[31] Brownell.

[32] Ibid.

[33] L. Todd Thomas and Thomas R. Levine, "Disentangling Listening and Verbal Recall: Separate but Related Constructs?" *Human Communication Research* 21 (1994): 103–127.

[34] Robert N. Bostrom, "The Process of Listening," in Owen D. W. Hargie (ed.), *Handbook of Communication Skills*, 2nd ed. New York: Routledge, 1997, 236–258. See also Elmore R. Alexander, Larry E. Penley, and I. Edward Jernigan, "The Relationship of Basic Decoding Skills to Managerial Effectiveness," *Management Communication Quarterly* 6 (1992): 58–73.

[35] Brownell.

[36] Ibid.

[37] Don Gabor, *How to Start a Conversation and Make Friends*. New York: Fireside, 2001.

[38] Brownell.

[39] Shelley D. Lane and Simon M. Lane, "Empathic Communication Between Medical Personnel and Patients," *Journal of the American Podiatry Association* 72 (1982): 333–336.

[40] Wendy Samter, Brant R. Burleson, and Lori B. Murphy, "Comforting Conversations: The Effects of Strategy Type on Evaluations of Messages and Message Producers," *Southern Speech Communication Journal* 52 (1987): 263–284.

[41] Sharon A. Ratliff and D. D. Hudson, *Skill Building for Interpersonal Competence*. Austin, TX: Holt, Rinehart, & Winston, 1988.

[42] Joseph B. Walther and Shawn Boyd, "Attraction to Computer-Mediated Social Support," in Carolyn A. Lin and David J. Atkin (eds.), *Communication Technology and Society: Audience Adaptation and Uses*. Cresskill, NJ: Hampton Press, 2002, 153–188.

[43] Andrew F. Wood and Matthew J. Smith, *Online Communication: Linking Technology, Identity, and Culture*, 2nd ed. Mahwah, NJ: Lawrence Erlbaum, 2005. See also Andrew M. Ledbetter, *Sex Similarities and Differences in E-Mail Social Support: Competing Perspectives*. San Antonio, TX: National Communication Association, 2006.

[44] Brian Carroll and Katie Landry, "Logging On and Letting Out: Using Online Social Networks to Grieve and to Mourn," *Bulletin of Science, Technology, and Society* 30, no. 5 (2010): 341–349.

[45] Ibid.

[46] Jimmy Sanderson and Pauline Hope Cheong, "Tweeting Prayers and Communicating Grief Over Michael Jackson Online," *Bulletin of Science, Technology, and Society* 30, no. 5 (2010): 328–340.

[47] Carroll and Landry, 347.

[48] T. Dean Thomlinson, "Intercultural Listening," in Deborah Borisoff and Michael Purdy (eds.), *Listening in Everyday Life: A Personal and Professional Approach*. Lanham, MD: University Press of America, 1991, 87–137.

[49] Michael W. Purdy, "Listening, Culture and Structures of Consciousness: Ways of Studying Listening," *The International Journal of Listening* 14 (2000): 47–68.

⁵⁰Richard D. Lewis, *When Cultures Collide: Managing Successfully Across Cultures*. Boston: Intercultural Press, 1999.

⁵¹Rod L. Troester and Cathy S. Mester, *Civility in Business and Professional Communication*. New York: Peter Lang, 2007.

⁵²Jerry L. Winsor, Dan B. Curtis, and Ron D. Stephens, "National Preferences in Business and Communication Education: Survey Update," *Journal of the Association for Communication Administration* 3 (1997): 170–179. See also Jan Flynn, Tuula-Riitta Valikoski, and Jennie Grau, "Listening in the Business Context: Reviewing the State of Research," *The International Journal of Listening* 22 (2008): 141–151.

⁵³Wolvin and Coakley.

⁵⁴Brownell.

⁵⁵Ibid.

⁵⁶Ibid, p. 311.

⁵⁷Ibid.

⁵⁸Beverly Sypher, Robert Bostrom, and Joy Seibert, "Listening, Communication Abilities, and Success at Work," *Journal of Business Communication* 26 (1989): 293-303.

⁵⁹Cheryl Hamilton, *Communicating for Results: A Guide for Business and the Professions*, 7th ed. Belmont, CA: Wadsworth, 2005. See also Charles Conrad and Marshall S. Poole, *Strategic Organizational Communication: Into the Twenty-First Century*, 5th ed. Orlando, FL: Harcourt Brace, 2002; and Beverly D. Sypher and Theodore E. Zorn, "Communication-Related Abilities and Upward Mobility: A Longitudinal Investigation," *Human Communication Research* 12 (1986): 420-431.

⁶⁰Peggy Klaus, *The Hard Truth About Soft Skills: Workplace Lesson Smart People Wish They'd Learned Sooner*. New York: HarperCollins, 2008.

⁶¹Deborah Borisoff and Lisa Merrill, "Gender Issues and Listening," in Deborah Borisoff and Michael Purdy (eds.), *Listening in Everyday Life: A Personal and Professional Approach*. Lanham, MD: University Press of America, 1991, 59-85.

⁶²Daniel N. Maltz and Ruth B. Borker, "A Cultural Approach to Male-Female Miscommunication," in John Gumperz (ed.), *Language and Social Identity*. New York: Cambridge University Press, 1982, 196-216.

⁶³Deborah Tannen, *You Just Don't Understand: Women and Men in Conversation*. New York: William Morrow, 1990.

⁶⁴Daena J. Goldsmith and Patricia A. Fulfs, "You Just Don't Have the Evidence: An Analysis of Claims and Evidence in Deborah Tannen's 'You Just Don't Understand,'" in Michael E. Roloff (ed.), *Communication Yearbook 22*. Thousand Oaks, CA: Sage, 1999, 1-49.

⁶⁵Graham D. Bodie, "Evaluating Listening Theory: Development and Illustration of Five Criteria," *International Journal of Listening* 23 (2009): 81-103.

Chapter 6

¹Nigel Farndale, "Kate Hudson Interview: Goldie's Girl on Scrabble, Nepotism, and her Shocking New Film," *The Telegraph*, May 17, 2010. www.telegraph.co.uk/culture/film/starsandstories/7723869/Kate-Hudson-interview-html (accessed June 23, 2011).

²Todd Plitt and Donna Freydkin, "Kate Hudson's Family Ties," *USA Today*, May 24, 2004. www.usatoday.com/life/people/2004-05-24-kate-hudson_x.htm# (accessed June 23, 2011).

³Carolyn Robertson, "Kate Hudson's Big, Happy Family," *Celebrity BabyScoop*, March 19, 2011. http://celebritybabyscoop.com/2011/03/19/kate-hudsons-big-happy-family (accessed June 23, 2011).

⁴"Kate Hudson and Matt Bellamy Name Their Baby Son [Poll]," *The Los Angeles Times*. July 14, 2011. http://latimesblogs.latimes.com/gossip/2011/07/kate-hudson-baby-name-bingham-hawn-bellamy-bing.html (accessed July 30, 2001).

⁵"Kate Hudson Talks About Her Unconventional Family and Happiness," *Babble: For a New Generation of Parents*, April 13, 2011. http://blogs.babble.com/famecrawler/2011/04/13/kate-hudson-talks-about-her-unconventional-family-and-happiness/ (accessed June 23, 2011).

⁶Cynthia L. Pickett, Wendi L. Gardner, and Megan Knowles, "Getting a Clue: The Need to Belong and Enhanced Sensitivity to Social Cues," *Personality and Social Psychology Bulletin* 30 (2004): 1096-1097.

⁷Roy F. Baumeister and Mark R. Leary, "The Need to Belong: Desire for Interpersonal Attachments as a Fundamental Human Motivation," *Psychological Bulletin* 117 (1995): 497-529.

⁸Malcolm Parks, "Personal Relationships and Health," in John Stewart (ed.), *Bridges Not Walls, A Book About Interpersonal Communication*, 11th ed. New York: McGraw-Hill, 2012, 42-52.

⁹William K. Rawlins, *Friendship Matters: Communication, Dialectics, and the Life Course*. New York: Aldine de Gruyer, 1992.

¹⁰James S. House, Kenneth R. Landis, and Debra Umberson, "Social Relationships and Health," *Science* 241 (1988): 540-545.

¹¹Chris Segrin and Stacey A. Passalacqua, "Functions of Loneliness, Social Support, Health Behaviors, and Stress in Association with Poor Health," *Health Communication* 25, no. 4 (2010): 312-322.

¹²Marianne Helsen, Wilma Vollebergh, and Wim Meeus, "Social Support from Parents and Friends and Emotional Problems in Adolescence," *Journal of Youth and Adolescence* 29 (2000): 319-335.

¹³Ed Diener and Martin E. P. Seligman, "Very Happy People," *Psychological Science* 13 (2002): 81-84.

¹⁴Steve Duck, *Understanding Relationships*. New York: Guilford Press, 1991. See also Shelley Taylor, *The Tending Instinct: Women, Men, and the Biology of Our Relationships*. New York: Times Books, 2002; and Colin T. C. Hargie and Dennis Tourish, "Relational Communication," in Owen D. W. Hargie (ed.), *The Handbook of Communication Skills*, 2nd ed. New York: Routledge, 1997, 359-382.

¹⁵Julia Wood, *Relational Communication: Continuity and Change in Personal Relationships*. Belmont, CA: Wadsworth, 1995.

¹⁶John Stewart, "Communicating and Interpersonal Communicating," in John Stewart (ed.), *Bridges Not Walls: A Book About Interpersonal Communication*, 11th ed. New York: McGraw-Hill, 2012, 14-41.

¹⁷Kathleen M. Galvin, Carma L. Bylund, and Bernard J. Brommel, *Family Communication: Cohesion and Change*, 6th ed. Boston: Pearson, 2004, 6.

¹⁸Dawn O. Braithwaite, Betsy W. Back, Leslie A. Baxter, Rebecca DiVerniero, Joshua R. Hammonds, Angela M. Hosek, Erin K. Willer, and Bianca M. Wolf, "Constructing Family: A Typology of Voluntary Kin," *Journal of Social and Personal Relationships* 27 (2010): 388-407.

¹⁹"Statistics—Living Together," *Alternatives to Marriage Project*, 2010. www.unmarried.org/statistics.html#living-together (accessed July 30, 2011).

²⁰Timothy W. Grail, "Custodial Mothers and Fathers and Their Child Support," *U.S. Census Bureau*, November 2009. www.census.gov/prod/2009pubs/p60-237.pdf (accessed July 30, 2011).

²¹Harriett Lerner, *The Dance of Anger*. New York: Quill, 2001.

²²Elaine Hatfield and Richard L. Rapson, "Love and Attachment Processes," in Michael Lewis and Jeannette M. Haviland-Jones (eds.), *Handbook of Emotions*, 2nd ed. New York: Guilford Press, 2004, 654-662.

²³Susan Sprecher and Diane Felmlee, "The Influence of Parents and Friends on the Quality and Stability of Romantic Relationships: A

Three-Wave Longitudinal Investigation," *Journal of Marriage and the Family* 54 (1992): 888–900.

[24]Kathleen M. Galvin and Pamela J. Cooper, "Friends," In Kathleen M. Galvin and Pamela J. Cooper (eds.), *Making Connections: Readings in Relational Communication*, 4th ed. New York: Oxford University Press, 2006, 327–328.

[25]Janet Yerby, Nancy Buerkel-Rothfuss, and Arthur P. Bochner, *Understanding Family Communication*, 2nd ed. Boston: Allyn & Bacon, 1990.

[26]Virginia Satir, "The Rules You Live By," in Kathleen M. Galvin and Pamela J. Cooper (eds.), *Making Connections: Readings in Relational Communication*, 3rd ed. New York: Oxford University Press, CA: Roxbury, 2003, 199–205.

[27]Elizabeth Stone, *Black Sheep and Kissing Cousins: How Our Family Stories Shape Us*. New York: Transaction Publishers, 2004.

[28]Beverley Fehr, "The Life Cycle of Friendship," in Clyde Hendrick and Susan S. Hendrick (eds.), *Close Relationships: A Sourcebook*. Thousand Oaks, CA: Sage, 2000, 71–82.

[29]Beverley Fehr, *Friendship Processes*. Thousand Oaks, CA: Sage, 1996. See also Rebecca G. Adams and Graham Allan, "Contextualising Friendship," in Rebecca G. Adams and Graham Allan (eds.), *Placing Friendship in Context*. Cambridge, UK: Cambridge University Press, 1999, 1–17.

[30]Steve W. Duck, *Meaningful Relationships*. Thousand Oaks, CA: Sage, 1994. See also Peter M. Nardi and Drury Sherrod, "Friendship in the Lives of Gay Men and Lesbians," *Journal of Social and Personal Relationships* 11 (1994): 185–199.

[31]Mchael Argyle and Monika Henderson, "The Rules of Friendship," *Journal of Social and Personal Relationships* 1 (1984): 211–237. See also Marianne Dainton, Elaine Zelley, and Emily Langan, "Maintaining Friendships Throughout the Lifespan," In Marianne Dainton and Daniel J. Canary (eds.), *Maintaining Relationships through Communication: Relational, Contextual, and Cultural Variations*. Mahwah, NJ: Lawrence Erlbaum, 2003, 79–102.

[32]Amanda Lenhart, Kristen Purcell, Aaron Smith, and Kathryn Zickuhr, "Social Media and Mobile Internet Use Among Teens and Young Adults," *Pew Internet & American Life Project*, February 2, 2010. www.pewinternet.org/~/media/Files/Reports/2010/PIP_Social_Media_and_Young_Adults_Report_Final_with_toplines.pdf (accessed April 3, 2010).

[33]D. Olanoff, "Facebook Announces Monthly Active Users Were at 1.01 Billion as of September 30th, an Increase of 26% Year-over-Year," *Tech Crunch*, October 23, 2012. http://techcrunch.com/2012/10/23/facebook-announces-monthly-active-users-were-at-1-01-billion-as-of-september-30th/ (accessed November 12, 2012).

[34]William Deresiesicz, "Faux Friendship," *The Chronicle of Higher Education*, December 6, 2009. http://chronicle.com/article/Faux-Friendship/49308/ (accessed December 7, 2009).

[35]Judith Donath, "Signals in Social Supernets," *Journal of Computer-Mediated Communication*, 13 (2007): article 12. http://jcmc.indiana.edu/vol13/issue1/donath/html (accessed July 30, 2011). See also Danah Boyd, "Friends, Friendsters, and Top 8: Writing Community into Being on Social Network Sites," *First Monday* 11 (2006). http://firstmonday.org/issues/issue11_12/boyd/index.html (accessed July 30, 2011).

[36]Donath.

[37]Keith N. Hampton, Lauren Sessions Goulet, Lee Ranie, and Kristen Purcell, "Social Networking Sites and Our Lives," *Pew Internet and American Life Project*, June 16, 2011. http://pewinternet.org/Reports/2011/Technology-and-social-networks.aspx (accessed June 16, 2011).

[38]Naeemah Clark, Shu-Yueh Lee, and Lori Boyer, *A Place of Their Own: An Exploratory Study of College Students' Uses of Facebook*, Presented at the International Communication Association convention, San Francisco, CA, May 24, 2007. www.allacademic.com/meta/p172779_index.html (accessed April 3, 2010).

[39]Clark et al. See also di Corinna Gennaro and William H. Dutton, "Reconfiguring Friendships: Social Relationships and the Internet," *Information, Communication, and Society* 10 (2007): 591–618 and Carlyne L. Kujath, "Facebook and MySpace: Complement or Substitute for Face-to-Face Interaction?" *CyberPsychology, Behavior, and Social Media* 14, nos. 1–2 (2011): 75–78.

[40]Aaron Smith, "Why Americans Use Social Media: Social Networking Sites Are Appealing as a Way to Maintain Contact with Close Ties and Reconnect with Old Friends," *PEW Internet and American Life Project*, November 14, 2011. www.pewinternet.org/Reports/2011/Why-Americans-Use-Social-Media.aspx (accessed November 14, 2011).

[41]Hampton et al.

[42]Ibid.

[43]Myron W. Lustig and Jolene Koester, *Intercultural Competence: Interpersonal Communication Across Cutures*, 6th ed. Boston: Allyn & Bacon, 2010.

[44]Judith N. Martin and Thomas K. Nakayama, *Intercultural Communication in Contexts*, 3rd ed. New York: McGraw-Hill, 2004.

[45]Mary Jane Collier, "Communication Competence Problematics in Ethnic Friendships," *Communication Monographs* 63 (1996): 314–346. See also Stanley O. Gaines, "Relationships Between Members of Cultural Minorities," in Julia. T. Wood and Steve Duck (eds.), *Under-Studied Relationships: Off the Beaten Track*. Thousand Oaks, CA: Sage, 1995, 51–88.

[46]Michelle Huston and Pepper Schwartz, "The Relationships of Lesbians and of Gay Men," in Julia. T. Wood and Steve Duck (eds.), *Under-Studied Relationships: Off the Beaten Track*. Thousand Oaks, CA: Sage, 1995, 89–121 and Gust A. Yep, Karen E. Lovaas, and John P. Elia, "A Critical Appraisal of Assimilationist and Radical Ideologies Underlying Same-Sex Marriage in LGBT Communities in the United States," *Journal of Homosexuality* 45 (2003): 45–64.

[47]Jeffrey A. Hall, "Sex Differences in Friendship Expectations: A Meta-Analysis," *Journal of Social and Personal Relationships* 28, no. 6 (2011): 723–747.

[48]Julia T. Wood and C. C. Inman, "In a Different Mode: Masculine Styles of Communicating Closeness," *Journal of Applied Communication* 21 (1993): 279–295.

[49]Malcolm Parks, *Personal Relationships and Personal Networks*. Mahwah, NJ: Lawrence Erlbaum, 2007. See also Erina L. MacGeorge, Angela R. Graves, Bo Feng, Seth J. Gillihan, and Brant R. Burleson, "The Myth of Gender Cultures: Similarities Outweigh Differences in Men's and Women's Provision of and Responses to Supportive Communication," *Sex Roles* 50 (2004): 143–175.

[50]Hatfield and Rapson.

[51]Sprecher and Felmlee.

[52]Martin Gross, "AP/Ipsos Poll: The Decline of American Civilization, or at Least Its Manners," *Ipsos*, October 14, 2005. www.ipsos-na.com/news/pressrelease.cfm?id=2827 (accessed October 14, 2005). See also "American Manners Poll: The Associated Press-Ipsos Poll on Public Attitudes About Rudeness," USATODAY.com, October 14, 2005. www.usatoday.com/news/nation/2005-10-14-rudeness-poll-method_x.htm (accessed January 28, 2006).

[53]Sven Wahloss, *Family Communication*. Boston: Macmillan, 1983.

[54]Laura Stafford and Marianne Dainton, "The Dark Side of 'Normal' Family Interaction," in William R. Cupach and Brian R. Spitzberg

(eds.), *The Dark Side of Interpersonal Communication.* Mahwah, NJ: Lawrence Erlbaum, 1994, 259–280.

[55]"American Manners Poll: The Associated Press-Ipsos Poll on Public Attitudes About Rudeness." See also "The Decline of Manners in the U.S.," CNN.com, October 14, 2005. www.cnn.com/2005/US/10/14/poll.rude.ap/index.html (accessed October 14, 2005).

[56]"1.5 Million Homeschooled Students in the United States in 2007," National Center for Education Statistics. Institute of Education Sciences, U.W. Department of Education, NCES 2009-030, December 2008. http://nces.ed.gov/pubs2009/2009030.pdf (accessed August 21, 2010). See also "American Manners Poll: The Associated Press-Ipsos Poll on Public Attitudes About Rudeness."

[57]Stephen L. Carter, *Civility: Manners, Morals, and the Etiquette of Democracy.* New York: HarperPerennial, 1998.

[58]John Cloud, "Sex and the Law," *Time*, March 23, 1998, 48–54.

[59]William K. Rawlins, *Friendship Matters: Communication, Dialectics, and the Life Course.* New York: Aldine de Gruyter, 1992.

[60]Patricia M. Sias and Daniel J. Cahill, "From Co-worker to Friends: The Development of Peer Friendships in the Workplace," *Western Journal of Communication* 62 (1998): 273–300. See also Stephen R. Marks, "Intimacy in the Public Realm: The Case of Coworkers," *Social Forces* 71 (1994): 843–858.

[61]Christine Pearson, Lynn M. Andersson, and Christine Porath, "Assessing and Attacking Workplace Incivility," *Organizational Dynamics* 29 (2000): 123–137. See also Christine Pearson and Christine Porath, *The Cost of Bad Behavior: How Incivility Is Damaging Your Business and What to Do About It.* New York: Portfolio, 2009.

[62]Pearson and Porath.

[63]Patrica M. Sias, Kathleen J. Krone, and Frederic M. Jablin, "An Ecological Systems Perspective on Workplace Relationships," in Mark L. Knapp and John A. Daly (eds.), *Handbook of Interpersonal Communication*, 3rd ed. Thousand Oaks, CA: Sage, 2002, 615–642.

[64]Robert L. Heath and Jennings Bryant, *Human Communication Theory and Research: Concepts, Contexts, and Challenges*, 2nd ed. Mahwah, NJ: Lawrence Erlbaum, 2000.

[65]Alan Feingold, "Gender Differences in Effects of Physical Attractiveness on Romantic Attraction: A Comparison across Five Research Paradigms," *Journal of Personality and Social Psychology* 59 (1990): 981–993.

[66]Frances E. Aboud and Morton J. Mendelson, "Determinants of Friendship Selection and Quality: Developmental Perspectives," in William M. Bukowski, Andrew F. Newcomb, and William W. Hartup (eds.), *The Company They Keep: Friendship in Childhood and Adolescence.* New York: Cambridge University Press, 1998, 87–112.

[67]Marjoijn L. Antheunis, Patti M. Valkenburg, and Jochen Peter, "Computer-Mediated Communication and Interpersonal Attraction: An Experimental Test of Two Explanatory Hypotheses," *CyberPsychology and Behavior* 10 (2007): 831–835.

[68]Kathryn A. Urberg, Serdar M. Degirmencioglu, and Jerry M. Tolson, "Adolescent Friendship Selection and Termination: The Role of Similarity," *Journal of Social and Personal Relationships* 15 (1998): 703–710. See also Donn Byrne, "An Overview (and Underview) of Research and Theory Within the Attraction Paradigm," *Journal of Social and Personal Relationships* 14 (1997): 417–431.

[69]Steven Nowicki and Susan Manheim, "Interpersonal Complementarity and Time of Interaction in Female Relationships," *Journal of Research in Personality* 25 (1991): 322–333 and Robert A. Neinmeyer and Kelly A. Mitchell, "Similarity and Attraction: A Longitudinal Study," *Journal of Social and Personal Relationships* 5 (1988): 131–148.

[70]Sharon S. Brehm, Rowland S. Miller, Daniel Perlman, and Susan M. Campbell, *Intimate Relationships*, 3rd ed. New York: McGraw-Hill, 2001. See also Leon Festinger, Stanley Schachter, and Kurt W. Back, *Social Pressures in Informal Groups: A Study of Human Factors in Housing.* Stanford, CA: Stanford University Press, 1963.

[71]Malcolm Parks and Kory Floyd, "Making Friends in Cyberspace," *Journal of Communication* 46 (1996): 80–97.

[72]Jochen Peter, Patti M. Valkenburg, and Alexander P. Schouten, "Developing a Model of Adolescent Friendship Formation on the Internet," *CyberPsychology and Behavior* 8, no. 5 (2005): 423–430.

[73]Helena Cole and Mark D. Griffiths, "Social Interactions in Massively Multiplayer Online Role-Playing Gamers," *CyberPsychology and Behavior* 10 (2007): 575–583.

[74]Charles R. Berger and Richard J. Calabrese, "Some Explorations in Initial Interaction and Beyond: Toward a Developmental Theory of Interpersonal Communication," *Human Communication Research* 1 (1975): 99–112.

[75]John F. Cragan and Donald C. Shields, *Understanding Communication Theory: The Communicative Forces for Human Action.* Boston: Allyn & Bacon, 1998.

[76]Berger and Calabrese.

[77]Charles R. Berger, "Communicating Under Uncertainty," in Michael E. Roloff and Gerald R. Miller (eds.), *Interpersonal Processes: New Directions in Communication Research.* Thousand Oaks, CA: Sage, 1987, 39–62.

[78]Lesa A. Stern and Kim Taylor, "Social Networking on Facebook," *North Dakota Journal of Speech and Theater* 20 (2007): 9–20.

[79]Paul Watzlawick, Janet Beavin, and Dan Jackson, *Pragmatics of Human Communication: A Study of Interpersonal Patterns, Pathologies, and Paradoxes.* New York: Norton, 1967.

[80]Deborah Tannen, *You Just Don't Understand: Women and Men in Conversation.* New York: Harper Paperbacks, 2001.

[81]Ibid.

[82]Ibid.

[83]Matt Richtel, "Using Their Cellphones to Dial Up Deception: Through Networks, Liars Find Strangers to Support Their Ruses," *Dallas Morning News*, June 26, 2004, 15A.

Chapter 7

[1]Scott Jackson, "Jack White and Karen Elson Throw Divorce Party," *LiveMusicGuide*, June 12, 2011. www.livemusicguide.com/blog/music-news/jack-white-and-karen-elson-throw-divorce-party.html (accessed July 17, 2011).

[2]Elizabeth Yun, "Jack White and Karen Elson Celebrate Their Divorce," *PopEater*, June 10, 2011. www.popeater.com/2011/06/10/jack-white-karen-elson-celebrate-divorce/ (accessed July 17, 2011).

[3]Jane Greer, "Jack White: Is There a Good Divorce?" *The Huffington Post*, June 16, 2011. www.huffingtonpost.com/dr-jane-greer/jack-white-is-there-a-goo_b_878405.html (accessed July 17, 2011).

[4]Jackson.

[5]Greer.

[6]Kristina Orth-Gomér, Sarah P. Wamala, Myriam Horsten, Karin Schenck-Gustafsson, Neil Schneiderman, and Murray A. Mittleman, "Marital Stress Worsens Prognosis in Women with Coronary Heart Disease: The Stockholm Female Coronary Risk Study," *Journal of the American Medical Association* 284, no. 23 (2000): 3008–3014. See also Salim Yusuf, Steven Hawken, Stephanie Ôunpuu, Tony Dans, Alvaro Avezum, Fernando Lanas, Matthew McQueen, Andrzej Budaj, Prem Pais, John Varigos, and Liu Lisheng, "Effect of Potentially Modifiable Risk Factors Associated with Myocardial Infarction in 52 Countries (the INTERHEART Study): Case-Controlled Study," *The Lancet* 364, no. 9438 (2004): 953–962.

[7] Malcolm Parks, "Personal Relationships and Health," in John Stewart (ed.), *Bridges Not Walls, A Book About Interpersonal Communication*, 11th ed. New York: McGraw-Hill, 2012, 42–52.

[8] Howard B. Kaplan, "Social Psychology of the Immune System: A Conceptual Framework and Review of the Literature," *Social Science and Medicine* 33 (1991): 909–923.

[9] Robert M. Kaplan and Richard G. Kronick, "Marital Status and Longevity in the United States Population," *Journal of Epidemiology and Community Health* 60 (2006): 760–765. See also Lamberto Manzoli, Paolo Villari, Giovanni M Pirone, and Antonio Boccia, "Marital Status and Mortality in the Elderly: A Systematic Review and Meta-Analysis," *Social Science and Medicine* 64, no. 1 (2007): 77–94 and Sally Macintyre, "The Effects of Family Position and Status on Health," *Social Science and Medicine* 35, no. 4 (1992): 453–464.

[10] Steven J. Stack, "New Micro-Level Data on the Impact of Divorce on Suicide, 1959–1980: A Test of Two Theories," *Journal of Marriage and the Family* 52 (1990): 119–127.

[11] David Popenoe, *The State of Our Unions: The Social Health of Marriage in America*. Piscataway, NJ: National Marriage Project, 2007.

[12] Hyoun K. Kim and Patrick C. McKenry, "The Relationship Between Marriage and Psychological Well-Being," *Journal of Family Issues* 23, no. 8 (2002): 885–911. See also Kathleen A. Lamb, Gary R. Lee, and Alfred DeMaris, "Union Formation and Depression: Selection and Relationships Effects," *Journal of Marriage and the Family* 65 (2003): 953–962.

[13] D. Eugene Mead, "Marital Distress, Co-Occurring Depression, and Marital Therapy: A Review," *Journal of Marital and Family Therapy* 28, no. 3 (2002): 299–314.

[14] Daniel Perlman and Beverly Fehr, "The Development of Intimate Relationships," In Daniel Perlman and Steve Duck (eds.), *Intimate Relationships*. Thousand Oaks, CA: Sage, 1987, 13–42.

[15] Roy F. Baumeister and Mark R. Leary, "The Need to Belong: Desire for Interpersonal Attachments as a Fundamental Human Motivation," *Psychological Bulletin* 117 (1995): 497–529.

[16] Mark T. Schaefer and David H. Olsen, "Assessing Intimacy: The PAIR Inventory," *Journal of Marital and Family Therapy* 7, no. 1 (1981): 47–60.

[18] Laura K. Guerrero, Peter A. Andersen, and Walid A. Afifi, *Close Encounters: Communication in Relationships*, 2nd. ed. Thousand Oaks, CA: Sage, 2007.

[19] Walid A. Afifi and Sandra L. Faulkner, "On Being 'Just Friends': The Frequency and Impact of Sexual Activity in Cross-Sex Friendships," *Journal of Social and Personal Relationships* 17 (2000): 205–222.

[20] Kathy J. Werking, *We're Just Good Friends: Women and Men in Non-romantic Relationships*. New York: Guildford, 1997. See also Afifi and Faulkner.

[21] Julia T. Wood, *Gendered Lives: Communication, Gender, and Culture*. Belmont, CA: Wadsworth, 1994.

[22] Myron W. Lustig and Jolene Koester, *Intercultural Communication: Interpersonal Communication across Cultures*, 6th ed. Boston: Allyn & Bacon, 2010. See also Judith N. Martin and Thomas K. Nakayama, *Intercultural Communication in Contexts*, 3rd ed. New York: McGraw-Hill, 2004.

[23] Ling Chen, "Communication in Intercultural Relationships," in William B. Gudykunst and Bella Moody (eds.), *Handbook of International and Intercultural Communication*, 2nd ed. Thousand Oaks, CA: Sage, 2001, 241–258.

[24] Ibid.

[25] David H. Demo, "Children's Experience of Family Diversity," *National Forum* 80 (2000): 16. See also Michelle Huston and Pepper Schwartz, "The Relationships of Lesbians and of Gay Men," in Julia T. Wood and Steven Duck (eds.), *Under-Studied Relationships: Off the Beaten Track*. Thousand Oaks, CA: Sage, 1995, 89–121; and Gust A. Yep, Karen E. Lovaas, and John P. Elia, "A Critical Appraisal of Assimilationist and Radical Ideologies Underlying Same-Sex Marriage in LGBT Communities in the United States," *Journal of Homosexuality* 45 (2003): 45–64.

[26] Charles A. Pierce and Herman Aguinis, "A Framework for Investigating the Link Between Workplace Romance and Sexual Harassment," *Group and Organization Management* 26 (2001): 206–229.

[27] Sean M. Horan and Rebecca M. Chory, "When Work and Love Mix: Perceptions of Peers in Workplace Romances," *Western Journal of Communication* 73 (2009): 349–369.

[28] Shelly Hovick, Renee A. Myers, and C. Erik Timmerman, "E-mail Communication in Workplace Romantic Relationships," *Communication Studies* 54 (2003): 468–480.

[29] Terrance L. Albrecht and Betsey W. Bach, *Communication in Complex Organizations: A Relational Approach*. Fort Worth, TX: Harcourt Brace, 1997.

[30] Horan and Chory.

[31] James Dillard, "Close Relationships at Work: Perceptions of the Motives and Performance of Relational Participants," *Journal of Social and Personal Relationships* 4 (1987): 179–193.

[32] Gerri Willis, "Managing an Office Romance," CNNMoney.com, February 9, 2006. http://money.cnn.com/2006/02/08/pf/saving/willis_tips/index.htm (accessed February 9, 2006).

[33] A. L. Sillars and William W. Wilmot, "Marital Communication Across the Life-Span," in Jon F. Nussbaum (ed.), *Life-Span Communication: Normative Processes*. Mahwah, NJ: Lawrence Erlbaum, 1989.

[34] Elizabeth B. Robey, Daniel J. Canary, and Cynthia S. Burggraf, "Conversational Maintenance Behaviors of Husbands and Wives: An Observational Analysis, in Daniel J. Canary and Kathryn Dindia (eds.), *Sex Differences and Similarities in Communication*. Mahwah, NJ: Lawrence Erlbaum, 1998, 373–392.

[35] Daniel J. Canary, William R. Cupach, and Susan J. Messman, *Relationship Conflict: Conflict in Parent–Child, Friendship, and Romantic Relationships*. Thousand Oaks, CA: Sage, 1995.

[36] Carolyn E. Cutrona and Julie A. Suhr, "Social Support Communication in the Context of Marriage: An Analysis of Couples' Supportive Interactions," in Brant R. Burleson, Terrance L. Albrecht, and Irwin G. Sarason (eds.), *The Communication of Social Support: Messages, Interactions, Relationships, and Community*. Thousand Oaks, CA: Sage, 1994, 113–135. See also Erich Kirchler, "Marital Happiness and Interaction in Everyday Surroundings: A Time-Sample Diary Approach for Couples," *Journal of Social and Personal Relationships* 3 (1988): 375–382.

[37] Laura Stafford and Daniel J. Canary, "Maintenance Strategies and Romantic Relationship Type, Gender, and Relational Characteristics," *Journal of Social and Personal Relationships* 8 (1991): 217–242.

[38] Kathryn Greene, Valerian J. Derlega, and Alicia Matthews, "Self-Disclosure in Personal Relationships," in Anita L. Vangelisti and Daniel Perlman (eds.), *The Cambridge Handbook of Personal Relationships*. Boston: Cambridge University Press, 2006, 409–427.

[39] Ibid.

[40] Namkee Park, Borae Jin, and Seung-A. Annie Jin, "Effects of Self-Disclosure on Relational Intimacy in Facebook," *Computers in Human Behavior* 27 (2011): 1974–1983.

[41] Greene et al.

[42] Harry T. Reis and Philip Shaver, "Intimacy as an Interpersonal Process," in Steve W. Duck (ed.), *Handbook of Personal Relationships: Theory, Research, and Interventions*. Chichester, UK: Wiley, 376–389.

[43] Irwin Altman and Dalmas Taylor, *Social Penetration: The Development of Interpersonal Relationships*. New York: Holt, Rinehart, & Winston, 1973.

[44] Wood and Duck.

[45] Steve Duck, *Meaningful Relationships: Talking, Sense, and Relating*. Thousand Oaks, CA: Sage, 1994.

[46] Mark L. Knapp and Anita L. Vangelisti, *Interpersonal Communication in Human Relationships*, 5th ed. Boston: Allyn & Bacon, 2005.

[47] Tamar Nordenberg, "Pick-up Lines That Work... or Will They?" *Discovery Health*, December 4, 2005. http://health.discovery.com/centers/loverelationships/articles/pickuplines.html (accessed December 5, 2005).

[48] Steven Duck, "The Essential Nature of Talk," in Karen M. Galvin and Pamela J. Cooper (eds.), *Making Connections: Readings in Relational Communication*, 2nd ed. New York: Oxford University Press, 2000, 147–152.

[49] Andrew M. Ledbetter, "Assessing the Measurement of Invariance of Relational Maintenance Behavior When Face-to-Face and Online," *Communication Research Reports* 27 (2010): 30–37.

[50] Laura Stafford and Daniel J. Canary, "Maintenance Strategies and Romantic Relationship Type, Gender, and Relational Characteristics," *Journal of Social and Personal Relationships* 8 (1991): 217–242.

[51] Marshall B. Rosenberg, *Nonviolent Communication: A Language of Compassion*. Encinitas, CA: PuddleDancer Press, 2001.

[52] John A. Bargh and Katelyn Y. McKenna, "The Internet and Social Life," *Annual Review of Psychology* 55 (2004): 573–590.

[53] Helena Cole and Mark D. Griffiths, "Social Interactions in Massively Multiplayer Online Role-Playing Gamers," *CyberPsychology and Behavior* 10 (2007): 575–583.

[54] Artemio Ramirez and Kathy Broneck, "'IM Me': Instant Messaging as Relational Maintenance and Everyday Communication," *Journal of Social and Personal Relationships* 26 (2009): 292–314.

[55] Borae Jin and Jorge F. Pena, "Mobile Communication in Romantic Relationships: Mobile Phone Use, Relational Uncertainty, Love, Commitment, and Attachment Styles," *Communication Reports* 1 (2010): 39–51.

[56] Jeffrey Boase, John B. Horrigan, Barry Wellman, and Lee Raine, *The Strength of Internet Ties*. Washington, DC: Pew Internet & American Life Project, 2006.

[57] Alan Garner, *Conversationally Speaking*, 3rd ed. Los Angeles: Lowell House, 1997. See also Daniel J. Canary and Laura Stafford, "Preservation of Relational Characteristics: Maintenance Strategies, Equity, and Locus of Control," in Pamela J. Kalbfleisch (ed.), *Interpersonal Communication: Evolving Interpersonal Relationships*. New York: Psychology Press, 1993, 237–259.

[58] Anne L. Weber, "Losing, Leaving, and Letting Go: Coping with Nonmarital Breakups," in Brian H. Spitzberg and William R. Cupach (eds.), *The Dark Side of Close Relationships*. Mahwah, NJ: Lawrence Erlbaum, 1998, 267–306.

[59] Leslie A. Baxter, "Trajectories of Relationship Disengagement," *Journal of Social and Personal Relationships* 1 (1984): 29–48.

[60] Leslie A. Baxter, "Strategies for Ending Relationships: Two Studies," *Western Journal of Speech Communication* 46 (1982): 223–241.

[61] Fran Dickson and Travis Cross, *Challenges Managing Facebook's Relationship Status Indicator*. Paper presented at the annual conference of the National Communication Association, New Orleans, LA, 2011.

[62] Jennifer Bevan, Jeanette Pfyle, Michelle Kermeni, William Miller, Brett Barclay, James Fearns, and Shea Ledetter, *Emotional and Cognitive Responses to Being Defriended on Facebook: An Exploratory Study*. Paper presented at the annual conference of the National Communication Association, New Orleans, LA, 2011.

[63] Leslie A. Baxter, "The Social Side of Personal Relationships: A Dialectical Perspective," in Steve Duck (ed.), *Understanding Relationship Processes: 3. Social Context and Relationships*. Thousand Oaks, CA: Sage, 1993, 139–165.

[64] Leslie A. Baxter, "Dialectical Contradictions in Relationship Development," *Journal of Social and Personal Relationships* 7 (1990): 69–88.

[65] Ruben C. Gur, Bruce I. Turetsky, Mie Matsui, Michelle Yan, Warren Bilker, Paul Hughett, and Raquel E. Gur, "Sex Differences in Brain Gray and White Matter in Healthy Young Adults: Correlations with Cognitive Performance," *Journal of Neuroscience* 19 (1999): 4065–4072. See also Helen Fisher, *The First Sex: The Natural Talents of Women and How They Are Changing the World*. New York: Ballantine Books, 1999 and Michael Gurian, *What Could He Be Thinking? How a Man's Mind Really Works*. New York: St. Martin's Press, 2003.

[66] Harry Weger, "Disconfirming Communication and Self-Verification in Marriage: Associations among the Demand/Withdraw Interaction Pattern, Feeling Understood, and Marital Satisfaction," *Journal of Social and Personal Relationship* 22 (2005): 19–31.

[67] John M. Gottman, *Why Marriages Succeed or Fail*. New York: Simon & Schuster, 1994. See also John M. Gottman and Nan Silver, *The Seven Principles for Making Marriage Work*. New York: Crown Publishers, 1999 and John M. Gottman, *What Predicts Divorce?* Mahwah, NJ: Lawrence Erlbaum, 1994.

[68] Michael Precker, "How Do I Love Thee? (Very Discreetly)," *Dallas Morning News*, June 5, 2005, 2E.

[69] Ibid.

[70] Gottman, *What Predicts Divorce?*

Chapter 8

[1] "Kansas Teen's Tweet of Dissent Goes Viral," *iClimberBlog*, November 28, 2011. http://blog.iclimber.com/kansas-teens-tweet-of-dissent-goes-viral/ (accessed January 16, 2012).

[2] Huma Kahn, "Tweeting Kansas Teen Gets Apology from Gov. Brownback, Her Following Soars," *ABC News*, November 28, 2011. http://abcnews.go.com/blogs/politics/2011/11/tweeting-kansas-teen-wont-apologize-to-gov-her-following-soars/ (accessed January 16, 2012).

[3] Ruth Marcus," Emma Sullivan's Potty-Mouthed Tweet Has a Lesson for All of Us." *The Washington Post*, November 29, 2011. www.washingtonpost.com/opinions/emma-sullivans-potty-mouthed-tweet-has-a-lesson-for-all-of-us/2011/11/29/gIQAG6CEAO_story.html (accessed January 16, 2012).

[4] Suzanne McCorkle and Janet L. Mills, "Rowboat in a Hurricane: Metaphors of Interpersonal Conflict Management," *Communication Reports* 5 (1992): 57–66.

[5] Jacqueline S. Weinstock and Lynne A. Bond, "Conceptions of Conflict in Close Friendships and Ways of Knowing Among Young College Women: A Developmental Framework," *Journal of Social and Personal Relationships* 17 (2000): 687–696.

[6] Glen H. Stamp, "A Qualitatively Constructed Interpersonal Communication Model: A Grounded Theory Analysis," *Human Communication Research* 25 (1999): 543.

[7] Fran C. Dickson, Patrick C. Hughes, Linda D. Manning, Kandi L. Walker, Tamara Bollis-Pecci, and Scott Gratson, "Conflict in Later-Life, Long-Term Marriages," *Southern Communication Journal* 67 (2002): 110–121.

[8] Ruth Anna Abigail and Dudley D. Cahn, *Managing Conflict Through Communication*, 4th ed. Boston: Pearson, 2011, 4.

[9] See, for example, Linda L. Putnam, "Definitions and Approaches to Conflict and Communication," in John

G. Oetzel and Stella Ting-Toomey (ed.), *The Sage Handbook of Conflict Communication: Integrating Theory, Research, and Practice*. Thousand Oaks, CA: Sage Publications, 2006.

[10] Joseph P. Forgas and Michelle Cromer, "On Being Sad and Evasive: Affective Influences on Verbal Communication Strategies in Conflict Situations," *Journal of Experimental Social Psychology* 40 (2004): 511–518.

[11] Herbert W. Simons, "The Carrot and the Stick as Handmaidens of Persuasion in Conflict Situations," in Gerald R. Miller and Herbert W. Simons (eds.), *Perspectives in Communication in Social Conflicts*. Englewood Cliffs, NJ: Prentice Hall, 1974, 172–205.

[12] Michael Roloff, *Interpersonal Communication: The Social Exchange Approach*. Thousand Oaks, CA: Sage, 1981.

[13] M. A. Rahim, "A Measure of Styles of Handling Interpersonal Conflict," *Academy of Management Journal* 26 (1983): 368–376.

[14] Stella Ting-Toomey, Ge Gao, Paula Trubisky, Zhizhong Yang, Hak Soo Kim, Sung-Ling Lin, and Tsukasa Nishida, "Culture, Face Maintenance, and Styles of Handling Interpersonal Conflict: A Study in Five Cultures," *International Journal of Conflict Management* 2 (1991): 275–296.

[15] Stella Ting-Toomey, "Intercultural Conflict Competence," in J. N. Martin, T. K. Nakayama, and L. A. Flores (eds.), *Readings in Cultural Contexts*. New York: Mayfield, 1998.

[16] William B. Gudykunst and Young Yun Kim. *Communicating with Strangers: An Approach to Intercultural Communication*, 4th ed. New York: McGraw Hill, 2003.

[17] Min Sun Kim, *Non-Western Perspectives on Human Communication: Implications for Theory and Practice*. Thousand Oaks, CA: Sage, 2002.

[18] William R. Cupach and Daniel J. Canary, *Competence in Interpersonal Conflict*. Long Grove, IL: Waveland Press, 1997.

[19] Jeannie Trudel and Thomas G. Reio, Jr., "Managing Workplace Incivility: The Role of Conflict Management Styles—Antecedent or Antidote?" *Human Resource Development Quarterly* 22 (2011): 395–423.

[20] See, for example, Deborah Tannen, *You Just Don't Understand: Women and Men in Conversation*. New York: Harper Collins, 1990.

[21] See, for example, Neil Brewer, Patricia Mitchell, and Nathan Weber, "Gender Role, Organization Status, and Conflict Management Styles," *International Journal of Conflict Management* 13 (2002): 78–94; Sheryl D. Brahnam, Thomas M. Margavo, Michael A. Hignite, Tonya B. Barrier, and Jerry M. Chin, "A Gender-Based Categorization for Conflict Resolution," *Journal of Management Development* 24 (2005): 197–208.

[22] Daniel J. Canary and Kimberly House, "Is There Any Reason to Research Sex Differences in Communication," *Communication Quarterly* 41 (1993): 129–144.

[23] Daniel J. Canary, William R. Cupach, and Susan J. Messman, *Relationship Conflict: Conflict in Parent-Child, Friendship, and Romantic Relationships*. Newbury Park: Sage, 1995. See also William R. Cupach and Daniel J Canary, "Managing Conflict and Anger: Investigating the Sex Stereotype Hypothesis," in Pamela J. Kalbfleisch and Michael. J. Cody (eds.), *Gender, Power, and Communication in Human Relationships*. Mahwah, NJ: Lawrence Erlbaum, 1995, 233–252; and J. T. Wood, "I Can't Talk About It Now," in Kathleen. M. Galvin and Pamela J. Cooper (eds.), *Making Connections: Readings in Relational Communication*, 4th ed. New York: Oxford University Press, 2006, 209–215.

[24] Abigail and Cahn.

[25] Carley H. Dodd, *Managing Business and Professional Communication*. Boston: Pearson Education, 2004.

[26] Uriel G. Foa and Edna B Foa, *Societal Structures of the Mind*. Springfield, IL: Thomas, 1974.

[27] Dudley D. Cahn, *Intimates in Conflict*. Hillsdale, NJ: Erlbaum, 1990, 16.

[28] Kristen Holland, "Pixel This: Dad Tells Son to Switch to GOP or Else," *Dallas Morning News*, March 11, 2006, 1B, 8B.

[29] "Pink on Landing Her *Cosmo* Cover: I've Been Told, 'You're Not Pretty Enough,'" NBC Washington, May 7, 2010. www.nbcwashington.com/entertainment/celebrity/Pink_On_Landing_Her_Cosmo_Cover__I_ve_Been_Told___You_re_Not_Pretty_Enough_-93164699.html (accessed May 8, 2010).

[30] Monique Mitchell, D. Urson, Caroline Rankin, and Patty Malone, *Cognition During Conflict: The Impact of Communication Medium and Perceived Intentions on Attributions*. Presented at the annual meeting of the International Communication Association, May 23, 2003.

[31] Elizabeth V. Hobman, Prashant Bordia, Bernd Irner, and Artemis Chang, "The Expressions of Conflict in Computer-Mediated and Face-to-Face Groups," *Small Group Research* 33 (2002): 439–465.

[32] Ana Zornoza, Pilar Ripoll, and José M. Peiro, "Conflict Management in Groups That Work in Two Different Communication Contexts: Face-to-Face and Computer-Mediated-Communication," *Small Group Research* 33 (2002): 481–508.

[33] Scott Caplan, Dimitri Williams, and Nick Yee, "Problematic Internet Use and Psychosocial Well-Being Among MMO Players," *Computers in Human Behavior* 25 (2009): 1312–1319.

[34] Roxane S. Lulofs and Dudley D. Cahn, *Conflict: From Theory to Action*, 2nd ed. Boston: Pearson, 2001.

[35] Mae Arnold Bell, "A Research Note: The Relationship of Conflict and Linguistic Diversity in Small Groups," *Central States Speech Journal* 34 (1983): 128–133.

[36] Lulofs and Cahn.

[37] Kathy Skuja and W. Kim Halford, "Repeating the Errors of Our Parents? Parental Violence in Men's Family of Origin and Conflict Management in Dating Couples," *Journal of Interpersonal Violence* 19 (2004): 623–638. See also Kerstin E. Edin, Ann Lalos, Ulf Högberg, and Lars Dahlgren, "Violent Men: Ordinary and Deviant," *Journal of Interpersonal Violence* 23 (2008): 225–244.

[38] Sonia Miner Salari and Bret M. Baldwin, "Verbal, Physical, and Injurious Aggression Among Intimate Couples over Time," *Journal of Family Issues* 23 (2002): 523–550; Dudley D. Cahn, "An Evolving Communication Perspective on Family Violence," in D. Cahn (ed.), *Family Violence: Communication Processes*. Albany, NY: SUNY, 2009, 135–153.

[39] Loreen N. Olson and Dawn O. Braithwaite, "'If You Hit Me Again, I'll Hit You Back': Conflict Management Strategies of Individuals Experiencing Aggression During Conflicts," *Communication Studies* 55 (2004): 271–286.

[40] Loreen N. Olson, "Exploring 'Common Couple Violence' in Heterosexual Romantic Relationships," *Western Journal of Communication* 66 (2002): 104.

[41] Dudley D. Cahn, "Family Violence from a Communication Perspective," in Dudley D. Cahn and Sally A. Lloyd (eds.), *Family Violence from a Communication Perspective*. Thousand Oaks, CA: Sage, 1996, 6.

[42] Belinda R. Walsh and Emma Clarke, "Post-Trauma Symptoms in Health Workers Following Physical and Verbal Aggression," *Work & Stress* 17 (2003): 170–181.

[43] Kelly A. Rocca, "College Student Attendance: Impact of Instructor Immediacy and Verbal Aggression," *Communication Education* 53 (2004): 185–195.

[44] Brenda Gieger and Michael Fisher, "Will Words Ever Harm Me? Escalation from Verbal to Physical Abuse in Sixth-Grade Classrooms," *Journal of Interpersonal Violence* 19 (2006): 337–357.

[45] "Section 14: Violence," *Health of Boston 2010*. www.bphc.org/about/research/hob2010/Pages/Home.aspx (accessed July 13, 2011).

[46] Loreen N. Olson, "'As Ugly and Painful as It Was, It Was Effective': Individuals' Unique Assessment of Communication Competence During Aggressive Conflict Episodes," *Communication Studies* 53 (2002): 171–188. See also Nathan C. Lowe and David C. May, "Responses to Scenarios That May Provoke Acts of Conflict and Aggression Among the General Public: An Exploratory Study," *Journal of Interpersonal Violence* 26 (2011): 1606–1627.

[47] Sandra Metts and William R. Cupach, "Responses to Relational Transgressions: Hurt, Anger, and Sometimes Forgiveness," in Brian H. Spitzberg and William R. Cupach (eds.), *The Dark Side of Interpersonal Communication*, 2nd ed. Mahwah, NJ: Lawrence Erlbaum, 2007, 243–266.

[48] Virginia Satir, "The Rules You Live By," in K. M. Galvin, and P. J. Cooper (eds.), *Making Connections: Readings in Relational Communication*, 3rd ed. New York: Oxford University Press, 2003, 199–205.

[49] For a discussion of the *Tendency to Forgive Scale* and its correlation with other personality measures, see Ryan P. Brown, "Measuring Individual Differences in the Tendency to Forgive: Construct Validity and Links with Depression," *Personality and Social Psychology Bulletin* 29 (2003): 759–771.

[50] See, for example, Everett L. Worthington, Jr., *Forgiveness and Reconciliation: Theory and Application*. New York: Routledge, 2006.

[51] Roxane S. Lulofs, *Swimming Upstream: Creating Reasons for Unforgiveness in a Culture That Expects Otherwise*. Presented to the Speech Communication Association Convention, San Antonio, TX, November 1995.

[52] Julie Juola Exline, Roy F. Baumeister, and Anne L. Zell, Amy J. Kraft, and Charlotte V. O. Witvliet, "Not So Innocent: Does Seeing One's Own Capability for Wrongdoing Predict Forgiveness?" *Journal of Personality and Social Psychology* 94 (2008): 495–515.

[53] See, for example, Scott R. Ross, Matthew J. Hertenstein, and Thomas A. Wrobel, "Maladaptive Correlates of the Failure to Forgive Self and Others: Further Evidence for a Two-Component Model of Forgiveness," *Journal of Personality Assessment* 88 (2007): 158–167; Everett L. Worthington, Jr., Charlotte Van Oyen Witvliet, Pietro Pietrini, and Andrea J. Miller, "Forgiveness, Health, and Well-Being: A Review of Evidence for Emotional Versus Decisional Forgiveness, Dispositional Forgiveness, and Reduced Unforgiveness," *Journal of Behavioral Medicine* 30 (2007): 291–302.

[54] Lulofs.

[55] Julie Juola Exline and Ray F. Baumeister, "Expressing Forgiveness and Repentance: Benefits and Barriers," in Michael E. McCullough, Kenneth L. Pargament, and Carl E. Thorsen (eds.), *Forgiveness: Theory, Research, and Practice*. New York: The Guilford Press, 2000, 133–155.

[56] Alexander G. Santelli, C. Ward Struthers, and Judy Eaton, "Fit to Forgive: Exploring the Interaction Between Regulatory Focus, Repentance, and Forgiveness," *Journal of Personality and Social Psychology* 96 (2009): 381–394. See also Robert J. Sidelinger, Brandi N. Frisby, and Audra L. McMullen, "The Decision to Forgive: Sex, Gender, and the Likelihood to Forgive Partner Transgressions," *Communication Studies* 60 (2009): 164–179.

[57] Jeremy C. Anderson, Wolfgang Linden, and Martine E. Habra, "Influence of Apologies and Trait Hostility on Recovery from Anger," *Journal of Behavioral Medicine* 29 (2006): 348.

Chapter 9

[1] "New Potter Book Topples U.S. Sales Records," *MSNBC*, July 18, 2005. www.msnbc.msn.com/id/8608578/ns/business-us_business/t/new-potter-book-topples-us-sales-records/ (accessed March 28, 2013).

[2] Charles J. Walker, "Experiencing Flow: Is Doing It Together Better Than Doing It Alone?" *The Journal of Positive Psychology* 5 (2010): 3–11.

[3] Gayle W. Hill, "Group Versus Individual Performance: Are $N + 1$ Heads Better Than One?" *Psychological Bulletin* 91 (1982): 517–539.

[4] Daniel Levi, *Group Dynamics for Teams*, 3rd ed. Newbury Park, CA: Sage, 2011.

[5] Hill.

[6] Levi.

[7] Susan M. Sorenson, *Group-Hate: A Negative Reaction to Group Work*. Presented at the Annual Meeting of the International Communication Association, Minneapolis, MN, May 21–25, 1981.

[8] Rod L. Troester and Cathy Sargent Mester, *Civility in Business and Professional Communication*. New York: Peter Lang Publishing, 2007.

[9] Adapted from Andrew F. Wood and Matthew J. Smith, *Online Communication: Linking Technology, Identity, and Culture*, 2nd ed. Mahwah, NJ: Lawrence Erlbaum, 2005, 91.

[10] Mei Alonzo and Melim Aiken, "Flaming in Electronic Communication," *Decision Support Systems* 36 (2004): 205–213.

[11] Joseph M. Kayany, "Contexts of Uninhibited Online Behavior: Flaming in Social Newsgroups on Usenet," *Journal of the American Society for Information Science* 49 (1998): 1141.

[12] Levi.

[13] Richard L. Moreland, "Are Dyads Really Groups?" *Small Group Research* 41 (2010): 251–267.

[14] Jennifer A. Stillman, Richard B. Fletcher, and Stuart C. Carr, "Netball Team Members, but Not Hobby Group Members, Distinguish Team Characteristics from Group Characteristics," *Journal of Sport & Exercise Psychology*, 29 (2007): 253–266.

[15] These ideas are summarized from a number of resources, including Levi; see also Roger N. Nagel, *Organizational Behavior and Organizational Change: Groups & Teams*, www.cse.lehigh.edu/~rnn0/bio/emba/EMBA04.pdf (accessed January 16, 2012); and Leadership Development Coaching, "Groups v. Teams." www.leadership-development-coaching.com/groups-v-teams.html (accessed January 16, 2012).

[16] Felicia Wu Song, *Virtual Communities: Bowling Alone, Online Together*. New York: Peter Lang Publishing, 2009, 1.

[17] James K. Scott and Thomas G. Johnson, "Bowling Alone but Online Together: Social Capital in E-Communities," *Community Development* 36 (2005): 1–18.

[18] Susan A. Wheelan, "Group Size, Group Development, and Group Productivity," *Small Group Research* 40 (2009): 247–262.

[19] Christopher O. L. H. Porter, Celile Itir Gogus, and Race Chien-Feng Yu, "When Does Teamwork Translate Into Improved Team Performance? A Resource Allocation Perspective," *Small Group Research* 41 (2010): 221–248.

[20] Bruce W. Tuckman, "Developmental Sequences in Small Groups," *Psychological Bulletin* 63 (1965): 384–399; Bruce W. Tuckman and Mary Ann C. Jensen, "Stages of Small Group Development Revisited," *Group and Organizational Studies* 2 (1977): 419–427.

[21] Moira Burke, Robert Kraut, and Elisabeth Joyce, "Membership Claims and Requests: Conversation-Level Newcomer Socialization Strategies in Online Groups," *Small Group Research* 4 (2010): 4–40.

[22] Marshall Scott Poole and Johny T. Garner, "Perspectives on Workgroup Conflict and Communication," in John G. Oetzel and Stella Ting-Toomey (eds.), *The Sage Handbook of Conflict Communication*. Thousand Oaks, CA: Sage, 2006.

[23] Ricky Griffin, *Management*, 8th ed. Boston: Houghton Mifflin Company, 2005.

[24] Information for this case retrieved fro, http://news.yahoo.com/s/nm/20100628/ts_nm/us_usa_christian_gays (accessed July 4, 2010).

[25] Ralph Warhman, "Status, Deviance, and Sanctions: A Critical Review," *Small Group Research* 41 (2010): 91–105.

[26] Jeroen Stouten, "Challenging the Leader or the Follower: Influence of Need for Emotion and Equality Violations on Emotional and Retributive Reactions in Social Dilemmas," *Journal of Applied Social Psychology* 38 (2008): 1378–1394.

[27] Rothwell, 2007.

[28] Rothwell, 135.

[29] Gary N. Powell, "Of Person–Organizational Fit and Diversity," *Organizational Dynamics* 26 (1998): 50–61.

[30] Powell.

[31] John R. P. French, Jr., and Bertram Raven, *Studies in Social Power*. Ann Arbor, MI: Institute for Social Research, 1959.

[32] Bertram H. Raven, "A Power/Interaction Model of Interpersonal Influence: French and Raven Thirty Years Later," *Journal of Social Behavior and Personality* 7 (1992): 217–244.

[33] Peter L. Wright, *Managerial Leadership*. London: Routledge, 1966.

[34] E. A. Fleishman, "The Description of Supervisory Behavior," *Personnel Psychology* 37 (1953): 1–6.

[35] D. L. Helmich and P. E. Erzan, "Leadership Style and Leader Needs," *Academy of Management Journal* 18 (1975): 397–402.

[36] T. R. Mitchell, A. Biglan, G. R. Onchen, and F. E. Fiedler, "The Contingency Model: Criticsim and Suggestions," *Academic of Management Journal* 13 (1970): 253–267.

[37] Dean Tjosvold and I. Robert Andrews, "Leadership Influence: Goal Interdependence and Power," *The Journal of Social Psychology* 132 (1992): 39–50.

[38] David M. Mayer, Mary Bardes, and Ronald F. Piccolo, "Do Servant-Leaders Help Satisfy Follower Needs? An Organizational Justice Perspective," *European Journal of Work and Organizational Psychology* 17 (2008): 180–197.

[39] Bradley L. Kirkman, Gilad Chen, Jiing-Lih Farhn, Zhen Xiong Chen, and Kevin B. Lowe, "Individual Power Distance Orientation and Follower Reactions to Transformational Leaders: A Cross-Level, Cross-Cultural Examination," *Academy of Management Journal* 52 (2009): 744–745.

[40] Melissa K. Carsten, Mary Uhl-Bien, Bradley J. West, Jaime L. Patera, and Rob McGregor, "Exploring Social Constructions of Followership: A Qualitative Study," *The Leadership Quarterly* 21 (2010): 543–562.

[41] Carsten et al., 545.

[42] Carsten et al.

[43] Troester and Mester, 191.

[44] Ira Chaleff, *The Courageous Follower*. San Francisco: Berrett-Koehler, 1995.

[45] Augustine O. Agho, "Perspectives of Senior-Level Executives on Effective Followership and Leadership," *Journal of Leadership & Organizational Studies* 16 (2009): 159–166.

[46] Rothwell.

[47] Rothwell.

[48] Alice H. Eagly and Steven J. Karau, "Role Congruity Theory of Prejudice Toward Female Leaders," *Psychological Review* 109 (2002): 573–598.

[49] Madeline E. Heilman and Aaron S. Wallen, "Wimpy and Undeserving of Respect: Penalties for Men's Gender-Inconsistent Success," *Journal of Experimental Social Psychology* 46(2010): 664–667.

Chapter 10

[1] "'No Labels' Group Wants Civility in Politics," *CBS News*, December 13, 2010. www.cbsnews.com/stories/2010/12/13/politics/main7146225.shtml (accessed September 22, 2011).

[2] "Talking Points," *No Labels*. www.nolables.org/talking-points (accessed September 22, 2011).

[3] "Lobbyists for Bipartisanship Want to Change Washington Politics," *No Labels*, 2001. http://nolabels.org/newsroom/lobbyists-bipartisanships-want-change-washington.politics (accessed September 22, 2011).

[4] Ibid. See also "Expect," *No Labels*, 2001. http://nolabels.org/what-we-expect (accessed September 22, 2011).

[5] John F. Cragan, David W. Wright, and Chris R. Kasch. *Communication in Small Groups: Theory, Process, Skills*, 6th ed. Belmont, CA: Wadsworth, 2004.

[6] Ibid.

[7] Ibid.

[8] Jonathan Levav and Shai Danziger, "Extraneous Factors in Judicial Decisions," *Proceedings of the National Academy of Sciences of the United States of America*. www.pnas.org/content/108/17/6889.full.pdf+html (accessed August 24, 2011).

[9] John Tierney, "Do You Suffer from Decision Fatigue?" *New York Times*, August 21, 2011. www.nytimes.com/2011/08/21/magazine/do-you-suffer-from-decision-fatigue.html (accessed August 24, 2011).

[10] Roy F. Baumeister and John Tierney, *Willpower: Rediscovering the Greatest Human Strength* (NY: Penguin Books, 2011).

[11] Alex Bavelas, "Communication Patterns in Task-Oriented Groups," *Journal of the Acoustical Society of America* 22 (1950): 725–730.

[12] Chuck Tryon, "Why You Should Be on Twitter," *AlterNet*, March 4, 2009. www.alternet.org/story/129319/ (accessed August 4, 2009).

[13] Steve Kolowich, "Tweeting in Class," *Inside Higher Ed*, November 5, 2009. www.insidehigher ed.com/layout/set/print/news/2009/11/05/twitter (accessed November 5, 2009).

[14] Patrick May, "Twitter's Becoming an Important Tool for Job Seekers and Employers," MercuryNews.com, October 5, 2009. www.mercurynews.com/ci_13474050 (accessed October 5, 2009).

[15] Dejin Zhao and Mary Beth Rossom, "How and Why People Twitter: The Role That Micro-Blogging Plays in Informal Communication at Work," in S. Teasley, E. Havn, W. Prinz, and W Lutters (eds.), *Proceedings of the ACM 2009 International Conference on Supporting Group Work*. New York: Association for Computing Machinery, 2009, 243–252.

[16] "Twitter Narrowcasting: Helping Groups Communicate Privately via Twitter," *GroupTweet*. www.grouptweet.com (accessed July 9, 2010).

[17] Kevin Bondelli, "Using Twitter for Your Organization," Kevin.Bondelli.com, May 5, 2008. www.kevinbondelli.com/2008/05/05using-twitter-for-your-organization/ (accessed July 9, 2010).

[18] David Carr, "Why Twitter Will Endure," *The Dallas Morning News*, January 17, 2010, 1P, 5P.

[19] Nancy Katz, David Lazer, Holly Arrow, and Noshir Contractor, "Network Theory and Small Groups," *Small Group Research* 25 (2004): 307–332.

[20] See, for example, Lee Humphreys and Tony Liao, "Mobile Geotagging: Reexamining our Interactions with Urban Space," *Journal of Computer-Mediated Communication* 16 (2011): 407–423.

[21] Katherine Adams and Gloria J. Galanes, *Communicating in Groups: Applications and Skills*, 6th ed. New York: McGraw-Hill, 2006.

[22] Ibid.

[23] Ibid.

[24] Elka Jones, "Career Solutions for Trained Problem-Solvers," *Occupation Outlook Quarterly*, Fall 2003, 12–21. www.bls.gov/opub/ooq/2003/fall/art02.pdf (accessed September 25, 2001).

[25] Marc Orlitzky and Randy Hirokawa, "To Err Is Human, to Correct for It Divine: A Meta-Analysis of Research Testing the Functional Theory of Group Decision-Making Effectiveness," *Small Group Research* 32 (2001): 313–343.

[26] John Dewey, *How We Think*. Lexington, MA: D. C. Heath, 1910.

[27] Keith Murnighan and John C. Mowen, *The Art of High Stakes Decision Making: Tough Calls in a Speed Driven World*. New York: John Wiley and Sons, 2002.

[28] Cain Burdeau, "BP Ad Campaign Following Gulf Oil Spill Deemed 'Propaganda' by Some," *The Huffington Post*, January 8, 2012, www.huffingtonpost.com/2012/01/08/bp-ad-campaign-gulf-oil-_n_1192600.html (accessed December 6, 2012).

[29] See, for example, Christopher O. L. H. Porter, Celile Itir Gogus, and Race Chien-Feng Yu, "When Does Teamwork Translate into Improved Team Performance? A Resource Allocation Perspective," *Small Group Research* 41 (2010): 221–248.

[30] Robert Weisberg, *Creativity: Genius and Other Myths*. New York: W. H. Freeman and Company, 1986.

[31] Charles E. Notar and Sharon Padgett, "Is Think Outside the Box 21st Century Code for Imagination, Innovation, Creativity, Critical Thinking, Intuition?" *College Student Journal* 144 (2010): 294–298.

[32] Tayloe Harding, "Fostering Creativity for Leadership and Leading Change," *Arts Education Policy Review* 111 (2010): 52.

[33] J. Mirowsky and C. E. Ross, "Creative Work and Health," *Journal of Health and Social Behavior* 48 (2007): 385–403.

[34] "Creativity in Small Groups," MHHE. www.mhhe.com/socscience/comm/group/students/creativity.htm (accessed July 4, 2010).

[35] Gayle T. Dow and Richard E. Mayer, "Teaching Students to Solve Insight Problems: Evidence for Domain Specificity in Creativity Training," *Creativity Research Journal* 16 (2004): 389–402.

[36] Ginamarie Scott, Lyle E. Leritz, and Michael D. Mumford, "The Effectiveness of Creativity Training: A Quantitative Review," *Creativity Research Journal* 16 (2004): 361–388.

[37] Jonali Baruah and Paul B. Paulus, "Effects of Training on Idea Generation in Groups," *Small Group Research* 39 (2008): 523–541.

[38] Robert J. Sternberg, "Creativity as a Decision," *American Psychologist* 57 (2002): 376.

[39] Edward de Bono, *Lateral Thinking: Creativity Step by Step*. New York: Harper and Row, 1970.

[40] de Bono, 14.

[41] Robert C. Litchfield, "Brainstorming Rules as Assigned Goals: Does Brainstorming Really Improve Idea Quantity?" *Motivation and Emotion* 33 (2009): 25–31.

[42] Tony Buzan with Barry Buzan, *The Mind Map Book*. New York: Plume Books, 1993.

[43] Joyce Wycoff, *Mind-Mapping: Your Personal Guide to Exploring Creativity and Problem-Solving*. New York: Berkeley Publishing Group, 1991, 43.

[44] Nancy Margulies and Nusa Maal, *Mapping Inner Space*. Chicago: Zephyr Press, 2002, 26.

[45] Irving L. Janis, *Victims of Groupthink: A Psychological Study of Foreign-Policy Decisions and Fiascoes*. Oxford, UK: Houghton Mifflin, 1972.

[46] See, for example, Clark McCauley, "The Nature of Social Influence in Groupthink: Compliance and Internalization," *Journal of Personality and Social Psychology* 57(1989): 250–260; and Ramon J. Aldag and Sally R. Fuller, "Beyond Fiasco: A Reappraisal of the Groupthink Phenomenon and a New Model of Group Decision Processes," *Psychological Bulletin* 113 (1993): 533–552.

[47] James K. Esser, "Alive and Well After 25 Years: A Review of Groupthink Research," *Organizational Behavior and Human Decision Processes* 73 (1998): 116–141.

[48] Paul 't Hart, *Groupthink in Government: A Study of Small Groups and Policy Failure*. Lisse, Netherlands: Swets & Zeitlinger Publishers, 1990.

[49] Gregory Moorhead, Richard Ference, and Chris P. Neck, "Group Decision Fiascoes Continue: Space Shuttle Challenger and a Revised Groupthink Framework," *Human Relations* 44 (1991): 539–550.

[50] Carol Tavris and Elliott Aaronson, *Mistakes Were Made, but Not by Me: Why We Justify Foolish Beliefs, Bad Decisions, and Hurtful Acts*. Orlando, FL: Harcourt Publishers, 2008.

[51] Jerry B. Harvey, *The Abilene Paradox and Other Meditations on Management*. San Francisco, CA: Jossey-Bass, 1988.

[52] Philip Zimbardo, *The Lucifer Effect*. New York: Random House, 2007.

[53] Ibid, 212.

[54] Ibid, 180.

[55] Karen A. Jehn, "A Qualitative Analysis of Conflict Types and Dimensions in Organizational Groups," *Administrative Science Quarterly* 42 (1997): 530–557; A. M. Passos and A. Caetano, "Exploring the Effects of Intragroup Conflict and Past Performance Feedback on Team Effectiveness," *Journal of Managerial Psychology* 20 (2005): 231–244.

[56] Carsten K. W. De Dreu, "When Too Little or Too Much Hurts: Evidence for a Curvilinear Relationship Between Task Conflict and Innovation in Teams," *Journal of Management* 32 (2006): 83–107.

[57] José M. Guerra, Inés Martinez, Lourdes Munduate, and Francisco J. Medina, "A Contingency Perspective on the Study of Consequences of Conflict Types: The Role of Organizational Culture," *European Journal of Work and Organizational Psychology* 14 (2005): 157–176.

[58] T. L. Simons and R. S. Peterson, "Task Conflict and Relationship Conflict in Top Management Teams: The Pivotal Role of Intragroup Trust," *Journal of Applied Psychology* 85 (2000): 102–111.

[59] Guerra et al.

[60] De Dreu, Carsten K.W. and Bianca Beersma. "Conflict in Organizations: Beyond Effectiveness and Performance." *European Journal of Work and Organizational Psychology* 14 (2005): 109, 105–117

[61] Karen A. Jehn and E. Mannix, "The Dynamic Nature of Conflict: A Longitudinal Study of Intragroup Conflict and Group Performance," *Academy of Management Journal* 44 (2001): 238–251.

[62] Maria T. M. Dijkstra, Dirk van Dierendonck, and Arne Evers, "Responding to Conflict at Work and Individual Well-Being: The Mediating Role of Flight Behaviour and Feelings of Helplessness," *European Journal of Work and Organizational Psychology* 14 (2005): 119–135.

[63] Bradford D. Smart, "Achieving Effective Meetings—Not Easy, but Possible," *Training and Development Journal* 28 (1974): 12–17.

[64] Shirley Fine Lee, "How Should Team Meetings Flow?" *Journal for Quality and Participation* 31 (2008): 25–28.

[65] David A. Harrison, Kenneth H. Price, Joanne H. Gavin, and Anna T. Florey, "Time, Teams, and Task Performance: Change Effects of Surface- and Deep-Level Diversity on Group Functioning," *Academy of Management Journal* 45 (2002): 1029–1045.

[66] Harrison et al.

[67] William L. Dunlop and Mark R. Beauchamp, "Does Similarity Make a Difference? Predicting Cohesion and Attendance Behaviors Within Exercise Group Settings," *Group Dynamics: Theory, Research, and Practice* 15 (2011): 258–266.

[68] Lynn Smith-Lovin and Charles Brody, "Interruptions in Group Discussions: The Effects of Gender and Group Composition," *American Sociological Review* 54 (1989): 424–435; Dina G. Okamoto and Lynn Smith-Lovin, "Changing the Subject: Gender, Status, and the Dynamics of Topic Change," *American Sociological Review* 66 (2001): 852–873.

[69] Dawn T. Robinson and Lynn Smith-Lovin, "Getting a Laugh: Gender, Status, and Humor in Task Discussions," *Social Forces* 80 (2001): 123–158.

[70] Robinson and Smith-Lovin.

[71] Jennifer L. Berdahl and Cameron Anderson, "Men, Women, and Leadership Centralization in Groups over Time," *Group Dynamics: Theory, Research and Practice* 9 (2005): 45–57.

Chapter 11

[1] Avinash, "Quoting the Famous: Brad Pitt Will Ease Your Pain," *omg!*, December 2, 2011. http://omg.yahoo.com/blogs/thefamous/style-icon-emma-watson-an-unknown-to-vivienne-westwood/666?nc (accessed March 28, 2013).

[2]J. E. Kopfman and S. Smith, "Understanding the Audiences of a Health Communication Campaign: A Discriminate Analysis of Potential Organ Donors Based on Intent to Donate," *Journal of Applied Communication Research* 24 (February 1996): 33–49.

[3]Barack Obama, "Remarks by the President at a Memorial Service for the Victims of the Shooting in Tucson, Arizona," Whitehouse.gov, January 12, 2011. http://www.whitehouse.gov/the-press-office/2011/01/12/remarks-president-barack-obama-memorial-service-victims-shooting-tucson (accessed September 12, 2011).

[4]G. W. Bush, "9/11 Address to the Nation," *Famous Speeches and Speech Topics*. © 2008. www.famous-speeches-and-speech-topics.info/presidential-speeches/george-w-bush-speech-9-11-address-to-the-nation.htm (accessed March 9, 2012).

[5]Jennifer Epstein, "Discouraging Jeerers," *Inside Higher Education*, October 26, 2009. www.insidehighered.com/news/2009/10/26/jeers (accessed February15, 2013).

[6]Dean Schabner and Ryan Creed, "Donald Trump 'Honored' to be Butt of Obama, Seth Meyers Jokes at Correspondents' Dinner," *ABC News*, May 1, 2011. http://abcnews.go.com/Politics/donald-trump-honored-butt-obama-seth-meyers-jokes/story?id=13503379#.T1qLmDHeDmM (accessed March 9, 2012).

[7]M. Krumboltz, "First Responder Fireman Co-writes 9/11 Book with Daughter," news.yahoo.com, September 6, 2011. http://news.yahoo.com/first-reponder-fireman-co-writes-9-11-book-with-daughter.html (accessed September 14, 2011).

[8]"History of YouTube," *Wikipedia*. http://en.wikipedia.org/wiki/History_of_YouTube (accessed January 14, 2013).

[9]Shane Richmond, "YouTube Users Uploading Two Days of Video Every Minute," *The (London) Daily Telegraph*, May 20, 2011; and Alexi Oreskovic, "YouTube Hits 4 Billion Daily Video Views," *Reuters*, January 23, 2012.

[10]Megan O'Neill, "5 Ways YouTube Has Changed the World Forever," *SocialTimes*, November 8, 2010. http://socialtimes.com/youtube-changed-the-world_b26201 (accessed January 14, 2013).

[11]L. Smith-Spark, "Why Is Italy Now at Center of Europe's Debt Crisis?" articles.cnn.com, August 11, 2011. http://articles.cnn.com/2011-08-04/world/italy.economy.explainer_1_italy-finance-minister-giulio-tremonti-prime-minister-silvio-berlusconi?_s=PM:WORLD (accessed March 13, 2012).

[12]David Zarefsky, *Strategic Public Speaking: A Handbook*. Boston: Pearson, 2007, 178.

[13]Ibid, 178.

[14]Ibid, 179.

[15]Ibid, 179.

[16]"Census Bureau Reports Hispanic Voter Turnout Reaches Record High for Congressional Election," *U.S. Census Bureau*, September 28, 2011. www.census.gov/newsroom/releases/archives/voting/cb11-164.html (accessed March 14, 2012).

[17]"Paradigm," *Merriam-Webster Online Dictionary*, © 2012. www.merriam-webster.com/dictionary/paradigm (accessed March 14, 2012).

[18]"Mark Zuckerberg Quotes," *Brainy Quote*, © 2001–2012. www.brainyquote.com/quotes/authors/m/mark_zuckerberg.html (accessed March 14, 2012).

Chapter 12

[1]Carnegie Mellon University, *University Lecture Series: Journeys*. www.cmu.edu/uls/journeys/ (accessed December 11, 2011).

[2]Randy Pausch, "Randy Pausch Last Lecture: Achieving Your Childhood Dreams," youtube.com, December 20, 2007. www.youtube.com/watch?v=ji5_MqicxSo (accessed 16 February 2013).

[3]Sal Gentile, "Interview with Phil Davison, the Man Behind One of the Most Intense Stump Speeches Ever," PBS.org, September 9, 2010. www.pbs.org/wnet/need-to-know/the-daily-need/anatomy-of-a-political-freakout-interview-with-phil-davidson/3433/ (accessed February 16, 2013).

[4]Sonja K. Foss and K. A. Foss, *Inviting Transformation: Presentational Speaking for a Changing World*, 2nd ed. Long Grove, Illinois: Waveland Press, Inc., 2003, 110.

[5]Ibid, 110

[6]Sandra R. Harris, R. L. Kemmerling, and M. M. North, "Brief Virtual Reality Therapy for Public Speaking Anxiety," *CyberPsychology & Behavior* 5, no. 6 (2002): 543–550.

[7]Ibid, 544.

[8]Ibid, 545.

[9]Ibid, 545.

[10]Ibid, 545.

[11]Ibid, 545.

[12]Ibid, p. 546.

[13]Ibid, 546.

[14]Ibid, 547.

[15]Ibid, 548.

[16]David Zarefsky, *Strategic Public Speaking: A Handbook*. Boston: Pearson, 2007, 237.

[17]Carnegie Mellon University, *Journeys*. www.cmu.edu/uls/journeys/ (accessed April 23, 2012). See also Pausch.

[18]I. Eibl-Eibesfeldt, "The Expressive Behavior of the Deaf-and-Blind-Born," in M. von Cranach and I. Vine (eds.), *Social Communication and Movement: Studies of Interaction and Expression in Man and Chimpanzee*. New York: Academic Press, 1973, 163–194.

[19]Ibid.

[20]Angela R. Garber, "Death by PowerPoint," *Small Business* Computing.com, April 1, 2001. http://www.smallbusinesscomputing.com/biztools/article.php/684871/Death-By-Powerpoint.htm (accessed April 29, 2013).

[21]Ibid, 109.

[22]J. K. Sawyer, *PowerPoint Reality: Slides in Real Time for Real Audiences with Real Easy Steps*. Boston: Allyn & Bacon, 2011, 30.

[23]Ibid, 30.

[24]Ibid, 30.

Chapter 13

[1]"First Lady Michelle Obama Observes National Breast Cancer Awareness Month," Komenadvocacy.com, October 25, 2009. www.komenadvocacy.org/newsArticles.aspx?id=2147483687 (accessed August 13, 2012).

[2]Ibid.

[3]Ibid.

[4]Ibid.

[5]Ibid.

[6]Glenn Kessler, "The RNC and Obama, Taking Quotes Out of Context," *The Washington Post*, May 14, 2012. www.washingtonpost.com/blogs/fact-checker/post/the-rnc-and-obama-taking-quotes-out-of-context/2012/05/13/gIQAV4BnMU_blog.html (accessed June 21, 2012).

[7]Ibid.

[8]Ibid.

[9]Ibid.

[10]Ibid.

[11] Dominique Enright, *The Wicked Wit of Winston Churchill*. London, UK: Michael O'Mara Books, 2001.

[12] Steve Lucas, *The Art of Public Speaking*, 9th ed. New York: McGraw-Hill, 2007, 470.

[13] Meghan Neal, "High School Teacher Tells Graduating Students: You're Not Special," *The New York Daily News*, June 8, 2012. http://articles.nydailynews.com/2012-06-08/news/32128878_1_david-mccullough-speech-teacher (accessed June 11, 2012).

[14] Ibid.

[15] B. Brown. "Wellesley High Grads Told: "You're Not Special," *The Swellesley Report*, June 6, 2012. www.theswellesleyreport.com/2012/06/wellesley-high-grads-told-youre-no-special/ (accessed June 6, 2012).

[16] Ibid.

[17] David McCullough, Jr., "You're Not Special: After My Commencement Speech That Stunned America," *Newsweek*, June 25, 2012, 26–27.

[18] Rachel Marsden, "Tough-Love Grad Speech Is on the Mark," *The Dallas Morning News*, June 14, 2012, 15A.

[19] "U of Alberta Dean Stole Speech: Med Students," *CBC News Canada*, June 12, 2011. www.cbc.ca/news/canada/edmonton/story/2011/06/12/edm-university-alberta-speech.html (accessed June 13, 2011).

[20] Ibid.

[21] Ibid.

[22] Ibid. See also "U of Alberta Dean Accused of Plagiarism Apologizes." *CBC News Canada*, June 12, 2011. www.cbc.ca/news/canada/edmonton/story/2011/06/13/edmonton-dean-apology-plagiary.html (accessed June 13, 2011).

[23] "University of Alberta Medical Dean Steps Down," *University of Alberta Express News*, June 17, 2011. www.expressnews.ualberta.ca/News-Articles/2011/06/2011067.Update.aspx# (accessed June 20, 2011).

[24] "U of Alberta Dean Stole Speech: Med Students."

[25] Anne Ryman, "ASU History Professor at Center of Plagiarism Debate," *USA Today*, May 7, 2012. www.usatoday.com/USCP/PNI/Front%20Page/2012-05-07-pni0501met-asu-plagiarsm_ST_U.htm (accessed June 22, 2012).

[26] Ibid.

[27] Ibid.

[28] Eriq Gardner, "Australian Political Leader Caught Plagiarizing 'The American President,'" *The Hollywood Reporter*, January 27, 2012. www.hollywoodreporter.com/thr-esq/anthony-albanese-australia-plagiarism-the-american-president-285277 (accessed June 21, 2012).

[29] Ibid.

[30] Patrick Lion, "Anthony Albanese Loses the Plot After Plagiarism of 'The American President,'" News.com.au, January 27, 2012. www.news.com.au/national/anthony-albanese-loses-the-plot-after-plagiarism-of-the-american-president/story-e6fr-fkvr-1226254834658 (accessed June 21, 2012).

Chapter 14

[1] Hillary Rodham Clinton, "Internet Freedom," *Foreign Policy*, January 21, 2010. www.foreignpolicy.com/articles/2010/01/21/internet_freedom?page=full (accessed January 23, 2012).

[2] Aristotle, *On Rhetoric: A Theory of Civic Discourse*. George A. Kennedy, trans. Oxford: Oxford University Press, 1991, 36–37.

[3] Simon Benson and Allison McMeekin, "Joe Hockey Accuses Julia Gillard of 'Lecturing' World on Economic Management," News.com.au, June 18, 2012. www.news.com.au/world-old/bus-crash-delays-julia-gillards-g20-meeting-in-mexico/story-e6fr-fkyi-1226398604587 (accessed August 10, 2012).

[4] Simon Benson, "Prime Minister Julia Gillard Pushes Her Numbers at G20 Summit in Mexico," *The Daily Telegraph*, June 19, 2012. www.dailytelegraph.com.au/news/national/prime-minister-julia-gillard-pushes-her-numbers-at-g20-summit-in-mexico/story-e6freuzr-1226399232050 (accessed June 23, 2012).

[5] Ibid.

[6] Ibid.

[7] Ibid.

[8] Stephen Toulmin, *The Uses of Argument*. Cambridge. UK: University Press, 1958.

[9] Richard E. Petty and John T. Cacioppo, "The Elaboration Likelihood Model of Persuasion," *Advanced in Experimental Social Psychology* 19 (1986): 123–190.

[10] Richard E. Petty and John T. Cacioppo, *Communication and Persuasion: Central and Peripheral Routes to Attitude Change*. New York: Springer-Verlag, 1986.

[11] Aaron Smith and Joanna Brenner, "Twitter Use 2012," *Pew Internet & American Life Project*, May 31, 2012, http://pewinternet.org/Reports/2012/Twitter-Use-2012/Findings.aspx (accessed April 3, 2013).

[12] Ibid.

[13] Janet Johnson, *Blogs and Dialogism in the 2008 United States Presidential Campaign* [PhD dissertation]. Texas Woman's University, 2010, 29.

[14] Ibid.

[15] Jennifer Golbeck, Justin M. Grimes, and Anthony Rogers, "Twitter Use by the U.S. Congress," *Journal of the American Society for Information Science and Technology* 61, no. 8 (2010): 1620.

[16] Frederic I. Solop, "'RT @BarackObama We Just Made History': Twitter and the 2008 Presidential Election," in John Allen Hendricks and Robert E. Denton, Jr. (eds.), *Communicator-in-Chief: How Barack Obama used New Media Technology to Win the White House*. New York: Lexington Books, 2010, 48.

[17] Ibid, 47.

[18] Alec R. Hosterman, "Tweeting 101: Twitter and the College Classroom," in Hana S. Noor Al-Deen and John Allen Hendricks (eds.), *Social Media Usage and Impact*. New York: Lexington Books, 2012, 108.

[19] Alan H. Monroe, *Monroe's Principles of Speech*, military ed. Chicago: Scott Foresman, 1943.

[20] Sonja K. Foss and Cindy I. Griffin, "Beyond Persuasion: A Proposal for an Invitational Rhetoric," *Communication Monographs* 62 (1995): 2–18.

[21] Cindy L. Griffin, *Invitation to Public Speaking*, 4th ed. Belmont, CA: Wadsworth, 2011.

[22] Ibid.

[23] Ibid.

[24] Ibid.

[25] Foss and Griffin.

[26] Jennifer E. Bone, Cindy L. Griffin, and T. M. Linda Scholz, "Beyond Traditional Conceptualizations of Rhetoric: Invitational Rhetoric and a Move Towards Civility," *Western Journal of Communication* 72, no. 4 (2008): 434–462.

[27] Ibid, 449.

GLOSSARY

Abilene paradox A barrier to problem solving that occurs because people fail to voice their opinions about the decision being made.

abstraction The levels of specificity in language. In general, highly connotative words tend to be highly abstract.

accenting A function of nonverbal communication. Nonverbal communication can accent or emphasize the spoken word.

accents The particular way that words are pronounced. Accents vary according to ethnicity, age, and geographic location.

active followers Followers who offer opinions when given the opportunity but also emphasize loyalty to the leader.

active listening A type of listening that features verbal and nonverbal responses to others that let them know we are paying attention and taking responsibility for understanding their meanings.

ad hominem A logical fallacy in which a speaker attacks the character of the opposition rather than address the substance of the other side's position.

affect blends A combination of one emotion evidenced in one facial area and another emotion shown in a different area; two different emotions illustrated in one part of the face; and a facial display that results from muscle action that is associated with two emotions.

affection In terms of relational communication, the force to become close with a relational partner.

agonism A ritualistic form of insult and nonliteral fighting. Agonism occurs among those who enjoy fighting for its own sake and who perceive trading insults as a type of game.

allness The incorrect idea that it is possible to know everything about a person, place, or thing. Allness results from the first stage in the perception process, during which we attend to some stimuli and filter out the rest. Allness also results from the multiple factors that can affect meaning.

ambushing Waiting to pounce the moment someone stops speaking.

anaphora Repetition of the first word or group of words from the beginning of a sentence in the next clause of the same sentence and/or are in subsequent sentences.

apology A statement that includes an admission of guilt, an expression of remorse, and a promise not to engage in damaging behavior again.

appreciation A relationship maintenance tactic of communicating that we feel grateful and that we are thankful for our relational partner and the relationship itself.

appreciative listening A type of listening in which we engage when we want to enjoy and appreciate the messages we listen to.

argumentation The process of forming reasons to support conclusions.

artifacts Items such as clothing, jewelry, and accessories that communicate about the person who wears them.

attitude An audience's tendency to view a speaker and a topic favorably or unfavorably.

attraction theory A theory which predicts that we are attracted to and may initiate relationships with people we believe are physically attractive, who are similar to us, and who are in physical proximity to us.

attribution theory A theory that explains how we create explanations or attach meaning to our own or another's behavior.

audience expectations What listeners anticipate the speaker will tell them and what they will learn or gain from the speech.

autonomy/connection dialectic A dialectic that reflects the tension between wanting to be independent and wanting to feel connected.

avoiding A conflict strategy that circumvents the conflict by physical means, as in not making contact with the other person in the conflict, or communicative means, as in refusing to talk about the conflict or changing the subject.

backing Additional evidence or support for a warrant.

belief What listeners accept as true or untrue.

body orientation and posture The extent to which we face or lean toward or away from others. Both body orientation and posture can indicate whether or not we are open to interaction.

brainstorming A problem solving technique in which group members quickly contribute as many ideas as they can think of without judging whether the idea is good or bad. Also a technique for generating ideas that involves freely associating words and ideas.

captive audience Listeners who have little choice but to listen to a speech.

channel The pathway used to convey a message between a sender and a receiver.

chronemics An environmental factor, *time*, that influences nonverbal behavior.

civil communication The choice we make to communicate on the basis of respect, restraint, and responsibility.

civil listening Also known as *confirming listening*, a listening style that communicates our belief in the quality of all people.

civility The choice we make to consider others' thoughts and feelings in our communication and general behavior. Also, a forgiveness strategy that involves respecting the other by restraining from a focus on the transgression and communicating responsibly, using neutral language.

claim The central argument of a speech.

claim of fact An assertion that a condition exists, did exist, or will exist.

claim of policy An assertion that an action should or should not be taken to address a given set of circumstances.

claim of value An assertion that something is preferable or not preferable.

climate The psychological atmosphere of a group.

cloaking A forgiveness strategy that consists of telling yourself that you don't want to forgive the other person but engaging in minimal interaction with the other.

closed-ended questions Questions that often evoke one-word responses and may not provide us with additional information we can use to keep a conversation going.

closing A forgiveness strategy that consists of telling yourself that you don't want to forgive the other person and refusing to engage in reconciliation behaviors that will restore the relationship.

co-culture A group within a larger dominant culture that has its own values and beliefs, which sometimes may be at odds with the dominant culture.

coercion Social influence involving force or threat of force.

coherence In terms of the Coordinated Management of Meaning theory, "making meaning" is the goal of conversation.

cohesiveness A set of factors that act to keep group members together and committed to the group.

collectivist culture A culture that focuses more on the group (e.g., the family, village, or organization) than the individual.

communication The process of creating and sharing meaning.

communication apprehension Nervousness or fear that interferes with a person's ability to communicate with another.

communication models Pictures of the structure and key components of communication. Models define and isolate specific elements in the communication process and show their relationship to each other and to the communication process itself.

communication network A pattern of interaction between group members that dictates who an individual may exchange information with.

comparative advantage organization An organizational strategy in which the speaker shows how one option is more effective than other alternatives.

competitive interrupting A kind of uncivil communication in which a listener doesn't allow others to finish, but starts in on his or her own idea before the speaker has finished his or her idea.

complementing A function of nonverbal communication. Complementing nonverbal communication adds meaning to verbal communication. Examples of complementing nonverbal behaviors include weeping while telling a sad story and blushing when communicating embarrassment.

comprehensive listening A type of listening in which we engage when we want to learn, understand, and recall information.

compromising A conflict strategy that focuses on finding a middle ground between what you want and what the other person wants in the situation.

concrete words Words based on sense data.

confirming listening Also called *civil listening*, a listening style that communicates our belief in the quality of all people.

confirming responses Civil verbal and nonverbal communication that expresses affection, respect, and concern.

conflict management The behavior a person employs based on his or her analysis of a conflict situation.

conflict situation A setting in which conflict occurs, which seems familiar to the participants and which helps to provide clues for managing the conflict that is occurring.

confrontation steps Actions taken to move through a conflict: preparation, arranging a time to talk, confrontation, considering the other's point of view, resolving the problem, and setting a time to follow up.

confrontational listening A type of disconfirming listening in which we listen carefully for flaws in a conversation partner's message to refute them or attack the speaker in response.

connotative meaning Meaning that is emotional and personal and that engenders disagreement.

consciousness raising A process of engaging listeners to become more aware of commitments they have taken for granted.

consensus The agreement that results when members come to a decision that is acceptable to the group; however, it doesn't mean that the decision is the best one of all or that it is everyone's first choice.

consequentialist ethics Ethics that examine the relationship between the ends and the means.

content-level meaning The content of the words and sentences that are communicated.

content paraphrase A confirming response in which you reword the speaker's message in terms of your understanding of the speaker's thoughts. Content paraphrasing can be used when you listen to a lot of information, when you are given complex directions and/or instructions, and when the information is technical and laden with unfamiliar jargon.

context The environment surrounding communication, including the physical environment, interpretation of a particular situation (e.g., the formality or informality of an occasion), frame of reference (e.g., culture, gender, expectations, past history, beliefs, attitudes, values), and significant others. It's easiest to communicate with others when our contexts overlap.

control The force to gain dominance. Control can be communicated at the relational level of meaning.

Coordinated Management of Meaning A theory that says that the application of syntactic, semantic, and pragmatic rules enables conversation partners to experience meaning based on coherence, coordination, and mystery.

coordination In terms of the Coordinated Management of Meaning theory, how meaning is created by the rules we use to manage talk and create our social realities.

coping A forgiveness strategy that consists of telling yourself that you want to forgive the other but do not want to continue a relationship with that person.

costs Features of a relationship that are considered negative.

creativity The process of making sense of some problem in a new way.

(re-)creating A forgiveness strategy that consists of self-talk that helps us reframe the transgression at the same time that we do things that communicate reconciliation to the other.

credibility A speaker's ability to earn the audience's trust.

critical listening Also known as *critical thinking*, a listening style in which we analyze and evaluate messages by delaying or suspending judgment before forming an opinion. Critical listening also includes separating fact from inference, assessing the source(s) of the information, and focusing on the form of reasoning.

cultural pattern The particular beliefs and values associated with a specific culture.

culture The shared assumptions, values, and beliefs of a group of people that result in characteristic behaviors.

deception cues Behaviors that are typically associated with lying, such as fidgeting behaviors and throat clearing.

decoding The mental process of interpreting a message.

defensive listening A type of disconfirming listening in which messages are interpreted as criticism and personal attack.

delivery The presentation of a speech, including use of gestures and body language, tone of voice, eye contact, volume, and rate.

delivery cues Notations on a presentation outline that tell a speaker *how* to say something. Brackets, underlined words, and/or words and phrases marked with a highlighter or written in different colors to note transitions, pauses, and/or specific citations and quotations are examples of delivery cues.

demographic characteristics Characteristics such as the size of the audience, group composition, cultural differences, age, and gender.

denotative meaning Meaning that is considered to be "correct" and that is found in dictionaries.

deontological ethics Ethics concerning principles, rules, and duties.

differentiation phase The phase of conflict in which the participants work out the problem using constructive or destructive strategies and tactics, presenting both sides of the story, moving back and forth, and escalating and deescalating.

direct persuasion An approach in which a speaker states the purpose in a very explicit way. In most cases, a speaker chooses this approach with an audience supportive of the message or with an audience in which support is likely to be mixed.

disconfirming communication Communication that does not validate others. We communicate disconfirmation when we ignore people, fail to acknowledge their thoughts and feelings, and refuse to accept their opinions and emotions.

disconfirming listening A type of uncivil listening that does not acknowledge and respect a speaker's verbal and nonverbal messages. Specific types of disconfirming listening are defensive listening, pseudolistening, confrontational listening, and literal listening.

display rules Rules that tell people how and when to display nonverbal behaviors. They vary by culture.

disruptive roles Informal roles in groups that include such things as demanding the center of attention, clowning around, and being cynical about all the tasks the group takes on.

dominating A conflict strategy that people use when they believe that getting their way with respect to the conflict issue is more important than the relationship they have with the other person.

dormant ties Social ties that were once potentially very important and active in someone's social network but for various reasons, such as moving or changing jobs, have become dormant.

doublespeak Language used deliberately to mislead and to manipulate.

elaboration likelihood model A framework in which speakers or listeners cooperate jointly to develop meaning and understanding.

emblems Nonverbal behaviors that can be translated directly in a word or two of verbal communication.

emotional appeal A speaker's attempts to arouse emotion in listeners to compel them to believe his or her claim or argument.

emotional residues Lingering emotional responses to the memory of a conflict.

empathic listening A listening style during which we listen to understand and experience the feelings of a conversation partner. We can engage in empathic listening by paraphrasing for feelings.

empathy Attempting to understand the thoughts and feelings of others and also vicariously experience the emotions of others.

encoding The process of translating thoughts, feelings, and ideas into symbols (words and nonverbal cues).

enunciation Articulating words clearly.

ethics A system of standards that defines what behaviors are "right" or "good" and that allows us to evaluate and decide among behavioral options. In terms of civil communication, ethics allow us to make good choices about what and how we communicate.

ethos appeal An appeal through the speaker's character to convince the audience of his or her claim.

euphemisms Words with positive or neutral connotations that are used to replace words associated with unpleasant and negative connotations. Many euphemisms in the English language concern natural body functions and taboo topics such as death and sex.

evaluative listening A type of listening in which we engage when we want to judge the soundness of a message.

expectancy The basis for perceptual interpretation when we perceive what we expect to perceive.

extemporaneous speech A speech given after some preparation but whose wording is composed at the time of delivery.

extending fit The result of a group emphasizing diversity over cohesiveness in group membership.

facial expression and eye behavior Nonverbal communication that is involved in opening, closing, and regulating the channels of interaction and that functions as the prime communicator of emotion.

fact Information that is independently verifiable by others. Facts are often, but not always, based on sense data, such as what we see, hear, taste, smell, and touch.

familiarity The basis for perceptual interpretations of perceiving or failing to perceive what we are familiar with.

family A group of people with a past history, a present reality, and a future expectation of interconnected, mutually influencing relationships.

family rules Rules that concern "shoulds" and "oughts" and that range on a continuum from explicit to implicit.

feedback The response to a sender's message, which can be verbal, nonverbal, or both. It is through feedback that the sender learns whether her or his message has been received as intended.

feelings paraphrase A confirming response in which you reword the speaker's message in terms of your understanding of the speaker's emotions. Paraphrasing for feelings requires you to monitor the speaker's nonverbal communication for clues about the speaker's emotions.

flaming Intense and/or negative language, swearing, and communication that is intended and perceived as hostile.

flow Being absorbed in a task while feeling competent to meet it.

followership The behaviors of a follower with respect to his or her leader, such as taking or refusing responsibility, communicating or failing to express opinions, and approaching problem solving proactively or reactively.

forgiveness An intrapersonal communication process that consists of self-talk that focuses on letting go of feelings of revenge and desires to retaliate.

formal role A role that arises out of a person's assigned position in a group.

forming The first phase of group development in which members come together to create a group.

fractionation The process of breaking down a problem into smaller pieces and then dealing with each piece, one at a time.

friends People who like each other, enjoy each other's company, and establish voluntary relationships.

friendship rules Rules that prescribe effective and appropriate communication in our relationships with friends.

fundamental attribution error Reasons for others' behavior that overemphasize inherent characteristics or personality and underemphasize situational factors.

gender The influence of the environment and socially constructed meaning of the similarities and difference between men and women.

general attractiveness and body shape A type of nonverbal communication used to judge others' backgrounds, characters, personalities, talents, and potential future behavior.

generalizing Reaching a conclusion by making sweeping and broad claims.

gestures Movements of the body used to communicate thoughts, feelings, and/or intentions.

gifts A relationship reward in the form of spontaneous or planned offerings of material items.

goal An outcome that a person or group wants to achieve.

gossip Communication about people (not necessarily against them).

grounds Evidence supporting a claim.

group A human communication system composed of three or more individuals, interacting for the achievement of some common goal(s), who influence and are influenced by each other.

grouphate A negative attitude toward working in groups.

groupthink A barrier to problem solving that occurs when people are so committed to the group and its integrity as a cohesive unit that they fail to engage in conflict when they should.

halo effect A perception influenced by positive qualities. The halo effect causes us to perceive that a person holds many positive qualities if we believe she or he possesses one or a few positive qualities.

haptics Touch. The meanings that are associated with touching behavior depend on what body part is touched, the intensity of the touch, the duration of the touch, the method of the touch (such as closed or open fist), and the frequency of the touch.

hasty generalization A logical fallacy that draws a conclusion from insufficient evidence.

hearing The reception and processing of sounds.

helping A relationship reward that involves receiving assistance from a partner on a difficult task.

high-context cultures Cultures that tend to communicate in an indirect manner. Members of high-context cultures focus on situational factors for meaning and do not rely solely on verbal communication when communicating or interpreting messages.

hostile audience Listeners who are strongly opposed to the speaker's position.

hyperpersonal communication Internet communication that is more sociable, personal, and intimate than what is found in face-to-face interaction.

I-statements Language we can use to personalize a conflict by owning up to our feelings rather than making them the responsibility of the other person.

identity-oriented conflict A type of group conflict that occurs when others treat a person contrary to the way that person sees himself or herself.

illustrators Speech-related gestures that are directly tied to speech. Pointing movements, movements that depict spatial relationships, and rhythmic chopping gestures are examples of illustrators.

immediacy In terms of nonverbal communication, physical or psychological closeness between people involved in interaction.

impersonal communication Communication with others as if they are objects or roles.

impersonal relationships Relationships in which we communicate with others based primarily on their social or occupational roles (e.g., nurturer, server, disciplinarian, cashier).

implicit personality theory A theory that explains one way to perceive others. According to implicit personality theory, we tend to perceive others based on a set of beliefs that tell us which characteristics relate to other characteristics.

impromptu speech A speech given with little or no prior preparation.

incompatible goals Goals that seek different outcomes; for example, we want to buy two different cars but can afford only one.

incompatible means Means that try to achieve the same goal but differ in how to do so; for example, we agree on the same car but on whether or not to finance it or pay cash.

indexing A communication skill that recognizes differences in thought and opinion that may be based on insufficient evidence. Indexing also communicates that we are open to different meanings and interpretations. Indexing-related words and phrases include *maybe*, *it could be*, and *perhaps*.

indirect persuasion An approach in which a speaker deemphasizes the purpose and/or thesis of the speech in some way.

individualist culture A culture that focuses more on the individual than the group. Individual needs come before group needs, and people take care of themselves before they take care of others.

inference An interpretation based on a fact.

informal roles Roles that arise from the way in which people actually interact with one another.

information A relationship reward in the form of advice, opinions, instructions, or enlightenment given through self-disclosure.

informative speech A speech that provides the audience with new information, raises awareness of some issue, or communicates additional information about a topic that the audience already knows about.

initiation phase The stage of conflict in which at least one person makes known to the other the presence of a felt conflict.

initiation strategies The ways we approach and initiate contact with a potential relationship partner to whom we are attracted.

instrumental/task-oriented conflict The assumption that a moderate amount of conflict, as opposed to very low or very high levels, results in cognitive flexibility, creative thinking, and problem-solving abilities.

integrating A conflict strategy that puts equal importance on the issue to be resolved and the relationship with the other person in the conflict, resulting in an outcome that satisfies both parties.

intent The speaker's desire for the audience to listen to and accept his or her message.

interaction management How we control the channels of communication. For example, making eye contact with someone indicates that communication channels are open, while avoiding eye contact suggests that communication channels are closed.

interdependence A relationship that is characterized by all involved in it as one that is important and worth the effort to maintain.

internal dialogue A natural and normal form of intrapersonal communication that helps us solve problems and work out our feelings.

interpersonal attraction A motivational state that brings people together by causing them to think, feel, and act in a positive manner toward each other.

interpersonal communication Communication between at least two people who establish a communicative relationship. Interpersonal communication involves partners who have the power to simultaneously affect each other through their behavior, either positively or negatively.

interpersonal conflict A problematic situation with the following four unique characteristics: the conflicting parties are interdependent; the conflicting parties perceive that they seek incompatible goals or outcomes or that they favor incompatible means to the same ends; the perceived incompatibility has the potential to adversely affect the relationship if not addressed; and there is a sense of urgency about the need to resolve the difference.

interpersonal violence A partner's imposing his or her will on another through verbal or physical intimidation.

interpretation The third stage of the perception process, during which we assign meaning to the stimuli that we have selected and organized from the environment.

intimate distance The distance used for touching and intimacy as well as physical aggression and threat (i.e., contact to 18 inches).

intimate relationships Relationships that can be characterized by one or more of five qualities: sharing emotions, socializing with friends, physical closeness, sharing ideas, and/or engaging in activities together.

intrapersonal communication Communication that takes place within us. Internal dialog and self-talk are examples of this form of communication.

invitational rhetoric (invitational speaking) Rhetoric in which a speaker enters into a public dialogue with an audience.

jargon A specialized vocabulary shared and understood by members of particular occupational groups. Jargon often functions as a "shorthand code" or quick method for sharing meaning.

kinesics Nonverbal behaviors that are associated with movement.

lateral thinking A problem-solving technique that is concerned with restructuring patterns (insights) and provoking new ones (creativity); it is a nonlinear problem solving approach.

leadership A communicative process that encompasses the ability to engage in mutual influence with others in the group in order to move toward the accomplishment of the task at hand.

leading questions Questions that suggest a "correct" answer and/or attempt to guide a respondent's answer.

listening A complex skill that does not have a widely accepted definition. However, a common definition posits that listening entails six stages that don't necessarily have to be enacted in order: hearing, understanding, remembering, interpreting, evaluating, and responding.

literal listening A type of disconfirming listening in which we listen to only the content of a message. Literal listening occurs when we overlook nonverbal communication and the emotional tone of a message.

loaded questions Closed-ended questions that typically provide only two alternatives and which presuppose something that has not been proven or accepted.

logical appeal A speaker's use of logical reasoning to persuade an audience of his or her position.

long-term groups Groups that members enter and remain with for indefinite time periods.

love A relationship reward with nonverbal expressions of intimacy, passion, and commitment in romantic relationships and nonverbal expressions of positive regard, warmth, and comfort in friendships.

low-context cultures Cultures that tend to communicate in a very direct manner. Members of low-context cultures focus on verbal communication for meaning and do not rely on situational factors when communicating or interpreting messages.

Lucifer effect A barrier to problem solving that is applied to situations where groups commit great harms due to the release of situational constraints that would otherwise keep them from behaving in such a manner.

maintenance roles Informal group roles that include supporting and encouraging others, helping relieve tensions in the group, and monitoring the feelings of the group.

maintenance strategies Behaviors used to sustain the meaning of a relationship held by the relational partners. Maintenance behaviors have been conceptualized as both nonstrategic and strategic actions that can prevent deterioration of the relationship.

Maslow's Hierarchy of Needs A theory of psychology proposed by Abraham Maslow in 1943. Maslow's hierarchy identifies several basic needs of all human beings: self-actualization, esteem, love/belonging, safety, and physiological needs.

mediated and technology-based communication Communication that is transmitted by some kind of technology, such as television, radio, mobile devices, or the Internet.

message The information (e.g., thoughts, feelings, ideas) a sender wishes to convey to a receiver. Both verbal (words) and nonverbal (e.g., body language, vocal behavior) communication are used to convey meaning.

metacommunication "Communication about communication" or "communication about relationships." We can metacommunicate about both the content of a message and the underlying relational message.

metaphor A comparison where the speaker does not explicitly state the similarity between two things that share at least one characteristic in common.

microexpressions Extremely fast facial movements that last less than one-fifth of a second and that can reveal emotions, especially those we are trying to conceal.

mind mapping A problem-solving technique for making your ideas visible.

money A relationship reward in the form of the financial contributions each person makes to a relationship.

monochronic time A time orientation that considers time as commodity. Individuals who have a sense of urgency, believe that time shouldn't be wasted, and believe that people should do things one at a time adhere to a monochromic time system.

Monroe's motivated sequence An organizational strategy developed by Alan H. Monroe that organizes a speaker's message according to the audience's motivations.

mystery In terms of the Coordinated Management of Meaning theory, mystery refers to the idea that coherence and coordination are arbitrary and are created by language. Mystery also suggests that the words we use not only create and name things in our experience of reality but also limit them and can make them invisible.

noise Any force that can interfere with the communication process in any communication context or situation.

nonverbal communication All forms of communication other than words themselves.

norm An expectation for behavior that all members of a group should observe.

norming The third phase of group development, in which the group begins to fall into regular patterns of behavior that allow members to plan effectively for the work they will do.

novelty/predictability dialectic A dialectic that concerns the tension between wanting predictability and routine in a relationship and the desire for novelty and newness.

obfuscation Use of obscure or confusing references that leave the audience feeling bewildered.

obliging A conflict strategy that involves giving in to the other person's requests without asking for much in return.

occasion The circumstances and events surrounding the moment of the speech as well as the tone of that moment (e.g., sorrowful, cheerful).

open-ended questions Questions that require more than a "yes or no" answer. Responses to open-ended questions tend to be descriptive and provide us with insight into what a conversation partner thinks and feels.

openness/closedness dialectic A dialectic that reflects the tension between wanting to self-disclose and engage in open communication and our desire for privacy.

organization The second stage of the perception process, during which we categorize the stimuli we have selected from the environment to make sense of the environment.

other-centered approach An orientation in conflict that leads us to choose strategies based on how well they will serve the needs and desires of the other person.

overstatement An argument that is an unqualified generalization.

owning our thoughts and feelings A way to accept responsibility for our thoughts and feelings and recognize that others may not think and feel as we do.

paralanguage Also known as vocalics, a category of nonverbal communication that includes tone of voice, accents, pauses, and silence. Vocalics refers to *how* something is said instead of *what* is actually said.

paraphrase A type of confirming response in which you reword the speaker's message in terms of your understanding of its meaning.

passive followers Followers focused on taking orders and following directions.

passive listening A type of listening that assumes that it's the responsibility of a speaker to ensure that the listener understands. Because passive listeners merely absorb information, they believe that any misunderstanding is the fault of the speaker.

perception A process that occurs when sense data—or what we see, hear, smell, taste, and/or touch—is transmitted to the brain. Perception occurs in three stages: selection, organization, and interpretation.

perception check A communication skill that includes three elements: a description of sense data, at least one interpretation (perception) of the sense data, and a request for feedback.

performing The fourth phase of group development, which occurs when members are aware that they are focusing on the presenting problem.

personal communication Communication that occurs when we interact with others on the basis of their uniqueness.

personal distance The preferred distance for informal conversation and to keep people "at arm's length" (i.e., 18 inches to 4 feet).

personal relationships Relationships in which we communicate with others based primarily on their uniqueness.

perspective-taking Imagining oneself in the place of another to understand how she or he perceives the self, others, and the world.

persuasion The process by which speakers engage audiences to move them to action or to change their minds.

persuasive speech A speech that seeks to change the attitudes, beliefs, values, or behaviors of an audience.

phase theory A theory which assumes that conflict unfolds in fairly predictable ways over a period of time and progresses through recognizable stages of interaction.

physical attraction A component of attraction theory that is based on the extent to which we view another person's physical self as attractive.

pickup line A rehearsed question or comment designed to make the communicator appear attractive to a potential relationship partner.

place The physical environment where a speech occurs.

plagiarism Presenting another person's ideas as our own.

polychronic time A time orientation that considers time as limitless and not quantifiable. Individuals who believe that time should be adjusted to peoples' needs; that it's acceptable to change schedules and deadlines; and that people can do several things simultaneously adhere to a polychronic time system.

post hoc, ergo propter hoc A logical fallacy that confuses causation and chronology. The speaker wrongly asserts that just because something negative followed an event, that event, therefore, caused that something negative to happen.

power A resource available to people in groups that allows them to influence others.

pragmatic rules Rules that help us interpret verbal communication in a given context.

prelude to conflict All the factors and events that lead up to a conflict.

proactive followers Followers who see themselves as partners of their leaders.

problem–solution organization An organizational strategy in which the speaker defines the present condition, or status quo, as unsatisfactory and then argues for a way to bring about needed change.

problematic situations Situations that occur when partners perceive that they seek different outcomes or favor different means to the same ends.

process Communication that is ongoing and continuous.

process-oriented conflict Disagreements over the working style that is typical of a group.

prompts Silence, sounds ("Mmm" and "Uh-huh"), or words ("Go on" and "I'm listening") that let a speaker know that you are listening and you want the speaker to continue.

pronunciation Saying words correctly.

proxemics How people use space and distance. Also called *personal space*, proxemics can reveal how we feel about ourselves and how we feel about others.

proximity The basis for perceptual organization of grouping together stimuli that are physically close to each other. Also, a component of attraction theory that is based on the idea that we are more likely to be attracted to people who are in closer proximity to us than to those who are not.

pseudolistening A type of disconfirming listening in which we pretend to listen even though we focus on our own thoughts and miss the speaker's message.

psychographics Relates to how a speaker and a subject can become even more important and relevant in relationship to the audience's attitudes, beliefs, and values.

public communication Communication that occurs when a speaker delivers a message to an audience.

public dialogue A civil and ethical exchange that includes sharing perspectives and facts, asking questions, and participating in thought-provoking discussions.

public distance The distance that is used by instructors in their classrooms and for other public speaking situations (i.e., 12 feet and beyond).

Pygmalion effect An effect that illustrates the way our significant others influence our self-concept.

qualifier An exception to a speaker's claim, signaled by words such as *usually* or *often*.

rate The speed at which a speaker speaks.

rebuttal A speaker's refutation of a competing claim.

receiver A person who receives a message conveyed by a sender. The receiver is responsible for interpreting or assigning meaning to the message and for responding to the sender.

reconciliation An interpersonal communication process in which we talk about a conflict and take actions to restore a relationship or create a new one.

red herring A logical fallacy that introduces some irrelevant point or issues into a debate.

refutational organization An organizational strategy in which the speaker responds to and counters the opposite position on an issue.

regulating A function of nonverbal communication. Subtle shifts in nonverbal behavior which signal that a speaker is finished with her or his turn and/or a listener desires a turn to speak.

reinforcing fit The result of groups choosing members that will maximize the cohesiveness of the group.

relational communication Communication in which people engaged in conversation not only interact about the content of communication but also about their association.

relational feedback A confirming response that involves a brief description of a situation that parallels a speaker's and points to a connection between the speaker's experience and your own.

relational transgression A conflict where those involved have broken important rules of the relationship.

relational-level meaning The unspoken meaning of a message that can be ascertained, in part, from nonverbal communication.

relationship A voluntary commitment that is constantly in process and marked by continuing, significant interdependence between specific individuals.

relationship-oriented approach An orientation in conflict that leads us to choose strategies based on how well they will serve the relationship with the other person.

relationship-oriented conflict A type of group conflict that occurs when people are unsure of or do not agree with the rules of interaction in the group.

repeating A function of nonverbal communication. This type of nonverbal communication can stand alone and convey the verbal meaning without the necessity of accompanying words.

resolution phase The stage when those involved in a conflict agree to some outcome.

respect In terms of relational communication, acknowledging others by listening well and validating their points of view.

revenge Behavior we take with the goal of getting even with the other person by harming that person in the same way we believe we have been harmed.

reversal A problem-solving technique that entails working backward from the goal or end result.

rewards Features of a relationship that are considered positive.

rhetoric Methods or strategies speakers and writers employ to persuade audiences.

role A collection of behaviors that a particular person is expected to have in a group.

romantic relationships Relationships based on intimacy, passion, and commitment.

S-TLC A conflict resolution process that has four steps: Stop, Think, Listen, and Communicate.

salience A characteristic of stimuli that are selected from the environment based on their interest, use, and meaning to us.

sanction A punishment for failing to follow a group norm.

Sapir-Whorf hypothesis A hypothesis that illustrates that culture influences language and language influences cultural differences in thought.

schemas Mental templates that enable us to organize and classify stimuli into manageable groups or categories.

selection The first stage of the perception process, during which we select from the environment the stimuli to which we will attend.

selective listening A type of disconfirming listening during which we attend to some parts of a message and ignore others.

self-concept How we perceive ourselves.

self-control A process that occurs when an individual overrides, inhibits, or stops a response to avoid a temptation, reach a goal, or follow a rule.

self-disclosure The deliberate communication of personal information to another person. In terms of social penetration theory, self-disclosure includes the breadth of information we share with others and the depth of information that we choose to self-disclose.

self-efficacy One's belief in his or her ability to manage prospective situations.

self-esteem The value or importance we place on our perceived characteristics.

self-image The characteristics we believe we possess.

self-oriented approach An orientation in conflict that leads us to choose strategies based on how well they will serve our needs and desires.

self-serving bias Reasons for our actions that include attributing our successful behavior to inherent characteristics or our personality and our unsuccessful behavior to situational factors.

self-talk Communication within us that is specifically about ourselves. Positive self-talk offers encouragement, support, reassurance, and sometimes a pat on the back. Negative self-talk is critical, evaluative, and devaluing.

semantic rules Rules that specify what symbols stand for or mean. Semantic rules are found in dictionaries and concern denotative meanings.

sender A person who conveys thoughts, feelings, or ideas to others.

sense of urgency A point in a conflict situation at which at least one person in the conflict feels it must be addressed because things cannot continue as they are.

sexual attraction A desire to engage in sexual activity with someone; this desire is heightened while in the company of the individual.

shared time A relationship reward in the form of time spent exclusively with loved ones where you are not distracted by work or people external to the relationship.

shift response A situation that occurs when a person turns a conversation to himself or herself rather than follow the expected course of the conversation.

short-term, task-oriented group A group that forms for a limited period to accomplish a particular goal and then disbands when the goal has been achieved.

significant others People who are important to us.

similarity The basis for perceptual organization of grouping together elements based on size, color, shape, and other characteristics.

simile A comparison where the speaker explicitly states a similarity between two different things.

six hats approach A problem-solving technique that requires one to ask questions from different vantage points.

slang A specialized vocabulary shared by people with similar experiences and interests. Slang establishes a sense of belonging and commonality among its users.

sledgehammer introduction A lackluster opening that needlessly states the intent of the speaker and the speech.

slippery slope A logical fallacy that suggests a domino effect on a given issue. A speaker contends that if a particular course of action is taken or that if something is permitted to occur, a series of terrible consequences will take place as a result.

small group communication Communication that occurs when a small number of people (sometimes characterized as 5 to 7 people or 3 to 12 people) share a common purpose and interact for a reason.

social comparison A comparison that provides us with knowledge about ourselves in terms of how we measure up to others.

social distance The distance that is appropriate for business discussions and conversations that are neither personal nor private (i.e., 4 to 12 feet).

social exchange theory A theory developed by psychologists John Thibaut and Harold H. Kelley, in which perceived rewards and costs determine whether people develop, maintain, or terminate their relationships.

social information Various types of interpersonal information communicated by people during interaction. We ask questions to seek social information and to reduce our uncertainty about new acquaintances and to predict their behavior.

social penetration theory A theory that explains how relationships develop and change in terms of the self-disclosure that occurs between relational partners.

specific purpose statement A statement that limits a topic by precisely identifying what the speaker intends to accomplish.

stage models Models that illustrate relationships in terms of following a trajectory. Stage models also classify relationships in terms of particular stages that illustrate integrating, maintenance, or termination.

status A relationship reward that involves verbal and nonverbal expressions of high or low prestige or esteem.

stereotypes Generalizations that lack validity because they ignore individual differences and contribute to perceptual inaccuracies.

storming The second phase of group development, which occurs as people begin to feel some identification with the group but don't really feel a sense of unity around its purpose.

strong ties Friends who are confidants, people with whom we share multiple interests, and people who can be called on in an emergency.

styles theory A theory which suggests that people have preferred means of dealing with conflict situations and generally use those preferred means whenever possible.

substituting A function of nonverbal communication; nonverbal behavior can function as a substitute for verbal communication.

symbolic interactionism A theory developed by sociologist George Herbert Mead that posits that our view of self is shaped by those with whom we communicate.

symbols Verbal (i.e., words) and nonverbal communication that stands for something else. Also words that stand for tangible objects or abstract concepts.

sympathy Feeling sorrow for another person or persons.

syntactic rules Rules that specify how symbols are arranged (e.g., a grammar).

talkover A situation that occurs when more than one person speaks at the same time in a group.

task roles Informal group roles that include giving and receiving information, helping information flow, and clarifying ideas.

termination The final phase of group development, in which the group itself may end, the particular task may end, or some members may depart or be replaced by newcomers to the group.

termination strategies Strategies used to end a relationship. Such strategies include manipulation, withdrawal/avoidance, and positive-tone strategies.

territoriality A stationary area or fixed geographic location to which one lays claim and that one protects from invasion by others. Your territory may include your room, your bathroom, and even your particular seat at the dinner table.

thesis statement One sentence that summarizes the central or controlling idea of a speech.

time The duration of a speech as well as the interval in which it occurs in the context of other events.

Toulmin Model A model for argumentation named after former University of Chicago English professor Stephen Toulmin. It is used to describe a basic structure of all arguments that includes the components of the claim, the warrant, and the support or evidence.

transaction The simultaneous communication between individuals who participate in face-to-face conversation and listen as a conversation unfolds.

transformational leader A person who is supportive of his or her followers and recognizes them as individuals.

triggering event A behavior that at least one person in a conflict points to as the "beginning" of the problem.

uncertainty reduction theory A theory that suggests that sharing information allows us to explain and predict human behavior. Uncertainty reduction theory postulates that when strangers meet, their primary concern is to reduce uncertainty or increase predictability about the behavior of both themselves and others in the interaction.

unforgiveness An intrapersonal communication process that consists of self-talk that focuses on feelings of revenge and desires to retaliate.

value A strong feeling of the audience related to the inherent worth of a concept or an idea.

verbal communication The use of words to create and convey meaning.

verbal pause Also known as a vocal pause, a noise such as a stammer that a speaker makes to fill moments of silence, usually while he or she is trying to gather thoughts.

vertical thinking A problem-solving technique that involves moving through a series of steps, making sure that one is completed before the next one is started.

virtual groups Groups composed of members who do not meet face-to-face but who interact with each other via the Internet or telephone conferences.

vividness A characteristic of stimuli that are selected from the environment because they are noticeable.

volume The relative loudness of a person's voice.

voluntary audience Listeners who freely choose to listen to a speaker and a speech.

warrant An unstated underlying assumption that connects a claim to the evidence supporting it.

weak ties Friends who are distance acquaintances, people we know in a particular context, and people toward whom we feel little responsibility.

workplace incivility On-the-job behaviors that are rude, discourteous, and disrespectful and display a lack of regard for others.

CREDITS

Text Credits

Chapter 1: p. 2 "Remarks by the President at a Memorial Service for the Victims of the Shooting in Tucson Arizona," Whitehouse.gov. Speeches and Remarks. January 12, 2011 http://www.whitehouse.gov/the-press-office/2011/01/12/remarks-president-barack-obama-memorial-service-victims-shooting-tucson (accessed March 29, 2013); p. 3 Stephen Carter, *Civility Manners, Morals, and the Etiquette of Democracy*, Harper Perennial, 1999; p. 7 Michael Josephson, *Making Ethical Decisions*, Los Angeles, CA: Josephson Institute of Ethics, 2002; p. 8 Rod L. Troester and Cathy Sargent Mester, *Civility in Business and Professional Communication*, NY: Peter Lang, 2007; p. 8 National Communication Association, www.natcom.org; p. 15 Nancy Baym, *Personal Connections in the Digital Age*, Malden, MA: Polity Press, 2010.

Chapter 2: p. 26 Ben Walker, "Selig Won't Overturn Call that Cost Perfect Game," Msnbc.com, June 3, 2010; p. 26 "Blown Call Ends Perfect Game Bid," *The Dallas Morning News*, June 3, 2010, C3; p. 29 P.M. Forni, *Choosing Civility*, New York: St. Martin's Griffin, 2002; p. 43 Scott Parks, "Work Together and No One Loses," *The Dallas Morning News*, May 12, 2003, 2B, 13B.

Chapter 3: p. 53 "Unfriend – A Feeling of Removal in 2009?" *The Dallas Morning News*, November 18, 2009, 8A; p. 61 (Figure 3.4) Shelly D. Lane, *Interpersonal Communications: Competence and Contexts*, 2nd ed., 2010, p. 127. Reprinted and electronically reproduced by permission of Pearson Education, Inc. Upper Saddle River, New Jersey.

Chapter 4: p. 85 (Table 4.1) Virginia Peck Richmond and James C. McCroskey, *Nonverbal Behavior in Interpersonal Relations*, 5th ed., 2004. Reprinted and electronically reproduced by permission of Pearson Education, Inc., Upper Saddle River, New Jersey.

Chapter 5: p. 90 Bernie Goldberg, "Opinion: Can Oprah Help Restore Civility?" AOL News.com, January 4, 2011; p. 91 Michael Josephson, "Listening: A Vital Dimension of Respect 635.4" Character Counts. September 9, 2009. Accessed September 9, 2009 from http://charactercounts.org/michael/2009/09Listening_a_vital_dimension_of_1.html; p. 104 (Table 5.1) G.M. Gazda, R.P. Walters, and W.C. Childers, *Human Relations Development: A Manual for the Health Sciences*, MA: Allyn & Bacon, 1975.

Chapter 6: p. 114 Kathleen M. Galvin, Carma L. Bylund and Bernard J. Brommel, *Communication: Cohesion and Change*, 6th ed. Boston, MA: Pearson, 2004, p. 6.

Chapter 7: p. 137 Mark L. Knapp and Anita L. Vangelisti, *Interpersonal Communication and Human Relations*, 5th ed., 2005. Reprinted and electronically reproduced by permission of Pearson Education, Upper Saddle River, New Jersey; p. 147 Michael Precker, "How Do I Love Thee (Very Discretely)," *The Dallas Morning News*, 2005, 2E.

Chapter 8: p. 151 Ruth Marcus, "Emma Sullivan's Potty-Mouthed Tweet Has a Lesson for All of Us, *The Washington Post*, November 29, 2011; p. 154 (Figure 8.1) M. Afzalur Rahim, "Conflict Styles: A Measure of Handling Interpersonal Conflict," *The Academy of Management Journal*, Vol 26, No. 2 (June 1983), 368-376; p. 157 (Figure 8.2) Ruth Anna Abigail and Dudley D. Cahn, *Managing Conflict through Communication*, 4th ed., 2011. Reprinted and electronically reproduced by permission of Pearson Education Inc., Upper Saddle River, New Jersey.

Chapter 9: p. 175 Joseph M. Kayany, "Contexts of Uninhibited Online Behavior: Flaming in Social Newsgroups on Usenet," *Journal of The American Society for Information Science* 49 (1998), p. 1141; p. 182 M. Krumboltz, "Christian Gays in the United States," News.yahoo.com, June 11, 2012; p. 186 (Table 9.1) Adapted from Kenneth D. Benne and Paul Sneats, "Functional Roles of Group Members," *Journal of Social Issues* 4 (1948), 41-49; p. 190 (Table 9.2) Used by permission, taken from *A History of Leadership Theory*.

Chapter 10: p. 198 John Tierney, "Do You Suffer from Decision Fatigue?" *New York Times*, August 17, 2011; p. 199 (Figure 10.1) Based on Nancy Katz, David Lazer, Holly Arrow and Noshir Contractor, "Network Theory and Small Groups," *Small Group Research* 25 (2004), p. 319; p. 200 Chuck Tryon, "Why You Should be on Twitter," AfterNet, March 4, 2009; p. 200 David Carr, "Why Twitter will Endure," *The Dallas Morning News*, January 17, 2010, 1P, 5P; p. 203 John Mowen, *The Art of High Stakes Decision Making: Tough Calls in a Speed Driven World*, John Wiley & Sons, 2002; p. 209 (Figure 10.2) Courtesy of Illumine Limited. http://mind-mapping.co.uk/enquiry.htm; p. 212 From *The Lucifer Effect* by Philip Zimbardo; Published by Rider; Reprinted by permission of the The Ramdom House Group Limited;

Chapter 11: p. 227 G.W. Bush, "9/11 Address to the Nation"; p. 233 (Figure 11.2) Google and the Google logo are registered trademarks of Google Inc., used with permission; p. 237 M. Krumboltz, "First Responder Fireman Co-Writes 9/11 Book with Daughter," News.yahoo.com, September 6, 2011. Reprinted with permission from Yahoo. 2015 Yahoo!

Chapter 12: p. 255 Sandra R. Harris, R.L. Kemmerling, and M.M. North, "Brief Virtual Reality" *CyberPsychology & Behavior*, Volume 5 (6), 2002, 544.

Chapter 13: p. 278 Glenn Kessler, "The RNC and Obama, Taking Quotes out of Context." The Fact Checker: The Truth Behind the Rhetoric, *The Washington Post*, May 14, 2012; p. 283 Meghan Neal, "High School Teacher Tells Graduating Students: You're Not Special," *The New York Daily News*. National. June 8, 2012. Retrieved June 11, 2012 from http://articles.nydailynews.com/2012-06-08/news/32128878_1_david-mccullough-speech-teacher; p. 283 B. Brown, "Wellesley High Grads told You're Not Special," *The Wellesley Report*, June 6, 2012; p. 285 Anne Ryman, "A History Professor at Central of Plagiarism Debate," *USA Today*, May 7, 2012; p. 286 Eriq Gardner, "Australian Political Leader Caught Plagiarizing the 'American President'," *The Hollywood Reporter*, January 27,2012. Retrieved from www.hollywoodreporter.com/th-resq/anthony-albanese-australia-plagiarism-the-american-president-285277.

Retrieved from www.hollywoodreporter.com/th-resq/anthony-albanese- australia-plagiarism-the-american-president-285277.

Chapter 14: p. 295 Simon Benson and Allison McMeekin, "Joe Hockey Accuses Julis Gillard of 'Lecturing' World on Economic Management," News.com, June 18, 2012; p. 302 Frederic I. Solop, "'RT @BarackObama We just Made a History': Twitter and the *2008 President Election Communicator-in-Chief: How Barack Obama Used New Media Technology to Win the White House*, ed. John Allen Hendricks and Robert E. Denton, Jr. (New York, Lexington Books, 2010), 48; p. 311 Jennifer E. Bone, Cindy L. Griffin and T.M. Linda Scholz, "Beyond Traditional Conceptualizations of Rhetoric: Invitational Rhetoric and a Move Towards Civility," *Western Journal of Communication*, 72(4), (2008), 434-462.

Photo Credits

Chapter 1: p . 1 Gary Hershorn/Reuters; p. 4 © Tyler Olson/Fotolia; p. 5 James Edward Bates/MCT/Newscom; p. 7 Stockbyte/Getty; p. 11 © Cla78/Fotolia; p. 13 CREATISTA/Shutterstock; p. 14 (c) Spencer Grant/PhotoEdit; p. 18 (top) © bst2012/Fotolia; p. 18 (bottom) © Odua Images/Fotolia; p. 19 Blaj Gabriel/Shutterstock; p. 20 Charles Dharapak/Associated Press; p. 21 © Rommel Canlas/Shutterstock; p. 23 © Marin Conic/Fotolia.

Chapter 2: p. 26 Kirthmon F. Dozier/MCT/Newscom; p. 28 © Scott Griessel/Fotolia; p. 30 wavebreakmedia/Shutterstock; p. 33 (bottom) © ZUMA Wire Service/Alamy; p. 36 © Mug Shot/Alamy; p. 38 © Anadne Van Zandbergen/Alamy; p. 40 © Brigette Sullivan/PhotoEdit; p. 42 (top) © Kathanne Andriotis/Alamy; p. 42 (bottom) © zoranm/iStock.

Chapter 3: p. 47 ©epa European pressphoto agency b.v./Alamy; p. 49 © ots-photo/Fotolia; p. 52 ©Leah-Anne Thompson/Fotolia; p. 55 Birgit Reitz-Hofmann/Shutterstock; p. 56 Malcolm Clarke/Associated Press; p. 59 © Homer W. Sykes/Alamy; p. 62 Getty Images; p. 63 David Bohre/AP Images.

Chapter 4: p. 67 © AF archive/Alamy; p. 71 Stuart Jenner/Shutterstock; p. 73 ©Friedrich Stark/Alamy; p. 74 © bst2012/Fotolia; p. 75 Valent/Shutterstock; p. 77 © Hyperstar/Alamy Stock Photo; p. 80 © saiva_l/Fotolia; p. 81 ©Cultura Creative/Alamy; p. 83 ©B.A.E. Inc./Alamy; p. 84 © Boris Karpinski/Alamy.

Chapter 5: p. 90 Stephan Savoia/AP Images; p. 93 ©Wavebreak Media Ltd/Alamy Stock Photo; p. 95 © PhotoAlto/Alamy; p. 98 © PhotoAlto sas/Alamy; p. 102 © Catchlight Visual Services/Alamy; p. 103 © Design Pics Inc./Alamy; p. 105 © Monkey Business/Fotolia; p. 106 © M4OS Photos/Alamy; p. 107 AVAVA/Shutterstock.

Chapter 6: p. 115 ABC Photo Archives via Getty Images; p. 116 © Sergey Galushko/Shutterstock ; p. 118 © Queerstock, Inc. Alamy; p. 119 ©Catchlight Visual Services/Alamy; p. 123 ©Westen61 GmbH/Alamy; p. 125 Justin Horrocks/iStock; p. 126 djedzura/Shutterstock; p. 127 © Blend Images/Alamy Stock Photo.

Chapter 7: p. 129 © WENN UK/Alamy Stock Photo; p. 133 © Maskot/Alamy; p. 135 © michaeljung/Fotolia; p. 139 © rilueda/iStock; p. 140 ©nensuria/iStock; p. 141 (c) Kathleen Smith/Alamy; p. 142 Lorraine Boogrich/iStock; p. 143 © DNY59/iStock; p. 145 © Doreen Salcher/Fotolia; p. 146 © Junial Enterprises/Fotolia.

Chapter 8: p. 150 Charlie Riedel/AP Images; p. 152 (c) Radius Images/Alamy; p. 159 (right) © Dan Wozniak/ZUMAPRESS/Alamy; p. 159 (left) Lynne Sladky/AP Images; p. 162 Allstar Picture Library/Alamy; p. 164 (c) Ian Dagnall Laptop Computing/Alamy; p. 167 ©Paramount/courtesy Everett Collection; p. 169 Cultura Creative Alamy.

Chapter 9: p. 172 PJA WENN Photos/Newscom; p. 175 eteimaging/Shutterstock; p. 176 © Steve Skjold/Alamy; p. 177 © BigPile Stock/Alamy; p. 178 © New Line Cinema/courtesy Everett Collection; p. 179 © Peter Titmuss/Alamy; p. 180 © Joggie Botma/Fotolia p. 183©Wavebreak Media Ltd/alamy Stock Photo; p. 191 © Cultura/Getty.

Chapter 10: p. 195 Seth Wenig/AP Images; p. 198 © Mikael Karlsson/Alamy; p. 203 ©ZUMA Press, Inc./Alamy; p. 205 ©Ilene MacDonald/Alamy; p. 208 Shelley Lane; p. 211 © Image Source Plus/Alamy; p. 213 © laflor/iStock; p. 215 © Radius Images/Alamy; p. 218 ©Klubovy/iStock.

Chapter 11: p. 221 JAF/Splash News/Newscom; p. 224 Kzenon/Shutterstock; p. 226 ©Blend Images/Getty; p. 227 Czarek Sokolowski/AP Images; p. 228 Dan Balilty/AP Images; p. 230 AF archive /Alamy; p. 231 Realistic Reflections/Alamy; p. 233 Google and the Google logo are registered trademarks of Google Inc., used with permission; p. 236 © saturno dona' ZUMApress/Newscom; p. 245 Kyndell Harkness /ZUMApress/Newscom.

Chapter 12: p. 251 Kaylin Bowers/AP Images; p. 254 © ZUMA Press Inc./Alamy; p. 256 Chris Fitzgerald/Candidate Photos/Newscom; p. 258 © Marmaduke St. John/Alamy; p. 259 © Richard Ellis/Alamy; p. 261 Hero Images Inc./Alamy; p. 262 ©Purestock Alamy; p. 269 Goodshoot/Thinkstock.

Chapter 13: p. 272 © PixelPro/Alamy; p. 274 © Jeff Greenberg/Alamy; p. 275 © GL Archive/Alamy; p. 276 © Jim West/Alamy; p. 280 (top) © Bill Bachman/Alamy; p. 280 (bottom) © Andres Rodriguez/Alamy; p. 281 © ZUMA Press, Inc./Alamy; p. 286 Dav & Les Jacobs/ZUMAPRESS/Newscom;

Chapter 14: p. 293 Alexis C. Glenn/Newscom; p. 295 Cris Bouroncle/AFP/Getty Images; p. 296 Panos Karas/Shuttertock; p. 297 © Sylvia Linares/Getty; p. 302 Newscom; p. 306 © ffotocymru/Alamy; p. 311 © OJO Images Ltd./Alamy.

INDEX

Note: Page numbers in **bold** denote definitions in margins, *t* is for tables, and *f* is for figures.

Abbott, Tony, 286
Abigail, Ruth Anna, 157
Abilene paradox, **210**–211
abstraction, **59**–60
accenting, **70**
accents, **76**–77
accessible, making information, 277–279
acronyms, social media, 53
action
 feedback model, 17–18
 inducing with persuasive speech, 297
 moving audience to, 303
active followers, **191**
active listening, 98–**99**, 101
active social information seeking, 123
adaptation, to audience, 242, 304–305
ad hominem, **308**, 309*t*
advertising, 297
affect blends, **75**
affection, **124**
Africa, 38, 58
African-Americans, 4
age, of audience for public speeches, 225–226
agenda, 217*f*
aggressive approach to conflict, 162
aggressive drivers, 83
aggressor, 187*t*
agonism, **21**
Agriculture, U.S. Department of, 56
Akihito, Emperor, 20
Albanese, Anthony, 286
Alberta, University of, Medical School, 284
Algeria, 133
all-channel network pattern, 199
Allegheny College Survey of Civility and
 Compromise in American Politics, 2–3
allness, **61**–62
al-Qaeda, 56
Altman, Irwin, 135–136
ambiguity, 158–159
ambushing, **184**
American Association of University Professors
 (AAUP), 64
The American President, 286
American Sign Language (ASL), 96
analogies, 248
anecdotes, 248
anger, 82. *See also* uncivil behavior
Anglo Americans, 38
Anti-Defamation League (ADL), 5
anxiety
 communication apprehension, 253–254
 nervousness, techniques for handling, 254–255
apology, **169**
appeals
 final to audience, 245–246
 persuasive speech, 295–296

appearance, 85*t*
appreciation, **140, 159**
appreciative listening, **95**
Arabs, 156
argumentation, **294**
Aristotle, 294, 295–296
Arizona
 Giffords shooting, 2, 5
 immigration law, 285
artifacts, **77**–79
Artinian, Peter and Nita, 96
Asia, 80–81
Ask the Ethicist
 diversity, 188
 fear appeals and personal attacks, 310
 impersonal relationships, 114
 influencing others' perceptions of self, 35
 listening, 94
 lying, 144
 online research, paying for, 285
 revenge, 169
 saying what I want, 60
 sharing resources, 249
 social gatherings, "mandatory," 71
 speaking up when group off track, 211
 visual aids, speakers using same, 265
 what's ethical?, 6
Asperger's syndrome, 275
assertive approach to conflict, 162
assurances, 140
attention, capturing, 241–242
attire, for public speaking, 260–261
attitudes
 audiences for public speeches, **223,** 224
 conflict and, 159
attraction, sexual, 132
attraction theory, 120–**121**
 interpersonal relationships, 120–122
attribution, source, 286–287
attribution theory, **35**–36
audience
 converting, with persuasive speech, 297
 demographics, 225–227
 example, 221–222
 hecklers, 228
 motivating with informative speeches, 276–277
 moving to action, 303
 needs, appealing to, 222–223
 occasion, 227–229
 psychographics, 223–225
 type, 227
audience expectations, **229**
Australia, 37, 286, 294
autographs, 67–68
autonomy/connection dialectic, **144**
avoidance, 142
avoiding, **155**
awards, accepting or presenting, 282
awareness, 275
Axelrod, David, 278

backing, **298,** 299*f*
Baker, Philip, 284, 285, 287
Barber, Ron, 5
bargaining, opportunity for. *See* conflict
Barrentine, Julie, 43
barriers, group problem-solving, 209–213
Barroso, Jose Manuel, 295
Barrows, Jeff, 161
Baumeister, Roy F., 29, 198
Bavelas, Alex, 198–200
Beef Products, 56
behavior. *See also* uncivil behavior
 conflict and, 159
 explanation for another's, 123
 facial expression and eye, 75
 forgiving, 22
 group meeting, 217–218
 immediacy, 84–87
 rules, conflict and, 159
Belgium, 37, 70
beliefs
 audiences for public speeches, **223,** 224–225
 conflict and, 159
belief systems, 57–58
Bellamy, Matt, 112
bickering, 119
Biden, Joe, 302
Blackfoot Indians, 107
black hat, 207
blocker, 187*t*
Bloomberg, Michael, 195
blue hat, 208
BMW, 81
body, speech, 239–240
body movement, 73–76, 85*t*
body orientation and posture, 74–75
body shape, **77**
boys, referring to African-American males as, 4
brainstorming
 for group problem-solving, **207**
 for speech ideas, **231**–232
Bratz dolls, 77
breast cancer treatment, 272–273
Brownback, Sam, 150–151
Bryant, Dez, 159
Bush, George W., 210, 227–228
Buzan, Tony, 208–209

Cahn, Dudley D., 157
California, University of, 182
Canada, 156
Canary, Daniel J., 82
captive audience, **227**
careers
 and confirming responses, 108
 group problem-solving, 202
 immediacy behaviors, 87
 interpersonal relationships, 120
 intimate relationship, 133–134
 work groups, 179
caring, 10

348

Carter, Stephen I., 3
Case Study in Ethics
    cell phone subterfuge, 126
    cochlear implants, 96
    cursing prof and "Conservative Coming Out Week," 64
    decision fatigue, 198
    gay marriage and Dollywood, 9
    hair in school, 78
    hecklers, 228
    loser sentences, 43
    parents and political parties, 161
    politics of exclusion, 182
    Secret Lover Collection, 147
    uncivil persuasion, 295
    uncivil speech delivery, 252
    you're not special, 283
causes, SCRIPTS conflict-resolution model, 204
cell phone subterfuge, 126
chain network pattern, 199
chair role, 186t
changing listeners' minds, 303
channel, **19**
character, 304
charisma, 304
Chautauqua movement, 279
Cheney, Dick, 63
Chicago, University of, 229
children, 119
China, 58, 118, 156
Choosing Civility: The Twenty-Five Rules of Considerate Conduct (Forni), 3
Christian Legal Society (CLS), 182
Christian Legal Society v. Martinez, 182
chronemics, **79**
Churchill, Winston, 279
CIA, 56, 75–76
circle network pattern, 199
civil communication, 2–**3**, 10
    about perceptions, 44–45
    civility and, 3–5
    criticism of, 4–5
    social media, 5
civility, **3**, 168
    conflict, 165
    definitions, 3, 10
    groups, 174–175, 197
    importance, 2
    interpersonal relationships, 119–120
    intimate relationship, 146–148
    speech audiences, engaging, 222–229
Civility: Manners, Morals, and the Etiquette of Democracy (Carter), 3
civil listening, **91**, 93
civil rights movement, 4
civitas, 7
claim, **298**
claim of fact, **299**
claims, persuasive speeches, 299–300
claims of policy, **300**
claims of value, **299**
clarifier-elaborator, 186t
clear language, 279
climate, **181**
    groups, creating, 181–187
Clinton, Hillary Rodham, 293–294

Clinton, J. R., 190t
Clinton, Bill, 259
cloaking, **168**
closed-ended questions, **102**
closing, **168**
clothing, 77–79
    for public speaking, 260–261
clothing mannequins, 77
clown, 187t
CMQ. *See* computer-mediated communication
CNBC, 302
cochlear implants, 96
co-culture, **38**
coercion, **294**
coercion power, **188**
coherence, **55**
cohesiveness, **185**
collaborating, **155**
collectivist culture, **37**–38. *See also* culture
College Republicans, 64
college students
    civility requirement at Queens University, 4
    jeers, discouraging, 228
Columbus, Christopher, 57
commercial advertising, 297
commitment
    in romantic relationships, 132
    strengthening, in persuasive speech, 296–297
    weakening, in persuasive speech, 297
common ground, 304
communication, **11**
    action and interaction feedback models, 17–18
    civil and ethical, 2–5
    competence assessment, 23
    contexts, 20–21
    culture context, 20
    defining, 11
    ethical, 6–10
    gender context, 21
    group patterns, 198–200
    groups, 174–175
    importance, 2
    inevitability, 22–23
    interpersonal, 12–13
    intimate relationship, 134
    intrapersonal, 11–12
    irreversible, 22
    mediated and technology-based, 14–17
    models, 17–20
    ongoing process, 22
    public, 14
    relationships, 113f
    small group, 14
    transactional model, 19–20
    workplace context, 21
communication apprehension, **253**–254
    Virtual Reality Therapy (VRT), 255
Communication Foundation for Southern Arizona, 5
communication models, **17**
communication network, **198**
communication style, gender and, 108
community, concern for, 10
comparative advantage organization, **305**–306
competence
    credibility, establishing, 304
    self-perceived, 23

competitive interrupting, 184
complementing, **70**, 71
composing persuasive speech, 303–307
comprehensive listening, **97**
compromiser, 187t
compromising, **155**
computer games, 52
computer-mediated communication (CMQ), 175
    conflicts, 163
    irreversible communication, 22
    nonverbal communication, 72
    physical attraction, 121
conclusion, 245–246
concreteness, in word choice, 61
concrete words, **61**
confidence, for public speaking, 254–255
confidences, 116
confirming listening, **91**
confirming responses, **101**–106, 184
    career and, 108
    and culture, 107
    gender, 108–109
    paraphrasing thoughts and feelings, 103–105
    prompting, 102
    questioning, 102–103
    reassuring and expressing concern, 103
conflict
    asking for forgiveness, 169
    causes of conflict in workplace, 158-159
    causes of conflict in relationships, 159–160
    civility, 165
    defined, 151
    emotional residues, 153
    forgiveness, 167
    in groups, 158–159
    identity-oriented conflict, 214
    incompatible goals or means, 152–153
    instrumental/task-oriented conflict, 213–214
    interdependence, 152
    interpersonal, 151–152
    intimate or romantic relationship, 145–146
    managing, 160–164
    messages, effective, 165
    offensive Twitter remark, 150–151
    in organizations or groups, 158–159
    options in conflict management, 160-164
    phase theory, 157–158
    process-oriented conflict, 214–215
    reconciliation, 169
    relationship-oriented conflict, 214
    in relationships, 159–160
    repairing relationships, 166–170
    revenge, 169
    rewards and costs, 153
    sense of urgency, 153
    situation, 152
    social exchange theory, 153–154
    S-TLC conflict resolution system, 164–165
    styles theory, 154–157
    theories, 153–158
    unforgiveness, 167
    violence, avoiding, 165–166
conflict management, **160**–161
Conflict Management Styles, 156
conflict situation, **152**
confrontation. *See* conflict

confrontational listening, **92**
confrontation steps, **165**
connotative meaning, **50**–51
consciousness raising, **296**–297
consensus, 201
consequential ethics, **6**
Conservative Coming Out Week, 64
Constitution, U.S., 29
contempt, 146–147
content-level meaning, **124**
content paraphrase, **105**
context, **20**
control, **124**
Coordinated Management of Meaning (CMM), **54**–55
coordination, **55**
coping, **168**
costs, **153**
courts, 77
   mandatory minimums sample student speech, 312–314
   Supreme Court, 182
creativity, **205**
   group problem-solving, 205–206
credibility
   establishing, 304
   public speaking, 242–243
"Credo for Ethical Communication," 8–10
Crist, Charlie, 195
critical listening, **98**
criticism, 146
Cronen, Vernon, 53
crude language, 63
"cues-filtered-out" approach, 72
cultural pattern, **37**
culture, **20, 37**
   audiences, considering, 226
   as communication context, 20
   confirming responses and, 107
   conflict styles, 155–156
   group meeting behavior, 217–218
   influences on perception, 37–38
   and interpersonal relationships, 116–118
   intimate relationship, 132–133
   and nonverbal communication, 72–73
   and thought, 57–59
cursing, 63–65
cynic, 187t

Davison, Phil, 252–253
Deaf culture, 96
"Death by PowerPoint," 262
deception cues, **83**, 83–84
decision fatigue, 198
decision making
   group, 197–201
   informative speeches, 275–276
decoding, **19**
Defense, U.S. Department of, 76
defensive listening, **92**
defensiveness, 147
definitions, 248
delivery
   anxiety, controlling, 253–255
   civility and ethics, 252–253
   practicing speech, 270

uncivil, 252
delivery cues, **268**–269
demographic characteristics, **225**–226
   audience, 225–227
   social information based on, 122
denotative meaning, **50**–51
deontological ethics, **6**
Depp, Johnny, 67–68
Dewey, John, 202–203
Dewey's Reflective Thinking Model, 203
dialectical tensions model, **143**–145
difference of opinion. *See* conflict
differentiation phase, **158**
dignity, 7
direct persuasion, **301**
disagreement. *See* conflict
disconfirming communication, **146**
disconfirming listening, **92**
display rules, **72**–73
disruptive roles, **185**
   groups, 187t
distracting gestures, 260t
divorce
   party, 129–130
   predicting, 146–148
Dollywood, 9
dominating, **155**
Donald, Jason, 26
dormant ties, 117, **118**
doublespeak, **56**

Einstein, Albert, 196, 275
Ekman, Paul, 75–76
elaboration likelihood model, **300**–301
Electronic Arts, 52
Elle Magazine Style Awards, 222
Elson, Karen, 129–130
email, 72
emblems, nonverbal, **69**, 70f
emotional appeal, **295**
emotional qualities, intimate relationships, 131
emotional residues, **153**
emotions
   conflict, 153
   display of, 72–73
   lying, 83–84
   public speaking, 261
   words associated with, 50
empathic listening, **98**
empathy, **100**
encoding, **19**
end of thought units, 76
energizer, 186t
"enhanced interrogation techniques," 56
enunciation, **258**
environment, 85t
   nonverbal communication, 79–81
equity, 116
ethical communication, 8–10
ethics, 7. *See also* Ask the Ethicist; Case Study in Ethics
   defined, 6, 10
   ethical communication, 7–8
   groups, 196
ethos appeal, **295**–296
euphemisms, **51**

Europe, 80–81
evaluating and critical listening, 98, 101
evaluative listening, **98**
evaluator-critic, 186t
EverQuest 2 (EQ2), 164
examples, 248
expectancy, **33**
expectations
   gender, 81–82
   performance and, 41
   role, conflict and, 158
expertise power, **188**
explanation, social information based on, 123
extemporaneous speech, **256**–257
extending fit, **185**
eye contact, 85t, 259–260

face, 85t
Facebook, 14–15, 40, 117
   proximity, 121
   research, 231
   virtual groups, 178
face-to-face (FTF) communication, 163
facial expression and eye behavior, **75**
fact, **44**
   claim of, 299
   inference, separating, 101
fairness, 7, 10
fallacies, 308–309
familiarity, **33**
family, **114**
   communication, 115
   influence of, 115
   interpersonal relationships, 114–115
FBI, 75–76
fear appeals, 310
federal mandatory minimum standards, 312–314
feedback, 17–18, **19**
feeling expresser, 187t
feelings, owning, 62
feelings paraphrase, **105**
fig gesture, 70f
figure-ground orientation, **31**
First Amendment, 29
five-person network patterns, 199f
flaming, **174**
   social media, 175
flow, 173, **174**
flowcharts, 281
followership, **191**
forgiveness, **167**
   asking for, 169–170
   uncivil behavior, 22
formal role, **184**
   groups, 186t
forming, **179**–180
Forni, P. M., 3
Foss, Sonja, 310–311
fractionation, **207**
France, 70, 79, 107
freedom, 311
freedom of speech, 29, 150–151
French, John R. P., 188–189
friends, **115**–116
friendship rules, **116**

friendships
    Facebook, 117
    interpersonal relationships, 115–116
functional leadership, 190*t*
fundamental attribution error, **35**–36
Fund for Civility, Respect, and Understanding, 5

G20 nations summit, 295
Galarraga, Armando, 26–27
Gallagher, Cathy, 147
Gambordella, Ted, 161
Gambordella, Teddy, 161
Garber, Angela R., 262
gatekeeper-expediter, 187*t*
Gawande, Atul, 284, 285
gay/lesbian/bisexual/transgender (GLBT) issues, 9
    family relationships, 114–115
    self-concept, 42
gaze, 85*t*
gender, **21**
    audiences, considering, 226
    as communication context, 21
    confirming responses, 108–109
    conflict styles, 156–157
    expectations, 81–82
    group meeting behavior, 218
    group situations, 192
    and interpersonal relationships, 118
    intimate relationship, 132
    and nonverbal communication, 81–82
    perceptual differences, 33–34
    self-concept, 42–43
    stereotypes, 81–82
    swaps in online gaming, 43
    troubles talk, 109
general attractiveness and body shape, **77**
generalizing, **308**, 309*t*
Germany, 81, 107
gestures, 74, 85*t*
    distracting, 260*t*
    public speaking, 259
Giffords, Gabrielle, 5, 47–48
gifts, **160**
Gillard, Julia, 294, 295
"give and take," 116
global plagiarism, 285
goal(s), **177**
    groups, 177
    incompatible, 152–153
Goddess clothing mannequins, 77
"golden rule," 6
good manners, 4–5
Gore, Al, 90
gossip, **53**
Gottman, John M., 146–147
graduation speeches, 283
grammatical breaks, 76
Greece, 70
green hat, 208
Griffin, Cindy, 310–311
grounds, **298**
grouphate, 173–**174**
group meetings
    culture and behavior, 217–218
    gender and behavior, 218
    guidelines, 215–216

    individual roles, 216–217
group(s), **176**
    audience composition, 226
    categorizing by, 30
    characteristics, 176–179
    civility, 197
    climate, creating, 181–187
    cohesiveness, 185
    communication and civility, 174–175
    conflict in, 158–159
    decision making, 197–201
    defined, **176**
    development, 179–181
    ethics, 196
    example, 172–173
    following, importance of, 191
    forming, 179–180
    goals, 177
    leadership, 189, 190*t*
    leadership emergence, 191–192
    long-term, relationship-oriented, 178
    meetings, 215–218
    norming, 180–181
    norms, 181–183
    performing, 181
    power, 188–189
    problem-solving, 196, 197*t*, 202–213
    processes, 202–218
    productivity, 179
    responding to one another, 183–184
    roles, members', 184–185, 186–187*t*
    short-term, task-oriented, 177
    storming, 180
    teams versus, 176–177
    terminating, 181
    virtual, 178–179
    work, 179
groupthink, **210**
Guatemala, 38

hair styles in school, 78
Hall, Edward T., 80–81
halo effect, **36**
hand signals, 70*f*
haptics, **75**
harmonizer-tension reliever, 187*t*
Harris, Sandra, 255
Harry Potter, 172–173
Harvard University, 50
Harvey, Jerry, 210–211
Hastings Law School, 182
hasty generalization, **308**
Hawn, Goldie, 111
headscarves, 79
hearing, **95**
hearing and appreciative listening, 95–97, 99
hecklers, 228
Heider, Fritz, 35
help, meaning of word, 61
helping, **160**
high-concept belief systems, 57–58
high-context culture, **58**
Hinds Community College, 64
HIV home testing sample speech, 288–290
home schooling, 119
hostile audience, **297**

Hudson, Bill, 111
Hudson, Kate, 111–112
hyperpersonal communication, 141, **142**

ideas, public speaking, 231–232
identity-oriented conflict, **214**
illustrators, **70**
immediacy, **84**
immediacy behaviors, 84–87
    career, 87
    nonverbal scale, 86
impersonal communication, **12**–13
impersonal relationships, **113**–114
implicit personality theory, **36**, 36–37
impromptu speech, 257*t*
incivility. *See also* uncivil behavior
    nonverbal communication, 82–83
    road range as example, 82–83
incompatible goals, **152**
incompatible means, **152**–153
incremental plagiarism, 286
indexing, **62**
India, 133
indirect persuasion, **301**, 303
individualist culture, **37**. *See also* culture
Indonesia, 38
inevitability of communication, 22–23
inference, **44**, 101
inflection, 76
informal roles, **184**
    groups, 186*t*
information, **160**
    insufficient, group conflict and, 158–159
    listening, 101
    for public speaking, 246–247, 273–274
information giver, 186*t*
information seeker, 186*t*
informative speeches, 229–230
    accessible, making information, 277–279
    appropriate supporting material, 280
    awareness, 275
    clear language, 279
    decision-making, 275–276
    motivating audience, 276–277
    providing new information, 275–276
    purpose, 174–175
    strategy, 279–280
    visual aids, 280–281
initiation phase, **158**
initiation strategies, **139**
initiator-contributor role, 186*t*
inspire, speeches to, 230–231
instrumental/task-oriented conflict, **213**–214
insufficient information, 158
integrating, **155**
intellectual qualities, intimate relationships, 131
interaction feedback model, 17–18
interaction management, **76**
interactive social information seeking, 123
interdependence, **152**
    conflict, 152
internal dialogue, **12**
internal previews, 244
internal summaries, 244
Internet
    intimate relationship, 141

number of people who use, 14
relationship initiation and maintenance, 141
research, 231, 247
interpersonal attraction, **120**–121
interpersonal communication, **12**–13
interpersonal conflict, **151**–152
interpersonal relationships, 112–113
    attraction theory, 120–122
    career, 120
    civility, 119–120
    culture and, 116–118
    example, 111–112
    family, 114–115
    friendships, 115–116
    gender and, 118
    impersonal and personal, 113–114
    metacommunication, 125–127
    relational communication, 124–125
    theories, 120–124
    uncertainty reduction theory, 122–124
interpersonal violence, **166**
interpretation
    empathic listening and, 98, 100
    nonverbal communication, 82
    perception process, **32**–33
interrupting, 119
intiation strategies, 139
intimacy, in romantic relationships, 131
intimate distance, **80**–81
intimate relationship, 130–**131**
    careers and, 133–134
    civility, 146–148
    communication, 134
    conflicts, 145–146
    culture, 132–133
    dialectical tensions model, 143–146
    example, 129–130
    gender, 132
    initiation strategies, 139
    Internet and social media, 141
    Knapp and Vangelisti's staircase model, 138
    maintenance strategies and skills, 139–140, 142
    self-disclosure, 135
    social penetration theory, 135–138
    termination strategies and skills, 142–143
intrapersonal communication, **11**, 11–12, 22
introduction
    public speaking, 241–243
    speech of, 281
intuition, SCRIPTS conflict-resolution model, 204
invitational rhetoric, 310–311
Iowa, University of, 64
Iran, 79
Ireland, Jeff, 159
isolate role, 187*t*
Israel, parole board in, 198
I-statements, **165**

Jackson, Michael, 106
Jacobson, Lenore, 41
Jacobson, Nancy, 195–196
Janis, Irving, 210
Japan, 58
jargon, **51**–52
jeerers, discouraging, 228
jihad, 50

Jobs, Steve, 260
Johns Hopkins Civility Project, 3
Johnson, Janet, 302
Joyce, Jim, 26–27
just, 7

Kargman, Harry, 126
Katz, James E., 126
Kelley, Harold H., 153
Kelly, Jesse, 48
Kemmerling, Robert, 255
Kessler, Glenn, 278
kinesics (body movement and position), **74**–76
Knapp, Mark L., 138*f*
Knapp and Vangelisti's staircase model, 138
"know-it-all," 61–62
Knowles, Beyonce, 1–2, 10
Korea, 58
KRC Research, 3

labels, food, 55–56
lab studies, 83
language
    clear, in informative speeches, 279
    special occasion speeches, 282
lateral thinking, **206**
    group problem-solving, 206–207
Latin America, 58
Latinos, 73, 118
leadership, **189**
    emergence, 191–192
    group decision-making patterns, 200–201
    groups, 189, 190*t*
    historical approaches, 190*t*
leading questions, **102**
Leahy, Patrick, 63
legitimacy power, **188**
Lewin, Ellen, 64
Lewis, Richard, 107
line, standing in, 79
listen, 165
listening, **91**–92
    civil, 93
    confirming responses, 101–109
    evaluating and critical, 98, 101
    hearing and appreciative, 95–97, 99
    importance of, 94
    improving abilities, 99–101
    interpreting and empathic, 98, 100
    remembering messages, 97–98, 100
    responding and active, 98–99, 101
    stages, 94–99
    types, 94–95
    uncivil, 92–93
    understanding and comprehensive, 97, 100
loaded questions, **103**
Logan, Michelle, 126
logical appeal, **295**
logical fallacies, 307–310
logos appeal, 295–296
loneliness, social media and, 15
long-term, relationship-oriented groups, 178
long-term relationships, 113*f*
Lord of the Rings, 178
loser sentences assignment, 43
love, 159

low-concept belief systems, 57–58
low-context culture, **58**
Lucifer effect, **212**–213
lying, 6, 83–84, 144

Machiavellian supervisors, 87
Madoff, Bernard, 36–37
maintenance roles, **185**
    groups, 187*t*
maintenance strategies, **139**–140
    intimate relationship, 139–140, 142
managing conflict, 160–164
Manchin, Joe, 195
mandatory minimums sample student speech, 312–314
mandatory social gatherings, 71
manipulation, 142
manuscript, speaking from, 256, 257*t*
marital happiness/unhappiness, 130
marriage
    culture, 132–133
    disconfirming communication as predictor of divorce, 146–148
    example, 129–130
    physical violence, 165–166
Maslow, Abraham, 222–223
Maslow's Hierarchy of Needs, 222–223
massively multiplayer online role-playing games (MMOPRGs)
    proximity, 121–122
    relationships, 141
    self-concept, 43
McCroskey, James, 253
Mead, George Herbert, 41
meaning
    coordinated management of, 54–55
    denotative and connotative, 50–51
    gender and, 52–54
    shortcuts (jargon and slang), 51–52
    triangle of, 49–50
means, incompatible, 152–153
Medal of Honor game, 52
media, social. *See* social networking
mediated and technology-based communication, **14**–17
memorializing online, 106
memory, 75
    speaking from, 256, 257*t*
Memory Test, 32
men. *See* gender
message, **19**
    conflict, 165
    remembering, 97–98, 100
metacommunication, **125**–126
    interpersonal relationships, 125–127
metaphor, **282**
Mexican-Americans, 38
Mexico, 156
microexpressions, **75**–76
Middle East, 38, 107, 228
Midwesterners, 77
Millennial Generation, 96–97, 283
Milward, H. Brinton, 64
mind mapping, **208**–209
MMOPRGs. *See* massively multiplayer online role-playing games
money, 160

Index

monochronic time, **79**
Monroe, Alan H., 306–307
Monroe's motivated sequence, **306**–307
moods, 115
movement, body, 73–76
movies, 63
Mowen, John C., 203–204
MTV Video Music Awards, 1–2, 10
Murnighan, Keith, 203–204
MySpace, 106, 121
mystery, **55**

names, remembering, 100
National Communication Association (NCA), 8–9
National Institute for Civil Discourse (NICD), 5, 64
National Prayer Breakfast (2010), 2
Native Americans, 57, 73, 80–81
    sympathetic listening, 107
naturalistic studies, 83–84
Navy SEAL, 52
NCA. *See* National Communication Association
needs
    audience, appealing to, 222–223
    fulfillment, friendships and, 116
negotiation, opportunity for. *See* conflict
nervousness, techniques for handling, 254–255
the Netherlands, 37, 156
net lingo, 53
network. *See* social networking
neutralization, 145
New Jersey, 77
new media, 15
Newseum, 293–294
New York, 77
NICD. *See* National Institute for Civil Discourse
9/11, 80, 227–228, 237
Nixon, Richard, 210, 297
NMMs. *See* nonmanual markers
noise, **20,** 95–97
No Labels political civility group, 195–196
nonassertive approach to conflict, 162
nonmanual markers (NMMs), 96
nonverbal communication, **68**–71, 259
    accenting, 70–71
    complementing, 71
    culture and, 72–73
    deception, 83–84
    environment, 79–81
    example, 67–68
    gender and, 81–82
    immediacy behaviors, 84–87
    incivility, road rage as example of, 82–83
    kinesics (body movement and position), 74–76
    paralanguage (vocalics), 76–77
    physical characteristics, 77–79
    regulating, 71–72
    repeating, 69
    substituting, 69–70
Nonverbal Immediacy Scale, 86
norming, **180**–181
    groups, 180–181
norms, **180,** 181–183
North, Max, 255
notes, speaking from, 256
novelty/predictability dialectic, **144**

Obama, Barack, 2, 20, 48, 229, 230–231, 278, 302
Obama, Michelle, 272–273
obfuscation, **279**
obliging, **155**
occasion, **227**–228
    public speeches, 227–229
    speaking audience, 227–229
Odgen, C. K., 49–50
Odgen's triangle of meaning, 49*f*
Odom, Olivier, 9
Oliver, Jamie, 55–56
Olmert, Ehud, 229
online games. *See* massively multiplayer online role-playing games
online research, 285
online support groups, 106
open-ended questions, **102**
openness, 140
openness/closedness dialectic, 144, **144**–145
opinion seeker, 186*t*
opportunities
    for bargaining or negotiation (*See* conflict)
    SCRIPTS conflict-resolution model, 203–204
Oprah Winfrey Network (OWN), 90–91
optimal self, 40
orations, 256
organization, **30**
    conflict in, 158–159
orienter, 186*t*
other-centered orientation, **162**
outline
    practicing speech, 268–269
    speaking from, 256, 257*t*
    speech, writing, 238–241
overstatement, **308**
Owens, Pete, 9
OWN. *See* Oprah Winfrey Network
owning our thoughts and feelings, **62**

Pakistan, 38, 80–81
Palin, Sarah, 48
paralanguage (vocalics), **76**–77
paraphrase, 103–**104**
    for content, 105
    for feelings, 105
    ways to begin, 104
parliamentarian role, 186*t*
passion, in romantic relationships, 132
passive followers, **191**
passive listening, 98–**99**
passive social information seeking, 123
patchwork plagiarism, 285–286
pathos appeal, 295–296
Pausch, Randy, 251–252, 261
pauses, 258
Pearce, W. Barnett, 53
perception, 27
    communicating civilly and effectively, 44–45
    differences, 33–34
    influencing others' perceptions of yourself, 35
    interpretation, 32–33
    mediated and technology-related communication, 16
    selection, 30–32
    self-control and civility, 29
    stages, 30–35

    theories, 35–38
perception check, **44**
performing, **181**
personal attacks, 310
personal beliefs, 122
personal communication, **13**
personal distance, 81
personal experience, 231
personal relationships, 113–114
perspective, 26–28
    SCRIPTS conflict-resolution model, 204
perspective-taking, 27, **28**
persuasion, **294**
persuasive speech, **230**
    appeals, 295–296
    composing, 303–307
    invitational rhetoric, 310–311
    logical fallacies, 307–310
    outcomes, 303
    process, 297–303
    purposes, 296–297
    rhetoric and argumentation, 294
    structuring message, 305–307
    student sample, 312–314
    uncivil, 295, 307–310
Pew Internet & American Life Project, 117, 302
PFLAG (Parents, Families and Friends of Lesbians and Gays), 114–115
phase theory, **157**
    conflict, 157–158
phrases, transitional, 244–245
physical attraction, **121**
physical characteristics, 77–79
physical environment, 79
physical preparation, for public speaking, 254
pickup line, **139**
Pink, 162
"pink slime," 56
pitch, speech, 76
place, **228**
plagiarism, 284–287
plane crash, 80
policy, claims of, **300**
politeness, 6
political parties
    civility group vs., 195–196
    family conflict over, 161
    Twitter, 302
    uncivil behavior, 278
polychronic time, **79**
position, body, 73–76
positive tone, 142–143
positivity, 140
post hoc, ergo propter hoc, **309**
Potter, Harry, 172–173
power
    groups, 188–189
    unequal distribution, conflict and, 158
power leadership, 190*t*
PowerPoint, 261–263
practicing speech, 254, 267
    delivery, 270
    outline, 268–269
    with presentation aids, 269
    simulating situation, 269–270
pragmatic rules, **54**

pregnant pauses, **258**
prelude to conflict, **157**
presentation aids
    practicing speech with, 269
    purpose, 261–262
    slides, 265–267
    software, 263–265
    when to use, 262
preview
    internal, 244
    topic, 243
Prezi, 263
privacy, 116
proactive followers, **191**
problematic Internet use (PIU), 164
problematic situation, **152**
problems, groups solving
    barriers, 209–213
    careers, 202
    conflict management, 213–215
    creativity, 205–206
    standard techniques, 207–209
    steps, 202–205
    vertical and lateral thinking, 206–207
problem-solution organization, **305**
procedural technician, 186*t*
process, **11**
    persuasive speech, 297–303
process-oriented conflict, **214**–215
productivity, group, 179
profanity, 63–65
prompts, **102**
pronunciation, **258**
proxemics, **80**–81
proximity, **31**, 31–32, **121**
pseudolistening, **92**
psychographics, audience, 223–225, **223**–225
public communication, **14**
public criticism, 116
public dialogue, **311**
public distance, **81**
public speeches
    audience, engaging with civility, 222–229, 251–252
    conclusion, 245–246
    delivering with civility and ethics, 252–270
    example, 221–222
    informative, 272–281, 284–287
    introduction, 241–243
    organizing information, 234–237
    persuasive, 293–314
    planning, 229–234
    purpose, 229–231, 232–234
    sample student, 288–290
    selecting topic and generating ideas, 231–232
    special occasion, 281–287
    supporting material, 246–249
    thesis statement, 234
    transitions, 244–245
    writing outline, 238–241
public swearing, 63
Pugh, Taylor, 78
purpose
    informative speeches, 174–175
    persuasive speech, 296–297
Pygmalion effect, **41**

qualifier, **298**, 299*f*
quarrel. *See* conflict
Queens University, 4
quotation, 248

radio shock jocks, 63
Rahim, M. Afzalur, 154–155
rate, **258**–259
Raven, Bertram, 188–189
Reagan, Ronald, 210
reasoning, 101
rebuttal, **299**, 299*f*
recognition seeker, 187*t*
reconciliation, 167
(re-)creating, **168**
recreational qualities, intimate relationships, 131
red hat, 207
red herring, **309**
reference power, 188
reframing, 145–146
refutation, 299*f*
refutational organization, **306**
regulating, **70**
    nonverbal communication, 71–72
reinforcing fit, **185**
relational communication, **124**
    interpersonal relationships, 124–125
relational feedback, **103**
relational-level meaning, **124**
    metacommunication, 127
Relational Maintenance Strategies, 140
relational transgressions, **166**
relationship, **113**
    conflict in, 159–160, 214
relationship-oriented approach, **162**
relationship-oriented conflict, **214**
remembering messages, 97–98, 100
repairing relationships after conflict, 166–170
repeating, **69**
    nonverbal communication, 69
Republican National Committee, 278
research
    interviewing, 247
    library, 247
    online, paying for, 285
    for public speaking, 246–247
    resources, sharing, 249
    speech topics based on, 231
    World Wide Web, 247
resolution phase, **158**
respect, 7, 10, **125**
responding and active listening, 98–99, 101
responding to one another, 183–184
response, anticipated, 304–305
responses, confirming, 101–106, 184
    career and, 108
    and culture, 107
    gender, 108–109
    paraphrasing thoughts and feelings, 103–105
    prompting, 102
    questioning, 102–103
    reassuring and expressing concern, 103

responsibility, 7, 10
restraint, 10
resumes, 35
revenge, **167,** 169
reverse brainstorming, **207**
reward power, **188**
rewards, **153**
rhetoric, **294**
Richards, I. A., 49–50
risk, SCRIPTS conflict-resolution model, 204
road rage, 82–83
Robinson, Chris, 111–112
Roiphe, Katie, 283
role, **180**
roles, members'
    in groups, 184–185, 186–187*t*
    unclear expectations, conflict and, 158
romantic relationship, 130–132, **131**
    career, 133–134
    civility, 146–148
    communication, 134
    conflicts, 145–146
    culture, 132–133
    dialectical tensions model, 143–146
    example, 129–130
    gender, 132
    initiation strategies, 139
    Knapp and Vangelisti's staircase model, 138
    maintenance strategies and skills, 139–140, 142
    self-disclosure, 135
    social penetration theory, 135–138
    stage models, 138–143
    termination strategies and skills, 142–143
Romney, Mitt, 278
Rosenthal, Robert, 41
Rowling, J. K., 173
rules for behavior, 159
Russell, Kurt, 111

safety, 311
salience, **30**
sanction, **183**
Sapir, Edward, 58–59
Sapir Whorf hypothesis, **58**–59
Sarkozy, Nicolas, 79
Scandinavia, 79
scent, 85*t*
schemas, **30**
    perception and, 30–31
school, hair styles in, 78
SCRIPTS model, 203–205
search engines, 232
Second Life nonverbal communication, 72, 73
secretary-recorder role, 186*t*
Secret Lover Collection, 147
selection, **30**–32, 145
selective listening, **97**
self-centered orientation, **162**
self-concept, **28**–29, 38–39
    culture and, 41–42
    gender, 42–43
    others' influence on, 41
    self-esteem, 39, 41
    self-image, 39
    workplace, 42
self-confessor, 187*t*

self-control, 29, **29**
self-disclosure, **135**
self-efficacy, **42**
self-esteem, 29, **39**, 41
　loser sentences, 43
self-image, **39**
Self-Monitoring Scale, 39
Self-Perceived Communication Competence (SPCC) scale, 23
self-serving bias, **36**
self-talk, **11**–12
semantic rules, **54**
Senate, U.S., 63
sender, **19**
sense of urgency, **153**
　conflict, 153
sensory fragments, 75
separation, 145
September 11, 2001, 80, 227–228, 237
sex. *See* gender
sexual attraction, **132**
sexual qualities, intimate relationships, 131
Shandwick, Weber, 3
shared time, **160**
sharing tasks, 140
Sheon, Nicolas, 288
shift response, **183**–184
shortcuts, 51–52, 198
short-term, task-oriented group, **177**
short-term memory, 97–98
short-term relationships, 113*f*
signaling the close, 245
significant others, **41**
silence, 76
silence, cultural interpretations of, 73
similarity, **32**
　friendships, 116, 121
simile, **282**
simulation, 269–270
situation, conflict, 152
situational ethics, 6
situational leadership, 190*t*
six hats method, **207**–208
size of audience, considering, 226
slang, **51**–52
sledgehammer introduction, **242**
slides, speech presentation aids, 265–267
slippery slope, **308**–309
small group communication, 16–17
Smith, Dennis, 237
social comparison, **41**
social distance, **81**
social exchange theory, **153**–154
social gatherings, "mandatory," 71
social influence/transformational leadership, 190*t*
social information, **122**
social networking
　civility, 3, 5
　conflict resolution, 163
　"cues-filtered-out" approach, 72
　effects, 15
　Facebook, 117
　flaming and group communication, 175
　gender, uses by different, 34
　group communication, 200
　intimate relationship, 141

number of people who use, 140
　political process, 302
　relationship initiation and maintenance, 140, 141
　supportive communication, 106
　taking words out of context, 278
　Twitter, 200, 302
　vocabulary, 53
social penetration theory, **135**, 135–138
social qualities, intimate relationships, 131
software, 263–265
solution, SCRIPTS conflict-resolution model, 205
source attribution, 101, 286–287
　World Wide Web, 247
South Americans, 80–81
Southern California, University of, 76
Southerners, 77
space, 85*t*
Spain, 133
SPCC. *See* Self-Perceived Communication Competence
special occasion speeches
　awards, accepting or presenting, 282
　delivering effectively and civilly, 282–283
　graduation, 283
　of introduction, 281
　language, using creatively, 282
　plagiarism, avoiding, 284–287
specificity, in word choice, 61
specific purpose statement, **233**–234
speeches, public
　audience, engaging with civility, 222–229, 251–252
　conclusion, 245–246
　delivering with civility and ethics, 252–270
　example, 221–222
　informative, 272–281, 284–287
　introduction, 241–243
　organizing information, 234–237
　persuasive, 293–314
　planning, 229–234
　purpose, 229–231, 232–234
　sample student, 288–290
　selecting topic and generating ideas, 231–232
　special occasion, 281–287
　supporting material, 246–249
　thesis statement, 234
　transitions, 244–245
　writing outline, 238–241
speech of introduction, 281
speed, speech, 76
stage models, **138**–143
staircase model, intimate relationship, 138
standing in line, 79
Star Trek, 167
Stark County Treasurer's Office, 252–253
State Department Protocol Office, 20
statistics, 248
status, **159**–160
stereotypes, **30**–31
　gender, 81–82
　schemas vs., 31
Stevens, Hampton, 27
S-TLC conflict resolution system, **164**–165
Stone, Eunice, 80
stonewalling, 147
stop, 164

storming, 180, **180**
strategy, informative speeches, 279–280
strong ties, **117**
student sample
　informative speech, 288–290
　persuasive speech, 312–314
student volunteering, 232
styles leadership, 190*t*
styles theory of conflict, **154**–157
substituting, **69**
　nonverbal communication, 69–70
Sullivan, Emma, 150–151
summary
　internal, 244
　main ideas in speeches, 245
SUNY-Albany, 83
supporter-encourager, 187*t*
supporting material
　informative speeches, 280
　for public speaking, 246–247
supportive communication, social media, 106
Supreme Court, 182
Swift, Taylor, 1–2, 10
symbolic interactionism, **41**
symbols, **11**, **49**
sympathy, **100**
syntactic rules, **54**

Tafoya, Melissa A., 82
Taiwan, 156
talking over, 119
talkovers, **183**–184
Tannen, Deborah, 109
task roles, **185**
tasks
　sharing, in relationships, 140
　short-term groups, 177
Tate, Powell, 3
Taylor, Dalmas, 135–136
teams, groups versus, 176–177
tech check
　nonverbal immediacy scale, 86
　self-perceived communication competence, 23
technology
　civility initiatives, 5
　conflict communication, 163
　"cues-filtered-out" approach, 72
　e-mail, 72
　Facebook, 117
　flaming and group communication, 72, 175
　groups, 200
　new media, 15
　political process, 302
　relationship initiation and maintenance, 141
　supportive communication, 106
　taking words out of context, 278
　Twitter, 200, 302
　Virtual Reality Therapy (VRT) and communication apprehension, 255
　vocabulary, 53
　YouTube and public speaking, 238
technology-based communication, 14–17
teleprompter, 256*f*
termination, group, **181**
termination, relationships, **142**
　intimate relationship, 142–143

territoriality, **79**–80
testimony, 248
thesis statement, **234**
    stating, 243
Thibaut, John, 153
think, 164
thought
    culture and, 57–59
    indexing, 62
    owning, 62
    strongly-influencing words, 55–56
    subtly-influencing words, 56–57
    verbal communication, 55–59
threats, SCRIPTS conflict-resolution model, 203
thumbs-up gesture, 70*f*
time, 86*t*, **160, 227**
    relationships, 113*f*
time frame, SCRIPTS conflict-resolution model, 204
Tipton, Jennifer, 9
touch, 85*t*
Toulmin, Stephen, 298
Toulmin Model, **298**–299
traits leadership, 190*t*
transaction, **11**
transactional model, 19–20
transformational leader, **189**
transformational leadership, 190*t*
transitions, 244–245, 259
treasurer role, 186*t*
triangle of love, 131–132
triangle of meaning, 49–50
triggering event, **157**–158
troubles talk, 109
trustworthiness, 7, 10
T-shirt messages, 9
Tuckman, Bruce, 179–181
Tucson, Arizona shootings, 2
Turkey, 70
TV, 63
Twitter, 302
    group communication, 200
    number of people who use, 11
    offensive remark, 150–151
    political process, 302
    research, 231
    supportive communication, 106

uncertainty reduction theory, **122**
    interpersonal relationships, 122–124
uncivil behavior, 22
    persuasive speech, 295, 307–310
    profanity and cursing, 63–65
uncivil listening, 92–93

uncivil speech delivery, 252
unclear role explanation, 158
understanding and comprehensive listening, 97, 100
unforgiveness, **167**
uniqueness, 113
United States
    hand gestures, 70
    individualist culture in, 37
    standing in line, 79
University of Alberta Medical School, 284
University of California, 182
University of Chicago, 229
University of Iowa, 64
University of Southern California, 76
university students
    civility requirement at Queens University, 4
    jeers, discouraging, 228
"unpacking" slides, 263
urgency, conflict, 153
U.S. Constitution, 29
U.S. Department of Agriculture, 56
U.S. Department of Defense, 76
U.S. Senate, 63
U.S. Supreme Court, 182

value, 311
value, claims of, **299**
values
    audiences for public speeches, **224**, 225
    conflict and, 159
Vangelisti, L., 138*f*
verbal communication, 48–**49**
    example, 47–48
    gender, 52–54
    improving, 59–62
    meaning, 49–55
    thought, 55–59
    uncivil language (profanity and cursing), 63–65
verbal immediacy, 85*t*
verbal pause, 258
vertical horn, 70*f*
vertical thinking, **206**
    group problem-solving, 206–207
violence, 5, 47–48, 165–166
virtual groups, **178**–179
Virtual Reality Therapy (VRT), 255
visual aids, 280–281
visual delivery, 259–260
vividness, **30**
vocalics, 76–77
vocal qualities, 76
    effective public speaking, 257–258
voice, 85*t*
volume, **258**

volume, speech, 76
voluntary audience, **227**
voting, decision-making in groups, 201
"v" sign, 70*f*

warrant, **298**
Watson, Emma, 221–222
weak ties, 117, **118**
web, 247
West, Kanye, 1–2, 10
West Africa, 38
Westwood, Vivian, 222
wheel network pattern, 199
When Cultures Collide: Managing Successfully Across Cultures (Lewis), 107
Whitaker, Matthew, 285–286
White, Jack, 129–130
white hat, 207
Whorf, Benjamin Lee, 58–59
Winfrey, Oprah, 90–91
withdrawal, terminating relationships, 142
women. *See* gender
words
    specific and concrete, 61
    strongly-influencing thought, 55–56
    subtly-influencing thought, 56–57
    transitional, 244–245
work groups, 179
workplace
    as communication context, 21
    conflict styles, 156
    inappropriate behavior, 5, 21
    mandatory social gatherings, 71
    romances, 133–134
    self-concept, 42
Workplace Bullying Institute (WBI), 5
workplace incivility, **21**
World Trade Center attacks, 80
World Wide Web, 247
writing persuasive speech, 303–307

Yahoo groups, 178
Yasin, Zayed, 50
yellow hat, 207
Y network pattern, 199
YouTube, 238

Zaozirny, Jonathan, 284
Zarefsky, David, 245
zealot, 187*t*
Zirnstein, Gerald, 55–56